ABOUT THE AUTHOR

James W. Loewen is the bestselling and award-winning author of *Lies My Teacher Told Me*, *Lies My Teacher Told Me About Christopher Columbus*, *Sundown Towns*, and *Lies My Teacher Told Me: Young Readers' Edition* (all from The New Press). He also wrote *Teaching What Really Happened* and *The Mississippi Chinese: Between Black and White* and edited *The Confederate and Neo-Confederate Reader*. He has won the American Book Award, the Oliver Cromwell Cox Award for Distinguished Anti-Racist Scholarship, the Cox, Johnson, Frazier Award of the American Sociological Association, the Spirit of America Award from the National Council for the Social Studies, and the Gustavus Myers Outstanding Book Award. Loewen is professor emeritus of sociology at the University of Vermont and lives in Washington, DC.

Also by James W. Loewen

The Mississippi Chinese: Between Black and White

Mississippi: Conflict and Change (with Charles Sallis et al.)

Social Science in the Courtroom

Lies My Teacher Told Me About Christopher Columbus

Lies My Teacher Told Me:
Everything Your American History Textbook Got Wrong

Sundown Towns:
A Hidden Dimension of American Racism

Teaching What Really Happened

The Confederate and Neo-Confederate Reader: The "Great Truth" About the
"Lost Cause" (editor, with Edward H. Sebesta)

LIES ACROSS AMERICA

WHAT OUR HISTORIC SITES GET WRONG

JAMES W. LOEWEN

THE
NEW
PRESS

NEW YORK
LONDON

© 2019, 1999 by James W. Loewen
All rights reserved.
No part of this book may be reproduced, in any form, without written permission from the publisher.

Requests for permission to reproduce selections from this book should be made through our website:
thenewpress.com/contact

Originally published in the United States by The New Press, 1999
This revised and updated edition published by The New Press, New York, 2019
Distributed by Two Rivers Distribution

ISBN 978-1-62097-506-0 (hc)
ISBN 978-1-62097-433-9 (pb)
ISBN 978-1-62097-493-3 (ebook)
CIP data is available

The New Press publishes books that promote and enrich public discussion and understanding of
the issues vital to our democracy and to a more equitable world. These books are made possible by
the enthusiasm of our readers; the support of a committed group of donors, large and small; the
collaboration of our many partners in the independent media and the not-for-profit sector; booksellers,
who often hand-sell New Press books; librarians; and above all by our authors.

www.thenewpress.com

Book design and composition by Bookbright Media
This book was set in Bembo and Scala

Printed in the United States of America

10 9 8 7 6 5 4 3 2 1

NOTE

At the end of each entry, a source note lists citations in the approximate order in which they are relevant to the entry, allowing the luxury of footnotes without letting them overpower the page. Abbreviations in the source notes include postal codes for state names, U for university, UP for university press, and GPO for Government Printing Office. Sites on the web are listed by title when appropriate and URL. If a URL is too long for one line, it wraps to the next line without a hyphen, to avoid ambiguity.

PHOTO CREDITS

Leon Waters, 10; James W. Loewen, 15, 22, 27, 28, 29, 49 (2), 65, 69, 116, 132, 149, 179, 184, 203, 288 (2), 312, 398, 404 (2), 438 (2), 446, Karen Osborne, 37; Alaska Division of Tourism, 61; Robert Weyeneth, 89; Nevada State Historic Preservation Office, 94; Lawrence Livermore National Laboratory/DOE, 97; Idaho State Historical Society, 101; Smithsonian Institution National Museum of American History Photo Office, 144; Muscatine Department of Parks and Recreation, 157; Hannibal Convention and Visitors Bureau, 163; Chicago Sun-Times, 169; National Park Service, 182; Library of Congress, 195, 206, 225, 234, 306; Times-Picayune, 231; Corbis/Bettmann, 258; Howard University Moorland-Springarn Center, 263, 290, 291, 331, 407; James B. Jones, Jr., 273; National Archives, 299; Metro Richmond Convention and Visitors Bureau, 329; The New Press, 353; University of Vermont Archives, 434.

Dedicated to the memory of the heroes portrayed in this book

—feet of clay and all—

whose examples may yet inspire this nation

to live out the meaning of its beliefs,

and to the activists and scholars,

whose numbers are increasing,

who work to get our public history

to become more accurate,

so our society can become more just.

CONTENTS

THE FAR WEST

THE MOUNTAINS

THE ATLANTIC STATES

ALPHABETICAL INDEX
OF STATES

PREFACE TO THE
SECOND EDITION

What a difference two decades have made! When the first edition of *Lies Across America* came out, some people considered it outlandish. To include an appendix that called for monuments to be toppled! To say that the signs at the edge of towns noting "First Settled" are off by thousands of years! To defend the vandalism of a statue in New Mexico! To suggest that Richmond has its history precisely backward—that it should celebrate, rather than mourn, its liberation by U.S. troops in April 1865!

Today these ideas have become, if not mainstream, at least commonplace. The SCV (Sons of Confederate Veterans) and UDC (United Daughters of the Confederacy), which looked as solidly influential in 1999 as the bronze and granite of their monuments, now seem feeble. Even then, new forces were at work; I wrote in 1999 that our landscape was "contested." States were beginning to put up markers for embarrassing events, not just comforting ones. And now, reactionary white supremacist monuments are beginning to tumble. Even Monument Avenue in the citadel of the Confederacy is no longer safe, not even after the addition of tennis great Arthur Ashe cleansed it of its sin of racial exclusivity.

Over the last twenty years, *Lies Across America* has become the country's consistently bestselling book in public history—the discipline that studies monuments, markers, museums, and the like. The book has been explicitly cited by, among others, New Orleans mayor Mitch Landrieu as influencing his thinking about monuments and has played some role in the changes that are now upending the field. My intention in creating this completely revised second edition is not only to bring the book up-to-date, noting the ongoing changes and how they occurred, but also to provide readers with examples of how they might do likewise. As I ended the first edition: this is our country, after all, our narrative, and our landscape upon which to tell it. Go be a troubadour!

IN WHAT WAYS WERE
WE WARPED?

When I was a boy on our annual summer vacation trips, the family car seemed to stop at every historic marker and monument. Maybe yours did, too. Dad thought it was "good for us," and I suppose in a way it was. Little did he suspect that it was also *bad* for us—that the lies we encountered on our trips across the United States subtly distorted our knowledge of the past and warped our view of the world. My sister and I needed to unlearn the myths we were learning in school, but the historic sites we visited only amplified them and taught us new ones.

My bestseller *Lies My Teacher Told Me* tells how American history as taught in most high schools distorts the past and turns many students off. One result is that only one American in six ever takes a course in American history after graduating from high school. Where then do Americans learn about the past? From many sources, of course—historical novels, PBS series—but surely most of all from the landscape. History is told on the landscape all across America—on monuments at the courthouse, by guides inside antebellum homes and aboard historic ships, by the names we give to places, and on roadside historical markers. This book examines the history that some of these places tell and the processes by which they come forward to tell it.

Markers, monuments, and preserved historic sites usually result from local initiative. Typically, a private organization—the chamber of commerce, a church congregation, the local chapter of the United Daughters of the Confederacy—takes the lead, but public monies are usually involved before it's unveiled. It follows that the site will tell a story favorable to the local community and, particularly, to that part of the community that erected or restored it. An account from another point of view might be quite different and also more accurate.

Americans like to remember only the positive things, and communities like to publicize the great things that happened in them. One result is silliness: the first airplane was invented not by the Wright Brothers but by Rev. Burrell Cannon, and the first flight was not in Kitty Hawk, North Carolina, but in Pittsburg, Texas. It must be true—an impressive-looking Texas state historical marker (chapter 38) says so! Meanwhile, Georgia, Massachusetts, and Rhode Island *all* claim the first use of anesthesia. And markers in Brunswick, Georgia, and Brunswick County, Virginia, battle over where Brunswick stew was born.

A more important result is racism. People who put up markers and monuments and preserve historic houses are usually pillars of the white community. The spate of Martin Luther King Jr. avenues and monuments in the 1970s and 1980s notwithstanding, Americans still live and work in a landscape of white supremacy. Especially in the South, but all across America, even on black college campuses (chapter 47), markers, monuments, and names on the landscape glorify those who fought to keep African Americans in chains as well as those who, after Reconstruction, worked to make them second-class citizens again. In 1999, when this book first came out, readers were amazed to learn that the person who got the most historical markers in any state was not Lincoln in Illinois or Washington in Virginia, but Nathan Bedford Forrest, Confederate cavalry general and first national leader of the Ku Klux Klan, in Tennessee. Moreover, those white Southerners misguided enough *not* to be racist were ignored entirely or converted into "good white Southerners" when remembered. Thus, Helen Keller's birthplace (chapter 49) flew a Confederate flag, while the real Keller was an early supporter of the National Association for the Advancement of Colored People (NAACP).

Other monuments expressed white domination over Native Americans. A later introductory essay, "Hieratic Scale in Historic Monuments," shows how sculptors typically place Native Americans physically lower than European Americans on historic monuments. Whites always wound up in positions of power and action, while people of color were passive on the bottom. Lame Deer, a Dakota leader, sees the same message in the four European American faces carved on Mount Rushmore:

> [T]hese big white faces are telling us, "First we gave you Indians a treaty that you could keep these Black Hills forever, as long as the sun would shine, in exchange for all the Dakotas, Wyoming, and Montana. Then we found the gold and took this last piece of land, because we were stronger, and there were more of us than there were of you, and because we had cannons and Gatling guns. . . . And after we did all this we carved up this mountain,

the dwelling place of your spirits, and put our four gleaming white faces here. We are the conquerors.

The language at historic sites is also warped. All across the country, Americans call Native Americans by tribal names that are wrong and even derogatory. According to these histories on the landscape, Indians are "savage," whites "discover" everything, and some causes portrayed as stainless today were drenched in blood in their own time.

Then there is the matter of who gets memorialized and who gets left out. All too often, memorials heroify people who should not be forgotten, but who should never have been *commemorated*—Jeffrey Amherst, for example, who initiated germ warfare in the Americas and for whom Amherst College and Amherst, Massachusetts, are named (chapter 85). Across America, the landscape has commemorated those men and women who opposed each agonizing next step our nation took on the path toward freedom and justice, while the courageous souls who challenged the United States to live out the meaning of its principles have lain forgotten or even reviled.[1]

Markers and monuments in many states left out women, sometimes so totally as to be unwittingly hilarious. As of the millennium, the only white woman to get a historical marker in Indiana (chapter 30), to take one offending state, got remembered for coming into the state minus a body part she lost in Kentucky! Kentucky, meanwhile, erected (the right word) a female Civil War horse (chapter 32) with an extra body part that turns her into a male! As the preface to this new edition noted, however, a new era has begun to dawn. Virginia is putting up statues of twelve female history-makers on the lawn of its capitol, exactly equaling the number of men already memorialized there. New York's Central Park is about to get Susan B. Anthony and Elizabeth Cady Stanton. Previously, the Park's only women were Mother Goose, Alice in Wonderland, and Juliet, along with some anonymous angels and dancers, compared to about 50 statues of men.

In 1999, historic sites routinely covered up or lied about the sexual orientations of people if those orientations were gay or lesbian. Sex lives, in general, were off-limits. In the late 1990s, when historian Richard Shenkman asked a tour guide at Franklin D. Roosevelt's family mansion in Hyde Park, New York, about Roosevelt's mistresses, she told him, "[T]he guides are specifically forbidden from talking about this." By 2019, we seem to have moved from flat denial to "If asked, will tell."

Just as "Don't ask, don't tell" proved an unstable resting point for the armed forces in the first decade of this millennium, I think many historic sites are about to make further changes in this regard. In 2016, President Obama designated the Stonewall Inn in Greenwich Village a national monument to recognize how its 1969 "riot" sparked the gay rights movement in New York City and nationally. The National Register of Historic Places took in a rowhouse in Washington, DC, because it housed the "Furies Collective," a lesbian group that "led the debate over lesbians' place in American society," according to the National Park Service. So we may be moving toward a public history that recognizes sites *because* of their gay or lesbian history—quite a remove from denial.

Another form of omission still takes place at historic homes, which often do not take their own history seriously enough to bother to tell it like it was. Instead of telling visitors what happened to the people who lived and worked there, guides prattle on about what the guests ate and the silverware they used. Guides almost always avoid negative or controversial facts, and most monuments, markers, and historic sites omit any blemishes that might taint the heroes they commemorate, making them larger and less interesting than life (high school history textbooks do the same thing). Presidents, especially, must be perfect. Woodrow Wilson's house in Washington, DC, says nothing negative about the man who segregated the federal government; a temporary exhibit even credited him with supporting women's suffrage, which he opposed. Even Franklin Pierce, arguably our least popular president, is lauded by the historical marker in his hometown (chapter 88).

But inventing blemish-free heroes has never really worked. High school students don't really buy that the founding fathers were flawless, so they don't think of them as heroes to emulate, even when they were! Instead, they conclude that history textbooks are dishonest. Similarly, adult Americans don't really believe that their exalted forebears were as perfect as their monuments claim. I have watched tourists grow passive while guides tell them quaint stories about dead presidents. They don't know enough to ask about what's being left out, and the social situation doesn't encourage visitors to ask substantive questions, so they just traipse from room to room on automatic pilot. A critical question to ask at any historic site is, "What does it leave out about the people it treats as heroes?"

A special form of these omissions still occurs at war museums, most of which present war without anguish and instead focus genially on its technology.

The battleship museum *USS Intrepid* in New York City mostly leaves out the Vietnam War—too "political" for its board of directors (chapter 82). Omissions such as this can be hard to detect, especially for visitors who come to a site to learn a little history without bringing some knowledge of the site with them. People don't usually think about images that aren't there.

And some images don't exist anywhere. "Pay attention to what they tell you to forget," poet Muriel Rukeyser once wrote, and this book does. Nowhere have I seen portrayed the multicultural nature of pioneer settlements, where Native Americans, European Americans, and often African Americans lived and worked together, sometimes happily. Only a few obscure markers—one each in Utah, Colorado, Louisiana, and Michigan, and two in South Carolina—offer any mention of the trade in Indian slaves that started in 1513 and continued in some places at least until the Emancipation Proclamation in 1863.[2] Yet enslaved Natives were a feature of life in New York City, Charleston, Detroit, and other cities. All across America, the landscape suffers from amnesia, not about everything, but about many crucial events and issues of our past. When the landscape does not omit unpleasant stories entirely, it often tells them badly, even by the mediocre standards set by U.S. history textbooks. Except for the Chief Vann House, a state historic site in Georgia, historic sites and museums in the United States rarely depict Native American farms, frame houses, or schools, compared to the enormous number of tipis on display. Thus, they portray American Indians as mobile and romantic—even when they weren't (chapter 23)! What tourists learn about slavery by visiting most historic sites (chapter 69) is trifling compared to the more accurate information that current textbooks provide to high school students. On Reconstruction, that period after the Civil War when the federal government tried to guarantee equal rights for African Americans, the landscape is almost silent; most sites that do mention it present a *Gone With the Wind* version of *black* bad behavior that never happened (chapter 43). Until the opening of the Montgomery lynching memorial in 2018, our landscape displayed little trace of the lynchings and race riots that swept the United States between 1890 and 1940, the "Nadir of race relations." All across America, monuments to the Spanish-American War, which was over in three months, are inscribed "1898–1902"; few visitors realize that those dates refer to the larger and longer Philippine-American War, which otherwise has mostly vanished from the landscape and from our historical memory (chapter 25).

The antithesis of omission is overemphasis, and the history written on the American landscape is largely the history of the federal governments—the United States of America and the Confederate States of America—and particularly of their wars. We infer much of what we know about the ancient Mayans and Egyptians from their public sculptures and monuments. What will archaeologists ages hence infer about us? That we venerated war above all other human activities?[3]

America has ended up with a landscape of denial. James Buchanan's house denies that our fifteenth president was gay. Fort Pillow denies that Nathan Bedford Forrest's Confederates massacred surrendered U.S. troops there. The National Mining Hall of Fame and Museum denies that mining today causes any environmental damage. And so it goes, from sea to shining sea. These misrepresentations on the American landscape help keep us ignorant as a people, less able to understand what really happened in the past, and less able to apply our understanding to issues facing the United States today.

The thoughtful visitor can learn to read between the lines of historical markers, however, and deconstruct the imagery on historic monuments. Then these sites divulge important insights not only about the eras they describe but also about the eras in which they were built. In short, the lies and omissions memorialized across the American countryside suggest times and ways that the United States went astray as a nation. They also point to unresolved issues in a third era—our own. That's why it may be more important to understand what the historical landscape gets wrong than what it gets right.

So, come along as we visit more than a hundred markers, monuments, houses, and other historic sites in all 50 states and the District of Columbia. Our journey will start in the West, mirroring the journey the first people made as they discovered the Americas and settled it from west to east. People got to the Americas by boat from northeast Asia or by walking across the Bering Strait during an ice age. Most Indians in the Americas can be traced by blood type, language similarity, and other evidence to a very small group of first arrivals. Thus, they may have come by boat. Either way, afoot or by boat, evidence suggests that Native Americans share some cultural and physical similarities with northern Asians to the west of Alaska.

Beginning in the West has the additional benefit of being unconventional. "How refreshing it would be," ethnohistorian James Axtell wrote, "to find a textbook that began on the West Coast before treating the traditional eastern colonies." The usual approach to the American past is from the vantage point of Boston, looking southwestward. Travel books, too, start in New England, even though four Asian countries (Japan, China, Korea, and India) send more tourists to the United States than the top four European nations (the United Kingdom, Germany, France, and Italy).[4] Europeans too—Spaniards—were living in New Mexico years before Anglos had moved to New England or Virginia, so it is doubly appropriate for us to make our trip from west to east. Therefore, we will begin in the state that extends farthest west, Alaska, and end in Maine, farthest east.[5] You don't have to go that direction, however. The Index of States invites you to proceed alphabetically by state or to begin with whatever state interests you, and cross-references within and at the end of entries encourage you to explore topically related entries.

On our journey, not only will we uncover new facts about the American past, but we will also catch indications of hidden fault lines in the social structure of the United States today. Some of these places are familiar to millions of Americans: Boston Common, Valley Forge, the Jefferson Memorial, Abraham Lincoln's log cabin, and Sutter's Fort. Other entries in this book will visit places and tell stories that have *not* been memorialized grandly on the landscape. You will meet people whose existence you may never have imagined—for instance, Elizabeth Van Lew, Robert and Mary Ann Lumpkin, and Patty Cannon—and perhaps learn some facts you never imagined about famous Americans you thought you knew well.

Some of these sites lie far off well-traveled tourist paths and never get into most travel guidebooks. Other markers or statues stand in oft-visited places, but unobtrusively, such as the plaques in the entry halls of state capitols. Although few writers have commented on most of these monuments and markers, they too make a difference, because they represent the thousands of other historic sites all across America that help frame the way we talk about the past yet have never drawn the attention of the historical profession.

These barely known but important sites bring up the critical distinction between what happened in the past versus what we say about it. The former is "the past," the latter "history." Ideally, I believe the two should match. Some people do not agree. In 1925, the American Legion declared that American history, at least when taught to children, "must inspire the children with patriotism," "must be careful to tell the truth optimistically," and "must speak chiefly of success." Since the American past is littered with failures as well as successes and since the past cannot be changed, the Legion would have history lie or say little about the failures. So would a lot of other people. It follows that sites that are important but little-known may have been left out of history because their stories would be unsettling to some Americans. Conversely, nothing much happened in actuality at some allegedly important sites—Valley Forge, for one—but history has made a great to-do about them.

Some monuments and markers tell their stories complexly and accurately, so not every entry will be critical of its site. Sites are also depicted favorably, I'm sure, when their bias matches my own—and my biases can be inferred from the list of heroes to whose memory this book is dedicated. I have chosen these sites to correct historical interpretations that seem profoundly wrong to me and to tell neglected but important stories about the American past. To be honest, I also included a few because they are funny.[6]

Americans share a common history that unites us. But we also share some more difficult events—a common history that divides us. These things too we must remember, for only then can we understand our divisions and work to reduce them. Markers and monuments could help, except too often they suffer from the same forces that created the divisions in the first place. Moreover, most historic sites don't just tell stories about the past; they also tell visitors what to think about the stories they tell. Many sites seek to transform our secular history—events that actually happened on earth, done by real people, with the usual mix of admirable and despicable characteristics—into hallowed milestones along the path of our sacred journey as a nation. But if a monument or marker misrepresents the past or tells it from only one biased viewpoint, then whatever moral imperative it suggests must be suspect. If we cannot face our history honestly, we cannot learn from the past.

Americans agree with this proposition when applied to *other* countries. We commend Germany for preserving concentration camps as monuments of remembrance. We commend the Russians for changing Leningrad back to St. Petersburg rather than continuing to honor a man whose political philosophy wreaked havoc on so many lives.[7] We understand when South Africans, after dethroning white supremacy, set about reevaluating their statues and museum exhibits honoring white supremacists. Surely the United States—like Germany, Russia, or South Africa—needs to rethink its past and reassess how it commemorates that past in stone. Surely we don't want to be people of the lie, complicit with the worst in American history because we cannot stand to acknowledge it. The way we heal is to come face-to-face with the truth, and then we can better deal with it and each other.

I wrote back in 1999 that this process was already underway. Since then, as the preface to this new edition tells, we have made great strides in making our public history more accurate and more candid. Throughout this book, entries will show how history, as remembered in town squares and on highway waysides, has changed over time. Even though monuments are written in stone, they are not permanent. Americans have forever been talking back to the landscape, whether by persuading a state to revise the wording on a historical marker or by vandalizing a statue. On the whole, it is a healthy process. The history written on the American landscape was written by people after all, and *we* the people have the power to take back the landscape and make it ours.

When a site tells an inaccurate or incomplete story, challenging what our public history commemorates can make a difference in our public discourse. Indeed, questioning the myths as told on the American landscape is intrinsically subversive, since the interrogation itself diminishes their power to motivate human behavior, a power that depends on shared belief. Questioning the myths requires serious historical research. Often, the viewpoint of the dominant faction not only rules the landscape but also permeates the history books. In the last 30 years, however, researchers have unearthed new voices from the past and allowed them to speak in their books and articles. Altering the landscape, then, involves expanding our public history by telling about the past from these "new" perspectives. In the process, new markers and monuments will establish new stories and extol new heroes—factually based, with feet of clay when appropriate, but role models

After U.S. forces took New Orleans during the Civil War, Union commander Ben Butler altered the monument to Andrew Jackson in the center of the French Quarter by having the words "The Union Must And Shall Be Preserved" carved into its base. Confederates fumed but had to admit that the phrase was Jackson's, spoken as a toast in the face of separatist John C. Calhoun.[8]

nonetheless. "American history is longer, larger, more various, more beautiful, and more terrible than anything anyone has ever said about it," wrote James Baldwin. The truth is also more wonderful and more terrible than the lies Americans have been telling themselves.

The next five essays provide some tools and provisions for our journey. "Some Functions of Public History" examines the roles that monuments, markers, and other historic sites play for individuals and our society. "The Sociology of Historic Sites" tells how historical markers get created in the first place and suggests that their local nature has both positive and negative implications for the history they relate. "Historic Sites Are Always a Tale of Two Eras" notes that every site can teach visitors not only about the event or person it commemorates but also something about the time of its erection or preservation. Therefore, visitors must consider *both* eras when thinking about what the site says. "Hieratic Scale in Historic Monuments" discusses how the nonverbal symbolism on monuments and memorials influences how visitors think and feel about the topics they commemorate. "Public History After Charlottesville" tells of the ongoing questioning of our white supremacist landscape, inadvertently triggered by two white supremacist events—the murders of nine parishioners in a historic black church in Charleston, South Carolina, in 2015, and the "Unite the Right" rally in Charlottesville, Virginia, two years later. Aided by these discussions and Appendix B, "Ten Questions to Ask at a Historic Site," readers will be better able to critique the next place they visit, even if it is not among the more than a hundred sites described here.

After our tour of lies across America, a final essay will provide some ideas on what to do about the biased texts, inappropriate names, and unfit statues we will have encountered. "Getting into a Dialogue with the Landscape" points out that even though history on the landscape looks permanent, revision constantly takes place. It tells how Americans have changed many sites already and suggests ways that readers can make our markers, monuments, and historic sites tell a fuller, more accurate history. Finally, Appendix C lists twenty candidates that still deserve immediate removal or revision.[9]

1. In the past twenty years, citizens have gotten a few of the worst names removed and exchanged for potential role models, memories of whom have been recovered.
2. Since Mormons broke up the Spanish and Native trade in Basin Indians, Utah is "free" to picture it, which a small marker does, north of Cedar City.
3. Virginia's new statues of women will help correct this overemphasis in one state.

4. More visitors may have arrived from Canada or Mexico, but separating tourists from Canadians and Mexicans who work or shop in the United States is difficult.

5. Within states, entries are in chronological order.

6. Appendix A tells more about selecting the sites.

7. Ironically, Peter the Great also wreaked havoc on individuals in the name of the state.

8. Jackson's precise words were probably, "Our federal union: it must be preserved."

9. Albert Boime, *The Unveiling of the National Icons* (Cambridge: Cambridge UP, 1998), 162–63; Muriel Rukeyser, "Double Ode," in *A Muriel Rukeyser Reader* (NY: Norton, 1994), 274; James Axtell, "Europeans, Indians, and the Age of Discovery in American History Textbooks," *American Historical Review* 92 (1987): 630; U.S. Department of Commerce, "International Visitation in the United States: Market Research," travel. trade.gov; James Baldwin, "A Talk to Teachers," *Saturday Review* (12/21/63), reprinted in Rick Simonson and Scott Walker, eds., *Multi-Cultural Literacy* (St. Paul, MN: Graywolf Press, 1988), 11; Joseph R. Conlin, ed., *Morrow Book of Quotations in American History* (NY: Morrow, 1984), 153; James M. Goode, *The Outdoor Sculpture of Washington, DC* (DC: Smithsonian Institution Press, 1974), 377.

SOME FUNCTIONS OF
PUBLIC HISTORY

Why have Americans put up hundreds of thousands of markers and monuments across the landscape? Why have we preserved thousands of historic houses, forts, and ships? "That the future may learn from the past" is the motto of Colonial Williamsburg. Surely that's a good justification, especially since 83% of all Americans—turned off by their high school history textbooks—never take a course in American history beyond high school.

Unfortunately, learning from the past is hardly the only reason for public history. It's not even the primary reason, including for Colonial Williamsburg itself, which has evolved into a powerful moneymaking machine. "Popular education in history is a market commodity," says Cary Carson, Colonial Williamsburg's Vice President for Research. Boston's Freedom Trail, taking visitors from plaque to building, marker to monument, has become the city's number one tourist attraction. It has been joined by a Women's Heritage Trail, Black Heritage Trail, Literary Trail, and Historical Map of Lesbian and Gay Boston, seeking more niche tourism dollars. It's revealing to examine the various functions—economic, political, social, and cultural, as well as educational—that preserving historic sites and erecting markers and monuments play for individuals and society.

First, there is the role that stories play in human culture. Human beings live by stories. Individuals who have not forged a heroic narrative of their own can nonetheless feel part of something important—in this case, our nation's progress—by identifying with others who performed heroic deeds. Remembering these deeds on the landscape meets this human need.

Putting up markers and monuments and preserving historic sites also allows affluent Americans to feel good about their wealth and fame, their knowledge and civic-mindedness, and often their ancestors. Usually, behind even the simplest aluminum plaque lurks someone who feels good about its installation. The efforts of the upper class to commemorate their history help them feel better psychologically; the results also help them stay upper. History is power. Those on top of society, including John D. Rockefeller and his social-classmates who started Colonial Williamsburg, know this. Therefore, they take the time to determine how history will be remembered.

Historic sites also help hold society together, providing a shared community heritage. Tenth-generation Americans and recent immigrants alike can glory in what the founders achieved in Philadelphia and feel sorrow for the dead listed on the Vietnam Veterans Memorial. Monuments and markers provide sacred sites for what sociologist Robert Bellah called America's "civil religion." Memorials, in particular, declare what is worth dying for, which turns out to be mostly the state, in war. In turn, most American war memorials transform their conflicts into noble causes decided by the will of the people. Consequently, public history, as it is called, usually fosters the civic status quo by praising the government and defending its acts. Rarely do historic markers and monuments criticize the state (chapter 11).

Instead, they make things that were problematic seem appropriate, ordained, even commendable. Why did the United States choose to fight in, say, World War I or Vietnam? Why did the Southern states secede? Why do men (and not women) rule? Why did this particular man rule? These are not easy questions—scholars have written whole books wrestling with them. Most monuments and markers ignore them and proclaim flatly, "Whatever happened was good." Things worth thinking about are converted into things taken for granted. Even a modest plaque on the side of a building helps set a tone that discourages thinking, for it speaks with authority, implying that the community agreed at some point that its message was not only incontestable but also important enough to be on permanent display. The usual emotion at the dedication of most monuments and markers is celebratory, even smug. But a rosy view of the past can help make injustice in the present seem more acceptable.

I have been told that public history doesn't matter. What difference do old monuments in the park really make? Who now even recalls who the county or high school was named after? The fact that Edgefield, South Carolina, dedicated a granite monument to veterans for "preserving our freedom and way of life during the Vietnam War" does not force residents of the town to agree that that was America's role in that war or our reason for intervening. And correcting a historical marker whose language and inaccurate history disrespect American Indians, for instance, doesn't send a single Native American child to college.

Most of us have felt the force of public history, however, written across

America in bronze, aluminum, marble, and granite and in buildings and battlefields preserved for us today. Being at the place where history was made has a certain power. "It may have been *this chair* where Abraham Lincoln sat when he had lunch here," a tourist I did not know whispered as we reached the parlor of the White House of the Confederacy in Richmond (chapter 61). "That gives me the shivers," he continued. The statue of Juan de Oñate in New Mexico (chapter 19) enables some Hispanic visitors to identify with a heroic forebear, while it arouses rage in some Native American visitors at the heroification of a bloody conquistador. The Lincoln Memorial in Washington, DC, prompts visitors to react with pride, regret, elation, sorrow, remorse, happiness, and rededication. The Jefferson Davis Monument in Fairview, Kentucky (chapter 15), prompts some of the same reactions among neo-Confederate sympathizers.

Sometimes, the historical marker becomes more important than the site itself. If the place has changed, plaques offer something to see, a way to connect with the event. For example, my home town, Decatur, Illinois, was the site of the 1860 statewide convention of the Illinois Republican Party. Here, for the first time, Abraham Lincoln's name was put forth for president. I knew this growing up, because in 1915, the Daughters of the American Revolution (DAR) had put a bronze tablet on the side of the bank on the street where a huge tent, "the wigwam," had housed the gathering. That plaque kept the memory of the event alive. In 1970, the DAR put up another plaque with a basrelief of the tent. Then in 2010, to mark its sesquicentennial, a Decatur artist created four bronze

These four stools and a portion of the counter were rescued from the wrecker at the Greensboro Woolworth's and now stand in the Smithsonian's National Museum of American History; four other stools are in the Greensboro Historical Museum.

silhouettes illustrating the event. Since Lincoln entered the convention after the tent was jammed by 2,500 people, he got to the front by being hoisted up and passed hand to hand over the heads of the crowd, so the silhouettes are dramatic and amusing. They keep alive the memory of the event, even though parked cars now occupy most of the street.

Even when the countryside hasn't changed much, as is the case for the monuments commemorating the Mountain Meadows Massacre in southern Utah, in itself the landscape reveals little of what happened at the site more than a century earlier. The story is told on the marker or monument—or it should be.

Historic sites even take on a celebrity of their own. Stone Mountain in Georgia is an obvious example, visited by tourists who have no interest in the Civil War, much less any leaning toward the Confederacy. They simply want to see what is reputed to be the world's largest monument (chapter 53). Even lowly historical markers can "put a town on the map"—I know of two different small towns whose residents hijacked and hid their only marker when they learned that the state had threatened to remove it because it was inaccurate.

The economic function of public history can provide a mechanism for civic improvement. For at least twenty years, the state of Alabama has been aware that black visitors spend green money, just as white visitors do. Its one-page handout to entice visitors is headed "Alabama: Fun and Games Begin Here," with five woodcuts below. The first is of Martin Luther King Jr., followed by a golfer. The juxtaposition of title and pictures is truly jarring: there is no way to fit the Birmingham church where the KKK bombed four girls at Sunday school, King's own church in Montgomery, or now the new museum about the Scottsboro Boys under the heading "Fun and Games." The order of the images, with King first, however, implies that the state believes that more visitors will come to see Civil Rights sites than to golf, visit historic homes, see Civil War battlefields, or learn about Alabama's role in the space program. Readers who want to create more accurate public history can use this awareness that it can be good for the bottom line in a community, not just for its residents' knowledge and humanity.

What a community erects on its historical landscape not only sums up its view of the past but also influences its possible futures. Returning to our Vietnam example, it is hard for residents of Edgefield to honor Americans who fought *against* the Vietnam War so long as their downtown monument credits those who fought *in* the war for being right. It will always seem right for whites to command our governments, law firms, and corporations, so long as whites are on top of our statues, "helping" and dominating African Americans and Native Americans on the bottom. It is hard for Southern whites today to emulate or even learn about white Southerners who enlisted in the Union armies or fought for black rights during Reconstruction, so long as every Southern courthouse town boasts a monument conflating the Confederate cause with "Deo Vindice" (God Our Vindicator) and "states' rights." It is harder for women to win election as president so long as many Americans believe that women have done little up to now, partly because monuments and markers omit their actions. What one generation puts on the landscape thus becomes a force imprisoning the minds of the generations that follow.

On the other hand, recognizing local history on the landscape helps empower people to make more local history. And, as Congressman Tip O'Neill said about politics, ultimately all history is local—it happened *here*. The first woman to win office in the community, the racial desegregation of the school, the town's response to a natural disaster, the most important people and ideas that have come from the area—all these are worthy of note, and noting them may make it more likely that townspeople will continue to do things worthy of note. In every locale, markers and monuments can define what that community has done and can symbolize its citizens' aspirations. Our challenge is to create a public history that functions for *us* as we go about our business as Americans, which is to bring into being the America of the future.[1]

1. Cary Carson, remarks at conference at National Museum of American History, 3/98; Archer H. Shaw, ed., *The Lincoln Encyclopedia*, Peoria speech, 10/16/1854 (NY: Macmillan, 1950), 364; John Bodnar, *Remaking America* (Princeton: Princeton UP, 1992), 19–20; William Graham Sumner, *Folkways* (NY: New American Library, 1940 [1906]), 80.

THE SOCIOLOGY OF HISTORIC SITES

Desperate to cause change in their city and nation, student demonstrators in Beijing in 1989 recognized the power of monuments to move people. Students erected a styrofoam and plaster statue, "Goddess of Liberty," opposite Mao's portrait in Tiananmen Square to symbolize their aspirations and legitimize their acts. The Chinese government likewise recognized the symbolic power of the Goddess. "This statue is illegal," blared government loudspeakers. "It is not approved by the government. Even in the United States, statues need permission before they can be put up."

Indeed, they do. Americans are not as free as Chinese students may have hoped we are, or as we ourselves might like to think. Statues, historical markers, and monuments *do* need approval before they can be put up on public property, and only certain kinds *have* gone up. Reviewing the process by which markers and monuments get erected and historic sites get preserved may help explain why so many tell bad history. We begin with historical markers.

Historians usually credit (or blame) Virginia for starting statewide highway marker programs in 1927, although New York started the same year; Colorado, Indiana, and Pennsylvania may have put up markers earlier; and Massachusetts had 234 markers in place by 1930. Of course, towns, local organizations, the Daughters of the American Revolution (DAR), and individuals were putting up plaques long before any states got involved.

Early state markers were usually the creation of the state marker office, which typically boasted a staff of one person who may or may not have earned a graduate degree in history. As a result, some early markers use offensive terminology and commemorate events that never happened.

In the late 1950s and early 1960s, many states hired staff members with backgrounds in history or set up review boards for marker texts or both. Consequently, in these states (Colorado, Georgia, Kansas, Mississippi, Texas, Virginia, and West Virginia, for example), recent markers are more accurate and more inclusive. Texas has been making a particular effort to ensure that women get included at sites where they played a role. Pennsylvania got a private foundation grant in 1990 for 66 new markers treating African American history in Philadelphia. The final essay in this book, "Getting into a Dialogue with the Landscape," tells of wording changes underway in Virginia and other states.

In the 1980s and 1990s, some states closed down their marker programs altogether. General governmental retrenchment was responsible, along with the realization that interstate highways, where stopping between exits is prohibited, now draw the bulk of travelers, especially from out of state. Some other states went to a pay-as-you-go basis: organizations can erect an official state marker only if they pay for it themselves. Usually, the content of such markers is negotiated between the local group and the state marker office.

Different states have different rules, but most require some passage of time before a marker can go up. Georgia, for example, requires an event to have taken place "generally at least 50 years ago" or, if the proposed marker is about a person, that they be dead at least "generally 50 years." Some states require as little as 20 or 30 years, and most allow for exceptions for especially important events or people, as Georgia does by saying "generally."

Most states have some criteria about the importance of the event or person to be honored. Georgia sets up four options:

a. A military operation, including . . . conflicts with Native Americans;

c. A meeting of persons, the results of which were of lasting historical importance;

c. An artistic creation . . . [or] mechanical device, which has been of lasting value to society; or

d. An act of such historic importance as to have changed the course of history of the state or nation.

The applicant is to meet this burden of proof "with documentation in the form of proper footnotes and a bibliography," preferably including references to primary sources. Proposed texts are vetted by the State Historical Marker Review Committee, which consists of members of the Georgia National Register Review Board. Review boards usually include people from different parts of the state and different racial and ethnic groups; some may have educational or occupational backgrounds in history. Under Billy Townsend, who directed the Georgia program from 1970 to 2001, Georgia put up "a lot of women's historic markers and black historic markers, because basically for the first 30 years it was white men," in Townsend's words. Nevertheless, his office and review board didn't have the final say. "If a legislator called with a complaint [about a marker]," he admitted, "we'd take it down!"

Unlike Townsend, most marker officers take no initiative. For instance, in the words of Jon Austin, executive director of the Illinois State Historical Society in 1999, "We are reactive, not proactive." It shows; Illinois still has only a handful of markers about individual women, for example, and none for such organizations as the General Federation of Women's Clubs founded in Chicago in 1890, which had a million members by 1910; the Woman's Christian Temperance Union, historically an extremely important organization, whose headquarters are in Evanston; or the League of Women Voters, founded in a Chicago hotel in 1920.

Michigan boasts three accurate markers about the 1936 General Motors sit-down strike, a good summary of the life of Malcolm X in front of his boyhood home in Lansing, and credible markers on Native Americans. But its historical marker for Orville Hubbard, the notorious racist mayor of Dearborn, never mentions Hubbard's lifelong segregationist policies (chapter 34). Robin Peebles, who ran Michigan's marker program when the marker went up in the mid-1980s, wanted Hubbard's marker to say he was a segregationist but was told, "We can't say that; let's just say everything that we *can* say." The result is a marker commending Hubbard as an "effective administrator"!

Markers and monuments are often written in stone, but they are not written by gods. People put them up. Although good texts do go up, the process has also gone awry on occasion in every state. When you see a roadside marker, take in what it tells but also ask, "How might this be wrong?" One giveaway is the use of qualifying phrases introducing statements of fact, as in, "According to tradition . . . " or "According to the legislature . . . " Visitors can count on the rest of such sentences to be unsubstantiated.

Monuments are even less likely than state historical markers to tell or symbolize impartial history, partly because no relatively disinterested statewide commission reviews what they say or portray. It is harder to summarize the process that creates monuments, because, unlike historical markers, each monument is different. But some general statements can be made. Much effort—personal, political, and physical—is required to put up a monument or preserve a house. Little plaques on their backs often disclose the monuments' sponsors, but monuments credited to private individuals or organizations also involve some public decision making and usually some public monies. Often, a private club raises part of a monument's cost and persuades a municipality, county, or state to pay the rest. Even when all the expense is borne privately, a public entity usually contributes to the site and maintains the monument thereafter. Conversely, even publicly funded monuments are often forced into being by pressure from private organizations. Visitors need to understand why those who put up the monument went to such trouble—choosing the location, getting governmental approval, mobilizing support, paying for, designing, building, and finally erecting it. Appendix B supplies ten questions visitors can ask wherever history is told to them. To ask these questions is to explore the sociological importance and ideological purpose of the monument, marker, or site.

My 1995 book *Lies My Teacher Told Me* examined how Americans present the past in high school history textbooks. Textbooks have no plaques on their backs revealing their sponsorship, but they too are written by people, not gods, despite their all-knowing monotone. Textbooks also pass through a process, not unlike that for markers and monuments: sales representatives lobby municipal, county, or state governmental bodies to get them adopted. Unlike markers and monuments, however, textbooks are developed as national products intended for the entire United States. Most historic markers and monuments are products of local discussions. This makes for several differences.

For example, I faulted textbooks for downplaying Indian wars, especially those in the East. Perhaps the most violent Indian war was King Philip's War, which ravaged New England in 1675–76. While many U.S. history textbooks leave it out entirely, 11% of the 234 markers that Massachusetts put up in 1930 for its 300th anniversary dealt with King Philip's War. Another 10% treated other Indian wars. By contrast, only 2.6% mentioned the Revolutionary War. That's because King Philip's War cost more American lives in combat in Massachusetts than the Revolution did throughout the entire United States.[1] King Philip's War touched virtually every Massachusetts town. The Revolutionary War did not. Conflict with Native Americans similarly gets much attention in West Virginia (20.1% of 750 historical markers[2]), Georgia, Ohio, North Dakota, and many other states. Indeed, the American landscape is filled with reminders of Indian wars that have almost vanished from our written history. Some of these markers exemplify what historian Francis Jennings calls "the cant of conquest" (chapters 7, 35, and 66), but no one reading

Unions have put up monuments in almost every state. Even on the grounds of state capitols, labor has demonstrated its power, erecting "The Coal Miner" in Springfield, Illinois, and Indianapolis, Indiana, and this fireman, toppled only temporarily during construction at the Texas capitol in Austin. Elsewhere a lumberman donated a monument of three loggers in Bangor, Maine; a bronze garment worker toils at his sewing machine on Seventh Avenue in Manhattan; and granite workers in Barre, Vermont, have memorialized a quarry worker in—what else?—granite.

them can fail to understand that Native Americans lived all across America and contested the seizure of their land and homes.

The landscape is also superior to American history textbooks in its portrayal of conflicts between workers and owners. I had expected to find that America's rather bloody history of strikes and strikebreaking would be invisible on the American landscape. But I had overlooked the power of labor unions. Chapter 9 tells how labor unions have marked the sites of many bloody confrontations with management and police forces across the United States. It also tells of the markers and monuments documenting some of the disasters that have killed scores of workers in factories and mines across America. On reflection, these representations of workers and labor issues should not have surprised me. Labor unions have precisely the three factors needed to influence state marker offices: political influence, some historical expertise, and money for the marker.[3]

If labor sometimes wins representation in stone, the upper class always does. According to Susan Schreiber of the National Trust for Historic Preservation, all of the first nineteen sites the trust acquired were originally "owned by the elite" except the Usonian house, which architect Frank Lloyd Wright created for the average American—and the Usonian house is displayed on the grounds of Woodlawn, a plantation mansion in Virginia![4] All across America, every town of any substance has its historic house museum, usually in a mansion. In some places, log cabins have been saved—and even invented!—but the upper class gets represented everywhere.

Although the localness of most historic sites can be a force for factual history, more often the resulting provincialism prompts fallacious history. The problem is, communities usually recognize only their happy history on the landscape—the impressive people, the events that most residents can take pride in. Vermont has stated the goals of its historical marker program:

> Provide the traveling public with an awareness of the contributions of Vermont in history and prehistory. . . . Foster a sense of the past and pride among Vermonters. Educate the public to an understanding of the factors influencing Vermont's development and the contributions Vermont has made to the development of the United States. Provide visitors who are entering the state with a sense of its past. Encourage positive attitudes toward historic resources.[5]

Fostering "pride among Vermonters" may foster other attitudes my thesaurus likens to "pride": arrogance, conceit, condescension, disdain, haughtiness, hubris, and immodesty. These by-products might reasonably result from presenting a state's past as a story of progress and goodness, something simply to be proud of.

Following this policy, one historical marker on Colchester Avenue in Burlington states, "The mortal remains of Ethan Allen, fighter, writer, statesman, and philosopher, lie in this cemetery beneath the marble statue. His spirit is in Vermont now." This is hardly a Native American perspective; Abenakis see Allen as a rapacious Indian-hater who manufactured pretexts to steal Indian land. Thus, a tale that arouses pride—with all its synonyms—in one Vermonter may offend and alienate another. Yale professor Robin Winks has criticized historical markers across America as "inert, pointless exercises in the most obscure forms of ancestor worship." This Vermont marker is a good example: its worship of Allen derails any attempt to convey concrete information about the man, so the visitor leaves with no idea of what he did in Vermont or even when he lived.

Our tour of historic sites will lead to many places affected by such local boosterism. Two different towns in Rhode Island claim the site of Massasoit's Spring, named for the great "friend of the white man," when the Pilgrims landed in Massachusetts (chapter 90). Kentucky and Missouri both claim Daniel Boone's bones. Sometimes these "local history wars" can get quite local, such as markers just eight miles apart in New Hampshire, each claiming to be the site of the first public library in the United States (chapter 87).

The sociology of knowledge studies what and how people think. By "knowledge," sociologists mean not only fact but also error, lies as well as truth, and also art, poetry, religion, law, and other intellectual products that can hardly be labeled "true" or "false." One approach the sociology of knowledge takes is to examine the institutional framework within which "knowledge" is produced. This chapter has begun to analyze the organizational and social contexts that influence what our markers, monuments, and historic places say about the past. The next chapter will look at the art, size, and location of historical monuments, which relate to the influence they wield. Understanding these issues can help visitors avoid being taken in by the lies our public history tries to tell. So can Appendix B, "Ten Questions to Ask at a Historic Site."[6]

1. I include lives lost on both sides of King Philip's War, since Wampanoags and Narragansetts are now U.S. citizens. Including only colonial deaths, King Philip's War was nevertheless more deadly than the French and Indian War, War of 1812, or Spanish-American War.

2. This figure is as of 1999.

3. For photographs and descriptions of labor memorials, see *Labor's Heritage* (spring 1995).

4. As of 2019, the Trust has broadened slightly to include three governmental structures: the Cooper-Malera Adobe in California, Gaylord Building on the Illinois-Michigan Canal, and "Lincoln's Cottage" in the Soldiers and Sailors Cemetery in Washington, DC. It also associates with a handful of other sites that are not rich mansions but does not own them.

5. I omit two goals advocating historic preservation.

6. "GA Historical Marker Application" (Atlanta: GA Parks, Recreation, and Historic Sites Division, typescript, 1996), 1–2; W.J.T. Mitchell, ed., *Art and the Public Sphere* (Chicago: U. of Chicago Press, 1992), 29; Francis Jennings, *The Invasion of America: Indians, Colonialism, and the Cant of Conquest* (Chapel Hill: U. of NC Press, 1975); *Labor's Heritage* (spring 1995): 40; Kenneth E. Foote, *Shadowed Ground* (Austin: U. of TX Press, 1997), 82–84; Billy Townsend, conversation, 1/96; Richard Shenkman, undated letter, 1996; Yvonne Farley, email, 5/4/96; Lawrence D. Weiss, "Hawk's Nest—The Murder of 764 Workers," *People's Daily World* 2/1/90; Susan Schreiber, letter, 4/96; Robin Winks, "A Public Historiography," *Public Historian* 14(3): 96–98, 105; William A. Haviland and Marjory W. Power, *The Original Vermonters* (Hanover, NH: UP of New England, 1981), 243.

HIERATIC SCALE IN
HISTORIC MONUMENTS

Monuments convey both less and more than historical markers. They tell less history because they usually have fewer words. In addition, their words are usually chosen to inspire rather than inform. Thus, monuments are more likely to instruct visitors on how to think and feel about the topic they commemorate. The word "monument" comes from the Latin *monere*, to remind, admonish, instruct. One way they do this is through their art. Since memory is an intensely visual medium, the images monuments show us often linger in memory long after we have forgotten the words they tell us.

Everything you see in a monument has been put there for a reason. Its size, the materials from which it was made, and its position relative to the viewer and to nearby buildings and surrounding elements result from a complex decision-making process that usually involves an artist, the committee that hired the artist, leaders of a sponsoring organization, public officials, and whoever is paying for it all. While pragmatic concerns like money and feasibility do enter into these decisions, the effort is calculated to make an impression upon the visitor. Understanding this allows one to view monuments more analytically. One can still be deeply moved by them—as I am by several monuments in this book—while identifying how they make their impact.

Monuments (and many markers) are intended to elicit more than an abstract interest in the past. To begin, most monuments say, "I am important." Some communicate this by being large, even huge—imagine the shout of "Timberrrr" that would be fitting for the toppling of the Washington Monument! Even small memorials are usually built for the ages, made of granite, marble, bronze, and the like. These materials assert, "This mattered and should be honored," because they imply that generations far into the future will still want to know about the persons or events they depict.

The grandeur of monuments intrinsically includes an element of consecration, which not only sanctifies the past but also sanctions future actions. Their very existence implies that the person or event portrayed is worth emulating

or the cause symbolized is worth advancing. They embody a moral imperative: go thou and do likewise.

Their landscaping also implies that the people and events remembered on
monuments were important and should be honored. In *The Theory of the
Leisure Class*, Thorstein Veblen suggests that the rich prove their affluence
and hence their worth partly by commanding others to do *useless* work for
them. Useless work is key, Veblen points out. After all, a middle-income
farmer can pay a full-time worker to help grow crops on his 240 acres without demonstrating high status—that's just how the farmer makes his living.
But a financier who pays a full-time gardener to mow and weed the ten acres
around his mansion in a wealthy suburb makes no money off his land. On
the contrary, keeping it nice proves he knows the aesthetic meaning of "nice"
and has the money to achieve it. The extensive lawns and plantings around
historic monuments represent similar expenditure on behalf of the persons
commemorated—money spent to declare and ensure their status.

When trash around a statue is not picked up and its landscaping goes to
weed, the person it commemorates probably no longer commands our historical imagination. In Chicago's Grant Park stands a splendid statue of John
Logan carved in 1897 by Augustus Saint-Gaudens. Logan was an important citizen-general during the Civil War who then helped found the Grand
Army of the Republic. When I visited it in 1999, only a few ducks paid any
attention to him. One plaque had been ripped off, probably for its scrap
value, and derelicts slept at the monument in broad daylight. Logan helped
establish Memorial Day to remember Civil War veterans, but his own monument lay forgotten.[1]

Many towns built massive monuments to the soldiers and sailors who
fought in World War I. But that "war to end wars" didn't, as Americans
found out in 1941. The result is visible across America in the neglect of
many World War I memorials. After World War II ended, most communities were not about to rush out to commemorate it because their experience
with World War I memorials had soured them on the enterprise. Moreover,
the Cold War began immediately, so no one could be sure that the fruits of
victory included peace. Monuments built for World War II are comparatively
modest. Some merely add plaques to World War I monuments even though
World War II lasted more than twice as long and took more than twice as
many American lives as World War I.

Size conveys importance. Monuments also communicate eminence by

In front of St. Cloud Hospital in St. Cloud, Minnesota, stands a major monument "Erected in 1952 to the memory of Reverend Francis Xavier Pierz, 'Father of the Diocese of St. Cloud,' 1785–1880." Father Pierz stands above a kneeling white parishioner, both of whom loom over a seated American Indian, who seems eager to take their instruction.

how they portray a person. Thus, the statue of George Washington in the National Museum of American History has the body of a Greek god even though he didn't. Similarly, Jefferson Davis sits on a horse at Stone Mountain, Georgia, alongside his generals Robert E. Lee and Stonewall Jackson even though as president of the Confederacy he spent most of his time behind a desk. We look up to men on horseback, physically and figuratively. Ever since the invention of the automobile, sculptors have scrambled to figure out ways to get passersby to look up to the people they are characterizing.

All across America, monuments depict whites in dominant positions over Native Americans. In front of Ysleta Mission in El Paso, Texas, is a monument put up by the Knights of Columbus that features an obsequious Native American kneeling at the feet of a conquistador. On the grounds of the Illinois State Capitol stands Father Menard, again with an Indian subservient to him. Further east, in Plattsburgh, New York, Samuel de Champlain stands on a pedestal, towering above a kneeling Native. This monument exemplifies European cultural imperialism in two additional ways. First, the sculptor did not bother to depict an Abenaki or Mohawk—Indians who lived and live yet on the shores of Lake Champlain. Instead, he sculpted a Plains Indian, complete with full feathered headdress! (A ten-minute walk through the woods near the lake would have disabused him of the appropriateness of such an item.) Also, Champlain is fully clothed with a cloak and cape, while the Indian is almost naked. Depending on the weather on that spring day in 1609 when Native Americans showed Champlain the lake he "discovered," either the Indian was freezing or Champlain was perspiring. Of course, the

Sometimes the pressure to conform to hieratic scale is so strong that it prompts artists to muddle the stories they purport to tell. On the grounds of the Iowa State Capitol in Des Moines are these three figures, entitled "The Pioneers." According to a clipping that probably dates to the monument's dedication in 1892, the triad represents a "father and son guided by a friendly Indian, in search of a home." Such is the power of the social archetype of the defeated Indian that the sculptor has shown him seated subserviently while the white man stands gazing capably ahead. The sculptor has removed what literary theorists call "agency" from the Native American. Only viewers who have read somewhere that the Indian is the guide will ever see him that way.[2]

two aren't supposed to be realistic; the clothing is simply part of the language of power. So is naming the lake for the leader of the first whites to visit it. (Chapter 7 suggests problems with "discover.")

All these artistic conventions are called "hieratic scale" in sculpture—"hier-" as in "hierarchy"—and date back to depictions of Pharaoh and Christ.

African Americans also look up to European Americans on monuments all across the country. In Washington, DC, in Lincoln Park, east of the Capitol, stands the first statue of Abraham Lincoln put up after his death. It reads:

FREEDOM'S MEMORIAL

In grateful memory of Abraham Lincoln, this monument was erected by the Western Sanitary Commission of St. Louis, Missouri: with funds contributed solely by emancipated citizens of the U.S. declared free by his proclamation January 1, A.D. 1863.

Crouched at Lincoln's feet, his chains still on but broken, is a semi-naked African American. The monument shows the respect African Americans felt for Lincoln and also plays the important role of representing Lincoln's role as Great Emancipator and his concern—often inconsistent, to be sure—for black civil rights. In the words of William G. Eliot, a friend of the escaped slave who was the sculptor's model, the slave in the monument "has grasped

For years the tomb of Ulysses Grant on Manhattan's Upper West Side languished under trash, graffiti, and neglect. Its sad condition precisely paralleled the lamentable reputation his presidential administration received in our history textbooks after 1890. Between 1896 and 1954, when America's legal and social systems agreed that African Americans "obviously" should be locked into second-class citizenship, any leaders who acted as if they believed otherwise "must have" done so for personal or political gain. Hence scandals, which did occur under Grant, came to define his administration. In 1997, after the Civil Rights Movement made it possible for historians gradually to again credit Grant's administration for its important early accomplishments in race relations, the National Park Service gave his tomb a splendid restoration. This photo shows it decked with bunting for its centennial. It remains to be seen whether textbook authors will follow suit.

the chain as if in the act of breaking it, indicating the historical fact that the slaves took an active part in their own deliverance." Inadvertently, however, the sculpture also shows the power of the cultural archetype over nonwhite as well as white minds, because it follows the conventions of hieratic scale.[3]

At Tuskegee Institute in Alabama, a similar statue varies the theme: Booker T. Washington stands, removing the cloak of ignorance from the young African American man who kneels before him. Aware of Washington's accommodationist stance vis-á-vis the white power structure around 1900, Tuskegee undergraduates joke about whether he is taking off or putting back the cloak.[4]

The huge Indiana State Soldiers' and Sailors' Monument dominates "The Circle" in downtown Indianapolis. The Civil War monument includes many figures—men fight in battle, reunited sweethearts kiss, etc. All are white except the lowest figure on the sculpture. He is a former slave, again semi-reclining. He holds up his arm with dangling broken chains, apparently in thankful supplication to the fair woman, presumably "Columbia," symbolizing the nation, who has smashed his shackles for him. No African American could possibly take pride in this representation. He lies passive, conveying no hint that nearly 200,000 African Americans, including some from Indiana, fought in the army and navy of the United States during the Civil War. Thus, although it celebrates the end of slavery and does allow an African American a bit part, the monument still conveys white supremacy. Whites built it in 1889, well after the end of Reconstruction, when the United States was pushing African Americans back into second-class citizenship. Thirty-five years later, the Ku Klux Klan dominated the state. The Klan would parade around and around the monument because its white supremacy was mirrored symbolically on the tableau.

Gender is an important element of social relations, and patriarchy is an important element of hierarchy in America. Does it show on the landscape? Some monuments do show women in inferior positions. The most common example is the generic plaque on many Spanish-American War monuments (chapter 25). It shows a native woman kneeling like the ex-slave, with her chains broken, facing the white Americans who seem to have smashed them. More often, women are at the top of monuments. But these women are neither specific individuals nor do they symbolize women generically. Instead, they usually represent the state, liberty, or angels of peace, comfort, or death. The woman of the Spanish-American War monuments kneels not because of her gender, but because she is native.

So far as I know, all but one of the women "on top" are white. The exception crowns the dome of the U.S. Capitol. She is a bronze woman called the "Statue of Freedom." Many tourists take her to be an American Indian because she wears a buffalo robe and her helmet is topped by an eagle's head and flowing plumage. Also, the colonies, and later the new nation, often used an Indian to represent liberty. Ironically her headdress is neither American Indian nor does it represent liberty. Jefferson Davis, secretary of war during the Pierce administration, objected to the original design, a "liberty cap" worn by French revolutionaries. He worried that this was a Yankee protest against slavery or might give slaves ideas of freedom. He ordered a feathered helmet encircled by stars instead. The "Statue of Freedom" figure has always been Roman, but if most Americans think she is an Indian, then for practical purposes she has become Native American.

Generic images of women do get on the landscape. The Daughters of the American Revolution put up "Madonna of the Trail" statues all across America, from Pomona, California, to Bethesda, Maryland, in 1928, commemorating women pioneers.[5] Other examples abound, such as "The Pilgrim Mother" in Plymouth, Massachusetts. Gender bias becomes clearer when we move from generic figures to individual women. Representations of real women from history are much less common than those of men, partly because so many monuments across the United States memorialize war. Even in peacetime, however, important specific women are not recognized on the landscape in many states, while less important men are (chapters 30 and 41).

Hieratic scale shows in other ways as well. At Manassas Battlefield in Virginia, Stonewall Jackson rides a horse that has muscles on its muscles. No horse ever looked like this, and Jackson's surely did not. Again we are to be in awe of the horse's power and, by extension, of Jackson. Chapter 32 tells how even mares must be male, and chapter 19 tells how even a lithe Spanish horse ends up a Budweiser Clydesdale.

As women, workers, people of color, and others whose stories have not been told on the American landscape gain recognition, a question arises: will they get the same type of embodiments as white men of high status, or will more humane conceptions replace the canons of hieratic scale? It is too early to tell. But there is something paradoxical about Martin Luther King Jr. towering over us as he emerges from a boulder—he who helped lead a movement of "ordinary" people and risked jail to gain equal rights for all.

Two recent monuments to famous women give hope that new conventions may replace hieratic scale. In Chicago, a series of interlinked hands represents Jane Addams, while the Eleanor Roosevelt statue in New York makes her life-sized and approachable. Perhaps bronze and marble will give way to new materials—holography, sound, mobile phone messages, websites. Perhaps Americans can put up enough new monuments honoring hitherto neglected people and events in enough new forms that we will relegate hieratic scale to a period in our past, like Art Deco. At that point, monuments will no longer have to be, well, monumental, to succeed in touching their visitors and revealing important aspects of our past.

The next chapter treats the chronological contexts of markers and monuments because *when* history was written or symbolized helps explain *how*.[6]

1. In 2012, a private citizen, Lawrence Pucci, a tailor, paid to spruce up the monument, and a rededication was held. Since then, Chicago has used the monument annually for a Memorial Day commemoration. See Susan Chandler, "Logan's Hero," *Chicago Tribune*, 2/15/2004.

2. The monument also leaves out females entirely, although we may doubt whether the father bore and raised his son by himself.

3. A similar statue entitled "The Emancipation" stands in Park Square, Boston.

4. A similar statue stands in front of Booker T. Washington High School in Atlanta. In *Invisible Man*, Ralph Ellison appropriated the student line.

5. Harry S. Truman was in charge of siting these statues.

6. Charles L. Griswold, "The Vietnam Veterans Memorial and the Washington Mall," in Harriet F. Senie and Sally Webster, eds., *Critical Issues in Public Art* (NY: Harper Collins, 1992), 74; Mike Teskey, email 9/96; Lee Friedlander, *The American Monument* (NY: Eakins, 1976), unpaginated; Philip T. Drotning, *Guide to Black History* (Garden City, NY: Doubleday, 1968), 46; Margo Gayle and Michelle Cohen, *Guide to Manhattan's Outdoor Sculpture* (NY: Prentice Hall, 1988); James M. Goode, *The Outdoor Sculpture of Washington, DC* (Washington, DC: Smithsonian Press, 1974), 60; William G. Eliot, *The Story of Archer Alexander* (Boston: Cupples, Upham, 1885), 1.

HISTORIC SITES ARE
ALWAYS A TALE OF
TWO ERAS

Whether monumental in scale or just a small plaque affixed to a building, every historic site tells two different stories about two different eras in the past. One is its manifest narrative—the event or person heralded in its text or artwork. The other is the story of its erection or preservation. The images on our monuments and the language on our markers reflect the attitudes and ideas of the time when Americans put them up, often many years after the event. Americans have typically adjusted the visible past on the landscape to make what we remember conform to the needs of the current time. To understand a marker or monument we must not only analyze what it says and how it looks but also when it was unveiled. To understand a historic site we need to know when its interpretation—what the guides show and tell—was established. Why was this story told then? What audience was it aimed at? How would the story differ if we were telling it today, or in another 50 years? Too often our historic sites relate inaccurate and misleading history owing to the ideological demands of the time and the purpose of their erection or preservation.[1]

One way to ferret out bias is to see what historians writing in *other* eras said about the event. What would people have thought if this had been put up when the person still lived or the event had just happened? Another approach is to return to primary sources, making sure to include sources from all acting groups. Learning about when the marker or monument went up takes us out of the present to reveal why people then chose that person or event to commemorate. Pondering what people will say 50 years hence about this site takes us out of the present in the opposite direction and can help disclose limitations in our vision today. When examined thoughtfully with these cautions in mind, historic sites always reveal something—accurate or inaccurate—about the period they describe and the period when they went up or were preserved . . . and perhaps about our own time as well.

The foregoing paragraphs form an introduction to the concept of historiography—perhaps the most important tool that historians offer the world. Unfortunately, very few Americans, even teachers of history and social studies in K-12 schools, know the concept, so they cannot teach it to others. Historiography, most simply, means the study of history, but not in the sense of, "Oh gosh, I'm behind, I've got to do historiography this weekend!" Historiography means the study of the *writing* of history. It asks us to look at a piece—an article, textbook, historical marker, even a photograph—and ask, who wrote this (or built it or painted it, etc.)? Who did *not*? Whose perspective is omitted? What was the author's purpose? And so on.

All this relates to the question of historical perspective. The passage of time, some people assume, somehow provides perspective. State historical marker programs implicitly make this assumption when they require that 30 or 50 years elapse after an event before a marker can commemorate it. Unfortunately, it is more common to invoke historic perspective than to think cogently about it.

I have found useful a distinction that some societies in East and Central Africa make. According to religious scholar John Mbiti, Kiswahili speakers divide the deceased into two categories: sasha and zamani. The recently departed whose time on earth overlapped with people still here are the sasha, living-dead. They are not wholly dead, for they live on in the memories of the living, who can call them to mind, create their likeness in art, and bring them to life in anecdote. When the last person to know an ancestor dies, that ancestor leaves the sasha for the zamani, the dead. As generalized ancestors, the zamani are not forgotten but revered. Many, like our George Washington or Clara Barton, can be recalled by name. But they are not living-dead. There is a difference. By extension, a person's sasha is that period when they were aware of societal happenings. For me, born in 1942, my sasha would be from about 1952 to the present. Before 1952, history is zamani for me.

Historical perspective does not always accrue from the passage from sasha to zamani. On the contrary, more accurate history—certainly more detailed history—can often be written while an event lies in the sasha. For then people on all sides still have firsthand knowledge of the event. Primary source material, on which historians rely, comes from the sasha. To assume that historians or sociologists can make better sense of it later in the zamani is merely chronological ethnocentrism.

Monuments lend little support to the idea of historical perspective. Many monuments and most tombstones are products of the sasha. Family members often erect memorials to their beloved dead within weeks of their passing from the living into the sasha. In a sense, this is the most local history of all, and sometimes the most accurate. Sasha monuments are often located in cemeteries or quiet parks. Sasha monuments and markers often simply remember an event and those who died in it, often listing them (and sometimes the living) by name.[2]

Zamani monuments are usually quite different. Not primarily motivated by loss or grief, zamani monuments and markers usually go up to serve the political exigencies of the time of their erection. They make the ideological point their erectors need to make to respond to those exigencies. They seek to influence how people behave by telling them what to think about the ancestor, event, or cause they commemorate. Often zamani monuments get put up downtown, where their presence on important public land at the courthouse or city hall implies that the community is united in the sentiments they express. People who do not share their sentiments and would not seek them out in cemeteries or parks will see them and presumably be influenced by them in these locations.

One reason to delay putting up markers and monuments is to avoid controversies about people and events still in the sasha. But the end of a controversy may not signal agreement on a disinterested consensus account. In *Political Influence*, Edward C. Banfield analyzed local governments as arenas of competing interest groups. Often no one group can get its way so long as other groups are strong enough to create a controversy. Thus, various groups have informal veto power. Decades after an event, however, some groups may have lapsed into inactivity, lost social power, died out, or moved on to other issues, leaving one individual or group to decide how an event is remembered. When only one segment of society—usually the white elite—controls public memory, distorted history is the result.

During the Nadir of race relations, from 1890 until about 1940, white supremacists had the power to determine how the Civil War and Reconstruction would be remembered in the South, having disfranchised African Americans outright and terrorized white Republicans into submission. After 1890, in an important sense, the South, or rather the white neo-Confederate South, won the Civil War. They won it because they won what secession was all about: white supremacy. Of course, the South had seceded specifically to maintain and extend slavery, but slavery was in the service of white supremacy. Some of the reasons Southern leaders gave for seceding had only to do with the latter: Mississippi, for example, said it was seceding partly because "It [the Republican Party] advocates negro equality, socially and politically." In 1890, Mississippi ended racial equality with its new, openly racist state constitution. People always put up monuments after they win. The new Confederate monuments also showed white supremacy by their placement next to the instruments of power—courthouses and state capitols.

Unfortunately, this was also the great period of monument building in the United States (and Europe), which also helps explain why so many Confederate and neo-Confederate statues went up then. These new monuments, put up by neo-Confederate organizations like the United Daughters of the Confederacy and Sons of Confederate Veterans, distorted why the South seceded (chapter 74) and made hash of Civil War history from beginning (chapter 60) to end (chapter 65). To these groups, erecting monuments was a way to continue the Civil War by other means. As a result, to this day, those who worked for civil rights in the nineteenth century, including ex-Confederate Gen. James Longstreet (chapter 44), get far less recognition on the landscape than people who worked against civil rights, such as ex-Confederate Albert Pike.[3]

Thus, objective historical perspective does not necessarily result from the passage of time. Instead, visitors must always ask what points of view dominated the period when the marker or monument went up or the site was preserved. The success of the Civil Rights Movement of the 1960s, not just the passage of a few more decades, prompted revisions in our public landscape of white supremacy. Not only Martin Luther King Jr., but also Frederick Douglass, Barbara Jordan, and other champions of equal rights for African Americans now have streets and schools named for them. Gen. Longstreet, too, has recently gotten more and kinder treatment on the landscape, including a statue at Gettysburg.

In 1948, Minnesota misremembered the Philippine-American War with a beautiful large bronze plaque in its state capitol containing phrases that some returning veterans from that war would have protested bitterly in 1899 (chapter 25). The United States was sending aid and military advisors all over the globe to help other nations stop communism in 1948, allegedly for their own good. Picturing American involvement in the Philippine-American War as a similar example of global civic-mindedness made sense in those Cold War years. But it does not in our time, and it did not in 1899.

The previous sentence invokes a third age that comes into play whenever one visits a historic site—the viewer's own era. Is it fair-minded of us to see these

Sometimes, who sits on the horse tells a great deal about who put up the monument. In front of the American Museum of Natural History in Manhattan, Theodore Roosevelt sits on a horse while beneath him on each side stand examples of America's "inferior races." Teddy's left hand rests on an African American's head; a Native American trudges along on his right. The ensemble calls to mind the words of Stephen A. Douglas in the first Lincoln–Douglas debate: "I would extend to the Negro, and the Indian, and to all dependent races every right, every privilege, and every immunity consistent with the safety and welfare of the white races; but equality they never should have,

either political or social, or in any other respect whatever." Some authorities claim the flanked figures are "guides" or "continents," but visitors without such foreknowledge internalize the monument, without even thinking about it, as a declaration of white supremacy. When the statue went up, the museum was openly racist; the eugenicist Madison Grant, author of *The Passing of the Great Race*, was a trustee. The statue echoes those old "races of mankind" posters that used to decorate college classrooms of physical anthropology, with whites highest on the evolutionary tree, furthest from the ape. Inside its doors the American Museum of Natural History still takes the same stance, putting American Indians and Africans closer to animals, whites furthest removed.

sites through the lens of the present? Some people argue that when we criticize historic monuments and markers, we are being anachronistic—judging people of the past by the standards of our time. Typically, however, when the proponents of change dig deeply, they find that those celebrated people and events from past eras, whose acts contravene standards of justice and conduct in our time, turn out to have been controversial figures in their own time as well.

When Americans choose to leave in place a monument or leave a street named for a controversial person, we continue to honor their actions in *our* time. We imply to future generations that by today's standards, we judge this person to be worthy of remembrance and emulation. When Americans let biased monuments stand with no plaques to balance or contextualize their stories, and when we fail to revise inaccurate or incomplete historical markers, we imply that we continue to endorse these accounts—even though we now know a fuller story. If we don't mean to do this, we need to revise the landscape in our time.

Sometimes, change is easy. King County, encompassing Seattle, Washington, was named for William Rufus King, vice president under President Franklin Pierce. (The next county to the south was named for Pierce; Washington became a territory during the Pierce administration.) King had been a senator from Alabama and, like Pierce, was a member of the extreme pro-slavery wing of the Democratic Party. In 1986, officials renamed King County . . . King County—for civil rights leader Martin Luther King Jr.! Not even a sheet of letterhead had to be discarded! But even that change wasn't easy; the vote was six to five.

Sometimes, change is hard, because reasonable people can differ about the historic merit and meaning of persons or events of the past. The 1995 controversy over naming a building at Iowa State University for an Iowa suffragist offers such a case. Carrie Chapman Catt was a national leader in the women's movement in the early decades of the twentieth century. Like some other feminists in those years (but not all), she said that women should be allowed to vote because "[w]hite supremacy will be strengthened, not weakened, by woman suffrage." She went on to argue that the United States should "cut off the vote of the slums and give it to woman." She was also outraged that the United States would let "brutal, treacherous, murderous Indians" vote and not white women.

Proponents of renaming Old Botany Hall "Carrie Chapman Catt Hall" argued that Catt was "a product of her times" and should be judged by the standards of those times, not our time. "The question is not whether she's a woman of our time," wrote Iowa State English professor Debra Marquart, criticizing the renaming, "but, rather, whether she's a woman for our time. When we put her name on a building and dedicate the building to her memory, she becomes a kind of artifact we have chosen . . . and a symbol we pass on to future generations." Surely Marquart was right about the principle. A case for Catt can nonetheless be made. Donna Lively, a self-identified "woman of color" writing her PhD dissertation on Catt, said, "I am disturbed, however, that Carrie Chapman Catt is being remembered only in terms of her racism. . . .[This] is an extremely monolithic view of her life." On some occasions after women won the right to vote, Catt did speak out *against* racism in the United States, and when the Nazis began persecuting Jews in Europe she organized a protest by non-Jewish women. The hall remains Carrie Chapman Catt Hall and arguments over the name continue at Iowa State.[4]

When proponents of change do their homework and show that a person or event was controversial in the past and has been idealized in the teeth of damning evidence ever since, their opponents cannot reasonably claim that correcting markers or removing monuments does violence to our *history*. Instead, they usually argue that the proposed revision does violence to "our *heritage*." "The heritage syndrome," as historian Michael Kammen calls it, is "an impulse to remember what is attractive or flattering and to ignore all the rest." Thus, history and heritage are not the same; indeed, the two are often at odds. When Edward Ball in the 1990s began to research his family's ownership of slaves, some older members of his family grew upset. While they reveled in the "heritage" of their links to the gentry of the antebellum South, they did not want Ball bringing out what actually *happen*ed—the family history—which Ball nevertheless presented in his interesting book *Slaves in the Family*.

The conflict between history and "heritage" goes still deeper. Too often, events that reek of dishonor and shame get abracadabra'd into a noble heritage. In the early 1990s, Governor Jim Folsom ordered Alabama to stop flying the Confederate battle flag from the state capitol. Immediately, neo-Confederates condemned him for what they called a "heritage violation." Folsom had no problem with the Confederate flag flying from the First White House of the Confederacy across the street, where its presence was historically appropriate. But the state capitol had flown the flag only since the day in April 1963 when Attorney General Robert F. Kennedy visited the building to meet with Governor George Wallace about desegregating the University of Alabama. Then Wallace had used it as a symbol of resistance and white supremacy. So the flag on the capitol did not really symbolize anything about the Civil War but rather a tawdry attempt to maintain white supremacy during the Civil Rights era.

The point to neo-Confederates is not to put the Confederacy into its proper historical context, but to maintain its symbols as sites for homage in the present. Thus, neo-Confederates charge "heritage violation" every time people in a community want to remove a monument to white supremacy (chapter 44) or stop naming a high school after KKK leader Nathan Bedford

Forrest (chapter 52). *History* gains by these kinds of changes. Now that the community no longer must defend its decision to honor such a person or cause, it can afford to tell more about them. Also, the public can develop a more sophisticated understanding of the nature of history from the change on the landscape, especially if a plaque leaves a record of the prior monument or name. The "heritage" lost is the tradition of decades of distorting an event or honoring a repulsive person. Losing this legacy is precisely the point. The next essay tells how two criminal acts by neo-Confederates coupled with ideological opposition to white supremacy led to a new era of public history in the second decade of the 21st century.[5]

1. Sometimes (chapter 44, for example) markers and monuments also tell stories about a third era—the intervening years when they were altered or vandalized.

2. The Vietnam Veterans Memorial is primarily a sasha monument, albeit on the Mall in Washington, DC. Over time its zamani function will predominate.

3. A Pike statue is treated in Appendix C.

4. An interesting "B.C." (Before Charlottesville) exchange about Catt among historians is at "Carrie Catt/Sanitized History Discussion," *H-Women*, 3–4/1996, networks.h-net .org/node/24029/pages/31420/carrie-cattsanitized-history-discussion-march-1996

5. John Mbiti, *African Religions and Philosophy* (Oxford: Heinemann, 1990); Edward C. Banfield, *Political Influence* (NY: Free Press, 1961); Debra Marquart, "No Sister of Mine: A Word from the Great Unwashed on Carrie Chapman Catt," uncited website, 6/98, quoting Catt from Aileen Kraditor, *The Ideas of Woman Suffrage 1890–1920* (NY: Columbia UP, 1965), 76; Kraditor, *Up From the Pedestal* (Chicago: Quadrangle, 1968), 261; and Jacqueline Van Voris, *Carrie Chapman Catt: A Public Life* (NY: Feminist Press, 1987) 21; Donna Lively, email to H-Amstdy, 4/4/96; Jane Cox, letter, 7/20/96; Edward Ball, *Slaves in the Family* (NY: Farrar, Straus and Giroux, 1998), 61–63; Michael Kammen, *Mystic Chords of Memory* (NY: Knopf, 1991), 626; Sanford Levinson, *Written in Stone* (Durham: Duke UP, 1998), 91.

PUBLIC HISTORY AFTER
CHARLOTTESVILLE

At least since the 1960s, our public history has been contested. Even before the first edition of this book came out in 1999, people were shooting historical markers full of holes in West Virginia, using dynamite to topple a monument in Chicago, sawing a foot off a statue in New Mexico (chapter 19), and changing offensive place names all over the country.

A few apologies were even beginning to appear on the landscape. In *Lies My Teacher Told Me*, I wrote that some racial atrocities "such as the 1921 riot in Tulsa, Oklahoma, in which whites even dropped dynamite from an airplane onto a black ghetto, killing more than 75 people and destroying more than 1,100 homes, have completely vanished from our history books." I visited Tulsa in 1996 expecting to find no hint of this horrendous event, only to discover an impressive new memorial put up by blacks and whites together, about to be dedicated on the 75th anniversary of the riot.

But Tulsa residents did a rare thing. In most places, Americans still have not shown the moral courage to tell what really happened there, let alone offer a hint of apology or rectification. Apologies are more common in Germany. In the Schöneberg quarter of Berlin for instance, "Places of Remembrance" signs detail the regulations that restricted Jewish life in the Third Reich. Signs point out benches that had been marked "No Jews," park areas saying "Jews, Forbidden," and other benches marked for "Jews Only," making graphically clear that the great bulk of Germans knew about and participated in segregating of and discriminating against Jews. The United States needs similar reminders to show how African Americans—and sometimes Native, Mexican, and Asian Americans—were restricted under segregation and by sundown towns.

Until about 1968, our monuments pretty much reflected white history. Very few African Americans had been memorialized on our landscape. Almost the only Native Americans we had commemorated were the "Tonto figures" on "our" side: Massasoit, who helped the Pilgrims; the Catawbas in South Carolina, who fought with the Confederacy; and above all, Sacagawea, who guided Lewis and Clark. Worst of all, many of the whites our statues lauded were celebrated precisely *because* they were white supremacists.

Then, beginning with Chicago in July 1968, city after city renamed streets after Martin Luther King Jr. Less than four months earlier, King had been assassinated. Later, other African Americans got noticed on the landscape, including tennis great Arthur Ashe in Richmond, Virginia; slain NAACP leader Medgar Evers in Jackson, Mississippi; and midwife and philanthropist Biddy Mason in Los Angeles. This we might call "inclusionist history"— incorporating notable African Americans as success stories, even though some of them had wound up assassinated. The white leadership of some communities deliberately allowed such memorials as a sort of quid pro quo: "you" don't challenge "our" monuments and markers (which are downtown, next to city hall, etc.), and we will let you tell "your" history in "your" part of town.[1]

The first edition of this book noted in 1999 that "merely grafting positive stories about people of color onto our national consciousness is only part of the job that needs to be done." If every group heroifies its past leaders and actions, we still end up honoring boring, perfect heroes while ignoring and forgetting the common history that divides us. For a time, we seemed to be winding up with parallel histories that did not speak to each other. Each group remembered the past in isolation from the others. The past, however, happened only once.

In many places, whites have ended up memorializing racists while blacks memorialized antiracists. The most famous example stands in Virginia, where tennis star and humanitarian Arthur Ashe offsets a host of Confederate leaders on Richmond's Monument Avenue. Such an array of heroes in bronze can only further persuade visitors that whites may be masters of what Germans call *zweckrationalität*—technical rationality—but are deficient in *wertrationalität*—"worth" or value rationality. Sociologists use these terms to describe differing human reactions to morally complex situations like slavery and secession. People display *zweckrationalität* when they do something well, such as, in this instance, organizing a new nation and fighting effectively, without regard to why. They display *wertrationalität* when they act in accord with their basic values.[2]

Although monuments and markers about people of color may not challenge the narrative of white supremacy directly, erecting them is imperative. They do tell important stories about the past. Moreover, when they wind up downtown or at interracial institutions, they also desegregate the landscape. Frederick Douglass was the first African American ever to get a monument: Rochester, New York, his home town, did that in 1899.[3] The 1899 statue remained the only outdoor representation of Douglass until 1989, when Lincoln University of Pennsylvania, a historically black college, put one up, now located near Frederick Douglass Hall, a male dormitory. After 2000, however, new Douglass statues kept foundries busy:

- having tea with Susan B. Anthony in Susan B. Anthony Square Park in Rochester in 2001;
- a huge head on Fells Point in Baltimore in 2006;
- at Hofstra University on Long Island in 2008;
- in Decatur, Illinois, with Abraham Lincoln, in 2009;
- on the campus of Hillsdale College, Michigan, in 2010;
- on the grounds of the Talbot County Courthouse in Easton, Maryland, in 2010;
- on Frederick Douglass Plaza in New York City in 2011;
- outside the New York Historical Society Museum in 2011; and
- on the main campus of the University of Maryland in 2015.

Then, in 2018, Rochester topped everywhere else by putting up thirteen more outdoor statues of Douglass! These monuments, unlike most memorials and street-namings for King, were not confined to the black part of towns.

Arthur Ashe does play a desegregative role in Richmond, precisely because he did not wind up in a black neighborhood, where some had proposed to put him. Since his statue went up on Monument Avenue in 1996, the United Daughters of the Confederacy (UDC) no longer celebrates "Our President's Day" at the Jefferson Davis monument nearby. Instead, they moved the event to Davis's grave in Richmond's Hollywood Cemetery. Thus, Ashe has changed the UDC's perception of Monument Avenue from "our space" to neutral space or even "their space." Ashe achieved this influence even though he is not even in sight of Davis but more than a mile away, with two other Confederate monuments in between!

Lauding people of color on our landscape is fine. There is nothing wrong with whites choosing as heroes Martin Luther King Jr. or Sojourner Truth— or Arthur Ashe, for that matter. Nevertheless, it is striking that white students never pick a white abolitionist, civil rights martyr, labor leader, or advocate, like Helen Hunt Jackson, for American Indian rights. These pioneers go overlooked on the landscape and in our history textbooks. The whites immortalized on the landscape are mostly famous for actions on the other side, from Jeffrey Amherst through Nathan Bedford Forrest to J. Edgar Hoover. Meanwhile, between 2000 and 2010, neo-Confederates continued to put up new Confederate monuments across the South.

Even in 1999, however, citizens were moving beyond mere inclusionist history toward authentic history—hard-hitting monuments and markers that seek to explain, for example, why we have had so few women presidents and governors, rather than just memorializing the few we have had. Examples in race relations include the Civil Rights Museum at the Lorraine Motel in Memphis, the African American Museum in Detroit, Kelly Ingram Park in Birmingham, and the new lynching memorial in Montgomery, described below. The National Museum of African American History and Culture, the new Smithsonian museum on the National Mall, could have merely taught inclusionist history—showing the lives of successful African Americans throughout our past. It does that, but it also takes on tougher stories, including the lynching of Emmett Till. It also faces some issues that might make African Americans uncomfortable, such as whether the success of black men in the National Basketball Association makes a bad impact on black boys.

Some groups have gone through governmental channels to rename sites (chapters 1 and 24) or get corrective plaques installed. In 2003, Native Americans won an evocative new memorial at Little Bighorn Battlefield in Montana. Arizona has put up bilingual historical markers in Apache or Spanish as well as English. After they got a casino and developed some economic clout, Pequot Indians in Connecticut were able to persuade officials in 1996 to move a statue of John Mason, who commanded the destruction of most of their tribe in 1637, from the massacre site to a less offensive location near his original home.

Recently, these efforts have multiplied. I completely revised this book, rather than just adding a new chapter or two, because our public history has advanced so much since 1999, when the first edition came out. Groups that formerly did not have the power to change insulting plaques even in their own neighborhoods are now putting up new public history "downtown." As a result, our landscape has been enriched by new markers and monuments that not only portray Native American history, African American history, women's history, gay and lesbian history, and the stories of other people and events previously ignored but also correct errors and omissions in our common history. Just in Mississippi, new museums include the Civil Rights Museum, Medgar Evers home, Canton Freedom House, and a host of others. And they are popular.

Among recent examples of our new willingness to portray real history are accurate treatments of lynching, a hitherto taboo topic. The opening essay in this book noted that lynchings were almost invisible in our public history landscape. In 1999, however, as this book came out, that omission began to get filled in. The Moore's Ford Memorial Committee worked with the Georgia Historical Society to put up an accurate state historical marker telling of the last mass lynching in Georgia—of two young black married couples, George and Mae Dorsey and Roger and Dorothy Malcom—in 1946. Since then, the committee has marked their graves, organized a scholarship contest requiring an essay on race relations, and, astonishingly, ritually reenacted the event.

In 2003, Duluth, Minnesota, site of the hanging of three black circus workers in 1920, put up an extensive monument to the victims: Elias Clayton, Elmer Jackson, and Isaac McGhie. They tried to draw as many spectators to the dedication—2,500—as attended the lynching itself. And like the Moore's Ford committee, they organized an ongoing scholarship contest requiring an "essay, video, poem, or speech" about racism.

We don't recognize lynching on the landscape for the same reason that the Atlanta History Center would not host the traveling exhibit of lynching photos and postcards, "Without Sanctuary," in 2002.[4] For the same reason that the only serious permanent museum exhibit of lynching until 2018, to my knowledge, was at the obscure black-owned Baltimore museum Great Blacks in Wax. For the same reason that white parents in Montgomery County, Maryland, objected to school field trips to Great Blacks in Wax. For the same reason that U.S. history textbooks still don't include lynching photographs. We might sum up the *stated* reasons as "white fragility." White children—adults too—might be upset. We can't have that!

For that matter, *black* children might be upset. I first encountered this argument against accurately portraying our history of lynching in federal court back in 1980. The case was *Loewen et al. v. Turnipseed et al.*, prompted by the state of Mississippi's rejection of a Mississippi history textbook I had co-authored, *Mississippi: Conflict and Change*. John Turnipseed, a member of the Textbook Rating Commission, refused to allow the school system to adopt our book partly because it had a lynching photo. As lynching photos go, ours was "tasteful." In the foreground, in silhouette, a man is being burned. Behind him, well-dressed white men and women pose for the camera. The photo did not show the victim in close-up; no one is hacking parts off his body. Nevertheless, when the assistant attorney general for the State of Mississippi asked Turnipseed why he had objected to *Conflict and Change*, he had the court turn to the page where we discussed lynching. Pointing to the photo, he said, "Now, you know, some ninth-graders are pretty big, especially black male ninth-graders. And we worried, or at least I worried, that teachers, especially white lady teachers, would have trouble controlling their classes, with material like this in the book."

We had pretested our book in an overwhelmingly white classroom and an overwhelmingly black classroom; both had preferred it overwhelmingly to "their" book, so we had material for rebuttal testimony at the ready, but we didn't have to use it. At that point, Judge Orma Smith, 83 years old, a white Mississippian, but a person of integrity, took over the questioning.

"But that happened, didn't it?" he asked. "Didn't Mississippi have more lynchings than any other state?"

"Well, yes," Turnipseed admitted. "But that all happened so long ago. Why dwell on it now?"

Smith replied, "Well, it is a *history* book!"[5]

Not talking about lynching amounts to white history. Judge Smith knew this. Refusing to recognize or discuss lynchings disguises their crucial characteristic: a public murder, done with considerable support from the community.[6] The impunity of the participants is precisely what is so ominous about the practice: the whole community knows that nothing is likely to be done about it. That's why perpetrators are happy to be photographed committing this felony. And that's why defenders of our past—as contrasted to students of our past or people trying to teach our past honestly—don't want to talk about lynchings. Doing so helps show the complicity of the entire white community in terrorism against African Americans. This, in turn, helps explain why African Americans still lag in income, wealth, life expectancy, even SAT scores. We don't avoid putting up historical markers because we're afraid of traumatizing high school students. We're afraid to make white America look bad. The judge was not afraid of making white America look bad.

Moore's Ford, in Georgia, and Duluth, in Minnesota, led the way in recognizing lynchings where they occurred. Then, in 2018, the National Memorial for Peace and Justice opened in Montgomery, Alabama. It is a national lynching memorial, displaying 800 columns, one for every county that had at least one lynching, complete with the victims' names. Its success is so great that it can be measured economically in its impact on the tourism industry in central Alabama. Its particular genius is that it also holds an identical column in storage for each county, waiting to go up on the site where each lynching occurred, as soon as an organization in the county has made adequate efforts to "address racial and economic injustice."[7]

Throughout this book, we shall see that improvements in our public history have been made, as Margaret Mead suggested, by small groups of people, usually sparked initially by one person. "Never doubt that a small group of thoughtful, committed citizens can change the world," she has been credited with writing. "Indeed, it is the only thing that ever has." Exactly *that* happened in Georgia and Minnesota, and now the Montgomery memorial, spearheaded by civil rights attorney Bryan Stevenson, is prompting groups to form around the nation to reconsider the way history is told on their local landscapes. Already, several places have taken this important step.

As important as the recognition of unpleasant events like lynchings, some citizens, since at least the sesquicentennial of secession (2010–11), have taken on the daunting task of delegitimizing the Confederacy on our landscape. In 1999, this book called for removing statues of John C. Calhoun, Jefferson Davis, Nathan Bedford Forrest, and other Confederate leaders, or at least explaining right next to them what was wrong with their cause. For this, many people considered me outlandish.

Simply getting Americans to realize why the South seceded proved a tough task. All primary sources show that Southern states seceded not because they were for states' rights, but because they were against them. Northern states were interfering in modest ways with attempts to re-enslave fugitives from the South. They also allowed abolitionists to distribute antislavery materials. They also no longer permitted temporary slavery, such when planters on vacation brought along their cook and coachman. Southern states cited as justification for seceding Northern states' exercising of states' rights like these. They also cited decisions by New England states to make African Americans citizens. During lectures I gave beginning in 1998 in the Greensboro (North Carolina) History Museum, I conducted referenda of my audiences, asking why the South left the United States. Audiences supplied four causes: for slavery, for states' rights, because of the election of Lincoln, and over tariffs and taxes. The first and third are correct, the other two flatly wrong. In talks in Greensboro, northern Minnesota, Cleveland, Long Beach, Memphis, New York City, and everywhere else, states' rights won absolute majorities, usually 60–65%. It took eleven years before an audience ever gave slavery, rather than states' rights, first position, and that was a fluke.[8] The next year, in 2010, I published this referendum process as the core of a chapter—"Why Did the South Secede?"—in *Teaching What Really Happened*. In 2011, for the sesquicentennial of secession, I wrote "Five Myths About Why the South Seceded." It became the most viewed article at *The Washington Post* that year and was reprinted in the *Chicago Tribune* and other major newspapers. I also replied to more than 1,800 emails about it, including 1,200 from neo-Confederates. Other historians wrote similar articles. Beginning in 2000 and culminating in the new visitors center at Gettysburg in 2008, the National Park Service revised its narratives at Civil War battlefields to highlight slavery as the key cause of the conflict. During the four-year sesquicentennial of the Civil War, 2011–15, national public opinion slowly changed about the nature of slavery, the reasons why Southern states seceded, and hence the morality of the Confederate cause. Gradually, audiences began to reply more accurately to my poll. But opinion shifted rapidly after 2015.

What happened in 2015?

On June 17, neo-Confederate Dylann Roof shot ten unarmed African Americans in a Bible study group at a historic church in Charleston, South Carolina, killing nine of them. He showed how esteem for the Confederacy, expressed in our public history, helped incubate murderous extremism on behalf of white supremacy. In the aftermath, the governor of South Carolina ordered the Confederate flag taken down from in front of the state capitol, and private citizens, as well as public officials, started to question Confederate public history across the country.

Gradually, the true history of these monuments became clear to people. They went up in two main groups. Shortly after the war, some went up in Confederate cemeteries (and a few other places). Mainly these monuments mourned the loss of life and listed the dead from that community.

Most Confederate monuments were erected later, during the Nadir of race relations, after 1890 and before 1940. Mainly they got placed next to centers of power—on the grounds of state capitols and county courthouses, in front of city halls, in downtown parks. Rarely did they mourn the dead; instead, they suggested the "Lost Cause" was right, using phrases like "Deo Vindice"

On the left is an unusual, late, and particularly interesting example of an early Confederate monument, put up in 1889. Titled "Appomattox," it still stands on the main street of Alexandria, VA. The soldier is pensive. The base lists the dead soldiers from Alexandria. On the right is an example of the monuments that went up after 1890, during the Nadir of race relations: Robert E. Lee on Monument Avenue in Richmond. It is hieratic; the feet of Lee's horse are 30 feet off the ground. His horse looks nothing like Traveler, but has muscles on its muscles. In short, it is triumphant. And why not? In 1890, the neo-Confederates won the Civil War.[9]

and "States' Rights." When they were dedicated, speakers openly celebrated white supremacy.[10]

After Charleston, and also triggered by a wave of videos, taken by citizens, of police shooting unarmed African American men and boys, private citizens began expressing their disregard for Confederate monuments by spray-painting them with "Racist" and "BLM" ("Black Lives Matter"). A few monuments came down, including a 70-foot tall one at the University of Louisville.[11] Mitch Landrieu, mayor of New Orleans, took down his city's four Confederate and neo-Confederate monuments a year after Charleston and gave an eloquent explanation for so doing.

Still, most politicians resisted taking these monuments down or moving them to museum settings where they might be contextualized with labels explaining what they signified and when and why they went up. In February 2017, I participated in a symposium sponsored by the American Civil War Museum at the Library of Virginia about Richmond's Confederate monuments. The mayor of Richmond had said that removing them from famed Monument Avenue was out of the question. Speaking last, I took care to put that alternative back on the table. When I suggested, as I had eighteen years earlier in the first edition of this book, removing the Confederate monuments from famed Monument Avenue, no longer was this notion considered outlandish. Indeed, favorable newspaper coverage of the conference made clear that my remarks now fell within the realm of acceptable public rhetoric.[12] My position had not changed; the culture had shifted.

Then, on August 11–12, 2017, ostensibly to protest the city's decision to take down statues of Robert E. Lee and Stonewall Jackson, far-right racists, many openly calling themselves "Nazis," staged a two-day "Unite the Right" rally and riot in Charlottesville, Virginia. The rally extended into the evening, with participants carrying flaming torches modeled after KKK rallies, initiating intimidating confrontations with counter-protestors and chanting racially charged slogans, including "Jews will not replace us." One of the white supremacists intentionally drove a car into a crowd of counter-protestors, killing one young woman, Heather Heyer, and injuring 35 other people. Charlottesville triggered a further change in public rhetoric. Now, arguments for the removal of Confederate statues carried the day in many places. Los Angeles removed its Confederate monument. San Diego took down its plaque marking the Jefferson Davis Highway. Bradenton, Gainesville, Tampa, and other Florida county seats removed their Confederate monuments. The mayor of Birmingham surrounded that city's monument with plywood; so did the county executive of Montgomery County, Maryland.

Prior to Charlottesville, Baltimore's four main Confederate monuments had endured vandalism and controversy, including spray-painted "BLMs." Its mayor had appointed a commission to study the issue, temporarily quelling the protests, but neither she nor the commission head had any stomach for action beyond talk. After Charlottesville, the (new) mayor took all four monuments down within days. The University of Texas similarly removed its four remaining Confederate statues in the middle of the night.[13]

Unlike Mayor Landrieu in New Orleans, officials who ordered removals in other cities typically did not take a position on their merits—that is, on the Confederate cause. Instead, they defended their decisions on the ground of *zweckrationalität*. The monuments had become flashpoints of protest, so it was only prudent to remove them. Since cities, counties, states, and even the U.S. government had spent at least $40,000,000 in the previous decade erecting and maintaining Confederate monuments and organizations, not including the escalating cost of protecting and restoring them, these officials had a point. Perhaps the Marriott Hotel chain supplied the purest example of *zweckrationalität*: it took down the historical marker on the Marshall House in Alexandria when it bought the property, simply because it *might* be an issue. They were right; it was. Chapter 60 tells what was wrong with the marker.

After this book came out in 1999, I tried to maintain a list of every instance of de-Confederatizing, but after Charleston, I couldn't keep up. Likewise, the editor at the History News Network tried to maintain such a list, but after Charlottesville, he couldn't keep up either. Now the forces of crowd-sourcing have been unleashed at "Removal of Confederate Monuments and Memorials" on Wikipedia.[14] But even this last omits some recent examples, so rapidly has the movement grown.

A single small town, Charles Town, West Virginia, exemplifies this reversal of neo-Confederate sentiment. In 1986, the United Daughters of the Confederacy put up a plaque on the Charles Town Courthouse:

> *In honor and memory*
> *Of the Confederate soldiers of*
> *Jefferson County, who served in the*
> *War Between the States.*

That last phrase is anachronistic, of course; no one used it while the war was going on. It's a *neo*-Confederate term from the Nadir of race relations that falsely implies that a number of states fought the war—South Carolina, Georgia, etc., on the Southern side, and Wisconsin, Maryland, etc., on the Northern. That's bad history, of course; actually, a faction of one nation tried to separate from the whole. Indeed, the entire plaque is questionable. After all, West Virginia never joined the Confederacy. On the contrary, it seceded from Virginia to stay with the United States, although almost as many residents fought for the Confederacy as for the United States. During the Nadir of race relations, however, like most states, North and South, West Virginia went under the thumb of white supremacists who were pro-Confederate, essentially joining the Confederacy retroactively!

In 2017, six African American women, all in their 60s and 70s, wrote a letter to the Jefferson County Commission seeking removal of the plaque. They pointed out that there was no plaque for Union soldiers. Nor did anything mark the buying and selling of their enslaved ancestors, which had occurred right in front of the courthouse. Why should the courthouse honor only the side that fought to preserve slavery? And why was it placed there so recently? "It is impossible to enter the courthouse to conduct business or to even vote without being taunted by its presence," they wrote. "The plaque perpetuates division at all levels on a wider scale." The local newspaper agreed and called for the plaque's removal. After a debate, the commission members split two to two, and the commission's head voted to keep the plaque up. The next year, however, after Charlottesville, and partly because of his vote, the head of the commission was voted out of office; a month later, the plaque came down.

We see a similar change in North Carolina. In 2000, an officer of the Chapel Hill campus of the University of North Carolina threatened me after my article "The Shrouded History of College Campuses" appeared in the *Chronicle of Higher Education*. The article showed that many universities, including UNC, misrepresented their own history. In Chapel Hill, during Reconstruction, a white supremacist resident, Cornelia Phillips Spencer, helped foment a student boycott of the university because it was led by white anti-racist Republicans and because it let African Americans attend events on campus. Having stayed open to a few students for two years, the university bowed to pressure and closed. After white supremacists regained control in 1874, it reopened; Spencer celebrated by ringing the campus bell. UNC later named its first women's dormitory Spencer Hall, complete with a plaque crediting her for *preserving* the institution! After my article pointed out this irony, a college official claimed I had Spencer wrong and directed me to post a correction to the *Chronicle* or face consequences. I refused, and he never actually did anything.

The rhetoric on his campus was already beginning to change. As its class gift, the graduating class of 2002 gave UNC $50,000 toward an "Unsung Founders Memorial" intended to honor the enslaved people who helped build and staff the university.[15] In 2004, the Cornelia Phillips Spencer Bell Award, for a woman who has made "outstanding contributions to the university," got renamed after Spencer's racist views were publicized. In 2015, UNC renamed another building that had carried the name of Spencer's friend William Saunders, because he had been head of the KKK and had led the ouster of Republicans in North Carolina and at the university. Three years later, students pulled down Silent Sam, the Confederate monument that had greeted visitors to the campus since 1913. I suspect Spencer Hall is on borrowed time. Certainly today, the official would be afraid for his job if he threatened me over my accurate article showing that Spencer had worked to close, not preserve, the university.

Many people still have not thought through the issues thoroughly and imagine that removing Silent Sam and other symbols of white supremacy and reverence for the Confederate cause amounts to "whitewashing" history. New Orleans Mayor Landrieu's speech shows what is wrong with these objections. As he puts it,

> These monuments purposefully celebrate a fictional, sanitized Confederacy; ignoring the death, ignoring the enslavement, and the terror that it actually stood for. . . . To literally put the Confederacy on a pedestal in our most prominent places of honor is an inaccurate recitation of our full past, it is an affront to our present, and it is a bad prescription for our future.

Monuments can interfere with rigorous thinking, as well as with remembering the past. An empty pedestal does prompt thought, perhaps more than a man on a horse captioned "Lee" ever did. Naming a school or a highway for a Confederate general teaches precious little history—only that he was a great man and should be honored. And it's precisely those last three words that we need to erase.

Every time a monument comes down or a name gets changed, a historical marker should go up explaining what had been here, when it went up, what it tells about the time it was erected, when it came down, and what its removal signifies.[16] That should result in good history on the landscape.

The African slave trade, too, is now getting attention. At the Royall House near Boston, at the Independence Seaport Museum in Philadelphia, in Alexandria (chapter 59) and Richmond, Virginia (chapters 62 and 63), at the African American History Monument in South Carolina, and other places, Americans are now portraying the slave trade on the landscape where it actually happened. New Orleans unveiled a new slave trade tour app, while Richmond put up a triangle trade monument. Recognition of the trade is becoming international: identical monuments went up in Liverpool and Benin. The history museum in Nantes, France, as well as an outdoor museum and a walking tour, now all treat the French slave trade.

Back in the United States, the movement to cleanse our public history of white supremacist bias has moved beyond the Confederacy. Back in 2002, ninth-grader Nathaniel Vogel sparked a movement to change the name of the elementary school in Cambridge, Massachusetts, from which he had graduated. Louis Agassiz Elementary School honored a nineteenth-century Harvard faculty member whose racist theories of human origins invalidated much of his scientific work. The school is now named for Maria Baldwin, its principal for 33 years and the first black principal of a mixed-race school in New England. "Calhoun College" (really a dormitory) at Yale was named for the great theoretician of slavery, white supremacy, and secession. So was Lake Calhoun in Minneapolis. Since Charleston, both names got changed. Then Charlottesville prompted a re-evaluation of still other figures across the North and West whose feet of clay, when fully exposed, turn out to reach up to their shoulders.

Criminal behavior has often led to renaming and removal of individual monuments, of course, but two recent movements are causing massive change: the investigations of sex abuse in the Catholic Church and the "MeToo Movement" against sexual harassment more broadly. James Clifford Timlin House at the University of Scranton became Oscar Romero House in honor of the Salvadoran bishop who spoke out against poverty, after an investigation showed that Bishop Timlin had covered up for priests guilty of rape. A bridge in Augusta, Maine, named for John J. Curran, a local priest posthumously found guilty of child abuse, was renamed Calumet Bridge.

Americans are also beginning to remove the white supremacy from our public history treatment of Native Americans. In 2018, the city councils of San Francisco and Kalamazoo, Michigan, decided to take down their hieratic statues showing whites towering over American Indians. Later chapters in this book show how states are revising markers and renaming places to use words like "discover" and "squaw" more accurately, if at all. In California, people who helped exterminate Natives are getting de-memorialized. Most Spanish missions, which have a mixed legacy regarding their "subjects," are no longer presented heroically but thoughtfully. Statues of Christopher Columbus have come down in San Jose and Los Angeles and are being questioned in St. Louis, New York City, and elsewhere. Some will stay, but perhaps with useful context added.

The federal government still has a long way to go. At West Point, in 2019, U. S. Grant finally got a statue, but the military academy still pays homage to his opponent, Robert E. Lee, who committed treason on behalf of slavery, in at least five places. As well, the army still names at least ten forts and other installations for Confederate officers, including arrant racists and incompetent generals. This is honoring the wrong side.[17]

No, we need not remove every statue of George Washington or rename every school named for Thomas Jefferson, even though both owned slaves. We did not honor them *because* they owned slaves, after all, but for other reasons. We honored Jefferson Davis, Robert E. Lee, and all the other Confederate generals, on the other hand, precisely because they led a rebellion on behalf of white supremacy as an ideology and slavery as a form of it. So we must stop honoring them. Similarly, Agassiz's work is intertwined with his white supremacy. So is Orville Hubbard's (chapter 34).

We cannot demand that the people we want future generations to remember be perfect, for then no one would qualify. We must note that Jefferson never lived by his own principles. Lincoln was a racist as well as an anti-racist. Martin Luther King Jr. plagiarized others while he also originated great speeches. We must not distort the historical record to create monuments that try to convince people to worship or blindly emulate figures from the past. Charlottesville gives new momentum to our work of getting the landscape right. We must not squander it by denying the good in our past. Public history is now the focal point for serious discussions of our past and our future. Let us have these discussions. Truth about the past, if we tell it on our landscape, can help bring forth justice in the future.[18]

1. Distinctions historian Vincent Harding drew between "white history," "Negro history," and "black history" helped my thinking about these matters.

2. I wrote "further persuade" because responses from hundreds of white college students have convinced me that they already believe this about the past. When I ask them in anonymous surveys to "tell me your heroes in history," few name European Americans. Often, they choose people of color—Martin Luther King, Jr., Malcolm X, Rosa Parks, Sojourner Truth, or perhaps Mahatma Gandhi or Nelson Mandela. Many reply "none." That is, they have *no* heroes in history—certainly none of the white people who get statues across America.

3. He had been honored with an indoor bust in Rochester twenty years earlier, now at the Rush Rhees Library of the University of Rochester.

4. Some History Center staff claimed they didn't say no but merely wanted to delay so they could include it as part of a larger exhibit about slavery. Of course, racial lynchings were rare during slavery, because an enslaved person was someone else's property. See Darryl Fears, "Atlanta, Ready to Revisit an American Evil," *The Washington Post*, 1/28/2002.

5. At this point, co-editor Charles Sallis and I nudged each other. "We're gonna win this case!" I murmured.

   See Charles W. Eagles, *Civil Rights, Culture Wars: The Fight over a Mississippi Textbook* (Chapel Hill: U. of NC Press, 2017).

6. To be sure, not all lynchings were of African Americans, though about two-thirds were. Especially in the West, Chinese Americans, Mexican Americans, Native Americans,

and, yes, European Americans were also lynched. Indeed, some whites were lynched because they refused to follow sundown town rules and fire their black employees, others for horse stealing or shooting a police officer.

7. In March 2017, before the lynching memorial opened, it helped a Georgia county put up a marker dealing with its own four lynchings; the process prompted considerable racial reconciliation. See Brad Schrade, "Family Reveals 76-Year-Old Secret in Georgia Lynching," *Atlanta Journal-Constitution*, 3/16/2017, ajc.com/news/family-reveals-year -old-secret-georgia-lynching/vH0uCAwkC4dKqEAnATj2II. For economic impact, see Keith Schneider, "Revitalizing Montgomery as It Embraces Its Past," *The New York Times*, 5/21/2019, nytimes.com/2019/05/21/business/montgomery-civil-rights.html

8. It occurred at the University of Nebraska simultaneously with the Missouri-Nebraska football game. Audience members enjoyed telling me that the yahoos who would have answered "states' rights" were watching the game!

9. The victorious nature of the Lee monument is further emphasized by "an elaborate granite pedestal with the east and west sides embellished with four gray marble columns and scrollwork at the north and south ends," quoting the description in its application for the National Register of Historic Places, dhr.virginia.gov/VLR_to_transfer/PDFNoms /127-0181_LeeMonument_2006_nomination_final.pdf

10. Some delegitimizing of the Confederacy predated 2015. For example, after hearing civil rights activist Rodney Hurst in 2013, the student body of Nathan Bedford Forrest High school in Jacksonville, Florida, voted two to one to rename their school. It had been named for Forrest in 1959, at the suggestion of the United Daughters of the Confederacy. As chapters 51 and 52 tell, after *Brown v. Board* triggered the Civil Rights Movement in 1954, neo-Confederates seized upon Forrest as their favorite Civil War general, not despite his having presided over the massacre of surrendered black (and white) POWs at Fort Pillow, but *because* he did so. When the school system desegregated, Forrest High wound up 65% black. After the student vote, the Duval County School Board voted unanimously for the name to be changed. Unfortunately, very few white students supported renaming. After Charlottesville, perhaps they would.

11. It remains on public display: Brandenburg, 40 miles southwest, erected it at their waterfront park.

12. See, inter alia, Katherine Calos, "Symposium Considers Standing of Confederate Monuments," *Richmond Times-Dispatch*, 2/25/2017, roanoke.com/news/symposium-considers -standing-of-confederate-monuments/article_f2c41f13-4160-58e5-9d93-b15baa79ac31 .html. My talk is at c-span.org/video/?423748-104/confederate-monuments-memorials

13. Jefferson Davis had come down after Charleston. Greg Fenves, president of the University of Texas, may have acted at night, but he gave a strong *wertrationalität* reason for their removal: "The events [of Charlottesville] make it clear, now more than ever, that Confederate monuments have become symbols of modern white supremacy and neo-Nazism. Erected during the period of Jim Crow laws and segregation, the statues represent the subjugation of African Americans. That remains true today for white supremacists who use them to symbolize hatred and bigotry."

14. en.wikipedia.org/wiki/Removal_of_Confederate_monuments_and_memorials

15. Unfortunately, the memorial wound up being a batch of tiny figures at ground level, about a foot tall, holding up a bowl or platter, which often gets used as a picnic table. It seemed out of scale, especially compared to "Silent Sam," the nearby Confederate monument, whose feet were ten feet off the ground and who towered another seven feet above that.

16. Virginia's historical marker program now informs local history museums when it retires a bad marker. They can get the old one, providing they agree to display it accompanied by text that corrects it. This provides the museums with tools to teach historiography!

17. Grant has also moved up from #33 to #22 as president, according to a recent C-SPAN poll, as historians begin to credit him for trying to improve race relations, instead of blaming him for so doing.

18. See Loewen, *Lies My Teacher Told Me* (NY: New Press, 1995), 158–59; *Facing History and Ourselves News* (winter 1993–94):19; Edmund Mahony, "Statue of Colonial Captain Who Killed Pequots to Be Moved," *Hartford Courant*, 4/29/95; Martha T. Moore, "Surging Interest in Black History Gives a Lift to Museums, Tourism," *Pew Trust*, 11/21/2018, pewtrusts.org/en/research-and-analysis/blogs/stateline/2018/11/21/surging-interest-in-black-history-gives-a-lift-to-museums-tourism; Mitch Landrieu, "Truth," *HNN*, 5/2017, historynewsnetwork.org/article/166085; Brian Palmer and Seth Freed Wessler, "The Costs of the Confederacy," *Smithsonian Magazine*, (12/2018), smithsonianmag.com/history/costs-confederacy-special-report-180970731; Claire Cardona, "UT-Austin Takes Down Confederate Statues on Campus," *Dallas News*, 8/2017, dallasnews.com/news/higher-education/2017/08/20/ut-austin-take-4-statues-leaders-confederacy; Rebekah Allen, "UT to Re-Erect Statue of James Hogg After Removing It in 2017 Because of Confederate Ties," *Dallas News*, 12/2018, dallasnews.com/news/higher-education/2018/12/06/ut-re-erect-statue-james-hogg-after-removing-2017-confederate-ties; Joe Heim, "A Controversial Civil War Memorial Faces Removal After West Virginia Election," *The Washington Post*, 11/20/2018; John K. Chapman, *Black Freedom and the University of North Carolina, 1793–1960* (Chapel Hill: UNC PhD, 2006, cdr.lib.unc.edu/indexablecontent/uuid:9797fe2f-6cb9-4e40-8674-619fa3a597b481), 116–18, 131; Jonathan Michels, "Who Gets to Be Remembered in Chapel Hill?" *Scalawag*, (10/8/2016), scalawagmagazine.org/2016/10/whats-in-a-name; Timothy J. McMillan, "Remembering Forgetting: A Monument to Erasure at the University of North Carolina," *Berghahn Journals*, 8/2017, berghahnbooks.com/blog/remembering-forgetting-a-monument-to-erasure-at-the-university-of-north-carolina-essay; Alissa J. Rubin, "'They Threw Themselves Into the Sea, 14 Black Women, All Together'," *The New York Times*, 10/30/2018; Lauren R. Dorgan, "Committee Renames Local Agassiz School," *Harvard Crimson*, 5/22/2002, thecrimson.com/article/2002/5/22/committee-renames-local-agassiz-school-the; Audra J. Wolfe, "The Unloved Naturalist," *C&EN* 91(20): 35–36, cen.acs.org/articles/91/i20/Unloved-Naturalist.html; Loewen, "Ten Questions for Yale President Peter Salovey," *Chronicle of Higher Education*, 6/10/2016, B11–13 (reprinted in "Confronting History on Campus," 2016, 19–22, chronicle-assets.s3.amazonaws.com/5/items/biz/pdf/ChronFocus_NameControv5_i.pdf); Ronald C. White, "The Growing Appreciation of U. S. Grant," *The Washington Post*, 4/24/2019.

LIES ACROSS AMERICA

THE FAR WEST

1. The Tallest Mountain—
The Silliest Naming
ALASKA *Denali (Mt. McKinley)*

Since people probably reached Alaska before any other part of the Western Hemisphere, they probably named North America's tallest mountain thousands of years ago. They didn't call it Mt. McKinley.

Replacing Native American names with those of European Americans is a form of cultural imperialism. The practice declares that the new rulers of the landscape can afford to ignore what Native names mean and connote in favor of new names that typically have no relation to what is named.

Low-profile conflicts have raged for many years between those who want

The mountain is Denali, "the great one." It does not deserve to be named for William McKinley, who was never "the great one."

to change the names of localities and geographic features back to their original Native names and those who want them named for European American people, towns, or words. To some degree, this is a contest between Native Americans and European Americans, but European Americans are usually found on both sides of the arguments. The battles might also be characterized as between traditionalists and those desiring change, except that both parties claim to have tradition on their side. Denali, or Mt. McKinley, dramatically embodies these disputes about names all across America, not only because it is such a dramatic place but also because the controversy at Denali went on for more than 30 years.

William A. Dickey renamed the peak, the tallest point in North America, Mt. McKinley in 1896. Why he got to name it is hard to fathom. Dickey had come to Alaska spurred by discoveries of gold in Cook Inlet. With three companions he made it to Talkeetna and saw Denali, "the great one" in the language of the nearby Tanaina Indians. According to C. H. Merriam, testifying before the U.S. Geographical Board in 1917, "[t]he right of the discoverer to name geographical features has never been questioned," but Dickey was no discoverer. Native people had discovered the mountain thousands of years earlier. Even if only *white* people "discover," Russians saw it in the 1770s or 1780s and named it Bulshaia Gora, "big mountain." Even if only *English-speaking* white people "discover," George Vancouver saw Denali in 1794. Dickey was not even the first white *American* to see it; other Americans had preceded him by a quarter century.

Dickey had no serious reason to name the mountain as he did. William McKinley had not yet been martyred when he received the honor; indeed he had not even been elected president. Nor had McKinley ever been to the mountain, or even to Alaska. William Dickey favored conservative fiscal policies, while most people in the West wanted to expand the amount of money in circulation by minting more silver coins and certificates. Dickey was irritated by arguments he had lost with "free silver" partisans on his trip and decided to retaliate by naming Denali after the gold standard champion.

"The original naming was little more than a joke," according to George R. Stewart, author of *American Place-Names*. From the first, some people preferred the Native name, and Dickey's frivolous reason for choosing McKinley gave them ammunition. Nevertheless, probably because he wrote about his trip in the *New York Sun*, Dickey's choice began to catch on. McKinley defeated William Jennings Bryan in 1896, so at least the mountain turned out to be named after a president and, when McKinley was shot in Buffalo in 1901, after a martyred president.

By 1999, however, when this book first came out, many Americans considered the Native name more melodious and objected to "McKinley" on aesthetic grounds—as if the Mississippi River had been renamed for, say, Zachary Taylor. They were coming around to the view expressed by an Apache man to museum curator Lucy Lippard: "The white man's names are no good. They don't give pictures to your mind." Others supported Native efforts to gain better recognition on the landscape. "It's time we listened to the Native people of Alaska," declared Senator Ted Stevens of Alaska in 1991. "This mountain is the largest in North America. It was named by the Natives long before we arrived."

For many years, a lone congressman from Ohio prevented the renaming of the mountain. In 1975, Rep. Ralph Regula from Canton, William McKinley's hometown, blocked a compromise proposed by the Alaska legislature to name the mountain Denali and leave the national park surrounding it named for McKinley. Five years later, the National Park Service agreed to a compromise Regula couldn't block: it changed the name of Mt. McKinley National Park to Denali National Park, but the mountain stayed Mt. McKinley. This resolution proved unstable, however. Finding its Native lobby more persuasive than Ohio's McKinley lobby, Alaska changed its name for the mountain to Denali, relegating the 25th president to the parenthetical statement, "(also known as Mt. McKinley)." Regula found a way to block any change on the national level, however. His aide told me, "The Board on Geographic Names won't change names so long as legislation on the subject is pending. Congressman Regula always has legislation pending."

When the Board on Geographic Names was considering a proposal to rename the mountain in 1977, Congressman Regula testified, "This action would be an insult to the memory of President McKinley and to the people of my district and the nation who are so proud of his heritage." But Americans *aren't*! That's the problem: most Americans don't rank William McKinley very high in the pantheon of presidents. They remember him if at all as a creation of political boss Mark Hanna, beholden to big business, and addicted to high tariffs. He also got us bogged down in a seemingly endless colonial war in the Philippines (chapter 25). In 2018, the town of Arcata, California, led by nearby Native Americans, protested Arcata's statue of McKinley, charging him with white supremacy. The city council voted 4-1 to remove the statue from Arcata Plaza; it will likely wind up a few blocks away on private land. This decision symbolized quite a change for Arcata, a former sundown town that had driven out its Chinese population in 1886.

After decades of gridlock, the Obama administration officially renamed the mountain Denali in 2015. Chapter 24 tells that Native groups want to change some other names all across America. They are winning some of these battles. Memphis renamed DeSoto Bluff "Chickasaw Heritage State Park." "Custer's Last Stand" is now "The Little Bighorn Battlefield." Places with "squaw" in their names are getting changed, since that word is a derogatory term for Native American woman. Also, the U.S. Board on Geographic Names adopted a policy in 1990 to favor names derived from American Indian, Inuit, and Polynesian languages.[1]

1. William E. Brown, *Denali: Symbol of the Alaskan Wild* (VA Beach, VA: Downing, 1993), 27–28; C.H. Merriam, "Shall the Name of Mount Rainier Be Changed?" statement before U.S. Geographical Board (DC: GPO, 1917), 3; William Harris and Judith Levey, *The New Columbia Encyclopedia* (NY: Columbia UP, 1975), 1650; Lucy R. Lippard, *The Lure of the Local* (NY: New Press, 1997), 45; Barbara Wainman, conversation, 9/3/97; Donald J. Orth and Roger L. Payne, *Principles, Policies, and Procedures: Domestic Geographic Names* (Reston, VA: U.S. Board on Geographic Names, 1997 [1987]), 14; 10/10/91 clipping in Ralph Regula's files, 9/97; Mark Monmonier, *Drawing the Line* (NY: Holt, 1995), 66–67.

---------------- ✴ ----------------

2. King Kamehameha I, The *Roman*!
HAWAII *Honolulu*

Kamehameha I was an extraordinary leader. Born on the Big Island of Hawaii about 1758, he died on Kona in 1819. Using his intelligence, courage in man-to-man combat, his own genealogy (very important in traditional Hawaiian culture), diplomacy, Western arms, and capable advisors and underlings, Kamehameha conquered all of the Big Island of Hawaii in the 1790s. He then moved northwest, conquering Maui, Lanai, Molokai, and Oahu. Finally, in 1810, by negotiation, he was acknowledged king over Kauai, unifying all the Hawaiian Islands for the first time.[1]

Kamehameha's imposing statue stands across South King Street from Iolani Palace in Honolulu. An identical statue stands near his birthplace. A third

statue, made from molds prepared from the one in Honolulu, stands indoors
in the U.S. Capitol. Eight-and-one-half feet tall with gold robes, it is "easily
the most striking in the National Statuary Hall" in the words of the guidebook for the collection. Kamehameha's likeness can thus be seen on the landscape at more places than that of any other Asian or Pacific Island American.

Only it's not Kamehameha's likeness.

The statue had its origin in 1878 when Walter Gibson, a non-Polynesian
member of the Hawaiian legislature, proposed it in connection with the centennial of Hawaii's "discovery" by Capt. James Cook. This had a certain
logic, since Kamehameha was among the many Hawaiians who had met
Cook during his two visits to the islands before Cook was killed there. The
legislature appropriated $10,000 for the project and made Gibson chair of the
monument committee, which included native Hawaiian members but soon
became a one-man show. Gibson chose Thomas R. Gould, a Boston sculptor, to craft the work.

Gould never went to Hawaii and seems never to have learned what Kamehameha looked like, although several portraits did exist, painted at different
points in his life. Photographs of native Hawaiians were mailed to Gould
as he worked on the statue in Florence, Italy, but they did not make much

Kamehameha I with his Roman nose and Roman pose. This copy is in the National
Statuary Hall in the U.S. Capitol.

impact either. Gould was in Italy, so he made the statue look like an Italian with a long Roman cloak. According to travel writer Hal Glatzer, "The statue is essentially that of a Roman general with dark skin. The features are more Caucasian than Polynesian. The pose, with the right arm extended, palm upturned, is 'supposed' to be a welcoming aloha gesture. But it is based on the Roman pose with an upright staff or spear."

David Kalakaua had become king of Hawaii in 1874, and in 1882 Hawaiians finished the Iolani Palace for him. The statue of King Kamehameha I, not ready for the 1878–79 centennial of Cook's visit, was scheduled as part of Kalakaua's belated coronation festivities connected with opening the new palace in 1883. Cast in bronze in Paris and then shipped to Hawaii via Cape Horn, the statue was lost before rounding the Cape when the ship wrecked at the Falkland Islands.

The Hawaiians had insured the statue for $12,000, and with that money, they ordered another one. Gould made a copy and sent it off to Hawaii. Before it could get there, however, a ship came into Hawaii with the original! Enterprising Falkland Islanders had recovered it from the sea and sold it to the captain for $500. He sold it to Gibson for $875. Now Hawaii had two statues, and neither looked anything like Kamehameha. The reordered statue was placed in front of Iolani Palace, while the original went up near the northernmost point of the Big Island, near Kamehameha's birthplace.[2]

Making Kamehameha look Roman is a classic example of Eurocentrism. Hawaiians do not look Italian. James King, lieutenant to Capt. Cook, said Kamehameha had "as savage a looking face as I ever saw." "Savage" of course was a Eurocentric way of saying "Polynesian"; Hawaiian women found Kamehameha quite attractive. Nevertheless, Native Hawaiian activist Poka Laenui points out that the statues do symbolize how Hawaiians of that era were finding ways to "walk in two worlds"—their own culture and the European-dominated world economy. In 1840, Hawaii adopted a written constitution and other accoutrements of modern nationhood.

Regardless, Europeans were taking over Hawaii as they were taking over Kamehameha's likeness. In 1887, whites forced Kalakaua to sign a constitution supporting white interests. Venereal disease, cholera, influenza, measles, typhoid, smallpox, and other diseases from Europe and Asia, including leprosy, which arrived in 1830, decimated the Hawaiians. Hawaii's Native population shrank from perhaps 650,000 when Capt. Cook arrived to about 35,000 by 1893. In that year American residents on Hawaii, aided by 162 U.S. sailors, overthrew Queen Liliuokalani, Kalakaua's successor. It seemed then that Native Hawaiians might disappear from their own country as thoroughly as the likeness of King Kamehameha had from his own statue. Beginning around 1970, in a development that paralleled Black Power and American Indian movements on the mainland, the number of Hawaiians who identified themselves as Native Hawaiian has soared. So has the number of Native Hawaiians learning Hawaiian music, dance, language, crafts, and navigation. In the 2010 census, about 135,000 people listed no other race but Hawaiian.[3] Although that is only one-tenth of the population of the islands, 527,000 additional people on the islands had some Hawaiian ancestry.[4]

Chapter 26 tells of a similar population decline and rebound among Native Americans and a corresponding rise in the number of those identifying themselves as American Indians.

1. Kamehameha never conquered the farthest-west island of Niihau, which has less than a hundred square miles.

2. In 1912, it was moved nearby to the lawn of the county building at Kapaau, where it still stands.

3. Other estimates are as high as 200,000; much depends on how the question is phrased, which has changed in almost every census. More than 75,000 Native Hawaiians live elsewhere in the United States, including at least 33,000 in California.

4. Jacob Adler, "The Kamehameha Statue," *Hawaiian Journal of History* 3 (1969): 87–91; Gavan Daws, *Shoal of Time* (Honolulu: U. of HI Press, 1968), 29, 34–46; Hal Glatzer, email, 8/97; Philip H. Viles Jr., *National Statuary Hall Guidebook* (Tulsa, OK: Viles, 1995), 45; Poka Laenui, emails, 7/98; West Hawaii Today, website, 7/98; Laura Steinhoff, *Cultural Identity Within the Hawaiian Sovereignty Movement* (Portland, OR: Reed College BA thesis, 1997), 11–12, 21–22, 33–34; Bureau of the Census, *1990 Census, HI* (DC: GPO, 1992); Gene Demby, "It Took Two Centuries, but the Native Hawaiian Population May Be Bouncing Back," NPR, 4/18/2015, npr.org/sections/codeswitch /2015/04/18/398578801/it-took-two-centuries-but-the-native-hawaii-ans-has -finally-bounced-back; "The Native Hawaiian and Other Pacific Islander Population: 2010" (DC: U.S. Census, 2012), census.gov/content/dam/Census/library/publications /2012/dec/c2010br-12.pdf

———— ✫ ————

3. The Flat Earth Myth on the West Coast
CALIFORNIA *Sacramento*

An 1883 statue of Christopher Columbus and Queen Isabella of Spain dominates the ground floor rotunda of the California State Capitol. At first glance, for California thus to honor Columbus seems absurd. After all, he never came within several thousand miles of Sacramento. Nor did Italian Americans in Sacramento cause the California Columbus monument to come into being, as they did elsewhere in the United States. D. O. Mills, a Sacramento banker, donated the statue; at its dedication, his brother declared "that California, more than any other state in the American Union, fulfills [Columbus's] visions of marvelous lands beyond the setting sun." Californians, like Columbus, had journeyed west to find their fortune. The nineteenth century was the time of "manifest destiny" as the United States conquered Indian nation after Indian nation and then went on to take Hawaii, Puerto Rico, Guam, and the Philippines, just as Columbus and the Spanish had done in the Caribbean.[1]

The nineteenth century was also the prime time for telling lies about Columbus. One was the flat earth myth. Most Americans learned in grade school that Europeans thought the world was flat until Columbus proved it round; the statue illustrates this myth. As *The American Pageant*, a high school American history textbook, told it, "The superstitious sailors, fearful of sailing over the edge of the world, grew increasingly mutinous."[2] My poster book *The Truth About Columbus* includes a photo of a 1492 globe made in Europe *before* Columbus sailed and points out that in 1491 almost no one thought the world was flat. It *looks* round. In a lunar eclipse, it casts a round shadow on the moon. The Catholic Church said it was round. Sailors are especially able to appreciate its roundness when ships disappear over the horizon hull-first as the roundness of the earth gets in the way. Columbus never had to contend with a superstitious crew worried about falling off the end of the earth.

American novelist Washington Irving, who invented Rip Van Winkle, popularized the flat earth fable in 1828 in his bestselling biography of Columbus. Irving probably thought it added a dramatic flourish. Writers of American histories soon picked up the story, and since textbooks tend to be

In the California State Capitol, Columbus holds up a sphere to persuade the queen of the roundness of the earth. The caption on the monument invokes another myth: "I will assume the undertaking," she said, "for my own crown of Castile, and am ready to pawn my jewels to defray the expenses of it, if the funds in the treasury shall be found inadequate." The words are from the 1837 *History of the Reign of Ferdinand and Isabella* by William Prescott, whose work *The Columbia Encyclopedia* calls, charitably, "outdated because of subsequent research." Kirkpatrick Sale's book on Columbus calls the jewel-pawning scene "pure fiction."

clones of each other rather than based on historical sources, his little hoax persists in some books to this day. Other elements of American culture still perpetuate it. A character in the movie *Star Trek V*, for instance, says, "The people of your world once believed the earth to be flat; Columbus proved it was round." This statue in Sacramento helps maintain the myth, as does a statue of Columbus holding up a globe at the Ohio State Capitol.

Irving himself probably thought it would do no harm. But it does. It invites us to believe that most people had only a crude understanding of the planet they lived on before a forward-thinking European man of science brought them out of ignorance. Such a story uplifts Columbus's voyages from mere passages for plunder and trade into scientific expeditions. It also makes the boss smarter than the "motley crew," in the words of *The American Pageant*. And it fits with the archetype of progress in American culture: we typically imagine our predecessors as primitives, exactly the kind of folk who would believe in a flat earth.

In the past, Americans invoked Columbus reflexively when celebrating progress. Columbus, Wisconsin, boasts a Columbus Museum mostly filled with objects from the 1893 Columbian World Exposition in Chicago. Forty years later, conjoined with its 1933 Century of Progress exposition, the Windy City was still celebrating Columbus. Near the downtown lakefront on newly built Columbus Drive, Chicago put up an elaborate Columbus monument whose four busts symbolize "faith, courage, freedom, and strength."

Often, Italian Americans lie behind the adoration of Columbus across the American landscape.[3] The 1933 monument in Chicago says it was "[c]ommissioned by Chicago-area Italian Americans." Local Italian Americans, rather than any historic incident, also gave us monuments to Columbus in Columbus Circle in New York City, along the riverfront in Philadelphia, on the grounds of the state capitols in Indiana and Iowa, and in other locales across America. As late as 1992, the 500th anniversary of his arrival, Italian Americans were still at it. The Sons of Italy in America paid for a new Columbus marker in Albany, New York, as part of that city's observance of the Columbus Quincentennial. Philadelphia donors with Italian last names put up a monolith to honor Columbus as "Explorer, Charismatic Leader, Mathematician, Cartographer, Navigator, Visionary, and Naturalist"!

Across America, Columbus probably gets more statues, monuments, and plaques in public places than any other individual. Many stand in locations named for him, for more cities, counties, and geographic features are named "Columbus" or "Columbia" than have been named for anyone except George Washington.

In Washington, DC, Columbus's monument in front of Union Station proclaims:

> To the memory of Christopher Columbus Whose high faith and
> indomitable courage gave to mankind a new world.

The Eurocentrism of that statement is breathtaking: only when Europeans arrived did "mankind" arrive. Historian William McNeill estimated that when Columbus arrived in the Americas in 1492, about 100,000,000 people already lived here. Were they not mankind? At the State Capitol in Indianapolis, a monumental bust of Columbus says:

CHRISTOPHER COLUMBUS

> Born in Genoa, Italy, 1451. Discovered America October 12, 1492. This
> land of opportunity and freedom was thus preserved for humanity by the
> perennial genius abiding in the Italian race.

Somehow the people living here were not "humanity" either, and somehow if Columbus had not gotten here to preserve it, the Americas might have vanished! But then, as the Bishop of Avila said to Queen Isabella in 1492, "Language is the perfect instrument of empire."

The people who were here first are no longer passively accepting these Eurocentric views. On October 14, 1991, demonstrators splashed the monument in front of Union Station with red paint, leaving the message "500 years of genocide." The next year, to mark Columbus's Quincentennial, Native Americans poured blood over it. In Denver, the American Indian Movement launched a 1992 counter-demonstration that included a "counter-memorial," consisting of 100 skeletal tipis, 25 feet tall, burned and scorched, accompanied by 29 official-looking historical markers with texts by American Indian Movement leader Russell Means, Native American author Leslie Marmon Silko, Spanish priest Bartolomé de las Casas, and others. Protesters wrote "stolen land" and "murderer" at the base of a 50-foot Columbus statue in Pittsburgh, also in 1992. "Killing the Indians," read a sign found at a Columbus statue freshly coated with red paint in Torrington, Connecticut. In Newport, Rhode Island, a statue of Columbus was sprayed with red paint on Columbus Day, 1993, and on January 16, 1998, a woman sprayed red paint on a sculpture of Columbus inside the White House. Throughout the Americas, from Chile to Canada, Bolivia to Honduras, paint-wielding protesters have repeatedly defaced statues of the fifteenth-century explorer. According to the protesters, the paint symbolizes the blood shed by Native Americans resulting from the conquest of the Americas that began with Columbus's second voyage in 1493.

After the questioning of Confederate monuments sparked the murders of nine African Americans by a neo-Confederate in Charleston, South Carolina, in 2015, other statues and monuments came under fire. It seems somehow appropriate to begin our summary of this phenomenon with the Columbus status in the Californian state capitol, about as far away from Charleston as possible, within the contiguous United States. In June 2018, thirteen protesters climbed on this Columbus statue, demanding its removal, claiming Columbus started the process of genocide of Native populations in the Americas.[4]

The flat earth myth and these Columbus statues and monuments help legitimize what Californians in the nineteenth century, Spaniards in the fifteenth century, and other Europeans in the centuries in between had done to Native Americans. They imply that only Europeans really matter, because only Europeans are really progressive. If Californians no longer wish to make this claim, now that California is less than 50% European American, they could add words or symbols to the flat earth statue that prove the story was a lie, and tell the Native side as well as the European side of Columbus's accomplishment.

Better yet, Californians might replace this tired cliché with a new statue representing *California's* difficult and marvelous history. When Americans put up yet another plaque or statue about Columbus, they are really admitting a failure of their own historical imagination. Why not bring to light a less-known figure of *local* importance? If Californians want to honor Italian American "explorers," they might choose Alejandro Malaspina or Paolo Emilio Botta. Malaspina was an eighteenth-century Italian navigator and naturalist in the Spanish navy who circumnavigated the globe three times. He led a scientific expedition between 1789 and 1794 that explored the Pacific Coast and tried to find a northwest passage to Asia. Botta served aboard *Le Héros*, the French vessel commanded by Auguste Duhaut-Cilly, in 1827–28. Botta described the people and fauna of California and translated Duhaut-Cilly's extensive book on California into Italian. These men are not familiar names from second grade on, so Americans might learn something from commemorating either person. Unfortunately, the California landscape is silent about these Italians, who did reach California. It shouts about Columbus, who did not.[5]

1. The United States didn't actually finish conquering the Philippines until the next century—about 1916. See chapter 25.

2. In 1994, in one of those typical textbook makeovers that corrects a mistake with the smallest change possible, *Pageant* replaced "fearful of sailing over the edge of the world" with "fearful of sailing into the oceanic unknown."

3. For the same reason, the Minnesota State Capitol boasts a statue of Norwegian explorer Leif Ericksson.

4. *Lies My Teacher Told Me About Christopher Columbus* (NY: New Press, 2014) gives a full analysis of Columbus's role in world history.

5. "The Columbus Group," *Sacramento Record-Union*, 12/23/1883; Kirkpatrick Sale, *The Conquest of Paradise* (NY: Knopf, 1990), 92; William H. Harris and Judith S. Levey, *The New Columbia Encyclopedia* (NY: Columbia UP, 1975), 2213; J. B. Russell, *Inventing the Flat Earth* (NY: Praeger, 1991), 43–51; Sherburne Cook and Woodrow Borah, *Essays in Population History: Mexico and the Caribbean, I* (Berkeley: U. of CA Press, 1971); Ira J. Bach and Mary L. Gray, *A Guide to Chicago's Public Sculpture* (Chicago: U. of Chicago

Press, 1983), 9; Clipping, 10/12/93 in Save Our Sculpture files, RI Historical Commission; "Columbus Statue Attacked," *The New York Times*, 10/13/97; Paul Duggan, "White House Vandalism Fits a Pattern of Protest," *The Washington Post*, 1/17/98; James D. Hart, *A Companion to California* (Berkeley: U. of CA Press, 1987), 139, 300; Miguel A. Bernad, "The Ascent of Canlaon," www.aenet.org/bernad/bernadb.htm 4/7/99; Cassie Dickman, "Protesters of Christopher Columbus 'Genocide' Climb Statue, Get Arrested at California Capitol," *Sacramento Bee*, 6/5/2018, sacbee.com/news/politics -government/article212594239.html

✷

4. Exploiting vs. Exterminating the Natives

CALIFORNIA *Sacramento*

At 27th and I Streets in Sacramento stands "Sutter's Fort," one of the oldest buildings in California, preserved and reconstructed. It comes with a state historic marker:

SUTTER'S FORT

John Augustus Sutter, born of Swiss parents in Germany, arrived in New York in July 1834 and in California in July 1839. He founded the fort in 1839 to protect "New Helvetia," his 76-square-mile Mexican land grant. Of the original fort, the two-story central building, made of adobe and oak remains; the fort's outer walls and rooms, which had disappeared by the 1860s, were reconstructed after the state acquired the property in 1890.

While the marker is not wrong, it does not tell the most important facts about the fort, including who built it and how Sutter's enterprise worked.

John Augustus Sutter talked the Mexican governor of California into granting him 76 square miles of the Sacramento Valley. Of course, it was already occupied: about 200 Miwok Indians were living about twelve miles south of what became Sutter's Fort, Kadema village was five miles west, and five miles north was the territory of the Maidus. Following a pattern used across the continent (chapter 78), Sutter negotiated with chiefs or men he considered chiefs. He honored these men with the title of "capitanos" and gave them blankets, sugar, alcohol, and other goods after they supplied him with workers.

Although unmentioned on the marker, Sutter's Fort was first and foremost a Native American site. "Except for a few overseers, Indians did all the work on Sutter's rancho," historian Albert Hurtado points out. "His" Miwoks and Maidus built the fort, plowed the fields, planted wheat and other crops, tended his livestock, wove cloth, ran a hat factory and blanket company, operated a distillery, worked in his tannery, staffed something of a hotel for immigrants to California from the East, and killed deer to get food for them all.

Equally missing from the marker is any mention of the amazingly interracial nature of Sutter's Fort. While predominantly American Indian, Sutter's "New Helvetia" also had Mexicans, Swiss, Hawaiians, Russians, Germans, and Americans. Sutter even brought eight or ten Polynesian workers with him to California from Hawaii in 1839—one as his common-law wife.[1] Two years later, he bought Fort Ross and all of its stores, the only Russian settlement in California, on credit. He then organized a 200-man Indian army—clothed in Tsarist uniforms and commanded in German!—and used this militia to seize children from distant or hostile tribes to maintain his labor supply.

Interpretation within Sutter's Fort does tell that Native Americans built the place, which marks an improvement over how history is presented at California's many missions. At least twenty state historical markers treat missions without mentioning Native Americans—although mission communities *were* Indian communities typically comprising 200 to 2,000 natives, a handful of Spanish or Mexican soldiers and their family members, and two priests. Half a dozen other markers mention Indians only as recipients of Spanish services—the most insulting is at San Juan Capistrano, which the marker describes as "seventh in the chain of 21 missions established in Alta California to Christianize and civilize the Indians." In San Luis Obispo County, a marker does tell that Mission San Luis Obispo was "built by the Chumash Indians living in the area"; another marker for its outpost, Santa Margarita Asistencia, states, "Here the mission padres and the Indians carried on extensive grain cultivation." No marker in any other county lets on that Indians made and laid virtually every brick in every mission in California. Instead, like the slave plantations we will visit later (chapter 69), the head man did all the work himself, as in this marker in Santa Clara County:

OLD ADOBE WOMAN'S CLUB

This adobe, among the oldest in Santa Clara Valley, was one of several continuous rows of homes built in 1792–1800 as dwellings for the Indian families of Mission Santa Clara. It links the Franciscan padres' labors with California of today.

When interpretation does mention Indians at missions maintained as museums—particularly at those still owned by the Catholic Church—it presents the missions as harbors of shelter and well-being built *by* the Spanish *for* the Natives, echoing the state markers. Guides and labels do not tell how overseers forced Indians to farm, build, and even worship under threat of lash and chain.

At Sutter's Fort, labels do better. An early panel says, "Everywhere he went, Sutter noted how others built and ran forts. . . . He saw Native Americans used as labor." The next label is titled, "Miwok and Nisenan People Did Most of the Work." A later label is titled, "California Indians had Many Reasons for Working at the Fort," but its second paragraph admits, "Sutter also used force. If a village wouldn't cooperate, his militia attacked until the people agreed to work for him." Still, it shies away from the full story. Sutter did feed and pay "his" Indians, but the system amounted to serfdom and verged on slavery. "I had to lock the Indian men and women together in a large room to prevent them from returning to their homes in the mountains at night," wrote Heinrich Lienhard, Sutter's manager. "Large numbers deserted during the daytime." Sutter armed men from "his" nearby villages to steal children from more distant villages and sold the captives in San Francisco to pay his debts. Sexual pleasure may also have played a role; writer William Holden suggests Sutter "was fond of the young Indian women." In 1844, Pierson Reading, Sutter's manager, extolled the easy life he led: "The Indians of California make as obedient and humble slaves as the Negro in the south. For a mere trifle, you can secure their services for life." One California Indian recalled a life not so easy: "My grandfather was enslaved by Sutter to help in building the Fort. While he was kept there, Sutter worked him hard and then fed him in troughs. As soon as he could, he escaped and with his family hid in the mountains." James Clyman, who visited Sutter's Fort in 1846, corroborated his account:

The Capt. keeps 600 or 800 Indians in a complete state of slavery and I had the mortification of seeing them dine. I may give a short description: 10 or 15 Troughs 3 or 4 feet long ware brought out of the cook room and seated in the Broiling sun all the laborers grate and small ran to the troughs like so many pigs and feed themselves with their hands as long as the troughs contain even a moisture.

Before condemning Sutter too roundly, however, we need to compare Native life under the Spanish and Mexicans (including Sutter) to what happened under the Anglos who followed him. Spanish and Mexican rule was brutal. Indians had revolted against the missions in 1771, 1775, 1810, 1812, 1824, and 1831 according to California historian David Wyatt. Nevertheless, Sutter's enterprises did connect the Indians to the world economy. The alternative, *not* to be so connected, meant extermination. Anthropologists are fond of saying that the French penetrated Native American societies, the Spanish acculturated them, and the British expelled them. Or, equally accurate, the French exploited the Indians, the Spanish enslaved them, and the Anglos killed them. And, of course, disease played a major role, regardless of the colonizers' nationality.

Sutter volunteered his Indian garrison to U.S. Army Lt. John C. Frémont in Frémont's 1846 campaign against the "Californios," the Mexicans on the coast, during the Mexican War. Frémont's victory helped secure California for the United States, but the new territorial government had no further use for Native Americans. A newspaper account related the 1849 massacre of a Pomo Indian village at Clear Lake, north of San Francisco: "The troops arrived in the vicinity of the lake and came unexpectedly upon a body of Indians numbering between two and three hundred. . . . They immediately surrounded them and as the Indians raised a shout of defiance and attempted to escape, poured in a destructive fire indiscriminately upon men, women, and children. They fell, says our informant, as grass before the sweep of the scythe." Sutter would surely have had his Indian army conquer and enslave the Pomos rather than massacre them, but Sutter was not long to be a factor in California. That same year, James Marshall discovered gold some 50 miles east of Sutter's Fort. Sutter tried to keep it secret, but soon, thousands of Americans, hundreds of Chinese, and other immigrants from Europe and Latin America surged to California to seek their fortune. Sutter's rule was not strong enough to withstand this rush. His Indians fled, leaving no one to harvest his wheat. Miners plundered his livestock and even stole his mill-stones. In the ensuing anarchy, even his legal claim to the land was challenged (though eventually upheld) and Sutter went bankrupt.

The Natives likewise had to deal with this anarchic white frontier. For a moment, it seemed they might benefit from the discovery of gold. In 1848, of 4,000 gold miners in the central mining district, more than half were American Indians. One white might hire 50 Indians, who received about $40 a month, four times what Sutter had paid two years earlier; yet whites made huge profits from their labor. Some Native Americans were able to mine on their own using willow baskets, and some became temporarily middle-class from their earnings. Almost immediately, however, whites began driving Native workers out of the labor force. Indian men were confined to panning gold at the edges of white society; many Indian women became prostitutes.

Even these alternatives did not last long. White Americans thought of California Indians as depraved because most wore little or no clothing, as "digger Indians" because they used "primitive" gathering technology and ate "disgusting" food, as "horrendously ugly and dirty," and heathen even if Catholic. As a result, in the words of historian Tomás Almaquer, "the California state government launched a systematic policy of sanctioned decimation." In January 1851, Governor Peter H. Burnett's message to the California legislature read, "A war of extermination will continue to be waged between the two races until the Indian race becomes extinct." A startling drop in native population ensued. In 1848, perhaps 150,000 Indians lived in California, compared to about 15,000 non-Indians, mostly Mexican Californians. Ten years later, just 16,000 Indians were left.

By 1910, "Sutter's Indians" had been ravaged. The Maidus, who had numbered at least 9,000, were reduced to 1,000 people, and the Miwoks, starting with like numbers, to 670. They did not disappear though, and even rebounded somewhat by 1990—the Maidus to 2,334. They have disappeared from the historical marker for Sutter's Fort, however, even though they built it.[2]

1. He also had a legal wife in Switzerland.

2. Santa Barbara Indian Center and Dwight Dutschke, "A History of American Indians in California," in CA Dept. of Parks and Recreation, Office of Historic Preservation, ed., *Five Views* (Sacramento, CA: Office of Historic Preservation, 1988), 42, 70; Albert Hurtado, *Indian Survival on the California Frontier* (New Haven, CT: Yale UP, 1988),

47–49, 75, 88–89, 104–7; Hurtado, "John A. Sutter and the Indian Business," in Kenneth N. Owens, ed., *John Sutter and a Wider West* (Lincoln: U. of NE Press, 1994); Jack D. Forbes, "What Do We Honor When We Honor Sutter?" email, 1/19/99; Heinrich Lienhard, *A Pioneer at Sutter's Fort, 1846–1850* (Los Angeles: Calafia Society, 1941), 67–68; James Clyman, quoted in Robert F. Heizer and Alan F. Almquist, *The Other Californians* (Berkeley: U of CA Press, 1971), 19–20; David Wyatt, *Five Fires* (Reading, MA: Addison-Wesley, 1997), 39; William Holden, "'Captain' John Sutter," *American History* (2/98): 34, 66; Joe Pitti, conversation, 1/14/99; Philip Burnham, *How the Other Half Lived* (Boston: Faber and Faber, 1995), 101–8; Tomás Almaquer, *Racial Fault Lines* (Berkeley: U. of CA Press, 1994), 5, 8, 26, 120–30; Francis L. and Roberta B. Fugate, *Roadside History of New Mexico* (Missoula, MT: Mountain Press, 1989), 14; Melanie Turner, "Yes, Street Will Remain Sutter Place," *Davis Enterprise*, 1/10/99.

------------------ ✭ ------------------

5. China Beach Leaves Out the Bad Parts

CALIFORNIA *San Francisco*

A cul-de-sac off El Camino Del Mar near 28th Avenue in San Francisco leads to a lovely stretch of publicly owned coastline. At the head of the trail down to the beach is a large trapezoidal stone marker placed by Chinese Americans in 1981:

CHINA BEACH

Since Gold Rush times, this cove was used as a campsite by many of the Chinese fishermen who worked in and around San Francisco Bay. Their efforts to supply the needs of a young city helped establish one of the area's most important industries and traditions.

It's proper to have some Chinese American history on the California landscape because Chinese Americans played a major role in the West, not just building the railroads but also in mining, farming, business, personal service, heavy construction, and, as this marker tells, fishing. Indeed, in the early 1880s Chinese Americans made up 50% of all fishing crews in the Bay area. But this marker tells only half the story.

During most of the twentieth century, the beach was not called China Beach but Phelan Beach.[1] That's because whites expelled Chinese people from the beach and from the fishing industry in the 1890s. In 1880, California passed "An Act Relating to Fishing in the Waters of this State": "All aliens incapable of becoming electors of this state are hereby prohibited from fishing, or taking any fish, lobster, shrimps, or shell fish of any kind, for the purpose of selling, or giving to another person to sell . . . " Conveniently, only Chinese were aliens not eligible to vote. Courts declared the bill unconstitutional under the Fourteenth Amendment, but the legislature continued to pass similar measures until the end of the century. California's senators got Congress to pass the Chinese Exclusion Act in 1882, which cut Chinese immigration from 39,500 in 1882 to just ten persons five years later. Meanwhile white fishermen resorted to extralegal strong-arm tactics. By 1890, only 20% of the fishing community was Chinese, and their numbers continued to dwindle. Between 1880 and 1900, more than 40 towns across California drove out their Chinese residents and became "sundown towns."

"By 1893, riots and boycotts in San Francisco and the farming districts of California created conditions approximating civil war," according to a 1997 exhibit at the Autry Museum in Los Angeles. White thuggery forced many Chinese Americans back to Chinatowns for protection. Prejudice against Chinese Americans ran so high that San Francisco's public schools admitted African Americans to desegregated schools in 1899 and Native Americans in 1921, but kept Chinese Americans out until 1929.

Renaming China Beach Phelan Beach was ironically appropriate because James Phelan, three-term mayor of San Francisco at the end of the century, argued for excluding all Asians from the United States. As mayor, he allowed a blockade and later a quarantine of Chinatown.

That Chinese Americans would note on the landscape their success in fishing but not their exclusion from it is not surprising. While doing research for my book *The Mississippi Chinese*, I found that some young Chinese Mississippians knew only vaguely that whites had until

As U.S. Senator from California, 1915–21, Phelan supported laws keeping Japanese from owning land in the state. This poster comes from his reelection campaign in 1920, which did not succeed.

recently kept them out of white public schools and other institutions. Their parents had never told them, perhaps feeling it would only disempower their children to know that dominant whites had oppressed them. Nor is this a uniquely Chinese trait: the chapter "In What Ways Were We Warped?" tells how working-class white families often do not inform their children of the trials they faced. African Americans in the 1990s expressed regret to family historian Edward Ball that the survivors of slavery didn't tell their "children things they should have told them." Shame may also be a factor—a group's sense that its members must have done *something* to cause the powers that be to oppose them so strongly.

Some might argue to leave the China Beach marker as it is—let bygones be bygones. But all too often, all across America, historic sites emphasize only the good parts of our past. Surely, historian Paul Gagnon is correct to say, "We do not need a bodyguard of lies. We can afford to present ourselves in the totality of our acts." Rather than leaving out the bad parts, as this marker does, hoping that anti-Chinese sentiments will never recur, San Franciscans could engage in a civic dialogue to formally declare the beach China Beach. In 2018, the city did discuss Phelan Avenue, named originally for Phelan's father but later associated with the mayor, and wound up renaming it for Mexican artist Frida Kahlo. Installing a plaque at China Beach completing its half-told story, including the Phelan interlude, would expose rather than continue to honor the anti-Chinese sentiments exemplified in Mayor Phelan's career.[2]

1. In about 1983, the National Park Service, which owns the site, reverted to "China Beach." By 1998, some San Franciscans knew it only as Phelan Beach while others knew it only as China Beach.

2. Robert F. Heizer and Alan F. Almquist, *The Other Californians* (Berkeley: U. of CA Press, 1971), 170–71; Jack Chen, *The Chinese of America* (San Francisco, CA: Harper and Row, 1980), 97–101; Arthur F. McEvoy, *The Fisherman's Problem* (Cambridge: Cambridge UP, 1986), 75–103; Ask Asia, "Linking the Past to Present: Asian Americans Then and Now," www.askasia.org/frclasrm/readings/r000192.htm; Autry Museum exhibit, 10/97; Hyung-Chan Kim, ed., *Dictionary of Asian-American History* (Westport, CT: Greenwood, 1986), 452; Franklin Odo, *In Movement* (Los Angeles: Visual Communications, 1977), 39; James D. Hart, *A Companion to California* (Berkeley: U of CA Press, 1987), 94, 384; Tomás Almaquer, *Racial Fault Lines* (Berkeley: U of CA Press, 1994), 163; Nancy Wey, "Chinese Americans in California," in *Five Views* (Sacramento: CA Office of Historic Preservation, 1988), 103–58; Loewen, *The Mississippi Chinese: Between Black and White* (Prospect Heights, IL: Waveland Press, 1988); Edward Ball, *Slaves in the Family* (NY: Farrar, Straus and Giroux, 1998), 18; Paul Gagnon, *Democracy's Untold Story* (DC: American Federation of Teachers, 1987), 19; Dominic Fracassa, "Citing Racist Connection, SF Changes Phelan Avenue to Frida Kahlo Way," *San Francisco Chronicle*, 6/19/2018.

★
---

6. Killing a Man Is Not News

CALIFORNIA *Downieville*

Downieville, a small town in the Sierra Mountains, is one of only three places in California, so far as I know, to have historical markers about lynchings.
In 1996, E Clampus Vitas, an organization in the western states whose major
function seems to be to mark historic places, put this plaque on the Craycroft
Building near the site of the Jersey Bridge in Downieville:

IN MEMORY OF JUANITA

*The Spanish woman also known as Josefa, was hung off the Jersey
Bridge, July 5, 1851, a short distance downstream from this spot, for the
murder of Frederick Alexander Augustus Cannon.*

*Cannon and his friends were celebrating Independence Day and after
closing of the saloons they passed Jose and Josefa's cabin.
He broke the door down. However, history did not tell what happened.
The next morning he came back, supposedly to apologize.
An argument ensued and Josefa stabbed Cannon fatally in the heart.*

*A mob trial was held and she was sentenced to death.
Josefa climbed the scaffold without the least trepidation and placed the
rope around her own neck. Her last words were, "I would do the same
again, if I was so provoked."*

In *Women of the Sierra* Anne Seagraves includes an entry on the person she
calls "First White Woman Lynched in California": "Juanita (no last name
was ever recorded) was considered attractive, with long, lustrous dark hair;
delicate features; and passionate black eyes. . . . She lived with her lover in a
small cabin, and although many men sought her favors, Juanita was content
with her man, José." In the early morning hours on the day after Independence Day in 1851, drunken revelers "went down the streets breaking open
the doors of houses," in Seagraves's words. Jack Cannon was one of these, a
big man, popular with his fellows, something of a camp rowdy. He broke

into Juanita's house, and she asked him to leave her alone. He called her a prostitute; she swore back at him. A few hours later he returned, perhaps to apologize, perhaps to continue his pursuit. José asked him to have his door repaired. Cannon began once more "to insult both Juanita and José. The argument became louder, and a crowd began to form." What happened next is not clear: either Cannon lunged at her or Juanita simply exploded. In any event, she grabbed a bowie knife and plunged it "into Cannon's chest, instantly killing him. The stunned spectators, realizing their friend was dead, started yelling 'Lynch them!'"

The mob dragged Juanita to the main plaza of Downieville and placed Cannon's body, with its ugly wound, nearby. Without delay, the crowd set up a mock trial. It was so unfair that when the young man chosen as defense attorney actually defended Juanita, the mob threw him off the barrel he stood on, broke his glasses, and kicked and beat him. The jury found her guilty and sentenced her to hang within the hour. She tossed her straw hat to a spectator in the crowd, and in Seagraves's words, her "thick dark hair came cascading down around her slender shoulders. She took the noose in her own hands and placed it around her neck." Within seconds of her hanging, Juanita was dead.

According to Seagraves, "this infamous miscarriage of justice was heard around the world," with newspapers in Europe commenting on American "border justice." Surely this ugly event deserves a marker. But we must pause a moment and analyze what the hanging and the marker teach us about gender in the United States. Seagraves makes ironic use of "Independence Day": "The speeches about equality and liberty for all obviously were not meant to include women, especially of the Mexican race." Juanita's status as a Mexican indeed made her vulnerable. White Americans have consistently singled out people of color as lynching victims, beyond the protection of the law. Many other lynchings occurred in California in the nineteenth century, disproportionately of Mexican Americans and Chinese Americans. But Juanita's status as a woman did not contribute to her death. The only other marker on lynching in California makes this evident: in Placerville, a city formerly called "Hangtown" because of its many lynchings, a state historical marker states that "In the days of 1849, when this city was called Hangtown, vigilantes executed many men for various crimes."

Across America, while four of every five lynching victims have been non-white, fewer than one in ten has been female.[1] The new lynching memorial in Montgomery, Alabama, shows this imbalance. Those numbers suggest that female status is quite different from nonwhite status. Seagraves implies this when she converts Juanita from "of the Mexican race" to "First White Woman Lynched in California" in her title, because to lynch a white or a woman is unusual and sensational. Because African Americans, Mexican Americans, and Chinese Americans have been lynched in numbers far greater than their proportion in the population, social scientists infer (correctly) that these groups have historically had lower status. Because males have been lynched in numbers far greater than their proportion in the population, should we infer that men have historically had lower status?[2]

The answer, surprisingly, is yes, we should, in certain ways. This is surprising because the women's movement of the 1970s correctly taught our society that women have been disadvantaged in politics, most occupations, and many different parts of our culture. The lack of a men's movement has kept us from seeing that men have been disadvantaged in other areas of our culture. One disadvantage has to do with violent death. Not just in frontier California but even today, men are four times more likely than women to be murdered. Men are also 2.6 times as likely to die from accidents. Even nature seems to have it in for men: lightning is seven times as likely to strike men as women! Nature, of course, doesn't check sex before sending a bolt; men are more likely to be exposed to storms. Our culture tells men it's not manly to take shelter or drive sedately on the one hand, and our occupational structure steers men toward dangerous all-weather jobs like telephone lineman and truck driver on the other. Either way, the culture has been and still is careless of male lives—most obviously in requiring only men to register for the draft. Consistent with this devaluation, men seek medical care later and less often than women suffering from similar ailments, and are also 4.3 times as likely as women to kill themselves.

Thus, although the text of "In Memory of Juanita" is accurate, in a sense the plaque's very existence implies that women's lives are more precious than men's. Most lynchings of men, even white men, go unremarked on the American landscape because the victims were male. Newspapers follow this rule every day. Thus, wire service reports in the 1990s about "ethnic cleansing" in the Balkans frequently emphasized that "women and children" were among the slain. Although male deaths were usually more numerous, they went unremarked so journalists could tap into the outrage that readers are supposed to feel when they learn that these perpetrators would stoop to kill women and children. Killing men is more common and more morally acceptable. In short, killing men is not news. Killing women is.

To single out the lynching of a woman for remarks on a plaque presents a double irony. The first involves women: only sixteen of about a thousand California state historical markers treat women. This is because California's social structure has not allowed women to play an equal part, and California's historical markers do not recognize many women who nevertheless did make history. This Downieville marker hardly makes up for those omissions.

The second irony involves men. Seagraves calls Juanita's hanging "one of the most shocking crimes in California history," but California had at least 59 lynchings between 1875 and 1935, and many more before 1875, almost all of men. None is noted on the landscape, though each was just as shocking in its way as Juanita's. This Downieville marker hardly makes up for those omissions, either.

The literal unremarkability of violence against men points to how unconscious these gender differences are. They lie deep in our mores. Sociologists use the term "intersectionality" to point to the combined effects of two or more sources of stigma or discrimination, but they have too easily assumed that gender discrimination disadvantages women in all areas. As this marker shows, American culture also discriminates against men, especially where violence is concerned.[3]

Chapters 41 and 30 tell how some states are even worse than California about leaving women off the American landscape.

1. This ratio is visible in Montgomery, AL, where Maya Lin's famous Civil Rights Memorial lists "Forty Lives for Freedom"—civil rights martyrs killed by white supremacists. All are male except Viola Liuzzo, killed by Ku Klux Klansmen after the 1965 Selma to Montgomery march, and the four little girls killed in the Sixteenth Street Baptist Church bombing in Birmingham.

2. Most lynchers have been white males who disproportionately victimize people in their racial/ethnic outgroup and their sexual ingroup.

3. Anne Seagraves, *Women of the Sierra* (Lakeport, CA: Wesanne, 1990), 29–31; James D. Hart, *A Companion to California* (Berkeley: U. of CA Press, 1987), 292; Arthur F. Raper, *The Tragedy of Lynching* (Montclair, NJ: Patterson Smith, 1969), 481; Kenneth D. Kochanek and Bettie L. Hudson, "Advance Report of Final Mortality Statistics, 1992" (Hyattsville, MD: National Center for Health Statistics), *Monthly Vital Statistics Report*, 43 no. 6 (supplement, 12/8/94), 1–4, 8–10; Roy U. Schenk, "Statement to the Wisconsin Supreme Court . . . ," *Transitions* 13 no. 1 (1/93):13–14.

———————— ✶ ————————

7. Don't "Discover" 'Til You See the Eyes of the Whites!

OREGON *La Grande*

A marker on Interstate 84 just south of La Grande used to tell how, in 1811,"The Wilson Price Hunt Astoria Expedition, after failing to find a route through Snake River Canyon, obtained the guidance of a Shoshone Indian and discovered the route over the Blue Mountains." Getting a Shoshone guide made sense—the Blue Mountains were their home, after all, so the Shoshones knew their way over them. But even though this marker said that a Native American showed European Americans the way, it still credits the Wilson Price Hunt Astoria Expedition with "discovering the route."

So far as I can tell, this marker has disappeared. Instead, at least two other historical markers tell of the Wilson Price Hunt Astoria Expedition, but they don't even mention that a Native was involved.

Bodies of water seem particularly vulnerable to "discovery." In Iowa, Jean Nicolet "discovered" Okamanpadu Lake according to a marker, which does not explain how the lake got its obviously Indian name. A plaque in Louisiana marks the death of Hernando de Soto, who "was buried in the Mississippi River, which he discovered." The Spaniards buried their leader furtively in the river *because* of the presence of earlier discoverers—American Indians whom de Soto had antagonized—lest they notice and take advantage of the now leaderless men.

Ironically, de Soto wasn't even the first *white* man to see the Mississippi. Henry R. Schoolcraft wasn't the first white to "discover" its origin either, but you can't tell that from the Minnesota marker that credits him unless you read carefully. "The long search [for the source of the Mississippi] came to a close with the discovery of Lake Itasca by Henry Rowe Schoolcraft in 1832," according to the marker. Then the marker ends by admitting that Schoolcraft had merely rechristened Lac la Biche, Lake of the Elk, as "it was known to Indians and traders," to Itasca, a name he made up.

Other lakes get similar treatment. According to Michigan markers, whites discovered Lake Michigan, Lake St. Clair, and Lake Superior. Lake Erie gets a more complex marker: "Named for the Erie Indians, this was the last of the

Great Lakes discovered by white men . . . " Actually, *none* of them was discovered by white men, but this marker at least admits that Native Americans existed and implies they knew of Lake Erie.[1]

This discovery problem begins with 1492, of course. All across America, plaques commemorate Christopher Columbus, "discoverer of America." Historians and educators denounced "discovered" rather thoroughly during 1992, the Columbus Quincentenary. Some commentators denounced the denunciations as mere exercises in political correctness. When historical markers emphasize explorers like Jean Nicolet just because they were white, they offend people of color. Worse is their effect on whites, who are invited to infer that only when whites see a place has humankind discovered it. The practice literally dehumanizes Native Americans. The plaque at Schroeppel, New York, even has a European discovering people:

KUH-NA-TA-HA

Indian fishing village 1654, known to the Indians as "Place of Tall Pines." Discovered by Father Le Moyne.[2]

The Portuguese Explorers Monument in Newport, Rhode Island, put up in 1988, makes the most grandiose discovery claim of all: it celebrates "the discovery by the Portuguese of two thirds of the world."

Inspired by such examples, Adam Nordwall, an Ojibwe, led a group of Native Americans to Rome in 1973 and "discovered" Italy! They demanded an audience with the Pope and otherwise comported themselves as explorers are wont to do. So far as I know, however, no plaque marks the spot at the Rome airport where they first set foot on Italian soil.

A museum in Capetown, South Africa, changed its account for Dr. David Livingstone from "discovered Victoria Falls in 1855" to "visited Victoria Falls in 1855." Immediately, we realize that "visited" is accurate while "discovered" was Eurocentric. Eurocentrism similarly distorts all the "discover" markers in the United States.[3]

Chapter 1 tells how Native Americans are removing from the American landscape some of the names European "discoverers" have imposed. Chapters 21, 24, 35, 66, and 89 lament other Eurocentric terms on markers and monuments across America.

1. In 2018, the Michigan Historical Commission vowed to remove and improve its share of these discovery markers. Sandra Clark, director of the Michigan History Center, noted,

"They say that so-and-so discovered Lake Michigan—of course, Native Americans, indigenous people, had known Lake Michigan was there for a very long time before the first Frenchman found out it was there." Quoted in Maxwell Evans, "Historical Markers Scrutinized: Narrow Focus, Euro-American Perspectives Subject of April 18 Meeting," Capital News Service, in *Traverse City Record Eagle*, 4/12/2018, record-eagle.com/news /go/historical-markers-scrutinized/article_d621fcff-fd87-5c62-b6a4-c3687384c6f1 .html

2. "Indians Claim Italy by Right of Discovery," *The New York Times*, 9/24/73; Loewen, *The Truth About Columbus* (NY: New Press, 1992), 5; Peter Hulme, *Colonial Encounters* (London: Methuen, 1986), 1.

3. An organization in Syracuse, Neighbors of the Onondaga Nation, whose slogan is "Working in Solidarity with the Onondaga Nation," notes my critique of this marker on their website, but they don't seem to plan any action to correct it. "Pendleton Historic Trail," Historical Marker Database, hmdb.org/marker.asp?marker=111565

————— ★ —————

8. No Communists Here!

WASHINGTON *Cowlitz County*

In the last half of the 1800s and the first three decades of the 1900s, many socialists, anarchists, and communists were among the Europeans coming to the United States. Fleeing persecution in Europe, they sought better opportunities here. After they became citizens, these people elected socialist mayors and legislators, most prominently the long-term mayor of Milwaukee. They set up self-help organizations and cooperative stores to get better prices from wholesalers and pass the savings on to their members. They also influenced to some degree the social programs of both political parties.

On today's landscape this history of left-wing politics is almost invisible.

Among all immigrant groups, Finns were probably the most radical.[1] "Finn Hall," a historical marker in Cowlitz County in southwest Washington, shows the cover-up in action. The association that built Finn Hall was communist; its official name translated as "Comrades Society." But the Washington state historical marker disguises this:

FINN HALL

In 1916 Finnish immigrants constructed a hall near the site under the name of a literary association (Kirjallisuus Seura), forming a lending library. Although they brought their diet, language, and saunas with them, some old country beliefs were left behind. These people found it

*necessary to meet where they could study the social customs of their new
country, challenge and question partisan politics, and reflect on new
technological insights. At this cultural center were held language classes,
meetings, athletic activities, wedding dances, funerals, and programs with
oratory, drama, poetry, vocal and instrumental music. Steaming kettles
of coffee and the warmth of dignified waltzes, pulsating polkas, and
schottisches brought togetherness to these rugged individualists.
Life to them was involvement.[2]*

The state put up this marker in October 1976. Writing twenty years later
about her role, Helmi Kortes-Erkkila, who chaired the local marker committee, admitted that leaving out the name of the organization in English
"was a factual omission." Members did not think saying "Comrades Society" would be prudent in 1976, when the United States was locked in a
struggle with the Soviet Union. "Memories of the McCarthy years were still
influencing the sons and daughters of the former sympathizers of Socialists,
Communists, and IWW's," Kortes-Erkkila explained, "so we resorted to
the popular and non-controversial term that was inscribed on the historical
marker."

Passionate political debates and intellectual controversies raged in this hall,
especially in its early years when the Woodrow Wilson administration had
declared war on all leftists. "Life to them was involvement"—well, yes. But
involvement in *what*? In a communist society in rural southwest Washington?
No one would envision *that* without help, and this historical marker hardly
provides the necessary assistance.[3]

*Chapter 49 is another example of how historic sites mystify left-wing politics all
across America. So is the next chapter.*

1. In 1915, Finns helped organize the Nonpartisan League in North Dakota, which dominated state government by 1918. In 1919, Finns helped form the Farmer-Labor Party,
   which was strong in Washington, Montana, and South Dakota; a related group won the
   governorship in Minnesota in the 1920s.
2. The Finn Hall historical marker is still up as of June 2018. Interestingly, the word
   "technological" on the marker has been carved out, making the marker a bit more accurate.
3. Helmi Kortes-Erkkila, "The Finn Hall Historical Marker" (Vancouver, WA: Typescript, 1996).

---✯---

9. Using Nationalism to Redefine a Troublesome Statue

WASHINGTON *Centralia*

In Washington Park (chapter 79), in the town square of Centralia, stands a statue that looks like all the other "doughboys"—lone infantrymen in helmets that honor World War I soldiers all across America. The American Legion put it up in 1924. On the front it reads:

THE SENTINEL

It was their destiny—rather it was their duty—the highest of us is but a sentry at his post.

In 1993, Centralia added a "Freedom Walk" to connect the statue with the street. Next to the walk a granite tablet declares the walk to be a memorial to the men and women who died in all American wars since World War I. It looks as if Centralia intended "The Sentinel" to take care of World War I and the "Freedom Walk" and granite tablet to memorialize World War II, Korea, Vietnam, and our smaller interventions.

Closer inspection reveals that "The Sentinel" has nothing to do with World War I, however. On its backside are the words "To the memory of Ben Casagranda, Warren O. Grimm, Earnest Dale Hubbard, Arthur McElfresh, slain on the streets of Centralia, Washington, Armistice Day, Nov. 11,

1919, while on peaceful parade wearing the uniform of the country they loyally and faithfully served." But why would anyone be slain "while on peaceful parade"? The answer is simple: that isn't what happened.

On Armistice Day, November 11, 1919, a year after the end of World War I, Centralia witnessed probably the most tragic event in its history. An armed confrontation between members of the American Legion and the Industrial Workers of the World—the IWW or "Wobblies"—ended with victims killed on both sides. Anti-labor writers dubbed the affair "the Centralia Massacre" and used it to destroy support for the IWW throughout the Northwest.

The IWW was a militant left-wing union especially strong in the West among loggers and miners. The American Legion had formed only recently, started by Teddy Roosevelt Jr. and by U.S. officers in Western Europe alarmed by growing support for leftist ideas among our victorious troops. Composed of veterans, its purpose according to its constitution was "to maintain law and order" and "to foster and perpetuate a 100% Americanism." Its ideology also matched the outburst of nativism and anticommunism whipped up by the Woodrow Wilson administration. Within months it had a million members.

In 1918, an anti-Wobbly mob had burned down the Wobbly union hall and beaten up union members. According to historian Robert Weyeneth, in 1919 "Centralia's American Legion post scheduled an Armistice Day parade with an unusual agenda: destruction of the [new] local IWW hall. The plan was an open secret in town for several weeks, but unbeknownst to Legion organizers, the IWW decided not to be intimidated and to defend the hall when attacked." Warren Grimm was a Centralia Legionnaire who had recently helped invade Siberia with the U.S. Army (chapter 75) and therefore considered himself an expert on communism. He called the Wobblies "the American Bolsheviki" and led the Legion against them. As the parade neared the hall, some Legionnaires rushed the building. Armed Wobblies opened fire from inside as well as from an adjacent boardinghouse and nearby hilltop. The gunfire killed Grimm, Casagranda, and McElfresh and wounded almost a dozen others but did not drive off the Legion, who broke into the building. The Wobblies scattered, and the Legion dragged the contents of the hall into the street and set them on fire. Wesley Everest, an IWW organizer, fled north towards the Skookumchuck River. Cornered at the river, he shot and killed Earnest Dale Hubbard, one of his pursuers. Everest was captured, beaten, and

put in jail. Some IWW members may also have been killed during the day;
historians differ.

That evening, a mob dragged Everest from the city jail and took him to the
edge of town. There they may have cut off his testicles, then his penis.[1] The
men hanged him from a bridge and then shot him.

Eleven union members were tried for killing the Legionnaires. Eight were
convicted and served prison terms of more than ten years. Some jurors later
filed an affidavit saying they had wrongly convicted the men, believing that
if they did not sentence them to prison, Legionnaires were likely to kill them
in the streets. No one was ever charged with lynching Wesley Everest.

For decades, the union was ignored on the Centralia landscape. Other than
Everest's tombstone in a paupers' cemetery at the edge of town, nothing told
the IWW's side of the story. In 1990, historian Weyeneth went to Centralia
to see how the town remembered the 1919 event. He found silence. The
nearby county historical museum had nothing about it. No plaques marked
the sites of either IWW hall or Everest's lynching. After some difficulty Weyeneth got "The Sentinel" and Wesley Everest's grave listed in the National
Register of Historic Places, deliberately choosing one site from each side.
Nominating them spurred useful civic discussion within Centralia and led to
coverage by the Associated Press and National Public Radio in 1991.

The next year, a project taking a pro-labor view of the Armistice Day confrontation was a statewide winner of "History Day," a national contest for high
school students. The winning student received a marble marker, which she
proposed to give to the city for placement next to "The Sentinel." The marker
featured a noose and a hammer and a long text suggesting "Incidents like the
Centralia Massacre" helped bring about "an eight-hour day, Social Security,
Worker's Compensation, Occupational Health and Safety, and job security."

Months of controversy followed. Residents pointed out inaccuracies in the
student's text. The local newspaper suggested a plaque "carefully and diplomatically worded, limited to known facts only." Instead, the town resorted to
bland nationalism and added the "Freedom Walk" and granite tablet. Implicitly, these additions conflated "The Sentinel" with conventional World War
I doughboys, despite the words to the contrary on its base. Clearly, in 1993
Centralia was still not ready to address the events of eight decades earlier.

The sites of many important events in labor history are well marked
across the United States, especially by the United Mine Workers of America

(UMWA). In Ludlow, Colorado, the UMWA put up an inspiring monument to the thirteen children and seven adults killed there on April 20, 1914, when company police and the Colorado National Guard burned the striking miners' camp. Michigan has accurate historical markers for the General Motors sit-down strike of 1936–37. Two plaques mark the 1911 Triangle Shirtwaist fire that killed 146 women in New York City, and there is an annual remembrance at the site. Indeed, disasters of all kinds, but especially mine fires and explosions, are memorialized all across America.

The Centralia event is more problematic. Afterward, Woodrow Wilson's attorney general, A. Mitchell Palmer, led raids and legal attacks that broke the back of the IWW nationally. Today, it exists only as a shell, hardly strong enough to underwrite a historical marker let alone win the public support needed to put it up. The rest of the labor movement might not want to honor such a left-wing union. And labor did draw the first blood that Armistice Day. What difference does it make that Centralia took the easy way out? Why not simply forget about it all, as some of Robert Weyeneth's interviewees suggested? A labor historian described how a recent union march in Centralia, unconnected with the Armistice Day events, met a very different reception than in nearby towns. "While neighboring towns had been warm and friendly . . . in Centralia the marchers were greeted by plain clothes police and warnings to get off the main street." Weyeneth concluded, "The new Freedom Walk suggests that the journey toward historical reconciliation remains unfinished." Resorting to nationalism to camouflage a one-sided statue is no substitute for honest history on the landscape and in the minds of the town.

On December 14, 1997, the owner of a Centralia antique mall dedicated a dramatic mural about the Armistice Day confrontation that showed Wesley Everest rising from his grave. This work by New Jersey artist Mike Alewitz provoked condemnation from the American Legion's national convention. Ironically, some IWW members outside Centralia also attacked the mural at first. Within Centralia, Alewitz's project did spur the formation of a Centralia Union Mural Project Committee and may yet prompt a civic dialogue that could result in historical accuracy, memory recovery, and even reconciliation.[2]

1. Writers differ: John M. Barry says they did; Tom Copeland says they didn't.
2. Robert R. Weyeneth, "History, He Wrote: Murder, Politics, and the Challenges of

Public History in a Community with a Secret," *Public Historian* 16 no. 2 (spring 1994): 51–73; John Helmer, *The Deadly Simple Mechanics of Society* (NY: Seabury, 1974), 223; John M. Barry, *Rising Tide* (NY: Simon & Schuster, 1997), 139; Tom Copeland, *The Centralia Tragedy of 1919* (Seattle: U. of WA P, 1993); William Pencak, *For God and Country* (Boston: Northeastern UP, 1989), 49–53; Julia Stein, "Thomas Churchill's *Centralia Dead March* and The Repression of Working Class Memory, Part I," email, 11/96; Scott Sunde, "Thanks to Mural, No Pushing Aside Centralia Conflict," *Seattle Post-Intelligencer*, 12/13/97.

———————— ✭ ————————

10. What We Know and What We Don't Know About Rock Art

NEVADA *Hickison Summit*

On U.S. 50, 24 miles east of Austin, a historical marker titled "Hickison Summit" tells about nearby petroglyphs left by prehistoric people: "About one mile northwest lies a natural pass between two buttes which, prehistorically, the aborigines may have used as a site of ambushing migratory deer herds. Three petroglyph panels are located in this pass." Unfortunately, the marker then tells us what the petroglyphs mean: "Petroglyphs suggest magical or ritual connections with hunting activities. They were added seasonally by the group's religious leader, or shaman, as omens to insure a successful hunt."

Actually, no one really knows what the petroglyphs mean. In the 1960s, many archaeologists believed that petroglyphs were done to "insure a successful hunt," but few believe it now. Today, most think that the art was created by shamans who were high on hallucinogenic drugs rather than tribal leaders before a hunt. But there isn't much evidence to support either hypothesis.

Although no tribe in the area today preserves a tradition of interpreting Nevada rock art, contemporary Native American names for these petroglyph sites do include "shaman's cache," "shaman's spirit helper place," and the like. Another bit of evidence comes from cultures in South Africa. There, drugs do cause people to "see" forms that have some commonalities with the images in some Nevada petroglyphs. On the other hand, Robert Bednarik, petroglyph expert from Australia, points out that rock art there, which also has images that resemble some similarities to the images in Nevada, is "conspicuously non-shamanistic." Indeed, "the Hickison petroglyphs," according to Nevada historian Ron Powers, "are mostly female genitalia."

In *The Imprint of Man: Rock Art of the North American Indians*, Campbell Grant sums up what he calls "a number of plausible explanations." In addition to the hunting and hallucinogenic hypotheses, Grant suggests that petroglyphs may be clan symbols ("signatures" of, for example, the turtle clan), images connected with religious rituals or puberty and fertility rites, drawings of constellations, references to important events, maps to mark hunting areas, or simple doodling by children or adults. To this list, I would add that they just may be "art"!

Archaeology is a difficult undertaking. Archaeologists must understand not only a society's technology, occupations, and kinship, but also its religious beliefs, architecture, the botany of the plants it used, even its disease history. Indeed, archaeologists must be experts on every aspect of the society they study—but they can't be. Moreover, they face the task of trying to reconstruct all the foregoing from the faintest evidence—those few objects that have survived for hundreds or thousands of years. On top of that, since most ideas come into a culture from other cultures, archaeologists need to be experts on more than one society.

The result is that archaeologists often end up projecting ideas from our culture onto the largely blank slate of the distant past, and this is why new hypotheses sweep the field from time to time. Rock art is particularly hard to decipher; Charles Lock concludes in "Petroglyphs In and Out of Perspective"

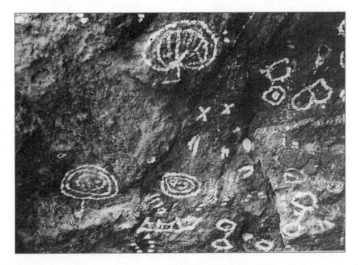

Are these Hickison petroglyphs signatures ("Kilroy was here!")? religious images? constellations? history? symbols of ownership? doodling? art?

that he is "less than enthusiastic about the possibility of learning anything about petroglyphs, even with the help of the most advanced technology."

This Hickison marker is not only out of favor with current thinking in archaeology, then, it is also far too sure of itself. Archaeologists cannot now date petroglyphs within several thousand years—radiocarbon dating doesn't work because organic material is the first to weather off the rocks. Nevertheless, this marker author seems to know the rock paintings were "added seasonally"! A more accurate marker would present a summary of the changing interpretations of petroglyphs. Thus, it would teach visitors to be skeptical of *all* archaeological hypotheses—whether of the Bering Strait crossing, the "disappearance" of "the Anasazi" (chapter 14), or the purpose of petroglyphs. Unfortunately, historic sites routinely present a single view of the past, with no room for ambiguity about the nature of the event itself or uncertainty over the evidence for differing views of it.[1]

1. Sue Ann Monteleone, "Who Made NV Rock Art? And When? That is What Rock Art Specialists are Trying to Find Out," *NV State Museum Newsletter* 25 no. 2 (1997): 2; David S. Whitley, "Shamanism and Rock Art in Far Western North America," *Cambridge Archaeological Journal* 2 no. 1 (1992): 91; Robert Bednarik, "On Neuropsychology and Shamanism in Rock Art," *Current Anthropology* 31 no. 1 (2/90): 77–79; see J. D. Lewis-Williams and Thomas A. Dowson, "Reply," Ibid: 80–83; Ron Powers, conversation, 1/99; Campbell Grant, *The Imprint of Man: Rock Art of the North American Indians* (Cambridge: Cambridge UP, 1983), 13–14; Charles Lock, "Petroglyphs In and Out of Perspective," *Semiotica* 100 no. 2/4 (1994): 405; Robert F. Heizer and Martin A. Baumhoff, *Prehistoric Rock Art of Nevada and Eastern California* (Berkeley: U. of CA Press, 1962), 225.

---------------★---------------

11. Don't Criticize Big Brother
NEVADA *Nye County*

At the junction of U.S. 95 and the road to Mercury, Nevada, is the historical marker for the "Nevada Test Site"—surely after Las Vegas, one of Nevada's most famous places. The site certainly merits a marker: larger than Rhode Island, it is surrounded by additional land larger than Connecticut "withdrawn from the public domain," as its website euphemistically puts it. Moreover, what happened here had worldwide significance.

The marker's text, written in 1971, seems straightforward enough:

NEVADA TEST SITE

Testing of weapons for defense and for peaceful uses of nuclear explosives is conducted here. The nation's principal nuclear explosives testing laboratory is located within this 1,350-square-mile, geologically complex area in the isolated valleys of Jackass, Yucca, and Frenchman Flats. Selected as on-continent test site in 1950, the first test took place on Frenchman Flat in January, 1951.

Unfortunately, this text conceals far more than it reveals. Its matter-of-fact tone is not appropriate for such a controversial site. No one would infer from this marker that nuclear tests detonated here gave leukemia to scores of residents in towns like St. George and Cedar City, Utah, and may be causing the premature deaths from cancer of hundreds more. No one could guess that among the places hit hardest by radiation from this site would be counties in the Midwest and upstate New York. No one would accuse the U.S. government of knowing about these dangers before the first 1951 test and taking care to protect its own workers at nuclear laboratories while neglecting even to measure carefully the radiation dangers to citizens living downwind of the tests. And no one would imagine that all the while, the government was conducting a disinformation campaign to reassure westerners that there was no danger when it knew better. As Richard Lamm, former governor of Colorado, and Michael McCarthy summarized in 1982, "the government acted recklessly and carelessly . . . [and then] covered up news of rising cancer rates in desert towns. When finally confronted with evidence that its tests were responsible, it began a long litany of denial."

From 1951 to 1962, 126 atmospheric "tests" of atomic "devices" took place at the Nevada site in addition to 828 belowground blasts. More than 40 of the underground tests vented radioactivity into the atmosphere, sometimes creating large mushroom clouds. Political scientist Howard Ball describes the scene: "Days sometimes began with bright white early-morning atomic explosions, followed by brownish-purple mushroom clouds . . . ; and children played in the grey radioactive dust as they would in snow." The explosions were seen and heard in San Diego, San Francisco, and southern Idaho; near the site, they knocked people off their feet.

In 1953, sheep ranchers in the area lost thousands of their animals to the blasts. Elevated levels of strontium 90, a radioactive isotope from the fallout,

The marker also fails to convey what the explosions were like. Political scientist Howard Ball describes the above-ground blasts as seen in southern Utah: "Days sometimes began with bright white early-morning atomic explosions, followed by brownish-purple mushroom clouds . . . ; and children played in the grey radioactive dust as they would in snow." This aerial photo shows subsidence craters from some of the 828 below-ground blasts, one of which, the Sedan crater, is nearly a quarter-mile wide and 320 feet deep and has been declared a national historic site. Below-ground explosions continued through September 1991.

began showing up across the United States and became a political issue in the 1956 presidential campaign. Protestors demonstrated at the site beginning in 1957, and in 1964 *The Wall Street Journal* reported that the fallout from Nevada had reached Canada. Thus, this 1971 marker, whose content might have been written by the Atomic Energy Commission itself, amounts to a whitewash on the federal government's behalf. Its tone is anachronistic—a product of 1950s thinking when most Americans trusted the government and distrusted its critics. Such views lasted longer in Nevada and Utah, but by 1973 the Watergate scandal and continuing Vietnam quagmire would make this mindset passé even in the Great Basin.

Nevada marker officials are hardly alone in their reluctance to criticize the government. Across the United States, virtually no historical marker criticizes any government—federal, state, or local—for any act since Reconstruction. Curiously, in this way markers resemble high school American history textbooks, which also make the government, especially the federal government, their biggest hero.

"Curiously" because from newspaper editorials to radio talk shows, post-Watergate Americans make something of a national pastime out of criticizing their governments—but not on markers or in textbooks. Some acts of criticism took place at this Nevada test site—and the marker needs updating to tell about them as well. It never hints that thousands of protesters have been arrested there over the years—over a thousand on single days in 1988 and 1989—while demonstrating for peace and against nuclear testing. Nor has Nevada revised the plaque to include the major lawsuit, *Allen v. U.S.*, that residents of southern Nevada and southwest Utah, harmed by radiation, filed in 1979, won in U.S. District Court in 1984, and then lost on appeal three years later.

Why did the Atomic Energy Commission test in Nevada? Because it was cheaper and easier than testing in the Pacific.[1] For the same reason, the AEC also often detonated at ground level, while Great Britain always used a tower, balloons, or airdrops in its Australian tests to minimize fallout. What American taxpayers saved in logistics, however, may cost much more in health care expenses and premature deaths. In 2012, the United States finally passed the Radiation Exposure Compensation Act, empowering the Department of Justice to pay $50,000 to every "downwinder" who developed a "specified compensable disease." By 2015, DOJ had awarded more than $2 billion, and the program will continue until at least 2022.

In all, according to Tomas Clark of *The Seattle Times*, the Nevada test site released 148 times as much radiation as the Chernobyl disaster in the Soviet Union. Rebecca Solnit tells how protesters in Kazakhstan, where the Soviet Union tested its bombs, named themselves the Nevada Semipalatinsk Antinuclear Movement in solidarity with the protesters in Nevada. In Kazakhstan, "more than a million people signed the Nevada Semipalatinsk statement opposing nuclear testing," Kazakhstan's miners threatened to strike, and tens of thousands of Kazakhs demonstrated in October 1989, Solnit writes. Partly in response, the USSR stopped testing later that month and declared a unilateral moratorium on further explosions. President George Bush followed suit two years later with a temporary halt since extended by his successors but without the force of law of the Soviet shutdown.

Perhaps American protesters never had a chance for equal success. Keeping the public uninformed and misinformed prevented American citizens from making educated choices over how much to test, where to test, and even whether to test at all. In a democracy, the people are supposed to learn about and think over such weighty matters. The bland text on this marker hampers that process by treating citizens as children who need to be shielded from all the historical issues related to the site. Governments are bigger and older than any citizen to be sure, but citizens should not be fooled into treating them like godlike parents. Like children, governments make mistakes and must be corrected. Nevada deserves credit for venturing to treat a recent, important, and controversial topic, but its reluctance to criticize the government only continues on the landscape the cover-up that the Atomic Energy Commission started in the 1950s.[2]

1. Testing in the Pacific was not without hazard to Pacific islanders and to the planet.
2. www.em.doe.gov/em94/swnts.html, 6/98; www.nv.doe.gov/nts, 11/98; Lorna Arnold, "The Elements of Controversy Project: A Review," *Public Historian* 18 no. 1 (winter 1996), 41; Tomas Clark, "50 Years from Trinity; Part II: Nevada Test Site," *The Seattle Times*, 1995; Howard Ball, *Justice Downwind* (NY: Oxford UP, 1986), 69–70, 77, 90, 128, 144, 155–61, 197; Richard D. Lamm and Michael McCarthy, *The Angry West* (Boston: Houghton Mifflin, 1982), 154–56; Rebecca Solnit, *Savage Dreams* (San Francisco, CA: Sierra Club Books, 1994), 26, 97, 105, 119; *Congressional Record*, 9/11/97, online, 59, 110; U.S. DOJ, "Radiation Exposure Compensation Act," justice.gov/civil/common /reca

THE MOUNTAINS

12. Circle the Wagons, Boys—
It's Tourist Season

IDAHO *Almo*

Opposite the post office in the little town of Almo stands a beautiful slab of stone carved into the shape of the state of Idaho. It memorializes a horrifying incident in the history of the West:

ALMO, IDAHO

Dedicated to the memory of those who lost their lives in a horrible Indian massacre, 1861. Three hundred immigrants west bound. Only five escaped.
—Erected by S & D of Idaho Pioneers, 1938.

The Almo marker, decorated with Christmas lights.

The local grocery store sells a pamphlet giving more details about this extraordinary event. Not only was it the most important incident in Almo's past, but it was also by far the most brutal massacre of white pioneers in all the history of the West.

At Almo, more European Americans died than in Custer's Last Stand at the Little Bighorn and the Fetterman Massacre in Wyoming combined!

The only trouble is, it never happened.

Proving that an event did *not* occur can be difficult. Regarding the Almo massacre, however, based on "over forty years of research," historian Brigham Madsen makes a compelling case. First, Madsen shows that the *earliest* mention of the massacre was in 1927—66 years after 1861! He notes that other much smaller hostile incidents won extensive newspaper coverage when they occurred. "Even the slightest Native American disturbance along the road received immediate notice from these various western newspapers," wrote Madsen. "The lack of any reference to an affair at Almo Creek can only mean that there was no 'Almo Massacre.'"

Next, Madsen confirms that the records of the Indian Service, the War Department, and state and territorial bureaucracies reveal no mention of the event. "A massacre involving the deaths of 294 emigrants would have engendered a massive amount of material," he argues. "There is none."

Then Madsen looks into the origin of the 1927 account. Its author, Charles Walgamott, cited "an old trapper who gave us a detailed account" when Walgamott had visited Almo some 50 years earlier. And in 1927, Walgamott talked with a "Mr. W. M. E. Johnston, whose family bought the land in 1887," when it "still bore evidence of the hard-fought battle." Johnston also claimed to have heard a version of the massacre "from an old Indian," which Walgamott incorporated into his story.

According to Walgamott's account, the Indians surrounded the train of more than 60 wagons, causing the pioneers to circle their wagons in traditional Hollywood style. The emigrants settled in for a siege, digging a trench under each wagon and throwing the dirt to the outside. Meanwhile, they tried to dig a well but found no water. "Men who undertook to bring water from the creek were shot down. Occasional shots from the Indians killed or badly wounded some white man, woman, or child, which threw the members of the besieged party into greater confusion and grief."

Walgamott added details to construct a scene out of Dante's *Inferno*: "The excitement grew intense as panic-stricken horses in their struggles broke their fastenings and ran frantically around the inclosure, while others in their attempt to break loose were snorting, rearing, and trampling the earth from which rose great columns of dust through which frantic women and children darted hither and thither in their aimless attempt for relief. This, with the constant yelling of the Indians and howling of their dogs, made a scene too wild and awful to contemplate."

As with any good massacre, there must be survivors to tell the story, and Walgamott told of six. First came a young couple: "It was on the fourth night that the guide employed by the train gave up all hopes and planned his escape. He was accompanied by a young woman who had displayed great courage and marksmanship. Under the protection of the darkness they crawled through the sagebrush, making their way to the mountain." The other four made for even better copy. "In the after part of the same night one man and two women, one with a nursing baby, secretly stole from the doomed camp, crawling for miles on their hands and knees. The mother of the child, in her anguish and endeavor to keep in company with the others as they crawled through the brush, was compelled to take the garments of the child in her teeth and carry it in that manner." Later, the four "lived on rose-buds and roots" until rescued by Mormons, who then found all the rest slain. The Mormons buried these unfortunates "in the wells which they had dug."

Madsen finds it hard to believe that in three or four days, while under siege, these people dug wells deep enough to accommodate 294 bodies. He also notes that no one has ever been able to come up with any information about the 300 emigrants before the attack or the six survivors afterward.

With all these inconsistencies in the "old trapper/old Indian" account, how did it get memorialized on the landscape? It fit with white Americans' stereotype of "savage Indians," of course. Historian John D. Unruh Jr. pains-takingly compared emigrants' diaries with their letters to friends and found that throughout the Western migration, pioneers embellished and invented hostile Indians for the folks back East. Unruh also found a rash of fictional massacre reports in newspapers in the 1850s.

By the 1930s, these stories resonated with the familiar American arche-type of whooping Indians racing their horses around the ring of wagons. Of course, Indians rarely circled like that—such action would merely expose them and their horses to danger. In fact, the "tradition" of circling Indians did not begin in the West but in 1883, in Buffalo Bill's Wild West Show, where Indians had to circle because they were riding in a circus ring! Buffalo Bill became the biggest show business act in the world; by 1893, 50 imitators were touring the United States. Hollywood picked up the tradition, and the rest was history—or, rather, myth. One-third of all Hollywood movies made before 1970 were westerns! Today, as western novelist Larry McMurtry put it, "Thanks largely to the movies, the lies about the West are more potent than the truths."

Madsen researched the specific genesis of this marker. Two Idaho newspaper editors, striving to put this part of Idaho on the map, concocted an "Exploration Day" set for October 17, 1938. They wanted tourists to visit the "City of Rocks," an interesting nearby formation of rock pinnacles, which they were trying to get designated as a national monument. They were also trying to interest government officials in diverting Snake River water to a huge irrigation project. The Almo Massacre marker was a way to draw visitors.

When "Exploration Day" dawned, a mix of rain and snow dampened enthusiasm for the Almo Massacre marker dedication, which ended up being attended mainly by its donors, the Sons and Daughters of Idaho Pioneers. Over time, however, even though the event never happened, the massacre marker won a place in the hearts of Almo citizens. A few years ago, the Idaho State Historical Society tried to remove it, but "was met with firm resistance" according to Larry Jones, a state historian. "Apparently, the majority of the fifty or so permanent residents still consider the marker to be accurate." The historical society placed its removal attempt on hold.

According to the Hollywood myth, now cast in stone at Almo, Native Americans were the foremost obstacle pioneers faced. Actually, though Natives did defend their homes and lands against intruders, on the whole, they proved more help than hindrance to westering white pioneers. Peter Boag studied the diaries of emigrants who passed through this part of Idaho, scene of more conflicts between Native residents and newcomers than any other part of the Oregon Trail. He found 105 references to Native Americans in 32 journals written between 1835 and 1850. Boag classified 41 as clearly positive, 35 as neutral ("saw an Indian"), and 29 as negative. The unfriendly comments were mostly disparaging physical descriptions of Native Americans or reactions to annoying trade relations. Only two diaries referred to actual or rumored attacks or nearly violent encounters. Instead, journals tell how Indians offered salmon in trade and helped whites ford rivers.

Relations did worsen over time. As more newcomers came they became a burden to the Natives, disrupting their hunting patterns and threatening their sovereignty. The trade nexus wore thin; later in the emigration, whites had less need for Indian guides or interpreters or even for Indian foods. Native Americans meanwhile had grown more dependent upon European technology, leading them to beg and even steal to get it. European Americans became more careless in their dealings with Native Americans: they refused to pay tributes, for example, and "physically abused the Indians," in Boag's words. Even so, according to Unruh, throughout the entire West between 1842 and 1859, of more than 400,000 pioneers crossing the plains, fewer than 400, or less than 0.1%, were killed by American Indians. And no one massacred anyone in Almo.[1]

1. Brigham Madsen, "The 'Almo Massacre' Revisited," *Idaho Yesterdays* 37 no. 3 (fall 1993): 59; Susan L. Franzen, *Behind the Facade of Fort Riley's Hometown* (Ames, IA: Pivot Press, 1998), 23, 27; Larry McMurtry, "Broken Promises," *The New York Review of Books*, 10/23/97, 16; Larry Jones, correspondence, 3/96; Lonn Taylor, "Frontiers Real and Mythical" (Houston, TX: ALHFAM , 1996), 8; John Unruh Jr., *The Plains Across* (Urbana: U. of IL Press, 1979), 156, 176, 185; Peter G. Boag, "'The Indians of This Place Are Snakes in the Grass'—the Overlander Perspective on Native Americans in Southern Idaho, 1836–1860," *Idaho Yesterdays* 37 no. 3 (fall 1993): 17–23.

-------------- ✶ --------------

13. Bad Things Happen in the Passive Voice, but Now the Church Is Facing the Truth

UTAH *North of St. George*

In 1990, 28 miles north of St. George off Utah Highway 18, leaders of the Church of Jesus Christ of Latter-day Saints and the state of Utah, along with descendants of the victims, dedicated a major monument to the Mountain Meadows Massacre. The memorial is a broad tablet of white granite made of several panels set into a hillside above a valley. Although it has many words, none says who put it up. In fact, no words tell *who* did anything; the key verb is in the passive voice:

IN MEMORIAM

In the valley below, between September 7 and 11, 1857, a company of more than 120 Arkansas emigrants led by Capt. John T. Baker and Capt. Alexander Fancher was attacked while en route to California. This event is known in history as the Mountain Meadows Massacre.

The monument lists the names of those who were killed and goes on to say, "The following children survived and were returned to their families in Northwest Arkansas in September 1859." Again, there is no clue as to *who* returned them to their families. "Historic Sites View Finders" direct your view "toward the historic campsite" and the "massacre site." The latter says, "Most of the Baker-Fancher Party were killed on September 11, 1857, as they were being escorted out of the valley heading north." Once more, the monument is silent on who did the killing and who did the escorting.

It's not that historians were in the dark. Years before the monument went up, Juanita Brooks examined the event closely in her book *The Mountain Meadows Massacre*. She concluded, as have others, that Latter-day Saints did it with help from their Paiute allies. In the words of historian Kenneth Foote, the Mountain Meadows Massacre was "the most shameful event in Mormon history," murdering more "gentiles" than all the Mormons killed by gentiles along the entire path of their exodus from New York through Missouri and Illinois to Utah. Latter-day Saints still dominate Utah, however, especially southwest Utah. Hence the passive voice. In 1990, the church and civic leaders who organized what proved to be a memorable reunion between descendants of attackers and victims could not bring themselves to be more candid on the landscape.

When coupled with the passive voice, the term "massacre," while perfectly appropriate, guaranteed that most tourists would infer that Native Americans did the grisly work. Across the United States, historic markers and monuments often use "massacre" when Native Americans kill European Americans, even when as few as one white died![1] Utah alone has at least five historical markers that use "massacre" for Indian attacks on whites and none for any white attack.[2] Latter-day Saints knew this.

How did it happen that Latter-day Saints, themselves European American pioneers, would engage in the mass slaughter of other European American pioneers? To understand this event we need to examine the prickly relations between the Mormon Church hierarchy, which was also the government of Utah Territory, and the United States in 1857.

For eight years, beginning with the 1849 California gold rush, Mormon settlers in Utah had hosted emigrants from the East. Often, the relationship was mutually beneficial: wagon trains got new oxen and supplies, and Mormons got household valuables not likely to make it over the mountains to California. But often the relationship was acrimonious: Mormons abused emigrants from Missouri and Illinois in revenge for having themselves been mistreated in those states, and wagon trains drove their cattle through Mormon towns and farms without regard for damages caused while trespassing. When disputes went to court, the judicial system inflamed rather than settled the quarrels because non-Mormons felt they received no justice from Mormon judges and juries.

Most Americans have no idea that among the official actions of the U.S. Army is the "Utah War" of 1857–58. The Buchanan administration was upset that many federal appointees in Utah Territory—judges and Indian agents—found it impossible to function in the theocracy that Brigham Young had created. The army took its campaign quite seriously. To an even greater extent, so did the Latter-day Saints. According to the *Encyclopedia of Mormonism*,

> A large contingent of United States troops was marching westward toward Utah Territory in the summer of 1857. Despite having been the federally appointed territorial governor, Brigham Young was not informed by Washington of the army's purpose and interpreted the move as a renewal of the persecution the Latter-day Saints had experienced before their westward hegira. "We are invaded by a hostile force who are evidently assailing us to accomplish our overthrow and destruction," he proclaimed on August 5, 1857. Anticipating an attack, he declared the territory to be under martial law and ordered "[t]hat all the forces in said Territory hold themselves in readiness to March, at a moment's notice, to repel any and all such threatened invasion."

Young, head of the Mormon Church, preached on the need for Mormons to declare independence from the United States and ordered Latter-day Saints not to sell "gentiles" a grain of wheat. He even made contingency plans to abandon and burn Salt Lake City and evacuate to the mountains.

Into this cauldron of suspicion came the unfortunate Fancher party en route from Arkansas to California. These emigrants were hardly diplomatic. Mormons refused to sell them supplies, so they "boasted of what they would do when the army came to set these people straight," according to Brooks. Mormons claimed that some in the Fancher group bragged about being in the mobs that had run the Saints out of Missouri. Probably they hadn't,[3] but these were explosive words in Utah. Latter-day Saint leaders had also been talking with nearby Paiutes, inflaming them to be allied with them against the United States. When the Fancher émigrés camped at Mountain Meadows to get their livestock ready for the trek across the dry lands to the west, the Indians and Mormons attacked. The initial assault killed several on each side; then the Fancher survivors hunkered down behind embankments. Several of them tried to dash for help, but Mormons and Paiutes killed them before they got far.

Then came the massacre. Mormon leaders in southwest Utah determined to wipe out the entire group. On the fifth day of the siege, they sent John D. Lee and William Bateman under a white flag to talk with the emigrants. Lee said the Mormons would escort the travelers to safety, but they would have to abandon their cattle and horses to the Indians and give up their arms to the Mormons. Desperate, the pioneers agreed. The young children were put in a wagon and driven ahead along with another wagon carrying two or three wounded men. Women and older children then walked out. Last came the unarmed men, each accompanied by an armed Mormon. "At the command 'Halt! Do your duty!'" Brooks tells that "each Mormon man was to shoot the emigrant at his side, the Natives hiding in the brush were to kill the women and older children, and Lee and the drivers were to finish off the wounded in the wagon." It went according to plan. Most of the Fancher men fell at the first volley. Within a few minutes, it was all over—except the cover-up.

Brooks established that two local Mormon leaders, Col. W. H. Dame and Lt. Col. I. C. Haight, had ordered the killing. (They had military titles because the Saints had organized a militia.) But the blame may belong at the top; according to historian David A. White, "Brigham Young cannot escape responsibility for setting the stage for the tragedy." His interpreter, apparently speaking for Young, promised the Paiutes the party's cattle in a meeting with Young beforehand, which helped incite them to attack. On the other hand, Young also sent orders to let the emigrants pass without harm, but the directive arrived after the massacre had taken place. Brooks and historian Will Bagley show, however, that Young ordered and participated in the cover-up.

If the army had kept coming, the United States might have witnessed an attack on a religious sect that would have dwarfed the 1993 assault on the Branch Davidians in Waco, Texas.[4] But that autumn, the crisis eased. An early snowfall coupled with the Mormons' scorched-earth policies in eastern Utah caused logistical problems for the army. Later, President Buchanan declared the emergency over.

The Latter-day Saints released the orphaned children they had adopted, and the United States reunited them with family members back in Arkansas.[5] The Mormon leadership concocted a cover-up that blamed the Paiutes, but as the United States established more control over Utah, some Mormon had to be held responsible for the massacre, because too many people knew that whites had done it. In 1870, the Mormon leadership excommunicated Haight, one of the men who had ordered the killings, and Lee, who had negotiated the surrender and directed the murders on site. Four years later the church readmitted Haight, but in 1876, after two trials, John D. Lee was sentenced to death. On March 23, 1877, he was shot to death by firing squad at the scene of the crime. Dozens of other church members in southern Utah breathed a sigh of relief when Lee's sacrifice appeased the national cry for justice. For decades, the event was simply not talked about openly in southern Utah. Juanita Brooks breached that wall of silence; her courageous research proved that Lee was hardly the only Mormon responsible for the massacre but had been made a scapegoat by the church hierarchy. In 1961, respecting her scholarship, the Latter-day Saints reinstated Lee posthumously, to the relief of his family.

The 1990 monument was, in fact, the third on the site. In 1859, Maj. James H. Carleton of the U.S. Army was ordered to investigate the massacre and bury the victims. His report blasted the Mormon perpetrators and tells how his men gathered 34 unburied corpses—skeletons by then—and buried them in a mass grave. Above it, his men built a rock cairn 50 feet around and twelve feet high, topped by a twelve-foot cedar cross. Two years later, Brigham Young visited the monument and watched as his entourage toppled the cross and destroyed the cairn. U.S. soldiers rebuilt it a year later, but Mormons tore it down again.

In 1932, the Utah Pioneer Trails and Landmarks Association and some nearby residents erected a stone marker at this burial site two miles off the highway. It stood until 1990 but was seen by few tourists, who had to brave a steep and narrow track to view it. Although it too used the passive voice and avoided the words "Mormons" or "Latter-day Saints," this marker admitted that the Fancher train "was attacked by white men and Indians." In the

1960s, the church bought the site and removed road signs telling of the 1932 marker, making it even harder to find. In 1990, it replaced the 1932 marker with a new one that removes any reference to who did it: "This stone monument marks the burial site for some of those killed in the Mountain Meadows Massacre in September 1857." The new 1990 marker also refers to the very first monument and states that it "was not maintained"—a passive-voice euphemism for "Mormons tore it down."

The truth about Mountain Meadows has long been available on the landscape—just not in Utah. In Harrison, Arkansas, where the Fancher train began its trek, a marker tells the saga in telegraphic style: "Camped at Mountain Meadows, Utah, in early Sept.—Attacked by Indians directed by Mormons—formed a corral with wagons—Fought several days till ammunition exhausted—approached by Mormons under flag of truce—promised protection—surrendered—all were killed except for seventeen small children—found later in Mormon homes—rescued by Army in 1859—taken to Arkansas . . . " This Arkansas marker tells much more history than Utah's. Another Arkansas marker at Caravan Spring is clearer still: "The entire party, with the exception of seventeen small children, was massacred at Mountain Meadows, Utah, by a body of Mormons disguised as Indians." But Arkansas is hardly forthcoming about its own massacres, such as the murder of surrendered black Union soldiers at Poison Spring (chapter 51). Meanwhile, in Virginia, a marker for the Warrascoyack Indian village notes that "their village was destroyed in 1623"—by whom is left obscure. All across the United States, when the dominant group has committed wicked deeds, historical markers either simply omit the acts or write of them in the passive voice.[6] Thus, the landscape does what it can to help the dominant stay dominant and the rest of us stay ignorant about who actually did what in American history.

Shortly after *Lies Across America* came out in 1999, however, and not sparked by its publication, the Mormon Church and survivors groups dedicated a new monument that was more forthright. They also put up two new historical markers on the path to the deficient 1990 memorial. These told the full story. Unfortunately, at the 1999 dedication, church president Gordon B. Hinckley declared, "That which we have done here must never be construed as an acknowledgement on the part of the church of any complicity in the occurrences of that fateful day," which bothered the descendants, as well as some truth-seeking Mormons.

★   ★   ★

By 2011, the church had bought more land and dedicated yet another monument, on the spot where the men and boys had been murdered. On September 11, 2011, for the first time, descendants were able to take a memorial hike along the path the men and boys from Arkansas had walked to their doom.[7]

1. Indeed, the previous essay commemorates a "massacre" in which no one died!

2. These are the Ephraim Massacre, Given Family Massacre, Gunnison Massacre, Pinhook Draw Massacre, and Salt Creek Canyon Massacre. Each of these attacks took the lives of between four and eight whites. The markers do not mention the number of Indian casualties, if known.

3. Jacob Forney, U.S. superintendent of Indian affairs in Utah, concluded that the Fancher "company conducted themselves with propriety." Friction also grew because Mormons refused to sell them food, and the Fancher train felt its cattle had a right to graze on Mormon hay and grazing grounds.

4. I use "sect" in its sociological sense—a small religious group with beliefs and practices distinctively different from the larger society and usually marginalized by it. The Mormon Church today is far too large and mainstream to be considered a sect.

5. Anna Jean Backus claims that her grandmother was an Arkansas child hidden by Mormons and raised in Utah. At the end of the list of survivors on the memorial is the sentence, "At least one other survivor remained in Utah." However, this is contested.

6. *Lies My Teacher Told Me* shows that high school U.S. history textbooks similarly insulate leaders from wrongdoing by putting their questionable acts in the passive voice.

7. Juanita Brooks, *The Mountain Meadows Massacre* (Norman: U. of OK Press, 1991[1950]), vi–viii, xx, 13, 46–57, 70–75, 110–11, 144, 184–87, 192–97, 290–91; John D. Unruh Jr., *The Plains Across* (Urbana: U. of IL Press, 1982), 252–84; David L. Bigler, *Forgotten Kingdom* (Spokane, WA: A. H. Clark, 1998), 161–79; Will Bagley, emails, 10/31/97, 12/31/98; "Mountain Meadows Massacre," *Encyclopedia of Mormonism, vol. 2* (NY: Macmillan, 1992), www.mormon.org,4/98; Kenneth E. Foote, *Shadowed Ground* (Austin: U. of TX Press, 1997), 246–63; David A. White, ed., *News of the Plains and Rockies, vol. 4* (Spokane, WA: A. H. Clark, 1998), 212–53; "Mountain Meadows Historic Site," National Register of Historic Places Inventory (DC: National Park Service); Anna Jean Backus, *Mountain Meadow Witness* (Spokane, WA: A. H. Clark, 1995), 16–20; Robert W. Coakley, *The Role of Federal Military Forces in Domestic Disorders, 1789–1878* (DC: GPO, 1988), 194–226; Mountain Meadows Association, "Plaques at 1999 Memorial Site," mtn-meadows-assoc.com/NewPlaques/plaques.htm; Mark Thiessen, "Statue Controversy Opens Old Wounds, Re-ignites Mormon Controversy," *Casper Star-Tribune*, trib.com/news/state-and-regional/statue-controversy-opens-old-wounds-re-ignites-mormon-controversy/article_3479fdf2-a248-5be3-ab6f-8c2f6a9313ff.html

———————— ★ ————————

14. Calling Native Americans Bad Names
ARIZONA *Navajo Reservation*

The names Americans use for many American Indian tribes are derogatory. European Americans often learned what to call one tribe from a neighboring rival tribe. Sometimes, whites simply developed their own contemptuous names for groups of Native people. Markers in Arizona are full of these wrong names. Some Native groups have responded to this confusion by accepting their new name even if it originally had negative connotations. Others are mounting determined efforts to be known by the name they call themselves. Arizona offers examples of both.

By far, the largest and most populous Indian reservation in the United States is the Navajo reservation, which occupies all of northeastern Arizona and extends into Utah and New Mexico. "Navajo" is the name given to these once nomadic people by the already-settled Tewa Pueblo Indians.[1] It may mean "thieves" or "takers from the fields." The Navajos came to the Southwest millennia after the Tewas and call themselves Diné, sometimes spelled "Dineh," which means "we the people."[2] Most Native American groups call themselves by names that mean "we the people." Like most societies, they were ethnocentric—seeing their own culture as the yardstick of sound human behavior—and these names reflect that certainty.

The name of another famous Arizona tribe, the Apaches, means "enemies." The Zunis named them that. Related linguistically to the Navajos, the Apaches, too, call themselves Diné. In southern Arizona, "Papagos" means "bean eaters," a name given by the nearby Pimas. The Papagos call themselves Tohono O'odam or "desert people." The Pimas, another southern Arizona tribe, refer to themselves as Ahkeemult O'odham or "river people." "Pima" actually means "I don't know," apparently their reply when asked their name in Spanish by an early explorer!

Americans have learned to call the people who built the ancient cliff dwellings at Canyon de Chelly in Arizona "the Anasazi." "Anasazi" is a Navajo word meaning "ancient enemies." Since the Anasazis have "vanished," according to anthropologists, we cannot now ask them what they called themselves. In reality, the Anasazi didn't "vanish" but merged into the various Pueblo peoples whose descendants still live in Arizona and New Mexico. Most Pueblo Indians prefer to call the Anasazi "ancestral Puebloans" and still know which pueblo includes descendants from which "Anasazi" site.

The use of derogatory names is hardly limited to Arizona. Native people living in far northern Canada and Alaska call themselves Inuits—again, "we the people"—while the Crees to their southeast called them Eskimos, "those who eat raw flesh." The Sioux call themselves Dakotas or Lakotas, meaning "allies" or "people," but their ancient enemies, the Ojibwes, called them Nadouwesioux, meaning "little snakes" or "enemies," and the French shortened it to "Sioux." In turn, the Ojibwes, sometimes written "Chippewas," refer to themselves as Anishinabes, "people of the creation." "Mohawk" means "cannibal" in Algonquian; they call themselves Kaniengehagas, "people of the place of flint."

Some names take note of physical characteristics of Natives. Thus, British Americans called the Salish ("we the people") the Flathead Indians. The French called two groups of Indians Gros Ventres, "big bellies," apparently derived from their name in Indian sign language. The French also renamed the Nimipus ("we the people") the Nez Percés, "pierced noses," because some of them wore nose pendants.

A few new names were complimentary. On the east coast, the British renamed the Lenape "Delawares." They didn't mind once the British explained that Lord De La Ware was a brave military leader. "Lenape" means—you guessed it—"we the people."[3] The most famous new name of all—"Indians," coined by Columbus for the Arawaks he met in the Caribbean—was complimentary in a sense: Columbus either thought he was in the East Indies or hoped to convince his supporters that he had reached that important trading destination by using the term.[4]

Some whites claim that their practice of naming sports teams for Native Americans is complimentary. Thus, we have the Florida State University Seminoles, Cleveland Indians, Atlanta Braves, and worst of all, Washington Redskins. Some Indians do consider some of these terms flattering. The Cleveland Indians defend their name on that basis, claiming it stems from a popular member of the team in the 1890s. "Chief Wahoo," the bucktoothed Indian caricature that still decorated Cleveland uniforms in 2018, offends many Native Americans, however. And Native American newspapers continue to react angrily to the "Washington Redskins" by portraying its team pennant next to ones for the "Atlanta Niggers," the "New York Kikes," and the "Chicago Polacks."[5] More positive terms like "braves" still trivialize Native Americans as mascots, some American Indians assert.

At least two tribes in Arizona are called by their own names. "Havasupai" means "people of the blue-green waters," referring to their homeland's beautiful waterfalls in a side gorge of the Grand Canyon, and "Hopi" means "peaceful ones." Some other Arizona Indians have given in to the renaming. Apaches now acquiesce to being called Apaches. Many Navajos accept "Navajo" rather than insisting on "Diné." Many Pimas now call themselves Pimas. Papagos, however, are making a concerted effort to be known as Tohono O'odam. In Minnesota, some Ojibwes now ask others to call them Anishinabes. Throughout the world, naming has been a prerogative of power. With colonialism on the wane, calling natives by the name they use for themselves is gradually becoming accepted practice. Thus when leaders in Upper Volta changed its name to Burkina Faso, mapmakers had to make the adjustment.[6] Native Americans who care may win similar respect in coming years.[7]

1. "Pueblo" means "town" in Spanish and is itself a misnomer as a proper noun; Pueblo Indians call themselves Zunis, Acomas, etc.

2. There is more than one English spelling for many native names, since they are attempted phonetic renditions of non-English words.

3. Some linguists would insist it means "we the *proper* people." "Lenape" was somehow repeated as "Lenni Lenape" by an early missionary. Native Hawaiians likewise call themselves kanaka maoli or "the real people."

4. Russell Means and some other Native Americans have claimed that "Indian" is a corruption of "in dios," "with God," because Columbus originally thought the Caribbean natives he met were peaceful, had "very good customs," and seemed religious. I have not found adequate confirmation for this. Columbus did speak positively of Native Americans at first; soon enough, when justifying his wars and enslavement of them, he called the Indians "cruel" and "stupid," "whose customs and religion are very different from ours."

5. In 2015, I got the Organization of American Historians to take a formal stand condemning the Washington NFL team; see Valerie Strauss, "Organization of American Historians Calls on Redskins to Change Name, Logo," *The Washington Post*, 4/30/2015.

6. Unlike Burkina Faso, Native American groups do not have the advantage of statehood. This may explain why spellcheck programs in computer word processors still have a long way to go: of the fourteen derogatory names I checked for this essay, nine were in my spellcheck program, but of the thirteen positive names, the program recognized only one—Dakota—a state!

7. Bill Bryson, *Made in America* (NY: Morrow, 1994), 24; S. L. A. Marshall, *Crimsoned Prairie* (NY: Scribner's, 1972), 8; Barbara A. Leitch, *A Concise Dictionary of Indian Tribes of North America* (Algonac, MI: Reference Publications, 1979); Kristen Hartzell, "Anasazi, Other Words Dropped," *The Denver Post*, 11/9/97; "Tribal Names: Meanings & Alternative Names," members.tripod.com/~Philkon/names.html

---
★
---

15. No Confederate Dead? No Problem! Invent Them!

MONTANA *Helena*

In 1916, the United Daughters of the Confederacy (UDC) dedicated a memorial fountain in what is now called Hill Park near the heart of Helena, Montana:

> *A loving tribute to our Confederate Soldiers*

Of course, Montana never *had* any Confederate soldiers. For that matter, Montana hardly had any *Union* soldiers. Most of Montana was still Indian country during the Civil War and for some time thereafter, as Lt. Col. George Armstrong Custer found to his sorrow at the Little Big Horn in 1876. The state was not admitted to the union until 1889, a quarter century after the war ended. Montana was not even a territory during most of the Civil War, getting organized in 1864.

The UDC may look silly dedicating a memorial to Confederate dead who never existed, but these ladies knew exactly what they were doing. UDC members used these monuments to demonstrate their own status—indeed, their dominion over the American landscape—and promote the respectability of the Confederate cause. Fifty years earlier most Northerners and many Southerners had seen the Confederacy as a failed attempt to break up the United States and perpetuate slavery—which it was. By 1916, this monument declared implicitly that the Confederacy was somehow patriotic and that whites agreed, even this far north, to honor it nostalgically. Thus, this monument really reflects the time when it was erected—the Nadir of race relations in the United States, from 1890 to about 1940, when segregation gripped the nation and lynchings reached their peak. (Chapters 80 and 81 tell how segregation swept the North as well.) Most Confederate monuments went up during these years. In the Nadir, as Charles Royster put it in *The Destructive War*, "[white] Southerners found it easy, or at least expedient, to forget a great deal of what they had known about the Confederacy, to reshape its history, and to remember things that had not occurred." And there is a direct connection between the neo-Confederate mythology erected on the landscape and the segregation and lynchings done to African Americans. As Voltaire put it, "If we believe absurdities, we shall commit atrocities."

A Confederate monument in Montana warns us that we need to think about where as well as when monuments are erected. The locations of some other Confederate monuments are equally but less obviously absurd. A Confederate monument dominates the lawn of the east Bolivar County courthouse in Cleveland, Mississippi, for example. It is the usual bronze sentry on a pedestal, on whose base are the words

BOLIVAR TROOP CHAPTER U.D.C. C.S.A.

To the memory of our Confederate dead
1861–65
Dead upon the field of glory Hero fit for song and story

But Cleveland, Mississippi, had no Confederate dead either. In fact, Cleveland did not exist during the Civil War or for some decades afterward. According to the *History of Bolivar County*, "until 1900 most of the interior of Bolivar County was a vast forest." The area around

"Through the efforts of the United Daughters, the Southland has become a land of monuments," boasted *UDC Magazine* in 1994. "In hundreds of communities, markers, tablets, and monuments have been erected by Divisions and Chapters." That is true, and to a degree, the UDC has been memorializing itself: prominent on the front of the Confederate monument's shaft in Cleveland, Mississippi, are the words "Bolivar Troop Chapter U.D.C."

Cleveland "was a wild country, abounding in bear, deer, wild turkey, and wolves."

Just like Montana!

Many communities now saddled with UDC monuments, even in the South, were predominantly Unionist during the Civil War. As historian George C. Rable put it, the UDC "managed to forget the unseemly parts—especially conflicts within the Confederacy—and eventually rewrote the history of the war." The Confederate monument in Ellisville, Mississippi, provides an example. In 1912, the UDC erected an imposing monument in front of the courthouse for the southern district of Jones County, even though most residents of Jones County opposed the Confederacy during the Civil War. Newt Knight, a white farmer with a black wife, even led a revolt that briefly took over the Ellisville courthouse and declared the county "The Free State of Jones"; Confederate officials had to dispatch troops to force the county back into line. Ellisville's Confederate monument is as misleading in its way as those in Cleveland, Mississippi, and Helena, Montana.

In the border states, the UDC and SCV (Sons of Confederate Veterans) erected pro-Confederate monuments and markers that made Maryland, West Virginia, Kentucky, and Missouri—states that were predominantly Unionist—look predominantly Confederate. Kentucky's legislature voted not to secede. Early in the war, Confederate Gen. Albert Sidney Johnston occupied Bowling Green, 40 miles east of Todd County, but found "no enthusiasm as we imagined and hoped but hostility was manifested in Kentucky." Eventually, 90,000 Kentuckians would fight for the United States as against 35,000 for the Confederate States. Nevertheless, the state now has ten times as many Confederate monuments as Union ones! West Virginia seceded from Virginia to stay with the Union, yet in 1910 the UDC erected a statue of Confederate Gen. "Stonewall" Jackson on the state capitol lawn,[1] and in 1959 an additional bust of Jackson went up inside the building. Maryland never seceded, but during the Nadir, Baltimore wound up with four major Confederate monuments as against just one U.S. monument.[2]

Pulitzer Prize-winning journalist Tony Horwitz recorded the impact of the Confederate monument in Todd County, Kentucky. "Todd County wasn't rebel country, at least not historically," he pointed out. "Most Todd Countians supported the Union in the Civil War." But this history has been lost. "Almost all whites I spoke to . . . proclaim[ed] their county rebel territory and believ[ed] it had always been so. As proof, they pointed to a 351–foot concrete spike soaring at the county's western edge. The obelisk marked the birth site of Confederate president Jefferson Davis."

Davis lived in Todd County only for the first two years of his life. Nevertheless, the Kentucky State Park system boasts that this monument is "the world's tallest concrete obelisk." The UDC raised the money and finished it in 1924 at a cost of $200,000. They consider it "the greatest of all monuments built to the Confederate cause." The state also puts out an astonishing brochure, "Jefferson Davis State Historic Site," that is an unabashed apologia for Davis. Every year on Davis's birthday, Todd Countians converge at it for what Horwitz calls "a bizarre rite: the crowning of a local teenager as 'Miss Confederacy.'" UDC and SCV members judge contestants on their "poise, hair, hooped skirt, and answers to questions such as, 'What will you do while holding the title to promote and defend Southern heritage?'"

Thanks to this monument, whites in Todd County invented a past in which their land was staunch rebel territory and their ancestors were brave Confederates. Their high school named its sports teams "the Rebels" and took as its mascot two cartoonish Confederates waving the battle flag of the Army of Northern Virginia. One result is racial polarization. In 1995, four young African Americans killed the driver of a pickup flying a large rebel flag, which led to even more polarization.

To be sure, not all racial tension in Todd County derives from its obelisk. But the fact that whites choose to celebrate the most racist figure in their past while ignoring their Unionist forebears can hardly help race relations in the present. Nationally, neither can the fact that even in petty ways, Confederate public history was white supremacist: it mostly ignored those few Confederate officers who proved "unreliable" on race during and after Reconstruction. James Longstreet, for example, was Lee's second-in-command at Gettysburg, but he got no statue or monument there until 1998. Nor did he gain recognition in Georgia or Louisiana for his anti-racist actions. William Mahone, hero of the Crater at Petersburg, got a monument there, lauding his service to the Confederacy, but his historical markers in Virginia studiously avoided that he worked for racial justice after the war.

Monuments simultaneously symbolize power and have a symbolic meaning of their own. Thus, the Confederate memorial in Helena was not as senseless as it seems. It was never intended as a "sasha monument," to use a term defined in the chapter "Historic Sites Are Always a Tale of Two Eras." As that chapter tells, sasha monuments help people who knew an event or person firsthand to remember it, with concomitant emotion. Often, sasha Civil War monuments list a community's dead and sometimes its living returned soldiers by name. That would be quite impossible in Montana, or in Cleveland, Mississippi, for that matter.[3] The white Southerners who moved to Helena and put up the granite fountain in 1916 or to Cleveland and erected the bronze soldier in 1908 were not remembering specific dead Confederate soldiers. They were making a statement.

Even in towns that did have Confederate dead, monuments put up in 1908 or 1916 were erected far too late to help most people grieve or remember the dead. These are zamani monuments, intended to instruct residents on how to think about the past. The Helena fountain implied that the Confederacy should be revered even as far north as Montana. The very size of the Cleveland monument tells what (white) residents of that town considered important. In comparison, its monument "Dedicated to the memory of those veterans who made the supreme sacrifice in the World Wars" is a stone slab about the size of the bottom half of a Dutch door. Similarly, the Jefferson Davis obelisk implies by its overt mimicry of the Washington Monument that the president of the Confederacy merits almost as much respect as the father of our country. (Never mind that Davis tried to divide what Washington tried to hold together.)

All across America, Confederate monuments have made their impact. President John Kennedy wrote, "The great enemy of truth is often not the lie . . . but the myth"—yet the tragically wrong treatment of Reconstruction in his *Profiles in Courage* shows how he himself (or his ghostwriter) was taken in by the neo-Confederate myth. Karen Cox, who wrote her doctoral dissertation on the UDC, summarized the organization's effect: "By transmitting Confederate culture—the ideology and symbols of states' rights and white supremacy—the Daughters . . . helped lay a foundation for massive resistance to desegregation at mid-century." Northerners too came to believe it proper to display Confederate symbols. In 1995, I talked with a flag vendor at a flea market near Brattleboro, Vermont. He displayed more Confederate flags than any other single item. Embroidered across them were the words, "If the South had won, we'd have no trouble now." "What does this mean?" I asked him. "I don't know," he parried. "It's my bestseller."

The embroidery was an example of "dog whistle racism," so called because racists know exactly what the words mean, but they can pretend that they don't. For that matter, displaying the Confederate flag itself is usually dog whistle racism. In 2016, in Bloomington, Indiana, some students pitched the whistle lower: upset when LGBTQ students organized the display of their rainbow flags, they came to school the next day wearing Confederate battle flag symbols. Heritage? No, hate. A *Washington Post* story in October 2018 showed how the flag remains a problem across the rural North. It featured the former mayor of Tolono, a sundown town in central Illinois, who flies Confederate flags inside and outside his home. He says that for him they stand for white grievances, not slavery, but of course, since almost no one in the United States has argued for the return of slavery since 1865, he would not be likely to embrace the original purpose of the Confederacy.

After the white supremacist riot in Charlottesville, Virginia, in August 2017, Confederate monuments clearly became liabilities. The Native American caucus in the Montana legislature asked Helena to take down its Confederate fountain. Within five days, it was gone. One more step remains: the posting of an accurate historical marker that explains what monument stood here, why and when it went up, and why and when it came down. Then passersby will learn that we began to misrepresent secession and the Confederacy during the Nadir, even in far-off Montana. After the murders by a neo-Confederate in Charleston, South Carolina, in June 2015, we began to get this history right on our landscape. And now, after 2017, they can infer that Helena no longer celebrates white supremacy, at least not in an important public space.[4]

1. Unionists retaliated the next year by erecting a Union mountaineer to honor the "Home Guard" who protected West Virginia from Confederate invasion as it seceded from the Confederacy.

2. One monument, of generals Lee and Jackson, didn't get finished until 1948 but it too was funded and planned in the Nadir.

3. No doubt, ex-Confederates moved to Montana and Cleveland long after the war. Nevertheless, no dead bodies came home from the Civil War to Helena or Cleveland, and no families in either city mourned casualty reports.

4. *The Monumental Works of the Daughters of the Confederacy* (Richmond, VA: Scrapbook at Museum of the Confederacy, c. 1916), 184; Charles Royster, *The Destructive War* (NY: Knopf, 1991), 94–172; Florence Sillers, compiler, *History of Bolivar County, MS* (Jackson, MS: Daughters of the American Revolution, 1948), 225, 282–83; James Chenoweth, *Oddity Odyssey* (NY: Holt, 1996), 143; Mrs. Ray Hunter, "South Carolina Division History," *UDC Magazine* (9/94): 111; www.nps.gov/delta/cwmile4.htm, 7/98; George C. Rable, *Civil Wars: Women and the Crisis of Southern Nationalism* (Urbana: U. of IL Press, 1989), 236–37; Tony Horwitz, *Confederates in the Attic* (NY: Pantheon, 1998), 95–105; Martha B. Carson, "World's Greatest Monument Builders," *UDC Magazine* (2/51): 12, 19; John Winberry, "'Lest We Forget': The Confederate Monument and the Southern

Townscape," *Southeastern Geographer* 23 no. 2 (11/83): 110; Gaines M. Foster, *Ghosts of the Confederacy* (NY: Oxford UP, 1987), 44, 194; Edward A. Pollard, *The Lost Cause Regained*, quoted in Rollin Osterweis, *The Myth of the Lost Cause* (Hamden, CT: Archon, 1973), 14; Karen Cox, *Women, the Lost Cause, and the New South: The United Daughters of the Confederacy and the Transmission of Confederate Culture* (Hattiesburg, MS: U. of Southern MS, PhD, 1997), i; Frances Sellers, "Flying the Colors for Racial Grievance," *The Washington Post*, 10/23/2018; Josh Delk, "Montana City to Remove Confederate Fountain," *The Hill*, 8/17/17, thehill.com/business-a-lobbying/347038-helena-to-remove-confederate-memorial-without-city-council-vote

———— ★ ————

16. A Woman *Shoulda* Done It!
WYOMING *South Pass City*

Sociologists have long postulated that a scarcity of women raises their status in society. Wyoming offers a case in point. In 1869, Wyoming Territory passed the first law in the United States giving women the right to vote. Since women were relatively rare on the frontier, men may even have advocated suffrage as a recruitment effort! Proud of this accomplishment, when Wyoming became a state in 1890 it took the motto "Equality State." Women's suffrage wasn't a national right until 1920, by which time women were already voting in most western states. Since then, unlike those states that slight the role women played in their past (chapters 30, 41), Wyoming has given a woman *more* space on the American landscape than she deserves.

During the push that led to the women's suffrage amendment to the U.S. Constitution, two Wyoming residents decided it would be nice if a woman were recognized for having something to do with Wyoming's pioneering statute. They chose Esther Morris, who had served for eight months as justice of the peace of South Pass City half a century earlier. Grace Hebard and H. G. Nickerson fabricated and popularized Ms. Morris as a campaigner for suffrage and even co-author of the suffrage law.[1]

The landscape reflects their hustle. In 1920, Hebard built a rock cairn in South Pass City to mark where Morris's cabin once stood, and Nickerson installed an inscribed sandstone slab in front of it. Later, an even more permanent granite marker replaced the sandstone slab. It reads, "Home and office site of Esther Hobart Morris. First woman justice of the peace in the world, Feb. 14, 1870. Author with W. H. Bright of the first equal suffrage law. Dec. 10, 1869." Her reconstructed cabin, a state historic site, stands nearby.

Unfortunately, the consensus among historians today is that Esther Morris had nothing to do with the law. Wyoming's Division of State Parks and Historic Sites has tried to correct matters by putting a bronze plaque nearby. It reads,

ESTHER MORRIS

Controversy exists concerning Esther Morris and woman suffrage. In 1869 the legislature passed and Governor Campbell signed a woman suffrage bill authored by William Bright, a South Pass City resident. As a result, Wyoming became the first territory or state to allow women the right to vote.

For eight months in 1870, Esther Morris served as South Pass City's justice of the peace, making her the nation's first woman judge. After her death in 1901, some historians claimed that Mrs. Morris had helped Bright write the suffrage bill. . . .

However, recent studies indicate that Bright was the only author of the suffrage bill. . . .

It further turns out that the granite marker does *not* mark the spot of Morris's office; she probably held court in the downtown county building. What about the cabin? Built in 1975–76, with the help of the Wyoming Professional Women's Club and "based on faulty research," it is located on the wrong lot! It is also much smaller than Morris's actual dwelling, which was a house, not a cabin.

The plaque concludes that the monument and "nearby 1870 period cabin" do honor Mrs. Morris, "who exemplified the spirit of frontier women." The plaque may revise the granite marker and errant cabin so gently as to be ineffectual, but we must credit Wyoming with the correction, a phenomenon all too rare at historic sites.

Wyoming has made no such correction on the grounds of its state capitol, however, where a Morris statue stands. She is also one of Wyoming's two entries in the National Statuary Collection in the nation's Capitol. The Hall's *Guidebook* credits her as being a good justice of the peace, if only for eight months and, trying to supply some reason for her inclusion, also notes that in 1895 "she was present at a dinner in Cheyenne given for Susan B. Anthony"![2]

1. Nickerson was a Republican, and when Wyoming Democrats claimed in 1919 that they had enacted women's suffrage in 1869, which they had, Nickerson may have settled upon Morris, also a Republican, to claim credit for his party.
2. L. E. Murphy and W. H. Venet, *Midwestern Women: Work, Community, and Leadership at the Crossroads* (Indianapolis: IN UP, 1997); Nancy Woloch, *Women and the American Experience* (NY: McGraw-Hill, 1994), 144–45, 233–34; Bruce Noble, conversation, 11/96; Todd Guenther, letter to Noble, 8/95; T. A. Larson, *History of Wyoming* (Lincoln: U. of NE Press, 1965), 89–94; Michael Massie, email, 12/98.

---- ★ ----

17. Tall Tales in the West

COLORADO *Pagosa Springs*

Some Westerners are amused or exasperated at the tall stories that people outside the region believe about the West. Others in the West perpetuate larger-than-life events and characters, often in the interest of tourism. In 1955, the Woman's Civic Club of Pagosa Springs did its part. On U.S. 160 west of town, they erected a rock cairn topped with a bronze marker, which commemorates an amazing feat that almost certainly never happened:

> *Near here in 1872, Col. Albert H. Pfeiffer, famous frontiersman,*
> *killed a Navajo in a knife duel. By agreement of watching Navajo and*
> *Ute warriors, Pfeiffer's victory won the Pagosa Hot Springs for his*
> *Ute friends.*

On its face the tale is hardly likely: why would the Utes choose a white man to represent them? More importantly, the story does violence to American Indians' common practice at places that benefited everyone, like hot springs. Across the country, Native Americans usually made such areas intertribal. If one society dominated such a site, it nonetheless typically declined to shut out others. In 1878, just six years after this alleged incident, Lt. C. McCauley reported to the U.S. government exactly this policy among the Utes: "All the Ute Indians . . . have always regarded the Springs with feelings akin to adoration, conceiving them to be the creation of the Great Spirit for the cure of the sick of all tribes. . . . The pipe of peace is said to have here had an unusual supremacy." Neither McCauley nor Pagosa historian John Motter mentions the knife fight incident, though both discuss the springs at some length.

If the values and policies of the Utes make the knife fight unlikely, so do the facts about the Navajos. In 1863–64, eight years before the alleged fight, Gen. James H. Carleton, Kit Carson, and the U.S. Army had subdued the Navajos and led most of them on the notorious Long March from their homeland in Arizona to Fort Sumner in eastern New Mexico. Many died on the way. The rest languished on the Bosque Redondo Reservation until 1868 and were then confined to the Navajo reservation, which did not extend into Colorado. No Navajo could possibly think about successfully contesting Ute claims in Colorado after these traumatic events.

In 1868, the United States had already forced Ute leaders to cede much of their Colorado land. By 1870, white miners were moving into the San Juan Mountains, the heart of Ute country. Rather than winning the springs against the Navajos, the Utes were losing them to the whites. The growing white presence thus also dictates against the knife fight story. According to Motter, the Utes tried to keep the springs open to all, in keeping with Indian values: "The Utes expressed their wish to Commission Chairman General Edward Hatch that the 'Great Father in Washington [the president, for the U.S. government] retain possession of the place, so that all persons, whether whites or Indians, might visit it, and when sick come there and be healed.'"

It was not to be, however. European Americans quickly found a way to make a profit from the property by claiming exclusive ownership of the Pagosa Hot Springs in the early 1870s. In May 1877, the United States did set aside from sale a square mile of land, including the Great Spring as its center, "because of the grandeur of the Great Hot Springs, and the medicinal qualities of its waters." Nevertheless, by 1879, and surely earlier, whites were building small private bathhouses at the springs. By 1881, the Denver and Rio Grande Railroad had a station 27 miles away with coach connection to the springs. Two years later various "capitalists," to use Motter's term, gained possession of the springs, paying a total of $5.09 for it. They and their various heirs held it until 1910, when it was sold at public auction to a Kansas company and then later to a wealthy Oklahoman.

Ironically, Col. Pfeiffer did play a role regarding ownership of Pagosa Hot Springs. Instead of "winning" it for the Utes, he was appointed to take it from them in 1878 on behalf of the United States. He got the tribe to agree to cede most of their land, including the springs, retaining a reservation east of Pagosa. Congress failed to ratify the agreement, however. Instead, the United States confined the Utes to land far to the southwest, leading to resentment that culminated in later violence against whites.

Pfeiffer's descendants believe the knife fight happened and, I was told, prompted the Woman's Civic Club to act. I could find no solid evidence to support the story, however. According to David Halaas, chief historian at the Colorado Historical Society, the folder documenting the marker contains nothing but a photograph of the marker itself. "I don't think it happened," Halaas concludes.[1]

1. Lt. C. McCauley, *Notes on Pagosa Springs, Colorado, December, 1878* (DC: GPO, 1879), 5; John M. Motter, *Pagosa Country: The First Fifty Years* (Pagosa Springs, CO: no publisher indicated, n.d.), 7–9, 20–21; Dee Brown, *Bury My Heart at Wounded Knee* (NY: Bantam, 1972), 350–51; conversation with David Halaas, 9/98.

★

---

18. Still Licking the Corporate Hand That Feeds You

COLORADO *Leadville*

Most of this book deals with how Americans remember history on the land-scape, but once in a while, we must go indoors. The National Mining Hall of Fame and Museum, first opened in 1988, cries out to be included in any discussion of how history is distorted in the United States. It is a blatant example of how corporate sponsorship dictates what is and is not presented.

A competent history of mining in the United States would have to con-sider these issues:

- Exploiting our rich mineral and oil deposits has helped the United States develop its enormous economy and our comfortable stan-dard of living.

- Ethnic and racial groups have often concentrated in mining jobs, flavoring the politics and lifestyle of mining communities.
- Workers have often not shared fairly in the profits from mining, particularly when they have not organized into unions.
- Mining profits have fueled unholy alliances between mining companies and politicians. Results include bribery, tax breaks, legal loopholes, economic colonialism, and archaic mining laws.
- Mining and drilling have caused immense environmental problems, some of which persist.
- Next to firefighting, mining is probably the most dangerous occupation in America; explosions and cave-ins have killed scores and even hundreds of miners at a time.

Of these six points, the National Mining Hall of Fame and Museum treats only the first! Its brochure bills itself as "The Showcase of American Mining," and showcase it is—not a true museum. Its Hall of Fame is equally skewed. Of its 240 inductees, more than half were mining executives. Most of the rest were engineers, geologists, and people who acquired vast mining properties. Only a handful represent individual miners, prospectors, explorers, journalists, politicians, labor leaders, philanthropists, and all others.[1]

The Mining Museum doesn't tell much about those who have done the actual mining in the United States; luminaries it does include are mainly white Anglo-Saxon Protestant men, like most mine owners. In reality, mining has been one of America's most multicultural occupations. Italian anarchists mined granite in Vermont. Cornish workers dug lead out of Wisconsin. Finnish socialists mined copper in Upper Michigan. Chinese Americans panned for gold across the West. So did some Native Americans, although generally mining wreaked havoc with Indian land and peoples. In the 1970s, mines hired women as miners. Almost none of their sagas are recounted in Leadville.

One Native American does make the Hall of Fame—Paddy Martinez, the Navajo who first found uranium in the San Juan basin in northwest New Mexico in 1950. The result was 30 years of frenzied mining "spurred by the world race to develop atomic energy and the U.S. government's need to develop new sources of uranium," according to his plaque. While Martinez cannot be held responsible for what happened to the Navajos who did much of the work in the uranium mines, both the government and the mining company, Kerr-McGee, knew by 1949 that the radioactive radon gas in the mines caused illness. Nevertheless, Kerr-McGee never bothered to ventilate the mines and the government never asked it to. By 1990, more than 450 miners had died of cancer, over five times the expected number. In that year Congress passed a compensation bill; 1,100 Navajos filed claims related to uranium exposure. The museum has not a word on any of this at the Martinez plaque or anywhere else; the plaque ends with the assertion that Martinez will be "remembered for his contribution to mining and to mankind." Nor does the museum mention the perils that mining has visited upon other miners across the country—silicosis, black lung disease, and the like.

Even if killing miners one at a time isn't worthy of notice, I had imagined that a few major mine disasters would get some attention. After all, mining company executives would agree with labor that mining disasters are to be mourned and learned from. Several disasters happened in Colorado, including the Hastings Mine Explosion in Ludlow, which killed 121 men in 1917. The museum is silent on the subject, however.

Organized labor is likewise largely missing from the Mining Museum. Only two labor union leaders are among the more than 125 plaques in the Hall of Fame—and one was a conservative labor leader whom mining executives liked. The plaque honoring John L. Lewis, long-time president of the United Mine Workers of America, is the only one in the museum to honor labor's side of the issues—hardly an accurate representation of labor's huge role in the mining industry. According to Carl Miller, the first executive director of the museum, Lewis was the Hall of Fame's most controversial inductee. In 1943, asserting that miners were not getting a fair share of the nation's wartime prosperity, Lewis called a strike. "Many mining executives consider him a traitor because of what he did during World War II," Miller told me.

In fact, terrible working conditions in the mining industry led to some of the most radical labor unions and best-known labor leaders in U.S. history, all of whom are absent from the hall of fame. The most famous was Big Bill Haywood, who began as a miner when fifteen years old. He joined the Western Federation of Miners and in 1900 became its national secretary-treasurer. He gave militant leadership to the union from its national office in Denver, and in 1904 led the nearby Cripple Creek strike. The next year Clarence Darrow won Haywood's acquittal on the charge of assassinating the former governor of Idaho; that year Haywood also helped found the Industrial

Workers of the World (IWW). Sentenced to twenty years in jail for sedition during the Woodrow Wilson administration, he skipped bail and lived the last seven years of his life in the Soviet Union. Haywood is better known than *any* member of the National Mining Hall of Fame except perhaps Lewis. So is IWW leader Joe Hill, executed in neighboring Utah in 1915 and subject of the famous labor song "I Dreamed I Saw Joe Hill Last Night." Nevertheless, they are not even mentioned.

Then there are the legendary conflicts between miners and owners. One of the best-known happened in the museum's home state of Colorado. In 1914, John D. Rockefeller prevailed on the governor to get the Colorado National Guard to fire on a camp of striking mine workers and their families. They killed thirteen babies and children along with seven adults. The "Ludlow Massacre," as it is called today, made national headlines—but goes unmentioned at the National Mining Hall of Fame and Museum.[2] Even closer to Leadville was the 1927 confrontation near Fort Collins, in which Colorado State Police fired on hundreds of unarmed men and women at the Columbine Mine. Six miners were killed and many others wounded, a tragedy that led mine owners to finally sign contracts with the United Mine Workers of America. In *The Great Coalfield War*, Senator George S. McGovern and historian Leonard F. Guttridge call these Colorado events "the most hard fought and violent labor struggle in American history," but the National Mining Museum ignores them. In 1896, Leadville itself was the scene of a "labor war," but the museum never mentions it. Indeed, the museum does not even show a peaceful picket line. On the other hand, several company executives won their place in the Hall of Fame because they opposed labor. According to their plaques, Samuel Warriner, president of Lehigh Coal, "left his mark on the anthracite industry through strong leadership and with a tough stance on unions," while George Wingfield "acted to suppress the mining unions in the riotous labor troubles in 1906–07."

Probably the most famous bribery scandal in U.S. history is Teapot Dome, which might have toppled Warren G. Harding's presidential administration if he hadn't died first.[3] Teapot Dome is an oil reserve in neighboring Wyoming, not far from Leadville, but the museum never mentions it. Nor does it treat what Colorado ex-governor Richard Lamm calls "the destructive effects of colonialism" all over the West. Indeed, the museum's only treatment of government and mining is an exhibit that lobbies for continued easy access to minerals on public land, and this exhibit never mentions that management of those minerals is still governed by a mining law passed in 1872! Like the Homestead Act and the railroad land grants of the nineteenth century, Congress passed this law to promote settlement of the West by European Americans. The settlement era is long past. Nevertheless, for a pittance, companies can still claim they have found minerals on public land and therefore "patent" this land more cheaply because it is more valuable! Areas patented under the 1872 mining law become private land, forever withdrawn from the public domain. According to William C. Patric, an authority on mining policy, "the fate of the mining law is one of the most controversial natural resource issues of the day." Not at the Mining Museum, however, which never mentions the controversy, surely because its sponsors like the law just as it stands.

The Mining Museum does mention the environmental problems of mining, but only to locate them in the distant past. One exhibit stresses the beautiful results from reclamation. "Such efforts are important on some sites," Patric acknowledges. Now the industry faces even larger challenges, however. Patric goes on to note, "Meaningful reclamation is simply impossible given the scale of mining today." The museum brags that companies now mine lower-grade ore "using new techniques." It never hints that these new techniques can cause new damage to the environment. On the contrary, the executive director of the museum blandly assured me, "That's all in the past. Today mining is an environmentally conscious industry."

Is it? The Summitville Mine, 150 miles south of Leadville, on patented land that had been part of Colorado's Rio Grande National Forest, shows the environmental dangers inherent in modern gold mining. At least two engineers earned their plaques in the Hall of Fame by pioneering the cyanide process to separate minute particles of gold from ore. A large modern gold mine may 1,000,000 pounds of cyanide in a year. Cyanide is extremely poisonous—hence its prominence in murder mysteries. In 1988, Galactic Mining opened the Summitville Mine, which quickly turned into an environmental disaster. Galactic declared bankruptcy in 1992 and abandoned Summitville. "American taxpayers have now spent more than $100,000,000 attempting to prevent 170,000,000 gallons of cyanide and acid-laden waters from further damaging the Alamosa River," Patric reports.

In 2011, the Hall of Fame continued its cover-up of environmental hazards by inducting Jeffrey Zelms, long-time CEO of The Doe Run Company, "the world's largest primary lead producer." Doe Run's smelter had just been found guilty of poisoning children in Herculaneum, Missouri, drastically decreasing their intelligence and causing them to suffer from attention deficit disorder. Company documents proved that Doe Run knew of the problem for years but did nothing about it. Partly owing to the bad impression Zelms made at trial, the jury awarded $320,000,000 in punitive damages on top of compensatory damages to the victims. In its write-up of almost 500 words, the Hall of Fame says nothing about the matter, of course. Instead, it called Zelms a "charismatic, approachable, and outspoken man of the people" who always "vowed to make tomorrow better than today."

Visitors need not stray beyond Leadville for evidence of mining's environmental damages. The city itself is an Environmental Protection Agency (EPA) Superfund cleanup site! Aluminum, cadmium, copper, iron, lead, manganese, and zinc from years of mining now pollute the soil in some Leadville neighborhoods and enter into the Arkansas River. Miller knows this, because in addition to being the first executive director of the museum, he was Leadville's elected state representative. In that capacity, he led a campaign to "get the EPA out of Leadville." He did not succeed, but he has kept any mention of the EPA out of the National Mining Museum.

The distortions in the "history" presented at the National Mining Museum are so flagrant that the only lesson to be gleaned here is that historic sites may falsify history owing to their sponsorship. At least the museum is honest about its corporate sponsors—logos of Phelps Dodge, Conoco, and other mining and petroleum companies adorn its entry. This frankness offers an important lesson, because every historic site, from the elegant Washington Memorial Chapel at Valley Forge to a lowly wooden highway marker, has sponsors, corporate or not, and sponsors' agendas usually have the potential to distort history. A responsible historic site, however, does not let its funders prevent it from telling its history. The National Mining Museum fails even to make clear *how* Americans mine, perhaps because some modern mining techniques are so destructive. Backers of the museum hope to lift Leadville by its tourist bootstraps; the town has been economically depressed since its large mines shut down. The museum would attract more visitors if it told more actual history, however. Spending an hour watching an industry pat itself on the back is, ultimately, boring.[4]

---

1. Elizabeth Nix, a professor of public history in Baltimore, helped review the Hall of Fame for this 2018 revision. We categorized each person once, but many could be listed in two or three categories: for example, engineers helped companies decide which mineral rights to buy and became high executives in the process.

2. The United Mine Workers has put up a memorial at the site in Ludlow.

3. In return for a large bribe, Harding's secretary of the interior, Albert Fall, persuaded the secretary of the navy to transfer Teapot Dome to Fall's department, who then leased it to Sinclair Oil.

4. "Tails of Woe", *Mining Journal* 325 no. 8341, www.info-mine.com, 5/98; Richard D. Lamm and Michael McCarthy, *The Angry West* (Boston: Houghton Mifflin, 1982), 9; Daniel Pinchbeck, "Guyana Gold," www.word.com/place/guyana/eco/ecobod.htm, 5/98; Donald A. Grinde and Bruce E. Johansen, *Ecocide of Native America* (Santa Fe, NM: Clear Light, 1995), 211–18; William C. Patric, "Between a Rock and a Hard Place," *Inner Voice* (5/97), www.afsee.org/publications/inner_voice/mayjune97/pg14. html, 5/98; "A Look Back at 1997," Leadville *Herald Democrat*, www.leadvilleherald .com/1997.html, 6/98; Charles N. Alpers, "Responsibilities and Activities of the U.S. Geological Survey Related to Mining and the Environment," *U.S. Geological Survey Mine Drainage Interest Group Newsletter* no. 4 (12/95), water.wr.usgs.gov/mine/sep /forum.html, 6/98; George S. McGovern and Leonard F. Guttridge, *The Great Coalfield War* (Niwot, CO: UP of CO, 1996 [1972]), xi; Jim Carlton, "Mining Fans Seek to Rescue Industry from History's Pits," *The Wall Street Journal*, 10/11/93; Donna Walter, "Doe Run Jurors Reflect on Three-Month Trial, $358 Million Decision," *Missouri Lawyers Weekly*, 10/3/2011, molawyersmedia.com/2011/10/03/doe-run-jurors-reflect -on-three-month-trial-358-million-decision

---

★

---

19. The Footloose Statue
NEW MEXICO *Alcalde*

In the rear patio of the Oñate Monument Visitors Center northeast of Española on New Mexico 68 stands the 1991 bronze statue of conquistador Juan de Oñate. In 1998, New Mexico celebrated the 400th anniversary of his arrival. Pueblo Indians and their partisans chose not to join the party. Instead, someone marked the quadricentennial by cutting off the statue's right foot.[1]

Why his foot?

Oñate was the original conquistador of New Mexico. In 1598, in the words of a New Mexico historical marker, "the viceroy of New Spain appointed Juan de Oñate as governor of New Mexico and directed him to settle the area along the upper Rio Grande." Oñate proceeded into what is now New Mexico with a sizable force: "some 200 settlers, including soldiers, families, and priests, and over 7000 head of livestock," the marker relates. He made San Juan Pueblo his base and from there sent out parties seeking gold, good land, and a route to the Pacific. They comported themselves as Spaniards usually did in the Americas: they assumed the right to tell the Natives what

The artist represents Oñate heroically—even his horse is sculpted to hieratic scale, bigger and stronger than Spanish horses ever were with a triumphal, flowing, larger-than-life tail.

to do in return for bringing them the benefits, to their way of thinking, of Christianity and Spanish trade goods.

Some Indians tired of their subservient role, and most in the Acoma Pueblo decided not to put up with the Spanish any longer. When Oñate's nephew Juan de Zaldívar went to Acoma again desiring to trade, the Indians told him to camp nearby and wait. On the assigned day, half of Zaldívar's men were in small groups trading in the pueblo when the Indians attacked with stones and clubs. They killed Zaldívar and some other Spaniards; the survivors staggered back to San Juan.

Oñate declared "war by blood and fire" and sent another nephew, Vicente, and 72 well-armed men to conquer the Acomas. Although about 400 Acoma men opposed them, Spanish arms were superior and included two cannons loaded with grapeshot. Hundreds died, only one of them a Spaniard, and Vicente brought a number of captives toward San Juan Pueblo. Oñate met them at another village, Santo Domingo, proceeded to put the captured Natives on trial, and ordered the Acoma to hand over all children under twelve for a Christian upbringing. According to Oñate's biographer, Marc Simmons, 60 small girls were sent to Mexico City and raised in convents there; "none ever saw their homeland or relatives again." Everyone over twelve years of age Oñate enslaved for twenty years. In addition, he ordered one foot cut off every male captive over age 25, some two dozen in all. Oñate had the punishment carried out at Santo Domingo, so villagers there would know and tell other Indians what happened to men who dared question Spanish rule.[2] Later, the Spaniards sacked two other pueblos, also as an exemplary punishment.

What happened to Juan de Oñate in 1998 was, thus, from a Native American viewpoint, a fitting tribute.

The sculptor, Reynaldo Rivera, managed to recast the foot based on the statue's left foot. In May 1998, close inspection still showed the unweathered seam. The incident symbolizes a larger conflict: groups in New Mexico today look at what happened in New Mexico 400 years ago from different perspectives.

Juan de Oñate "is the George Washington of New Mexico," says biographer Simmons. "Everything starts from there." Not so according to television newsman Conroy Chino, a member of the Acoma Pueblo. "He inflicted tremendous pain and suffering, death, and destruction, especially among Acoma people." "From our viewpoint, we would prefer that it never did happen," says Herman Agoyo, a member of the San Juan Pueblo tribal council. Nevertheless, "good, bad, or indifferent, it's still part of our history."

The dismemberment of Oñate's statue outraged the *Santa Fe New Mexican* newspaper. It called the maiming "a cowardly act against art" and asked, "has art-loving Northern New Mexico become a place whose citizens must fear for every unguarded work?"—deliberately downplaying the history and revenge that this act symbolically expressed. In a sense, so long as the statue is complete, the story it tells is incomplete. The statue honors Oñate, but honoring Oñate this way tells only one side of what he did. The historical marker for the Española Valley hardly makes good the omission; it says merely, "Juan de Oñate established New Mexico's first colony here in 1598." The pamphlet that the Oñate Monument Visitors Center distributes is even less satisfactory, saying nothing negative about him on any of its eight pages.

Some commentators charge that critics judge Oñate unfairly by applying the standards of our very different time. Actually, although many Hispanics praise Oñate unreservedly today and his monument reflects their political influence, the Spanish in the area at the time did not praise him. At the end of his term as governor of New Mexico, he faced his *residencia* or "performance review." Charged with, among other things, abusing the natives, he was fined and sentenced to perpetual banishment from New Mexico.[3]

After the statue's amputation, several newspaper writers suggested leaving Oñate maimed. His missing foot symbolically presented the Acoma side, they pointed out. Certainly, the maiming increased people's knowledge of the statue and the past. Before the amputation the monument often went unnoticed; the perpetrators even had to contact the local newspaper to get the public to notice their deed! Afterward, "a lot of people have come up just to see the destruction of it," according to the artist. They saw two views of Oñate: honoring and dishonoring. They also saw that people still care passionately about how the man and his enterprise are portrayed on the New Mexican landscape 400 later.[4]

1. The perpetrator came forward in 2017, but required anonymity. See Simon Romero, "Statue's Stolen Foot Reflects Divisions Over Symbols of Conquest," *The New York Times*, 9/30/2017.

2. Some believe the Spanish only cut off toes.

3. He appealed and years later won partial reinstatement.

4. Marc Simmons, *The Last Conquistador* (Norman: U. of OK Press, 1991), 125–46; Alvin M. Josephy Jr., *The Patriot Chiefs* (NY: Viking Press, 1958), 82–83; Donald A. Grinde and Bruce E. Johansen, *Ecocide of Native America* (Santa Fe, NM: Clear Light, 1995), 60–61; "Group Releases Photo of Oñate's Foot," *Albuquerque New Mexican*, 1/14/98; Thomas E. Chávez, "La Historia de la Nueva México," *El Palacio* 102 no. 2 (winter 1997), 37–43; Richard McCord, "The Scars of History Take Time to Heal," unidentified newspaper clipping in Oñate Monument Visitors Center, n.d.; Rick Romancito, "Oñate's Foot and the Changing Face of History," *Taos News*, 1/22/98.

THE GREAT PLAINS

20. The Oklahoma State History Museum Confederate Room Told No History; Finally, They Closed It

OKLAHOMA *Oklahoma City*

Although this book mostly treats outdoor remembrances of history, the Confederate Room in the Oklahoma State History Museum was so incompetent as to demand attention. Although I have not visited every state history museum, I have seen many, and this was the worst exhibit I have encountered in any state museum in the United States. Next door was the Union Room, which was only modestly better. The two rooms might make for a rare comparison of Civil War history as told by both sides. Instead, they revealed more about when they went up than about the war itself.

The rooms had quite different tones and purposes. The Union Room housed an exhibit entitled "War Comes to the Indian Nations." It told of the fierce battles in Indian Territory, now Oklahoma, in which Native Americans fought on both sides, taking more casualties, military and civilian, than any other group as a percentage of the population.

The larger Confederate Room told no history! It didn't even bother to have a subject. It merely worshiped the Confederacy. A shrine on one wall exhibited Confederate medals and implied God was on the Confederate side with the label,

LORD GOD OF HOSTS BE WITH US YET

Lest we forget—Lest we forget.

One exhibit told nothing about the Civil War but lauded the United Daughters of the Confederacy. It displayed old UDC ribbons; a label told that the organization was founded in 1894.

Another exhibit consisted of a photograph of a Confederate flag with a small photograph of Robert E. Lee placed like a sacred image in front. A label proclaimed,

THE FLAG THAT NEVER SURRENDERED

The Confederate battle flag of Brig. Gen. Joseph O. Shelby's Missouri Cavalry Brigade, Major General Sterling Price's Division, C. S. A. At the close of the War Shelby refused to surrender and led his brigade into Mexico. When he crossed the Rio Grande he ordered the flag thrown into the river where it was retrieved by Jarrett Todd of the 4th Missouri Cavalry. Years later Mr. Todd donated the flag to the Oklahoma Historical Society.

The exhibit had nothing to do with Oklahoma. Lee commanded troops in Virginia. Shelby's brigade fought in Missouri, Kansas, and Arkansas. Presumably, visitors were supposed to be impressed that Shelby and his men fled rather than surrendered. In fact, the tawdry Mexican escapade was nothing to brag about. Shelby's men tried to become mercenaries for the "Emperor" Maximilian in the civil war then raging in Mexico. France had foisted Maximilian on Mexico. Most Mexicans supported Juárez. When U.S. pressure in 1866 compelled Napoleon III to withdraw his French soldiers, the Mexicans toppled Maximilian and shot him. Shelby's escapade was just another Confederate attempt to use armed force on behalf of anti-humanitarian goals.

What was this sham of a collection doing in the Oklahoma State History Museum? Between 1865 and 1895 no such exhibit of Confederate triumphalism could have gone up. In those years Oklahoma had good race relations. Majority factions of the "five civilized tribes"—Cherokees, Chickasaws, Choctaws, Creeks, and Seminoles—had supported the Confederacy during the Civil War. Therefore, the United States imposed Reconstruction on them, as it did on the defeated Confederate states. The tribes had to grant freedom, tribal membership, and land allotments to their former slaves. The result offers insight into what Reconstruction might have accomplished in the South if the United States had ordered white Confederates to do the same. When Southern blacks entered Oklahoma in the late 1870s, during what historians now call the "exodus" from the Deep South that followed the end of Reconstruction there, they found the American Indians' freedmen farming their own land throughout eastern Oklahoma. Often, African Americans served on tribal councils or as town chiefs.

Indeed, race relations were so good that African American leaders circulated advertisements in the Deep South that urged blacks to move to Indian Territory, start businesses and towns, and maybe even create the first black state. Eventually, African Americans formed 10% of the population of Indian Territory, many living in some 27 majority-black towns, some of which still exist. "Oklahoma was possibly the first place in the US where African Americans had a fair shot at the American dream," according to "The African American Oklahomans," a pamphlet put out by the Oklahoma Tourism and Recreation Department. "Freedmen and new African-American settlers in Oklahoma could vote, study, and move about with relative freedom."

All this changed when whites took control from the Native Americans. In 1889, Oklahoma Territory was carved from the western half of Indian Territory. The next year its government permitted school systems to segregate black and white students; by 1897, they required it. American Indians finally lost their autonomy over the rest of Indian Territory in 1907 when Oklahoma became a state. The first law the new state passed segregated public transportation. According to Mark Cantrell, curator of the Confederate Room, a year or two later the legislature passed the law setting up the Oklahoma Historical Society and providing for Union and Confederate Rooms. Since then the Confederate Room has been under the control of first the UDC and more recently the SCV (Sons of Confederate Veterans). Laws passed in 1935 require that the rooms exist and that their curators be descendants of Union and Confederate veterans, and an act of the legislature might be required to change them.[1]

In 2005, Oklahoma opened a new history museum "with world-class museum exhibits," according to its website. The Union and Confederate Rooms were not world-class. So, even though the agency now has much more space, the Confederate and Union rooms have closed. As best I can tell, they have been consolidated into one collection which is open by appointment only, and people will rarely make appointments, since the website offers no hint that it exists. Surely, that's a positive outcome for public history in Oklahoma.[2]

1. For that matter, the SCV collected the funds to refurbish the *Union* Room as well, since Union veterans' groups are much weaker. According to Cantrell, an SCV member, it did so partly to make it harder for the museum to abolish both rooms.
2. The African American Oklahomans" (OK City: OK Tourism and Recreation Dept., 1995); Jay Monaghan, *Civil War on the Western Border, 1854–1865* (Lincoln: U. of NE Press, 1955), 347–49; Kenneth T. Jackson, *The Ku Klux Klan in the City: 1915–1930* (NY: Oxford UP, 1967), 85–86; Scott Ellsworth, *Death in a Promised Land* (Baton Rouge: LA State UP, 1982); Mark Cantrell, conversations, 11/98, 5/99; *Oklahoma Laws*, 1935, 65 §8–9; conversation with staff member, 7/2018; www.okhistory.org/historycenter /index and nested pages, 8/2018

★

---

21. Which Came First: Wilderness or Civilization?

KANSAS *Gardner*

At Gardner, the great westering route divides into the Oregon and Santa Fe trails. A state historical marker marks the spot with these words: "Over these two roads branching here into the wilderness, traveled explorers, traders, missionaries, soldiers, forty-niners, and emigrants, the pioneers who brought civilization to the western half of the United States."

This is hardly a Native perspective or even a Spanish one. The text perpetuates on the landscape the old primitive-to-civilized continuum already all too available in our culture. Obviously, its authors have never taken introductory anthropology, where professors disabuse undergraduates of this line of thinking in the first two weeks.

The marker takes for granted that civilization is an urban Eastern Anglo phenomenon. In 1927, an organization called the Grand Council Fire of American Indians challenged this assumption. "What is civilization?" they asked. "Its marks are a noble religion and philosophy, original arts, stirring music, rich story and legend. We had these. Then we were not savages, but a civilized race."

An old conundrum—"Which came first, wilderness or civilization?"—helps show the bias in this marker. The unthinking answer is, of course, wilderness, since wilderness gave way to farms, towns, and finally urban civilization. But if by "civilization" we mean differentiated urban society as anthropologists define the word, the correct answer, surprisingly, has to be civilization! For, in the beginning, the natural world was no wilderness—it was home.

The archetype of progress, by now embedded deep in the American psyche, prompts Americans to reply to the riddle thoughtlessly. In reality, unthinking belief in progress is nothing but a chronological form of ethnocentrism. Things "must be" getting better, so we must have evolved from a "wilderness." Actually, only differentiated urban society creates the alienation from the world that converts nature into wilderness. "Wilderness" is thus a "civilized" concept, a product of cities and large-scale agriculture. Indeed, the land that Americans today perceive as still wilderness was, in fact, better known to Natives centuries ago than it has ever been since they were dispossessed. In this sense, America is more wilderness now than then. Seeing nature as wild is no advance—just a different view. Similarly, urban civilization is not more civilized as we mean the term in everyday parlance—just different.[1]

Chapters 7, 24, 35, 66, and 89 tell of other terms on markers and monuments across the country that subtly bias the thinking of those who read them.

1. Rupert Costo and Jeanette Henry, *Textbooks and the American Indian* (San Francisco, CA: Indian Historian Press, 1970); Loewen, *Lies My Teacher Told Me* (NY: New Press, 1995), chapter 10.

---------------⋆---------------

22. Lesbians Begin to Appear on the Landscape

NEBRASKA *Red Cloud*

Willa Cather's novels and short stories are Nebraska's premier legacy to the world of literature. She gets a major state historic marker on U.S. 281 fifteen miles north of Red Cloud:

CATHERLAND

Here on the Divide between the Republican and the Little Blue lived
some of the most courageous people of the frontier. Their fortunes and
their loves live again in the writings of Willa Cather, daughter of the
plains and interpreter of man's growth in these fields and in the valleys
beyond. . . .

Willa Cather wrote from her heart the wonderful tales she heard and the
vital drama she saw in her growing years. In her books those she knew
and admired live forever. My Antonia, earth mother of the plains, grew
to maturity, loved, worked, and died within a few miles of this spot, yet
she is known and cherished all over the world.

"The history of every country begins in the heart of a man or a woman,"
and the history of this land began in the heart of Willa Cather.

Although extensive, this marker tells nothing at all about Willa Cather's
life. Nebraska may avoid her biography because she was lesbian, indeed, a
"butch" lesbian. She arrived at the University of Nebraska dressed as William
Cather, her imaginary opposite-sex twin. She had three major relationships
in her life, all with women, and lived her last 40 years with her companion,
Edith Lewis, in New York City.

This marker exemplifies how homosexuality is written out of the American
landscape. "A compact marker can't tell everything," might be one
response. But Red Cloud also boasts the "Willa Cather Thematic District"
with more than 190 historical sites, "possibly the largest historic district dedicated to an author in the United States" according to its website. It includes
the "Willa Cather Pioneer Memorial," which offers tours of five restored
buildings, among them Cather's childhood home. Surely there's room to
mention her sexual orientation somewhere!

"Do you learn that she was lesbian at the Willa Cather Pioneer Memorial?" I asked Patricia Phillips, its director in 1999. "No, you don't," she
replied. "We don't think she was lesbian. I don't think there's anything in
her writing that indicates that. Not at all." But Phillips volunteered that her
bookstore does sell studies of Cather that assert she was lesbian.

Another response might be, "So what?" Knowing that Aaron Copland was gay does not contribute much to understanding or appreciating his music. Sexual orientation often seems irrelevant to one's accomplishments. We don't talk much about the heterosexuality of Charles Ives, after all, or Georgia O'Keeffe.

Sometimes sexual orientation does make a difference, however. In *The Reader's Companion to American History*, Eric Foner and John A. Garraty note that Cather, Walt Whitman, Langston Hughes, Bayard Rustin, Cole Porter, "and many other notable Americans of the past were gay men and lesbians whose homosexuality, though hidden, deeply influenced their sensibility, their values, and their careers." Most recent critics agree that Cather "must be approached as a lesbian writer," as Frances Kaye wrote in *Isolation and Masquerade: Willa Cather's Women*, ". . . because so many of the nuances of the work are unintelligible unless we read it as being by and about a lesbian consciousness." In some works, according to Cather's biographer Sharon O'Brien, Cather created female characters whose sort of strength and determination had usually been attributed only to men.[1] Kaye believes that *My Antonia* itself can and perhaps should be read as a lesbian novel.

Even if Cather's sexual orientation did not influence how she saw the world, it still might be worthwhile to know she was a lesbian. In 1999, when this book first came out, lesbians were invisible on the landscape. In Greenwich Village, the Stonewall Rebellion of gays against the police was memorialized by the only marker I know that used the word back then:

STONEWALL INN

Site of the Stonewall Riots June 27–29 1969
Birth of Modern Lesbian and Gay Rights Liberation

On the West Coast, gay city council member Harvey Milk got a San Francisco park named for him and a plaque. Otherwise, our public history kept gay or lesbian people and events locked in the closet. But if Americans knew that some of the historical figures the landscape celebrated were lesbian or gay, public discourse might be improved. In the early 1990s, for example, Americans debated whether gay men could or should serve in the armed forces. They already had, of course, including my uncle, a "confirmed bachelor"—my family's euphemism for a gay man—who served in the Aleutians during World War II. And they have been everything else, from president (chapter 73) and first lady to star athlete to common laborer.

By 2018, Cather's pioneer village was a bit more forthright. Its new director of education, Tracy Tucker, said that the staff now believes she was lesbian, but since "there is not a lot of evidence," they still don't say much about it. Online, their biography does say she "cropped her hair short, referred to herself as 'Willie,' 'William,' or 'Wm Cather, M.D.,' and adopted a generally male form of dress." The Cather scholar who wrote it told me in 2018, "Pretty much everybody accepts it now"—but he doesn't plan to revisit the bio.

A similar collection of historic buildings, Pendarvis, in Mineral Point, Wisconsin, was saved by two gay men. The Wisconsin Historical Society focuses on the buildings, but if asked about the founders, they do take one step beyond Catherland, calling their policy, "If Asked, Will Tell."

Elsewhere, the landscape is beginning to take bolder steps. An official Ohio historical marker in Dayton, put up in 2009, tells of Natalie Barney, who lived an openly lesbian lifestyle in the late 1800s and published love poems to women. At Independence Hall in Philadelphia, a new marker claims that the nation's "first organized and annual gay and lesbian civil rights demonstration" took place here, on July 4, 1965. A sidewalk of fame in San Francisco has plaques for many openly LGBTQ people of note from across the country.

Telling these stories is important. As Martina Navratilova put it in 1997, speaking to the Gay, Lesbian, and Straight Education Network in New York City, "In too many schools, students find little or no information about lesbian or gay people in their libraries or in the curriculum. It's time that schools told the truth. . . . so that young people will realize that those of us who have been lesbian or gay are part of America and always have been." For that matter, communities in America, even small towns like Mineral Point and Red Cloud, sometimes provided supportive environments for people of different sexual orientations, ignoring rather than repressing what they didn't understand. That's part of America's story too.[2]

Buchanan (chapter 73) is a site that still refuses to treat sexual orientation.

1. On the other hand, her criticism of other women writers was unusually harsh, partly because she had contempt for "traditional" women, believing them to be inferior to men in intelligence and creativity. Knowing about her sexual orientation provides a context for understanding her attitude.

2. "Catherland," Explore Nebraska History, mynehistory.com/items/show/524, 8/18;

Willa Cather Pioneer Memorial website,www.willacather.org, 1/99, 8/18; Patricia Phillips, conversation, 1/11/99; Eric Foner and John A. Garraty, eds., *The Reader's Companion to American History* (Boston: Houghton Mifflin, 1991), 514; Frances W. Kaye, *Isolation and Masquerade: Willa Cather's Women* (NY: Peter Lang, 1993), 2–5, 31, 99, 186–88; sunsite.unc.edu/sheryb/women/Willa-Cather, 2/98; U. of IL Chicago, Lesbian/Gay/Bisexual/Transgender, website, www.uic.edu/depts/quic/history /willa_cather.html, 2/98; Sharon O'Brien quoted in Sheryl Meyering, *A Reader's Guide to the Short Stories of Willa Cather* (NY: Macmillan/Hall, 1994), 239–41; Elsa Nettels, *Language and Gender in American Fiction* (Charlottesville: UP of VA, 1997), 122, 146; Betsy Nix, interview with WCF staff member, 7/2018; Robert Thacker, interview, 8/2018; "Natalie Clifford Barney," hmdb.org/Marker.asp?Marker=104542; Martina Navratilova, "The Genocide of Gay Youth," www.universal way.org/gaygenocide .html, 5/98.

---------------★---------------

23. American Indians Only Roved for About a Hundred Years

SOUTH DAKOTA *Brookings*

On the eastern border of Brookings County is a historical marker that reads, "You Are About to Enter Brookings County—Home of roving Indians until 1862." It is true that Dakota Indians lived in Brookings County when immigrants from the United States arrived in 1862, and they did rove about on their horses, a classic example of the Plains Indian culture. Most Americans do not realize, however, that Indian "roving" in South Dakota—as in most of the United States—started with the white man.

Most Native Americans did not rove until roving Europeans forced them to. After his 1779 raid on the Iroquois league during the American Revolution, for example, Gen. John Sullivan bragged, "We have not left a single settlement or field of corn in the country of the Five Nations." Helen Hunt Jackson (chapter 85) tells that in the Ohio Valley in 1795 the United States destroyed the cornfields of the Delawares three times in one year. The Ohio Indians now had to rove, given the impossibility of farming or settling. Some anthropologists believe that even the "primitive" gathering and hunting peoples of the Amazon jungle had an agricultural past until Spanish and Portuguese immigrants forced them to rove.

Similarly, in the late 1600s, the Dakota or Sioux people, after whom South Dakota is named, lived in settled communities in eastern Minnesota and

The Mandans of South and North Dakota were a settled agricultural people who never took up the new Plains Indian culture and thus showed how some Plains Indians lived in the Dakotas before the advent of the horse and "roving." Karl Bodmer, noted Swiss artist, went up the Missouri River in 1833–34 and painted these Mandan boaters and their village, made of permanent sod and wood houses. Three years later, a small steamer inadvertently brought smallpox to the Mandans, reducing their population from 1,600 to just 31. Epidemics were particularly virulent in settled villages with this kind of housing. Thus disease was another white-initiated process that favored roving.

Wisconsin. There they harvested wild rice from canoes, farmed corn and squash, made maple syrup, fished the land of 10,000 lakes, and hunted on foot through the north woods. Then pressure from the British and French invasion of what is now the eastern United States and Canada forced natives there to move westward. By 1690, the Ojibwes in Wisconsin were trading with the French for guns and bullets, which they used to drive the Dakotas west across the Mississippi River.

Luckily for Dakota survival, wild horses and horse culture ideas flowed northward from the Spanish in Texas shortly thereafter. The Dakotas, like several other Native American groups, adopted horses and horse culture ideas and transformed them into a new tradition: Plains Indian culture. They learned to hunt buffalo from horseback. Using horses to pull long poles, the Dakotas created large movable tipis, which made "roving" possible. Now the Great Plains could support large groups of American Indians without their reliance on agriculture. The movement was from place to place within one's home territory, usually repetitive with the seasons, not really "roving."

All around the Plains, previously settled Native cultures were in flux caused by the European newcomers. Cheyennes had lived in Minnesota just east of the Dakotas, but pressure from the Ojibwes and Dakotas forced them westward into North and South Dakota, where they built earth-lodge villages and raised crops. When the horse culture appeared, the Cheyennes adopted it and began roving westward and southward into Colorado, Wyoming, and Montana. Some Shoshones, meanwhile, moved the opposite direction. They began as a branch of the Utes, gathering and hunting people living in small groups in difficult terrain in the Utah Basin. Some adopted the new Plains culture, moved southeast, and became known as Comanches. Plains Indian culture was an exhilarating example of syncretism—blending elements from American Indian and European cultures to come up with something new. It drew Dakotas, Cheyennes, Comanches, Pawnees, and Apaches, each from different language and culture families, into a new societal convergence.

Agricultural societies usually have an advantage over gathering and hunting peoples because their greater density allows them to mobilize more people. For defense, the Arikaras, for example, had lived in earth lodges in South Dakota since at least the 1300s, raising corn, beans, and other crops, and operating as a major trading center for native groups from the Great Lakes to the Rocky Mountains. The new Plains technology disadvantaged the Arikaras. By the 1830s, the Dakotas had forced them northwest into what is now North Dakota.[1] "Roving" worked for the Plains Indians for about a century—worked so well in fact that it took the U.S. Army to force them into reservations.

South Dakota boasts a rich history of rapid cultural change that recapitulates within its borders a process that took place all across the Americas. Condensing this story into "home of roving Indians" fits with our national archetype of American Indians as roving people, contrasted with Europeans who settled. It does violence to the truth of a much larger and more important narrative, however, that begins with settled Indians and roving Europeans.[2]

---

1. Smallpox and other diseases then decimated the Arikaras, Mandans, and other previously "settled" South Dakota peoples.
2. Sullivan quoted in "George Washington, An American Hero?" in Bill Bigelow and Bob Peterson, eds., *Rethinking Columbus* (Milwaukee, WI: *Rethinking Schools*, 1998), 58; Helen Hunt Jackson, *A Century of Dishonor* (Boston: Roberts, 1888),41–44.

★

---

24. The Devil Is Winning, Six to One

NORTH DAKOTA *Devils Lake*

On the south side of the lake, the Devils Lake Sioux Tribe changed their name to Spirit Lake Dakotah Nation. On the north side, the overwhelmingly white town of Devils Lake, with a population of 9,000, is sticking with Devils Lake, partly out of loyalty to its high school football team, the Satans.

Native Americans are upset with names like "Devils Lake," "Heathen Meadow," "Devils Tower," and the like. They realize that European Americans often gave such names to sacred sites precisely when they learned that these places figured in Native religions. American Indians near Devils Tower, the stunning rock column in Wyoming, consider the name blasphemous. To them, it is a holy site, "The Bear's Lair." "It's like calling the Vatican the 'house of the Devil,'" said one Native American.[1]

Native Americans also insist that "squaw" is a derogatory term. Some believe it derives from a French corruption of an Iroquois epithet for vagina, analogous to "cunt" in English. Others believe it meant "bitch" in Algonquian dialects spoken in Virginia. Some linguists say it is merely an Algonquian prefix meaning "female" but has taken on contemptuous overtones over the centuries. All three hypotheses might be true, but there is no doubt that today the term in English is a derogatory reference to a Native woman or wife, also sometimes connoting prostitution. Whites know this; in Minnesota for example, white high school students have harassed Native girls by calling them "squaws." Hence Native Americans are also unhappy with Squaw Island, New York; Squaw Valley, California; Squaw Mountain, Colorado, and Maine; Squaw Butte, Idaho; and most repugnant of all, Squaw Tits, Arizona.[2]

In Minnesota, Native Americans and those concerned for the feelings and image of Native Americans passed a law against place names containing "squaw." Not everyone agreed—residents of Lake County in the far northeastern part of the state reacted sarcastically by renaming Squaw Creek and Squaw Bay "Politically Correct Creek" and "Politically Correct Bay." Indeed, to some non-Indians concern about "squaw" or "devil" on the American landscape seems like an arcane exercise in political correctness. Nevertheless, several other states have followed Minnesota's lead.

Renaming can be distressing and expensive. Maps, telephone directories, legal documents, and corporate names must be changed. Ponder just the stationery costs of residents who live on a peninsula in Lake Ontario in Wayne County, New York, once named Niggerhead Point. In 1955, as whites achieved new sensitivities owing to the Civil Rights Movement, it was renamed Negrohead Point. After the Black Power movement, African American thinking came to disparage "Negro" and favor "black," but no one proposed "Blackhead Point." Finally, in 1977 the peninsula was renamed Graves Point.

Not renaming poses other costs. Retaining terms like "squaw" and "nigger" on the landscape surely announces that whites are in charge, whites who have no consideration for the feelings of others. In the late 1980s, the Board of Geographic Names, at last, got around to renaming at least 102 places in 34 states with "nigger" in their names. "Jap" also became "Japanese" across the United States. A Chinese American vacationing at Yellowstone took offense at "Chinamans Spring" and got it renamed "Chinese Spring." Surely all this is appropriate. Would we still want place names like Niggerhead Mountain to decorate the state map of Vermont? What of Dago Gulch, Montana? Chinks Peak, Idaho? Dead Nigger Bayou, Mississippi? All these were all too real; all have now been corrected.

"Devils Lake" ought to be corrected too, nationally and in North Dakota. Across the United States in 1998, "devil" outnumbered "spirit" on the American landscape by 1,672 to 287, or six to one.[3] The next time you pass Heathen Meadow, Devil's Gap, or, in North Dakota, Devils Lake, consider: these names were deliberate attempts to stigmatize the religions of Native Americans as heathen. They made it easier to look down on Native Americans as primitive and savage. In a nation that prides itself on freedom of religion, Native American religions have not usually been included and are still subject to interference. And why not, if they are truly, as the landscape implies, the work of the devil. If non–Native Americans no longer believe that Native religions are the devil's work, it is time to remove that implication from names all across America.[4]

Chapter 1 tells of other successful Native renamings.

1. For those who haven't been to Wyoming, Devils Tower was the landing site for a spaceship in the movie *Close Encounters of the Third Kind.*

2. Other mammarial offenders include Squaw Tit, California; Squaw Tit Butte, Nebraska; Squaw Tit, New Mexico; Squaw Teat Butte and Squaw Teat Creek, South Dakota; Squaw's Teat, Texas; Squaw's Tit, Washington; Squaw's Teat, Wyoming, and, it turns out, Milk Shake, Washington! And that's not counting Montana, which has Squaw Teat, Squaw Teats, Squaw's Teat, and Squaw Nipple. In all, some 934 places (with some multiple counting, particularly of creeks) in the U.S. Geological Survey were named "squaw" as of 1999, from Squaw Bay, Maine, to Squaw Harbor, Alaska. "Chinaman" remained on the map in 29 places and "Dago" in 26. As of 2018, because of more double listings and more complete research, "squaw" got 1,176 entries, "Chinaman" 37, and "Dago" 41. All this use of "tit" and "teat" implies the dominance of men over women, too. "Breast" is used in only two places, White Breast, Iowa, and Virgin's Breasts Islands, Maine. "Nipple" and "Nipples" are used 99 times, including for one of the Virgin's Breasts. "Penis" does not appear, nor could I find any slang terms for "penis" used as place names. Interestingly, "women" and "woman" are used some 611 times, but many are mere buildings; "squaw" far outpolls them.

3. By 2018, the ratio had improved a bit: 1,881 to 805, or 2.3 to one.

4. James Brooke, "Spirit Lake Tribal Members Had a Devil of a Time Redeeming Their Good Name," *St. Paul Pioneer Press*, 11/20/96; Associated Press story on Lake County, pharos.uwc.edu/~dcleek/courses/geo110/whomp.txt, 8/97; Mark Monmonier, *Drawing the Line* (NY: Holt, 1995), 50–52; U.S. Geological Survey website, mapping.usgs .gov:8888/gnis/owa/gnisquery?, 1/20/99; "School Problems in Minnesota," *Minneapolis Star and Tribune*, 4/21/93, www.bioc09.uthscsa.edu/ natnet/archive/nl/9306/0003. html, 8/97; Cindy Bloom, "Honoring Our Grandmothers," *Midwest Soarring Wings* 1 no. 6 (fall 1996), www.usd.edu/anth/soar/wings2.html, 10/10/97; files from Soarring; George R. Stewart, *American Place-Names* (NY: Oxford UP, 1970), 135, 201, 270, 322, 458; Frank T. Siebert Jr., "Resurrecting Virginia Algonquian from the Dead," in James M. Crawford, *Studies in Southeastern Indian Languages* (Athens: U. of GA Press, 1967), 316; Ives Goddard, "Since the Word Squaw Continues to be of Interest," *News from Indian Country* (mid-April 1997): 19A; several dictionaries; Shirl Kasper, "Signs of the Times," *Kansas City Star* (c. 1995); Lisa Blekin, "On Geographic Names and Cleaning Them Up," *The New York Times*, 2/14/90; William Least Heat Moon, *PrairyErth* (Boston: Houghton Mifflin, 1991), 118–22; Bill Bryson, *Made in America* (NY: Morrow, 1994), 24; George R. Stewart, *Names on the Land* (NY: Random House, 1945), 218; S. L. A. Marshall, *Crimsoned Prairie* (NY: Scribner's, 1972), 8; Donald J. Orth and Roger L. Payne, *Principles, Policies, and Procedures: Domestic Geographic Names* (Reston, VA: U.S. Board Geographic Names, 1997 [1987]), 18–19.

THE MIDWEST

25. "Serving the Cause of Humanity"

MINNESOTA *St. Paul*

America is full of statues and plaques that seem to commemorate the Spanish-American War. Just as "the doughboy"—the lone infantryman wearing a heavy metal helmet—became the symbol for World War I, "the hiker"—a bare-headed GI casually holding a rifle—appeared on many Spanish-American War memorials. The National Association of Spanish War Veterans is said to have placed at least 50 copies of this statue all around the country.[1]

Combat in the Spanish-American War began on May 1, 1898, and ended August 13 of that year. The U.S. Navy destroyed the Spanish Pacific fleet in

On the base of most Spanish-American War monuments is a bronze plaque with the war's standard memorial symbol, a circle over a Maltese cross. Around the circle are the words "Spanish-American War, 1898–1902"; on the four arms of the cross are "Cuba," "Puerto Rico," "Philippine Islands," and "U.S.A."[2] Inside the circle a bare-armed "native woman" with her chains

broken kneels before the U.S. soldier and sailor who ostensibly liberated her. This scene inverts history: any rational Filipina would have bolted for the woods when American soldiers or sailors came near, knowing full well she might be shot or see her house burned and her male children killed.

Manila Bay on May 1 and the Spanish Atlantic fleet off Santiago de Cuba on July 3. Two weeks later Teddy Roosevelt's Rough Riders helped compel the surrender of Santiago de Cuba, effectively ending the war. Troops under Nelson Miles took Puerto Rico with almost no opposition. In the entire war, only 379 Americans died in battle; 1,604 were wounded.

How did a hundred-day war wind up with a five-year timespan on its monuments?

The answer to this puzzle points to one of America's least-happy foreign adventures—our war with the Philippines. Hostilities in the Philippine-American War began on February 4, 1899, half a year after the Spanish-American War ended. On July 4, 1902, Theodore Roosevelt, who became president upon McKinley's assassination, declared the war won. Hence the "1898–1902."

Except for the curious dates on our Spanish-American war memorials, the Philippine-American War lies almost forgotten on our landscape. One of the few places that openly recognizes this war is a large bronze plaque in the rotunda of the Minnesota State Capitol. It honors the Thirteenth Minnesota All Volunteer Infantry as "one of the first regiments to carry the American flag across the seas." It mentions how this unit "participated in Battle of Manila, August 13th, 1898, ending the War with Spain." The plaque then details where the men fought next, as part of the U.S. Army in the Philippine-American War: "Military Police of Manila, August 22nd [1898] to March 17th, 1899. Volunteered for the Philippine Insurrection on March 25th. Sent to the front in the campaign against insurgent Filipinos under Chief Aguinaldo." In one way, this marker is a good thing: Minnesota at least recognizes that the Philippine-American War took place. But almost every phrase on it is a lie.

The Thirteenth Minnesota never volunteered for "the Philippine Insurrection." John Roberts, a bugler in the unit, said on his return, "We enlisted to fight the Spaniards, to fight them for two years if necessary, but we did not enlist to fight niggers in the Philippines, and if we had been asked to do so I, for one, would have refused." The McKinley administration sold the Spanish-American War to the American people on the grounds that the Spanish were colonial overlords and the oppressed people of Cuba, in particular, deserved to govern themselves. So the volunteering done by the Thirteenth Minnesota, although couched in racist terms by Roberts, involved a good measure of idealism.

Moreover, there was no "Philippine Insurrection." This term suggests that the United States held legitimate power in the Philippines, against which some Filipinos rebelled. Nothing of the sort was true. This was a war of conquest by an outside power, not an insurrection by a subordinate faction. The Filipino independence movement controlled most of the nation including all of the main island of Luzon except Manila when the United States attacked. Filipinos date their independence from June 12, 1898, before the American army even got there, and celebrated their centennial in 1998. They are clear about the role of the United States as an invader. American historians, too, now agree on the more accurate "Philippine-American War." So does the Library of Congress.

The plaque's last two words, "Chief Aguinaldo," are sillier yet. The Filipinos were not American Indians; Emilio Aguinaldo was no "chief"; he was president of the Philippine Republic. After the United States attacked the Filipinos, U.S. leaders tried to portray the war as some kind of uprising limited to a few "tribes." Earlier, when the Filipinos were our allies against Spain, American officials had considered Aguinaldo the leader of all Filipinos.

The United States sent some 125,000 troops to the Philippines. About 10,000 lost their lives including 4,234 who died in combat. Another 2,818 were wounded. Thus, the war was almost ten times as hurtful to our population as the Spanish-American War. Indeed, in absolute numbers, more Americans died in combat in the Philippine-American War than died in the American Revolution or the War of 1812—more, in fact, than in all but six of our wars.[3] Still, more Americans died of disease in the Philippines. For the other side, it was "the bloodiest conflict in Philippines history, including World War II," according to historian Leon Wolff. Americans killed and counted the bodies of 16,000 Filipino soldiers; total Filipino combat deaths exceeded 20,000. Among the civilian population, deaths from combat, disease, and starvation exceeded 200,000 and possibly reached 700,000. Thus in duration, effort, and losses at least, the Philippine-American War far overshadows the Spanish-American War. Since monuments are expressly intended to recognize effort and losses, every Spanish-American War monument in the United States might reasonably be renamed. Even the images on them didn't come from the Spanish-American War. "The hiker" and "hiking" were terms used by U.S. soldiers in the Philippine-American War to describe themselves and their campaigns to root out Filipino guerrillas from their mountain strongholds. In the Spanish-American War, the United States mostly attacked *cities*.

If more memorials noted the Philippine-American War, Americans might remember it better.[4] As a citizen who came of age politically during the war in Vietnam, I have come to regret that neither I nor most Americans recalled the Philippine War in the 1960s, for it was a lost memory that might have prevented the war. Parallels between the two wars are many. In both countries the United States initially allied with a colonized people and then turned on them, reestablishing colonialism. The Filipino independence movement had been our ally against Spain, just as Ho Chi Minh's forces in Vietnam had been our allies against Japan during World War II. In the Philippines, the United States simply replaced Spain as the colonial master. In Vietnam, after Japan fell, the United States first tried to prop up France, the previous European colonial ruler, before installing its own puppet regime in South Vietnam after the Vietnamese ousted the French.

Even more than in most wars, truth was the first casualty in the Philippines and in Vietnam. Deception began from the outset when U.S. officials lied to explain why our troops were now fighting the Filipinos. (Chapter 75 tells how we actually came to attack them.) In Vietnam, the United States claimed to be "defending" the "nation" of South Vietnam against "outside aggression," while in reality, American forces were the outside aggressors.

In both wars, the administration lied to the American people about the "progress" of the war. In the Philippines, army officials kept journalists from many parts of the islands and censored their reports to the United States. Eleven correspondents sent a joint news story to their papers, charging that official dispatches "err in saying 'the situation is well in hand'" and had given Americans "an ultra-optimistic view that is not shared by the general officers in the field." In Vietnam, veteran correspondents labeled the armed forces' daily briefings "the five o'clock follies" and laughed when officials continued to see the "light at the end of the tunnel." This report to the *New York Post* from the Philippines by Albert Robinson could have been filed 70 years later from Vietnam by merely changing the last word to "Saigon": "There are towns here which have been 'captured' again and again, each time with a 'glorious victory.' Today it is unsafe for an American to go even ten miles from the city of Manila."

As in Vietnam, there were no front lines in the Philippine War, and as in Vietnam, soldiers could not easily discern friend—"amigo"—from foe. The results were not surprising: GI's adopted the slogan, "There are no more amigos." Generals declared that all civilians must enter "reconcentration camps" (in Vietnam, officials would call them "strategic hamlets"), and anyone outside them would be fair game. In both Vietnam and the Philippines, American troops called the enemy "gooks"; white Americans also used the term "nigger" for Filipino enemies.

The Minnesota plaque lists twenty battles in which the men participated and ten generals under whom they fought, followed by details of their mustering out. To the left of the list is a beautifully done scene of American soldiers attacking a village on Luzon. The typical sightseer, not having read accounts by participants, would have no idea what happened after the soldiers took that generic Luzon village. "We have been vastly more cruel than the Spanish," said Roberts. "I have known of orders being given which, if put in writing, would read, in effect: *Let there be no wounded among the enemy.*" Pvt. A. A. Barnes of the Third Artillery wrote from Luzon to his brother in Indiana: "Last night one of our boys was found shot and his stomach cut open. Immediately orders were received from General [Frank] Wheaton to burn the town and kill every native in sight; which was done . . . " L. F. Adams from Missouri wrote home about another campaign in Luzon: "In the path of the Washington regiment . . . there were 1,008 dead niggers and a great many wounded. We burned all their houses. I don't know how many men, women, and children the Tennessee boys did kill. They would not take any prisoners."

These were no isolated incidents. After a Filipino attack on a U.S. army post on Samar killed 38 of 74 men and wounded another 30, Brig. Gen. Jake Smith was told to "pacify" the island.[5] He ordered all civilians out of the island's interior and confined them in stockades. "Turn the entire island into a howling wilderness," he told his troops. "I want no prisoners. I wish you to kill and burn; the more you kill and burn the better it will please me." All male persons over age ten who had not already surrendered were to be shot. "Within six months Samar was as quiet as a cemetery," concluded historian Leon Wolff. Wolff quoted an observer, "Even the Spaniards are appalled at American cruelty."

As in Vietnam, war crimes committed by U.S. personnel in the Philippines "seldom saw the light of day," in Wolff's words; "those that did were systematically denied or minimized." In Vietnam, except for one man, Lt. William Calley, who drew a few years of house arrest for ordering and administering the murders of civilians in the My Lai massacre, no American received significant punishment for war crimes. In the Philippines, there was not even a Calley. The army brought up several officers and men on charges, but officials realized that the responsibility for the outrages led straight up the chain of command, so most got off with reprimands, some with small fines.

There are still more parallels with the war in Vietnam. American soldiers despised their assignments, so rot appeared in the army, and a serious antiwar movement arose at home. As in Vietnam, hawks then claimed that antiwar agitation was raising enemy morale, hence prolonging the war. Neither war stemmed from direct pressure by American commercial interests, which had no significant investments to protect in either country. Individual political leaders—McKinley and Roosevelt in the Philippines; Kennedy, Johnson, and Nixon in Vietnam—made the fateful decisions to send and maintain troops to subjugate the Asians we claimed to be helping.[6]

Another parallel between the wars was the popularity of the Filipino and Vietnamese revolutionary leaders compared with the unpopularity of the puppet leaders the United States installed. Dwight Eisenhower admitted that in a fair election, Ho Chi Minh would win 80% of the votes in Vietnam. John Bass, writing in *Harper's* decades earlier, said the same about Aguinaldo: "The whole population of the islands sympathizes with the insurgents; only those natives whose immediate self-interest requires it are friendly to us." And for that reason, both wars lasted a long time.

Until our recent never-ending war in Afghanistan, Vietnam was often called our longest war, but depending upon the date chosen for its ending, the Philippine-American War arguably lasted longer. When President Roosevelt declared victory on July 4, 1902, nobody really celebrated. Military historian John Collins judged that the war dragged on to 1913. Serious incidents continued as late as 1916.

When Americans swept the Philippine-American War under the rug of our Spanish-American War memorials, we lost our collective memory of it. In 1926, Moorfield Storey and Marcial Lichauco published a farsighted critique of the war, *The Conquest of the Philippines by the United States, 1898–1925.* They asked, "Why revive these memories that we would fain obliterate?" They answered by pointing out that Americans were still lying about the war: "With all this history behind him, the President of the United States [in 1925] still asserts that the islands came to us 'unsought.'" Finally, they argued that if we stay ignorant of this history, "what American representatives have done in the past may be done again." They meant in the Philippines, but their words had wider prophetic implications. Americans on all sides of the Vietnam War invoked various analogies to campaign for or against our involvement there—Munich, the domino theory, Korea, and the like. Few referred to the Philippine War, however—a pity, because that analogy would have been so close.

The Minnesota plaque, only slightly superior to total amnesia, employs an astonishing paragraph to summarize the war: "They served the cause of humanity. They battled to free the oppressed peoples of the Philippines Islands, who suffered under the despotic rule of Spain." If soldiers from the Thirteenth Minnesota All Volunteer Infantry coming home on October 12, 1899, could have seen it, they would have laughed those words off the wall. On that day, President McKinley joined Minnesota Governor John Lind to welcome the troops home to Minneapolis. In the presence of the president, Lind used the occasion to raise troubling questions about American imperialism: "By our growth and development the mission of the American volunteer soldier has come to an end. For purposes of conquest and subjugation he is unfit, for he carries a conscience as well as a gun. The volunteer soldier has always stood for self-government, liberty, and justice."

By 1948, when the plaque went up, American imperialism apparently no longer troubled anyone. Half a century of U.S. interventions had made sending troops into other countries seem routine. But in 1998, a group of Filipino Americans and other Minnesota citizens got a temporary exhibit installed in the rotunda of the Capitol that presented accurate information about the Philippine-American War.[7] Then they got a permanent corrective plaque placed below the bad plaque. It gets the dates right:

Spanish-American War, 1898
Philippine-American War, 1899–1902

Then it gently points out, "Most of the battles listed above were fought against Filipinos in a subsequent conflict now known as the Philippine-American War." It notes that the Filipinos had established "the Philippine Republic" before American ground forces arrived. Unfortunately, it then lapses into passive voice: "The Philippine-American War erupted on February 4, 1899. . . .

After the U.S. victory, the Philippines remained under American rule. Independence was granted in 1946."

I wish the corrective plaque flatly stated that it *is* a correction. I also wish it told more of the problematic history of our war against the Philippines. But at least it gets that war onto the wall. Maybe it will spark visitors to learn more.

Our Vietnam debacle, and our other wars since Vietnam, demonstrate that ignorance of this war has hardly been bliss.[8]

1. At least 26 hikers by Theodora Ruggles Kitson still stand along with at least 24 by other sculptors.

2. Sometimes "China" is added instead of "Puerto Rico" or "U.S.A.," adding in another unrelated war, the Boxer Rebellion.

3. In order, America's ten deadliest wars have been the Civil War, World War II, World War I, Vietnam, Korea, the Mexican War, the Philippine War, King Philip's War, the Revolution, and the War of 1812.

4. American history textbooks also promote amnesia; they devote almost eight pages to the Spanish-American War and only a paragraph or two to the Philippine War. The army also needs to recall the Philippine War more honestly. Its website lists the Spanish-American War but not the Philippine War among its "major wars." The army really knows better; another inventory, "Campaigns of the United States Army," lists eleven different campaigns under "Philippines Insurrection," while only three under Spanish-American War.

5. Another account lists 48 dead and 22 wounded.

6. I would grant that American commercial interests played a "cultural" role in both interventions. Some American political leaders saw the Philippines as a base that could be used to further U.S. interests in China and throughout the Far East. Some American political leaders believed that our intervention in Vietnam would further U.S. interests in other Third World countries.

7. An early draft of this chapter helped their cause.

8. Leon Wolff, *Little Brown Brother* (Garden City, NY: Doubleday, 1961), 40–48, 58, 67–69, 100, 221–62, 274–76, 305–7, 319–63, Lawton quoted on 290; Moorfield Storey and Marcial Lichauco, *The Conquest of the Philippines by the U.S., 1898–1925* (NY: Putnam, 1926), 121–29, 152–54; "As Cruel As Spain," probably from *Minneapolis Times*, 1900, from soldier's scrapbook, Minnesota State Historical Society, courtesy Kyle Ward; Robert Tomsho, "Death Toll," *The Wall Street Journal*, 11/19/97; James C. Thomason Jr., Peter W. Stanley, and John C. Perry, *Sentimental Imperialists* (NY: Harper & Row, 1981), 115; Jim Zwick, www.rochester. ican.net/~fjzwick/centennial/war.html, 9/97, 4/98; mcs.net/~flip/usrp.html, 9/97, 5/98; *Philippine Historical Markers* (Manila: Republic of Philippines Bureau of Public Schools, 1958), 42; William Bruce Wheeler and Susan D. Becker, *Discovering the American Past* (Boston: Houghton-Mifflin, 1990), 99; Julius W. Pratt, *America's Colonial Experiment* (Gloucester: Peter Smith, 1964), 80; John Collins, *America's Small Wars* (DC: Brassey's, 1991), 17; www.army.mil/cmb-pg/campaigns, 4/98; Daniel B. Schirmer, "U.S. Racism and Intervention in the Third World, Past and Present," *FFP Bulletin* (winter 1994); Oscar V. Campomanes, "Grappling with the Filipino as Primitive: The American Soldier in Love and War (1903)" (New Orleans: Society for Cinema Studies Conference, 1993), 17; Arthur M. Schlesinger, ed., *The Almanac*

of American History (NY: Putnam, 1983), 392; William McKinley, speech to Methodists, 11/21/1899, in Joseph R. Conlin, ed., *Morrow Book of Quotations in American History* (NY: Morrow, 1984), 138; Richard Hofstadter, "Manifest Destiny and the Philippines," in T. P. Greene, ed., *American Imperialism in 1898* (Boston: D. C. Heath, 1955), 59–60; George Stephenson, *John Lind of Minnesota* (Minneapolis: U. of MN Press, 1935), 174; Ken Meter, emails, 1/3/98; Leonard Inskip, "For War's Centennial, A Useful Second Look," *Minneapolis Star Tribune*, 6/11/98; Peg Meier, "Capitol Plaque Puts Philippine War's Hurtful History to Rest," *Minneaplolis Star-Tribune*, 2/4/2002; "Philippine Study Group of Minnesota," crcworks.org/?submit=philippine, 8/2018.

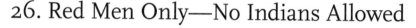

26. Red Men Only—No Indians Allowed

IOWA *Muscatine*

In Muscatine's Riverside Park a handsome bronze half-clad Native American male gazes toward the Mississippi River. A plaque on the statue reads, "Presented to the city by the 'Muscuitine Tribe #95, Improved Order of Red Men,' and 'dedicated to the Mascoutin Indians in 1926.'" Fifty years later, Muscatine used this image on its medallions issued to commemorate the U.S. bicentennial. And Iowa is not alone. In 1921, the Red Men put up the famous statue of Massasoit on Cole's Hill facing Plymouth Rock in Massachusetts to commemorate the 300th anniversary of the landing of the Pilgrims. In Charlemont in western Massachusetts stands a magnificent bronze Native American with upraised arms. Entitled "Hail to the Sunrise," its base read, "Erected by the Tribes and Councils of the Improved Order of Red Men, October 1, 1932." It is the centerpiece of Mohawk Park, a large park on Route 2, also known as the "Mohawk Trail," and is surrounded by dozens of plaques from the order's different lodges. I asked residents of a home across the road from Mohawk Park about the Red Men. They assured me that its members were Native Americans. "Every stone you see there was placed by a different tribe of Indians who used to live in this area," one told me. Although they were quite sincere, this information is hard to credit since the plaques on the stones were put there by chapters of Red Men from places like Barre, Vermont; Jacksonville, Florida; and even Honolulu, Hawaii. Similarly, there was no "Muscuitine Tribe" of Indians in Muscatine in 1926.

It turns out that the Improved Order of Red Men (IORM) is indeed a white fraternal organization. Organized in the 1840s, it claims to trace its roots to the Sons of Liberty in the 1770s.[1] Its members have included Samuel Adams, John Hancock, Patrick Henry, Thomas Jefferson, Paul Revere, Theodore Roosevelt, Franklin D. Roosevelt, and Richard Nixon. The Red Men venerated American Indians as exemplars of liberty who helped white Americans develop democracy.

However, the Red Men didn't let their admiration interfere with their racism. According to an exhibit at the Abbey Rockefeller Folk Art Museum in 1997, the Improved Order of Red Men "claims to be the nation's oldest secret society of purely American origin. Although founded in part 'to perpetuate the beautiful legends and traditions of a vanishing race and to keep alive its customs,' Native Americans are barred from membership."

In the first three decades of the twentieth century, when the Red Men were actively putting up their statues, there was a reason to believe that American Indians were a vanishing race. Native Americans had dropped in number from perhaps 14,000,000 in 1491 in what is now the United States to just 244,000 by 1920, a decline of 98% (chapter 89). Meanwhile, the Red Men had grown to 150,000 members by 1875 and to more than half a million by 1920.

What accounted for the popularity of the Improved Order of Red Men? Maybe white Americans wanted to inherit the aura and spiritual strength of the American Indian. Maybe whites wanted to feel a closer kinship with the land and with nature. Maybe they simply wanted justification for taking Indian land, which was still going on between 1875 and 1920. Over the centuries, whites have repeatedly taken pride in America's Native past while justifying Indian removal. Often, whites named elements of the landscape for Indian leaders or nations as they deported them. Lafayette Bunnell, a leader of the Mariposa Battalion in California that deported Native Americans from Yosemite, tells of their chief's reaction when he learned that Bunnell had just renamed Lake Tenaya in his honor:

> I called him up to us, and told him that we had given his name to the lake and river. At first he seemed unable to comprehend our purpose, and pointing to the group of glistening peaks, near the head of the lake, said "It already has a name; we call it Py-we-ack." Upon my telling him that we had named it Ten-ie-ya, because it was upon the shores of the lake that we had found his people, who would never return to it to live, his countenance fell and he at once left our group and joined his family circle. His countenance indicated that he thought the naming of the lake no equivalent for his loss of territory.

Likewise, historian James M. Mayo notes what he calls "this contradictory pattern" near Plymouth, in northern Indiana. A 1908 statue of Chief Menomonee is inscribed, "In memory of Chief Menomonee and his band of 859 Potawatomi Indians, removed from this reservation Sept. 4, 1838. . . ." According to Mayo, these remembrances demonstrate "local pride in Indian history," while giving "an air of legitimacy to the removal of the Indians."

For that matter, consider Thanksgiving, our national origin myth, complete with a ritual origin banquet that symbolizes the supplanting of natives by Europeans. The Pilgrims even take over Indian foods and then serve them back to the Indians, thus earning their undying good will.

The Red Men honored American Indians like Massasoit (chapter 90) and Pocahontas, allies of the Europeans whose memory helps to legitimize the white takeover. Or they honored tribes like the Mohawks and the Muscatines, who had had the grace to leave the area. There are few Mohawks left in Massachusetts and few Muscatines in Iowa. It would be harder to honor

Mohawks at the St. Regis Reservation in northern New York or idolize Indians as a dying race in places where living Indians still form a vibrant part of society like South Dakota, New Mexico, or even Chicago. Doing so would require consulting with living American Indians . . . perhaps an awkward duty for officials of an organization that wouldn't let them join.

Although one objective of the Improved Order of Red Men is still "perpetuating the beautiful legends and traditions of a vanishing race," today Native Americans are rapidly growing in number. In the 2010 census, they totaled more than 4,000,000. The Red Men are the vanishing race, down to just 28,000 members as of 1998. In 1920, there were more than two Red Men for every American Indian, not even counting the Daughters of Pocahontas. Today, there are more than 140 Native Americans for every Red Man. In the 1970s, perhaps realizing, at last, the incongruity of an all-white organization formed ostensibly to pay homage to members of a different race, the Red Men finally opened their ranks to Native Americans and other men of color (so far as the national office knows, no Native Americans have yet joined).[2]

As the Red Men die off, American Indians are symbolically taking over at least one of the Red Men monuments from them. In 1970, Wampanoags and other Native Americans in Massachusetts began to recognize Thanksgiving Day as a "National Day of Mourning." Participants typically gather at the statue of Massasoit in Plymouth on that day to listen to speakers and perform acts that challenge the traditional European American Thanksgiving legend. In 1995, for example, they and their supporters went down to nearby Plymouth Rock and symbolically buried it in the sand.[3]

1. The IORM says it was founded in 1847 but claims continuity with local groups dating to the Sons of Liberty, Sons of Tamina, and Red Men. That is how it claims Revolutionary figures as members. Other sources date its origin to 1813, 1834, 1841, and 1845.

2. In 1999, a staff member didn't think any Native Americans were members, but since the Red Men no longer ask about race on their application forms, they don't know for sure. In June 2018, staff declined to answer any questions about membership numbers and whether or not they have any Native American members.

3. R. Francis, *Cyrus E. Dallin: Let Justice Be Done* (Springville, MA: Press Publishing, 1976); Donald A. Grinde Jr. and Bruce E. Johansen, *Exemplar of Liberty* (Los Angeles: American Indian Studies Center, 1991), 214; Exhibit on fraternal organizations (Lexington, MA: Museum of Our National Heritage, 1996); Exhibit Label at Abbey Rockefeller Folk Art Museum (Colonial Williamsburg, VA, 1997); Bureau of the Census, *1990 Census* (DC: GPO, 1992); conversations with staff at the Red Men Museum & Library, 4/98; members.xoom.com/redmen, 4/98; Rebecca Solnit, "Up the River of Mercy," *Sierra* 11/92: 53; James M. Mayo, *War Memorials as Political Landscape* (NY: Praeger, 1989), 145. As of June 2018, I could find no evidence of criticisms of the statue.

★
---

27. Domesticating Mark Twain
MISSOURI *Hannibal*

With lumber milling wound down and the shoe factory closed, Hannibal's principal industry today is tourism and its principal attraction is, of course, Mark Twain. Samuel Clemens, his name when he lived here, spent his boyhood in Hannibal where his experiences provided the backdrop for and inspired many of the characters in *Adventures of Huckleberry Finn*, *The Adventures of Tom Sawyer*, and other beloved Twain writings.

Hannibal knows this all too well. 350,000 visitors come each year to a place that's not near anywhere else and drop $13,000,000 annually at places like the Mark Twain Boyhood Home and Museum Annex, John Marshall Clemens Law Office, Becky Thatcher House, Twainland Express, Mark Twain Wax Museum, Mark Twain Family Restaurant, Mark Twain Dinette, Mark Twain Fried Chicken, Mark Twain Book and Gift Shop, Becky Thatcher Book and Gift Shop, Mark Twain Card Shop, Tom Sawyer Dioramas, Mark Twain Cave, *Mark Twain* Riverboat, Tom 'n' Huck Motel, Best Western Hotel Clemens, and Mark Twain Outdoor Theater. And that's not counting the Huck Finn Shopping Center, Mrs. Clemens Antique Mall, Becky Thatcher Girl Scout Council, Mark Twain Elementary School, Mark Twain Jeep-Eagle Dealer, Mark Twain Citgo, and perhaps most incongruously, Mark Twain Redi-Mix. In 1999, however, Hannibal was selling Mark Twain, but only *part* of Mark Twain. The town presented a genial Twain, content-free, much like the Mark Twain robot that Coca-Cola uses to co-narrate (with Ben Franklin) its 23-minute, bland-as-pablum "American Adventure" at Epcot Center in Disney World.[1] This was not the Mark Twain that influenced black writers from Richard Wright to Toni Morrison. This was a Twain without irony.

It was also a Twain without a moral center. Not just Aunt Polly's fence got whitewashed in Hannibal—so did Mark Twain. For Twain was a writer fiercely involved in trying to make the United States a better nation. His most passionate concern was race relations, and in *Huckleberry Finn*, *Pudd'nhead Wilson*, and several shorter works, he raised the question, can the United States be moral and racist too? Twain's stories and essays questioned other occurrences in his America, from the Philippine-American War to the Christian Science religion. Perhaps Hannibal does not need to get involved in these matters, which happened long after Clemens left town. On the matter of slavery and America's subsequent treatment of African Americans, however, Twain's anti-racist writing is based on what he experienced here, in slaveholding Missouri.

On slavery, Hannibal was silent. Twain scholar Shelley Fisher Fishkin visited the tourist traps, from the otherwise informative Boyhood Home to the Mark Twain Cave. None explained that Twain had grown up in a slave society. None told that his own father had casually sold a slave to a buyer in Mississippi, away "from his home, his mother, and his friends, and all things and creatures that make life dear," in Twain's words. Fishkin did notice some classified ads selling slaves in the fine print of antebellum newspapers on display at the Boyhood Home Museum Annex, but no label directed visitors' attention to them. No site pointed out that Hannibal had been a slave market. None mentioned that Hannibal had also been a stop on the underground railroad or that Twain's own father as a juror helped send three white would-be slave emancipators to prison. A Missouri historical marker at the Visitor's Center in Mark Twain State Park, 30 miles southwest of Hannibal, tells that Clemens was born in nearby Florida, provides details of his life, and mentions statues of Twain, Sawyer, and Finn in Hannibal. Its text makes no attempt to characterize Twain's work or evaluate its moral or literary importance. The marker does say, "It was from his boyhood in Hannibal and here that he drew material for *Tom Sawyer* and *Huckleberry Finn*," but it never hints that Twain's exposure to slavery as part of that boyhood led to its centrality as a theme of *Huckleberry Finn*.

The "living history" sites were worse yet. The guide who narrated the *Mark Twain* Riverboat excursion pointed to Illinois but never mentioned its importance as free soil. The two-hour pageant at the Mark Twain Outdoor Theater even rewrote *Huckleberry Finn* to eliminate Jim, the black character whose struggle to win freedom provides Huck with the ethical dilemma that is the moral center of the novel!

Slavery, Mark Twain wrote, "was maintained by the lie of silent assertion—the silent assertion that there wasn't anything going on in which humane and intelligent people were interested." In 1999, Hannibal still maintained that silence. A newer historical marker, "Mark Twain: Remembrance of An American Past," was also content-free:

> *When Twain created stories based on his past, he did more than explain himself. He explained something about all of us, something true about human beings.*

Not only has Jim been edited out of Hannibal, but the town's visitor's guide takes care to omit his racial group. This photograph, used as the cover of the 1998 guide, exemplifies all the images found inside: of the 122 people whose race I could identify—role-playing Tom and Becky, eating at restaurants, gawking at attractions—all were Caucasian. Such an outcome would occur owing to chance much less than once in a billion! Either Hannibal draws only whites or it draws reasonable numbers of nonwhites but keeps them off its brochure.[2] All-white brochures, in turn, are more likely to draw all-white audiences. In 2018, these brochures had migrated to the web, but again, every person in them was Caucasian.

By 2018, a closure and an opening had improved Hannibal's portrayal of Mark Twain. Both involved Jim. The Mark Twain Outdoor Theater had closed, and Jim's Journey: The Huck Finn Freedom Center, a new museum, had opened. Its exhibits tell the story of Hannibal's black community from slavery to the present. In the process, it also tells more about Twain's thinking and writing than any other place in town. It ventures to use the r-word, telling how Clemens "absorbed the racist views of his church, community, and slave-owning parents." But then it discusses "the unlearning that contributed to his change of heart and his attempts to change America through satire and humor as he brought to light pressing social issues of his time both in the United States and abroad." For a black museum, this takes some courage, because Twain's use of irony to attack racism and classism has been taught so poorly in high school that some African American parents have been misled into trying to remove *Huckleberry Finn* from high school English courses because it uses "the n-word." This museum offers the corrective, promising that visitors will "[k]now Samuel Clemens as more than an author and a humorist. [They will] get to know him as a man who fought for human rights and against racism." Unfortunately, this new museum is only open during the summer and only on Fridays, Saturdays, and Sundays. That's because it is largely the creation of volunteers, sparked by one person, Faye Dant.

Mark Twain's writings still have the power to help bring racial and economic justice to our nation today. But only if we read Twain seriously. Most folks in Hannibal seem afraid to.[3]

1. Hannibal has changed, some. To my surprise, as best I can infer from Disney's website, "American Adventure" hasn't changed a bit!

2. Entry 49 tells the statistical methodology. Here, (.8)122 is <1 in 100 trillion. I excluded three photographs of named whites (Twain, Molly Brown, and a potter) whose racial makeup was determined before anyone composed the brochure.

3. Peter S. Prescott, "A Legend Sold Down the River," *The Washington Post Book World*, 3/9/97; Rita Stein, *A Literary Tour Guide to the United States: West and Midwest* (NY: William Morrow, 1979), 129–36; Ron Powers, *White Town Drowsing* (Boston: Atlantic Monthly Press, 1986), 47, 68, 186; Mark Twain, "My First Lie and How I Got Out of It," in *The Man That Corrupted Hadleyburg* (NY: Oxford UP, 1996 [1900]), 170; Shelley Fisher Fishkin, *Lighting Out for the Territory* (NY: Oxford UP, 1997), 13–67, 201; "Mark Twain: Remembrance of an American Past," hmdb.org/marker.asp?marker=58819; Jim's Journey: The Huck Finn Freedom Center, jimsjourney.org

———————— ✫ ————————

28. Not the First Auto

WISCONSIN *Racine*

Five miles north of Racine on State Highway 32, a "Wisconsin Official Marker" would have the world believe "In 1873 the Rev. Dr. J. W. Carhart of Racine designed and operated the first light self-propelled highway vehicle in the United States, and probably the first in the world."

Not even the Wisconsin Historical Society thinks so. "We sent corrections to the marker staff years ago, and they threw them out," an expert on Wisconsin history at the State Historical Society told me. "Didn't want to admit they'd been wrong. The vehicle was not light; it was not a real car."

A "real car" is a matter of definition, it turns out. Obviously, internal combustion engines are not a requirement—ask anyone who has ridden in a Stanley Steamer or a new (or old) electric car. Many historians credit France's Nicholas Cugnot with the first self-propelled vehicle. In 1763 or 1765 or 1769 (accounts differ), his steam-propelled vehicle carried four passengers at an average speed of two mph and a top speed of (gasp) nearly six mph.

Nor was Rev. Carhart's the first self-propelled vehicle in the United States, for in 1790 Nathan Read's steam carriage had astounded the citizens of Philadelphia. More than a century later, Carhart's "Spark" was also steam driven and went just five mph. Wisconsin historian Bruce Mohs claims that Carhart did build the earliest known steam-powered vehicle made for highway use *in Wisconsin*, and this distinction I cannot refute. But "[f]irst in the United States, and probably in the world" is strictly local boosterism.

Carhart's vehicle did attract interest within Wisconsin, however. The state legislature offered a $10,000 prize to whoever built "a self propeller . . . which shall be a cheap and practical substitute for the horse and other animals on the highways and farms." The legislature went on to require that it perform a north-south journey of at least 200 miles within the state "at an average rate of at least 5 mph."

According to Mohs, Rev. Carhart entered a vehicle in the competition, named it "Oshkosh," and competed against the rival "Green Bay." A 201-mile route was laid out from Green Bay to Madison and the race began on July 16, 1878. "Green Bay" broke down, but "Oshkosh" drove triumphantly into Madison 33 hours and 27 minutes later. Even though it had averaged slightly more than six mph, state officials argued that "Oshkosh" was hardly "a cheap and practical substitute for the horse." After considerable debate, the legislature awarded just $5,000 to Rev. Carhart. Nevertheless, another state historical marker north of Waupun commemorates the race.

Indiana has *three* historical markers celebrating Elwood Haynes of Kokomo, "the designer and builder of America's first mechanically successful automobile," but he wasn't first either. A 1939 article in the *Indiana History Bulletin* admits as much and warns "against the general use of the word 'first' in inscriptions and on markers"; nevertheless, the markers have stayed up. States just wannabe first, whether they were or not.[1]

---

1. Marco Ruiz, et al., *One Hundred Years of the Motor Car* (London: Willow, 1985), 101–102; Bruce Mohs quoted in Richard P. Scharchburg, *Carriages Without Horses* (Wearendale, PA: Society of Automotive Engineers, 1993), 119–21; "Duryea, Haynes, and the First American Automobile," *Indiana History Bulletin* 16 no. 3 (3/39): 145; J. W. Carhart, "An Early Doctor's Steam Carriage," *Horseless Age* 2 no. 2 (1/14/03): 100.

———— ✯ ————

29. America's Most Toppled Monument
ILLINOIS *Chicago*

When the people of Eastern Europe threw out their communist rulers they also toppled their statues of them. During the American Revolution, colonials toppled a statue of King George III and melted it into musket balls. Since then, we Americans haven't done much in the way of toppling. In part, this may be due to our remarkable political continuity.

What is the most toppled monument in the United States? That dubious award must go to the Haymarket monument in Chicago.

During the first four days of May 1886, workers in Chicago demonstrated for an eight-hour workday. (In 1867, Illinois had passed a law mandating an eight-hour day, but it had never been enforced.) A May Day (May 1) parade drew 80,000 workers up Michigan Avenue. Then on the afternoon of May 3, August Spies, editor of a left-wing German-language labor newspaper, spoke to several thousand workers near the McCormick Reaper Plant. Cyrus McCormick had locked his workers out two months earlier and was running the plant with strikebreakers. Some of Spies's audience left his talk to heckle the strikebreakers during the shift change. Police opened fire, killing at least two workers.

On the evening of May 4, some 2,000 workers assembled in Haymarket Square at the corner of Randolph and Des Plaines Streets, listening to speeches protesting the McCormick killings. Mayor Carter Harrison had issued a permit for the meeting. He came to the scene and stayed until about ten that evening. By this time a light rain had started to fall and most of the workers had gone home. Harrison declared the meeting peaceful, told the police to send their men home because the meeting was nearing an end, and went home himself.

Instead, police commanders ordered 176 policemen to enter the square. About 300 workers remained. A police captain raised his hand and ordered, "In the name of the people of Illinois, I command you to disperse in peace." Police began clubbing nearby members of the audience.

Immediately, someone in the crowd threw a bomb at the police. It exploded, killing seven policemen and wounding many others. As many as six policemen may have been killed by "friendly" fire; according to Eric Foner and John Garraty, "the police responded with wild gunfire, killing seven or eight people in the crowd and injuring about a hundred, half of them fellow officers." The crowd then scattered.

The bomb aroused public opinion against organized labor and set back the campaign for an eight-hour day. Eight labor organizers were charged with "conspiracy" to commit the police murders. Their case became a notorious travesty of justice, for several defendants who proved that they had not been in the square at all were sentenced to die anyway. Seven were condemned to hang; the eighth got fifteen years at hard labor. Protests poured in from around the world. On November 10, 1887, the day before their execution date, then Governor Richard Oglesby commuted the death sentences of two of them to life imprisonment. That same day, one of the men was killed in his cell, probably a suicide. The other four were hanged on November 11. Later, Governor John Peter Altgeld would pardon the three who had not been executed, an act that he felt wrecked his political career.

On May 4, 1889, third anniversary of the riot, Chicago dedicated a statue in Haymarket Square of the captain with his upraised arm as a memorial to the slain policemen. On the front of its large base were the words, "In the name of the people of Illinois, I command peace." Workers protested that this monument was one-sided and an affront. William Garvey, chief of the Haymarket Square Workers Memorial Committee, proposed erecting a statue of Governor Altgeld also, as a compromise, but Chicago said no. The city would not let workers memorialize their dead anywhere within its borders. Four years later, labor erected its own memorial—a woman standing over a dying anarchist martyr—in Waldheim Cemetery in suburban Forest Park. Another monument to Haymarket stands in Matehuala, Mexico, and a mural by Diego Rivera at the Palace of Justice in Mexico City depicts the "riot," trials, and executions. Throughout the world, May Day has become "Labor Day" in remembrance of the Haymarket events.[1] Over the years, many radical labor leaders have chosen to be buried or have their ashes scattered near the Waldheim monument, including Elizabeth Gurley Flynn, Emma Goldman, Big Bill Haywood, Joe Hill, and Lucy Parsons.

Between 1889 and 1900, the police statue in Haymarket Square took abundant abuse from working-class Chicagoans. Finally, the city moved the monument to a "safer" location, in Union Park. But on May 4, 1927, the 41st anniversary of the riot to the day, a runaway streetcar jumped its tracks, hit the statue, and knocked the captain off his pedestal. This may have been an accident, but according to labor historian William Adelman, the driver "said he was sick of seeing that policeman with his arm raised." Whatever his motive, that was the first toppling.

City fathers then moved it to another site in the park, away from streetcars. But in the 1950s, police agitated for its return to Haymarket Square, complaining that nothing marked the spot where seven of their brethren had died. Damage was also a concern: "At its present location," according to descendants of the police who had been at the riot, "the Haymarket Riot statue is slowly being destroyed by vandals." So in 1958, the city moved it back to the square, 200 feet west of the original site. The Haymarket Businessmen's Association paid for the move, hoping the statue would draw tourists.

In 1968, the Chicago Police Department earned the enmity of Students for a Democratic Society and other left-wing groups as a result of Mayor Richard J. Daley's notorious "shoot to kill" order during the April riot that followed the assassination of Martin Luther King Jr. Vandals showed their feelings about the police by smearing the statue with black paint on May 4, 1968, the anniversary of the original event. After Daley ordered the police to attack demonstrators outside the Democratic National Convention that summer, on October 5, 1969, a radical SDS splinter group called the Weathermen put dynamite between the statue's legs, blew them over a hundred feet onto the nearby expressway, and toppled the statue for the second time in its history.

Mayor Daley proclaimed the act "an attack on all the citizens of Chicago." The patrolmen's association and the city had new legs cast and re-erected the statue. On May 4, 1970, at the ceremony rededicating the statue, Mayor Daley asked for "law and order"; he went on to proclaim, "Let the younger generation know that the policeman is their friend." Some from the younger generation noted that policemen's behavior in 1968 was later called a "police riot" by the commission appointed to investigate the affair.

On October 5, 1970, one year to the day after the first explosion, the same young radicals, now calling themselves the Weather Underground, toppled it again. With a blast heard four miles away, they again blew both its legs off for toppling number three.[2]

"We'll rebuild the statue," swore Mayor Daley, and they recast the legs yet again. The city re-unveiled it in January, and the police mounted an around-the-clock vigil to prevent a fourth assault. Columnists had a field day, pointing out that the Weather Underground had succeeded in immobilizing five of Chicago's finest as well as a squad car. Police officers too were not excited at the prospect of spending an eight-hour shift watching a statue. Finally, after a year of statue surveillance, the city decided to move it once more to a locale that would presumably be safe—inside central police headquarters.

As time went on, it dawned on the police that instead of making the statue safe, they may have made themselves unsafe.
If terrorists mailed a bomb to police headquarters, they could still blow the statue up "and them too!" as a sergeant told me. So in 1976, the police moved it to a location where the public could not even see it—the atrium of the Chicago Police Academy at the corner of Jackson and Loomis Streets. "It's safe here," the desk sergeant told me. "After-hours, this building is tighter than a drum. You'd have to demolish the building to get to it." I neglected to point out that it was still vulnerable to helicopter attack, but in 2007, the police captain moved again; he now stands with his arm raised outside the new police headquarters on the South Side.

Back at the old site, in 1972, leftists tried to put up a statue of one of the four men the city hanged after the riot. Police nixed that. Instead, activists repeatedly sprayed slogans like "Resist Imperialism" on the substantial base. Then a nearby resident used the base for a small statue of the Virgin Mary. In 1996, I

The Haymarket statue leaves its base on its way to a new home at central police headquarters in 1972. This was the fourth of its six moves (so far), not including its several topplings.

visited Haymarket Square to photograph her . . . only to find her gone—the fourth and perhaps final toppling. A few months earlier, the city had removed her, taken away the base as well, and pulverized it, leaving only a circle of paving stones.[3] When I asked why the base was removed, a city official told me, "A woman was putting the Madonna on it, and it was becoming a bit of a problem." Statues of Our Lady stand everywhere in Chicago of course, and indeed throughout the world, creating no problem. I think his embarrassment stemmed from the fact that in all the world, Chicago boasted the only statue of the Blessed Virgin Mary that declared, "In the name of the people of Illinois, I command peace."[4, 5]

1. Workers in the United States and abroad have often engaged in other demonstrations on or near May 1, sometimes leading to other martyrs. Ironically, only Canada and the United States celebrate Labor Day in September; the rest of the world uses May Day.

2. One of the bombers was Bill Ayers, who later achieved notoriety as an ally of Barack Obama. Republicans used their relationship against Obama when he ran for president in 2008.

3. On March 25, 1992, another Mayor Richard Daley, son of Richard J., dedicated a small plaque in Haymarket Square that gives a reasonable synopsis of events: "Site of the Haymarket Tragedy, 1886 / A decade of strife between labor and industry culminated here in a confrontation that resulted in the tragic death of both workers and policemen. On May 4, 1886, spectators at a labor rally had gathered around the mouth of Crane's Alley. A contingent of police approaching on Des Plaines Street were met by a bomb thrown from just south of the alley. The resultant trial of eight activists gained worldwide attention for the labor movement, and initiated the tradition of 'May Day' labor rallies in many cities."

4. In 2004, the city dedicated a sculpture by Mary Brogger that represents labor. Because it's art, it's ambiguous and so far has avoided toppling. See cityofchicago.org/city/en /depts/dca/supp_info/chicago_s_publicartthehaymarketmemorial.html

5. Reader's Digest, America's Historic Places (Pleasantville, NY: Reader's Digest, 1988), 10; William Adelman, Haymarket Revisited (Chicago: IL Labor History Society, 1986 [1976]); "Haymarket Martyrs' Monument," National Register of Historic Places Inventory (DC: National Park Service); Kenneth E. Foote, Shadowed Ground (Austin: U. of TX Press, 1997), 12, 134–41; Clement H. Silvestro, "The Haymarket Riot Monument" (Chicago, IL: Chicago Historical Society typescript, n.d.); "Wacker Drive Site Urged for Haymarket Statue," Chicago Sun-Times, 4/26/50; Harlan Draeger, "Mayor Hits Bombing of Police Statue," Chicago Daily News, 10/7/69; "Daley Asks for Law, Order at Haymarket," Chicago Tribune, 5/5/70; Barry Felcher, "Explosion Heard 4 Miles Away," Chicago Daily News, 10/6/70; photo, Chicago Sun-Times, 1/27/72; "Police Block Substitute Haymarket Statue," Chicago Sun-Times, 5/2/72; Eric Foner and John A. Garraty, eds., The Reader's Companion to American History (Boston: Houghton Mifflin, 1991), 395; James R. Green, "Workers, Unions, and the Politics of Public History," Public Historian, 11 no. 4 (fall 1989): 31–33; Bruce C. Nelson, Beyond the Martyrs (New Brunswick, NJ: Rutgers UP, 1988), 188–90; Stephen Kinzer, "In Chicago, an Ambiguous Memorial to the Haymarket Attack," The New York Times, 9/15/2004.

———————— ✶ ————————

30. Coming into Indiana Minus a Body Part

INDIANA *Graysville*

In 1998, I asked Judy Rippel, manager of Indiana's Historical Marker Program, if Indiana had any plans to put up more markers about women, pointing out that the state seemed to have few if any mentions of women on its landscape. "No, we really don't," she replied. She continued with some embarrassment, "The only woman I can think of was the subject of the first successful gall bladder operation."

It turns out that Rippel's memory was slightly off: Jane Crawford had an ovary, not her gall bladder, taken out. One mile north of Graysville on Highway 63, a marker tells her story:

GRAVE OF JANE TODD CRAWFORD

Pioneer Heroine of Abdominal Surgery
Jane Todd was born in Virginia in 1763. In 1805 she and her husband,
Thomas Crawford, moved to Green County, Kentucky. Suffering from
a huge abdominal tumor, she rode 60 miles to Danville, Kentucky, to
submit to an operation never before performed. On Dec. 25, 1809, Dr.
Ephraim McDowell performed this, the first ovariotomy, in his home.
The ordeal lasted 25 minutes. There was no anesthesia. Mrs. Crawford
recovered completely. Years later she came to Graysville to live with her
son, Thomas, a Pres. minister. She died in 1842 at age 78. She is buried
here. The restored McDowell home in Danville is a surgical shrine.

So far as Indiana history is concerned, all Ms. Crawford did was cross its borders without an ovary! Yet she was the only white woman Indiana commemorated![1] Moreover, she gets a nearly identical marker near her home in Lexington, Virginia, which makes some sense, since that's where she was when she developed the tumor. Dr. McDowell gets a marker where he is buried in Kentucky that also tells of Crawford and her "22-pound ovarian cyst."

Indiana achieved such male dominance only by leaving important women out of the story. For example, in 1894 Helen Cougar tried to vote; when forbidden, she sued the election board for $10,000 damages and appealed to the Indiana Supreme Court, but lost. In 1891, Antoinette Leach qualified to practice law; two years later she became the first woman certified to practice law in Indiana. Indiana even left out Amelia Earhart, for heaven's sake, a visiting faculty member at Purdue University from 1935 to 1937. Each week she commuted to class from upstate New York flying her own plane! As part of her terms of employment, the Purdue Research Foundation gave her a Lockheed Electra in 1936. In 1937, Earhart flew it to Miami and from there took off in it on her final attempt to fly around the world.[2]

Leaving out women was hardly unique to Indiana. Only seven of Virginia's first 700 markers treated women, and most of those were appendages to men, such as the mother of the Wright brothers. Page Putnam Miller, director of the National Coordinating Committee for the Promotion of History, pointed out that in 1993 only 3% of the 2,000 national historic landmarks in the United States focused on women. Her group and the Organization of American Historians started a Women's History Landmark Project to increase the number of these sites. However, their method does risk what I call the "Jane Byrne problem" in representing women of the past. An American history textbook finds space to tell high school students that Jane Byrne was the first woman mayor of Chicago. Byrne was not America's first woman mayor though, and her single term in office was hardly distinguished. The same book never mentions Big Bill Thompson, flamboyant three-term mayor in the 1920s, Anton Cermak, who took a bullet probably intended for President-elect Franklin D. Roosevelt in the 1930s, Richard J. Daley, the city's "boss" in the 1950s and '60s, or any other mayor of Chicago. I do not suggest that Indiana should go around finding its own Jane Byrnes to reach some quota, such as half of all Indiana markers.

Nevertheless, for almost all of U.S. history, societal norms and laws have prevented women from attaining the same goals as men. Therefore, women's achievements are much more noteworthy. For example, after Antoinette Leach qualified to practice law in 1891, the Sullivan County Court denied her admission to the bar because she was not a voter. In turn, like Cougar, she could not vote because she was a woman. Leach appealed to the Indiana Supreme Court, which reversed the lower court in 1893.

Besides lacking markers for important women, Indiana also left women

out of the stories its markers *did* tell, even when women were equal participants. Consider this example from Zionsville:

PATRICK H. SULLIVAN 1794–1879

was the first white settler in Boone County, 1823, and built the first log
cabin. In 1857 he bought this site and lived here until 1872. He served in
the War of 1812.

When Patrick Sullivan first came to this part of the country, however, his
wife and son accompanied him! Unless he leaned forward to breast the tape
as their wagon crossed the county line, surely *she* was *also* "the first white settler in Boone County." Unless she sat outdoors knitting doilies, probably *they*
rather than *he* "built the first log cabin." It is true that she didn't "serve in the
War of 1812," but it turns out that he didn't either. He was in the army for six
months while the War of 1812 went on elsewhere, and he never saw action.

Another Indiana woman who needs to share a marker with her husband is
Catharine Coffin, Levi Coffin's wife. She was his partner in his underground
railroad activities. *Their* house, not *his*, sheltered runaway slaves. *He* credited
her in his autobiography; Indiana does not. What should be *their* marker in
Franklin City refers only to him.

Some states do even worse than Indiana. According to a 1995 study by the
Colorado Historical Society, "no markers interpret women or women's experience in Colorado," no woman is the subject of Colorado's thirteen biography markers, and no marker "interprets women even in a general sense."
Colorado has put up a few new markers and converted a historic house into
a new state museum on women in the state's history, but as of 2019, it was
a work in progress. Some states do better. We noted that Virginia is adding
twelve new statues of women to its state capitol grounds. To be sure, one is
Martha Washington, but the rest made history themselves, not just through
whom they married.

Indiana too now does better. A marker for an abolitionist household, "John
H. and Sarah Tibbets," includes them both, even though John "piloted [the
escapees] to the next safe haven," and why not? Both sheltered the fugitives; hence both risked imprisonment. "Pioneer Medical Doctors" tells of
George Osborn and his wife, both of whom became medical doctors before
the Civil War. If the main reason for their mention is their more famous son

Chase, nevertheless her becoming a doctor in 1860 remains a remarkable feat. Actress Irene Dunne gets a marker, as do writers Sarah Bolton and Gene Stratton-Porter. Women's organizations get markers, including the Women's Christian Temperance Union, Girl Scouts, and the Little Sisters of the Poor. Most indicative of change: pioneering suffragists are recognized, including Helen Cougar.[3]

Chapter 41 tells how Arkansas also leaves out women.

1. I stressed "white" because Indiana *did* have historical markers for at least two other women: Madam C. J. Walker, African American cosmetics entrepreneur, and Frances Slocum, raised by Indians and wife of a Miami chief. It may also have markers for Sarah T. Bolton, "pioneer poet," and Mary Bryan, "pioneer woman." They were not in the file at the time, and Ms. Rippel did not know of them. Many more African American women are included in the markers put up since 2000. I also missed two other markers that do not challenge my critique: Esther Wallace, wife of Governor David Wallace and mother of Gen. Lew Wallace, who "influenced the lives of two important Hoosiers," and Hannah Milhous Nixon, "mother of President Richard M. Nixon," who lived in Indiana as a girl. Counting the mall, 1.7% of Indiana's 477 markers treated women.

2. Earhart gets at least a dozen historical markers in other states, including "Amelia touched down here" at several airports.

3. Jennifer R. Loux, "Virginia's Historical Marker Program: Its History and Growth," *Notes on Virginia*, 54 (2016), 5; Page Putnam Miller, "Women's History Landmark Project," *The Public Historian* 15 no. 4 (fall 1993): 82; David Halaas and Dianna Litvak, *Point of Interest* (Denver, CO: Historical Society, 1995), 16–17; Petula Dvorak, "Breaking the Grip of Men and War on the Way We Memorialize History," *The Washington Post*, 8/6/2018; *Susan B. Anthony Slept Here*, by Lynn Sherr and Jurate Kazickas (NY: Times Books, 1994), 137–44, tells of other women's history sites in Indiana, many still unmarked on the landscape.

———— ✫ ————

31. The Invisible Empire Remains Invisible

INDIANA *Indianapolis*

At least 50 markers, monuments, and other historic sites in the United States laud actions and leaders of the Ku Klux Klan, from the Albert Pike monument in downtown Washington, DC, to the Walter Pierce Library in La Grande, Oregon. Chapters 47, 52, and 53 treat some of these tributes. In contrast, as of 1999, I uncovered just four historical markers (and no monuments or historic sites) that portrayed the Klan in a negative light. One is on Maryland Street in downtown Indianapolis, three blocks from Monument Circle.[1] It lauds a defunct daily newspaper: "The Indianapolis Times, begun as The Indianapolis Sun in 1878, was published here from 1924 until it ceased publication October 11, 1965. The Times won journalism's highest award, the Pulitzer Prize, in 1928 for exposing the Ku Klux Klan."

Since critical treatments of the Klan are so rare, Indiana deserves credit for this marker. The newspaper is obviously its principal subject, however, and this tangential mention doesn't begin to tell the remarkable story of the Ku Klux Klan in Indiana.

The full story of the Ku Klux Klan needs to be told. Northerners, in particular, think of the Klan as a terrorist organization from long ago and far away. The KKK has had three incarnations, but only the first—after the Civil War—was long ago and Southern. The most recent Klan, a white supremacist response to the Civil Rights Movement of the 1960s, still comes to life sporadically, mostly in rural areas, and enjoyed a brief[2] revival in 2017–18 during the presidency of Donald Trump. The second Klan, however, which boomed in the 1920s, was national. It was also the most powerful.

In 1920, David C. Stephenson moved to Indiana. He became a successful coal dealer, joined the Ku Klux Klan, and rapidly developed into "the most dynamic and colorful Klan leader in the United States," according to historian Kenneth Jackson. Stephenson became Grand Dragon of Indiana and recruited for the Klan throughout the East. Under his leadership, in Jackson's words, "from 1922 to 1925, Indianapolis was the unrivaled bastion of the Invisible Empire in Mid-America."

Stephenson had a fine home in Irvington, a 98-foot yacht on Lake Huron, and ambitions to be president. The Indiana Klan stressed law enforcement, motherhood, virtue, patriotism, and temperance. It also practiced vigilante violence against people suspected of violating those principles as well as Jews, Catholics, and African Americans. The Fiery Cross, Stephenson's newspaper, reached a weekly circulation of 125,000 by late 1923. At that point the Indianapolis chapter had 28,000 members, making it the largest single chapter in the nation. Its women's auxiliary enrolled another 10,000.

Many Protestant ministers openly lauded the Klan, but S. L. Shank, mayor of Indianapolis, opposed the secret organization. He prohibited masked parades, arrested news dealers selling The Fiery Cross, and tried to stop cross-burning within the city. In 1924, he ran for governor, but Klansman Ed

Jackson defeated him for the Republican nomination and went on to win the office. KKK candidates also won for sheriff and Congress, and the Klan elected a majority of the Indiana state legislature.

Besides winning almost complete control of Indiana, in 1924, the Klan elected governors in Colorado and Maine and helped elect them in Ohio and Louisiana. The organization also elected a U.S. senator from Oklahoma and dominated politics for a time in Arkansas, California, Georgia, Oregon, and Texas. In that year's Democratic National Convention, the Ku Klux Klan was strong enough to prevent the party from passing a statement condemning it.

Then Stephenson took eighteen-year-old assistant Madge Oberholtzer on a trip to Hammond. During the trip, he assaulted her. She grew so upset by his physical advances that she poisoned herself. Stephenson refused to let her see a doctor until they returned to Indianapolis, where at length she died. Authorities charged Stephenson with rape and murder.

Despite the scandal, in November 1925, most Indiana Klan candidates won, including those for mayor of Indianapolis and the city's school board. After their sweeping victory, thousands of the new mayor's supporters marched around Monument Circle in the heart of the city while a band played Klan songs.

Monument Circle, of course, displays no memory of the Klan today.

Shortly after the election, a jury found Stephenson guilty. At first, he didn't worry, confidently expecting that Governor Jackson—his Klan subordinate—would pardon him. When that didn't happen, he began to spill political secrets about the organization. As a result, the mayor, sheriff, and many others went to jail for violating the Corrupt Practices Act. The governor himself escaped indictment for bribery only by invoking the statute of limitations. Stephenson remained in jail, however, and his outrageous conduct with Oberholtzer hardly endeared him to the Klan's Puritanical membership. During 1925, the organization split and fell apart. In 1928, the *Indianapolis Times* won its Pulitzer for a series of articles exposing the Klan. Kenneth Jackson points out however that the campaign was "almost unnecessary, for there were fewer than 7,000 paid-up members in the state of Indiana in 1928."

By 2018, a few more sites mentioned the Klan, but most, like this Indiana site, mark opposition to it. Texas, which has by far the most historical markers of any state (chapter 40), has five. One, like this site, tells of a newspaper.

The Klan opposed Ma and Pa Ferguson, governors of Texas, so their marker tells of their opposition to the KKK. Other Texas markers tell of a Catholic priest and two prosecutors opposed to the Klan. Paducah, Kentucky, celebrates the "Duke of Paducah," who did the same. All these are thus "happy" markers, easy to put up.

Other than this *Times* marker, the Ku Klux Klan is invisible on the Indiana landscape. Judy Rippel, manager of Indiana's Historical Marker Program, admitted to having no KKK markers, "which we probably should, since the Klan was big in Indiana." A Klan marker, she added, "would be a difficult text to do." Nonetheless, Indianapolis should have a marker, probably at Monument Circle, its symbolic center, telling how the KKK briefly dominated the state and its capital city. So should Portland, Oregon; Portland, Maine; Montpelier, Vermont; Oklahoma City; Denver; Atlanta; and all the other sites of Klan dominance in the 1920s. Until those markers exist, citizens across the United States can say to themselves, "It can't happen here," unaware that in many cases it already has.[3]

Chapter 44 tells of the first Ku Klux Klan. Chapter 53 tells of the second and third.

1. The Civil Rights Movement sparked Southern markers and monuments telling of Klan deeds, such as Mississippi's marker noting the "Freedom Summer Murders" of 1964. The Equal Justice Initiative in Alabama is helping get up many markers about lynching; some of them will doubtless mention the Klan, including in the North. Chapter 47 tells of a name-change in Oklahoma that implies that the Klan was a negative force in that state.

2. I hope.

3. Kenneth T. Jackson, *The Ku Klux Klan in the City: 1915–1930* (NY: Oxford UP, 1967), 144–60; Carl Degler, "A Century of the Klans," *Journal of Southern History* (11/65): 442–43; Wyn Craig Wade, *The Fiery Cross* (NY: Simon & Schuster, 1987); Charles C. Alexander, *The Ku Klux Klan in the Southwest* (Lexington: UP of KY, 1965), 165–69; John S. Ezell, *The South Since 1865* (NY: Macmillan, 1963), 372.

---✷---

32. Putting the *He* in Hero
KENTUCKY *Lexington*

When this book first came out in 1999, in front of the Fayette County Courthouse in downtown Lexington stood a monument to Confederate "General

John H. Morgan and his Bess." After Charlottesville—that is, after the racist riot that protested the planned removal of the statue of Robert E. Lee from that Virginia city—Louisville decided to move Morgan to the cemetery, along with another statue of Confederate leader John C. Breckinridge. Both men are buried there.

In such a location, I have no problem with the monument, except for one thing. Look closely, and you'll see the lie—it might even be called a whopper.

Many states leave women off their historical markers; chapters 42 and 30 single out Arkansas and Indiana for this offense. Monuments are even more phallocentric. To many minds, Helen Hunt Jackson interviewing Native Americans seems less heroic than Jeffrey Amherst killing them with smallpox. (Chapter 85 makes this comparison.)

At this monument in Lexington, however, there can be no issue about what the two genders did; in war, male and female horses perform the same functions. Nevertheless, although Morgan's favorite horse was, in fact, a mare, the sculptor turned her into a stallion. According to an eighteen-stanza poem about the statue, "The Ballad of Black Bess" published anonymously, the sculptor insisted on the change because, "No hero should bestride a mare!"

The nameless Kentucky poet saluted Bess for the serene way she adapted to her new condition:

> Proud the eye of good Black Bess
> With shamelessness uncanny,
> She just ignores the testicules
> That hang beneath her fanny.

Morgan's "military career was not of lasting significance," according to historian James B. Jones Jr. He did lead the only significant Confederate foray into the Midwest, a cavalry raid into Ohio and Indiana in June of 1863, but succeeded mainly in getting most of his 2,640 men captured. "He was later shot behind enemy lines in Greeneville, Tennessee, while running from a Union patrol," Jones writes. "The married Morgan was, some insist, visiting a lady-friend and was caught unaware by the Yankee soldiers." Declining to surrender, he dashed out of the home of Mrs. Catharine Williams, lest he shame her, ran toward a fence, and was shot.

His gesture bespeaks a sense of chivalry that seems sadly wanting in Ken-

Bess is hardly the only mare with testicles. The same modification happened to
Gen. Winfield Scott's horse in Scott Circle in Washington, DC. Scott's grandchildren
were horrified to see their grandfather astride a mare, even though she was
his preferred mount, so they got the sculptor to add on "stallion attributes," as
evident here.

tucky today. For it became a tradition for undergraduates at the University of
Kentucky to paint Bess's testicles in brilliant colors.[1] The bard closed his epic
with a verse lamenting the practice:

> *So sorrow comes to Bluegrass men—Like darkness o'er them falls—*
> *For well we know gentlemen should show, Respect for a lady's balls.*

All across America, other bronze mares have undergone similar sex changes.
So we must end with this question:

> *How can women take their place*
> *In hist'ry in due course,*
> *When monuments don't even let*
> *A lady be a horse?* [2]

1. Perhaps the practice has stopped, now that Bess is nearly three miles from campus.
2. David Lowenthal, conversation, 8/96; Judith Schafer, conversation, 1996; Alex Jonas,
   ed., *Program Instructor Sourcebook* (Alexandria, VA: Close Up Foundation, n.d.), 56; James
   M. Goode, *The Outdoor Sculpture of Washington, D.C.* (DC: Smithsonian Institution
   Press, 1974), 287; James B. Jones Jr., *Every Day in Tennessee History* (Winston-Salem, NC:
   Blair, 1996), 117–18, 173.

———— ✭ ————

33. Abraham Lincoln's Birthplace Cabin— Built Thirty Years after His Death!

KENTUCKY *Hodgenville*

Thomas Lincoln bought Sinking Spring Farm near Hodgenville in December 1808. His son Abraham was born in a small cabin on the farm on February 12, 1809. A little more than two years later the family moved to another farm ten miles away. By the time Lincoln was assassinated, according to three different people who visited the farm looking for it, the cabin had disappeared. Either it had fallen into ruin or nearby farmers had recycled its logs into their buildings. In 1895, New York entrepreneur Alfred Dennett bought Sinking Spring Farm and instructed his agent, James Bigham, to build a log cabin on it, according to National Park Service historian Dwight Pitcaithley. Bigham bought a two-story cabin from a neighboring farm and used the best of its logs to build a cabin on the Lincoln farm.[1] Dennett then circulated widely photographs of this new cabin, which he tried to pass off as the actual cabin in which Lincoln was born. "Lincoln was born in a log cabin, weren't he?" said Bigham, defending himself to a skeptical newspaperman. "Well, one cabin is as good as another!"

Despite Bigham's efforts, few made the trek to rural Hodgenville to see the "historic" structure. Undaunted, Dennett and Bigham decided to take the cabin to the people, so they took it apart and reassembled it at the Tennessee Centennial Exposition in Nashville in 1897. To make the exhibit even better they bought another old log cabin and proclaimed it the birthplace of Jefferson Davis! Davis wasn't even born in a log cabin!

Next, the cabins traveled to the 1901 Pan-American Exposition in Buffalo, where they found themselves between "Bonner, The Educated Horse" and Esau, a trained chimpanzee billed as the "Missing Link." As an added feature, 150 African Americans billed as "Old Uncles and Aunties, formerly slaves," were on display "living in the genuine cabins in which Abraham Lincoln and Jefferson Davis were born."

Then the cottages went to Coney Island, where the "Lincoln cabin" was to become an attraction. "But alas," as Pitcaithley puts it, "during the journey to Coney Island the logs of the cabins became intermingled," so it became much larger and was briefly known as the "Lincoln and Davis Cabin!"

Meanwhile, Robert Collier, publisher of *Collier's Weekly*, acquired the farm in Hodgenville, set up a Lincoln Farm Association, bought the logs for $1,000 and shipped them to Kentucky. The train stopped in major cities along the way to let people touch the logs. The association then selected architect John Russell Pope to design a memorial building in which to enshrine the reassembled cabin and engaged lawyers to produce affidavits from three residents that claimed the cabin was authentic. (No one now believes these affidavits, collected a century after the original cabin's construction.)[2]

The logs arrived in Louisville in June 1906, and the cabin was built in a local park. Because its logs were originally from two cabins, it was twice as large as might be expected, in the tradition of the "Lincoln and Davis Cabin." Nevertheless, it was so popular that an armed guard had to be posted to stop visitors from taking pieces off it as souvenirs. After just a week, it was dismantled for safekeeping.

Three years later, the association used some of the logs to re-erect the cabin, now back to solo cabin size, at Hodgenville for the centennial of Lincoln's birth in 1909. President Theodore Roosevelt came to lay the cornerstone for the Greek temple that Pope had designed to house it. "The rude log cabin in which Lincoln was born in Hodgenville, Kentucky, is a symbol of his bonds with the common people, and it has come to mean to them as Americans what the humble stable in Bethlehem means to them as Christians," Roosevelt proclaimed. "But just as the world's faithful have sanctified the birthplace of Christ by housing it within an impressive Church of the Nativity, so the American people have ennobled the birthplace of Lincoln by housing it within a marble Temple of Fame."

When the temple was finished in 1911, however, it was too small to let visitors move around easily outside the cabin. Rather than enlarge the temple, Pope shrank the cabin! He took a couple of feet off its length and three or four feet from its width. Now just twelve by seventeen feet, it fits fine. It also fits well with the nation's ideological needs. Americans *want* to believe in the "log cabin myth," and the tinier the cabin, the bigger the myth. Now the site offers the ultimate expression on the landscape of the "rags to riches" story that Lincoln's life exemplifies: the cabin is even smaller than that in which he was born, and the Greek marble-and-granite temple makes a grander effect

Cut down to fit, the cabin looks a bit like a playhouse. For decades, the National Park Service still handed out what it called "sufficient "instructions for the building of an accurate replica of the Lincoln cabin." Although NPS knew full well that the actual cabin was probably about 18 feet x 16 feet, its diagrams showed the cut-down size, 12 x 17. Taking into account its thick walls, the shrinkage makes a big difference: the original cabin probably had more than 240 square feet of usable interior space, about half again as large as the 165 square feet in the counterfeit.

even than the White House to which he rose. Also, the 56 imposing steps—one for each year of his life—symbolize Lincoln's upward mobility.

Harold Holzer, writing in *The New York Times*, confirmed the power of the two structures in combination: "The shrine's almost oppressive formality cannot mask the rawness and shockingly tiny size of the airless, one-room cabin it contains. Picturing a family living in such a place tests the imagination, and touches the heart." But Lincoln's own son, Robert Todd Lincoln, discouraged preserving the cabin, complaining that it falsely bore the "stamp of poverty" when in fact the Lincolns owned two farms, livestock, and a lot in nearby Elizabethtown.

In the 1990s, the Park Service pretended the cabin was real, even admonishing visitors not to use flash cameras—as if their light could damage logs that have seen so many journeys. It labeled the little building "Traditional Lincoln Birthplace Cabin," which gave "traditional" a new definition: "hoax over time."[3] This fit in with what seemed to be America's *need* for this structure.

Long ago, a lad at the University of Wisconsin answered a class assignment for Professor Helen White with the blooper, "Abraham Lincoln was born in a log cabin which he built with his own hands." The reality is even sillier: Abraham Lincoln had been dead 30 years when his birthplace cabin was built! Even more bizarre, Americans built more birthplace cabins for him throughout the twentieth century—in Fort Wayne, Indiana; in heiress Mary Forbes's backyard in Milton, Massachusetts—indeed, the National Park Service used to give out hand-outs so everyone could build one in their own backyards! Beginning in 1920, children built miniature replicas all across the country: in that year, John Lloyd Wright, son of Frank, invented Lincoln Logs, named after these logs in Kentucky. Lincoln Logs originally came with instructions on how to build Uncle Tom's cabin as well as Lincoln's log cabin!

Sometime after the first edition of this book, probably because of Pitcaithley's scholarship, NPS stopped referring to the little structure as the "Traditional Birthplace Cabin." Now they say "Symbolic." An improvement? It's a step. But if NPS showed each step of the cabin's tortuous journey, visitors would learn something about how Americans sometimes fabricate history on the landscape to match their conception of how it *should* appear. That would be a lesson in candor which "Honest Abe" would surely approve.[4]

1. A few diehards have claimed that logs from the original Lincoln birthplace cabin might have found their way into the larger log home Bigham bought.

2. Pitcaithley exposes inconsistencies among the affidavits. He also notes that a local judge, who was born on a portion of the Lincoln farm in 1836 and sold it to Dennett in 1894, provided a fourth affidavit. The judge agreed that a cabin had been moved from the property in 1860, but said it was relatively new and therefore had no connection with Abraham Lincoln.

3. The NPS brochure "Abraham Lincoln Birthplace" does say, "Because its early history is obscure, there is a lack of documentation to support the authenticity of the cabin enshrined in the Memorial Building as the birthplace cabin of Abraham Lincoln." Unfortunately, "*lack* of documentation" is not the problem. The sources I cite document enough evidence that the cabin is *not* authentic. Another NPS handout is even less forthright: "While lacking absolute proof, oral tradition and available documentation support the belief that this cabin has been reconstructed with some of the original logs on or very near the birth site."

4. Dwight Pitcaithley, "A Splendid Hoax: The Strange Case of Lincoln's Birthplace Cabin" (DC: National Museum of American History Colloquium), 4/30/91; Pitcaithley, "Abraham Lincoln's Birthplace Cabin: The Making of an American Icon" (DC: typescript, n.d.); Fred Knieffen and Henry Glassie, "Building in Wood in the Eastern United States," in Dell Upton and John Michael Vlach, *Common Places* (Athens: U. of GA Press, 1986), 159–81; Vlach, conversation, 5/98; Merrill D. Peterson, *Lincoln in American Memory* (NY: Oxford UP, 1994), 179; Barry Schwartz, "The Reconstruction of Abraham Lincoln," in David Middleton and Derek Edwards, eds., *Collective Remembering* (London: SAGE, 1991), 100; Harold Holzer, "Lincoln's Early Years," *The New York Times*, 2/8/98; Edward Pessen, *The Log Cabin Myth* (New Haven, CT: Yale UP, 1984); Rick Schenkman, conversation, 4/98; Dixon Wecter, *The Hero in America* (NY: Scribner's, 1972 [1941]), 228.

---------- ★ ----------

34. Honoring a Segregationist No More?

MICHIGAN *Dearborn*

In front of city hall at 13615 Michigan Avenue a bronze statue of Orville Hubbard, Dearborn's infamous mayor, stood for 31 years.[1] Nearby still stands a Michigan historical marker:

ORVILLE L. HUBBARD

> *Orville Liscum Hubbard, LL.B. (1903–1982), was mayor of Dearborn from 1942 to 1978. . . . Often working twelve or more hours a day, Hubbard was an effective administrator who paid close attention to small details and the public's opinion. He made Dearborn known for punctual trash collection, speedy snow removal, Florida retirement facilities, and a free recreational area. . . .*

Dearborn under Hubbard may have been known locally for punctual trash collection and speedy snow removal, but it was famous nationally (and locally) for its racial segregation. In the words of David L. Good, on whose dazzling biography *Orvie: The Dictator of Dearborn* this entry relies, "For most of his 36 years as mayor of the Detroit suburb of Dearborn, the late Orville L. Hubbard was known as the most

A plaque on the base of the statue of Orville Hubbard once reproduced the famous saying by Etienne de Grellet: "I shall pass through this world but once. Any good therefore that I can do or any kindness that I can show to any human being, let me do it now . . . for I shall not pass this way again." Visitors passing by this place will no longer see this bizarre tribute to Hubbard, because the base was demolished when Hubbard's statue left City Hall on September 29, 2015.

outspoken segregationist north of the Mason-Dixon line." As the Detroit metropolitan area grew increasingly diverse, Hubbard's leadership helped Dearborn get increasingly white.

In 1944, two years after Hubbard first became mayor, an African American family moved into an all-white neighborhood in Detroit. To buy their home they had to break a restrictive covenant. The resulting case went all the way to the Supreme Court and had national implications. It gets a historical marker at 4626 Seebaldt Avenue in Detroit:

ORSEL MCGHEE HOUSE

In 1944 the Orsel McGhees, a black family, moved here into what was then an all-white neighborhood. A neighboring family won a court order revoking the McGhees' purchase of the house on the basis of a restrictive covenant forbidding non-white residents.

The McGhees, aided by the NAACP and represented by Thurgood Marshall, appealed the case to the U.S. Supreme Court. The court's 1948 decision in favor of the McGhees upheld the principle of freedom from discrimination in the enjoyment of property rights.

But Detroit was not Dearborn. In the 1930 census, well before Hubbard took office, Dearborn had 43 black residents out of a population of 50,000. By 1978, when Hubbard left office, fewer than twenty African Americans lived in Dearborn out of 90,000 people, an astonishing figure, for this is no obscure or distant burg. The edge of Dearborn is less than five miles from downtown Detroit, where three of every four people are black. Indeed, Detroit borders Dearborn on three sides. The Dearborn campus of the University of Michigan has 8,400 students. The world headquarters of Ford Motor Company is in Dearborn along with its huge River Rouge assembly plant. Dearborn houses two famous tourist destinations—the Henry Ford Museum and Greenfield Village. African Americans learned at the University of Michigan, worked at Ford, and visited Greenfield Village. They just didn't live in Dearborn.

Hubbard accomplished this with little subtlety. In 1948, he helped run a campaign to defeat a rental housing development with the slogan "Keep Negroes Out of Dearborn." During the race riots in Detroit in the mid-1960s he ordered Dearborn police to "shoot looters on sight." When a new black family moved into town, Hubbard was said to have provided excessive police and fire "protection," including wake-up visits every hour or so through the night in response to alleged trouble calls. "They can't get in here," Hubbard said in a notorious interview with the *Montgomery* (Alabama) *Advertiser* in 1956. "We watch it. Every time we hear of a Negro moving in—for instance, we had one last year—we respond quicker than you do to a fire."

Hubbard once said to his assembled department heads, "I'm not a racist, but I just hate those black bastards." "I just don't believe in integration," he told the *Detroit News* in 1967. "When that happens, along comes socializing with the whites, intermarriage and then mongrelization." In 1985, three years after his death, his influence lingered as Dearborn residents voted "yes" on a resolution to make most of its city parks off-limits to nonresidents, a measure clearly intended to keep out nonwhites.[2] In 1989, his statue went up.

Hubbard's biographer cautions us not to see him as unique. "In a sense, Orville Hubbard's view was no different from that in any of a dozen or more other segregated suburbs that ringed the city of Detroit—or in hundreds of other such communities scattered across the country," he points out. Within Dearborn it wasn't just working-class "hardhats" who supported him; most engineers at Ford were for Hubbard "because of his attitudes towards the colored," in the words of a pollster. Today, Dearborn has joined its more circumspect suburban neighbors. Its website, which offers a history of Dearborn with no mention of race, claimed in 1998, "You will find great diversity in our neighborhoods, people, and worship." By 2010, 3,965 blacks lived in Dearborn, 4% of the city's total population.

Living in an overwhelmingly white area still conveys status (chapter 83). Suburbs even whiter than Dearborn such as nearby Grosse Pointe have even higher social status. In 1960, *Time Magazine* told how Grosse Pointe hired private investigators to screen would-be owners. The investigators used written forms that completely excluded nonwhites and rated whites for "swarthiness," "descent," and "accent," among other characteristics. Religion was a final hurdle: Jews had to score higher than others to be allowed to buy. In 1990, Grosse Pointe had just twelve black households, most of them live-in domestic couples, according to political scientist Andrew Hacker. Grosse Pointe's status explains why Dearborn still honored Hubbard instead of being ashamed of him.

After a neo-Confederate murdered nine black churchgoers in Charleston, South Carolina, in June 2015, Americans across the country realized they no longer wanted to honor overt racists. Hubbard was one of the first to go, three months later. After some time in storage, he got put up near the entrance to the Dearborn Historical Museum early in the morning on March 31, 2017. This installation, unannounced, with no ceremony, sparked controversy immediately, because no historical marker accompanied him to tell that he personified racial exclusion during the Nadir of race relations. Absent "contextualization," the city was not putting him at the museum so people would muse but was instead again honoring him. At a City Council meeting a few days later, Mayor Jack O'Reilly hastened to explain that this was "just getting it over there"; the City planned to move Hubbard again to a less prominent spot and would be accompanied by "very brief" explanatory signage. Sure enough, Hubbard was moved, yet again, to behind a parking lot at the side door to the museum. At his new location, he has no polished base, but he does have a plaque, which contains this sentence: "A self-described segregationist, he periodically gained negative national attention for comments that disparaged African Americans."

In 1999, I ended this essay with this prediction: not until white suburbanites are embarrassed rather than delighted to live in all-white neighborhoods will Orville Hubbard's statue come down. Twenty years later, many white suburbanites are still delighted to live in *almost* all-white neighborhoods, because then they can deny any racism while still reaping the status that comes with the whiteness. So it seems appropriate that Orville Hubbard's statue has *kind of* come down.[3]

1. The building has been repurposed as an art space.
2. The NAACP called for a boycott of Dearborn businesses; the ordinance got bogged down in court and was never really enforced.
3. David L. Good, *Orvie: The Dictator of Dearborn* (Detroit, MI: Wayne State UP, 1989), especially 40–41, 264, 386–87; Good, "Orville Hubbard—The Ghost Who Still Haunts Dearborn," *The Detroit News*, 1/3/97; "Inventory of American Sculpture," www.siris.si.edu/webpac-bin/wgbroker 9/98; Bureau of the Census, *1990 Census* and Earlier Years (DC: GPO, 1992 and earlier years); "Dearborn Online," www.dearborn -mi.com, 2/98; Jean H. Hatch, "Capsule History of Dearborn," www.dearborn-mi .com/cityhall.htm, 2/98; R. J. King, "Dearborn Builds on its Housing," *The Detroit News*, 2/2/97; George Hunter, "Booming City Has Home to Fit Every Need, Price Range," *The Detroit News*, 2/2/97; Andrew Hacker, "Grand Illusion," *The New York Review of Books*, 6/11/98, 28; "Dearborn Removes Hubbard's Statue from Former City Hall," *Arab American News*, 9/29/2015, arabamericannews.com/news/news/id_11124 /Dearborn-removes-Hubbards-statue-from-former-city-hall.html; Good, "Hubbard Statue's Move to a New Home Rekindles an Old Controversy," *The Dearborn Historian* 54 no. 2 (summer 2017), 8–10; Perry A. Farrell, "Plaque Depicts Former Dearborn

Mayor Orville Hubbard as a Racist Who Hated Black People," *Detroit Free Press*, 2/6/2018, freep.com/story/news/2018/02/06/orville-hubbard-late-dearborn-mayor -plaque-shows-hubbard-racists/310121002/; Good, email, 8/26/2018.

———————— ✷ ————————

35. Who Menaced Whom?

OHIO *Delaware*

At the corner of Lincoln and Sandusky Streets in the town of Delaware, a state historical marker used to announce,

Two blocks east

SITE OF PLUGGY'S TOWN

A large Mingo town of the Revolutionary period, and a constant menace to settlers east and south of the Ohio. Here the noted Indian Chief Logan lived for some years.

The marker raised the question: who menaced whom?

Shortly after the first edition of this book came out, this marker disappeared. No one professed to know how or why it came down.

In 2008, the Delaware County Historical Society put up a new marker with the same title. It avoids the word "menace" and contains more information than the missing marker but does not try to tell the more complex story this entry relates. "The British Commander," it says, "had won the support of Pluggy and his warriors and convinced them to attack settlers living east and south of the Ohio River," but it does not tell why.

Logan's biography offers an answer. He was born about 1725 to parents who were members of the Iroquois Confederacy. After the French and Indian War (1754–63) he moved to Ohio. Although eminent, he was never an "Indian Chief." Indeed, most American Indian "chiefs" were never chiefs. Europeans projected chiefdom onto Native Americans because they could not easily conceive of people living in a civil society without permanent formal ranks. Also, making a "chief" of a respected Native (and sometimes any

Native who happened to be handy) gave a European leader an opposite with whom to deal—someone who could sell land, for instance.

For his part, the Native American gained not only flattery but also guns, trade goods, and increased influence within his tribe if he had not conceded too much to the newcomers. So it was with Logan: his friendship with whites gave him renown among Natives.

In 1774, one of those acts of violence occurred that particularly plagued friendly Native Americans in the zone of white-Indian contact. According to Henry Jolley, a white living nearby, half a dozen Indians were camped on the northwest bank of the Ohio near the mouth of Yellow Creek. A party of whites was camped on the opposite side of the river. Six of the Natives came over to visit. "The whites gave them rum, which three of them drank, and in a short time they became very drunk. The other two men and the woman refused to drink. The sober Indians were challenged to shoot at a mark, to which they agreed, and as soon as they emptied their guns, the whites shot them down. The woman attempted to escape by flight, but was also shot down; she lived long enough, however, to beg mercy for her babe. . . ." Back at their camp, the remaining Indians tried to escape by descending the Ohio, but a party of whites under Michael Cresap overtook them and took the scalp of at least one more.[1]

The slain Indians were members of Logan's family, and the incident converted Logan to an intense hatred of whites. Many Shawnees and Iroquois in Ohio had favored war against the white intruders; Logan now joined them. The result was a "mourning war, limiting the number of white victims to the number of their own people killed at Yellow Creek," according to historian Michael McConnell. Whites named it Lord Dunmore's War, after the colonial governor of Virginia who led two columns against the Native Americans and defeated them at Point Pleasant, Ohio.

At the end of Lord Dunmore's War, Logan refused to attend the peace negotiations. Instead, he sent an explanation that circulated widely throughout the colonies. Thomas Jefferson included it in his *Notes on Virginia*, and I include it here:

> I appeal to any white to say if he ever entered Logan's cabin hungry and he gave him not meat; if ever he came cold and naked, and he clothed him not. During the course of the last long bloody

war [French and Indian War], Logan remained idle in his cabin,
an advocate for peace. Nay, such was my affection for the whites,
that my countrymen hooted as they passed by and said "Logan is
the friend of white men." I had even thought to have lived with
you, but for the injuries of one man. Col. Cresap, the last spring,
in cold blood and unprovoked, cut off all the relations of Logan,
not sparing even my women or children. There runs not a drop
of my blood in the veins of any human creature. This called on
me for revenge. I have sought it; I have killed many; I have fully
glutted my vengeance. For my country, I rejoice at the beams of
peace. . . . Who is there to mourn for Logan? Not one.

White newcomers continued to be "a constant menace to [Indian] settlers,"
and not just at Pluggy's Town. Eventually, whites forced the Shawnees into
Indiana, then Missouri, Kansas, and finally, Indian Territory, now Oklahoma. Nor is this reversal of terminology confined to "Pluggy's Town." Near
Bandera, Texas, a state historical marker lauds the Texas Rangers who in
1841 "helped remove the Indian menace and open the frontier across Texas."
Further east and further back in time, in Aurora, New York, a monument
tells how the 1779 "expedition against the hostile Indian nations . . . checked
the aggressions of the English and Indians on the frontiers of New York and
Pennsylvania, extending westward the dominion of the United States." Since
the Natives were hardly trying to extend their dominion eastward, defining
their acts as "aggressions" is contradictory.

Still further east, these markers have a beginning in the tablet on a boulder
on Cape Cod in Eastham, Massachusetts, which reads,

On this spot
Hostile Indians
had their
First Encounter
December 8, 1620

with the Pilgrims (who are named individually). Historians might question
who was hostile first, but on the landscape from sea to shining sea the victors got to apply terms like "aggression," "hostile," and "menace" to Indian
behavior. The result of all this bad history is that Americans today simply do

not understand the texture of white violence that Native Americans living on the border of white control had to endure.[2]

Chapter 89 criticizes another term this Ohio marker misuses, "settler."

1. This brutality was probably not merely wanton; colonies and later states usually paid bounties for Indian scalps. Authorities weren't always careful whose scalp they were paying for, friendly or hostile, so long as it was Indian.

2. Wayne Moquin, ed., *Great Documents in American Indian History* (NY: Praeger, 1973), 126; Emily Foster, *The OH Frontier* (Lexington: UP of KY, 1996), 38–40; Michael McConnell, *A Country Between: The Upper OH Valley and Its Peoples* (Lincoln: U. of NE Press, 1992), 275; "James Logan," www.eb.com:180/cgibin/g?DocF=micro/354/50. html, 5/98; Anthony F. C. Wallace, *Death and Rebirth of the Seneca* (NY: Knopf, 1970), 134–48; Colin Calloway, *The American Revolution in Indian Country* (Cambridge: Cambridge UP, 1995), 51.

THE SOUTH

36. "No Nation Rose So White and Fair; None Fell So Free of Crime"

TEXAS *Gainesville*

On the Cooke County courthouse lawn in Gainesville, Texas, stands an impressive Confederate monument with this inscription:

> *God holds the scales of Justice; He will measure praise and blame; And*
> *the South will stand the verdict,*
> *And will stand it without shame. Oh, home of tears, but let her bear*
> *This blazoned to the end of time; No nation rose so white and fair,*
> *None fell so free of crime.*

Throughout America, Confederate memorials insist that their cause was without blemish (chapter 74). But this verse in Gainesville is particularly troubling, since something grim happened at this very site. When this monument went up in 1911, Gainesville already had a Confederate Soldiers' monument in Leonard Park, erected in 1908. This second monument at the courthouse was an obvious bid to put up a counterfactual statement to cover over the awful crime that Confederates carried out on these very grounds in October 1862.

During the early morning hours of October 1, Confederate militia scattered through Cooke and neighboring counties arresting Texans suspected of favoring the United States. In all, they arrested more than 200 people. By noon, they had locked 70 of them in a vacant store on the courthouse square in Gainesville. In the words of Richard McCaslin, whose fine book *Tainted Breeze: The Great Hanging at Gainesville, Texas* is the standard history of the event, "vigilantes executed at least 42 of these prisoners for conspiring to commit treason and foment insurrection." It was the largest mass hanging in

American history.[1] According to McCaslin, "few of the victims had plotted to usurp Confederate authority, and most were innocent of the abolitionist sentiments of which they were accused."

Many North Texans had opposed secession. In the 1859 election for governor, which became something of an early plebiscite on secession, staunch Unionist Sam Houston won 73% of the votes in Cooke County. Fewer than one Texan in four voted for the Union in the secession referendum of February 1861, but 61% of Cooke County voters did so. The Confederacy further alienated Cooke County residents in the spring of 1862 when it passed the first conscription law in American history. The final straw came when Confederate officials then sent North Texas draftees into battle east of the Mississippi, far from Texas, after promising not to.

We can learn what happened next from a Texas historical marker, "The Great Hanging at Gainesville, 1862," located about six blocks east of the courthouse monument.[2] The marker begins with an extended excuse:

> Facing the threat of invasion from the north and fearing a Unionist uprising in their midst, the people of north Texas lived in constant dread during the Civil War. Word of a "Peace Party" of Union sympathizers, sworn to destroy their government, kill their leaders, and bring in Federal troops caused great alarm in Cooke and neighboring counties. Spies joined the "Peace Party," discovered its members and details of their plans.

Actually, Texas was considered safer from the threat of invasion during the Civil War than any other part of the Confederacy, which is why hundreds of planters took their slaves there. On the contrary, since most Cooke County voters had opposed secession, it would be more accurate to claim that "the people of north Texas lived in constant dread" of Confederate draft officials.

Was there a Peace Party "sworn to destroy their government, kill their leaders, and bring in Federal troops?" Well, there was a Peace Party, and Samuel McNutt was one of its leaders. He circulated a petition against the draft, and he and like-minded citizens did speak against the Confederacy, but their actions hardly amounted to the ominous acts the marker implies were in the works. Some Northerners acted similarly on behalf of the Confederacy in southern Indiana and other "butternut" sections in the North but prompted no comparable Union treatment.

Having implicitly agreed with the Confederates on the existence of an extensive Unionist conspiracy, the Texas Historical Commission went on to defend the kangaroo court that decreed the hangings:

> Under the leadership of colonels James Bourland, Daniel Montague, and others, citizens loyal to the Confederacy determined to destroy the order; and on the morning of Oct. 1, 1862, there were widespread arrests "by authority of the people of Cooke County." Fear of rescue by "Peace Party" members brought troops and militia to Gainesville, where the prisoners were assembled, and hastened action by the citizens committee. At a meeting of Cooke County citizens, with Col. W. C. Young presiding, it was unanimously resolved to establish a citizens court and to have the chairman choose a committee to select a jury. 68 men were brought speedily before the court. 39 of them were found guilty of conspiracy and insurrection, sentenced, and immediately hanged. Three other prisoners who were members of military

The 42 hangings were far from the extent of the violence. Confederates hanged five more men in Wise County on October 18. Still others were hanged in nearby Grayson and Denton counties. Historian Richard Brown believes as many as 171 people may have been killed in all. This detail is from a larger print done by Frederick Sumner, a Grayson County Unionist, in the spring of 1864. It shows the hanging of the wife of another Union sympathizer, who himself avoided hanging by agreeing to join the Confederate Army. She was heard saying she wished the United States would overrun Texas so her husband could stay home and provide for his family. In McCaslin's words, "six women—some say men dressed as women—came to her house and lynched her while her three young children watched." To the right swing the bodies of 30 more Unionists.

units were allowed trial by court martial at their request and were
subsequently hanged by its order. Two others broke from their
guard and were shot and killed. . . .

The marker excuses the extralegal character of the hangings: "fear of
rescue" was responsible. Besides, "a meeting of Cooke County citizens"
"unanimously" supported the proceedings. In fact, a mob assembled at the
courthouse, aided by the Confederate militia, and intimidated opponents
from saying anything.

To some extent, the tragedy can be seen as one result of a struggle between
planters and small farmers over who would dominate North Texas. Most
homesteaders in the area in the 1850s were subsistence farmers who held no
slaves. Only 11% of all Cooke County households owned slaves. Nevertheless, slaveowners dominated the makeshift jury that ordered the October
hangings. Forty-three of the 44 condemned men, on the other hand, owned
no slaves.

Confederate authorities did nothing to stop the 1862 violence or punish
its perpetrators, which "allowed Texas officials and Confederate officers . . .
to crush dissent in North Texas," according to McCaslin. So, it continued:
during the next year or two, Confederates killed almost everyone who had
signed McNutt's petition against conscription. Nor were these North Texas
events unique. In the words of historian William C. Davis, "the Confederate experience is dotted with episodes that are not particularly admirable."
Two hundred seventy-five miles south of Gainesville, another Confederate
atrocity was memorialized on the landscape in 1866 when the residents of
Comfort, Texas, mostly German Americans, put up an obelisk, "Treue der
Union," "True to the Union." It honors the German Americans from central Texas who refused to take loyalty oaths to the Confederacy. In August
1862, 80 Unionist German Americans fled toward Mexico, hoping to evade
Confederate conscription and perhaps join the U.S. Army in New Orleans.
Confederates caught them encamped on the West Fork of the Nueces River.
Half escaped; Confederates shot the rest, including the wounded, who were
executed. Other mass killings of Confederate dissenters happened elsewhere
in Texas and in Kansas, Tennessee, North Carolina, and other states. None of
the perpetrators were ever charged with crimes by the Confederacy; several
were even promoted.

The Union never executed Northerners who were caught trying to reach Confederate lines. Historian Mark Grimsley points out that the United States took a softer course: "The Federal government deliberately chose to conduct the war largely as a contest between two nations, despite the fact that it explicitly denied the Confederacy's right to exist. It applied the insurrectionary principle sparingly. Had it done so broadly and consistently, captured Confederate soldiers and civilians who gave aid and comfort to the Confederate regime might well have faced execution." The United States did expel some dissenters to Canada and to the Confederacy and locked up others without trial for a time. On the whole, however, in the words of historian James McPherson, "the Lincoln administration's policy toward Confederate sympathizers, antiwar activists, and saboteurs behind the lines was remarkably lenient, under the circumstances. No Northern civilians were executed for such activities."

Even after the war, the intimidation persisted in North Texas and elsewhere in the former Confederate States. When Unionists thought about going to court to gain redress for the murders of their relatives and destruction and theft of their property, ex-Confederates disguised themselves as American Indians and terrorized them. The Texas Constitution passed under ex-Confederate rule during Presidential Reconstruction (1865–67) mandated "that no one was to be prosecuted or sued for any acts performed under Confederate authority." This made matters worse by implying there would be no legal redress. Violence against Unionists, white and black, increased; 550 were killed from June 1865 through 1867, resulting in only five convictions.

The case of the Allen Hill family living near Spring Hill, Texas, shows what could happen to people loyal to the United States. Allen C. Hill was lynched as a Unionist in the winter of 1863. In 1869 or 1870, his oldest son was killed. In 1872, his oldest daughter was hanged. Then two other daughters were lynched. Then Hill's widow's home was burned, and she and her four remaining children fled. A posse rode them down and shot her and her two oldest daughters.

After the Civil War, these methods finally achieved in North Texas what secessionists never could accomplish before or during the contest: now a majority there supported the Lost Cause. The erection of the Confederate monument shows that neo-Confederates controlled the Cooke County courthouse in 1911. The text of the historical marker shows their lingering power in 1963. Thirty-five years later, white Gainesville was still gathering to celebrate its Confederate heritage. Speakers at the Confederate Soldiers' monument "profess[ed] reverence for Southern history by those who wrote it in sacrificial blood," praised those who supported "a heritage of freedom and democracy" and recognized "those who fought and died for a just cause." Speakers included the mayor of Gainesville, a Cooke County judge, a state representative, a nearby professor of history, and commanders of the Sons of Confederate Veterans. The *Gainesville Daily Register* gave the event front page coverage on March 10, 1998. The monument at the courthouse had worked its spell: not one speaker mentioned the Confederate history that really happened in Gainesville.

However, descendants of the hanged and defenders of the truth finally came to the fore in 2014. In October, they dedicated two new stone monuments on a previously vacant lot close to the spot where most of the hangings took place. One stone lists those killed under four categories, including "Acquitted by Citizens Court, Lynched by Mob." It therefore joins the few mentions of "lynching" on the American landscape before the new lynching memorial went up in Alabama in 2018. The other stone gives a far more extensive and accurate account of the hangings than does the state historical marker. This remarkable resurrection of memory shows how a few residents can get truth upon the landscape for the edification of generations to come.[3]

1. The second largest, the execution of 38 Dakotas in Mankato, Minnesota, also took place in 1862. Since the Indians were hanged on a single day, theirs is often considered the largest mass hanging in American history.

2. "Those who had opposed the Confederacy refused to be forgotten," according to McCaslin. Descendants met every year for 50 years in the shadow of the courthouse. If not at the courthouse, the deceased achieved some recognition on the landscape: a simple stone slab titled "The Great Hanging at Gainesville 1862" commemorates them. It has moved about and is now located north of Main Street and east of Schopmeyer.

3. Richard B. McCaslin, *Tainted Breeze* (Baton Rouge: LA State UP, 1994), 1, 10–15, 27–49, 57–73, 100–14, 127–44, 169–70, 192–93; Wanda Fleitman, correspondence, 3/98; Richard M. Brown, *Strain of Violence* (NY: Oxford UP, 1975), 241; William C. Davis, *The Cause Lost* (Lawrence: UP of KS, 1996), 178; Richard Selcer and William Paul Burrier, "What *Really* Happened on the Nueces River?" *North & South* no. 2, 1/98: 60–64; Mark Grimsley, *The Hard Hand of War* (Cambridge: Cambridge UP, 1995), 223; James McPherson, correspondence, 10/98; "Sons of Confederate Veterans Honor Soldiers Lost," *Gainesville Daily Register*, 3/10/98; Abby Rapoport, "How Do You Memorialize a Mob?" *Texas Observer*, 11/17/2014, texasobserver.org/great-hanging-gainesville; Johnathan Paul Martin, "The Great Hanging," MFA thesis, U of North TX, 5/2016.

———————— ✯ ————————

37. The Only Honest Sundown Town in the United States

TEXAS *Alba*

America is dotted with towns that for many decades refused to let African Americans live in them. Some even posted billboards at their city limits that read, "Nigger, don't let the sun set on you in _____"—hence becoming known as "sundown towns." Those signs are long gone, but one remnant remains—the city limits sign with "Alba, Texas," on it at the edge of a small town in east Texas.

According to George R. Stewart's classic *American Place-Names*, Alba, which means "white" in Spanish, was so named because it was "a post-Civil War foundation where Negroes were not allowed."[1] Alba was laid out in 1881 during the reactionary period after Reconstruction ended in Texas. By 1884, its population was 50, all white, and it has remained all white ever since. A coal discovery shortly before 1900 led to a population boom. According to Alba historian Saundra Burge, "There [were] people of many different nationalities here, but predominating were Mexicans, Bohemians, and Armenians." But not African Americans—by 1910, Alba's population had reached about 1,500, all white.[2] By 1990, the population had dropped to 489, all white. The population of the town's zip code was larger: 2,595, consisting of 2,520 whites, 7 Native Americans, 68 "other" (probably mostly Mexican Americans choosing "other" rather than "white"), and, again, zero blacks.

East Texas is something of a center of sundown towns. Among others, Cumby had 571 whites, Grand Saline 2,510 whites, and Vidor 10,844 whites—and not one African American in all three, according to the 1990 census. In 2016, the census still estimated Alba's black population as zero, although it now had 708 people. In 2010, Cumby's population was up to 777, but it still had not one black family. Grand Saline had four families and may be getting past its sundown heritage. Vidor, a suburb of Beaumont, earned national notoriety in 1993 when African Americans moved into a public housing project there—the first black residents of the sundown town. Ku Klux Klan demonstrations and threats from local residents persuaded the

African Americans to flee. But by 2010, five black families were braving it out. Each of these towns, even tiny Alba and Cumby, has public housing. For many years each public housing department served whites only. In 1982, partly as a result of these sundown towns, the United States brought the largest desegregation lawsuit in the history of public housing against 72 public housing authorities in east Texas. Informants told me as late as 2006, however, that Vidor still had all-white public housing. So, of course, did Alba and Cumby.

Segregated public housing is hardly unique to east Texas. Indeed, experts say most of the nation's public housing projects are segregated. Sundown towns are not limited to east Texas, either. To be sure, in the twenty-first century it is harder to keep a town all white. Overt violence gives a town a bad name, and courts struck down formal covenants that used to forbid property sales to blacks. "Steering" by realtors and lenders can still keep out most people of color. So can "DWB" ("Driving While Black") policing that singles out African American motorists for stopping, ticketing for minor offenses, and abuse. Towns usually welcome Asian Americans and Latinos more readily than African Americans. Sometimes, African Americans may be allowed only in certain parts of town, especially those where rentals predominate. Thus, sundown neighborhoods still exist inside larger towns that appear integrated.

In 1844, Oregon passed laws excluding "blacks and mulattoes" from entering the entire territory. In 1851, Indiana passed a law that stated only blacks who already lived in Indiana and their children could remain in the state.[3] During the Civil War, a regiment of Indiana soldiers enforced this regulation by blocking a group of African Americans from crossing the Ohio River from Kentucky. In the twentieth century, Valparaiso, Linton, and scores of other communities in Indiana were sundown towns complete with billboards.

Sometimes, Chinese Americans, Mexican Americans, Jews, or American Indians have been the victims of sundown policies. Humboldt County, California, expelled all its Chinese residents in 1885.[4] In 1937, the Humboldt County newspaper bragged, "Although 52 years have passed since the Chinese were driven from the county, none have ever returned. On one or two occasions offshore vessels with Chinese crews have stopped at this port, but the Chinamen as, a rule, stayed aboard their vessels, choosing not to take a chance on being ordered out." Thomasville, Georgia, expelled its Jews during the Civil War, accusing them of profiteering; half a century later no Jews lived in Thomas County.[5]

Another type of sundown town is more recent. After World War I and continuing to 1968, new all-white suburbs sprang up around big cities such as Dearborn, Michigan (chapter 34), and Darien, Connecticut (chapter 83), two towns notorious for their racial policies.

In 2005, I published a book on sundown towns. Originally, I thought I would discover "at least ten" sundown towns in Illinois, my home state, as the original edition of this essay predicted. To my astonishment, I found more than 500—a 70% majority of all incorporated municipalities in the state. I believe similar proportions went sundown in Oregon and several other northern states. Some remain all-white even today.

Although the United States doesn't seem to have the courage to end sundown towns, it might curtail all federal spending in such jurisdictions. After all, every dime spent in a sundown town is by definition not available to African Americans.[6]

Many sundown towns derive from white attacks that killed or drove out all people of color; chapter 54 gives one example: Cedar Key, Florida.

1. Sources differ as to whether Alba got its name from the adjective "alba," "white" when applied to a feminine noun, to recognize and avow that only whites could live there. Most authorities, like Stewart, hold that it did. In *The New Handbook of Texas*, Rachel Jenkins gives two stories for the name: first, that it was intended for white settlers only, and second, that it was named for the son of a railroad official. The town was first named Simpkins Prairie. Saundra Burge, great-great-great-granddaughter of Joseph Simpkins, the 1843 pioneer who named it, believes both stories: "I have always heard that Alba means white in Spanish. It was first spelled Albia, then changed to Alba in honor of a railroad executive's son." I have not confirmed the spelling change, but the adage by sociologist W. I. Thomas applies here: "If a situation is defined as real, it is real in its consequences." If Burge, "considered the local historian," and other residents of Alba believe that their town was named "white" because it was intended solely for whites, then for all intents and purposes it was. Many African Americans believe that towns with "white" in them—White County, Indiana; Whitesboro, Texas; Whitesburg, Kentucky—signify places where only whites can live. In fact, most such places were named after someone named White, though all three of the foregoing probably did keep out African Americans. White Settlement, Texas, on the other hand, was meant to convey a town for white people, as opposed to (in the mid-nineteenth century) Native Americans. White Settlement never did become a sundown town, so far as I can tell, although it came close in the 1940s.

2. As the census states, "Hispanics may be of any race"; most Hispanics, including all in Alba, defined themselves as "white."

3. Around this time Illinois, Iowa, and Missouri also passed laws to keep African Americans from immigrating into their states, but they were rarely enforced.

4. About twenty Chinese men hung on in rural areas but were forced out the next year.

5. The U.S. Census stopped asking about religion around 1910, so I do not know whether Jewish Americans moved back into the county subsequently. Eureka, the county seat of Humboldt County, repealed its anti-Chinese ordinance in 1959, and a few Chinese Americans now live in the county.

6. George R. Stewart, *American Place-Names* (NY: Oxford UP, 1970), 6; Saundra Burge, correspondence, 10/97; Rachel Jenkins, "Alba, Texas," in Ron Tyler, et al., eds., *The New Handbook of Texas* (Austin: TX State Historical Association, 1996), 92; Census, *1990 Census* for towns listed (DC: GPO, 1992); Park Potok, "Town Wrestles with Past, Present," "Pioneer for Change Says Overall, Things Haven't," "In TX, a New Struggle against Old Hatreds," and "Lawsuit May Bring Change in Housing," *USA Today*, 11/22/93; Richard Stewart, "Desegregation at Public Housing Ripped by Audit," *Houston Chronicle*, 7/11/97; Bruce Tomaso, "Audit Says HUD Failing to Integrate East Texas," *The Dallas Morning News*, 7/10/97; William L. Barney, *Flawed Victory* (NY: Praeger, 1975), 154; John C. Miller, *The Wolf by the Ears* (NY: Free Press, 1977), 248; *Comprehensive Handbook to Indiana in the Civil War: Away from the Battle* (Indianapolis: IN State Historical Museum, 1995), 19; Census, "ACS Demographic and Housing Estimates, 2012–16," (DC: Census, c.2016), factfinder.census.gov/faces/tableservices/jsf/pages/productview.xhtml?src=CF; James Marten, *Texas Divided* (Lexington: UP of KY, 1990), 179; Richard M. Brown, *Strain of Violence* (NY: Oxford UP, 1975), 277; Lynwood Carranco, "Chinese in Humboldt County, California: A Study in Prejudice," *Journal of the West* 12 (1/73):139–62; Carranco, "Chinese Expulsion from Humboldt County," in Roger Daniels, ed., *Anti-Chinese Violence in North America* (NY: Arno Press, 1978), 339; Census: *Special Reports, Religious Bodies, 1906* (DC: Census, 1910); Loewen, *Sundown Towns* (NY: New Press, 2005; 2018).

———— ✯ ————

38. It Never Got Off the Ground

TEXAS *Pittsburg*

Attention, ye of little erudition, ye who learned in fourth grade that the Wright brothers invented the airplane and first flew it at Kitty Hawk, North Carolina. The State of Texas tells quite another story. A Texas Historical Commission marker in downtown Pittsburg announces:

THE EZEKIEL AIRSHIP

Baptist minister and inventor Burrell Cannon (1848–1922) led some Pittsburg investors to establish the Ezekiel Airship Company and build a craft described in the Biblical book of Ezekiel. The ship had large fabric-

covered wings powered by an engine that turned four sets of paddles. It
was built in a nearby machine shop and was briefly airborne at this site
late in 1902, a year before the Wright brothers first flew. En route to the
St. Louis World's Fair in 1904, the airship was destroyed by a storm. A
second model crashed and the Rev. Cannon gave up the project.

In 1987, the Pittsburg Optimist Club built a full-scale model, based on
Cannon's plans. I saw it on display at Warrick's Restaurant in downtown
Pittsburg, but now it has moved to the Depot, the town's museum. A handout available in the restaurant claimed that Cannon built a second airship in
Chicago, "and a pilot by the name of Wilder flew it off the earth. But as the
airship lifted into the air, it struck the top of a telephone pole and knocked
the bottom of the airship out. This catastrophe caused Cannon to give up his
flying machine."

However, neither flight story can withstand even a moment's thoughtful
scrutiny of the model. For the paddles behave as paddles do when attached to
a wheel: they move forward and down, then backward and up. This principle
of a vertically rotating paddle works fine aboard ship, where a clear demarca-
tion exists between water and not-water. Paddling backward through water
propels a steamship forward; the paddle returns forward through air. In an
airship, however—even the Ezekiel Airship designed according to principles
found in the Bible—after a paddle moves down to generate lift and backward to generate forward movement, it, unfortunately, moves up, negating
any lift, and forward, nullifying any for-
ward motion. The model is beautiful—
but even optimists agree it could never
get off the ground.

The Ezekiel Airship has
become something of
a logo for Pittsburg,
Texas, even though
it never got off the
ground.

Rev. Cannon recognized as much, concluding, "God never willed that this airship should fly." Despite the marker's claims, the Ezekiel Airship was never "briefly airborne at this site" or any other site, "late in 1902" or any other year. We can chalk up the error to local boosterism, like in chapter 28, the "first" automobile, and chapter 87, "local history wars." I understand that the museum does not actually claim that the Ezekiel flew, but the model's new location—in the air! suspended from the ceiling!—nevertheless gives it more legitimacy.

———————— ✦ ————————

39. The Real War Will Never Get into the War Museums
TEXAS *Fredericksburg*

Museums exist in part to show us things we don't get to see in ordinary life; natural history museums show us stuffed cheetahs, not housecats. Combat is wrenchingly unlike civilian life; paradoxically, however, war museums domesticate war. The only exception I know in the United States is the Holocaust Memorial Museum in Washington, DC, which by no coincidence, for ten years after its opening, still had long lines for tickets. Located in Fredericksburg, Texas, more than 1,200 miles from the Pacific Ocean, is the Museum of the Pacific War. There is a reason for its unmaritime location: Chester Nimitz, admiral of the Pacific fleet in World War II, grew up here in the steamboat-shaped hotel that used to be the museum's main building. The Nimitz Museum (as it is usually called) claims to be "America's only museum of the Pacific War." It pits enthusiasm for a local hero against the bloody and sometimes controversial history of our conflict in the Pacific.

When I visited, in 1998, history lost. The boosterism was apparent at the start. I joined a contingent of schoolchildren at the Nimitz. A lecturer began by proclaiming, "Admiral Nimitz commanded more men and more military power than all the commanders in all previous wars of human history combined." An early exhibit label echoed, "He commanded thousands of ships and aircraft and millions of men—more military power than all commanders in all previous wars." Nonsense! The various sides in World War I alone had more than 65,000,000 men in the field at one time or another, compared to about a million under Nimitz. German Gen. Erich Ludendorff commanded more men in a single battle, the Second Battle of the Somme, in March of 1918, than Nimitz controlled in the entire Pacific theater.[1]

Not all labels in the Nimitz Museum were this silly. Visitors encountered useful information about the reasons Japan started the war, race riots during the war, women's roles, Japanese Americans, and other topics. However, the museum provided no real sense of what the Pacific War was like—no feel for the horror and brutality of combat. Its twenty-minute video "The War in the Pacific" showed no bodies. Bombing was shown but not its effects. Surely, a museum about the Pacific War—particularly savage and racist on both sides—should make some attempt to present the reality of twentieth-century combat.

Paul Fussell, whose book *Wartime* is based on his combat experience as well as the literature of World War II, shows how most written and visual portrayals of war prettify the carnage, especially in this war. Writers disguise the reality of combat with evasions and euphemisms: kitchen terms like "mopping up" and "battle fatigue," where "insanity" is meant. Fussell laments that the home front never sees photos of body parts and never grasps such horrors as the fact that a soldier may be wounded by the head or foot of his buddy being blown at him. He quotes John Steinbeck, who was a war correspondent during World War II: "It is in the things not mentioned that the untruth lies."

The museum came closest to representing the reality of combat in its exhibit on Tarawa, a major atoll among the Gilbert Islands held by the Japanese. One label called Tarawa "a carefully coordinated [American amphibious] assault that completely snafued." Even here though, the museum fudged: it never explained that Tarawa was a bloodbath on both sides. On D-day on Tarawa, U.S. Marines suffered a far higher percentage of casualties than U.S. forces did in France later in the war, earning it the sobriquet "Bloody Tarawa." Fussell's *Wartime* portrays a scene from the battle of Tarawa: "One Marine battalion commander, badly wounded, climbed above the rising tide onto a pile of American bodies. Next afternoon he was found there, mad." This incident and all others like it are among the "things not mentioned" at the Nimitz Museum.

Tarawa taught Robert Sherrod that "probably no amount of shelling and bombing could obviate the necessity of sending in foot soldiers to finish the job." In 1944, Sherrod wrote that many Americans had been led to expect "an

In his best-seller *Tarawa*, which the Nimitz reprinted in 1993, Robert Sherrod began his caption of this photograph: "Amphibious tractors, knocked out after they landed troops ashore." On display at the Nimitz, it showed just about the only dead bodies anywhere in the museum. But the Nimitz left out the next two sentences of Sherrod's caption: "The bodies of several Marines float near the sea well after tide has come in. Of 500 men in the amphibious tractor battalion, 323 became casualties." Because the exhibit used only the first sentence, few visitors noticed the bodies, at least four of which are visible on close inspection.

easy war"—"that machines alone would win the war for us"—and lamented that the home front did not understand that this was not true. Fussell claims that war gets sanitized because "the morale of the home front must not be jeopardized." Half a century later, however, the need for home front morale could not excuse the Museum of the Pacific War's cheerful emphasis on the machines rather than the horrific nature of the war.

The largest exhibit at the Nimitz, "History Walk of the Pacific War," featured "three acres of World War II artifacts, tanks, guns, and large relics" in the words of its brochure. This "Walk" avoided the history of the war in favor of an obsession with the nuts and bolts of the war's machines and of obtaining and preserving these specimens. I watched as a veteran of our armed forces (but not of combat) demonstrated an LVT (landing vehicle, tracked) and a flamethrower for a group of elementary school students. The museum claimed that its living history "programs try to convey the day to day reality of life for the American soldier in the Pacific theater, the complexity of the U.S. war effort, and the harsh truths of modern war." They failed. The children's response—"Ooh, that's neat"—was perfectly appropriate to the spirit of the presentation.

Civil War battlefields similarly make war seem attractive by their very nature—they are parks with picnic tables and nicely mown grass. Gone are the briers and vines to be hacked through, the muck and flies to be endured, the smells and sounds and turmoil and fear, the illness and the blood. Compare William Tecumseh Sherman's famous 1880 warning to schoolchildren: "There is many a boy here today who looks on war as all glory, but, boys, it is all hell. You can bear this warning voice to generations yet to come." And Sherman was referring to a war fought by the far more civilized rules of the nineteenth century.

Excising death and insanity from a war in favor of a "neat" display of tanks and guns is not just a matter of taste. Our resulting innocence entails human costs. For one, home-front ignorance about war's brutal truths makes it harder for veterans to reenter society. It also leaves Americans unable to use knowledge from past wars to guide us in current and future conflicts. In Fussell's words, "America has not yet understood what the Second World War was like, and has thus been unable to use such understanding to re-interpret and redefine the national reality and arrive at something like public maturity." Thus, although the Nimitz Museum claimed to consider education important, it failed as a true educational institution.[2]

Besides avoiding the reality of war, the Museum of the Pacific War tried not to have visitors think about its morality. Since the Pacific War ended with two events that raised profound moral issues around the world—the atomic bombings of Hiroshima and Nagasaki—this evasion isn't easily accomplished. The Nimitz Museum distorted the facts to avoid the moral issues. "Fearing a million American casualties, committed to unconditional surrender, and faced with Japanese obstinance," said a Nimitz label, "Truman saw no point in delay." Each of the three subordinate clauses in that sentence is factually debatable, but not at the Museum of the Pacific War.

Army brass gave Truman low figures for American casualties in an invasion of Japan—perhaps partly so they would get the job and win the war. The Navy endorsed higher figures—perhaps partly to deter an invasion so they could win the war with their naval blockade. Air Force leaders claimed no invasion would be necessary, because air power would win the war by eliminating Japan's ability to fight on. If the Nimitz Museum provided some of these competing estimates and delved into why they differed, visitors could learn how history involves evaluating primary sources and making careful judgments. Interestingly, at the time, Chester Nimitz himself did not believe that the atomic bombings of Hiroshima and Nagasaki averted an invasion of Japan. According to Adm. Harry Hill, commander of the Fifth Amphibious Force, which would have been directly involved in any invasion, "neither

Admiral Nimitz or [Raymond] Spruance [Nimitz's chief of staff] considered that it would ever be necessary to invade the homeland of Japan." Now the Nimitz Museum serves up what Gar Alperovitz in *The Decision to Use the Atomic Bomb and the Architecture of an American Myth* calls "American myth" rather than Adm. Nimitz's own view!

Second, was the United States "committed to unconditional surrender"? Certainly, Japan never accepted unconditional surrender. Truman acceded to Japan's key conditions: that it be allowed to retain its imperial system and that Emperor Hirohito remain on the throne. Why Truman had said he would insist on unconditional surrender is at the core of another historical controversy. Adm. Nimitz was among the many high-level U.S. officials who had urged him to modify his policy.[3]

Third, was Japan obstinate? Undoubtedly, it had been, but by the summer of 1945, Japanese leaders were very aware of their hopeless military position and had contacted Soviet diplomats in an attempt to enlist Stalin as an intermediary to end hostilities with the United States. Since we had broken the Japanese code, American officials knew this. Again, the Nimitz Museum would better serve the cause of truth if it quoted Adm. Nimitz, who said in October 1945, "The Japanese had, in fact, already sued for peace before the atomic age was announced to the world with the destruction of Hiroshima and before the Russian entry into the war." On the other hand, historian Stanley Weintraub gives evidence of obstinacy within the Japanese cabinet and believes that the atomic bombs "did bring the war to an end." Other historians believe that Stalin's declaration of war against Japan on August 8 and his troops' invasion of Manchuria the next day were more important factors. Again, a historical debate, and again, the Nimitz Museum chose a (minority) position and presented it flatly as fact.

The museum depicted Hiroshima and Nagasaki in such a way as to remove them as a controversy or a moral issue—a sad decision for the nation's only Museum of the Pacific War. At the time—and afterward—the U.S. decision was both a controversy and a moral issue. Adm. Nimitz, in the words of his biographer E. B. Potter, "considered the atomic bomb somehow indecent, certainly not a legitimate form of warfare." And he specifically said that its use caused "an unnecessary loss of civilian life" when "we had them beaten." Once again, Nimitz's views and words on this issue were absent from the Nimitz Museum. So were Eisenhower's, Herbert Hoover's, and those of anyone else who questioned the bombings.[4, 5]

Those on the other side of the controversy were a large majority on August 7, 1945. Most soldiers, sailors, and fliers in the service of the United States had no reservations about dropping the atomic bomb on Hiroshima. Fussell didn't; he pointed out later that Allied casualties were running more than 7,000 each week in July and August 1945. Many veterans of the Pacific War think that the atomic bomb may have saved their lives.

Justifying the nuclear destruction of Hiroshima and Nagasaki wasn't hard for our airmen, soldiers, or President Truman, because it was merely an extension of what was already going on in the Pacific War. This understanding could not occur at the Nimitz Museum, however, because how military conduct grew increasingly savage during World War II is yet another topic that the museum left out. Nations are not supposed to bomb civilian targets. When German planes allied with the Spanish Fascists bombed the Spanish town of Guernica in 1937, the world cried shame. Early in World War II, Americans condemned the Nazis for bombing the residential neighborhoods of London. In Japan, the United States did the same thing and on a larger scale. The conventional bombing of Tokyo was morally indistinguishable from and prepared the way for the atomic bombing of Hiroshima and Nagasaki. Indeed, about as many people died in the firestorm in Tokyo on March 9–10, 1945, as in Hiroshima, and many more than in Nagasaki.

The Nimitz Museum takes for granted that our unlimited bombing of Japanese (and German) cities was a good thing. Besides the moral issue, however, the destruction of Japanese cities also raises an important strategic question: did this bombing help destroy Japan's will to fight on? Here is another historical controversy. Chapter 82 suggests that destroying cities from the air, especially cities with little military significance, stiffened rather than undermined enemy resolve in Germany and later in Vietnam. In Japan, such a policy probably hurt civilian morale and certainly crippled war production. When does such bombing work? When does it fail? It's an important question, and again, one the Nimitz Museum ducked.

Other rules of war went by the boards in the Pacific War. Our unrestricted submarine warfare was exactly what the United States had denounced Germany for in World War I and early in World War II (chapter 76). A veteran told me how he and his comrades bayoneted wounded Japanese soldiers on the beach at Iwo Jima. In earlier wars, even in most European theaters in World War II, such behavior was a war crime (chapter 51), but in the Pacific

War it was "normal." My point is not that the United States alone became bestial during the Pacific War. So did Japan, even earlier: Japan's treatment of U.S. prisoners of war flouted international law, as did its attacks on civilians in China. The Pacific War does show that the United States is not more moral than other nations in warfare. War is hell, and when the United States conducts it, just like any other nation, we too become the devil. The Nimitz Museum not only prettified the Pacific War, it also prettified America's role in it. Both distortions left the museum unable to raise and rationally discuss war's effects on our society or the changing rules of war throughout the world.

Readers will note that I used past tense for most of this entry. That's because since I visited, the museum has expanded dramatically. In 2001, its curator wrote to me that the new exhibits "confront many of the harsh realities of the conflict." I think this is true and invite you to visit and let me know your appraisal. However, recently, the museum added an outdoor event that is supposed to resemble Tarawa: four times each month, volunteers and staff reenact that battle! I suspect this tourist event avoids reality, because, in the words of a staff member, its "main focus" is "on heroism."

Why don't museums raise serious issues about World War II today? To facilitate the *next* war? In this sense, their staffs still seem concerned with maintaining civilian morale. Or perhaps curators maintain a cheery approach to war as curators do to other topics—quilting, vice presidents, even slavery—because they somehow believe that buoyant presentations make visitors feel good and come back. The Holocaust Museum refutes that notion. Hopefully, visitors come out of the expanded Museum of the Pacific War more able to think about the breakdown of civilized rules in modern warfare than when they went in.[6]

1. For that matter, though not a previous war, Dwight Eisenhower in Europe commanded more men and military power than Adm. Nimitz in the Pacific, and the Soviet Union under Mar. Stalin had more men in the field than all American forces in Europe *and* the Pacific combined. This declaration may originate in the opening sentence in *Nimitz* by E. B. Potter, which credits Nimitz with commanding "more military power than had been wielded by all previous commanders in all previous wars." Although per-soldier firepower did increase between the wars, this slightly more limited statement is also false, as John Ellis, Michael Clodfelter, and Anthony Bruce have shown.

2. The museum has put online some 5,000 oral interviews about World War II that are a marvelous teaching resource.

3. Alperovitz shows that many leaders in the military and state department believed that a statement from Truman allowing Japan to keep its emperor "would be likely to produce

a surrender." Alperovitz also shows that Secretary of State James F. Byrnes favored using the atomic bombs because of the leverage they would give the United States vis-à-vis the USSR in the postwar period. Whether the latter explains Truman's reluctance to issue the former probably can never be known.

4. "I voiced to [Secretary of War Henry L. Stimson] my grave misgivings, first on the basis of my belief that Japan was already defeated and that dropping the bomb was completely unnecessary, and secondly because I thought that our country should avoid shocking world opinion by the use of a weapon whose employment was, I thought, no longer mandatory as a measure to save American lives . . . "—Dwight Eisenhower, in an unconfirmed 1963 remembrance of a mid-July 1945 meeting, three weeks before Hiroshima.

5. "The use of the atomic bomb, with its indiscriminate killing of women and children, revolts my soul."—Herbert Hoover, August 8, 1945, two days after Hiroshima, one day before Nagasaki.

6. E. B. Potter, *Nimitz* (Washington, DC: U.S. Naval Institute, 1988), 1; John Ellis, *World War II: A Statistical Survey* (NY: Facts on File, 1993), 227–28; Michael Clodfelter, *Warfare and Armed Conflict: A Statistical Reference, vol. 2* (Jefferson, NC: McFarland, 1992), 731, 782–87; Anthony Bruce, *An Illustrated Companion to the First World War* (London: Penguin, 1989), 89, 116; Paul Fussell, *Wartime* (NY: Oxford UP, 1989), 270–73, 285–86 (Steinbeck quote); Fussell, *Thank God for the Atom Bomb, and Other Essays* (NY: Summit, 1988), 4–5; Robert Sherrod, *Tarawa* (Fredericksburg, TX: Nimitz Foundation, 1993), 149; Charles Royster, *The Destructive War* (NY: Knopf, 1991), 253; Gar Alperovitz, *The Decision to Use the Atomic Bomb and the Architecture of an American Myth* (NY: Knopf, 1995), 329–30 (Nimitz quotes), 355–56 (Eisenhower quote), 515–21, 626, 633–38 (Hoover quote); Jeffrey Underwood, review of Stephen McFarland, *America's Pursuit of Precision Bombing*, in *Journal of American History* 82 no. 4 (1996): 1609–10; Stanley Weintraub, "Letters," *The New York Times*, 12/7/97; "History Comes to Life at the National Museum of the Pacific War," KXAN, kxan.com/community/events/history-comes-to-life-at-the-national-museum-of-the-pacific-war/1031530544

★

---

40. This Building Used to Be a Hardware Store

TEXAS *Galveston*

In 2018, Texas had 16,250 historical markers—far more than any other state. When I remarked on this to various Texas officials, they shrugged as if to say, "Well, we've had more history!" But Texas hasn't. Moreover, like other states, Texas refrains from recognizing events that might embarrass or offend local communities. To place so many historical markers within one state while still avoiding all manner of important but taboo topics, Texas resorts to such minutiae as this plaque on a main street in downtown Galveston:

MAGALE BUILDING

A fire . . . in 1869 destroyed an earlier structure at this site. John F.
Magale (d. 1880) built this edifice in 1870 to house his wholesale liquor
business. . . .From 1889 until the late 1960s, this building was occupied
by J. F. Smith and Brother, a well-known paint and hardware store.

Not all these ubiquitous markers are official. Two different private companies sell mock markers. They incorporate the official top part of Texas's
round markers, changing "Historical Commission" to "Histerical Committee"; the lower rectangle then offers a choice of texts. One says, "On March 2,
1836, Texas declared her independence from Mexico, while the Comanches
roamed the Prairie, Rangers protected frontier settlements, and this building was not here yet." I suppose it's wrong to encourage these things, but I
learned about as much history from it as from the Magale Building marker.
Another reads, "On April 21, 1836, Texas troops under Sam Houston won
independence, as they shouted out, 'Remember the Alamo.' When we tried
that here, the neighbors complained about the noise."

Reporter John Kelso interviewed John Van Horn, one of the entrepreneurs,
who said, "We think the Historical Commission is just a big joke"—perhaps
because of markers like "Magale Building." "We just feel like people need a
chance to take history into their own hands, if they want to. Everybody feels
like their house needs a little extra attention. And people can designate their
house any way they want to this way." The Texas Historical Commission
isn't amused; they referred the matter to the attorney general's office.

In the first edition of this book, I wrote that Texas's official state markers might look less like "a big joke" if the state marked the sites where the
following events happened, none of which was then commemorated on the
landscape:

- Reconstruction violence (not one site marked).
- The notorious Brownsville race riot of 1906.
- The hundreds of lynchings in Texas, including the killing of at
  least eighteen African Americans in Slocum on July 29–30, 1910.
- *Sweatt v. Painter*, the first successful school desegregation lawsuit
  in modern Texas history and an important precursor in 1950 of
  Brown v. Board of Education.

- The first woman juror in Texas, in 1954.
- The founding of La Raza Unida, the first major Chicano political party, in Crystal City in 1969.

These are all matters of statewide if not national importance. Since then, Texas did add markers for the Slocum Massacre and *Sweatt v. Painter.* That's good, but still, Texas is adding about 300 markers a year—ten times as many as other states with active marker programs. Surely, it can treat more important events than "a well-known paint and hardware store."[1]

Chapter 91 tells of another well-known satirical marker.

1. "East Texas Race Riot; Eighteen Negroes Killed," *The Dallas Morning News,*7/31/10; Judy Newton and Michael Newton, *Racial and Religious Violence in America* (NY: Garland, 1991), 241; "A Report From Aztlan: Texas Chicanos Forge Own Political Power," clnet.ucr.edu/research/docs/razaunida/report.htm, 9/98.

41. Men Make History; Women Make Wives

ARKANSAS *Little Rock*

Halls of fame dot the American landscape. If the Baseball Hall of Fame in Abner Doubleday's hometown of Cooperstown, New York, is the most famous tourist destination, Cleveland's Rock and Roll Hall of Fame is certainly catching up. Many states have their own halls of fame, usually in the form of portraits hung in the state capitol or a nearby building. When I was first researching this book, Arkansas was no exception. Its collection of portraits of famous Arkansans was in the Arkansas History Commission on the mall behind the state capitol and in the capitol itself. The history commission tied the collection together with a handsome eight-page brochure, "The Arkansas History Commission Portrait Gallery." While its layout was attractive, the gallery was the most erratic display of eminent personages in any state hall of fame.

Its images implied that men made history in Arkansas, while women only made wives. Of the 88 individual portraits, only thirteen were of women. This proportion, about one in seven, might be defensible—after all, our society has not allowed women to be as prominent as men. However, the portrait gallery presented ten of its thirteen women as remoras. The remora, you'll recall, is a fish that attaches itself to a shark and gets carried along without much effort. When the shark kills something, the remora detaches and enjoys the feast.

The very first entry in the portrait guide, "Mary Morris Bertrand. Wife of Charles P. Bertrand," supplied no independent reason why Ms. Bertrand should be in the gallery. Compare her husband's entry: "Charles P. Bertrand. Lawyer, founder and editor of the *Arkansas Advocate* (1830), the second newspaper in the territory; secretary, 1836 Arkansas Constitutional Convention; member, Arkansas House of Representatives, 1840–41, 1844–49; mayor, City of Little Rock, 1855–56; president, Memphis Telegraph Company, the first to bring its lines to Little Rock in 1860."

Similarly, we learn that Elizabeth Johnson Pope was "Wife of John Pope," while Elizabeth Pope was "Niece of John Pope." Abbe Washburn Langford was "Daughter of Cephas Washburn," but at least Margaret T. Gibbs Rose *did* something: "Married U. M. Rose, 1863."

Martha E. R. Fones gets by far the longest entry of her gender: "Wife of James Amon Fones, vice president of Fones Brothers Hardware Company of Little Rock. Mr. Fones was the first president of the Little Rock Board of Trade, which he helped to establish." The portrait gallery includes her portrait instead of his, but she did nothing but be his wife so far as the visitor can infer. Writer Mary Daly makes a distinction between "foreground" and "background": in the foreground are the public events that newspapers usually cover, but the background is where life is truly lived, where "the depths of the self abide and find nourishment." Part of the reality of our past is that our male-dominated society has not given women an equal chance to become famous in the foreground. All ten of these women may have made important contributions in the background, but one would never guess it from these walls.

Only three women got in on their own. Two were long-time stalwarts of the Arkansas History Commission itself. The third, Willie Hocker, designed the Arkansas flag. That's all, folks!

Women have done things in Arkansas history. Let us compare some impressive women who are in the Arkansas Portrait Gallery with those who aren't.

IN: Maria Toncray Watkins Stevenson: 1793–1874. Wife of Isaac Watkins and sister of Silas T. Toncray.

OUT: Louise Thaden: 1905–79. Learned to fly in 1927; in 1928 flew at nearly twenty feet, higher than any woman previously. Won the first Women's Air Derby (California to Cleveland), in 1929, beating Amelia Earhart and others. 1932, set a new women's endurance record, staying aloft for more than 196 hours. 1936, the first woman to win the Bendix Trophy Race, Los Angeles to NYC. Wrote autobiography, *High, Wide, and Frightened.*

IN: Clara B. Eno: 1854–1951. Member Arkansas History Commission, 1909–51; collector of Arkansas materials.

OUT: Bernie Babcock: 1868–1962. Helped establish Arkansas Museum of Science and History, crusaded for women's suffrage and prohibition, wrote 26 novels. First woman from Arkansas listed in *Who's Who.*

IN: Abbe Washburn Langford: 1827–81. Daughter of Cephas Washburn.

OUT: Ella King Newsom: 1838–1919. An affluent young Arkansas widow, Newsom learned to nurse early in the Civil War in Memphis City Hospital. She then ran Confederate hospitals in Bowling Green, Kentucky, Nashville, Chattanooga, and finally Atlanta.

IN: Johanna Krause Hotze: 1847–81. Daughter of a Little Rock merchant, wife of Peter Hotze.

OUT: Hattie Caraway: 1878–1950. U.S. Senator, 1932–45. The first woman elected to a full term in the U.S. Senate, first to preside over the Senate, and first to chair a Senate committee. Opposed equal rights for blacks but co-sponsored Equal Rights Amendment (for women) in 1943.

Or we might consider the most famous incident in Arkansas history in the twentieth century—the desegregation of Central High School in Little Rock. This series of events made Little Rock and Governor Orval Faubus familiar names throughout the world. Two women played key roles in the struggle against Governor Faubus to desegregate the public schools and keep them open: Daisy Bates and Adolphine Terry. Bates organized the Little Rock Nine, students who volunteered to enroll at formerly all-white Central High School. She helped them face violence from white mobs and persuade President Dwight D. Eisenhower to send in federal troops. White supremacists bombed her home and organized economic reprisals against the newspaper she and her husband ran, but she later reestablished the *Arkansas State Press.* Bates received honorary degrees from at least three universities, including the University of Arkansas, but she didn't get on the wall of the portrait gallery.[1]

Her counterpart in the white community was Adolphine Terry. Despairing of the course taken by Governor Faubus, who suggested closing the schools rather than integrating them, Terry organized the Women's Emergency Committee to Open Our Schools. She helped mobilize enough support that Faubus, not the racial moderates, ended up isolated. Adolphine Terry died in 1976, and she is also forgotten at the portrait gallery.

Unlike Louise Thaden and Bernie Babcock, Bates and Terry may have been omitted not only because of their gender but because they were on "the wrong side." Similarly, the gallery guide's first section, "Territorial Days," leaves out any Native American. No leader of the Caddoes, the Quapaws, or the Osages—they were on the wrong side. The Civil War section is not only all-male but also all-white and all-Confederate! Yet many counties in Arkansas sent more soldiers to the Union Army than to the Confederate side. Arkansas had two governors simultaneously during the Civil War because the United States held part of the state, the Confederate States the rest. Harris Flanagin, "Confederate governor of Arkansas, 1862–65," is on the wall, but not Isaac Murphy, Unionist governor of Arkansas. Murphy had led the Huntsville Female Academy before the war. Elected to the secession convention in 1861 from an area that held few slaves, he voted against the secession ordinance. The convention president asked the five dissenters to change their votes to secure unanimity. All except Murphy acceded to the request. Murphy replied, "I have cast my vote after mature reflection . . . and cannot conscientiously change it." For his independence, he and his family were so persecuted that he fled to Union lines, according to historian Clement

Eaton. After the United States took Little Rock, however, delegates from across the state met on January 8, 1864, to frame a free state constitution. Arkansas voters ratified the result and elected Isaac Murphy governor. Gen. C. C. Andrews, who led Union forces in Arkansas, characterized Murphy as an "incorruptible and enlightened patriot." Although he certainly made Arkansas history, Governor Murphy never got on the walls of the portrait gallery—apparently, he too made history on the wrong side.

Even among Confederates, "right" and "wrong" ideology seems to play a role. Unrepentant Confederates get on the wall no matter how tenuous their Arkansas connection. Confederate William L. Cabell came to Arkansas during the Civil War and left the state in 1872. No matter—he participated in Confederate veteran organizations after the war and gets into the gallery due solely to his Confederate service. James F. Fleming was also a Confederate general and, unlike Cabell, came from Arkansas. He refused to surrender until June 1865, one of the last holdouts, and would seem to be a fine candidate for the portrait gallery. During Reconstruction, however, he became a Republican and favored equal rights for black people; President Grant appointed him U.S. marshal in 1875. Apparently, these activities disqualify him. Even more blatant, the gallery includes portraits of those famous "Arkansans," Jefferson Davis and Robert E. Lee! The history commission includes Lee and Davis as Arkansas heroes not because of what they did in Arkansas—they never did anything—but simply because they led the Confederate States.

The Reconstruction section similarly excludes Republicans and African Americans, which means it must leave out *all* office holders from 1866 through 1876. Undoubtedly the most famous governor in Arkansas history during the nineteenth century *not* to be included is Powell Clayton, who governed during Reconstruction and faced unusual challenges. White Democrats killed more than 200 blacks and white Republicans between July and October 1868. The violence escalated even further as the November 3 election neared, so Clayton raised a predominantly black militia to restore order. The day after the election he declared martial law in the ten counties where Ku Klux Klan night-riding had been most serious. Both white Unionists and African Americans responded to the governor's call and served in separate companies. "Refusing to retreat from assassination threats," wrote historian George C. Rable, "Clayton's courageous declaration of martial law had succeeded in crushing the Klan in Arkansas and setting an example of firmness for other southern governors." Clayton then wrote an important work of history, *Aftermath of the Civil War in Arkansas*. No matter; as a Republican who favored civil rights for African Americans, he does not get on the wall.

The "Twentieth Century" section is weakest of all. Most of its portraits are of people who became famous before World War I, some even before 1900. Perhaps the recent past is too controversial. Before William Jefferson Clinton, Senator J. William Fulbright was probably Arkansas's most prominent leader on the national scene in this century. Fulbright Fellowships are one part of his legacy. He also opposed the Vietnam War before it was politic to do so. H. L. Mitchell helped found the Southern Tenant Farmers Union, probably Arkansas's most famous contribution to labor history, but his passionate analysis of plantation economics might still affront rich landowners. Winthrop Rockefeller was a high-profile Arkansas governor, but his Republican Party membership might offend present-day Democrats. Maya Angelou is Arkansas's best-known author, but she was black and outspoken. The Arkansas History Commission failed to recognize individuals like these who made history. Instead, it honored people who merely recorded history: eight of the twelve citizens it commemorated since World War I were its own staff members and commissioners![2]

I put that last sentence in the past tense because, in 2006, Arkansas removed its portrait gallery from public view. The History Commission has received donations of portraits of Bates and Thaden, as well as other women, but it no longer exists, so they are not on display.

However, in 2019, Arkansas replaced its two statues in the National Portrait Gallery in the U.S. capital, both of white supremacists, choosing country music singer Johnny Cash and, yes, Daisy Bates.

1. John L. Ferguson, a state historian, told me in a phone conversation in February 1997 that Daisy Bates is in the collection. I didn't see her image on the wall and she is not in the guide by Lynn Ewbank. Dr. Ferguson himself wrote to me on February 25, "We have added no items to our portrait gallery since the Lynn Ewbank guide was published." If she is in the gallery, Miss Bates simultaneously gives the collection its only person of color and its only woman known for actually making history.

2. Lynn Ewbank, "The AR History Commission Portrait Gallery" (Little Rock: AR History Commission, distr. 1996); Kenneth Ames, "Anonymous Heroes," *Museum News*, 9/94, 34; Lynn Sherr and Jurate Kazickas, *Susan B. Anthony Slept Here* (NY: Times Books, 1994), 32; Jon L. Wakelyn, *Biographical Dictionary of the Confederacy* (Westport, CT: Greenwood, 1977), 120–21, 182–83, 232; Robert P. Broadwater, *Daughters of the Cause* (Martinsburg, PA: Daisy Publ., 1993), 5; Edward T. James, ed., *Notable American Women, vol. 3* (Cambridge, MA: Harvard UP, 1971), 475–76; Gen. C. C. Andrews, "Narrative of the Third Regiment," in *Minnesota in the Civil and Indian Wars*, 1861–65 (St. Paul, MN: Pioneer Press, 1890); www.genealogy.com/eggertj /genealogy/3rdmn/3rdmn8.html, 12/97; Clement Eaton, *The Freedom of Thought Strug-*

gle in the Old South (NY: Harper, 1964 [1940]), 391–92; George C. Rable, But There Was No Peace (Athens: U. of GA Press, 1984), 105; Peter F. Stevens, The Mayflower Murderer and Other Forgotten Firsts in American History (NY: Morrow, 1993), 232–39; Julienne Crawford, email, 7/2018.

———— ✶ ————

42. Suppressing a Slave Revolt for the Second Time

LOUISIANA *Laplace*

Historical markers and monuments in Louisiana supply a condensed tour of what has gone wrong in black-white race relations in American history—and how whites have lied about it. Four consecutive sites exemplify the problem in successive periods: slavery, Reconstruction, the overthrow of Reconstruction, and segregation.

The historical marker for this south Louisiana town says only,

TOWN OF LAPLACE

Named when a railroad stop was established on the Bazile Laplace plantation in 1883.

No matter how small, most towns in the United States have made headline news at some point in their history. No matter how dull the result, too many markers in America leave out precisely those important stories that captured national headlines. This marker for Laplace achieves perhaps a record in dullness, yet there was a time when the town and its surrounding area made big news.

Laplace is the principal city in St. John the Baptist Parish, where possibly the largest single slave revolt in U.S. history began. State historians in Louisiana know this. A marker at nearby Woodland Plantation reads,

WOODLAND PLANTATION

Acquired in 1793 and 1808 by Manuel Andry, a commandant of the German Coast. Major 1811 slave uprising organized here.

Louisiana records show that the state intended that its marker for Laplace treat the revolt. The state proposed the following text:

LAPLACE

The town of Laplace was named after plantation-owner Bazile Laplace. In this area about 500 slaves participated in an uprising in 1811.

This marker was "never ordered," however, according to a note in state records. Instead, Louisianans put up the shorter "privately funded marker" cleansed of all mention of the slave rebellion.

On January 8, 1811, slaves revolted at the Andry Plantation near Laplace. They killed at least two whites and marched down the river road toward New Orleans, "burning, pillaging, and killing as they went." At every plantation, other slaves joined until they numbered from 180 to 500. They flew flags, marched to the beating of drums, and shouted African chants. The next day, they continued toward the Crescent City, recruiting more support at the Destrehan Plantation, the largest in the area. Just ahead of them, white men and women, warned by a few house slaves or slave drivers, fled toward New Orleans in carts and wagons.

Although armed mainly with pitchforks and other farm implements, on January 9, they stood their ground against an attack by the local white militia. Then at 4 a.m. on January 10, reinforcements in the form of U.S. troops under the authority of Gen. Wade Hampton appeared. The African Americans retreated to the Bernoudy Plantation, upriver from Destrehan, but were nearly out of ammunition. At midmorning, U.S. troops attacked with muskets and cannon. The battle became a massacre; one historian described it as "open season on black people in the vicinity." On January 10, 66 resisters died in the fighting or were summarily executed afterward. "In addition," according to the official report, "the swamps were littered with beaucoup cadavers." By January 11 or 12, whites captured Charles Deslondes and other leaders of the insurrection, although some held out in the swamps until early February.

Thirty recaptured slaves were tried at the Destrehan Plantation, 30 miles above New Orleans. Its owner, Jean Nöel Destrehan, was one of the five presiding magistrates. The judges sentenced 21 to death. Whites shot them, beheaded them, and placed their heads on pikes at various points along the

Mississippi River to serve, in the court's words, "as a terrible public warning to those who would disturb the public tranquility."

The new Louisiana State History Museum (the Cabildo) in New Orleans tells this story. On the site, however, as of 1999, except for the six words in bronze at Woodland Plantation, the landscape was silent about the rebellion. No plaque marked where the battle took place.

One place to tell the story would be the Destrehan Plantation, a popular tourist destination. The plantation displays objects belonging to Jean Nöel Destrehan, but no one at his home in 1999 used the objects or the site to tell about the slave revolt. Destrehan presented a video that told of Jean Nöel's life at some length but never hinted at the slave revolt or his role in its aftermath. Destrehan's brochure also omitted the revolt. The Destrehan website boasted of its architecture, its "fine collection of early to mid-19th century furnishings and decorative arts," and even that the ballroom scene in *Interview with the Vampire* starring Tom Cruise and Brad Pitt was filmed there—but never mentioned the slave revolt. As at most plantation mansions, Destrehan tour guides mentioned slavery as little as possible; "sometimes the institution of slavery is left unmentioned altogether," according to a journalist. Instead, guides expounded on the tableware and furniture. According to Marian Hébert, chief tour guide at Destrehan, paraphrased by the journalist, "some white people don't want to hear about slavery, because it conflicts with their benevolent view of U.S. history, while some black people don't want to hear about it because it leaves them embarrassed, ashamed, or simply angry." Back in 1811, white Louisianans tried to keep blacks from learning about the revolt at Destrehan, lest they get ideas. In 1999, I noted that they were trying to keep tourists from learning about it, lest *they* get ideas about the reality of slavery. But even in 1999, when this book first came out, African Americans were trying to give a more accurate presentation of slavery, including the 1811 revolt. Leon Waters and the African American History Alliance in New Orleans gave talks and organized annual commemorations. In Donaldsonville, 50 miles upriver, Kathe Hambrick organized the River Road African American Museum, "dedicated to the lives, deaths, and contributions of the Africans enslaved along the River Road plantations." Then in 2014, just 25 miles from Destrehan, John Cummings opened Whitney Plantation. Its brochure is titled, simply, "The Story of Slavery." Cummings is white, but he participated in the Civil Rights Movement and never lost his anti-racist idealism. With assistance from Ibrahima Seck, its director of research, Whitney has developed remarkable exhibits, including sculptures of child slaves representing individuals in "the slave narratives," and elderly people interviewed by the Works Progress Administration (WPA) during the Depression. The Whitney Plantation's website has a rich page telling of resistance to slavery, including the 1811 revolt. An art exhibit even includes symbolic black heads on poles.

Immediately, Whitney became a hit. African American tourists became big fans; I have talked with black professionals in Houston who make an annual trek to Whitney. White tourists too proved thirsty for this new (to them) perspective. Nearby plantations have had to change to keep up; tourists now complain, "Aren't you going to tell us anything about the people who worked here?!" Laura Plantation had already exhibited something of the lives of its enslaved and now does more. Even Destrehan has added a small exhibit titled "1811 Slave Revolt." I knew that Americans were ready for more than the tired monologues most plantation homes still provide about their owners and the wallpaper (chapter 69), and now, Whitney has shown the world that we are.[1]

1. Albert Thrasher, *"On to New Orleans!": LA's Heroic 1811 Slave Revolt* (New Orleans, LA: Cypress Press, 1995); Plato Robinson, "LA Slave Revolt," Pacifica Network News, 2/12/97; LA State History Museum (Cabildo), permanent exhibit on LA history (New Orleans: LA State History Museum, 1997); Herbert Aptheker, *Essays in the History of the American Negro* (NY: International, 1964), 35–36; John Wilds, Charles Dufour, and Walter Cowan, *LA Yesterday and Today* (Baton Rouge: LA State UP, 1996), 62; Destrehan Plantation, "Destrehan Plantation Video Script" (Destrehan Plantation, n.d.); River Road African American Museum home page, africanamericanmuseum.org; David Amsden, "A Peculiar Institution," *The New York Times Magazine*, 3/1/2015, 48–53, 57.

———————— ★ ————————

43. Mystifying the Colfax Riot and Lying About Reconstruction

LOUISIANA *Colfax*

During Reconstruction(1866–76), "America tried democracy," as Lerone Bennett put it in *Black Power U.S.A.: The Human Side of Reconstruction*. He goes on to tell how "all over the South, in these years, Negroes and whites shared streetcars, restaurants, hotels, honors, dreams." Indeed, Bennett believes "the right reading of [Reconstruction] might still mark a turning point in our history."

The American landscape conspires to make sure that Americans don't get that reading. Indeed, Reconstruction is almost invisible all across the nation. Guides at antebellum plantations tell nothing about the remarkable changes that took place in the South during that time. Reconstruction governors of Southern states get no statues; few even get historical markers. Instead, monuments, markers, and historic sites across the South commemorate the white racist Democrats who during the 1880s and 1890s reversed the democratic policies that interracial Republican administrations had enacted during Reconstruction.

Colfax has one of the few historical markers that treats Reconstruction, but its text can most charitably be described as outrageous:

COLFAX RIOT

On this site occurred the Colfax Riot in which three white men and 150 Negroes were slain. This event on April 13, 1873, marked the end of carpetbag misrule in the South.

Calling the Republican government of Louisiana "misrule" is ludicrous compared to the racist policies and fiscal scandals of subsequent Democratic officeholders, including the horrifying violence perpetrated by Democrats to end Republican control in the first place. The old tag "carpetbag" implies that Republicans who came to Louisiana from the North were paupers carrying all their belongings in carpetbags, intending to plunder the state. The term is an affront to the whites and blacks, schoolteachers, and government workers who came to Louisiana during Reconstruction to make it better. For that matter, the Colfax Riot *did not* mark the end of Reconstruction in the South. Republican administrations continued in Florida, Mississippi, North Carolina, South Carolina, and even in Louisiana for two to three more years. The riot might be considered the beginning of the end of Reconstruction, however. At any rate, it showed how the end would come.

Colfax (named for Schuyler Colfax), vice president during Ulysses S. Grant's first administration, was the seat of Grant Parish (named for Gen. Grant). How did it come to pass that Louisianans might name a parish (county) and

town after these Republicans so soon after the Civil War? The answer is
that black men were in on the naming. African Americans were voting during Reconstruction, and voting freely. So were white Republicans, a sizable
fraction of the white electorate. Based on "one man, one vote," Republicans
were narrowly in the majority. But developments in Grant Parish indicated
that Democrats were organizing to take away that privilege.

In the 1872 Louisiana elections, two candidates for governor claimed vic-
tory. Each party certified different winners in local Grant Parish elections.
In February 1873, President Grant told Congress that he would recognize
William Kellogg, the Republican, as governor. Kellogg replaced the sheriff and parish judge, already installed by his rival, with two Republicans.
They took office but feared that white Democrats would oust them by force.
Determined not to let that happen, African Americans around Colfax raised
a militia under the command of black veterans, posted pickets at the major
roads, fashioned two makeshift cannons from pipes, and fortified the courthouse against attack. At least 150 black farmers flocked to the town with their
families, seeking safety in numbers. According to historian Eric Foner, "they
held the tiny town for three weeks."

Eventually, white Democrats mobilized superior firepower. On Easter
Sunday, armed with Winchester repeating rifles and a small real cannon and
led by ex-Confederate Capt. C. C. Nash, they overpowered the defenders.
"An indiscriminate slaughter followed," according to Foner. The authors of
a standard Louisiana history provide details:

> After a few blasts from the cannon, the blacks broke. One large
> group ran for the river. Mounted whites gunned them down at
> the water's edge, killing all but one. Riders also chased down and
> shot those attempting to reach the woods, although a few man-
> aged to escape that way. About 60 blacks took shelter in the court-
> house. The attackers torched the roof. When the blaze forced the
> men out, they were cut down by volleys of rifle fire. During the
> fight some 40 blacks . . . were taken prisoner. That night, their
> captors shot them all. Only one, an old man who feigned death
> after bullets struck his back and face, survived.

The Colfax massacre was "the bloodiest single act of carnage in all of
Reconstruction," according to Foner. That is saying a lot, because violence

This engraving of African Americans carrying off one of the people killed in the Colfax Riot to be buried ran in *Harper's Weekly* a month later. White Democrats in Louisiana bragged about the bloodbath; lurid stories of the Colfax massacre "sparked something of a small renaissance in Louisiana tabloid journalism," according to historian James Hogue.

was emblematic of the period. In Louisiana, in just the summer and fall of 1868, white Democrats killed 1,081 persons, mostly blacks and white Republicans. Across the Mississippi state line, whites slew an average of one African American a day in Hinds County alone, especially targeting servicemen. White Democrats mounted similar violent attacks from Virginia to Texas.

The Colfax massacre was also a turning point because it showed the inability or at least the unwillingness of the United States to enforce Reconstruction laws, including the Fourteenth and Fifteenth Amendments. The United States did eventually indict 97 alleged perpetrators for conspiracy to deprive the victims of their civil rights but managed to obtain only three convictions. The Supreme Court overturned even those three, holding that the Fourteenth and Fifteenth Amendments only prohibited violations of black persons' rights by *states*, not by individuals or organizations. Thus, it gave a green light to private terrorism. In the words of James Hogue, "Colfax thus became not only the spark, but also the blueprint for the overthrow of Radical rule."

Democrats promptly formed the "White League," which assassinated Republican officeholders, disrupted court sessions, and drove black families from their homes. In August 1874, Democrats murdered six Republican officials in nearby Coushatta. In September, the White League defeated black militiamen and New Orleans Metropolitan Police in the so-called "Battle of Liberty Place" (chapter 44). During the election of 1876, racists killed white

Republicans in Ouachita, Red River, Caddo, Natchitoches, and East Baton Rouge parishes. All across the state, black Republicans were also targeted. After that election, as part of the deal that made Republican Rutherford B. Hayes president, the United States made clear that its troops would not enforce fair elections, and white Democrats took over Louisiana. Violence continued of course, now with state sanction.[1]

Thus perished what Bennett calls "the first and last real attempt to establish a truly interracial society in the white-obsessed regions of the Western world."[2] Nevertheless, it is vital to understand that Reconstruction was destroyed not because white and black Republicans failed to establish viable governments and an interracial society, but because they were succeeding. That is the truth about Reconstruction, a truth that the Colfax Riot marker takes pains to obscure.

Two blocks away, a marble obelisk is even more blatant. It says,

IN LOVING REMEMBRANCE

Erected to the memory of the heroes,
Stephen Decatur Parish, Jame West Hadnot, Sidney Harris,
who fell in the Colfax Riot fighting for white supremacy
April 13, 1873

As of 2019, neither of these ahistorical expressions of racism has received criticism in Louisiana, so far as I can tell.[3] Nor is there any monument to the approximately 150 African Americans killed, even though Colfax is two-thirds black.[4]

1. In November 1887, the White League, now incorporated into the Louisiana state militia and aided by prominent citizens, shot 35 black sugar cane workers who were striking for a dollar-a-day minimum wage. In 1891, 1896, and 1899, mobs lynched groups of Italian Americans, nineteen in all. In 1896, Louisiana reported 21 lynchings, more than any other state in any single year. The state punished no one for them.

2. Bennett overstates his case. Many mixed-race peoples (chapter 66) and several American Indian nations achieved truly interracial societies. Some later political movements in the nineteenth century such as the Regulators in Virginia and the Republican-Populist coalition in Louisiana also made real attempts. So did the Civil Rights Movement, underway when Bennett wrote.

3. The National Park Service (NPS) has declared that it will devote some attention to the accurate history of Reconstruction between now and 2027, since the sesquicentennial of the era lasts until then. Its Cane River Creole National Historical Park does a much

better job discussing Colfax. Maybe NPS can influence the town to put its marker and monument into a museum as exhibits of white supremacist history.

4. Lerone Bennett, *Black Power U.S.A.: The Human Side of Reconstruction* (NY: Penguin, 1969), 22; Eric Foner, *Reconstruction* (NY: Harper & Row, 1988), 437, 530–31, 550; Robert W. Coakley, *The Role of Federal Military Forces in Domestic Disorders, 1789–1878* (DC: GPO, 1988), 322–24; James K. Hogue, "The 1873 Battle of Colfax" (Princeton: Princeton U. typescript, 1997), 14, 19–20, 30–31; George C. Rable, *But There Was No Peace* (Athens: U. of GA Press, 1984), 126–127; Morgan Kousser, "The Voting Rights Act and the Two Reconstructions" (DC: Brookings Institution, 10/19/90); W. E. B. Du Bois, *Black Reconstruction* (Cleveland, OH: World Meridian, 1964 [1935]), 681; John Wilds, Charles Dufour, and Walter Cowan, *LA Yesterday and Today* (Baton Rouge: LA State UP, 1996), 55, 188; Joel Sipress, *The Triumph of Reaction* (Chapel Hill: U. of NC PhD, 1993); William Ivy Hair, *Carnival of Fury* (Baton Rouge: LA State UP, 1976), 104–105; Mark Potok, "Is This the Nation's Nastiest Monument?" *The Daily Beast*, 8/17/2017, thedailybeast.com/is-this-the-nations-nastiest-monument

---

★

---

44. The White League Begins to Take a Beating

LOUISIANA *New Orleans*

"The Central Theme of Southern History," according to Southern historian U. B. Phillips in a much-quoted article by that title, has been "a common resolve indomitably maintained—that it shall be and remain a white man's country." Not only in the South but all across America (see chapter 15 for example), the landscape perpetuates this mentality by commemorating white racists. In 1891, at the foot of Canal Street in New Orleans, where the business district meets the Mississippi River, the white civic leadership of New Orleans erected the most overtly racist icon to white supremacy in the United States. This monument celebrated the White League in what it called "The Battle of Liberty Place." The monument's checkered history offers something of a barometer showing the relative power of blacks and whites in this part of America, and the importance each group places on control of the landscape.

A chilling battle is enshrined here: an armed insurrection in 1874 against city and state governments. During Reconstruction, a biracial Republican coalition had won election to most state and city offices. The White League, white New Orleans Democrats determined to replace those officials with their own men, had planned their takeover at the elite Boston Club. Their platform made their objective clear: "Having solely in view the maintenance of our hereditary civilization and Christianity menaced by a stupid African-ization, we appeal to the men of our race . . . to unite with us . . . in an earnest effort to re-establish a white man's government in the city and the State."

On the morning of September 14, 1874, thousands of white Demo-crats gathered at the statue of Henry Clay then located in the Canal Street median at St. Charles Street. After incendiary speeches, at four in the after-noon about 8,400 whites attacked 3,000 black members of the state militia, 500 mostly-white members of the metropolitan police, and 100 other local police officers, all under the command of Gen. James Longstreet. Longstreet had been a Confederate general; indeed, he was Lee's senior corps com-mander at Gettysburg. After the war, he came to believe, in accord with the Fourteenth and Fifteenth Amendments, that blacks should have full rights as citizens, including voting rights.

In fifteen minutes, the White Leaguers routed Longstreet's forces and cap-tured him. Eleven metropolitans and their allies were killed and 60 were wounded. Twenty-one White Leaguers were killed, including two bystanders, and nineteen were wounded. White League officials then took charge of all state offices in New Orleans and appealed to President Grant for recognition.

Grant refused to recognize the new group, and a few days later federal troops restored the Republican governor to office. League members had no choice but to vacate the government posts they had seized. However, the "Battle of Liberty Place" was an important event that presaged the end of Reconstruction, which white Democrats accomplished in 1876–77 using similarly violent methods.

In 1882, with the city now under white Democratic control, the median strip at the foot of Canal Street was renamed "Liberty Place." The Orwellian name celebrates the liberty that racist whites had finally seized in 1877 to suppress black voting rights. The City Council passed an ordinance to erect a monument there commemorating the events of September 14, 1874, and for several years on that date, white supremacists paraded through the streets to the site. But crowds dwindled as the "battle" receded in memory, and no monument was erected.

In 1891, another "racial crisis" hit New Orleans. Nineteen Italian immi-grants accused of the 1890 execution-style slaying of the police chief were acquitted. White League veterans called for a mass meeting, and on March 14, a huge crowd gathered again at the Clay monument on Canal

Street. "Not since the 14th day of September 1874 have we seen such a determined looking set of men assembled around this statue," shouted a White
League descendant. "Then you assembled to assert your manhood. I want
to know whether or not you will assert your manhood on the 14th day of
March." The mob responded by marching on the city jail and shooting nine
of the prisoners, dragging two others outside, and hanging them in view of
the crowd. The mass lynching caused an international incident that did not
end until the U.S. government paid Italy an indemnity of about $25,000. It
also reinvigorated the effort by local whites to erect a monument at "Liberty
Place."

That year, an obelisk went up, supported by a shaft and four polished
granite columns, inscribed with the names of sixteen White Leaguers killed
in the original battle and the date, September 14, 1874. No additional text
appeared, perhaps because white Democrats were still wary in 1891 of upset-
ting Northern Republicans, who had recently almost passed a strong voting
rights bill (chapter 81).

In 1932, in a reflection of the further deterioration of black rights, the
monument did acquire an overtly racist text. By then, as the Nadir of race
relations intensified, Louisiana let few African Americans vote, and the
U.S. government was clearly not going to do anything to help them, so
the white supremacist regime was now more secure than in 1891 when the
monument had been erected. Upper-class white citizens of New Orleans
faced a new threat, however: former Louisiana governor and then-U.S. Senator Huey Long seemed to be putting together a coalition of white farmers
and workers, including also those blacks who could vote. Again, the New
Orleans elite appealed to white supremacy, hoping to ward off the threat by
reminding white voters how they closed ranks behind the white elite before.
A commission of white citizens appointed by the mayor added the following
inscription to the White League monument:

> *[Democrats] McEnery and Penn having been elected governor and
> lieutenant-governor by the white people, were duly installed by this
> overthrow of carpetbag government, ousting the usurpers, Governor
> Kellogg (white) and Lieutenant-Governor Antoine (colored). United
> States troops took over the state government and reinstated the usurpers
> but the national election of November 1876 recognized white supremacy
> in the South and gave us our state.*

As segregation began to come under attack after World War II, the landmark was again used as a symbol of intolerance. Disgusted by the civil rights
plank in the now-more-liberal Democratic platform and by President Harry
Truman's desegregation of the armed forces, in 1948, racist Democrats ran
"Dixiecrats" Strom Thurmond of South Carolina for president and Fielding
Wright of Mississippi for vice president (chapter 47). Their supporters rallied
at the obelisk, and they carried the state. After the Supreme Court outlawed
school segregation in 1954, the site was invoked to remind white Louisianans
of what allegedly took place during Reconstruction, the last time the federal government "meddled" in Southern affairs. White supremacists rallied
repeatedly at the monument in the 1950s and 1960s.

By the 1974 centennial of the "Battle of Liberty Place," however, African
Americans again were voting in large numbers in New Orleans, thanks to
the Civil Rights Movement and the 1965 Voting Rights Act. New Orleans
businessmen even hosted the national NAACP meeting that year. Now the
city government felt compelled to add a "counter-marker" next to the original, which read,

> Although the "Battle of Liberty Place" and this monument are
> important parts of New Orleans history, the sentiments in favor of white
> supremacy expressed thereon are contrary to the philosophy and beliefs of
> present-day New Orleans.

Over the 1932 white supremacy language, the city cemented blank marble
slabs.

When I saw the monument in April 1988, however, it was clear that the
continuing battle of Liberty Place was far from resolved, and the "philosophy and beliefs" of New Orleans were still in dispute. Someone, probably
white supremacists, had removed the marble slabs, and the 1932 inscriptions
showed through the thin cement. Someone else had covered its phrases with
handwritten "Black Power" and "Fuck You White People" in yellow spray
paint.

A year later, major street construction on Canal Street gave New Orleans
an excuse to remove the obelisk "for safe keeping." For two years, it languished in a warehouse; then a New Orleans druggist filed suit to force it
back up. His lawsuit led to interesting debates. Supporters of the monument
claimed they weren't racist and were merely good historians, while its detrac-

tors were "revisionists" trying to erase history. The monument's opponents pointed out that knowing about the incident was different from celebrating it. Some politicians proposed what they termed a compromise: instead of reerecting the obelisk at its prominent place at the foot of Canal Street, it would be placed in a "more appropriate location" in a white residential neighborhood—implying that different histories are appropriate for different races and that those white supremacy memorials are okay in white areas.

In February 1993, the city finally reerected the monument at the foot of Iberville Street, only a block from the old location but out of the way behind a parking garage. First, workers obliterated the 1932 lettering. A new inscription honored those "on both sides of the conflict" and concluded vaguely, "A conflict of the past that should teach us lessons for the future."

Despite the tranquil new text, the controversy continued. The druggist

What the landscape says about the past can still arouse strong feelings today. Fifty supporters of the obelisk attended the rededication ceremony in March 1993, while almost as many protesters demonstrated against it. Speakers, including former Ku Klux Klan Grand Wizard David Duke, strained to be heard over demonstrators' shouts and spirituals. A local reporter recorded the event: "Organizers began the ceremony . . . by waving a Confederate flag alongside American and Louisiana flags. That led to shouts of 'Down with white supremacy!' from protesters, who tried to push their way to the monument, but were held back by eight police officers." In this photo, officers grab protester State Representative Avery Alexander in a choke hold; in the background a white woman holds a placard saying "Down With White Supremacy" while a white man on the other side waves a Confederate flag. Afterwards, Duke said, "We may be a minority in this city, but I tell you, we still have rights." Alexander called the monument "a badge of slavery" and said, "it should be removed." In all, one person attending the ceremony and four people protesting it were arrested.

sued to remove the new wording. Vandals tore out the four columns that, along with a central shaft, supported the obelisk. In retaliation, a man representing the "Monument Preservation Army" put white paint on a bust of Martin Luther King Jr. in February 1993. He said he would continue to deface black monuments "until they leave ours alone." Soon after that, African Americans asked the city to remove the White League monument, saying it met the criteria for a "public nuisance." Later that year, the city's Advisory Committee on Human Relations held hearings and found that it did meet those criteria,[1] since it:

- honors those who took part in killing city or state public employees;
- suggests the supremacy of one ethnic, religious, or racial group;
- praises actions wrongfully taken to promote ethnic, religious, or racial supremacy of one group over another;
- has been or may become the site of violent demonstrations that threaten life or property; [and]
- will present an unjustifiable expense to maintain or secure.

David Duke, a self-professed admirer of Adolf Hitler, enlivened one hearing by protesting that the city was using "Nazi tactics" to remove the monument.

Later that summer, the city council ordered the monument removed to a museum. No major museum volunteered to house it, however, and more legal battles loomed immediately. The obelisk still stood at the foot of Iberville Street, and I concluded this essay in 1999 by saying that the second battle of Liberty Place, the battle of the monument, is far from over.

After the neo-Confederate murders of nine African Americans at a church in Charleston, South Carolina in 2015, cities across the United States began questioning not only their Confederate monuments but also other monuments to white supremacy. This obelisk is the most overt of these (along with the monument in Colfax, up the river). Mayor Mitch Landrieu took down all of New Orleans's major Confederate monuments, and this one too, in May 2017. As he did, he gave an eloquent speech, titled simply "Truth," explaining why. It spoke to the simplistic claim that taking down a monument is an attempt to erase the past:

We have not erased history; we are becoming part of the city's history by righting the wrong image these monuments represent

and crafting a better, more complete future for all our children
and for future generations.

At long last, after almost 150 years, the Battle of Liberty Place had ended.[2]

1. It should; the public nuisance ordinance had been written with the monument specifically in mind.

2. Lawrence Powell, "A Concrete Symbol," *Southern Exposure* (spring 1990): 41; John
Wilds, Charles Dufour, and Walter Cowan, *LA Yesterday and Today* (Baton Rouge: LA
State UP, 1996), 57–58, 185–89; Herbert Aptheker, *Afro-American History: The Mod-
ern Era* (NY: Citadel, 1971), 18; "Anniversary of Battle Ending Carpetbag Reign to
Be Marked Wednesday," *Times-Picayune*, 9/11/32; Judith K. Schafer, "The Battle of
Liberty Place," *Cultural Vistas* 5 no. 1 (spring 1994): 9–17; Lawrence Powell, "A Con-
crete Symbol," *Southern Exposure* (spring 1990): 41; Edward J. Cocke, *Monumental New
Orleans* (Jefferson, LA: Hope Publications, 1974), 16–17; Bruce Eggler, "Judge Lets
Liberty Statue Gather Dust in City Storage," *Times-Picayune*, 2/20/92; Kevin Bell,
"Council Takes Step Against Monument," *Times-Picayune*, 4/16/93; Michael Perl-
stein, "5 Arrested at Monument Ceremony," *Times-Picayune*, 3/8/93; Eggler, "Lib-
erty Statue Is Replaced," *Times-Picayune*, 2/11/93; "Rev. King State Spray-Painted
White," *Times-Picayune*, 3/22/93; Susan Finch, "Duke Blasts 'Nazi' Tactics to Remove
Monument," *Times-Picayune*, 6/16/93; Finch, "Liberty: Store Monument, Panel Says,"
Times-Picayune, 7/1/93; Mitch Landrieu, "Truth," *HNN*, 6/4/17, historynewsnetwork
.org/article/166085

————————— ✴ —————————

45. The Toppled "Darky"

LOUISIANA *Baton Rouge*

In the grassy circle in the center of the road as one arrives at the Rural
Life Museum, east of Louisiana State University on Essen Lane, visitors
are welcomed by "a bronze figure of an old Negro—hat in hand, smiling,
with shoulders bent," in the words of the *WPA Guide to Louisiana*. For four
decades, it stood at the corner of Washington and Lafayette Streets in downtown Natchitoches. Long known as "The Good Darky," this monument
raises an important question: what should we do with statues that have outlived their usefulness? Topple and destroy them? Retire them to a museum?
Replace them?—and with what?

Actually, suggesting that "The Good Darky" has "outlived his usefulness"
is far too kind. This statue was, from the start, intended to be useful only to

"The Good Darky" is modeled after a photograph of "the ancient Negro gatekeeper" at Middleton Plantation outside Charleston, South Carolina, that ran in *National Geographic* in 1926. Famed Farm Security Administration photographer Marion Post Wolcott took this photograph in Natchitoches during the Depression, along with a series of "white" and "colored" signs across the United States.

the cause of white supremacy. S. R. Cunningham, founder and editor of the magazine *The Confederate Veteran*, floated the proposal in 1894:

> It seems opportune now to erect monuments to the Negro race of the war period. . . . What figure would be looked upon with kindlier memory than old "Uncle Pete" and "Black Mammy," well executed in bronze? By general cooperation models of the two might be procured and duplicates made to go in every capital city in the South. . . . There is not of record in history subordination and faithful devotion by any race of people comparable to the slaves of the Southern people during our great four years' war for independence.

In Louisiana his idea was carried out. The inscription reads, "Erected by the City of Natchitoches in Grateful Recognition of the Arduous and Faithful Service of the Good Darkies of Louisiana. Donor, J. L. Bryan, 1927." At its dedication, the Natchitoches Rotary Club adopted a resolution connecting the statue with slavery:

Resolved, that the faithful and devoted service rendered by the
old Southern slaves, in working and making crops and taking
care of the [white] women and children, while their masters were
away for many years, fighting to keep them in slavery, has never
been equaled. . . . Those who are old enough to remember . . . can
tell you how the slaves remained at home and took care of everything, and worked and made crops as they had always done. . . .

In reality, during the Civil War, many African Americans in Louisiana
flocked to New Orleans after the Union took the city. After Confederates
rejected them, the Louisiana Native Guards became the first black troops
to fight for the United States in the Civil War, and they were virtually the
only black soldiers to serve under African American officers. In all, more
than 180,000 African Americans, most of them slaves when the war broke
out, served in the U.S. Army during the Civil War, including more from
Louisiana than from any other state. A considerable number came from the
Natchitoches area. However, these African Americans are left off every Civil
War monument in the state, which commemorate only those Louisianans
who fought for the Confederacy.

Many African Americans did stay put until freedom came, of course, some
faithfully, others watchfully, aware of the dangers of flight. Emphasizing
those who remained faithfully on the plantation during the Civil War was
another way for white Louisianans to keep African Americans in their place
in the 1920s and convince themselves that blacks preferred it that way. The
function of "The Good Darky" was to commemorate, symbolize, and help
maintain white supremacy, particularly that rigid form of racial subordination known as segregation. As historian Gaines Foster put it, portrayals of
"good slaves" and "faithful blacks" were "intended to teach the 'new Negro'
born since slavery how to behave."

Right after the Civil War, African Americans had behaved as citizens—
they voted, served on juries, and ran for and sometimes won public office.
Their citizenship in Natchitoches stopped with the end of Reconstruction.
During the next election, in 1878, a white mob "herded the colored people
together and made them vote contrary to their wishes," according to a report
made later to the Louisiana Colored Citizens' Convention. As he left the
polls, each African American was given a badge, "Voted the Democratic
Ticket," which protected him and his family from the "ruthless mobocrats

patrolling the streets" of Natchitoches. In 1890, the overwhelmingly Democratic legislature passed a law requiring segregation on railroads and streetcars. Segregation in Natchitoches forced appalling inequalities on African Americans—"Separate but equal" never meant equal. In 1927, when whites erected "The Good Darky" in Natchitoches, black children were attending vastly overcrowded, crudely built schools for shorter school terms under less-educated teachers than white children. But at least they had schools. Natchitoches had just one hospital, which served only whites.

The era of segregation might be demarcated legally as 1890 through 1954, although it lingered through 1969. "The Good Darky" was emblematic of that era. People who did not themselves experience racial segregation have difficulty understanding its staying power. Segregation was a system of norms that dictated every aspect of human behavior from how one drove to whether one shook hands to how one person glanced at another when the two were of different races. In those years, blacks did not look whites squarely in the eye. Blacks called whites "Mr.," "Mrs.," "sir," and "ma'am." In return, whites called blacks by their first name, "boy," and "gal." Even when the African American was far senior in years and accomplishment, the European American was not to use "sir" or "ma'am." Whites who did not know blacks' first names might substitute "perfessor" or "auntie."[1]

At first, the rules of segregation seem confusing. A white housewife might be horrified at the idea of a black butcher—"putting his hands on the meat my children are going to put in their mouths"—yet employ a black cook whose hands were the last to touch that same dish. Whites kept blacks separate only when they did the same task as whites, such as learning arithmetic in second grade or working as a butcher alongside white butchers. When the situation was intrinsically hierarchical, blacks could come as close as a cook or even a wet nurse in a white household. Thus, segregation was an etiquette system whose purpose was always to imply that blacks were inferior to whites. And there were no passive onlookers. Everyone who sat on a bus, for example, had to sit in the white section or the black section. Thus, everyone was required to participate.

In 1963, "everyone" included me. I, a white undergraduate sociology major, went to Starkville, Mississippi, in January of that year, to see a section of the United States I had never experienced. On the campus of Mississippi State University, I had a classic "good darky" encounter. That spring, Mississippi State was in its last semester as a segregated all-white institution. Besides janitors, the only African Americans on campus were two families whose houses were at the rural edge of the campus and who walked through it to get home. I was walking toward my residence hall, a new dormitory set on the raw clay soil of east Mississippi. A path through the clay afforded a short-cut, but one had to stay on the compacted path to avoid the reddish muck on either side. Some distance in front of me trudged an elderly black man, not large, and stooped over like the "good darky." Probably he wasn't 60, but he seemed older and walked slowly. Then he heard my footsteps. Looking back and seeing that I was white, at once he moved to his right and trudged along in the mud, that I might pass.

At first, I walked more slowly, hoping he would understand that I didn't mean to pass, but I saw that he would walk beside the path forever if I didn't proceed. Then I hastened to get by. As I passed him I wanted to say, "You don't understand, you didn't have to do that for *me*." I knew that no brief conversation could suffice to prove me trustworthy for real interchange, however, so I just said, "Nasty weather we've been having." He agreed and laughed, and I walked on ahead.

Although the North was segregated too, the formal segregation in Dixie was qualitatively different. Because it was sanctioned by law, those who broke a segregation taboo in the South could be punished by the law, or by anyone, with the full authorization of the white community. Ultimately, Southern segregation rested on legal and extralegal terror. I saw the extralegal terror firsthand; inadvertently, I even caused it. As part of my informal research in Mississippi, I visited the office of the area's only black physician. He was also the head of the Starkville NAACP. As I stepped toward the reception window in the small waiting room to learn when I might talk with him, a black woman waiting to see the doctor cautioned her toddler daughter, playing with blocks on the floor, to "*Come here*," away from my path. The strained urgency in her voice bespoke the gravity of the situation, and I realized she was getting her daughter out of harm's way. I was the harm. The fear in her voice and the tension in her body told me that she didn't know what I might do. She did know that she would have no real recourse if, for any reason, we had an altercation.[2]

Although I am white, when I violated segregation rules I too felt anxious about the possibility of a violent white response. At the end of my college term in Mississippi, when I took the train home, I had to decide whether to buy my ticket at the "white" or the "black" side of the Illinois Central station. The ticket office was in the middle, so the (sole) clerk could wait on either side. Not wanting to be complicit in maintaining the system, I chose the black side. Externally, all I had to put up with was the clerk's waiting on all other white customers first, on the white side, of course, then glaring at me as he sold me the ticket. Internally, as I sat quietly in the black waiting room, I also had to endure twenty minutes of uncertainty, not quite knowing if the police would come to haul me away for sitting there.[3]

Today's reader may conclude that I have overinterpreted these segregation incidents—the old man just didn't want to delay me, the young mother was merely concerned that her daughter act politely. I can reply only that every adult who lived in the segregated South knew the terror on which segregation rested. All over the South, from about 1890 to 1970, African Americans faced the possibility of a harsh white response if they violated segregation rules, weren't sufficiently obsequious, or simply were too successful. Daniel Russell, ex-governor of North Carolina, made this clear in 1904: "The Negro who gets very prosperous is to be pitied, for straightway he is in a situation where danger confronts him. Let him own a fine farm, blooded horses and cattle, and dare to ride in a carriage, and if I were an insurance agent I would not make out a policy on his life. In plain English, to get above his ordained situation in life is, generally speaking, to invite assassination." Three parishes near Natchitoches—Ouachita, Caddo, and Bossier—led all other counties in the United States in assassinations (recorded lynchings).[4] That's why "The Good Darky" bows his head; ultimately, he doesn't want to be killed.

"From the end of Reconstruction well into the second half of the twentieth century, white Louisiana devoted incalculable effort to keeping blacks intimidated, submissive, and 'in their place,'" note the authors of *Louisiana Yesterday and Today*. "Few relics of the period express its prevailing atmosphere as clearly as this statue." Whites needed to convince themselves not only that it was somehow equitable to keep blacks out of hospitals, hotels, and jury boxes, but also that African Americans *liked* it that way and *deserved* the discrimination they received. Then European Americans could tell themselves that they had only positive feelings for the African Americans they mistreated. "The Good Darky" statue does all these things. His smiling, obsequious pose, bent over but happy, presents no threat and implies he is content to be inferior. As John Dollard wrote in *Caste and Class in a Southern Town*, blacks had to go beyond mere compliance: "they must be actively obliging and submissive." Or as poet Paul Lawrence Dunbar put it in 1896, "We wear the mask that grins and lies." Thus, the servile pose of the statue was no myth but a rational response by African Americans to an untenable situation. The response, like the statue, was nevertheless a white creation.

A 1927 article in *The New York Times* about "The Good Darky" statue employed the nouns of address used under segregation: "Many white people in the parish have been nursed or served by the old-time 'uncles' and 'aunties,' and a warm regard remains on each side." The white community in Louisiana even came to call the statue "Uncle Jack." Meanwhile, blacks who chafed at the bigotry implied by the unequal nouns of address camouflaged their frustration with "warm regard"—sometimes genuine, sometimes feigned.

"The Good Darky" entry in the *WPA Guide to Louisiana*, which I quoted at the beginning of this essay, went on to include a legend about the statue that took root in the white community within a few years of its erection. The anecdote manifested the same affable contempt that whites meant the monument itself to convey: "Plantation Negroes, inebriated after a spree in town, go to the statue to ask the way home and the Good Darkey never fails to tell them the right direction." The tale amused whites and helped convince them that blacks like "Uncle Jack" hardly deserved equal rights.

By the late 1960s, owing to the Civil Rights Movement, segregation was on its last legs and "The Good Darky" was losing its social power to stay in Natchitoches. In 1968, it "ended up in the nearby Cane River," according to the authors of *Louisiana Yesterday and Today*. Its toppling signified an end to the fawning servility that the statue symbolized. Rescued from the river, for several years "The Good Darky" languished in storage. Finally, Mr. Bryan's daughter donated a new base for it at the Rural Life Museum.

Americans rejoiced when Poles and East Germans toppled their statues of Lenin. Within our shores, however, we are not so sure. When statues become controversial, such as the White League memorial treated in the previous chapter, civic leaders sometimes suggest that they be carted off to a museum. The statue of "The Good Darky" shows what can go wrong with that solution. Although run by a university, the Rural Life Museum has not used "The Good Darky" to "provide insight into the largely forgotten lifestyles and cultures of pre-industrial Louisiana," the museum's avowed purpose. Instead, it situated the statue in a place of honor. No plaque gives any information about its history or symbolic meaning, and on the layout of the museum given to every visitor, it is identified by the familiar segregationist form of address, "Uncle Jack." In 2015, historian Nick Sacco visited the museum and concluded that my indictment of its treatment of "The Good Darky" was still valid. On its website, the museum threw up its hands, hoping someone else would come along to fix the problem: "In the future [it] is hoped that an accurate interpretation of the statue will be revealed not only to our visitors but also to ourselves."[5]

1. In *A Country of Strangers* (NY: Knopf, 1997), 419, David Shipler tells how blacks were still sometimes denied courtesy terms in the late 1990s.

2. In *Let Us Now Praise Famous Men* (Boston: Houghton Mifflin, 1969 [1941]), 39–41, James Agee described a similar encounter: running after a young black couple in Alabama to ask them something, he realized he had inadvertently terrified them. Like me, Agee had no intention of causing distress, yet was powerless to explain.

3. Segregation bred fear in white Southerners too, especially among white women—fear of black males.

4. No Louisiana marker hints at any of this.

5. S. R. Cunningham, editorial, *Confederate Veteran* 2 (1894): 336; Marion Post Wolcott, "The Keeper of the Outer Gate," photograph, *National Geographic* (5/26): 529; *The Civil War Book of Lists* (Conshohocken, PA: Combined Books, 1993), 28; Gaines Foster, *Ghosts of the Confederacy* (NY: Oxford UP, 1987), 194; Patricia Storace, "The Scripture of Utopia," *The New York Review of Books*, 6/11/98: 64; Leon Litwack, *Trouble in Mind* (NY: Knopf, 1998), 150; John Wilds, Charles Dufour, and Walter Cowan, *LA Yesterday and Today* (Baton Rouge: LA State UP, 1996), 65–68; "Old Time Slaves Honored by Club," *Natchitoches Enterprise*, 5/28/27; "Memorial to 'the Good Old Darkies,'" reprinted from *Dallas Journal* in *Natchitoches Enterprise*, 8/31/27; *The Shreveport Times*, 8/31/27; *WPA Guide to LA* (NY: Hastings House, 1941), 310; E. Franklin Frazier, *The Negro in the United States* (NY: Macmillan, 1949 [1957]), 669; Genevieve Fabre and Robert O'Meally, *History and Memory in African-American Culture* (NY: Oxford UP, 1994), 160; Stephen J. Whitfield, *A Death in the Delta* (NY: Free Press, 1988), 18; John Dollard, *Caste and Class in a Southern Town* (Garden City, NY: Doubleday, 1949), 185; Paul Lawrence Dunbar, "We Wear the Mask," in (*inter alia*) Joan R. Sherman, ed., *African-American Poetry of the 19th Century* (Urbana: U. of IL Press, 1992), 402; Nick Sacco, "Louisiana's 'Uncle Jack' Statue and the Problem of Interpreting Iconography in History Museums," *Exploring the Past*, 10/1/2015, pastexplore.wordpress.com/2015/10/01/louisianas-uncle-jack-statue-and-the-problem-of-interpreting-iconography-in-history-museums

---

★

---

46. Let Us Now Praise Famous Thieves

LOUISIANA *Fort Jackson*

Fort Jackson, which guarded the river entrance to New Orleans and was the site of an egregious Confederate defeat in 1862, is securely back in Confederate hands today. Three large bronze markers on the brick arch over its entryway venerate the most reactionary neo-Confederate of them all, Leander Perez. The plaques honor him not only for his efforts to restore the fort, but also for his "dedicated service to the people of Plaquemines Parish, the State, and Nation, all marked by unsurpassed courage and fortitude." Perez was indeed a figure of state and even national significance. Few citizens of Plaquemines Parish would use words like "statesman," "friend," and "dedicated service" to describe him, however—not if they knew much about his career.

Leander Perez ran Plaquemines Parish from 1919, when he was first appointed district judge, to his death in 1969. During most of those 50 years, he ruled adjoining St. Bernard Parish as well. He died at the peak of his power and passed his throne on to his sons. Although an intensely local man with no ambition to become governor or senator, Perez acquired a national reputation in the early 1960s.

According to his biographer Glen Jeansonne, Perez was the closest thing the United States had to a local dictator. He didn't bother having his parish council pass laws, he simply drew them up and put them in the minutes! "He concluded that honest elections were more trouble than they were worth and made sure none was held in his bailiwick." He didn't bother with believability either: his rolls of fake voters included names like Babe Ruth, Herbert Hoover, and Charlie Chaplin! In one precinct, his clerks recorded voters as having voted in alphabetical order! His candidates often won more than 90% of all votes cast; sometimes, Perez kept opponents from even getting on the ballot. He sent "large tough individuals" into the booths to "help" voters vote, and he even testified that he paid voters $2, $5, and $10 to vote his way depending on who they were. He paid no African Americans, however. "Most Negroes are just not equipped to vote," he claimed. "If the Negroes took over the government we would have a repetition here of what's going on in the Congo."

During the 1950s and 1960s, Leander Perez became Louisiana's most famous opponent of the Civil Rights Movement. He said of African Americans, "Do you know what the Negro is? Animals right out of the jungle. Passion. Welfare. Easy life. That's the Negro." The Civil Rights Movement can be traced, he declared, "back to all those Jews who were supposed to have been cremated at Buchenwald and Dachau but weren't, and Roosevelt allowed two million of them illegal entry into our country."[1] He forged an alliance with Strom Thurmond, George Wallace, Ross Barnett, and other segregationists across the South. He then guided Louisiana's resistance to school desegregation and equal rights so effectively that in the decade after the 1954 school desegregation decision, Louisiana enacted 131 anti-desegregation laws, far more than any other state.

Perez ruled Plaquemines so severely that civil rights workers often literally could not get into the county. Plaquemines Parish, with about 25,000 residents, is cut by bayous and tributaries of the Mississippi. At several points, ferries run by the county provided the only links across these streams. Ferry crews under Perez simply refused to carry civil rights workers and other outsiders who had unacceptable explanations for wanting to visit Plaquemines.

A charter member of the [White] Citizens' Council, the racist organization started in Mississippi to maintain segregation, he helped organize by far the largest local council in the United States, the Citizens' Council of Greater New Orleans, which had 50,000 members at its peak. His patronage kept the movement going in Louisiana after interest began to dwindle in the early 1960s. When school desegregation came to New Orleans in the fall of 1960, Perez played a key role in its opposition as he led protestors from Plaquemines Parish to a rally in the Crescent City. "Don't wait for your daughter to be raped by these Congolese," he shouted. "Don't wait until the burrheads are forced into your schools. Do something about it now." The next morning, November 16, 2,000 whites stormed the school board buildings, but policemen with fire hoses contained them. So they roamed the city throwing rocks at blacks in cars and buses. When the schools opened anyway, Perez helped organize whites to boycott them. Racists attacked white parents whose children attended desegregated schools, throwing rocks through their windows every night, slashing their tires, and firing them from their jobs. Volunteers who drove the white children to school were threatened with death, arson, and disfigurement. Perez personally arranged for white children to attend an all-white school in St. Bernard Parish without charge, so their parents couldn't claim poverty as an excuse for sending them to school with black students. Then he helped finance a private school in New Orleans for white children.

Eventually, desegregation reached even Plaquemines Parish. The parochial school for whites at Buras took in a handful of African American children. Leander Perez led what became bitter opposition. Parents who kept their children in school were fired from their jobs. Finally, all parents withdrew their children, and the Catholic Church kept the school open with *no* students for 249 days as a symbolic gesture. In the fall of 1963, arsonists torched the school, and it never reopened. The Catholic Church excommunicated Perez for his opposition to desegregation. Undaunted, Perez continued to oppose Catholic desegregation policies and attend mass; the Church was "being used as a front for clever Jews," he claimed.

His extreme racism, rather than disqualifying him for a marker or monument in his honor, seems to provide the basis for it. One plaque at Fort Jackson even displays the crossed Confederate and U.S. flags that the White Citizens Council used as its symbol and praises him in Citizen Council language: "This arch dedicated to Judge L. H. Perez by the people of Plaquemines Parish in appreciation of his leadership in restoring Fort Jackson and for his efforts to preserve our liberties, freedoms, and way of life." "Our way of life" was a code phrase for segregation.

Formal segregation has ended, but the Perez legacy lives on in Plaquemines Parish: the median black income is just 40% of the median white income, one of the lowest ratios in the United States. The median white income is nothing to brag about, and this too is partly Perez's doing. It turns out that he was also dishonest, according to Jeansonne. In 1936, he came up with a scheme to rake in millions of dollars for himself and his family. At the time, as district attorney, he used his position as legal adviser to the Plaquemines levee boards to negotiate payoffs between corporations he set up and the big oil companies that leased the levee board lands for drilling. After his death in 1969, when his grip on the area finally relaxed, the parish sued his heirs, seeking to reclaim an estimated $82,000,000 paid wrongfully to the Perez family. The paper trail set up by Perez was tough to follow, however, and in 1987, the parish settled for $12,000,000.

Although Plaquemines Parish runs Fort Jackson, Fort Jackson honors Leander Perez still; its bronze markers are unsurpassed in effrontery and misrepresentation. The fort *should* recognize Perez's importance not only in restoring the fort but also in the life of the parish. An accurate plaque might say:

LEANDER PEREZ

District attorney, judge, and president of Plaquemines Parish Council. A proponent of white supremacy, he helped keep public schools in the parish and the state segregated and unequal until court orders forced their desegregation; then he favored all-white private schools. He blighted the lives of African Americans in the parish by keeping them from voting and enjoying equal rights. He worked for the preservation and restoration of this fort. However, he made this task more difficult by diverting millions of dollars from parish governments to himself in secret land rights deals between 1936 and his death in 1969.[2]

1. Actually, to Roosevelt's shame, the government allowed just 20,000 Jewish refugees into the United States each year, or 185,000 from 1937 to the end of the war.
2. Glen Jeansonne, *Leander Perez* (Lafayette: Center for LA Studies, 1995), xiii–xxiii, 105–108, 226–70, 399; John Wilds, Charles Dufour, and Walter Cowan, *LA Yesterday and Today* (Baton Rouge: LA State UP, 1996), 44 et passim; U.S. Holocaust Memorial Museum, staff conversation, 4/7/99. As of 2018, according to a spokesman for the parish, the plaques were in storage, because Hurricane Katrina damaged them; then Hurricane Isaac damaged the fort, causing it to close to the public. The parish intends to reopen the fort to the public as a museum and to display the plaques again at that time. Unless they surround them with labels showing how wrong they are, this idea bodes ill for accurate history and for social justice.

---⋆---

47. A Black College Celebrates White Racists

MISSISSIPPI *Itta Bena*

College dormitories and classroom buildings are usually named for people, but most students who live and study within their walls have no idea who those people were, what they did, or what principles they embodied. Some buildings are named for major benefactors, but others are named for people who, in the minds of those who control the schools, exemplify ideals to which students and professors should aspire. Unfortunately, all too often these principles are shameful.

The buildings at Mississippi Valley State University (MVSU) resemble the one- and two-story elementary schools thrown up quickly in the 1950s as school districts struggled to cope with the baby boom. MVSU opened in 1950, timed to contain the educational aspirations of blacks in the Mississippi Delta in anticipation of the 1954 U.S. Supreme Court decision outlawing school segregation. The Delta, the prehistoric floodplain of the Mississippi and Yazoo rivers, stretches almost from Memphis to Vicksburg and at its widest point extends from Greenville on the Mississippi to Carroll County east of Greenwood. Almost perfectly flat, the Delta contains some of the richest farmland in America. Following a pattern that has prevailed in the South since slavery, African Americans have comprised most of the people who live on, but do not own, this rich soil. White supremacists hoped these African Americans would not want to attend the predominantly white University of Mississippi, just 70 miles to the northeast, or Delta State, less than 30 miles to the northwest, if they had "their own school."

Part of the college's problem is location. MVSU was first proposed to be in Greenwood, whose 20,000 people made it a relatively large city in the Mississippi Delta. White business leaders in Greenwood worried about having so many young African Americans in their town, so the state proposed to put the school in little Itta Bena, some eight miles "out from" Greenwood. Amazingly, although Itta Bena's business district was already dying, its leaders too didn't want the college in their town, so it ended up a mile or so "out from" Itta Bena. The school was located on "buckshot land," so called because it doesn't drain well, hence wasn't good cotton land, hence was inexpensive.

White politicians never intended for MVSU to compete with Ole Miss intellectually. The V in its name didn't always stand for Valley—originally MVC meant Mississippi Vocational College. "Moderate" white supremacists in the state used "vocational" as a sweetener to persuade more extreme racist legislators to swallow the idea of another college for African Americans. Vocational training could even be construed as a prudent investment, preparing African Americans for low-level positions, especially since cotton plantations were mechanizing, so planters no longer needed a huge reserve of underemployed impoverished workers to hire at chopping and picking times. And no white leader wanted blacks applying to the state's white colleges and universities.

Throughout MVSU's history, its administrators have had to walk a narrow and tortuous line. If they tried to do a good job—to build an institution that truly served the needs of the Delta, one of the neediest areas in the United States—they would only incur the wrath of the Board of Institutions of Higher Learning and the white politicians who appointed it. MVSU's first president, J. H. White, an African American, grasped the situation. He assured the white power structure that he would never let his students rock their boat and symbolized his servility by naming the college's two most prominent buildings for two of the most racist white political leaders in Mississippi's history: Walter Sillers Jr. and Fielding Wright.

Sillers's family owned cotton plantations near the Mississippi River. His father was one of the Red Shirts, Ku Klux Klan clones who armed themselves and intimidated African American voters to end Reconstruction in 1876. The younger Sillers was elected to the Mississippi House in 1916 and became speaker in 1944. Throughout his long tenure as speaker of the house, perhaps the most powerful single position in Mississippi, no one can remember him sponsoring any progressive initiatives. He opposed compulsory school attendance, for example, because blacks stayed out of school more than whites, which saved the state money.

Fielding Wright was another wealthy planter from the Delta. Governor of Mississippi from 1946 to 1952—years which saw the founding of MVSU—he grew outraged in 1947 because President Harry Truman proposed a civil rights bill. "Promotion of such measures constitutes a greater menace to the nation" than communism, he fumed. Early the next year he convened a meeting of white Democrats from ten Southern states. They agreed that unless the national Democratic Party turned its back on civil rights, they would walk out of the 1948 national convention. When the convention passed a civil rights plank, Wright led a walkout of the Mississippi delegation, joined by half of the Alabama delegates. Later, racist Democrats from across the South met to nominate Strom Thurmond of South Carolina for president and Wright for vice president on what became known as the Dixiecrat ticket. They didn't expect to win but hoped to carry enough states to throw the election into the House of Representatives.

Thurmond and Wright won nearly 88% of the votes in Mississippi in 1948, because most blacks were not allowed to vote and most whites were racial extremists. Truman won reelection, however, and most Dixiecrats later joined the Republican party. Despite Wright's white supremacist career, decades after his death, Fielding Wright Hall remains one of the two largest buildings on the MVSU campus. It honors a man who gave this advice to black Mississippians seeking integration: "If any of you have become so deluded as to want to enter our hotels and cafes, enjoy social equality with whites, then kindness and true sympathy requires me to advise you to make your home in some state other than Mississippi."

University president White agreed with Governor White. After the 1954 decision requiring school desegregation, Mississippi Governor Hugh White convened 90 African Americans from across the state and asked them to support a voluntary segregation plan. He was shocked when several black leaders spoke in favor of abolishing segregation. MVSU president White was one of only two African Americans at the meeting to support the governor's plan. In accord with state policy, he hired only black faculty members and allowed only black students to attend MVSU. When an African American named Clyde Kennard dared apply to a white state university, President White even tried to talk him out of it.[1]

In February 1970, students at MVSU revolted against President White's regime in the name of academic excellence. They boycotted classes to protest White's repressive campus regulations and demanded a better library, better facilities, and a better faculty. To halt the demonstrations, police arrested more than 900 students—about half the student body—probably the largest mass arrest in the history of American higher education.[2] MVSU's neglect of its library during President White's tenure was the foremost reason the school went unaccredited for decades. Despite these problems, in 1973, MVSU named it the J. H. White Library.

A majority black institution honoring men like Sillers and Wright by naming buildings after them might be excused in view of the desperate political circumstances under which it operated in the 1950s. For the college to retain these names and White's well into the next millennium, however, shows an absence of leadership or historical knowledge or both. MVSU has never labeled a single building after an African American whose name would be recognized off campus. No Medgar Evers Hall, even though the NAACP leader slain in 1963 lived for years just 25 miles northwest of MVSU. No Fannie Lou Hamer Hall, even though the famed civil rights pioneer lived less than twenty miles from the college. No B. B. King Hall of Music, even though the popular bluesman grew up almost within shouting distance of the campus. And no Blanche K. Bruce Hall of Political Science, to honor the first African American to serve a full term in the U.S. Senate, even though Bruce lived in the same nearby Delta county as Walter Sillers.

This problem is not unique to MVSU. All across America, institutions of higher learning honor people whose lives, described candidly, would warrant contempt. The University of North Carolina (Chapel Hill) commemorates Cornelia Phillips Spencer. During Reconstruction, Spencer helped foment a boycott of the university by white students lest it be integrated. After staying open for a mere handful of students for two years, the university finally closed. Ironically, Spencer then gets credited for "preserving" the institution, partly because she celebrated its white-only reopening by ringing the campus bell. UNC named its first women's dormitory Spencer Hall. It also named Saunders Hall for William L. Saunders in 1922. Saunders spent much of his last twelve years collecting and publishing records of North Carolina from the colonial period. He was better known, however, as the statewide leader of the Ku Klux Klan during Reconstruction and also founded a nativist anti-immigrant society.

Way back in 1988, the University of Oklahoma showed that colleges can do better. DeBarr Hall of Chemistry was named for Edwin DeBarr, its first professor of chemistry, who was also a statewide KKK leader. The University might have stonewalled. After all, DeBarr had served longer than any other member of the original faculty. Or it could quietly have renamed the building; over time, no one would recall that DeBarr had ever graced or disgraced the campus. Instead, the University renamed the hall "Chemistry Building" and put up a marker to tell why. The marker explains that the building "was originally named DeBarr Hall." The plaque goes on to tell that DeBarr chaired the chemistry department for 31 years. It concludes, "The strong campus reaction to the revelation that DeBarr had been involved with the Ku Klux Klan led to the removal of his name from the building." Thus, Oklahoma, unlike MVSU and Chapel Hill, used the issue of a problematic name to educate.

After a white supremacist professing a neo-Confederate ideology murdered nine African Americans in Charleston, South Carolina, in 2015, more colleges began to question the names and statues on their campuses. Yale University had a dormitory ("college") named for America's prime defender of slavery and secession, John C. Calhoun. After a surprisingly difficult series of discussions and actions, led by students with help from some alumni, the name changed. Princeton has had a still harder time wrestling with Woodrow Wilson. As the University's president, he kept Princeton white, and when he went on to the White House, he segregated the federal government. Students asked that his name come off a dormitory and the School of Public and International Affairs, and some thought a compromise might change the first while leaving the latter. As of 2018, however, Princeton had changed neither.

Across the eastern half of the nation, north as well as south, other colleges have begun wrestling with their support for slavery and their use of slave labor. Georgetown University renamed two buildings on campus that were named for university presidents who had sold slaves to pay off campus debts. All across the nation, buildings named for arrant racists now face scrutiny. The student union at the University of Minnesota, for example, is named for President L. D. Coffman, who between 1920 and 1938, during the Nadir of race relations, excluded African Americans from college dormitories. In 2018, the student government came out unanimously to remove his name. Dunn Hall at the University of Oregon was named for a classics professor who was also the statewide leader of the Ku Klux Klan in Oregon, one of five states briefly dominated by the KKK. His name came down in 2016.

Opponents of change invoke two main arguments: "erasing history" and "slippery slope." Of course, a building's name tells almost no history, merely that Frederick Dunn (or whoever) was great and we should honor him. If Oregon, like Oklahoma, puts up a plaque explaining what Dunn did, why and when he was honored, and why and when the school then removed the honor, that tells far more history.

The slippery slope claim is, "Once you remove the statue of Robert E. Lee, say, from the University of Texas (UT), where do you stop? What about Washington? He owned slaves too, didn't he? Why doesn't Washington College take his statue down on their main campus?" The answer to that line is simply to ask, "Why do we honor him?" Do we honor Washington *because* he owned slaves? Surely not. Surely we honor him because he held the army together during a long and difficult war, helped hold the nation together during its early years, and then set an important and generous precedent by relinquishing power after eight years.[3] Lee is quite another matter. His statue was on the UT campus not for his service in our Mexican War, nor for any other accomplishment other than leading the Confederate army as it committed treason on behalf of slavery and white supremacy. That's also why sculptures of Confederate president Jefferson Davis, Confederate general Albert Sidney Johnston, and Confederate postmaster John Reagon were on the campus. All of them now have come down.

Walter Sillers Jr. and Fielding Wright were similarly identified with white supremacy throughout their political careers. Surely, it's time for a black college to choose other Americans to honor.[4]

The next chapter shows another site in need of renaming.

1. To eliminate him as a threat to the segregated system, Kennard was framed for a theft he did not commit and sent to Parchman Penitentiary. There, he contracted stomach cancer, was denied medical attention, and was finally released to die in a Chicago hospital.

2. Like most other examples of civil disobedience, this protest and these arrests go unmarked on the landscape.

3. For the record, he did wrestle with slavery and set in motion freedom for his household's slaves after his wife's death.

4. Loewen, testimony in *Ayers v. Fordice* (U.S. Dist. Ct., N. Dist. [#4:75CV009-B-D]), 6/7/94, 5101, 5127–28; Frank Smith, conversation, 1993; V. O. Key Jr., *Southern Politics in State and Nation* (NY: Random House, 1949), 334; Loewen and Charles Sallis, eds., *MS: Conflict and Change* (NY: Pantheon, 1980), 252; Erle Johnston, *Politics: MS Style* (Forest, MS: Lake Harbor Publishers, 1993), 94; Anthony W. James, "A Demand for Racial Equality: The 1970 Black Student Protest at the U. of MS," *Journal of MS History* 57 no. 2 (summer 1995): 101; John Dittmer, *Local People* (Urbana: U. of IL Press, 1994), 27–28; Armand Derfner, conversation, 1/19/99; Loewen, "Ten Questions for Yale President Peter Salovey," *Chronicle of Higher Education* (6/10/2016): B11–13; Ashley F. G. Norwood. "As Ayers Settlement Winds Down, Anxiety Escalates at Universities," *Mississippi Today*, 9/12/2017, mississippitoday.org/2017/09/12/ayers-settlement-winds-anxiety-escalates-universities; Rilyn Eischens, "U Students: Remove Coffman Name from Coffman Memorial Union," *Minneapolis Star Tribune*, 3/9/2018, startribune.com/u-students-remove-coffman-name-from-coffman-memorial-union/476305893; "UO Picks 4 Finalists for Renaming Building Honoring KKK," *Oregon Live*, 5/12/2017, leaderoregonlive.com/today/index.ssf/2017/05/uo_picks_4_finalists_for_renam.html

———— ★ ————

48. If Russia Can Do It, Why Can't We?

ALABAMA *Calhoun County*

The center of Jacksonville boasts a historical marker that tells an interesting story about American heroes falling in and then out of favor. It reads,

JACKSONVILLE—FIRST COUNTY SEAT CALHOUN COUNTY, 1833–99

. . . Calhoun Co. originally was Benton Co., named for Col. T. H. Benton, Creek War officer, later U.S. Senator from Missouri. Renamed in 1858 for John C. Calhoun, champion of South in U.S. Senate. Benton's views by then unpopular in South.

Calhoun County thus offers a nineteenth-century example of renaming. Of course, Americans have been renaming the landscape for centuries. When the Pilgrims resettled the abandoned American Indian village of Patuxet in 1620, they renamed it Plymouth. (Chapter 1 tells how Alaska's Denali has shed the name Mount McKinley.) Notwithstanding this tradition of change, when names get challenged today some people raise a generic objection: "We can't rewrite history." Rewriting history is hardly the issue. The question is, whom do we choose to honor from our history? Comparing the man Calhoun County now honors with the man whose name was taken off the landscape in 1858 provides a useful lesson.

John C. Calhoun never set foot in Calhoun County, while Thomas Hart Benton probably did. Otherwise, the careers of the two men show several parallels. Both were wealthy slaveowners, both were important U.S. senators and national leaders of the Democratic Party, and both were considered for the presidency—Calhoun served as vice president under Andrew Jackson.

Gradually, however, Calhoun and Benton diverged in political philosophy until they became archenemies. Calhoun took ever more extreme positions favoring the South as a region and slavery as a cause. Over and over, he used the threat of disunion to blackmail national leaders to get what he wanted. Calhoun explained his strategy in a letter to a friend in 1847, "You will see that I have made up the issue between North and South. If we flinch we are gone, but if we stand fast on it, we shall triumph either by compelling the North to yield to our terms, or declaring our independence of them."

Opposed to the high tariffs of 1828–32, Calhoun prompted a national crisis when he got South Carolina to "nullify" them. Andrew Jackson refused to back down, declaring, "Our Federal Union—it must be preserved." Calhoun's threats did get congressional leaders to lower the tariff, however. Having browbeaten his way on the tariff, Calhoun later threatened disunion if Texas was not annexed, if the United States extended diplomatic recognition to Haiti, and even if citizens in Northern states continued to agitate for abolition. In the 1840s, Calhoun insisted that because the Constitution protected slavery, slaveowners had the right to take their property into any of the territories. This meant that Congress had no right to pass the Northwest Ordinance, which outlawed slavery in the land that would become Ohio, Indiana, Michigan, Illinois, Wisconsin, and part of Minnesota. Calhoun also labeled unconstitutional the Missouri Compromise, which he had supported in 1820, and which admitted Missouri as a slave state but banned slavery from all other territories north of Arkansas's northern boundary.

Calhoun's purpose must have been disunion or, in the words of Teddy

Roosevelt, who wrote a biography of Benton, "wanton malice." He knew
that if the federal government forced slavery into the territories, regardless
of what their inhabitants desired, Northerners would not tolerate it. In 1837,
he had noted that states' rights allowed Northerners to distance themselves
morally from slavery: "A large portion of the Northern States believes slavery
to be a sin, and would consider it as an obligation of conscience to abolish it
if they should feel themselves in any degree responsible for its continuance."
Nevertheless, he now threatened that the South would secede unless the federal government passed and enforced a harsh fugitive slave law.

Meanwhile, Thomas Hart Benton, Missouri senator from 1820 through
1850, became more and more convinced that the United States should be
preserved. Always a slaveowner, he insisted that he would always defend
slavery against the abolitionists. Increasingly, however, he came to believe
that slavery was wrong and should not be allowed to expand. In 1849, he
declared, "If there was no slavery in Missouri today, I should oppose its coming in; if there was none in the United States, I should oppose its coming
into the United States; as there is none in New Mexico or California, I am
against sending it to those territories." Benton pointed out that Southern
Democrats had opposed secession when New England Federalists had threatened to secede during the War of 1812. "The leading language . . . south of
the Potomac was that no state had a right to withdraw from the Union," said
Benton, ". . . and that any attempt to dissolve it, or to obstruct the action of
constitutional laws, was treason."

Despite Benton, by 1850, Calhoun's agitation for secession had borne fruit
beyond his home state of South Carolina. After complicated maneuvering,
a compromise between sectional interests emerged in which the North won
acceptance of California as a free state in return for a harsh fugitive slave
law. Benton and Calhoun both opposed the Compromise of 1850, but from
opposite perspectives. Benton argued that California met the requirements
for statehood and should be admitted without bargaining with radical slaveholders like Calhoun. He denied that the Constitution protected slavery and
urged Congress to exclude slavery from the territories. A dying Calhoun
threatened disunion one last time, claiming that the compromise didn't go far
enough in guaranteeing slavery forever. It is doubtful that *any* compromise
would have satisfied Calhoun at this point in his life.

In 1858, in keeping with the growing secessionist sentiment in the plantation areas of the Deep South, pro-slavery extremists in Alabama renamed

Benton County for John C. Calhoun. They took this step precisely *because* Benton stood for the United States, while Calhoun did not. As Roosevelt put it, "the extreme proslavery men honor[ed Benton] with a hatred more intense than they harbored toward any Northerner."[1]

Am I making too much of a name? Who cares for whom a county is named? Who even knows what Calhoun did these days? To this point, except for its parenthetical statement about Denali, this chapter stands unchanged from its original, published in 1999. Twenty years later, in 2019, many people know what Calhoun did. They grasp that neo-Confederates honored Calhoun during the Nadir of race relations, precisely because he was so intertwined with white supremacy. As the previous chapter notes, students finally pressured Yale University to rename Calhoun College. Minnesotans persuaded that state to rename Lake Calhoun in Minneapolis. Even in his home state of South Carolina, serious discussions now take place about taking him off his pedestal in Charleston and contextualizing his plantation at Clemson. Taking history seriously requires taking Calhoun seriously, which probably means taking his name and his statues down.

Another viewpoint is that even though Calhoun was a malevolent force in our history, he is "part of our heritage" after all. Why not just "respect the past" by leaving it be?

We take our heritage seriously when we learn about it, think about it, and debate it. In 1991, when Russians changed the name of Leningrad back to St. Petersburg, they were respecting their past. The policies, writings, and beliefs of V. I. Lenin had caused much harm in the world, especially in Russia. Leninism now stands discredited in many minds as well as on the Russian landscape. The policies, writings, and beliefs of John C. Calhoun similarly caused much harm in the world, but they hardly stand equally discredited partly because, unlike St. Petersburg, Benton County is not yet known again as Benton County.

To be sure, we can't change what *happened* in the past. We *can* change what we think and say about it. Renaming Benton County in 1858 told more about the white men who did it than about Thomas Hart Benton or John C. Calhoun. The renaming reveals them, like Calhoun, as advocates of slavery at any price. Leaving it "Calhoun" respects their long-discredited position today. Indeed, every year the name remains Calhoun County, it declares on the landscape that John C. Calhoun was a hero worthy of having a county named for him. Of course, this is an insult to every black resident of the

county and every white resident who does not believe that treason on behalf
of slavery made moral or political sense then or now. Benton, on the other
hand, struggled with and wrote about issues of race relations, politics, and
economics. Though he never attained consistency, his ideological movement
was heroic for his time, and studying his interesting life and books would be
time well spent for anyone interested in race relations, politics, or economics today. Perhaps when Calhoun County is again named Benton County,
students will be motivated to spend this time.[2]

Chapters 1, 24, 47, and 85 treat other renaming issues.

1. At about the same time and for the same reason, slaveowners changed Benton County,
   Florida, to Hernando County.
2. Kathryn Childress, Jacksonville, AL, correspondence, 2/10/97; Ann O'Hanlon, "Racial
   History Fuels Growing Debate Over School Names," *The Washington Post*, 2/10/98;
   Maggie Gallagher, "Small-Mindedness Reflects Historical Distortions," *St. Paul Pioneer
   Press*, 11/18/97; Mary Frances Berry, "Ashamed of George Washington?" *The New York
   Times*, 11/29/97; James McPherson, *Drawn With the Sword* (NY: Oxford UP, 1996), 41;
   William N. Chambers, *Old Bullion Benton* (Boston: Atlantic/Little, Brown, 1956), 345;
   Joseph R. Conlin, ed., *Morrow Book of Quotations in American History* (NY: Morrow,
   1984), 153; Theodore Roosevelt, *Thomas Hart Benton* (NY: Scribner's, 1926 [1887]), 22,
   108, 208; Dixon Wecter, *The Hero in America* (NY: Scribner's, 1972 [1941]), 143; John C.
   Calhoun, U.S. Senate speech, 2/6/1837; *The Jacksonville Story . . . An Enduring Heritage*
   (Jacksonville, AL: First National Bank, distr. 1996), 12; Abigail Darlington, "Proposed
   John C. Calhoun Plaque in Limbo after Charleston City Council Can't See Eye to Eye
   on It," *Charleston Post and Courier*, 1/9/2018, postandcourier.com/news/proposed-john
   -c-calhoun-plaque-in-limbo-after-charleston-city/article_2a798a66-f58c-11e7-b4ef
   -73fa27cd5008.html

---------- ✫ ----------

49. Confining Helen Keller Under House Arrest

ALABAMA *Tuscumbia*

Ivy Green, Helen Keller's birthplace in Tuscumbia, disables Helen Keller more
completely than the childhood fever that made her blind and deaf. The site
presents her as a bland source of optimistic inspiration to our youth—while
omitting everything she stood for, every cause she cared about.

Ivy Green begins misrepresenting her before visitors arrive. Its website reveals nothing whatever of the extraordinary content of Keller's adult life. About her radicalism, her support for trade unions, racial justice and integration, the First Amendment, birth control, women's rights and suffrage, and communism, the brochures say not a word. The Helen Keller they present, devoid of content, does not challenge visitors to think.

Once visitors arrive at her birthplace, Ivy Green continues to misrepresent Helen Keller. She joined the Socialist Party of Massachusetts in 1909. Gradually, Keller moved further left and became a Wobbly—a member of the IWW, the Industrial Workers of the World. Early in the life of the NAACP, she sent $100 to the organization and wrote a letter of support that appeared in its magazine, *The Crisis*, edited by W. E. B. Du Bois. In 1920, that was a radical act for a white Alabaman. Ivy Green says not a word about Keller's racial idealism, however.

Keller's commitment to socialism stemmed from her experience as a disabled person and from her sympathy for others with handicaps. She became interested in blindness and came to realize that to help the blind was to treat the symptom, not the cause. Through her research, she learned that blindness was not distributed randomly about the social strata but was more prevalent in the lower class. Poor men were more likely to be blinded by industrial hazards and inadequate medical care; poor women who became prostitutes faced the additional danger of syphilitic blindness. Thus, Keller learned how deeply the social class system controlled people's life chances, even determining their level of

In 2009, Alabama replaced its statue of secessionist J. L. M. Curry in the U.S. Capitol with this likeness of Helen Keller at age seven. This scene at the well was a high point of the play and movie *The Miracle Worker*. It is the only statue of a child in the entire Capitol and symbolizes the way textbooks and U.S. popular culture have ignored Keller's life after she learned to read and speak.

medical care and ultimately whether they could see. Nor was her research all book-learning: "I have visited sweatshops, factories, crowded slums. If I could not see it, I could smell it."

What does a tour of Ivy Green tell about Keller's lifelong convictions? Nothing! Even when asked point-blank about Keller's socialism and support of the NAACP, guides reply, "I don't know."

Having fought so hard herself to speak, she helped found the American Civil Liberties Union to fight for the free speech of others. (The ACLU is anathema to many white Southerners today, which may explain why Ivy Green leaves this out.) Keller supported the socialist candidate Eugene Debs in each of his campaigns for the presidency. (Again, since socialism is unpopular throughout the United States, especially in the South, Ivy Green may leave it out lest visitors think badly of Keller.) After the Russian Revolution, she sang the praises of the new communist government of the U.S.S.R. She wrote essays on the women's movement, politics, and economics, and she believed human beings should never be handicapped owing to their color. Visitors may not agree with all of Keller's positions, but that is no excuse to silence her. Helen Keller, who struggled so valiantly to communicate, is being held incommunicado in her own home! Nor is the North kinder to her: a plaque where she lived for 21 years in New York City says only that she "wrote, lectured, and inspired others to succeed."[1]

1. Loewen, *Lies My Teacher Told Me*, chapter 1; Nancy Murray, correspondence, 7/97, conversations, 8/97.

★

---

50. Famous Everywhere but at Home
ALABAMA *Scottsboro*

From 1931 through 1939 and beyond, the little town of Scottsboro was in the news because of the notorious affair that became known throughout the world as the Case of the Scottsboro Boys. Their trials prompted hundreds of magazine articles, at least two major histories, several autobiographies and biographies, at least two plays, and an international outcry against the American system of justice, at least as applied to African Americans. Alan

Axelrod and Charles Phillips list the Scottsboro Case as one of "200 Events that Shaped the Nation" in *What Every American Should Know About American History.*

Nevertheless, in 1999, the Scottsboro landscape was silent about the Scottsboro Case. Around the courthouse square in Scottsboro were four historical markers. Not one mentioned the event that made Scottsboro famous.

What an event for markers to ignore, for it would make a cliffhanger of a movie, complete with sex, violence, narrowly averted lynchings, a last-minute surprise witness, and even a communist conspiracy of sorts! And because so many people wrote about the case from so many perspectives, historians know exactly what happened.

On March 25, 1931, nine black youths were riding a freight train through northern Alabama along with several white boys and two white women, prostitutes as it turned out. The white and black youths got in a fight, triggered when one of the whites told Haywood Patterson, an eighteen-year-old African American, "Nigger bastard, this is a white man's train. You better get off." The white boys proceeded to stone Patterson and one or two of his friends. When the train made a short stop, the black youths joined forces with several other African Americans. As the train started up, the whites resumed their bombardment. Now, superior numbers confronted them, however, and after a short fight, all the white youths but one jumped or were thrown off the train.

Angry, the white boys walked bleeding to the next town and told their story, conveniently omitting their role in starting the dispute. The tale grew, and when the train reached Paint Rock, Alabama, a posse of armed white men rushed the freight cars, grabbed all nine African Americans, and drove them to the Scottsboro jail. Members of the posse also encountered the two white women. Perhaps to avoid the suspicion that they themselves had been up to no good, the women claimed that the blacks had raped them.

This set in motion the trial of all nine blacks on the charge of rape. A white mob almost lynched them from the Scottsboro jail. On April 6, having met with two hastily appointed defense attorneys for only a few minutes, the first two went on trial for their lives. All-white juries soon found all nine boys guilty. Eight were sentenced to death and one, just thirteen years old, life in prison.[1]

At this point, two national organizations—the National Association for the Advancement of Colored People (NAACP) and the Communist Party of the United States (and its International Labor Defense, or ILD) entered the fray. The ILD appealed to the Alabama Supreme Court and then to the U.S. Supreme Court, which called for new trials because the boys had not had adequate legal representation in their hurried first hearings. Letters now poured into the court and to the Alabama governor from novelists Thomas Mann, H. G. Wells, and Theodore Dreiser; conductor Leopold Stokowski; Albert Einstein; and hundreds of other well-known intellectuals. The communists organized Scottsboro Defense Committees in cities across the United States.

For the second set of trials, the ILD engaged Samuel Leibowitz, probably the best-known defense attorney in the country following the retirement of Clarence Darrow. The retrials were moved 50 miles west to Decatur, which also displayed no marker about the case in 1999. Haywood Patterson was first to be retried. During his trial, one of two physicians who had examined the women 90 minutes after the alleged attack told Judge James Horton privately that he did not believe they had been attacked. The women showed no signs of the physical or emotional upset to be expected in victims of multiple rapes. Moreover, the only semen found in one of them was lifeless, from a deposit many hours before. The doctor didn't want to say any of these things in open court, however, lest he loses his white clientele.

In Harlem, thousands of angry African Americans demonstrated in protest. Around the world, demonstrators denounced American justice and broke windows at American consulates in Europe and at an American-owned bank in Havana. In May 1933, 3,000 paraded in front of the White House; Ruby Bates was among the leaders, pictured between the signs at the left.

Just as the defense was about to rest, one of the two female accusers, Ruby Bates, came forward as a last-minute defense witness. To a hushed courtroom, she recanted her previous testimony and said that neither she nor her companion had been raped. Nevertheless, the jury again sentenced the first defendant to die. The verdict shocked many Americans.

In Alabama, Judge Horton concluded that the testimony of the sole remaining white complainant was not only uncorroborated but internally inconsistent and contradicted by evidence "which greatly preponderates in favor of the defendant." Convinced that all the boys were innocent, he set aside Patterson's conviction. In turn, the chief justice of the Alabama Supreme Court removed Horton from the case, and in the next election, voters removed Horton from office.

Late in 1933, under a new judge, Patterson was convicted and sentenced to death for the third time. The retrial of a second defendant, Clarence Norris, resulted in his conviction and death sentence, but in 1935, the U.S. Supreme Court again set aside the convictions, owing to the systematic exclusion of African Americans from Alabama juries. Although many juries in the Deep South continued to exclude blacks for another three decades, this decision, in *Norris v. Alabama*, was an important precedent for attacking all-white juries.

Alabama prosecutors slogged on. By using challenges, they kept their juries white. In 1936, they convicted Patterson a fourth time. This time he received a sentence of 75 years in prison, and the U.S. Supreme Court refused to review his case a fourth time. Clarence Norris was again sentenced to die, but Alabama Governor Bibb Graves commuted this to life imprisonment. Three more trials resulted in three long jail terms, but in 1937 Alabama dropped all charges against four of the boys, now young men. In 1943 and 1944, Alabama finally freed three more defendants. Two fled the state, violating their parole; when they returned voluntarily, Alabama rejailed them. Haywood Patterson escaped from prison and fled to Michigan in 1948, and the governor of Michigan refused to extradite him to Alabama. Finally, on June 9, 1950, the last "Scottsboro Boy" walked out of Alabama's Kilby Prison on parole. In all, the nine defendants spent a combined total of more than 100 years in jail for a crime that never happened.

The Scottsboro Case highlighted the impossible legal situation African Americans faced during the segregation era. Keeping blacks off juries was easy: juries were drawn from lists of registered voters, and whites used various "legal" subterfuges to keep blacks from voting. Without political or legal rights, African Americans had no hope for real economic advancement. Socially, segregation labeled African Americans as less than human; the term "boy" itself, applied to the Scottsboro defendants even as they became elderly, implied that they were less than men.

Yet the Scottsboro Boys were eventually freed. Moreover, Scottsboro and Decatur have now done a fine job of facing this past candidly. In 2004, more than 200 people turned out to unveil a new marker at the Jackson County Courthouse: "Jackson County Courthouse and the Scottsboro Boys." It is accurate and puts the local cases into a national legal context.[2]

Shelia Washington, who grew up in Scottsboro, took a vacant church building and converted it to the "Scottsboro Boys Museum and Cultural Center." On March 31, 2011, the 80th anniversary of the arrests, an extraordinary set of talks and performances brought people from all over the United States to dedicate the museum. It also puts out a comprehensive driving route to all the historic sites connected with the case.

In 2013, the Morgan County Archives in Decatur assembled some of the remarkable photographs of the trials by Fred Hiroshige, a local photographer, and displayed them at the nearby Carnegie Art Center. Titled "Scottsboro Boys: Outside the Protective Circle of Humanity," they are now on permanent display in the archives; a traveling exhibit teaches people across Alabama and in other states about the trials.

That same year, the nearby town of Paint Rock dedicated a marker that was truly integrated: one side tells the history of that hamlet, while the other is headed "Paint Rock Arrests in 1931 Began 'Scottsboro Boys' Cases." The marker is accurate but ends "happily": "In 2013, the State of Alabama exonerated the nine men, the last of whom died in 1989, and issued pardons."

Posthumous pardons don't accomplish a lot, but the steps people in northern Alabama have taken to remember rather than cover up the racism in their justice system deserve respect. They seem also to have whetted residents' appetites for more untold stories and prompted some reconciliation across the black/white divide. Previously, "nothing much" had been said about the Battle of Decatur during the Civil War, surely because black troops had helped defeat white Confederates. In 2014, the mayor of Decatur declared October 28 "USCT Day," marking the sesquicentennial of the Battle of Decatur. One hundred fifty years earlier, a bold charge by U.S. Colored Troops captured and disabled Confederate artillery, which helped convince Gen. John Bell Hood, commanding five times as many troops, to retreat and find another place to cross the Tennessee River. Decatur now honors Asa Gordon, Secretary General of the Sons and Daughters of the USCT, who in turn presented medallions to Peggy Towns and Jonathan Baggs, who had sparked Alabama to put up a historical marker, "The Charge of the 14th U.S. Colored Infantry."

Who knows where all this truth-telling might end![3]

1. Technically, the young boy's jury hung because it did not agree on the penalty, with nine of twelve jurors seeking death, the other three a long prison term.

2. *Lies Across America* helped spark Decatur (and perhaps Scottsboro) to remember the Scottsboro "Boys" on the landscape. The editor of the *Decatur Daily* wrote on April 7, 2000, "Author James W. Loewen's attempts to prick our community conscience . . . apparently worked. He got the mayor's attention." See "Scottsboro Boys: City Should Remember Case." This chapter helped Judge John Graham spur the Alabama State Bar and the Jackson County Historical Association to put up the Decatur marker. Of course, Graham, Sheila Washington, archivists, and other residents of Decatur and Scottsboro deserve all the credit for the markers, library photography exhibit, driving route, and museum that now tell this story fully and honestly.

3. Dan T. Carter, *Scottsboro: A Tragedy of the American South* (NY: Oxford UP, 1969); James Goodman, *Stories of Scottsboro* (NY: Vintage, 1995); Robin Winks, "A Public Historiography," *The Public Historian* 14 no. 3: 96; Eric Foner and John A. Garraty, eds., *The Reader's Companion to American History* (Boston: Houghton Mifflin, 1991), 971; William Harris and Judith Levey, eds., *The New Columbia Encyclopedia* (NY: Columbia UP, 1975), 2457; Ellen Spears, "'Rights Still Being Righted': Scottsboro Eighty Years Later," *Southern Spaces*, 6/16/2011, southernspaces.org/2011/rights-still-being-righted-scottsboro-eighty-years-later; Carol Codori, "Report from Decatur," *TVC-WRT Newsletter* (11/2014); Jonathan Baggs, "Welcome to Commemoration of 150th Anniversary of the Charge of the 14th United States Colored Troops," 10/28/2014, asagordon.byethost10.com/sdusct/JBAGGS14thUSCT150.pdf; Jonathan Baggs, "Black Troops Won Honor in Decatur in the Civil War," *Huntsville Times*, 2/19/2012, blog.al.com/times-views/2012/02/black_troops_won_honor_in_deca.html; City of Decatur, "Resolution," asagordon.byethost10.com/sdusct/alusct%20resolution.pdf

---------------------★---------------------

51. Remember Fort Pillow!

TENNESSEE *Fort Pillow*

Overlooking the Mississippi River some 40 miles north of Memphis is Fort Pillow, the scene of a disastrous Union defeat on April 12, 1864. But something more portentous than mere defeat happened here. From April 1864 to the end of the war a year later, black U.S. regiments charged into battle with the cry of vengeance, "Remember Fort Pillow!" Something grim happened to Union soldiers at Fort Pillow, especially to African Americans, something that inflamed people all across the North. But what? Unless today's visitors already know, they won't find out from this site.

Visitors first see the Tennessee historical marker for Fort Pillow, located eighteen miles away on a main highway in Henning:

FORT PILLOW APRIL 12, 1864

Federal forces captured this important Confederate work,
18 miles west, in 1862. To end depredations committed
by the Federal garrison, Forrest, with a force from his Confederate
Cavalry Corps, attacked and captured the fort. Of the garrison
of 551 white and Negro troops, 221 were killed.
The rest, some wounded, were captured.

The marker provides a place to start. Its numbers reveal that 40% of the garrison was killed. The overall ratio of dead to wounded in the Civil War was 1 to 6. At Fort Pillow, that ratio was almost inverted: 4.4 to 1. Moreover, there was a striking discrepancy by race: among whites at Fort Pillow, the ratio of dead to wounded was high, 2.25 to 1, but among blacks, it was an astounding 6.5 to 1. In all, 64% of the black defenders and 33% of the whites died.[1] Among the 1,500 attacking Confederates, just 14 died.

How could this happen? The battle itself was neither fierce nor protracted. Fort Pillow's low earthen walls offered little protection from Confederate sharpshooters, who approached through ravines and then fired into the fort from higher ground. After a pause during which the Union commander refused a surrender demand, Gen. Nathan Bedford Forrest's men over-whelmed the defenders in about twenty minutes. It was what happened *after* the battle that explains the casualty rates.

People who were there have left a record of testimony. Five days after the battle, a Union soldier wrote in a letter home: "As soon as the rebels got to the top of the bank there commenced the most horrible slaughter that could possibly be conceived. Our boys when they saw they were overpow-ered threw down their arms and held up, some their handkerchiefs and some their hands in token of surrender, but no sooner were they seen than they were shot down, and if one shot failed to kill them, the bayonet or revolver did not." A Confederate newspaper correspondent explained the difference in death ratios by race: "The whites received quarter, but the Negroes were shown no mercy." And a Confederate sergeant wrote to his sisters seven days after the battle,

> The slaughter was awful—words cannot describe the scene. The poor deluded Negroes would run up to our men, fall upon their knees, and with uplifted hands scream for mercy, but they were ordered to their feet and then shot down. The white men fared but little better. Their fort turned out to be a great slaughter pen—blood, human blood stood about in pools and brains could have been gathered up in any quantity. I with several others tried to stop the butchery and at one time had partially succeeded, but Gen. Forrest ordered them shot down like dogs and the carnage continued. Finally our men became sick of blood and the firing ceased.

This illustration of the massacre, surely based on verbal accounts rather than eye-witnessed, ran in *Harper's Weekly* and helped Northern readers visualize and remember Fort Pillow.

"Surviving Federals claimed the killing went on sporadically into the next day," according to Jack Hurst, another Forrest biographer. Soldiers testified before the Congressional inquiry that Confederates buried some wounded soldiers alive and crucified others by nailing them onto tent frames and then setting the tents afire. A day or so after the battle, Forrest's men, who had Maj. Bradford, the Union commander at Fort Pillow, in custody, killed him too.

At first, Confederates exulted in the slaughter. In his initial report, Forrest claimed that his men killed 71% of the Union forces. Other Confederates there suggested 80%. "The river was dyed with the blood of the slaughtered for 200 yards," Forrest boasted to his superiors; he "hoped" Fort Pillow would "demonstrate to the Northern people that Negro soldiers cannot cope with Southerners." The Memphis *Appeal* rejoiced in the "Capture of Fort Pillow. General Slaughter of the Garrison," and went on to exult, "One hundred prisoners were taken and the balance slain. The fort ran with blood." Gen. James Chalmers, Forrest's second-in-command, bragged that his troops had "taught the mongrel garrison of blacks and renegades a lesson long to be remembered." Chalmers's term "renegades" helps explain the murder of surrendered whites, most of whom were from Tennessee and were regarded by Forrest and Chalmers as traitors to the Confederate cause.[2]

Statements like these, reported proudly in newspapers across the South, led to an outcry in the Northern press. According to the rules of war, a nation goes to war with another nation (or would-be nation, in the case of the Confederacy), not a people. The point of war is not to eliminate the people—that is genocide, not war. This means that when an army has eliminated a person as an opponent—by death *or* capture—it has accomplished the aim of removing him as a fighting force. Therefore, captured soldiers are not killed.[3] Prisoners of war were also spared because, for much of the Civil War, they could be exchanged for captives of the other side.

Confederate atrocities at Fort Pillow violated these rules of war. Leaders of the United States from Abraham Lincoln to local commanders were outraged and threatened to retaliate against surrendered Southern troops. Congress set up a joint committee to investigate the incident. The uproar surprised Confederate leaders and the threats alarmed them. "By early May," in the words of historians John Cimprich and Robert C. Mainfort Jr., "the tone of Confederate newspaper accounts of the battle shifted dramatically from gloating over slaughter to denying it." Now, Confederates tried to hide or explain away the massacre.

The result was a controversy in the first half of the twentieth century as to just what took place after the surrender at Fort Pillow. Neo-Confederates developed five defenses against the charge that rebel troops massacred black soldiers (and civilians, as it happened) who had surrendered:

- there was no exceptional number of deaths;
- if there were, the dead died in battle;
- if many were killed after surrendering, "guerrillas and robbers" did it, not Confederate soldiers;
- if Confederate soldiers did it, Forrest wasn't at fault because his men were out of control;
- if Forrest did authorize the massacre, it was justified by prior "Union depredations."[4]

There is considerable tension among these explanations; according to Cimprich and Mainfort, modern historians disregard them all.

A sixth explanation makes more sense than any of the foregoing. The actions of Forrest's men at Fort Pillow were in line with stated Confederate policy. Immediately after the battle, Gen. Chalmers told a *New York Times* correspondent "that . . . it was against the policy of his Government to spare Negro soldiers or their officers." Forrest became something of a scapegoat in the North, Hurst points out, for similar acts that took place in many Confederate commands. Fort Pillow requires no special explanation or justification, because the massacre was not special. "Killing all captured blacks wearing U.S. uniforms was the declared policy of . . . Lt. Gen. Kirby Smith," Hurst points out, and Kirby Smith, who commanded all Confederate forces west of the Mississippi, far outranked Forrest.

In Louisiana, a Confederate regiment captured a squad of black soldiers. After some of them tried to escape, the regiment's colonel reported, "I then ordered every one shot, and with my Six Shooter I assisted in the execution of the order." Farther east, after the Confederate victory at Saltville, Virginia, Capt. Edward Guerrant wrote, "Our men took no Negro prisoners." After Confederates took Plymouth, North Carolina, in April 1864, in the words of one Union sergeant, "All the Negroes found in blue uniform or with any outward marks of a Union soldier upon him was killed. I saw some taken into the woods and hung. Others I saw stripped of all their clothing, and they stood upon the bank of the river with their faces riverwards and then they were shot." Similar incidents were reported at Milliken's Bend and Jackson, Louisiana; Poison Spring, Arkansas; Flat Rock Creek in Indian Territory; Olustee, Florida; and various other places, including the Crater during the siege of Petersburg, Virginia, late in the war.

The Confederacy never charged anyone with any wrongdoing as a result of any of these events. On the contrary, six weeks after the Fort Pillow massacre, the Confederate Congress passed a joint resolution commending Forrest and his men "for their late brilliant and successful campaign in Mississippi, West Tennessee, and Kentucky," a campaign which, they said, "has conferred upon its authors enduring fame." Thus, in his own mind and in the assessment of his government, Forrest and his men did no wrong, but right. Three weeks later at the Battle of Brice's Cross Roads in north Mississippi on June 10, Forrest's men again shot down African Americans who had already surrendered.[5]

Forrest biographer Brian Wills notes that black opponents always inflamed Forrest. After Forrest's successful raid at Murfreesboro, Tennessee, for instance (see the next chapter), a Confederate officer brought before Forrest "a mulatto man, who was the servant to one of the officers in the Union forces." Forrest cursed him and asked what he was doing there. The man replied that he was a free man, not a slave, and came out as the servant to an officer, whom he named. Forrest drew his pistol and blew the man's brains out. The Confederate officer, who knew the man came from Pennsylvania and had never been enslaved, "denounced the act as one of cold-blooded murder and declared that he would never again serve under Forrest."

Union uproar about the Fort Pillow massacre, Forrest, and this criminal Confederate policy never caused the policy to change, but it did make Confederate leaders more circumspect. In April 1864, for example, Gen. Braxton Bragg wrote the governor of North Carolina, "To avoid as far as possible all complications with the military authorities of the United States in regard to the disposition which will be made of this class of prisoners, the President respectfully requests Your Excellency to take the necessary steps to have the matter of such disposition kept out of the newspapers of the State, and in every available way to shun its obtaining any publicity."

To understand how massacring wounded prisoners can seem right, we must grasp the ideological context in which the Confederate government operated. To Confederate leaders, officers, and soldiers, African Americans were not legally people but property. Before secession, Southerners had hailed the 1857 *Dred Scott* decision of the U.S. Supreme Court, which stated "that [blacks] had no rights which the white man was bound to respect." Although perhaps not intended literally, *Dred Scott* implies that whites need not respect blacks' right to life.

Confederate leaders were outraged when the Union enlisted black troops. "No people . . . could tolerate . . . the use of savages." Confederate Secretary of War James A. Seddon fulminated in an early directive, "We ought never to be inconvenienced with such prisoners. . . . Summary execution must therefore be inflicted on those taken." In November 1862, Confederate raiders seized four African Americans in Union uniforms on a South Carolina island; Secretary Seddon and President Davis approved their "summary execution" as an "example" to discourage the arming of slaves. White Union officers commanding black troops were also targeted for death. Jefferson Davis's message to Congress on January 12, 1863, promised to turn officers of black regiments over to state governments as "criminals engaged in inciting servile insurrection" for the death penalty. The Confederacy never agreed to exchange black POWs for white POWs because that would imply a black soldier equaled a white soldier; this was one reason for the breakdown in POW exchanges. However, the Confederacy never achieved a consistent policy about black POWs or white officers of black regiments. Sometimes they were enslaved, sometimes kept in POW camps, and sometimes put to death.

In 1999, Fort Pillow, as a Tennessee State Historic Area, could not possibly argue that it was right to kill surrendered U.S. troops, so it was in denial. The brochure handed out at the fort claimed that Union troops got VIP treatment:

> After the Confederates successfully assaulted and occupied the main redoubt, Gen. Forrest lowered the Union flag and ordered all firing stopped.
>
> Wounded of both sides were treated by Confederate doctors.
>
> Forrest ordered equipment and firearms be collected, prisoners be secured, that wounded federals be transferred to first available steamer. . . .

The only hint of a problem came from one label in the small museum at
the fort:

> *Immediately after the Southern capture of Fort Pillow, the North labeled
> it a massacre. Cited were Forrest's reputation for giving his enemies little
> quarter, the Union's overwhelming losses, and survivors' accounts of the
> killing of captured troops. . . .*
>
> *The South claimed that [Union] panic and inexperience caused the huge
> loss of Union lives. Despite their threats, Grant, Sherman, and other
> Union leaders never carried out reprisals.*
>
> *To this day, the controversy remains.*

While it sounds scholarly to aver that "controversy remains," it isn't. His-
torians have uncovered and published the facts of the massacre in plain view.
This label, like the brochure and historical marker, merely continued the
Confederate cover-up that began in May 1864.

Nathan Bedford Forrest was a brilliant commander; the next entry tells
how he indeed achieved the "enduring fame" the Confederate Congress
foretold. Few Americans remember Fort Pillow for what it was—"a race
riot, a mass lynching," according to Richard Fuchs, author of a book-length
study of the battle. When I visited in 1996, the gift shop at Fort Pillow sold
souvenirs, flags, and items of clothing, all Confederate. One T-shirt pictured
Forrest against a faded Confederate flag with his words, "Keep firing until
nothing stands from ground to sky . . . " At the bottom was the legend,
"Nathan Bedford Forrest, Ft. Pillow, Tennessee, April 12, 1864." Surely, if
more Americans did "remember Fort Pillow," fewer would celebrate it with
T-shirts and flags.

Or maybe not. Tony Horwitz speaks of "a hardening ideological edge
to Confederate remembrance" in his 1998 book *Confederates in the Attic*. In
past decades, neo-Confederates bought more T-shirts of Robert E. Lee than
any other Confederate hero; by 1999, one manufacturer sold five Forrest
T-shirts to every Lee. In 2019, the largest online seller of neo-Confederate
goods featured Forrest above Lee and the Forrest shirts often had an edge,
such as "No Country For Yankees" or "Grey Lives Matter," while the Lee
shirts were simply his image. Neo-Confederates do know what Forrest did at
Fort Pillow and may be choosing his likeness precisely because they like his
"solution" to the "race problem."[6]

The next chapter (52) is more optimistic about our chances to tell the truth about Forrest on the landscape.

1. The marker underestimates the slaughter; Cimprich and Mainfort conclude that 285 of about 600 men were killed, or 48%. David Ndilei notes that two days after the attack, Confederate surgeon Samuel H. Caldwell wrote, "The fort was garrisoned by 400 white men and 400 Negroes and out of the 800 only 168 are now living." The difference may have been noncombatants who fled to the fort and were killed, including new would-be recruits waiting to be mustered into the army.

2. The *Appeal* was publishing "in exile" in Atlanta, since Memphis was under U.S. control.

3. There are other pragmatic reasons for this rule: if opponents expect to be executed if captured, they may fight all the more fiercely, which is hardly in one's own interest. Conversely, soldiers do not like to imagine that if captured they would likewise be executed; in this sense, the Golden Rule holds. Indeed, two months after Fort Pillow, Forrest was complaining to Union commanders that combat in his area "was far more bloody than it would otherwise have been but for the fact that . . . both sides acted as though neither felt safe in surrendering." He sought to learn "whether my men now in your hands are treated as other Confederate prisoners"—but he still did not agree to treat black soldiers or their officers like other Union POWs.

4. The Tennessee historic marker implicitly takes this approach.

5. Forrest's policy worked in the short run: it did intimidate some blacks from enlisting and some Union commanders from exposing them to combat. After Fort Pillow, Forrest's threats also prompted commanders of small mostly-black garrisons protecting Sherman's railroad lines in Alabama to surrender without a fight rather than have all their troops killed. On the other hand, black soldiers did "remember Fort Pillow" after several battles, killing captured Confederates in retaliation. Confederates also showed they were afraid of black U.S. soldiers on some occasions when the latter attacked shouting "Remember Fort Pillow!" At Fort Blakely, Alabama, for example, Confederates "ran for their lives over to the white troops on our left, to give themselves up" in the words of a lieutenant commanding black Union soldiers.

6. John Cimprich and Robert C. Mainfort Jr., "The Fort Pillow Massacre: A Statistical Note," *Journal of American History* 76 no. 2 (12/89): 832–37; Brian S. Wills, *A Battle from the Start* (NY: Harper, 1993), 77–78, 178, 186–93, 215, 373; Jack Hurst, *Nathan Bedford Forrest* (NY: Knopf, 1993), 161, 169–80; David Ndilei, *Extinguish the Flames of Racial Prejudice* (Gainesville, FL: IEF Publishing, 1996), 40, 91, 131, 157–58, and email 12/98; John L. Jordan, "Was There a Massacre at Fort Pillow?" *TN Historical Quarterly* 6 (1947); Nathan Bedford Forrest, 4/15/1864 dispatch, from *War of the Rebellion . . . Official Records vol. 32, pt. 1* (DC: GPO, 1891), 609–610; Richard Nelson Current, *Lincoln's Loyalists* (NY: Oxford UP, 1992), 139–43; Richard L. Fuchs, *An Unerring Fire: The Massacre at Fort Pillow* (Rutherford, NJ: Fairleigh Dickinson UP, 1994), 23, 116–17, 144–46; James McPherson, *Battle Cry of Freedom* (NY: Oxford UP, 1988), 565–66, 793–95; McPherson, *The Negro's Civil War* (NY: Pantheon, 1965), 186–87; Joseph T. Glatthaar, *Forged in Battle: The Civil War Alliance of Black Soldiers and White Officers* (NY: Free Press, 1990), 133–34; James Hollandsworth, "The Execution of White Officers from Black Units by Confederate Forces During the Civil War," *LA History* 35 (1994): 475–89; Hollandsworth, "LA Native Guards," www2.netdoor.com/~jgh, 7/97; Weymouth T. Jordan Jr. and G. W. Thomas, "Massacre at Plymouth," NC *Historical Review* 72 no. 2 (4/95): 189–92; Edward A. Miller Jr., *The Black Civil War Soldiers of IL* (Columbia: U. of SC Press, 1998), 76–82; David J. Coles, *Far From Fields of Glory* (Tallahassee: FL State U. PhD, 1996), 155–65, 172; Tony Horwitz, *Confederates in the Attic* (NY: Pantheon,

1998), 294; David Royer and Stacy Jacobson, "New Historical Marker Updates Nathan Bedford Forrest's Role in Slave Trade," Channel 3 News, 4/4/2018, wreg.com/2018/04 /04/new-historical-marker-updates-nathan-bedford-forrests-role-in-slave-trade

———— ★ ————

52. Forrest Rested Here

TENNESSEE *Woodbury*

In 1999, Nathan Bedford Forrest stood as the paramount hero on the Tennessee landscape. He got a bust in the state capitol, a statue in Nathan Bedford Forrest Park in Memphis, obelisks at his birthplace in Chapel Hill and at Nathan Bedford Forrest State Park near Camden, and 32 different state historical markers, far more than any other person in any other state in America. Tennessee supplied three U.S. presidents—Andrew Jackson, James K. Polk, and Andrew Johnson—but Forrest got more markers than all three put together. Another plaque "Erected to the memory of Gen. Nathan Bedford Forrest" on the Murfreesboro Courthouse thanks him "for heroic services rendered the citizens of Murfreesboro on July 13, 1862." His entire farewell address to his men in Alabama at the war's end is reprinted on the Confederate Monument in Beech Grove, Tennessee. The Tennessee National Guard established and named Camp Nathan Bedford Forrest near Tullahoma in 1926; during World War II, the camp became a federal base where African American soldiers trained. Forrest is also the subject of a statue and historical marker in Gadsden, Alabama, eight other Alabama historical markers, and at least two historical markers in Mississippi. From Florida to Texas, parks, streets, and schools were named for Forrest, as is a city in Arkansas and a county in Mississippi.

Forrest did not get all these honors because he made more history than any other American. The marker in Woodbury will suffice to disprove that idea:

FORREST RESTED HERE, JULY 12, 1862

Here Forrest, with his newly organized brigade of about 1400 cavalrymen, halted for a short rest before making his successful raid on Federal forces at Murfreesboro . . .

Even George Washington had to spend the night before meriting a "Washington Slept Here" marker—Forrest had but to rest!

Forrest was a brilliant cavalry leader, but his career looks better on the landscape than it was in reality because his defeats get no attention or are marked so ambiguously that they look like victories. Jim Jones of the Tennessee Historical Commission notes that the following marker, though perfectly accurate and much more important than "Forrest Rested Here," will never go up on the Tennessee landscape:

FORREST WHIPPED HERE

On August 29, 1862, Gen. N. B. Forrest, commanding Terry's Texas Rangers and Tennessee, Alabama, and Kentucky cavalry, attacked a Federal force they outnumbered nine to one. After three charges led by Forrest himself, the Confederates were repulsed. The federal force, two companies of the 18th Ohio Infantry, defended their stockade here at Short Mtn. Crossroads.

Since this chapter was first published, Tennessee did see fit to put up a marker for the above battle. It reads,

SKIRMISH AT GUEST HOLLOW AUGUST 29, 1862

At 1:00 p.m. Gen. Nathan Bedford Forrest's Cavalry attacked the federal stockade located next to the railroad. In the short but fierce struggle, Gen. Forrest's command suffered 180 casualties. Twelve Confederates were buried on the field of battle. Confederate forces withdrew and destroyed railroad bridges between Guest Hollow and McMinnville.

A careful reader can infer that Forrest lost, but the marker is not clear. Certainly "whipped" is not used, though correspondence about this skirmish in the Official Records used that term four times. Here is the vivid account by the U.S. captain in charge of the stockade:

On Friday, August 29, the troops under my command, numbering 100 effective men . . . had just completed the inclosure of a stockade at this place 30 by 40 feet square, of round timber, 12 feet high. The men were eating dinner at about 1 o'clock p.m. in a grove, distant from the stockade about 100 yards . . . when the enemy, 1,500 strong, made his appearance. . . . My men ran rapidly to the stockade, and at the same time the enemy, with a terrific yell, fired a volley and rushed to cut us off from the stockade. The attacking force consisted of 900 dismounted cavalry, commanded by Gen. Forrest, and led to the charge by him. My men kept up a sharp running fire on the way to the stockade, checking the impetuosity of the enemy, and all but some 10 of Company I and the men on picket got inside the fort before the enemy. The men cut off kept up a constant fire from the railroad and woods during the engagement and got in safely. The race to the stockade was a desperate one. On getting within the stockade I at once sent three parties of 6 men each, one from each company, to bring in the ammunition. . . . They ran to the thicket under a terrible fire from the enemy's skirmishers and succeeded in bringing in the ammunition.

The enemy now made an attack from three directions with great desperation, approaching within 50 feet of the stockade. I kept up a constant and well-directed fire upon him for ten minutes, when, finding it impossible to dislodge us or seriously injure our men and his own falling rapidly around, he made a rapid retreat to the woods in great confusion. His men ran in every direction before our fire, throwing down their arms, and immediately fell back out of range. Soon after an attempt was made to destroy the railroad above us. I went out with a party and drove them away.

Again, nowhere in Dixie does a historical marker say anything like that about Forrest. Across the South, historical markers would have us believe that the Confederacy won every skirmish and most battles—mystifying the outcome. Liston Pope, who grew up in the South, said it best: "I never could understand how our Confederate troops could have won every battle in the War so decisively and then have lost the war itself!"

Forrest's military career simply cannot explain the extraordinary homage the Tennessee landscape pays him. His operations in Tennessee were on a modest scale, far less important than those of Confederate Gen. Brax-

White Southerners still honor Forrest.
In the early 1970s, after judges required
public schools in the South to desegregate
fully, segregated "academies" sprang up
across Dixie, and several were named
for him. And in July 1998, the "League of
the South" dedicated a big new statue of
Nathan Bedford Forrest at a "Confederate
Flag Park" on private property south of
Nashville.

ton Bragg, say, or Ulysses S. Grant.
Yet Bragg and Grant get far less recognition. The key to the veneration
accorded Forrest is to be found in what
he did in Tennessee *after* the Civil War.

After the war, Forrest became the
first national leader of the Ku Klux
Klan. Jack Hurst begins his recent biography of Forrest, "A dozen years after
the Civil War, the South overturned its outcome," referring to the Klan and
the larger class of violent actions that it epitomized. Thus, these markers
and monuments pay tribute to Forrest *as a victor*, as markers and monuments
usually do.

In so doing, the landscape honors one of the most vicious racists in U.S.
history. Forrest had been a slave trader before the Civil War and sold people
brought in illegally from Africa half a century after Congress supposedly
ended that trade in 1808. During the war, he presided over massacres of surrendered black troops at Fort Pillow (chapter 51) and Brice's Cross Roads.
After the war, he hired black convict labor, the closest thing to slave labor,
for his cotton plantation near Memphis.

In 1999, I went on to write this paragraph as a conclusion: hopefully, the
day will come when few white Tennesseeans revere Forrest. "We need to
understand what the Confederacy stood for," says Tom Turnipseed, formerly campaign director for George Wallace and now an antiracist attorney
in South Carolina. "It's all been romanticized. The whole thing was based
on white supremacy, but we're in a state of denial." Certainly, Nathan Bedford Forrest, whose career was based on white supremacy, has been romanticized. "We've got to take on the Confederacy," urges Turnipseed. The

markers and monuments praising Nathan Bedford Forrest would be a good place to start.

The very next year, yet another Forrest monument went up, outside the history museum in Selma, Alabama. Immediately, it drew complaints, however, and in 2012 someone stole it. In 2015, the United Daughters of the Confederacy put up a replacement but in a cemetery. At Parkers Crossroads, Tennessee, a new kiosk gives Forrest's entire biography, claiming about Fort Pillow, "He lost control of his troops, and a number of Union soldiers, most of them black troops, were killed as they attempted to surrender." Note how the text excuses Forrest and puts the murder of the POWs into the passive voice.

However, across the South, worshipping Forrest on the landscape is finally beginning to ease. In 2013, Jacksonville, Florida, took Forrest's name off of what is now Westside High School. Students had voted about 64% to 36% for the removal. To those of us who try to remain optimistic about race relations, however, it was sad to see that the vote went along racial lines. Almost no white students voted against Forrest. At the end of 2017, after the race riot in Charlottesville, Memphis took down its statue of Forrest on a horse from Forrest Park. The city had already renamed the park. In 2018, three white-controlled organizations—Calvary Episcopal Church, Rhodes College, and the National Park Service—combined to put up an accurate marker, "Forrest and the Memphis Slave Trade," which helps balance some of the laudatory Forrest markers elsewhere in Tennessee. WE ALL BE, a black group in Memphis and Mississippi that concerns itself with how history is told today, also got a new Tennessee state marker up in Memphis. Titled on one side "Remember Fort Pillow," it portrays the battle and its aftermath accurately, making use of the dead-to-wounded ratio provided above. From a major intersection in Memphis, a worshipful marker claiming that Forrest "fought like a Titan and struck like a god, And his dust is our ashes of glory," has thankfully come down. Busts and statues of Forrest continue to draw protests and vandalism. Perhaps within another twenty years, our worship of Forrest will be a distant and unpleasant memory.[1]

1. League of the South, www.dixienet.org/ls-press-releases/nbf, 6/98; Pope quoted in Rollin Osterweis, *The Myth of the Lose Cause* (Hamden, CT: Archon, 1973), 113; Civil War Centennial Commission of TN, *Directory of Civil War Monuments and Memorials in TN* (Nashville: CWCC, 1963); Jack Hurst, *Nathan Bedford Forrest* (NY: Knopf, 1993); Brian S. Wills, *A Battle from the Start* (NY: Harper, 1993), 192, 215, 373; James B. Jones

Jr., "An Analysis of National Register Listings and Roadside Historic Markers in TN," *The Public Historian* 10, no. 3 (summer 1988): 29; Jones, email, 2/96 and 2/98; *Official Records of the War of the Rebellion*, Series F, 16, Part F (Philadelphia, PA: National Historical Society, 1872), 900–905; Tom Turnipseed, conversation, 4/96; "Forrest the Butcher," *The Intercept*, 9/2/2017, theintercept.com/2017/09/02/memphis-wants-to-remove-statue-honoring-KKK-grand-wizard-nathan-bedford-forrest

———————— ☆ ————————

53. A Confederate-KKK Shrine Encounters Turbulence

GEORGIA *Stone Mountain*

Every year 4,000,000 tourists visit Stone Mountain, a five-square-mile park sixteen miles east of Atlanta. They come to picnic, golf, watch the laser show, ride the paddlewheel riverboat and the steam railroad, look at the "reconstructed" antebellum plantation and grist mill, visit the petting zoo, and hear entertainers, but most of all they come to gawk at what Stone Mountain's website calls "the largest relief sculpture in the world." This sculpture, 90 feet high and 190 feet across, portrays three key leaders of the Confederacy—Robert E. Lee, Stonewall Jackson, and Jefferson Davis—carved in granite some 400 feet above the ground. Visitors walk to a viewing patio, visit a museum about the carving, and for an extra charge can get closer to its face by riding a cable car to the top of the mountain.

Older residents know but few out-of-towners realize that this tourist trap was from its inception a Ku Klux Klan site—indeed, *the* sacred site to members of the second and third national klans. The first incarnation of the Ku Klux Klan was founded in Tennessee immediately after the Civil War. Made up of ex-Confederates under the leadership of Nathan Bedford Forrest (chapter 52) and later John B. Gordon, the KKK terrorized African Americans and white Republicans, particularly in Tennessee and Georgia. Clones sprang up in other states, calling themselves Knights of the White Camellia, Red Shirts, White League, and the like. They made voting Republican a life-endangering act, leading to the overthrow of Republican rule in every Southern state by 1877.

Stone Mountain later became identified with the Confederacy and the first Klan. In 1915, Helen C. Plane, president of the United Daughters of the

Confederacy, hired the famous sculptor Gutzon Borglum, who would later go on to carve Mount Rushmore, to make Stone Mountain into a huge Confederate monument.[1] She asked him to include mounted Klansmen, since, as she put it, "they had saved us from Negro domination and carpetbagger rule." Plane was right to suggest a unity between Confederates and the original Ku Klux Klan: most original Klansmen came from the ranks of the Confederate Army, and most Klan leaders from its officer corps, and both organizations sought to keep African Americans in slavery or peonage. Borglum balked at including Klansmen in his battle scene, but he did incorporate an altar to the Klan into his plan. Instead of mounted Klansmen, Borglum proposed to carve a central group of key Confederate leaders including Jefferson Davis, Robert E. Lee, Stonewall Jackson, and four others to be chosen later. Above them and on both sides, he proposed what he called "a panorama representing the Confederate armies," with artillerymen, cavalry, and infantry.

The second Klan was born at Stone Mountain on Thanksgiving Day, 1915. William J. Simmons gathered 34 white men there who called themselves the "Knights of Mary Phagan." Phagan, a young white factory worker, had been murdered in Atlanta two years earlier. Leo Frank, a Jewish industrialist, was (erroneously) convicted of the crime. In August 1915, a band of whites took him from prison and hanged him. Spurred by their success and inspired by the recently released film *Birth of a Nation*, which told a tale of purported Reconstruction horrors, the men, some of whom had participated in lynching Frank, met on top of Stone Mountain to form the second national Klan. In the words of *Six Wars at a Time*, a biography of Borglum, "they slipped into bedsheet robes and pointed, hooded caps provided by Simmons, and formed a semi-circle in front of a crude stone altar on which lay an open bible and an unsheathed sword." Simmons lit a huge cross, whereupon Nathan Bedford Forrest's grandson, Nathan Bedford Forrest II, administered the Klan oath to each man. Like his grandfather, who oversaw the first den of the original Klan, Forrest II headed "Nathan Bedford Forrest Klan No. 1"; later he became grand dragon of Georgia and national secretary. As its genesis in the Frank lynching foretold, the new Klan would not be only antiblack but anti-Jewish and, eventually, anti-Catholic.[2]

The following year, Sam Venable, one of the fifteen new Klansmen, deeded the north face of the mountain to the UDC on behalf of the Venable family, its owners, with the stipulation that the Daughters complete the monument within twelve years. "No sculptured figures of ancient or modern times can be compared to these in magnitude or grandeur," Borglum waxed about his plans and promised assistance with fundraising. World War I put the project on hold, but after the war the Klan volunteered to help raise the money for the carving. Borglum himself became a member of the Klan, winding up as a close adviser of David C. Stephenson, leader of the Klan in the Midwest (chapter 31).

Amazingly, Borglum got the federal government to issue 50-cent coins with Robert E. Lee and Stonewall Jackson on them. The United States then authorized the Klan-related Stone Mountain Confederate Monumental Association to sell the coins for a dollar each, the profits going to the project. So deeply had Confederate ideology penetrated the United States by 1924 that even Republicans like Senator Henry Cabot Lodge supported this scheme. (Chapter 81 tells how antiracist idealism among Republicans deteriorated in the 1890s.) In that year, with Klan support, Congress also passed a harsh new immigration law designed to keep out Jews and Catholics from southern and eastern Europe and people of color from everywhere.

Borglum was a good Klansman. He wrote, "If you cross a pure bred with a mongrel dog you get a mongrel. So it is in races. . . . It is curious that the lowest race in civilization is the strongest physically and breeding (crossed) is always down. A Negro and Jew will produce Negro, but Hindu and Jew— Jew; Chinese and Jew, offspring Jew; Italian and Jew, offspring Jew; any European race and Jew, offspring Jew." His head of Robert E. Lee, finished early in 1924, garnered general acclaim. However, Borglum's support of Stephenson against the KKK leadership in Georgia, along with his general arrogance and a dispute over the coin money, led to his dismissal as sculptor in 1925. In a scenario combining Keystone Kops Komedy with melodrama, Borglum destroyed his models for Stone Mountain and escaped from Georgia literally moments before the sheriff came speeding after him.

His successor, Augustus Lukeman, obliterated Borglum's head of Lee and started from scratch. He scaled back Borglum's plan to emphasize Lee, Jackson, and Davis, but by the 1928 deadline, only Lee's head was complete again, funds were running low, and the Venables took back their property. Sam Venable had granted the Klan an easement for unrestricted access to the mountain for its activities, and that stayed in effect until the family sold the property in 1958. In May 1946, Dr. Samuel Green held a rally on Stone Mountain to reorganize the Klan, but it kindled little enthusiasm nationally or regionally.

The third phase of Stone Mountain, like the third phase of the Klan, was ignited by the 1954 *Brown v. Board of Education* decision of the U.S. Supreme Court requiring school desegregation, and the Civil Rights Movement it helped trigger. Many white Southerners vowed to maintain white supremacy. As part of that resistance they used Confederate imagery. In 1956, the Georgia legislature redesigned its state flag "to thumb its nose at federal court desegregation rulings," in the words of reporter Eric Harrison. Two-thirds of the new flag consisted of what is now called "the Confederate flag"—the battle flag of the Army of Northern Virginia. Two years later, the state of Georgia bought Stone Mountain and set out to finish what Borglum had started. Not by accident did Martin Luther King Jr. include in his 1963 "I Have a Dream" speech a call to "let freedom ring from Stone Mountain of Georgia." Instead, the next year, sculptor Walker Hancock was back at work using thermojet torches to carve away the granite. Nor by accident did Georgia officially open the park on April 14, 1965, the centennial—to the *day*—of the murder of President Lincoln. Hancock finally finished in 1972.

During the Civil Rights Movement, James R. Venable, heir to the Venable estate and the Venable legacy of Klan membership, had become imperial wizard of the National Knights of the Ku Klux Klan, one of the organizations claiming to follow in the bloody footsteps of the first two Klans. In the 1970s and 1980s, Georgia added memorial stones in the viewing patio that commemorate famous white male Southerners with passages from their speeches. Mostly these laud Confederates, Klansmen, or both such as John B. Gordon, Confederate general, Klan leader, and later governor of Georgia, but the passages are innocuous and no one is identified as a Klansman. The third Klan approved. In 1975, it held a major organizational meeting at Stone Mountain. In 1981, Klansmen symbolized their connection with the second KKK by painting swastikas on mailboxes of Jewish families in Marietta, Mary Phagan's hometown. Every Labor Day weekend, Venable, who for a time was mayor of Stone Mountain, invited the Klan to his property at the base of the mountain for rallies that included burning three 60-foot crosses.

Venable died in 1993. At about the same time the town was becoming a bedroom community for Atlanta and changing in racial composition: in 1990, 85% of the voters in Stone Mountain were white, but by 1997 only 50% were. Among its new African American residents was Chuck Burris, who got elected to the Stone Mountain City Council. In 1996, Venable's daughter sold the family home to Burris! In November of the next year, with biracial support, Stone Mountain elected Burris its first black mayor.

The state has since distanced itself from the fray: in 1998, Georgia privatized Stone Mountain's hotels, restaurants, water slide, golf and tennis center, and other attractions, in return for $9,500,000 million each year plus 3% of all revenue beyond $44,000,000. The park is also trying to distance itself from its past—tour guides no longer wear Confederate gray, and its website devotes four pages to the history of the mountain from 1567 to the present without ever mentioning the Ku Klux Klan![3] Journalist Tony Horwitz describes its laser show as an unfortunate mix of Coca-Cola, the Beatles, the Atlanta Braves, and Elvis singing "Dixie," followed by the "Battle Hymn of the Republic." Television ads end with the inclusive slogan, "Stone Mountain: A Different Day for Everyone." Eventually the desire for everyone's dollars may accomplish what the physical elements cannot: eradicating Stone Mountain as a Confederate-KKK shrine.

Over the last twenty years, the park has become more and more anachronistic. CNN hosted a group of international TV journalists at its headquarters in Atlanta and took them to Stone Mountain for an outing. "My colleagues from South Africa and I were stunned!!!" one wrote to me. "We joked to each other 'See you next year at Botha Park,'" referring to P. W. Botha, diehard supporter of apartheid.

After the murders of black churchgoers by a neo-Confederate in Charleston in 2015 and the race riot at Charlottesville in 2017, various groups floated different proposals for Stone Mountain. The NAACP suggested simply eradicating the bas relief. The Atlanta City Council suggested adding more people, perhaps including Martin Luther King Jr. or Jimmy Carter. Other political leaders proposed placing a giant liberty bell atop it, so freedom could ring, echoing King's famous phrase. But the Sons of Confederate Veterans made a key legal point: state law set up the park and the monument as a Confederate memorial, so all these ideas would be illegal unless that law was changed. As of 2019, the carving remains a flashpoint, drawing rallies by the NAACP, the KKK, and everyone in between.[4]

1. The KKK adopted Mount Rushmore as another shrine; in the woods around the mountain, hikers tell me they still encounter KIGY—"Klansman, I Greet You"—carved into tree trunks.

2. In the 1980s and 1990s, some neo-Confederates tried to claim that the Confederacy had nothing to do with the overt white supremacy of the three Klans. They need to read

Confederate Veteran, the official organ of the UDC and the SCV, between 1914 and 1918, which ran articles, advertisements for *Birth of a Nation*, and reviews that described the Ku Klux Klan in glowing terms as a continuation of the fight waged by the Confederate army. This support helped recruit new members into the second Klan. On this point, current Klansmen who revel in the connection between the Confederacy and the KKK are more accurate historically. See also such historians as Lerone Bennett, *Black Power U.S.A.: The Human Side of Reconstruction* (NY: Penguin, 1969); Paul Escott, *After Secession* (Baton Rouge: LA State UP, 1978); and Richard Zuczek, *State of Rebellion: Reconstruction in SC* (Columbia: U. of SC Press, 1996).

3. However, I'm told that an exhibit in their museum, new since I visited, does tell of the Klan connections.

4. Minna Morse, "The Changing Face of Stone Mountain," *Smithsonian*, 58: 61; Stone Mountain website, www.globolnet.com/online/stonemountain.html, 4/98 and 8/98; Jack Hurst, *Nathan Bedford Forrest* (NY: Knopf, 1993), 386–87; Howard Shaff and Audrey K. Shaff, *Six Wars at a Time* (Sioux Falls, SD: Center for Western Studies, 1985), 149, 213–14; Sion Schama, *Landscape and Memory* (NY: Knopf, 1995), 393–94; John S. Ezell, *The South Since 1865* (NY: Macmillan, 1963), 372; Charles Rutheiser, *Imagineering Atlanta* (NY: Verso, 1996), 38–40, 243; John Dittmer, *Black Georgia in the Progressive Era, 1900–1920* (Urbana: U. of IL Press, 1977), 185; Alex Heard, "Mount Rushmore: The Real Story," *New Republic* (7/15/91): 17; Lucy S. Stewart, *The Reward of Patriotism* (NY: Walter Neale, 1930), 412–13, 437–38; Eric Harrison, "GA Flag's Rebel Emblem Assumes Olympian Proportions," *Los Angeles Times*, 2/11/93; Michael Newton and Judy Ann Newton, *The KKK: An Encyclopedia* (NY: Garland, 1991), 106; Donald L. Grant, *The Way It Was in the South* (NY: Carol Publishing, 1993), 556–57; Ralph L. Eckert, *John Brown Gordon* (Baton Rouge: LA State UP, 1989), 145–46; Kevin Sack, "Mayor-Elect Declares New Clan in Georgia Town Where Klan Was Born," *Dallas Morning News*, 12/19/97; "The United Daughters of the Confederacy, The Sons of Confederate Veterans, and the Old Confederate Veteran Magazine's Role in the Revival of the Ku Klux Klan," www.anetdfw.com/~crawfsh/sefrose.htm, 9/98; Ben Smith III, "Stone Mountain Concessions Now Privatized," *Atlanta Constitution*, 1/3/98; Tony Horwitz, *Confederates in the Attic* (NY: Pantheon, 1998), 286–88; "NAACP DeKalb Calls for Changes at Stone Mountain Park," *Crossroads News*, 4/11/2018, crossroadsnews.com /news/naacp-dekalb-calls-for-changes-at-stone-mountain-park/article_392b105a -3da0-11e8-8fb2-9bc921708f58.html; Tia Mitchell, "Speakers Say King Still Relevant, Call for Monument at Stone Mountain," *Atlanta Journal-Constitution*, 4/4/2018, myajc.com/news/speakers-say-king-still-relevant-call-for-monument-stone-mountain /mfX9ZS2j22lsEt5XjVKgpO; Katie Leslie, "Atlanta Council Asks Deal to Consider Changes to Stone Mountain Relief," *Atlanta Journal-Constitution*, 7/20/2015, ajc .com/news/local-govt--politics/atlanta-council-asks-deal-consider-changes-stone -mountain-relief/pNDzM8sNVKQpUJIOT7txxL/; Debra McKinney, "Stone Mountain: A Monumental Dilemma." *SPLC Intelligence Report*, 2/10/2018, splcenter.org /fighting-hate/intelligence-report/2018/stone-mountain-monumental-dilemma

———————— ✭ ————————

54. The Missing Town of Rosewood

FLORIDA *Near Cedar Key*

Driving on State Highway 24 toward Cedar Key and the Gulf of Mexico, motorists encounter a sign, "Rosewood," and a little further on, another facing the opposite direction, indicating the departure from Rosewood. The signs look like ordinary city limit signs. However, other than a single two-story house and a tiny trailer park, there is no town.

The story behind these signs is one of the atrocities of American history. Rosewood was a reasonably thriving community, almost entirely African American, until the tragic week that began January 1, 1923, when whites in Levy County eradicated it.

The drama began when Fanny Taylor, a white woman living in nearby Sumner, claimed a black man assaulted her. Her bruises confirmed that someone had indeed beaten her. Whites blamed Jesse Hunter, a black convict recently escaped from a road crew. Blacks believed her white boyfriend did it and that she only blamed an African American to mislead her husband.

The sheriff deputized a posse of scores of whites to search for Hunter, including many Ku Klux Klansmen. On January 4, whites concluded that blacks in Rosewood were protecting him. Two white men tried to force their way into the house where they believed he was secreted and were killed. Whites outside opened fire, killing several inside the house.

The next day, hundreds of whites converged on Rosewood. They burned every black home and killed several people. Some African Americans hid out in the swamps for days, only to be murdered when they emerged. Survivors fled; all but one family were too afraid ever to return.

In 1994, the state of Florida finally recognized that this tragedy had occurred by enacting the "Rosewood Claims Act." This law admitted that state and local officials "had sufficient time and opportunity to act to prevent the tragedy, and nonetheless failed to act." Moreover, the state acknowledged, "officials thereafter failed to reasonably investigate the matter, failed to bring the perpetrators to justice, and failed to secure the area for the safe return of the displaced residents."

Like our national apology for interning Pacific Coast Japanese Americans during World War II, the Rosewood Claims Act compensated any survivor "who was present and affected by the violence . . . and was evacuated the week of January 1, 1923." Only a few old-timers, children during the massacre, could claim this payment, but the bill also provided college scholarships for descendants of these families and payments to heirs who could prove property damage. The bill was a courageous act, partly because the destruction of Rosewood was far from unique, so it set a precedent. White violence has destroyed perhaps 40 other black communities in American history including at least two more in Florida: Negro Fort, obliterated July 27, 1816, by Andrew Jackson, and the black part of Ocoee, destroyed in November 1920, after two African Americans dared to try to vote.[1] Florida also led the United States in the rate at which it lynched African Americans in the Nadir of race relations, from 1890 to 1940.

When this book first came out, no historical marker explained the lack of Rosewood between the two "Rosewood" signs. In 2004, however, the state put up a reasonably accurate historical marker. Telling of the expulsion was made easier because most of the second side focuses on the reparations. Thus, we see that achieving justice in the present makes it easier to tell the truth about the past.[2]

1. Other sites of destruction, some of which require more research, range from Torrance, California, through Tulsa, Oklahoma, to Ellenton, South Carolina. Midwestern sites include part of East St. Louis, Illinois, and Pierce City, Missouri. Several black communities in Texas were wiped out. Such attacks were often the genesis of "sundown towns" (chapter 37) that remain all-white or nearly all-white to this day, including the island of Cedar Key a few miles southwest of Rosewood. See my book *Sundown Towns* (NY: New Press, 2018) for more on these expulsions.

2. Harriet Frost, "The Rosewood Massacre" (DC: Petworth Library, 2/97); www.discovery .com/area/history/rosewood/rosewood1.8.html, 3/97; John Singleton, director, *Rosewood* (feature film, 3/97); Michael D'Orso, *Like Judgment Day: The Ruin and Redemption of a Town Called Rosewood* (NY: Gorsset, 1996); Maxine D. Jones, et al., *A Documented History of the Incident Which Occurred at Rosewood, Florida, in January, 1923* (12/93 report), www .freenet.scri.fsu.edu/doc/rosewood.txt, 9/98; Michael Gannon, *Florida: A Short History* (Gainesville: UP of FL, 1993), 86.

————————— ★ —————————

55. The Beech Island Agricultural Club Was Hardly What the Marker Implies

SOUTH CAROLINA *Beech Island*

On U.S. 278 in South Carolina, just east of Augusta, Georgia, stands the only historical marker in the United States, so far as I know, that treats the notorious "patroller" system that controlled slaves when they left their owners' plantations. Its text is so cryptic however that no passerby would guess its true topic. The marker says,

BEECH ISLAND AGRICULTURAL CLUB

On January 5, 1856, Governor James H. Hammond and eleven other farmers of this area organized the Beech Island Agricultural Club for the diffusion of agricultural knowledge and the regulation of illegal slave traffic. Monthly meetings and barbecues have been held almost without interruption since the club's founding.[1]

The first thing the marker gets wrong is the full name of the "club," which was the Beech Island Agricultural and Police Society. The society did share ideas about agriculture—fertilizers, new crops, and the like—but its primary purpose was to keep slaves in line. The phrase "the regulation of illegal slave traffic" seems to refer to the international slave trade made illegal in 1808,[2] but that's not what the "club" really sought to regulate at all. In fact, slaveowners founded the "society" as a "patroller" organization. What they wanted to stop was slaves who were moving about, going to town, and even making money by taking goods from the plantation and selling them.

As the club's full name implies, slavery was a police system. Like prison inmates, enslaved persons are under the control of others, and as with convicts, that control ultimately is physical and potentially violent. A large plantation might have only five or ten whites, including young children and an overseer or two, to control a hundred slaves. Mostly owing to fear of slave revolt and largely at government expense, South Carolina was militarized, from The Citadel—the state military college—down to local militias and patrollers. Despite these precautions, whites rarely felt secure. Because planters always feared slave uprisings, they formed police societies for mutual support. Indeed, South Carolina laws in force from the 1690s required whites to organize patrol systems in all jurisdictions where blacks were a majority. In the Beech Island area, in 1856, more than 60% of all people were enslaved.

Since whites had freedom of movement, they could usually mount sufficient force quickly enough to quell a budding slave rebellion. The patrol system, meanwhile, confined slaves to their own plantation unless they had passes and specific errands. Even a wife visiting her enslaved husband on the next plantation had to have a written pass to see him. Patrollers—volunteers and paid—stopped all African Americans to ask their business and see their passes.

In the 1850s, planters' anxiety grew more acute; they worried that abolitionist ideas, growing more popular, might reach their enslaved workers. Before his election as governor, Congressman James Hammond had made headlines by advocating the death penalty for abolitionists to keep their ideas out of the state and away from slaves. Hence, this new organization. The Society's founding document makes clear that its purpose was to control slaves. Part of it reads, "We, whose names are herewith subscribed, do hereby join, to form ourselves into a Society, for the purpose of communicating our opinions on subjects immediately connected with our best interests, and of acting in concert with each other, and with the fine and determined object of assisting the regular constituted authorities, in enforcing the laws relative to the government of colored persons. . . ."

Maintaining slavery was easier in isolated rural areas where everybody knew everybody, so anyone out of place could readily be challenged. But the founders of the Beech Island Agricultural and Police Society worried about the nearby towns of Augusta, Georgia, and Hamburg (now North Augusta), South Carolina, where dangerous ideas like freedom might flourish:

> The irregularities of our Negroes have become so serious, as not only to affect our interests, as planters materially, but also to endanger the peace and tranquility of the country, and as it is known that these evils arise particularly from the unrestrained manner in which these people are allowed to ramble about the neighborhood and the free unrestricted intercourse they have with the cities of Augusta and Hamburg, it becomes a duty highly

incumbent on us, to put a timely check upon them, and to establish that order so essential to our immediate benefit and future prosperity.

James Hammond was always trying to eliminate "irregularities" in the deportment of his slaves. He had acquired them by marriage, taking over his wife's Beech Island plantation with its mansion, 10,800 acres, and 147 slaves. He started taking control by stopping black church services, substituting white ministers and white passive church style. Hammond tried to convince fellow planters to join him in suppressing black religion by bringing up the specter of a slave revolt. "No very extensive insurrection can take place except through their churches," he argued during a meeting of the police society. "It is very easy to convert a religious organization into a military one, and these Negro churches we must put down."[3]

Hammond also struggled to change the labor system at the plantation. His wife's slaves had grown accustomed to being assigned tasks to complete. If they chose, they could take no breaks or lunch and finish by late afternoon to have time for their families. Hammond favored gang labor—groups of slaves working directly under overseers from sunup to sundown with specified breaks—and tried to implement it through frequent floggings. At least 53 people tried to escape from the Hammonds' plantations, although none succeeded permanently. It was clear why Hammond needed to organize the Beech Island Agricultural and Police Society.

Nevertheless, Hammond actually believed that his slaves "love and appreciate me." Indeed, Hammond's theories about slavery as a "positive good" became cornerstones of the white Southern defense of the institution. To his face, slaves acted the part of course, because a happy master was much less dangerous than an angry one. Many antebellum plantations still present that story today. At Monticello, for instance, guides tell how the slaves would crowd about to welcome Thomas Jefferson home from trips, even pulling his coach to the house by hand to show how much they liked him. During the Civil War, however, according to historian Drew Gilpin Faust, "as Union victory drew ever closer, sullen and unmanageable slaves made clear to James Henry Hammond that their now abandoned 'cheerful greetings' had been not a sign of acceptance of his legitimate domination . . . but a charade."

Hammond theorized that slavery was appropriate for blacks because, among other reasons, it controlled their otherwise untamed carnal instincts, an irony in light of his own inclinations. He had sex with his wife, his wife's sister's four young daughters, his slave mistress Sally Johnson, her twelve-year-old daughter Louisa, at least two white men according to historian Martin Duberman, and perhaps other women and male slaves.[4] Nevertheless, he was a stern moralist toward his slaves. If a slave couple wanted to divorce they had to convince him that sufficient cause existed; even then, each got a hundred lashes and could not remarry for three years.

Hammond's extensive diaries detail his treatment of the people he owned. In 1834, for example, he wrote that he had a slave "flogged . . . slightly. Left him unable to walk scarcely"—and that from a *slight* flogging! A hundred lashes would be life-threatening. His reputation for cruelty lasted more than a century in the black community: Amelia Dorsey, an old woman by the time she was interviewed by the WPA Writers Project in the 1930s, still remembered how when she was a child, "the old people tell about how Governor Hammond chastised his hands."

James Henry Hammond exemplified what Thomas Jefferson called "the most boisterous passions, the most unremitting despotism" of the slave system (chapter 68). The Beech Island Agricultural and Police Society extended his control and that of his class into the surrounding countryside. Patrollers were "generally intensely Negrophobic nonslaveholders," according to historian William Barney, who "meted out terrible punishments." Legislators tried to curb "irregularities" "arising chiefly from their drinking too much liquor before or during the time of their riding on duty." A white South Carolinian, writing after the Civil War, told of hearing acquaintances brag "with great gusto how in the good old times they used to hunt down runaway Negroes with hounds and guns, brand them, beat them till senseless, and while patrolling at night flog Negroes who had passes 'just to hear them beg.'" Throughout the South, even slaves on errands for their owners with legitimate passes feared the patrollers.

Historian Richard Zuczek tells that South Carolina planters briefly reinstated the patrol system in 1865, even though the Civil War had supposedly ended slavery! During Reconstruction, the night riding of the Ku Klux Klan and Red Shirts was a further extension of patrolling, Zuczek notes, involving some of the same men. A marker about the Beech Island Agricultural and Police Society, featuring Governor Hammond, that *accurately* portrayed his relations with his laborers would convey important information about how the antebellum South really worked.[5]

1. The marker's second side tells of the club in the twentieth century.

2. Some white South Carolinians had never been happy that Congress shut off the slave trade with Africa in 1808. They continued to smuggle in Africans as slaves and, in the 1850s, agitated to reopen the African trade.

3. Hammond was never able to eradicate black services entirely, including the practice of West African religion.

4. "Sex" as defined by the Clinton impeachment. He did not have intercourse with the nieces but had children by his wife, Sally Johnson, and Louisa Johnson, and perhaps other women.

5. Orville Vernon Burton, *In My Father's House Are Many Mansions* (Chapel Hill: U. of NC Press, 1985), 130, 140, 155–56, 182–87, 391; Burton, email, 1/99; H. M. Henry, *The Police Control of the Slave in SC* (NY: Negro UP, 1968 [1914]), 28–40; William L. Barney, *Flawed Victory* (NY: Praeger, 1975), 136–37; B. O. Townsend, "SC Morals," *Atlantic Monthly* 39 (4/1877): 471; "Beech Island file," SC Marker Office; Parks, Recreation, and Historic Sites Division (Atlanta); Carol Bleser, ed., *The Hammonds of Redcliffe* (NY: Oxford UP, 1981), 9; Drew G. Faust, *James Henry Hammond and the Old South* (Baton Rouge: LA State UP, 1982); *Southern Stories* (Columbia: U. of MO Press, 1992), 9, 54–66; James McPherson, *Drawn with the Sword* (NY: Oxford UP, 1996), 45; Martin Duberman, "'Writhing Bedfellows' in Antebellum SC," in Martin Duberman, Martha Vicinus, and George Chauncy Jr., *Hidden from History* (NY: NAL, 1989), 158; Richard Zuczek, *State of Rebellion: Reconstruction in SC* (Columbia: U. of SC Press, 1996), 18, 55.

★

---

56. To the Loyal Slaves

SOUTH CAROLINA *Fort Mill*

Across the former Confederacy from the 1890s on, whites put up markers and monuments honoring slaves who served the Confederacy and their owners loyally throughout the Civil War. Sometimes, it seems that neo-Confederates want to remember by name each and every African American who fought, dug ditches, cooked, or otherwise aided the Confederacy. In Darlington, South Carolina, a Confederate monument honors Henry "Dad" Brown, a drummer for Confederate troops. A museum in Plymouth, North Carolina, displays small wall exhibits for one or two African Americans in each nearby county who accompanied their owners to war as "body servants." In a black neighborhood in Canton, Mississippi, stands a twenty-foot obelisk erected by William Howcott, a Confederate officer, honoring Willis Howcott, the slave who accompanied him in the Civil War as "A colored boy of rare loyalty and faithfulness." In Greenville, Mississippi, a state historic marker tells of Holt Collier, an African American who "served as a Confederate sharpshooter and cavalryman." Near the Hermitage, Andrew Jackson's mansion just east of Nashville, a marker for a cemetery that holds 483 Confederate veterans singles out by name only "Ralph Ledbetter, former slave and bodyguard to a Confederate officer during the war." The Confederate monument in Arlington National Cemetery includes an African American man marching off to war behind two Confederate soldiers.

In "Confederate Park" in downtown Fort Mill, "With approval of the Jefferson Davis Memorial Association," Samuel W. White erected an obelisk in 1895 that purports to tell what African Americans did during the Civil War on the home front. On its front is the legend,

1860

DEDICATED TO THE FAITHFUL SLAVES
who, loyal to a sacred trust, toiled for the support of the army, with
matchless devotion, and with sterling fidelity guarded our defenseless
homes, women, and children, during the struggle for the principles of our
"Confederate States of America."
1865

On the base of the Fort Mill obelisk are carvings of a field hand resting under a tree and a black woman holding a white child on the steps of the "big house." Neither panel quite depicts work, and work was what slavery was all about. Instead, the illustrations invite visitors to think of slavery as a time of relaxation and interracial caring.

On the back, "In grateful memory of earlier days," the monument lists ten slaves "Among the many faithful," seven of whom are named White! This, of course, exemplifies the practice, common among dominant groups, of singling out a few "loyal" ones within the subordinate group for recognition (chapters 69 and 90).

In reality, as the Civil War continued, slaves on the home front acted with increasing independence, even impudence. "Although Confederate memorialists later praised the 'faithful darkies' who stood by their mistresses," according to historian George Rable, "contemporaries knew better." He tells that many slaves simply stopped work or at least ceased working for their absent owners. A South Carolina planter voiced in 1862 what became a widespread complaint after the Emancipation Proclamation of January 1, 1863: "We have had hard work to get along this season; the Negroes are unwilling to do any work." W. E. B. Du Bois called this "the general strike" and said it contributed mightily to the downfall of the Confederacy.

When Union armies came near, work slowdowns and stoppages gave way to mass escape. "We went to sleep one night with a plantation full of Negroes, and woke to find not one on the place," wrote Myrta Avary. "We had thought there was a strong bond of affection on their side as well as on ours." In the words of historian William Barney, "Southern whites were shocked to discover that the average domestic slave would be far more likely to lead Union soldiers to the family silver rather than to hide and guard it." White women took to burying their silver and other valuables secretly, at night, lest slaves betray the treasure to the Union. African Americans also betrayed the Confederacy in more important ways. In January 1864, Confederate Gen. Patrick Cleburne called slavery "an omnipresent spy system," and in *Spies and Spymasters of the Civil War*, Donald Markle tells about African Americans who provided U.S. commanders with important information.[1] And of course, some 130,000 slaves escaped and fought in the U.S. Army and Navy, including more than 5,000 from South Carolina.[2]

From the 1890s on, Confederate apologists denied all this. If African Americans served willingly in the Confederate cause, neo-Confederate thinking goes, then white Southerners could hardly have established the Confederacy to preserve and enlarge racial slavery. Indeed, as of 1999, neo-Confederates were still at it: Magnolia Plantation outside Charleston, South Carolina, told of the trusty slave who refused to reveal the location of his master's silver, and Terrell's Texas Cavalry, a Confederate reenactment group, was trying to raise funds for a new monument to Confederate soldiers

African Americans helped the U.S. Army in innumerable ways—providing food and water, supplying intelligence about Confederate forces, and suggesting the best roads, fords, and bridges. Some 25,000 ex-slaves worked around camp as cooks, firewood gatherers, general laborers, and body servants to officers. *Harper's Weekly* titled this illustration "Contrabands Washing Clothes for the Soldiers of the Union Army." Blacks also helped the army move forward by clearing trees the Rebels had felled across the roads, digging fortifications at new camps, and driving the horses and mules. They worked so hard that onlookers concluded "the labor of one freeman is worth that of two slaves—or three soldiers!"[3]

of color, which they hoped to erect in Richmond, Virginia.[4] (As of 2019, they had not succeeded; as far as I can tell, they have shifted views and now believe that the Afro-Confederate story is a hoax.)[5] It is a curious argument. Thousands of Jewish soldiers served in Hitler's army during World War II, far more than the number of African American soldiers who served in the Confederacy's army, but no one uses their memory to deny that Germany was anti-Semitic.

Markers and monuments like the Fort Mill obelisk must swim upstream against a torrent of facts. First, they grossly overstate the Confederacy's acceptance of black soldiers. Confederate Secretary of War James A. Seddon was perfectly clear: "Our position with the North and before the world will not allow the employment as armed soldiers of Negroes." The Confederate Congress adamantly refused to let African Americans enlist until March 13, 1865, less than three weeks before the liberation of Richmond.[6] Thus, "Dad" Brown was not allowed to carry a firearm because of his race.

This illustration from *Harper's Weekly* for May 10, 1862, shows a Confederate captain forcing two slaves at gunpoint to load a cannon within range of a Union sharpshooter who shot them, one after the other. Neo-Confederates could cite them as examples of African Americans who gave their all for the Confederate cause, except that in this case a Northern newspaper artist observed the coercion through a telescope.

Probably, Ledbetter's marker should read "former slave and body servant," not "bodyguard"; he was not buried in the circles of Confederate veterans but lies under a tree outside the outermost ring. Most of the many slaves who accompanied their owners were limited to performing menial tasks like foraging for food, washing laundry, and throwing up earthworks. Historian James K. Hogue at Princeton concluded, "The evidence of body servants actually fighting is so thin, and they are mentioned so infrequently, that perhaps the only reasonable judgment the historian can make is that they actually took up arms only very rarely." Historian Robert Krick, who has studied the records of 150,000 Confederate soldiers, "found fewer than a dozen were black."

Even more telling, these neo–Confederate markers and monuments over-look African Americans' service to the Union. In Columbia, North Car-olina, for example, an otherwise standard Confederate monument says on its reverse side, "In appreciation of our faithful slaves." Actually, more than 10,000 blacks in eastern North Carolina slipped away from their owners to coastal areas controlled by Union forces, according to *A History of African Americans in North Carolina*. Several thousand of them enlisted and fought for the Union cause; others worked for the Union, digging fortifications, clearing roads, and unloading ships. On the Confederate side, things were very different. R. B. Johnson, the agent for getting slave labor for the defense of South Carolina, complained, "the slaves themselves are very adverse to this labor." Confederate Gen. Joseph E. Johnston wrote in early 1864, "The impressment of Negroes has been practiced ever since the war commenced, but we never have been able to keep the impressed Negroes with an army near the enemy. They desert."

As the war ended in 1865, in the words of historian Stephen Ash, "many whites were profoundly shaken by the revelation that slaves hated slavery and resented their masters." This might seem obvious to us now, but as Ash notes, "the belief that blacks were content in their bondage was a cornerstone of proslavery ideology." Ash quotes a white Confederate when she learned the contrary: "As to the idea of a *faithful servant, it is all a fiction.*" Another over-generalized in despair, "There is not *one Negro* in *all the South*, who will remain faithful *from attachment to their master & mistress*—not one." Every commemoration of slave loyalty on the landscape, like this obelisk in Fort Mill, represents a dishonest effort, decades later, to mystify that truth. Moving the obelisk to a museum could prompt the writing of labels pointing out that it went up during the Nadir of race relations in service of the "Lost Cause" defense of the Confederacy. But South Carolina made it hard to correct bad public history when it passed its "Heritage Act" in 2000. No longer do towns like Fort Mill have autonomy over their own public history. Now, only the legislature can move or alter a monument, and it can do so only by a two-thirds supermajority of both houses.[7]

1. Chapter 61 tells of spies even in the White House of the Confederacy: "In contrast to the Negro spy efforts for the Union," Markle writes, "there is no available evidence that the Negro served as a spy for the Confederacy at any point in the war."

2. For that matter, poor whites also fled to Union areas in eastern North Carolina, especially to Plymouth. They showed little loyalty to the planter elite and sometimes raided nearby abandoned plantations or squatted on them and claimed the land for themselves. One African American, Robert Smalls, gets a South Carolina marker in Beaufort that says in part, "He commandeered and delivered to Union forces the Confederate gunboat *Planter*, on which he was a crew man."

3. Union Gen. I. N. Palmer related a different result: "The Negroes will not go voluntarily, so I am obliged to force them," but his was decidedly a minority report; another coastal North Carolina commander reported blacks "consider it a duty to work for the U.S. government" and "tabooed" any slackers.

4. As of 2018, Magnolia's main narrative at its website still focuses entirely on minutiae of the owning family and their gardens and health, with no mention of anyone else. However, in about 2015, Magnolia did open an exhibit in five cabins that treats African American life "from the 1850s to the 1990s," when the buildings were rehabilitated. I have not taken this tour, which costs an additional $8 on top of the garden tour

charge. I suspect most visitors avoid the extra expense. See magnoliaplantation.com /PDF/FromSlaverytoFreedomProjectOverview.pdf

5. One neo-Confederate leader tried to use this prospect to head off the statue of Arthur Ashe, the black tennis star, that Richmond added to its Monument Row of Confederate leaders in 1996. On Terrell's see Andy Hall, "37th Texas Cavalry Capitulates to Yankee Revisionism," *Dead Confederates* blog, 7/28/2011, deadconfederates.com/2011/07/28 /37th-texas-cavalry-capitulates-to-yankee-revisionism

6. African Americans recruited in Richmond probably never saw combat. According to one Confederate observer, they may have joined simply to get new clothes: "One company of Negroes was formed, and I witnessed their drill in the capitol square, but I understood that as soon as they got their uniforms they vanished in one night." Thomas Morris Chester, the black Civil War journalist, learned a very different motive from an African American who escaped from Richmond about six weeks before the Confederate Congress made its decision to accept blacks into the military. He told Chester that African Americans had secretly pledged to enlist when the Confederacy actually went through with the idea, but then if the opportunity arose, they would turn on Confederate troops and catch them in a crossfire.

7. George C. Rable, *Civil Wars: Women and the Crisis of Southern Nationalism* (Urbana: U. of IL Press, 1989), 117–18, 155; William L. Barney, *Flawed Victory* (NY: Praeger, 1975), 139, 141; James McPherson, *Negro's Civil War* (NY: Random House Vintage, 1965), 242; McPherson, *Battle Cry of Freedom* (NY: Oxford UP, 1988), 837; Donald E. Markle, *Spies and Spymasters of the Civil War* (NY: Hippocrene, 1994), 64; "Hitler Knew Some Army Officers Had Jewish Origins," *San Francisco Examiner*, 12/2/96; Lissa Hofbauer, "Monuments Honor the Blacks Who Wore Gray," *Charleston Post and Courier*, 2/2/97; Amelia Reece, conversation, 2/97; Douglas Demmons, "Monument Honors Slaves Who Served Confederate Cause," *Jackson [MS] Clarion-Ledger*, 11/27/82; "Ceremonies Rededicate Monument," *Madison County [MS] Herald*, 5/3/84; Jeffrey Crow, Paul Escott, and Flora Hatley, *A History of African Americans in NC* (Raleigh, NC: Division of Archives and History, 1992), 72–74; Ira Berlin, et al., *The Wartime Genesis of Free Labor* (Cambridge: Cambridge UP, 1990), 20; C. E. Cauthen, *SC Goes to War 1860–1865* (Chapel Hill: U. of NC Press, 1950), 184; American Social History Project, *Freedom's Unfinished Revolution* (NY: New Press, 1996), 65; James K. Hogue, "Did Blacks Fight for the Confederacy?" (Princeton, NJ: Princeton U. History Department, n.d.); 17, 25; James Ronald Kennedy and Walter Donald Kennedy, *The South Was Right!* (Gretna, LA: Pelican, 1994), 142; "Confederate Ordinance During the War," *Confederate Veteran* 12 (1904): 23; *Thomas Morris Chester, Black Civil War Correspondent*, ed. by R. J. M. Blackett (Baton Rouge: LA State UP, 1989), 247–48; Edward Sebesta, email, 6/14/98; Benjamin Quarles, *The Negro in the Civil War* (Boston: Little, Brown, 1953), 275; Stephen V. Ash, *When the Yankees Came* (Chapel Hill: U. of NC Press, 1995), 190–92, 223; Tony Horwitz, *Confederates in the Attic* (NY: Pantheon, 1998), 251; Bell Wiley, *Confederate Women* (Westport, CT: Greenwood, 1975), 163.

---------- ★ ----------

57. Who Burned Columbia?

SOUTH CAROLINA *Columbia*

At least nine different state historical markers in Columbia leave no doubt about who burned the capital of South Carolina. They tell how Union Gen. William T. Sherman's soldiers set fire to various buildings in town. The Washington Street Methodist Church was "burned by Union troops in 1865," the First Baptist Church building on Sumter Street was "burned Feb. 17, 1865, by Union troops," Ebenezer Lutheran Church was "burned by Union troops in 1865," the site of the old State House was "burned by Sherman's troops, Feb. 17, 1865," and the "Site of Gibbes House," which, "with his notable library, art treasures, and scientific collections was burned by Union troops February 17, 1865."

Sherman's men did burn several smaller towns in South Carolina. Who burned Columbia is not so simply answered, however. The issue has occupied Carolina historians and polemicists for decades. At the South Carolina Department of Archives and History, the controversy recurred in front of me. I asked one staff historian, "Who burned Columbia?" "It wasn't Sherman," he replied, "and a lot less burned than most people think." A few minutes later, a second historian, older and more senior at the archives, joined our conversation. Without prompting, he went off on a tirade: "Some historians have written revisionist nonsense, arguing that Sherman never burned Columbia. He said he was going to burn it, and he burned it. Period." My first informant quailed at his passion and said nothing. I said little. I didn't know.

Now, I do. Marion Lucas, a historian who grew up and got all his education in Columbia, devoted years of research to an entire book on the subject, *Sherman and the Burning of Columbia*. Aware that he is jousting against the received doctrine of a century of Confederate interpretation, Lucas carefully backed his conclusions with information from primary sources. He told that as they abandoned Columbia, Confederate soldiers and stragglers burned two railroad stations, the Congaree River bridge, and piles of cotton on Richardson Street, in accord with Confederate policy, as U.S. troops arrived on February 17, 1865.[1]

Lucas gave almost an hour-by-hour account of what happened next. An accidental fire broke out in the red-light district just west of the capitol and destroyed many houses, but firefighters and U.S. troops extinguished that blaze. Then, at eight that evening, what Lucas calls an "inexplicable blaze" broke out on Richardson Street. More than 2,000 U.S. soldiers tried to put it out. One general and his staff barely escaped from the hotel that he had taken for his command post and residence.

Lucas reached a conclusion about what caused the "inexplicable blaze." Fires in stacks of cotton bales are notoriously hard to put out. At least one smoldering pile had already burst into flames earlier in the afternoon. Lucas thinks that a high wind then roared in that rekindled the cotton and caused the fire to spread to nearby wooden buildings.

Lucas is careful to add that drunken Union soldiers as well as "the local criminal element" looted houses for souvenirs, set fires in them, and intimidated residents. One marker is correct: drunken U.S. soldiers did burn Gibbes's House, but Lucas doubts that their actions extended the general conflagration. The wind over the cotton bales did that, and when the wind died down in the early morning hours, exhausted firefighters and U.S. troops finally got the fire under control.

It turns out that Lucas's judgments weren't all that new; the famous historian James Ford Rhodes had arrived at much the same conclusions in an article written in 1902. After rigorously assessing the damage, Lucas concluded that the fire destroyed "about one third of Columbia," "confined chiefly to the business district." Nevertheless, ignoring his scholarship, an exhibit titled "The Burning of Columbia" in Columbia's "Confederate Relic Room and Museum" claims, "With no CSA troops to resist, General Sherman's men burned 80% of the city." The Relic Room, a state agency started in 1895 owing to pressure from (and with curatorial assistance by) the United Daughters of the Confederacy, may be the least accurate museum operated by a state government anywhere in the United States.[2]

What about other evidence of Sherman the brute? On February 18 and 19, U.S. forces destroyed Confederate rolling stock, Confederate printing presses, the arsenal with 10,000 muskets and rifled muskets, and all the cotton not already consumed, but these were legitimate military targets. After the War, white citizens collected testimony of misconduct by Union soldiers and Lucas examines it meticulously. He finds just six cases of specific acts of violence against civilians by U.S. soldiers, "all of which consisted of pushing, shoving, and striking." Union commanders did order two persons shot—both

U.S. soldiers, found guilty of looting. Even pro-Confederate historian E. Merton Coulter admitted, "There is no evidence that . . . [Sherman] ever permitted his army to slay non-combatants or that his army ever desired to do so."

When Sherman's forces moved north out of Columbia, thousands of African Americans left with them to avoid re-enslavement and to help the cause of freedom. They were wise, because when Confederates regained control of the city, they punished and even shot blacks who had supported the U.S. Army. At least 800 whites left as well—men avoiding Confederate conscription, women who had made attachments with soldiers, and especially Unionists who had never supported secession. As the troops left, Union Gen. O. O. Howard, later to run the Freedmen's Bureau, left 500 cattle on the green of the University of South Carolina for the people of Columbia, under the mayor's control. He also provided transport for citizens made homeless by the blaze to the abandoned Methodist Female College and gave them blankets and rations. A state marker tells the history of the University of South Carolina in the war but omits Howard's gesture.

Of course, Sherman also marched through Georgia and North Carolina. Thirty markers in Georgia have as their primary theme the destruction wrought by Sherman's soldiers, according to geographer Harold Gulley, and many more mention it. Again, although his army did make war hell, tales of the destruction it wrought grew with every retelling. According to William Surface of the Museum of the Cape Fear in Fayetteville, North Carolina, "it became a badge of honor for some Southerners to have an ancestor whose house was burned by Sherman's troops." Betty McCain, Secretary of the North Carolina Department of Cultural Resources, exemplified this mindset while testifying before the North Carolina Historical Commission in opposition to a proposed memorial to Sherman's troops at Bentonville Battleground (chapter 58). She declared that her foremother fought off Sherman's men with a broom three different times when they tried to burn down her house near Wilmington. With no McCain ancestors to stop them, Sherman's men *did* burn the warehouses in Wilmington, McCain claimed, as part of their swath of destruction across the state. Apparently, McCain did not know that *Confederates* set the Wilmington warehouses ablaze before pulling out of the town, to deny materiel to the Union. Nor did she know that Sherman's men never came within a hundred miles of Wilmington! Never mind—if it happened in Carolina and was bad, Sherman did it!

A Georgia geographer painstakingly mapped Sherman's route and found that many homes alleged to have been reduced to ashes in 1865 were standing in 1955! "The actual destruction of private dwellings was rare indeed," he concluded. In 1995, historians for the North Carolina Department of Archives and History assessed Sherman's advance through that state and came to much harsher conclusions, particularly as to the conduct of the "bummers" not under close supervision. Certainly, Sherman's men did torch the houses of Confederate leaders in Georgia and the Carolinas.

Confederates inflicted much of the damage done to the Southern countryside, however. A Savannah newspaper editor wrote in October 1864, well before Sherman took his city, "It is notorious that our own army, while falling back from Dalton [in northwest Georgia], was even more dreaded by the inhabitants than was the army of Sherman. The soldiers, and even the officers, took everything that came in their way, giving the excuse that if they did not, the enemy would." Similarly, in the Carolinas, much of the damage now credited to Sherman was done by Confederate cavalrymen under Maj. Gen. Joseph Wheeler. North Carolina Governor Zebulon Vance remarked that if, having visited seven plagues upon the wicked land of Egypt, the Lord needed an eighth plague, he would have used the Confederate cavalry. Directly after the war, Wheeler became something of a scapegoat. Some white Southerners were irate about the acts of his men, but Wheeler's orders from Gen. John Bell Hood were clear: "If Sherman advances to the South or East destroy all things in his front that might be useful to him." Because Wheeler was not always sure which route Sherman would take, his swath of scorched earth often had to be wider than Sherman's.[3]

White Southerners knew this in 1866. As a result, Sherman was much less reviled in the nineteenth century than in the twentieth. Today, some 600 historical markers in Georgia and scores more in the Carolinas give details of Sherman's progress and Confederate opposition. Written from a neo-Confederate viewpoint, the markers pretend that civilians were united in opposition to Sherman. Even after reading *all* of them, Civil War buffs would not learn several crucial facts about Sherman's campaign.

First, it was an extended experience in forging new race relations. For days on end, some of Sherman's units never saw white inhabitants. Many white males were away in the Confederate army, of course, and other whites had evacuated to safer areas. Sometimes, the experience was grim—white and black Southerners were shocked when some of Sherman's soldiers ransacked slave cabins. More often, the encounter was joyful. According to historian Joseph T. Glatthaar, "everywhere soldiers went, crowds of ecstatic blacks came out to see and encourage them." Planters tried to convince their slaves that the Yankees were going to sell them into slavery in Cuba or kill them outright, but most blacks put no stock in such tales. Sherman wrote that when he entered Covington, Georgia, "The Negroes were simply frantic with joy. Whenever they heard my name, they clustered about my horse, shouted and prayed. I have witnessed hundreds if not thousands of such scenes." From Tennessee through Georgia to the Carolinas, not one historical marker tells about the jubilation Sherman's arrival occasioned among most of the people who witnessed it—black people. The few markers that do mention African Americans honor those individuals who behaved heroically on the Confederate side.

No marker notes that Sherman's men freed many of the people they encountered. Sherman himself didn't always want to, and his officers tried to convince slaves that the army could not feed them and the war would soon free them anyway. Conditions for freedmen in the army camps were so squalid and disease-infested that historian William L. Barney estimated one inhabitant in four died before the war was over. Nevertheless, "the niggers was mighty glad to have the Yankees take them," said an ex-slave, and went on to tell why: "They wanted to get out from under that rough treatment. Georgia was about the meanest place in the world." On at least one occasion, Union Gen. J. C. Davis ordered a pontoon bridge over a flooded creek removed after his troops had passed but before allowing its black entourage to cross. Many of his men seethed, and some African Americans drowned trying to swim the river, knowing that pursuing Confederate soldiers would re-enslave them.

It is not too much to say that the blacks in Georgia and the Carolinas made Sherman's march possible. Their help meant that Sherman's forces would not be traveling through hostile territory without supply lines. Rather, the soldiers were more like a huge guerrilla force in friendly territory. When Gen. Sherman entered Columbia, Union prisoners of war who had escaped their Confederate jails met him joyfully. Free blacks in Columbia had secreted them in their homes for months, a remarkable feat because it required unanimous support of all who knew. But no historical marker tells that African Americans aided Sherman's march in any way. Instead, as the previous entry shows, the landscape teaches that African Americans sided with the South.

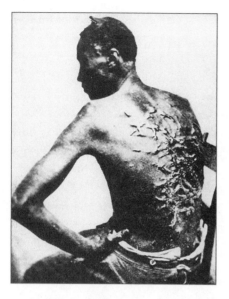

Taken in Baton Rouge, Louisiana, April 2, 1863, this photo showed the result of a whipping "Gordon" had received the previous October. Gordon had escaped slavery ten days earlier and was receiving a physical; he later became a corporal in the Union Army. The doctor, J. W. Mercer, stated that many of the 400 runaway slaves he examined that season were "as badly lacerated as the specimen presented in the enclosed photograph." When soldiers saw the backs of slaves who had been whipped, some converted instantly to an anti-slavery position. Units then made a point of burning the whipping post and shooting the bloodhounds at each plantation they encountered. Union soldiers were much more likely to loot plantations than small farms, and if the newly freed African Americans told them their owner had been particularly cruel, they were likely to burn the "big house" as well. No marker hints at this abolitionist tinge to the damage Sherman's men caused.[4]

Many whites in Georgia and the Carolinas also aided the Union columns. As Sherman marched to the sea from Atlanta to Savannah, his army grew in numbers because hundreds if not thousands of white Southerners joined him along the way. As he continued through the Carolinas, more whites including Confederate deserters volunteered for service. What were their motivations? War weariness can explain desertion but not joining the other side. Hunger was not a factor; Confederates, like Union soldiers, fed themselves by foraging in the countryside, which was adequate to the task. Probably, some soldiers simply wanted to be on the winning side. Others who had never supported slavery now saw a way to oppose the slave aristocracy without being hanged as deserters. Whatever their reasons, most thought they were doing the right thing to join Sherman, and the landscape should tell about these converts. Instead, all along Sherman's route, historic markers and sites maintain the myth of whites united behind the Confederacy.

Some markers heroify the Confederate opposition to Sherman's steamroller. Actually, there was little resistance. Four Confederate generals in South Carolina commanded 40,000 men, but they never united their forces to mount real opposition against Sherman. Several reasons accounted for this poor showing. Morale was low; after Lincoln won reelection in November 1864, Confederates had little to hope for. The success of black U.S. troops and slaves' clear dissatisfaction with bondage had thrown Confederate ideology into considerable confusion. Almost two-thirds of the grey-clad army that did oppose Sherman disappeared through desertion. Often, those who remained no longer fought hard, having little to fight with and no clear aims to fight for. Thus, historians record a number of Confederate debacles during the march, such as the capture of 73 Rebel cavalrymen by one Union lieutenant and two orderlies. None gets a marker.

Historic houses in the South use Sherman's march and "the ravages of Reconstruction" to explain their economic hard times after the war. Poplar Grove, for example, just north of Wilmington, North Carolina, puts out a brochure that invokes the traditional storyline of federal brutes trampling on the hapless white South: "Prosperous until the Civil War, Poplar Grove experienced many of the hardships inflicted by Union armies on the home front populace throughout the Confederacy." It turns out that the Union Army took "four horses, 50 bushels of peanuts, and 20 beehives of honey." That's it! Northerners never occupied the house, never burned a building. Furthermore, they left a receipt, and several years after the Civil War, the plantation owner succeeded in collecting payment for everything the army took. Blaming Poplar Grove's postwar economic woes on the "hardships inflicted by Union armies" is convenient but wrong. Plantation agriculture was typically uneconomical, partly because it encouraged neither owners nor slaves to innovate. It was often enormously profitable, but only because plantation owners didn't have to pay their workforce. The antebellum profits that built the Poplar Grove manor house and bought its furnishings dried up after the Civil War because landowners now had to pay their laborers. Seen this way, the postwar hard times show how slavery, not Sherman, was oppressive.

Finally, Betty McCain's foremother notwithstanding, a full history of gender relations during Sherman's trek remains to be written. In *Marching Through Georgia*, Lee Kennett records only one incident of a white woman being raped, near Milledgeville, and it cannot be authenticated. He points out that Confederate women felt secure enough in their persons to hide valuables in their clothes, and he found only one case in which U.S. soldiers were accused of stripping a woman and taking her jewelry.[5] According to historian Drew Gilpin Faust, "the privileges of gender did in fact provide considerable protection for Confederate females and served also as the foundation for their much vaunted belligerence." Faust might have added "the privileges of race," for Kennett found solid evidence that at least two or three black women were raped by Union soldiers, and Bell Wiley in *Confederate Women* concluded that such acts were probably fairly common. But Wiley also says, "in some instances wholesome relationships developed between black women and white Yankees."

Leaving the viewpoints of Union soldiers, African Americans, and Unionist white Southerners off the landscape distorts the historical record of Sherman's march and has unfortunate consequences for the present. The myth of a united Confederacy obliterates the memory of those whites who argued against slavery, objected to secession, and fought for the United States when they could. After the war, some of these Southerners worked for equal rights for all. Ignorance of their actions helps explain the obstinate resistance neo-Confederates display today to any proposed change in the pro-Confederate slant of the Southern historical sites. The Confederacy is the only heritage they know, so they want to hang on to it. They cannot take pride in the efforts of white Carolinians to end slavery, because they do not know about them. Nonetheless, the story of dissenting whites is an important part of Southern heritage. Conversely, portraying Sherman and his men as monsters who wantonly burned Columbia helps neo-Confederates perpetuate the idea that their cause was right. Thus, who burned Columbia still makes a difference—and Sherman didn't do it.[6]

Chapter 61 tells how some white Southerners spread similar misinformation about who burned Richmond.

1. Two markers do state that bridges were "burned to delay the advance of Sherman's Army in 1865 and rebuilt in 1870 and 1867," respectively.

2. After the murders of nine African Americans at a church in Charleston in 2015, Governor Nikki Haley brokered a compromise that took down the Confederate flag in front of the Capitol and was to put it on display in the Relic Room. Relic Room staff tried to expand that gesture into a $3,000,000 expansion but failed. Even a $350,000 plan to convert two offices in the museum into a display space for the State House flag failed to get funding in 2018.

3. Georgia Governor Joseph Brown complained that Wheeler's men had strayed far from their mission and farther from Sherman's path, becoming mere looters across the state. Wheeler defended himself by blaming "sixteen organized parties," *not* under his command but claiming to be, preying on the citizens of Georgia. Both were probably right; either way, the home front suffered at the hands of Confederate looters.

4. Not all Union soldiers became anti-slavery; many disliked and mistrusted blacks, and some even took bribes from white planters for returning of their fugitive slaves who had come into Union camps. Other Union soldiers set up informal schools to teach African Americans how to read and write. Seventy-seven of 86 black soldiers in a company recruited along the Georgia-Tennessee border were illiterate. By the end of the campaign in North Carolina every soldier had learned to read.

5. The soldiers fell into the hands of Wheeler's cavalry men, "who shot them forth with."

6. Marion B. Lucas, *Sherman and the Burning of Columbia* (College Station: TX A&M UP, 1976); Richard M. McMurry, review of foregoing in *American Historical Review* 82 no. 3 (6/77): 747; Joseph T. Glatthaar, *The March to the Sea and Beyond* (Baton Rouge: LA State UP, 1995 [1985]), 40–65, 142–46, 162–63; Charles Royster, *The Destructive War* (NY: Knopf, 1991), 31–33, 331–45, 419. (Glatthaar, 142–46, says Sherman's men "torched the capital of South Carolina," but his account is far less rigorous and detailed than Lucas's. Royster blames Sherman's men but begins his note supporting that conclusion by citing Lucas "for a careful study of the origins and extent of the fire"—which he then disregards! Perhaps Royster could not bring himself to give up the established neo-Confederate line even while recognizing Lucas's meticulous scholarship.) Relic Room staff member, conversation, 2/97; William Surface, correspondence, 1/97; Mark Grimsley, *The Hard Hand of War* (Cambridge: Cambridge UP, 1995), 1; Park ranger, Bentonville Battlefield, conversation, 3/97; George P. Rawick, ed., *The American Slave, vol. 18* (Westport, CT: Greenwood, 1972 [1941]), 105; Harold Gulley, "Roadside Reminders of the Civil War: Historical Markers in GA" (Oshkosh: U. of WI Department of Geography typescript, 1995?); Bell Wiley, *Confederate Women* (Westport, CT: Greenwood, 1975), 164; Lee Kennett, *Marching Through GA* (NY: Harper, 1996), 36–37, 84–85, 92, 276–79, 289–93, 306–307, 312; Ira Berlin, et al., *The Wartime Genesis of Free Labor* (Cambridge: Cambridge UP, 1990), 20, 54; Bertram Wyatt-Brown, "America's Holy War," *The New York Review of Books*, 11/6/97, 43; William L. Barney, *Flawed Victory* (NY: Praeger, 1975), 143–48; Drew Gilpin Faust, *Mothers of Invention* (Chapel Hill: U. of NC Press, 1996), 199; Tony Horwitz, *Confederates in the Attic* (NY: Pantheon, 1998), 312–31; James K. Hogue, "Did Blacks Fight for the Confederacy?" (Princeton, NJ: Princeton U. History Department, n.d.); Wilson Angley, et al., *Sherman's March Through NC* (Raleigh: NC Archives and History, 1995); Lucy S. Stewart, *The Reward of Patriotism* (NY: Walter Neale, 1930), 195–202, 226; John G. Barrett, *Sherman's March Through the Carolinas* (Chapel Hill: U. of NC Press, 1956), 75, 85–86, 189–90, 250–51; Eugene D. Genovese, *Roll, Jordan, Roll* (NY: Pantheon, 1974), 153; Stephen V. Ash, *When the Yankees Came* (Chapel Hill: U. of NC Press, 1995), 31; Barrie Stavis, *John Brown: The Sword and the Word* (NY: A. S. Barnes, 1970), 101–102; James McPherson, *Battle Cry of Freedom* (NY: Oxford UP, 1988), 832–38; Theodore Rosengarten, "New Views on the Burning of Columbia" (USCS Annual Meeting, 1993); Jeff Wilkinson, "Confederate Flag from SC State House Will Be Displayed. Here's Why Supporters Are Mad," *The State*, 8/16/2018, thestate.com/news/local/article216809930.html. In 2018, Lucas told me he stood by his conclusions, which had not been shaken by others' research.

———————— ✲ ————————

58. The Last Major Confederate Offensive of the Civil War

NORTH CAROLINA *Bentonville Battlefield*

In March of 1865, Gen. Joseph E. Johnston's 30,000 Confederates were trying desperately to stop Sherman's advance through North Carolina toward Virginia with 60,000 men. Sherman had divided his army, so Johnston attacked half the force at Bentonville. On March 19, he routed a Union division. Late in the afternoon, Confederates launched an all-out assault but were thrown back by Union reinforcements, so they pulled back to their lines. More Union troops arrived, and on March 21, U.S. forces drove in the Confederate left flank. Nevertheless, Sherman let Johnston withdraw during the night; five weeks later, Johnston surrendered near Durham.

The Bentonville Battlefield, marking the largest battle fought in North Carolina, is a North Carolina historic site whose brochure, slideshow, exhibits, and knowledgeable staff tell this story competently. Invisible to the visitor is the most recent battle there, however—the battle of the monuments, fought in 1995.

By 1990, Bentonville Battlefield already had four major monuments, all honoring Confederate participants: in 1893, Confederate veterans put up an attractive stone memorial listing the leader of each North Carolina regiment and stating that "[a]bout 360 unknown Confederate dead are buried here." In 1927, the United Daughters of the Confederacy, those intrepid monument builders, helped get the state to erect another stone a few hundred yards to the east. In 1965, Texas put up a monument to its soldiers who fought here, and in the early 1980s, the Sons of Confederate Veterans erected a brick entryway with plaques listing the North Carolina groups who participated on the Confederate side.

Nonetheless, the local chapter of the UDC had been collecting money for 30 years, much of it profits from the battlefield gift shop. In 1992, they spent some $26,000 on a new stone "[i]n memory of the North Carolina soldiers who fought and died so courageously and the civilians who suffered so grievously during the Battle of Bentonville."

The redundancy of these Confederate monuments helped mobilize sentiment for the other side. A nearby "Living History Society"—people who reenact the Battle of Bentonville every year—suggested it was time for a memorial to the *Union* soldiers who had fought at the site, some of whom even hailed from North Carolina. The Living History Society raised the money and petitioned the state for permission to erect a stone.

William S. Price Jr., director of the North Carolina Division of Archives and History, tells what happened next: "The Raleigh *News and Observer* published a letter from a concerned citizen implying that the proposed monument would be a statue of Gen. Sherman and would be paid for by the state. All hell broke loose. Hundreds of phone calls, letters, and petitions, mostly in opposition to any monument, came pouring in."

The North Carolina Historical Commission tabled the request and asked for a study on what Sherman's men did in the state. The pause allowed the storm of opposition to brew further. The Sons of Confederate Veterans were particularly incensed that *North Carolinians* could propose such a thing. "Monuments should be erected to heroes," said their state commander. "[Sherman's men] were no heroes. They were thieves, murderers, rapists, arsonists, trespassers." In the end, the commission voted down the proposal.

By omission, Bentonville, thus, joined the many sites throughout the South that portray Georgia, South Carolina, and North Carolina as victims of Sherman's barbaric horde. In 1865, the United States won at Bentonville. During Reconstruction, North Carolinians with Union sentiments controlled the area. The battle at Bentonville in the 1990s made clear, however, that neo-Confederates controlled the North Carolina landscape. As historian James McPherson put it, "The American Civil War is a highly visible exception to the adage that victors write the history of wars."

In 2013, citizens who wanted to honor the U.S. soldiers who fought and died at Bentonville finally managed to dedicate a modest monument on site. It didn't feature Sherman on a horse; it merely listed the four corps that fought and the states from which U.S. soldiers hailed. But it sufficed to give the Union a toehold on a battlefield where they actually won 150 years earlier. The battle for Civil War memory in North Carolina was far from over, however. In 2018, students toppled "Silent Sam," the Confederate statue that dominated the main entrance to the campus of the University of North Carolina, but some trustees want him back up. The governor and some other political leaders suggested moving the large Confederate monuments that dominate the public history of Raleigh, the state capital. As of 2019, who won the Civil War on the landscape of North Carolina was still up for grabs.[1]

Chapter 57 tells more about Sherman's campaign.

1. Wilson Angley, et al., "Foreword," *Sherman's March Through NC* (Raleigh: NC Archives and History, 1995); James M. McPherson, "Götterdämmerung," *The New York Review of Books*, 12/21/95: 10; George C. Rable, *Civil Wars: Women and the Crisis of Southern Nationalism* (Urbana: U. of IL Press, 1989), 155; Joseph T. Glatthaar, *The March to the Sea and Beyond* (Baton Rouge: LA State UP, 1995 [1985]), 40–65, 162–63; James Reston Jr., *Sherman's March and Vietnam* (NY: Macmillan, 1984), especially chapter 4; Marion B. Lucas, *Sherman and the Burning of Columbia* (College Station: TX A&M UP, 1976).

--------------------- ✶ ---------------------

59. The Invisible Slave Trade Now Becoming Visible

VIRGINIA *Alexandria*

At 1315 Duke Street in Alexandria, conveniently near the railroad, stands a dignified and well-constructed brick building marked by a plaque that says simply, "The Franklin and Armfield Office, Designated a National Historic Landmark by the United States Department of the Interior." The building is handsome and strong, but its history is more important than its architecture. For this was the headquarters and slave jail for the largest slave dealer in Virginia and one of the largest in the United States—Franklin and Armfield—with branches in Richmond, Natchez, and Texas.

Before the Civil War, slave trading was big business—one of the biggest in the United States—and was very visible then. Although it enriched men (and women), the sale and transport of human beings discomfited not just Yankee abolitionists but also many white Southerners, including slaveowners. In the nineteenth century, as the nation debated the morality of slavery, its defenders preferred to think of plantations as stable happy communities. On their home plantations, of course, few slaves had to be kept under lock and key. There they had family ties, friendships, and routines that were hard to break. Moreover, rural life afforded fewer options for escape. Owners could mobilize their neighbors, and any African American traveling without a pass would be challenged as a potential runaway. Other than the patrol system (chapter 55), rural slavery did not *look* like a police state.

Although I had read and taught about slavery for years, only in doing research for this book did I realize that people in the hands of slave traders lived in jails. Of course, it makes sense. How else could traders control them? Slave dealers had particular reason to fear escape by their charges, for their slaves' ties to family, friends, and locale had already been torn apart. Indeed, keeping African Americans in slavery was always more of a problem in cities. The anonymity of urban life made it harder for whites to know whether a black person was free, rented out, or absent from their owner without leave. In addition, free blacks tended to wind up in cities. In 1830, Alexandria had 1,381 slaves and 1,201 free blacks.[1] To make it easier to tell them apart, the city passed an ordinance requiring free blacks to register and carry their registration with them. Nonetheless, whites could hardly challenge every African American they saw, so slaves still required confinement. Many Southern hotels had some rooms with barred windows and externally locked doors to draw the trade of plantation masters who traveled with one or more slaves. Owners could lock their slaves in for the night, then retire to their own quarters secure in the knowledge that none could run away. Franklin and Arm-

field also provided this service for slaveowners visiting Alexandria, advertising "safe keeping at 25¢ per day." So did sheriffs with vacant cells in their jails. When an owner took newly purchased slaves home, they formed them into a coffle—a single file of handcuffed people with iron collars around their necks linked to each other by heavy chains— so none could run away.

This barred doorway, no longer extant, led to the cells that Franklin and Armfield built to the side and rear of their office to confine their slaves.

As the 1800s wore on, the myth of the plantation as a happy community became especially hard to maintain in Virginia. Repeated tobacco crops had depleted Virginia's soil. Meanwhile, planters in Alabama, Mississippi, Arkansas, Louisiana, and east Texas wanted more slaves to clear new land for growing cotton and sugar. So, Virginia planters turned to slaves as products. Beginning in 1828, John Armfield bought slaves in Virginia at relatively low prices and shipped them to his partner, Isaac Franklin, in Natchez, who sold them for much more. In 1832, Armfield and Franklin purchased the Duke Street location, from which they sent thousands of slaves to the Deep South. Both men became millionaires.

By the 1830s, Alexandria had become the largest port for the coastal slave trade in the upper South. Later, as part of the Compromise of 1850, the United States banned slave trading in the neighboring District of Columbia. As a result, Alexandria's importance as a slave market surged when the District's slave traders moved there from across the river. In the 1840s, other traders, including two who had to leave the District of Columbia after the 1850 law, bought the Armfield and Franklin property and continued operating as Price, Birch & Co. They not only sold slaves but also, on at least one occasion, sold free blacks into the Deep South as well: James Birch was the slave trader who bought Solomon Northup from his kidnappers, beat him when he claimed to be a free man, and sold him into slavery in Louisiana (chapter 70). Price and Birch bragged that their prison compound had witnessed only one escape and gave tours to show visiting abolitionists how impressive it was and how clean they kept it.

Many Virginians objected to the slave trade. "The exportation has averaged 8,500 for the last twenty years," said Thomas Jefferson Randolph, nephew of Thomas Jefferson, to the legislature in 1832. "It is a practice and an increasing practice, in part of Virginia, to rear slaves for market. How can an honorable mind, a patriot and a lover of his country, bear to see this ancient dominion converted into one grand menagerie, where men are to be reared for market, like oxen for the shambles?" Another Virginian wrote to the *Alexandria Gazette* in 1827,

> Scarcely a week passes without some of these wretched creatures being driven through our streets. After having been confined, and sometimes manacled in a loathsome prison, they are turned out in public view to take their departure for the South. The

children and some of the women are generally crowded into a
cart or wagon, while others follow on foot, not unfrequently
handcuffed and chained together. Here you may behold fathers
and brothers leaving behind them the dearest objects of affection,
and moving slowly along in the mute agony of despair—there the
young mothers sobbing over the infant . . .

Some dealers made their coffles walk through cities at midnight to the
waiting ship or railway to avoid drawing public notice. It was hard to speak
out against slave traders, however, since many, like Armfield and Franklin,
were wealthy members of the community.

In the 1980s, hoping to learn more about the people housed here, archaeologists did a study of the site, published as *The Alexandria Slave Pen.* While
the researchers accomplished much examining historical sources, they found
their archaeological work focusing on the site's material culture barren. In
an account reminiscent of descriptions of Auschwitz, they told why: "Slaves
arrived at the pen with only those personal items carried on their person or
in a knapsack," and even these were often confiscated. Consequently, the
prisoners left nothing for archaeologists.

Slavery finally ended here on the morning of May 24, 1861, when elements of the U.S. Army surprised the Confederate Cavalry while they were
having breakfast in the Slave Pen. They captured the horsemen but found
that Price, Birch & Co. had fled with their slaves, leaving only one "old man
chained to the middle of the floor by the leg." The United States used the
compound during the Civil War as a prison, mostly for drunks and Union
deserters. Late in the war, the building was used as L'Ouverture Hospital for
black soldiers and as housing for slaves seeking freedom behind Union lines
in Alexandria.

As of 1999, none of its past could tourists surmise from the building's bland
exterior, which mirrored the desire of nineteenth-century white Virginians
to keep the slave trade out of sight so they could put it out of their minds. But
visitors who ventured inside Franklin and Armfield could now learn something about the place. For in 1998, the Urban League bought it to house its
Northern Virginia chapter. Now an interior corridor displays a Franklin and
Armfield ad: "We will give cash—for one hundred likely young Negroes of
both sexes, between the ages of 8 and 25 years." On request, staff members

will let visitors see the basement windows, still barred from the building's days as a prison.[2]

Then, in 2005, Virginia put up a state historical marker, "Franklin and Armfield Slave Office," which does a fine job telling of the trade to Mississippi. In about 2016, the city of Alexandria put up another marker two blocks north, telling about the building, now renamed Freedom House Museum, and including historic photos. Here in Alexandria, as in some other places across the nation, the slave trade, at last, has begun to see the light of day on our historic landscape.[3]

1. Alexandria's whites numbered 5,681.

2. Visitors to the basement can also read a plaque commemorating Lewis Henry Bailey, the only slave of the thousands who passed through Franklin and Armfield who has been identified by name. Bailey was a slave in Texas when the Civil War freed him. He walked back to Alexandria, where he reunited with his mother. Eventually, he graduated from Wayland Seminary in Washington, DC, and became an ordained Baptist minister. During an extraordinary life, he organized schools for African Americans and helped found several Baptist churches.

3. Janice Artemel, Elizabeth Crowell, and Jeff Parker, *The Alexandria Slave Pen: The Archaeology of Urban Captivity* (DC: Engineering-Science, 1987), 35; WPA, *The Negro in Virginia* (NY: Hastings House, 1940), 162, 166–67; Michelle Genz, "Solomon's Wisdom," *The Washington Post*, 3/7/99; Steven Deyle, "Competing Ideologies in the Old South," paper at American Historical Association, 1/99; John Wilds, Charles Dufour, and Walter Cowan, *LA Yesterday and Today* (Baton Rouge: LA State UP, 1996), 61; Richard C. Wade, *Slavery in the Cities* (NY: Oxford UP, 1967); Northern VA Urban League, "Freedom House" (Alexandria: Northern VA Urban League, n.d.).

———— ✯ ————

60. The Clash of the Martyrs

VIRGINIA *Alexandria*

In 1999, on the side of the Holiday Inn in Old Town, Alexandria, a bronze plaque put up by the Sons and Daughters of Confederate Soldiers told this story:

> *The Marshall House stood upon this site, and within the building on the early morning of May 24, 1861, James W. Jackson was killed by Federal soldiers while defending his property and personal rights, as stated in the verdict of the coroner's jury. He was the first martyr to the cause of*

Southern independence. The justice of history does not permit his name
to be forgotten. Not in the excitement of battle, but coolly, and for great
principle, he laid down his life, an example to all, in defense of his home
and the sacred soil of his native state Virginia.

The plaque completely omitted Elmer Ellsworth, killed at this site moments before Jackson and one of the first "martyrs to the cause" of the United States in the Civil War. Coupled with the equally deceitful marker put up by the United Daughters of the Confederacy at Appomattox (chapter 65), this marker gave neo-Confederates the distinction of misrepresenting the beginning and the ending of America's most important war, at least in Virginia.

After the fall of Fort Sumter, Union commanders knew they could not defend Washington without controlling the land across the Potomac. Accordingly, in late May 1861, they decided to take Alexandria. As the first U.S. offensive against the Confederacy, it "at once attracted the attention of the whole nation," according to Julius C. Burrows, who gave the oration at the dedication of the monument honoring Ellsworth at Mechanicville, New York, in 1875. Col. Ellsworth, stationed in Washington that May, learned of the plan to attack Alexandria and asked to be included.

The night before the offensive, Col. Ellsworth wrote a last letter to his parents. It is the first of those poignant personal records that the Civil War seems particularly to have inspired.

My Dear Father and Mother:

The regiment is ordered to move across the river tonight. We have no means of knowing what reception we are to meet with. I am inclined to the opinion that our entrance to the city of Alexandria will be hotly contested, as I am just informed that a large force has arrived there today. Should this happen, my dear parents, it may be my lot to be injured in some manner. Whatever may happen, cherish the consolation that I was engaged in the performance of a sacred duty; and tonight, thinking of the probabilities of tomorrow, . . . I am perfectly content to accept whatever my fortune may be, confident that He who noteth even the fall of a sparrow, will have some purpose even in the fall of one like me. My darling and ever-loved parents, good bye, God bless, protect and care for you.

By two the next morning, Union troops were in motion; Ellsworth's regiment landed at the Alexandria waterfront just after dawn. In the light winds of the sunny May morning, a rebel flag waved over Jackson's inn, so large it was said to be visible from the White House. The Virginia militia had evacuated Alexandria. Meeting no resistance, Ellsworth's patrol was en route to seize the telegraph office when he spied Jackson's Confederate flag. "That flag must come down!" he cried; some historians claim he acted to forestall his men from shelling or burning the inn; others say he had promised President Lincoln to give him the flag in person. He entered the inn, climbed the stairway to the roof, and seized the flag. Descending the stairs, he was met by the innkeeper, who shot him through the heart. Immediately, one of Ellsworth's men, in turn, killed Jackson.

Ellsworth had worked in Abraham Lincoln's Illinois law office. He accompanied the president-elect east, was in charge of his security, and lived for a while at the White House. Lincoln wept openly at the news of his death and ordered Ellsworth's body brought to the White House for a military funeral. Mary Lincoln, to her horror, was presented with the blood-spattered Confederate flag that Ellsworth had taken down. Lincoln wrote personally to Ellsworth's parents,

> In the untimely loss of your noble son, our affliction here is scarcely less than your own. . . .
>
> In the hope that it may be no intrusion upon the sacredness of your sorrow, I have ventured to address this tribute to the memory of my young friend, and your brave and early fallen child. May God give you the consolation which is beyond all earthly power.
>
> Sincerely your friend in a common affliction,
> A. Lincoln

The incident attracted the attention of the nation. "Remember Ellsworth!" cried Union soldiers in early Civil War battles. Ellsworth's bloody shirt went on tour as a relic to rally money and troops for the Union and was used to recruit a new regiment named the Ellsworth Avengers. The Civil War Soldiers Museum in Pensacola has identified 149 different philatelic covers depicting or mentioning Col. Ellsworth. Poets, professional and amateur, hastened to commemorate him. In 1875, a monument to his memory was

Fort Ward, a Civil War fort three miles west of the inn, is now a museum. In 1997, it displayed Col. Ellsworth's uniform, with its blood-stained hole still over his heart. On permanent display is a huge star from Jackson's flag.

erected in Mechanicville, New York. On it is engraved, "He who noteth even the fall of a sparrow, will have some purpose even in the fall of one like me." According to Edward L. Cole, one of the speakers at its dedication, "His death was the call for a hundred thousand men to spring to arms." Cole compared Ellsworth and Jackson: "The one dying in defense of the principles of human freedom, his country and its laws, a martyr. The other, dying the death of a traitor, his name given an infamous notoriety by the cowardly assassin act, that brought its retribution in his instant death."

Meanwhile, Confederates named their children after Jackson and used his death as a recruiting tool. On-site, the Sons and Daughters of Confederate Soldiers continued this tradition, honoring and converting him into a martyr. Two blocks to the west, on the base of Alexandria's interesting 1889 Confederate Memorial, in 1900 they even added "James W. Jackson" to the 99 names of Confederates from Alexandria who were killed in battle. Although Jackson's name was inscribed just eleven years after the statue went up, because a different bezel was used, it looks like it was added just yesterday. The statue itself is under duress: the city council voted to move it across the street, in front of Alexandria's history museum, but the United Daughters of the Confederacy got Virginia to pass a law back in 1890 requiring that it "shall perpetually remain . . . at the intersection of Prince and Washington streets."

Shortly after I wrote this original essay, the Holiday Inn changed hands and became Hotel Monaco. The new management ran with the Confederate theme, decorating guest rooms with photos of Confederate soldiers as late as 2014. But some guests complained. At the same time, a descendant of

Ellsworth repeatedly contacted the Office of Historic Alexandria, asking that a plaque telling his ancestor's story be placed next to the plaque for Jackson.

Then the hotel changed hands again and got renamed The Alexandrian. At this point, the new Marriott management took down the plaque. Surprisingly, hotel employees deny this; one told me he personally saw a City of Alexandria van parked outside while city workers removed it. The United Daughters of the Confederacy confirmed that Marriott gave them the plaque. The city then put up a new marker on a pole at the corner of Pitt Street. Titled "Marshall House," it gives an accurate account of both deaths. On the opposite side, it reprints a story about Ellsworth from *Harper's* published at the time. So, Alexandria has done the right thing, even if Marriott won't take credit for so doing.[1]

1. *Exercises Connected with the Unveiling of the Ellsworth Monument at Mechanicville* (Alba, NY: Munsell, 1875); Patricia Sullivan, "Despite Alexandria Council Vote, Little Chance 'Appomattox' Statue Will Be Moved," *The Washington Post*, 9/25/2016; conversations with "The Alexandrian" staff, 9/2018; conversations with Dan Lee, research historian, Office of Historic Alexandria, and with Planning and Zoning staff and other employees, 9/2018; Alexandria, "Marshall House," hmdb.org/marker.asp?marker=115753; UDC official, conversation, 9/2018.

---------------- ✯ ----------------

61. "One of the Great Female Spies of All Times"

VIRGINIA *Richmond*

White Richmond built the Bellevue Elementary School at 2301 E. Grace St. deliberately to obliterate the home of, in the words of Donald E. Markle, author of *Spies and Spymasters of the Civil War*, "one of the great female spies of all times."[1] It didn't quite work, because after federal courts desegregated Richmond's schools, Bellevue became majority African American, and neo-Confederates lost control over how Richmond remembers Elizabeth Van Lew.

Van Lew was born in Richmond in 1818, where her father ran a successful hardware business. Her family sent her to a Quaker school in Philadelphia, which introduced her to abolitionism. After her father died, she persuaded her mother to free their nine slaves, including Mary Bowser, and Elizabeth used some of her endowment to buy several of their relatives and free them. John Brown's 1859 raid at Harpers Ferry and his eloquent last words increased her determination to fight against slavery.

When the Civil War began, Van Lew did not hide her Unionist sympathies. Owing to her family's prominent standing, however, and probably also because she was "only a woman," Confederate officials didn't interfere with her. When Confederates converted a Richmond tobacco warehouse into Libby Prison, she prevailed on administrators to let her bring the POWs "food, clothing, writing paper, and even furniture," according to A. A. and Mary Hoehling, Richmond historians. She also nursed the wounded and brought the prisoners information about safe houses in case they escaped. When 109 POWs tunneled out of the prison on February 9, 1864, 59 were never recaptured, partly due to her aid. Van Lew also got a Unionist sympathizer appointed at Libby Prison who helped individual prisoners escape, whom she then hid in a concealed room in her mansion.

So many white residents of Richmond questioned the Confederate cause that in March 1862, Jefferson Davis declared martial law in the city. Confederate authorities rounded up dozens, later hundreds, of citizens suspected of disloyalty. Despite this counter-surveillance, Van Lew was able to develop a spy ring of at least twelve persons including clerks in the Confederate war and navy departments, her own mother, and other well-off white residents. One, Martin M. Lipscomb, ran for mayor of Richmond while a spy for her!

Before the war, Van Lew may have paid for Mary Bowser to attend the Quaker School for Negroes in Philadelphia. Van Lew later prevailed upon an intermediary to get Varina Davis, First Lady of the Confederacy, to hire Bowser, who then became a Union spy within the Confederate White House. Thomas McNiven, who recruited Richmond loyalists as spies for the United States, said Bowser was a great help. He reported she had a photographic memory: "Everything she saw on the Rebel President's desk she could repeat word for word." Her color probably helped her undercover work, for many Confederates assumed that most blacks were loyal, could not read, were incapable of much initiative, and liked slavery anyway. In 1995, the Military Intelligence Corps inducted Bowser into its Hall of Fame.

The Confederate White House was a hotbed of espionage and sabotage. William A. Jackson, President Davis's coachman, escaped early in the war. In June 1862, his interviews with Northern journalists made headlines across the United States, telling how he had had to leave his wife and three children behind when he made his bid for freedom. Confederates vowed to hang him if they caught him, because for a month before his escape he had been slipping through their lines to pass information he had overheard in the coach and the White House to U.S. operatives. Eighteen months later, on January 9, 1864, the Confederate president's manservant and Mrs. Davis's maid ran away. Ten days later, on the evening of January 19, during a reception at the White House of the Confederacy, someone kindled a fire in a woodpile in the basement in an attempt to burn the house down. Smoke led to its discovery in time. In the excitement, two more slaves escaped to the North and someone robbed the mansion—all in the same night. People were inclined to blame "Yankee plotters," and according to historian Richard M. Lee, "Miss Van Lew was later known to be involved."

To get information to the Union Army, Van Lew set up five relay stations on the route to Union headquarters at Hampton Roads, Virginia. Her system worked so well that, on at least one occasion, she used it to send fresh flowers and a copy of the Richmond morning newspaper to Gen. Grant! One old black man in her employ carried baskets of eggs for sale. One egg in each basket was empty and contained messages to the Union Army. According to Markle, "Not one of her couriers were ever caught." Markle credits her with developing, on her own, several tools of the espionage trade including hidden rooms, invisible ink, and a cipher system to make her notes undecipherable if discovered.

To avoid Confederate interference, Van Lew let her hair grow wild and mumbled to herself on the streets, and Confederate officials regarded her as eccentric rather than dangerous. Union officers knew better. George H. Sharpe, chief of intelligence for the Army of the Potomac, said of her, "The greater portion of our intelligence in 1864–65 in its collection and in good measure in its transmission we owed to the intelligence and devotion of Elizabeth Van Lew." When Grant first visited Richmond after the war, he spent little time with officials but made time for tea with Van Lew at her home. During his presidency, he appointed her postmaster of Richmond.

After Reconstruction, however, which ended in 1870 in Virginia, ex-Confederates took control of the state again. They passed new laws reestablishing white supremacy (chapter 66) and redefined what the war had been about. Gradually, as the myth of the Lost Cause intensified, many white residents of the city forgot that they had not supported the Confederacy wholeheartedly. Now, snubbing Elizabeth Van Lew was a way to be patriotic in white Richmond. After the war, Van Lew persuaded the War Department to give her all its records about her operations so her white neighbors could not know the extent of her work. Nonetheless, her life in Richmond became increasingly lonely. In the 1890s, Van Lew wrote in her journal, "I live here in the most perfect isolation. No one will walk with us on the streets, no one will go with us anywhere; and it grows worse and worse as the years roll on and those I love go to their long rest."

Van Lew continually sought money from the federal government, pointing out that she had spent the family's fortune on her espionage tasks. She also became something of a feminist, always including with her city tax payments a note protesting Richmond's right to collect taxes from someone who had no right to vote. No white resident of Richmond came to her funeral in 1900—only African Americans and relatives of a Union soldier she had aided.

At first, her grave went unmarked. Then, friends and relatives of Maj. Paul Revere, a Massachusetts soldier to whom she had slipped mail and money from home when he was a prisoner, donated a granite block and bronze plaque which reads, "Elizabeth Van Lew, 1818–1900. She risked everything that is dear to man—friends, fortune, comfort, health, life itself—all for one absorbing desire of her heart, that slavery might be abolished and the Union preserved." Historian Ernest Furgurson writes that even her tombstone was defaced "in retribution for her role in the war." The damage has been repaired and the stone is easy to find in compact Shockoe Cemetery at the corner of Hospital and Fifth Streets, toward the center of the graves north of the main east-west drive. When I saw it, in 1999, someone had recently decorated it with a small U.S. flag.[2]

The city tore down her family mansion in 1912 "to get rid of all traces of her," according to Furgurson. In my repeated tours of the White House of the Confederacy, no guide has ever mentioned the espionage or sabotage that went on there; for that matter, none ever said anything about the African Americans who worked in the house.[3] Black espionage does not fit the traditional storyline (chapter 69) in white culture—that slaves actually liked slavery. Ironically, this ideology would prompt the Davises to believe they had good relationships with their slaves, leaving them open to spying by black agents of Elizabeth Van Lew.

The African American community honored Van Lew's memory, however.

Just inside the front doors of Bellevue School was a room dedicated as the Maggie Walker Museum. Walker, who started a bank for African Americans in the late nineteenth century and became the most important black woman banker in the United States, grew up in Van Lew's household. A bronze plaque in the museum read, "Maggie Lena Walker, born on this site in the Van Lew Mansion, 1867." Another honored Mary Elizabeth Bowser with the words, "Freed slave of the Van Lew family and indispensable partner to Elizabeth Van Lew in her pro-Union espionage work, she worked at the Confederate White House gathering and passing on military intelligence to the Union through Van Lew to General Grant." Several labels, portraits, and news stories told of Van Lew.

Outside, in 2005, Virginia put up a historical marker, "Adams-Van Lew House." It tells some of the stories of Van Lew and Bowser:

> During the Civil War, Elizabeth Van Lew led a Union espionage operation. African Americans, such as Van Lew's associate Mary Jane Richards (whose story closely parallels that of legendary spy Mary Elizabeth Bowser), served in Richmond's Unionist underground.

It also notes that Van Lew was postmaster of Richmond.

Her life as a spy, which she minimized so as to get along as the Nadir of race relations intensified, was then minimized by neo-Confederates after her death, so they could maintain the myth that Richmond was united for the Confederacy. Now that their power is waning, four different historical markers in Richmond treat Van Lew. When the school celebrated its centennial in 2013, it opened an expanded new museum. A next step might be to name the school for her![4]

1. Markle credits "knowledgeable experts in the field of espionage" with this appraisal. Edwin Fishel, a student of Civil War espionage, calls the Richmond underground "the most productive espionage operation of the Civil War, on either side, that has ever been documented."

2. Closer to the entrance is the stone of another defiant Unionist, John Minor Botts, who died in early 1869. "He was under all circumstances an inflexible friend of the American Union," it proclaims, and quotes, "I know no North, no South, no East, no West, I only know my country, my whole country, and nothing but my country." Again, many whites shared this sentiment in Richmond in 1869, but by 1890 such admitted Unionists would have been few. Although a slaveholder, Botts deplored slavery, and like Van Lew, spied for the United States during the war. Along with Van Lew, he is noted on a historical marker that Virginia Civil War Trails put up in 2014, marking the sesquicentennial of the Civil War.

3. My tours were all before 2000. In the late 1990s, the Museum of the Confederacy put a small array of labels on the walls of the basement corridor in the White House where visitors assemble to await their guided tour. Titled "In Service to the President: The Staff of the Confederate Executive Mansion," this display did speak of the discontent that seethed within arm's reach of President Davis.

4. I suggest naming for Van Lew because almost nothing in the United States gets named for anti-racist whites and because "Van Lew-Bowser Elementary School" is a bit long. It is always hard to know just what a spy did. Some writers are too certain Bowser never existed, others too certain every exploit credited to her is true. I rely on Lew's memoir, *A Yankee Spy in Richmond*, ed. David Ryan (Mechanicsburg, PA: Stackpole, 1996); Donald E. Markle, *Spies and Spymasters of the Civil War* (NY: Hippocrene, 1994), 58, 180–85; Edwin C. Fishel, *The Secret War for the Union* (Boston: Houghton Mifflin, 1996), 551–53; A. A. Hoehling and Mary Hoehling, *The Day Richmond Died* (San Diego, CA: A. S. Barnes, 1981), 36–42; Richard M. Lee, *General Lee's City: An Illustrated Guide to the Historical Sites of Confederate Richmond* (McLewan, VA: EPM, 1987), 69, 99–101; Ernest B. Furgurson, *Ashes of Glory: Richmond at War* (NY: Knopf, 1996), 94–95, 113–17, 339, 361; Robert W. Waitt Jr., "Recollections of Thomas McNiven and His Activities in Richmond During the Civil War" (Richmond, VA: Museum of Confederacy vertical files, typescript of remembrance in 1952 of conversations with Jeannette B. McNiven); "VA Profiles—Mary Elizabeth Bowser," gateway-VA.com/pages/bhistory/1998/bowser.htm, 9/98; Lois Leveen, "A Black Spy in the Confederate White House," *The New York Times*, 6/21/2012; and John Reid Blackwell, "Bellevue Elementary Celebrates Centennial; Historic School Now Has Museum to Call Its Own," *Richmond Times-Dispatch*, 1/20/2013, richmond.com/news/local/city-of-richmond/bellevue-elementary-celebrates-centennial/article67d9b7a3-f298-5b25-a010-62b16f41affd .html

---

★

---

62. Slavery and Redemption

VIRGINIA *Richmond*

Richmond was one of the great centers of the slave trade, but as of 1999, the city contained not one historical marker or site alluding to the buying and selling of human beings. Of course, the slave trade is not a happy topic for feel-good historical markers. Not all accounts of the trade tell of unrelieved suffering, however. Some incidents show the potential for growth—even redemption.

If you stand today where Broad Street passes over Interstate 95, formerly 15th Street, you are in the heart of Richmond's famous slave market. Until April 3, 1865, local African Americans called this area "the Devil's Half Acre." One reason was Robert Lumpkin's prosperous slave trading business located on Lumpkin Alley, which intersected Broad opposite 15th Street coming in from the north. Today, Lumpkin Alley is the parking and industrial area visible below Broad Street.

Among the buildings on the alley stood Lumpkin's jail, where he housed his "property." A young visitor from Syracuse gives us a glimpse of Lumpkin and his jail a few years before the Civil War: "I entered a large open court. Against one of the posts sat a good-natured fat man, with his chair tipped back. It was Mr. Lumpkin. . . . [He] received me courteously and showed me over his jail. On one side of the open court was a large tank for washing, or lavatory. Opposite was a long, two-story brick house, the lower part fitted up for men and the second story for women."

Slave trading was a big industry: in the 1850s, Richmond's biggest export was not tobacco, flour, or iron, but slaves. A Scandinavian tourist named Fredrika Bremer visited several slave jails in Richmond in 1851. Historian Frederic Bancroft relates what Bremer saw: "[In one jail] sat a strong-limbed Negro, silent and gloomy, who had cut off the fingers of his right hand as a strange revenge against his master, for separating him from his wife and children and ordering him sold South, on account of some offense, as was alleged." In another jail, Bancroft continues:

> She saw a room where the slaves of both sexes were flogged. There were the iron rings in the floor to which they were tied down before they were beaten with that paddle, a broad strip of cow-hide, which looked rather harmless. "Oh, yes, yes; but," replied the keeper, grinning with a very significant glance, "it can cause as much torture as any other instrument, and even more, because one can give as many blows with this strip of hide without its leaving any outward sign; it does not cut into the flesh."

The Confederate decision to abandon Richmond on April 2, 1865, caught Lumpkin by surprise as he had not yet managed to sell his latest shipment of slaves. During that confused evening, Lumpkin marched his coffle—some 50 people, chained together—to the train station, could not get passage on the last train out, marched them back to the jail, and locked them in for the night. It was to be their last night in bondage.

The next morning the Union Army set them free. (The next entry tells about this event.) Robert Lumpkin's occupation—slave dealer—abruptly ceased to exist. We do not know how he spent that day, April 3, when his world turned upside down. But soon he realized that he loved Mary Ann, the black woman he had bought a decade earlier who had already borne him two children. Not long after the liberation of Richmond, he married her.

In 1866, Rev. Nathaniel Colver, a Boston minister, came to Richmond to establish a school to train African Americans to be ministers. No white would rent him a suitable building, but Mary Ann Lumpkin offered to lease him Lumpkin's jail, a solid two-story structure with barred windows. "With unconcealed enthusiasm," historian Leon Litwack writes, "black workers knocked out the cells, removed the iron bars from the windows, and refashioned the old jail into a school . . . Before long, children and adults entered the doors of the new school, some of them recalling that this was not their first visit to the familiar brick building."[1]

The transformation of the building reflected an equally extraordinary metamorphosis within Robert Lumpkin, who died in 1867. Had he lived, many whites would have despised Lumpkin for abetting black education, the particular target of white vigilante violence during Reconstruction. The school, Richmond Theological Seminary, survived, and after mergers, name changes, and relocations, endures today as Virginia Union University.

Since the turn of the millennium, a small band of citizens has transformed public history in Richmond, including about the slave trade.[2] The James River Park System put up markers about the slave trade along the river, where much of it took place. It also created walking tours with guides, some from Hope in the Cities, who helped visitors grasp some sense of the inhumanity of the coffle, the uncertainty, and the lack of control over one's destiny. In 2007, not far from Lumpkin's jail, Richmond dedicated a somber stone monument to the victims of the "triangular trade" in slaves, sugar, rum, and other products; identical monuments went up in Cotonou, Benin, and Liverpool, England, two other cities that had prospered from the trade. In 2008, archaeologists uncovered the foundation of Lumpkin's jail and the beautifully preserved paving stones of his slave yard nearby. For a while, visitors could see and tour the site; temporary historical markers told the story. Then, for preservation, the site got covered again by dirt. Just to the north is the African Burial Ground, whose marking is another part of the rediscovery of Richmond's full history. In 2011, Richmond erected seventeen Slave Trail markers throughout its East End. In 2015, the sesquicentennial of the liberation of Richmond prompted events all over the city. Here at the jail site and the burial ground were ceremonies, concerts, walking tours of the area, and the world premiere of Ashby Anderson's jazz composition "Undertones." Nor has all of this been forgotten now that the sesquicentennial has passed. When conventions meet in Richmond, in their welcome kit is a flier, "Freedom Tales and Historic Trails," that includes the Richmond Slave Trail, stretching from the Manchester Docks along the river to Lumpkin's jail and the burial grounds, with markers all along the way.

Richmond got more entries in the first edition of this book than any other city, because it got its history more wrong. Now, at least with respect to the slave trade, Richmond is beginning to get it right.[3]

Chapter 59 tells of a slave jail still standing in Alexandria. The next chapter tells more about the liberation of Richmond, including Lumpkin's slaves, by U.S. troops. The opportunity for alliances across racial lines—marital or political—proved all too fleeting; chapter 66 tells how, in the 1960s, Virginians would have to go to the U.S. Supreme Court to win again the small victory over prejudice—the right to marry across racial lines—that the Lumpkins had exercised a century before.

1. Another account places this rental in 1867, after Lumpkin's death, in which case Mrs. Lumpkin inherited his holdings.
2. I would particularly emphasize the Sacred Ground Historical Reclamation Project led by Ana Edwards, Hope in the Cities, and Ralph R. White, who got the first slave trade markers placed on his own, risking his job in the process.
3. Michael B. Chesson, *Richmond After the War* (Richmond: VA State Library, 1981), 3; A. A. Hoehling and Mary Hoehling, *The Day Richmond Died* (San Diego, CA: A. S. Barnes, 1981); Ernest B. Furgurson, *Ashes of Glory: Richmond at War* (NY: Knopf, 1996), 325–46; Leon F. Litwack, *Been in the Storm So Long: The Aftermath of Slavery* (NY: Random House Vintage, 1980), 168–72; WPA, *The Negro in VA* (NY: Hastings House, 1940), 101–103, 164–65, 201, 241, 266–67; David Ryan, ed., *A Yankee Spy in Richmond* (Mechanicsburg, PA: Stackpole, 1996), frontispiece; *The New York Times,* 4/11/1865; Joseph T. Glatthaar, *Forged in Battle: The Civil War Alliance of Black Soldiers and White Officers* (NY: Free Press, 1990), 208; Abigail Tucker, "Digging up the Past at a Richmond Jail," *Smithsonian Magazine,* 3/2009, smithsonianmag.com/history/digging-up-the-past -at-a-richmond-jail-50642859; Virginia Foundation for the Humanities, "Lumpkin's Jail," 2018, aahistoricsitesva.org/items/show/256

★

---

63. The Liberation of Richmond

VIRGINIA *Richmond*

"Richmond is a city in thralldom to its past," is how Michael B. Chesson began his 1981 study *Richmond After The War.* Not all of its past, however— only the events and leaders of the Confederacy. In most cities, visitors' brochures tout some recent economic development or current cultural happening. When I visited Richmond in 1997, the *Richmond Guide* given to tourists at hotels and visitor centers contained just two articles. The lead essay was a worshipful study entitled "Robert Edward Lee." "The Flags of the Confederacy," by the same local business professor, supplied the names of the young ladies who sewed each of the first three "Battle Flags of the Army of Northern Virginia"—"Miss Constance Cary and her two cousins, Miss Hetty Cary and Miss Jennie Cary." The essay even ended with Abraham Ryan's nineteenth-century lament, "Furl that Banner, softly, slowly! Treat it gently—it is holy . . . "[1]

Like its visitors' guide, many of Richmond's markers and monuments still revere those four short years that ended April 2, 1865, when the Confederate government fled. At least two monuments apiece glorify Gen. Robert E. Lee, Gen. Stonewall Jackson, Gen. J. E. B. Stuart, and Jefferson Davis. Largest of all is the Confederate Soldiers and Sailors Monument. Even at the Harry F. Byrd Airport, the monument is of "Civil War Balloonists." Yet although some of the most dramatic moments in Richmond's history happened just after April 2 of that year, the landscape ignores them.

Poor whites, free blacks, Southern civilians imprisoned by the Confederacy, and Union POWs joined slaves in celebrating freedom the next morning. A retreating Confederate, Clement Sulivane, wrote that he "heard the very welkin [vault of heaven] ring with cheers as the U.S. forces reached Capitol Square." A soldier with the eleventh Connecticut wrote,

> Our reception was grander and more exultant than even a Roman emperor, leading back his victorious legions with the spoils of conquest, could ever know. We brought Government, Order, and Heaven born Liberty. The slaves seemed to think that their day of jubilee had fully come. How they danced, shouted, waved their rag banners, shook our hands, bowed, scraped, laughed all over, and thanked God, too, for our coming. Many heroes have fought for this day and died without the sight. . . . It is a day never to be forgotten by us, till days shall be no more.

Richmond forgot it nevertheless. Its markers and monuments ignored what took place after the city fell, stories at least as dramatic, heroes at least as heroic, as those that Richmond did commemorate in bronze and stone.

Many people believe avenging Union troops burned Richmond when they entered the city. A librarian at the Virginia State Library told me of an 1876 map that shows "everything they didn't burn." "Everything *who* didn't burn?" I asked. "Everything *we* didn't burn," she admitted, also letting slip her Confederate identification; "I try not to get into that." All historians agree that the Confederates burned the city. After the war, many white Southerners condemned the decision, which made no military sense. The laws of the Confederacy allowed commanders no discretion, however: supplies, especially cotton and tobacco, must be destroyed to prevent their capture by Federal forces.

Confederates torched Richmond's warehouses and bridges when they left the city and tried to burn the famed Tredegar iron mill, but its owner and armed workmen stopped them. Then, shortly before dawn, terrific blasts shook the city as Confederates exploded the magazines of seven gunboats

Most American history textbooks include a photograph of "the burned ruins of Richmond," as *Life and Liberty* captions this view. No caption explains that the departing Confederates burned it, or that Union forces saved much of the city. *Triumph of the American Nation* entitles its scene, "The impact of war is clear in this photo, taken in Richmond, Virginia, the once-proud capital of the Confederacy. During the war it was the target of Union attack . . . " The caption contains no literal error, yet implies that Union forces caused the destruction, which is a lie. *The American Pageant* exaggerates the extent of the destruction in its caption: "Richmond Devastated: Charleston, Atlanta, and other Southern cities looked much the same, resembling bombed-out Berlin and Dresden in 1945." Most blatant of all is the question posed in the caption in John Garraty's *American History*: "Why were major cities of the South destroyed?" Garraty's *Teacher's Edition* supplies the answer: "To break the Southerner's will to fight." Considering that white Confederates destroyed Richmond and other major cities of the South, this answer is preposterous and demonstrates how neo-Confederate mythology has captured our national historical narrative. Chapter 57 tells of the similar falsehood about Columbia, South Carolina.

packed with powder in the James River followed by a still louder blast as the army's central powder magazine blew up. The destruction was senseless because the United States already had abundant powder, according to historian Rembert Patrick. "The gain from destroying the ammunition in the Richmond magazine could never justify the danger to the city."

Chaos and riots broke out. People ran to loot the warehouses. In the words of historian Leon Litwack, "black and white women together raided the Confederate commissary, while the men rolled wheelbarrows filled with bags of flour, meal, coffee, and sugar toward their respective shanties." Buildings caught fire. Prisoners freed themselves in the state penitentiary. Whites particularly formed a mob the morning of April 3, angered by the abundant stores they found, when they as well as Lee's army had been hungry. They blamed the Confederate central government and "the Jews."

Col. A. G. Draper's colored infantry of the 25th Corps took the lead and were the first U.S. troops to reach the outskirts of Richmond. Sensitive to whites' feelings, however, Union generals halted their advance to let white troops march into Richmond ahead of them. Confederate deserters, tired and hungry, seemed as willing to surrender to black troops as to whites, and U.S. forces met no resistance. Even die-hard pro-Confederate civilians experienced the Union forces' arrival with some relief after the nightmare night. Two Union officers raised a U.S. flag on the state capitol amid cheers from the crowd below.

At 8:15 a.m., the mayor surrendered the city to Union officials and requested that the Federals occupy it. U.S. troops, black and white, mobilized quickly to put out the flames and reestablish order. Within four hours, they had contained the fires. "Even the most anti-Unionist Richmonder admitted that the Federal soldiers labored hard and bravely," according to Patrick. Other Richmond residents were less restrained, he continues: "Thousands of Negroes danced with joy on seeing their brothers-in-arms. Bands playing 'Yankee Doodle,' 'John Brown's Body,' or the 'Battle Hymn of the Republic' were greeted with ear-shattering cheers."

Garland H. White, born a slave in Hanover County, Virginia, in 1829, had escaped to Canada years before the war. There he became a minister. When the war began, White helped recruit Ohio blacks into what became the 28th U.S. Colored Infantry and became its chaplain. He described the scene as the regiment marched into Richmond on Broad Street: "I marched at the head of the column, and soon I found myself called upon by the officers and men of my regiment to make a speech, with which, of course, I readily complied. A vast multitude assembled on Broad Street, and I was aroused amid the shouts of ten thousand voices, and proclaimed for the first time in that city freedom to all mankind." They reached Lumpkin's Alley, where stood the slave jail of Robert Lumpkin, hated "negro trader." From behind the barred windows his imprisoned African Americans began to chant,

> Slavery chain done broke at last!
> Broke at last! Broke at last!
> Slavery chain done broke at last!
> Gonna praise God till I die!

The crowd outside took up the chant and the soldiers opened the slave cells. The prisoners came pouring out, shouting and praising God and "master Abe" for their deliverance. Chaplain White found himself unable to continue, "overcome with tears."

Later in the day, black soldiers took turns swiveling in the speaker's chair in the Hall of Delegates where the Confederate Congress had recently met. Meanwhile, an old woman forced her way through the throngs of rejoicing African Americans in search of Garland White. "A black soldier overheard the woman and brought her to see his regimental chaplain," according to historian Joseph Glatthaar. She asked the chaplain question after question until at last, she said, "This is your mother, Garland, whom you are now talking to, who has spent twenty years of grief about her son."

In the eastern and poorer parts of the city, whites too cheered U.S. forces as they entered Richmond. Even during the Confederate reign over the city, many German Americans and Scottish Americans had been secret and sometimes not-so-secret Union supporters (chapter 61). By the afternoon of April 3, in the words of the French consul, who might be considered a neutral observer, whites were openly fraternizing with Union troops, "especially when it was understood that there was nothing to fear. Moreover, there was a strong bitterness against the Confederate authorities who, in spite of all promises, persisted in destroying the properties and the principal city of a people who had bent every effort in their behalf." Now at least as many white Richmonders despised Davis as supported him, according to historian Ernest Furgurson.

In the next few days, thousands of African Americans crowded into Richmond tasting freedom, many hoping for reunions with loved ones like Chaplain White's. U.S. troops put on a military band concert on the grounds of the state capitol. To appease local whites, they barred blacks from attending. Notwithstanding this extraordinary gesture, most whites did not come to celebrate the demise of their cause. African Americans, meanwhile, organized their own celebration. On April 7, 1,500 African Americans, including many soldiers, packed the First African Church on Broad Street for a jubilee meeting. In 1876, this congregation rebuilt its church, slightly renamed, in a grand style. The result, now part of the Virginia Commonwealth University Medical College, still proclaims "First Baptist Church Colored" above its imposing columns at the corner of College and Broad streets.

Thus, Richmond's history hardly came to an end when the Confederates left. Indeed, the ashes of Richmond kindled new possibilities for the flowering of the human spirit as shown in the jubilee meeting, the reunion of Chaplain White and his mother, and thousands of other incidents in the lives of Richmond citizens and soldiers that we no longer remember.

When this book went to press in 1999, the places where the story of Richmond's liberation was told, such as the Siege Museum in Petersburg or the visitor center at the Richmond National Battlefield Park, were openly pro-Confederate. Exhibits and videos played funereal music when they reached April 3, 1865. "To the very end, the people of Petersburg had believed in their cause and their ultimate victory," said the Petersburg video, assuring us that this was "what *all* of them felt." Actually, no one in the town had believed in Confederate victory since the previous November, when Lincoln had won reelection. Visitor center guides refer to "the fall of Richmond," never "the liberation of Richmond." A. A. Hoehling and Mary Hoehling even titled their 1991 book on the Confederate abandonment of Richmond *The Day Richmond Died*—but for the greater part of the populace, it was the day the city began to live.

Since 2000, however, the neo-Confederate stranglehold on Richmond's public history, which affected even the National Park Service, has broken. During the sesquicentennial of these events in early April 2015, Richmond put on an astonishing series of lectures, reenactments, and performances. U.S. Colored Troops (USCT) reenactors came into the city to liberate it a second time. Scenes from the war were projected on buildings in the burned district. National Park Service rangers led lantern tours of the burned areas. Asa Gordon, a USCT reenactor and Secretary of the Sons and Daughters of the USCT, spoke on the "Legacy of National Redemption and Democracy" resulting from the USCT's actions. The Virginia Union University choir sang.

Richmond needs to make these changes permanent. What if the landscape told these stories? Imagine if a historical marker pointed to where retreating Confederates blew up the ammunition dump and set fires in the city. Imagine if other markers showed where U.S. troops put them out. Imagine if a marker told about the march of the 28th U.S. Colored Infantry down Broad Street stopping to liberate the slaves who were singing "Slavery chain done broke at last!" Technology can help historical markers tell these stories with sound and video, playable on visitors' own smartphones. When Richmond marks events like these permanently, then its public history will become a force not only for increased tourism but also for better race relations.[2]

The next two chapters tell more of this transformation, still ongoing as of 2019.

1. Some issues of the *Richmond Guide* may not emphasize the Civil War, but I've been to Richmond three times and all three did.

2. Frederic Bancroft, *Slave Trading in the Old South* (Columbia: U. of SC Press, 1996 [1935?]); Ernest B. Furgurson, *Ashes of Glory: Richmond at War* (NY: Knopf, 1996), 325; Gary Nash and Julie Roy Jeffrey, *The American People* (NY: Harper & Row, 1990), 535; Paul Lewis Todd and Merle Curti, *Triumph of the American Nation* (Orlando, FL: Harcourt Brace Jovanovich, 1990), 427; Thomas A. Bailey and David M. Kennedy, *The American Pageant* (Lexington, MA: D. C. Heath, 1994), 488; John A. Garraty with Aaron Singer and Michael Gallagher, *American History* (NY: Harcourt Brace Jovanovich, 1982), 487; Leon F. Litwack, *Been in the Storm So Long: The Aftermath of Slavery* (NY: Random House Vintage, 1980), 168–72; WPA, *The Negro in Virginia* (NY: Hastings House, 1940), 101–103, 164–65, 266–67; Rembert Patrick, *The Fall of Richmond* (Baton Rouge: LA State UP, 1960), 43–56, 68–71; Mary W. Scott, *Old Richmond Neighborhoods* (Richmond, VA: William Byrd Press, 1975 [1950]), 72; Burke Davis, *To Appomattox* (NY: Rinehart, 1959), 139–47; A. A. Hoehling and Mary Hoehling, *The Day Richmond Died* (Lanham, MD: Madison, 1991); Katherine Calos, "Marking Richmond's Fall and Rise from Ashes," *Richmond Times-Dispatch*, 4/1/2015, richmond.com/entertainment /weekend/article_5f9a2e05-daca-521a-8df8-b1cf56743bcb.html

---- ★ ----

64. Abraham Lincoln Walks Through Richmond

VIRGINIA *Richmond*

On April 4, 1865, Abraham Lincoln, with his young son Tad, came up the James River to visit the former capital of the Confederacy. The idea was risky, for his army had entered Richmond only the previous morning, but

Lincoln wanted the personal satisfaction of seeing the city that had eluded Union capture for so long. His trip is one of the great walks in American history, full of little incidents rich with larger meaning. Richmond needs to recognize it on its landscape.

In 1999, others did not think so. I suggested to Teresa Roan, librarian at the Valentine Museum, the museum of Richmond history, that they might offer a tour of Lincoln's route. She hesitated. "It's an exciting part of Richmond history," I pointed out. "Yes," she replied, "but [pause]." "But it's not a *Confederate* part?" "I was trying to think how to put that," she agreed. Virginia, which marks every site where George Washington sneezed, had not one historical marker for Abraham Lincoln.[1] The landscape cried out for markers to commemorate his landing, the site where he spoke to black workers, Castle Thunder (a Confederate prison), his visit to the Confederate White House, and his speech at the capitol.

On the 150th anniversary of his walk in 2015, Richmond finally promoted it as an attraction. An upscale market/café and Coca-Cola sponsored "Lincoln's Richmond Walk," with fourteen manned stops telling what happened from Rockett's Landing to the Confederate White House. Rdml. David Dixon Porter's flagship had borne Lincoln up the James, but the water grew too shallow, so Porter assigned twelve sailors to row the presidential party ashore in a naval barge. At Rocketts Landing, Lincoln came ashore wearing a long black overcoat, black pants, and a high silk hat, "giving his form a very commanding appearance" in the words of a newspaper report. A dozen African American workmen were working nearby with spades. One of them, 60 years old, recognized the president and ran to the barge shouting, "Bless the Lord! The great Messiah . . . Glory, hallelujah!" He fell on his knees and kissed the president's feet, and the others crowded about. The president seemed embarrassed. "Don't kneel to me," Lincoln said. "That's not right. You must kneel to God only, and thank him for the liberty you will hereafter enjoy. I am but God's humble instrument; but you may rest assured that as long as I live no one shall put a shackle on your limbs, and you shall have all the rights which God has given to every other free citizen of this Republic." These words, repeated later on this walk and also spoken from the White House balcony, offer a glimpse into what Lincoln's Reconstruction policies might have been, had he lived.[2]

Atop the hill on the right is Libby Hill Park with its Confederate Soldiers

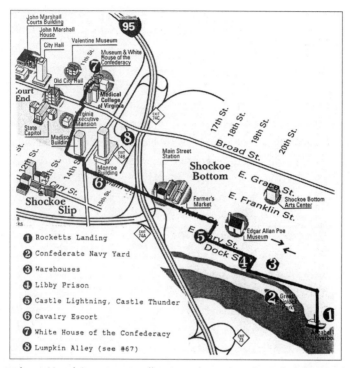

This map shows Lincoln's route, as well as I can determine, through today's Richmond. Many buildings remain from Lincoln's time, so visitors can gain some sense of what his walk was like.

and Sailors Monument, erected in 1894. Ahead on the river to the left, looking toward Richmond, stood the Confederate Navy Yard. Here, before dawn on April 3, 1865, Adm. Raphael Semmes had blown up his warships and set fire to buildings before abandoning the yard to the Union.

Lincoln walked west, probably along Dock Street, past tobacco warehouses, some of which still stand. After the South's victory at First Manassas, Confederates used them as prisons for troops captured in that early Union debacle. After the Union won some victories and had a comparable number of captured Confederates, prisoners were exchanged for a time, which freed the buildings to store tobacco and cotton again. As Richmond fell, official Confederate policy still held that the North and the world hungered for tobacco and cotton, so keeping it out of Union hands would still somehow help bring victory. Therefore, retreating Confederates burned some of these warehouses to deny their contents to the Union. When Lincoln came, some of these buildings would have been in ruins, perhaps still smoldering.

Lincoln then turned toward downtown Richmond, and word of his arrival spread like wildfire. Ernest Furgurson writes in *Ashes of Glory: Richmond at War* that hundreds of other African Americans now flocked around "laughing, weeping, shouting 'Glory, hallelujah!' and 'Thank you, Jesus!'" Several ex-slaves touched the president to make sure he was real. Adm. Porter wrote later, "The crowd poured in so fearfully that I thought we all stood a chance of being crushed to death." Porter ordered his sailors to fix bayonets and form a circle around the small party. Lincoln then told the crowd: "You can cast off the name of slave and trample upon it; it will come to you no more. Liberty is your birthright . . . " According to historian Donald Pfanz, "As Lincoln spoke you might have heard a pin drop, but now that he was through the crowd cheered and roared as if it would split the firmament."

Adm. Porter had hoped that U.S. troops in Richmond would meet and escort their party, but they were nowhere to be found. J. J. Hill, a soldier in the 29th Connecticut Volunteer Infantry, an African American unit with white officers, tells how the admiral positioned the scant forces at his disposal: "Six soldiers [sailors] dressed in blue, with their carbines, were the advanced guards. Next to them came President Lincoln and son, and Adm. Porter, flanked by the other officers right and left. Then came a correspondent, and in the rear were six sailors with carbines. Then followed thousands of people, colored and white. What a spectacle! I never witnessed such rejoicing in all my life." Holding hands with his son Tad, whose twelfth birthday it was, Lincoln walked toward Jefferson Davis's former mansion in downtown Richmond, which the Union Army was using as its headquarters. An African American man acted as guide.

President Lincoln walked in silence, occasionally acknowledging the salutes of officers and soldiers and the greetings of citizens, black and white. Some sources claim that few whites welcomed Lincoln; one historian describes an atmosphere "charged with menace," and one guard thought he saw a rifle held behind an upstairs window. According to Adm. Porter, however, "Many poor whites joined the throng and set up their shouts with the rest." Reporters agree that a beautiful young white girl pushed through the crowd and gave Lincoln a bunch of roses. When an elderly African American removed his hat and bowed, Lincoln paused, faced him, and silently returned

This engraving, published in 1866, was probably not by an eyewitness but does show the euphoric mood of the crowd and the want of security as the little party slowly made its way through the city.

the gesture. The crowd stirred noticeably; the courtesy was "a death-shock to chivalry, and a mortal wound to caste" one Union soldier wrote later.[3]

Between 21st and 20th Streets stood an enormous warehouse renamed Libby Prison by the Confederacy. A plaque on the nearby concrete floodwall has the words "On this site stood Libby Prison C.S.A." Fourteen months earlier, 109 Union officers had escaped from Libby Prison. Many made it to the North, where they told of the pathetic conditions they had endured. In response, within a month of the escape, a Union cavalry force descended on Richmond to free the remaining prisoners. The rescue effort failed, whereupon guards packed enough powder below the prison to blow it up if the North ever tried again, in effect holding the prisoners hostage. It took the president half an hour to get this far owing to the press of the crowd. When Lincoln passed it, a group of black workers following him called, "We'll pull it down!" "No," he said, "leave it as a monument."[4] Lincoln visited the prison and "by one account," according to Furgurson, he "'gave way to uncontrollable emotions' as he saw how Union captives had lived."

The president now turned right on 19th Street. To his left, on the river side of Cary Street, stood Castle Lightning; on the uphill side stood Castle Thunder—two other former tobacco factories turned into prisons. Many Richmonders suspected to be Union spies ended up in Castle Thunder, "the most dreaded political prison in the South" in Furgurson's words, partly owing to the many hangings ordered by its commander. Departing Confederates had emptied the prison, taking the POWs with them and releasing the common criminals back into the general population. U.S. troops were already filling it up again with looters when Lincoln passed by. Castle Thunder lives on in the nearby "Castle Thunder Cafe" at Main and 18th. Lincoln continued northwest on Main Street. At 17th Street, he could see the James River again, where engineers were beginning to construct a pontoon bridge they would finish a day or so after his visit. During the next six weeks, regiment after regiment from Meade's Army of the Potomac and then Sherman's triumphant army from Carolina would march north across this bridge on the way to their final encampment in Washington before going home.

At 15th Street, Lincoln reached the region blackened by the fire Confederates had set as they evacuated the city two days before. On his left from Main Street to the river, most buildings had burned. He turned right on 14th Street. Somewhere along here, the presidential party picked up an escort of black U.S. cavalrymen. He continued to Governor Street. Turning right, he could see Richmond's imposing public buildings.

Lincoln then walked northeast, past the former seat of the Confederate government, the Virginia Capitol, two more blocks to Clay Street. Here, he went inside the Davis house, visitable today as the White House of the Confederacy. He sat briefly at Davis's desk, drank a glass of water, and toured the building. He went to the door and bowed to three cheers from the crowd that had gathered outside, then ate a light lunch with Union commanders.

By coach, Lincoln next retraced his steps to the Rebel capitol. From its steps, he delivered a short speech, according to historian Herbert Aptheker, including these remarks directed to the African Americans in his audience: "In reference to you, colored people, let me say God has made you free. Although you have been deprived of your God-given rights by your so-called masters, you are now as free as I am, and if those that claim to be your superiors do not know that you are free, take the sword and bayonet and teach them that you are—for God created all men free, giving to each the same rights to life, liberty, and the pursuit of happiness." The crowds had additional chances to cheer Lincoln as he then went by coach to see other sights that afternoon before leaving the city.

The day was surely one of the more satisfying of his presidency, if not his whole life, which had only eleven days remaining. On April 15, "it is said that no Negro in Richmond spoke above a whisper," according to the WPA history *The Negro in Virginia*. "Remembering the tall gaunt man who had waved and smiled at them, men and women walked the streets, asking one another, 'Is it really true?'" John Wilkes Booth had acted, however, and Abraham Lincoln would walk no more.

On April 5, 2003, with National Park Service consent, entrepreneur Robert Kline dedicated a statue of Lincoln and his son Tad at Tredegar Iron Works, an NPS site that now houses the main museum about the Civil War in Richmond. The statue was surprisingly controversial, because neo-Confederate ideology holds Lincoln responsible for the Civil War.[5] During the dedication, the Sons of Confederate Veterans made clear their approval of John Wilkes Booth by paying a small airplane to circle overhead towing a banner that read, "Sic semper tyrannis." Now the statue has become a tourist attraction.

VisitRichmond.com suggests that tourists can also "Walk in the steps of Abraham Lincoln, who visited Richmond just ten days before his assassination." However, although its website boasts beer trails, garden trails, food tours, and a "liberty trail," it gives no guidance for those seeking to follow its advice and retrace Lincoln's route. A diligent search of the web did not reveal any map, so I retain mine from the first edition. NPS did put up a marker, "President Lincoln Visits Richmond," but it is not very accurate and says almost nothing about his walk itself. A marker at the White House mentions Lincoln's visit. Surely, it is time for Richmond to place markers along the route, telling what happened at each important spot and pointing to the next marker.[6]

1. Lincoln also walked in Petersburg the day before, only hours after its last Confederate defenders pulled out, but you cannot learn that in the Siege Museum in Petersburg or anywhere else on the landscape.

2. When the president repeated these sentiments from the White House balcony a week later, one listener, John Wilkes Booth, snarled to his companion, "That means nigger citizenship. Now, by God, I'll put him through. That is the last speech he will ever make." Three days later Booth shot Lincoln.

3. White supremacy as a formal system consisted in large part of a pattern of etiquette, every component of which denied the equality of the person of color. Chapters 45 and 50 tell of that system and what happened when it was violated. Owing to his presidential power, nothing happened to Abraham Lincoln on this occasion of course, but he must have known that he was violating racial protocol; the violation must have been deliberate.

4. An entrepreneur dismantled it in 1892, however, shipped it to the Chicago World's Fair, and reassembled it as an exhibit. Then it was demolished again; some bricks and beams were used to build a large barn that still stands in Hamlet, Indiana.

5. Neo-Confederates claim Lincoln should have turned the other cheek after Confederates took Fort Sumter, even though no president could have done so without facing charges of dereliction of duty. They also claim, against all evidence, that he never cared about slavery or holding the nation together but mainly wanted Southern tariff monies.

6. Accounts of Lincoln's walk vary as to details. I base this composite account on Noah Trudeau, *The Last Citadel* (Boston: Little, Brown, 1991), 410; "The Visit of his Excellency President Lincoln," *Richmond Whig*, 4/5/1865; Donald C. Pfantz, *Abraham Lincoln at City Point* (Lynchburg, VA: H. L. Howard, 1989), 58–67; John S. Barnes, "With Lincoln from Washington to Richmond in 1865," *Appleton's Magazine* 9 (1907): 746–49; Tony Horwitz, *Confederates in the Attic* (NY: Pantheon, 1998), 242; Richard M. Lee, *General Lee's City* (McLean, VA: EPM, 1987), 96, 107, 110; Ernest B. Furgurson, *Ashes of Glory: Richmond at War* (NY: Knopf, 1996), 113–21, 328, 343–47; James McPherson, *Battle Cry of Freedom* (NY: Oxford UP, 1988), 847, 852; Virginius Dabney, *Richmond: The Story of a City* (Charlottesville: UP of VA, 1990), 195–96; Henry J. Raymond, *The Life and Public Services of Abraham Lincoln* (NY: Derby and Miller, 1865), 681–83; Herbert Aptheker, *And Why Not Every Man?* (NY: International, 1961), 270–71; Elizabeth Van Lew, *A Yankee Spy in Richmond*, ed. David Ryan (Mechanicsburg, PA: Stackpole, 1996), 7–8; Neil November, "I Remember When . . . ," newspaper article (full citation not available); Alfred Hoyt Bill, *The Beleaguered City: Richmond 1861–65* (NY: Knopf, 1946), 279–80; Burke Davis, *To Appomattox* (NY: Rinehart, 1959), 184–85; A. A. and Mary Hoehling, *The Day Richmond Died* (San Diego, CA: A. S. Barnes, 1981); WPA, *The Negro in VA* (NY: Hastings House, 1940), 214; Robert W. Waitt Jr., remembrance in 1952 of conversations with Jeannette B. McNiven about "Recollections of Thomas McNiven and His Activities in Richmond During the Civil War" (Richmond, VA: Museum of Confederacy vertical files). On a website put up long after this essay first appeared, Richard J. Behn weaves several primary sources into an absorbing narrative, "Entering Richmond," Lehrman Institute, mrlincolnandfreedom.org/civil-war/black -soldiers/entering-richmond

---------- ★ ----------

65. Getting Even the Numbers Wrong

VIRGINIA *Appomattox*

At Appomattox cemetery, where the Civil War ended for the Army of Northern Virginia, the United Daughters of the Confederacy put up a marker with the words, "Here on Sunday April 9, 1865 after four years of heroic struggle in defense of principles believed fundamental to the existence of our government Lee surrendered 9000 men, the remnant of an army still unconquered in spirit, to 118,000 men under Grant." The marker gets the date right, and the Confederacy did put up "four years of heroic struggle." Otherwise, like most markers and monuments put up by the Daughters, it cannot be relied on for accuracy.

We might begin with "defense of principles believed fundamental." Three weeks before the Confederacy attacked Fort Sumter, Confederate Vice President Alexander Stephens expounded, "Our new government's foundations are laid, its cornerstone rests, upon the great truth that the Negro is not equal to the white man, that slavery—subordination to the superior race—is his natural and normal condition." UDC leaders doubtless hoped that if they left those principles vague, readers would infer something nobler.

Were Lee's troops "unconquered in spirit?" Much contemporary scholarship emphasizes that the Confederacy eventually fell because of a failure of spirit. In the months just before Appomattox, thousands of desertions sucked the life from Lee's army and Confederate armies everywhere. A month before Appomattox, Confederate soldier Harry Hammond wrote from Petersburg, "We have had some 60 or 70 desertions recently from the Brigade, most of them going over to the enemy at night while on picket." These men did not desert for lack of food, for Hammond went on to note, "Our supplies continue sufficient." Carleton Beals notes that the Confederate army was breaking up by the spring of 1865 in Texas and other states, even in the absence of Union approaches. He concludes that its ideological contradictions were the Confederacy's gravest liabilities, ultimately causing its defeat. White Southerners fought to preserve slavery partly because they believed it was right, or at least they maintained they did. Yet during the war, slaves behaved in ways that expressed their clear dissatisfaction with slavery (chapter 57). The success of black U.S. troops led to proposals by Confederate leaders to arm slaves, which threw Confederate ideology into further confusion.

Then there are the numbers. When Lee surrendered he asked that some sort of parole slip be given to his men so they would face no problems going through Union lines. The passes also entitled ex-Confederates to travel free on Union-controlled railroads and to draw rations from Union troops they met along the way. Moreover, men with paroles would not risk being shot as deserters by Confederates still in the field. Grant approved, and during the next five days, a small printing press churned out more than 28,000 slips that were signed and given to individual soldiers in Lee's surrendered army. Between 2,000 and 2,500 men who lived nearby just went home without waiting for their slips. To say "Lee surrendered 9000 men" is preposterous.

On the Union side, Grant did have about 120,000 men in his final Petersburg-Appomattox campaign, but only about 63,000 were at Appomattox Court House. His other forces were occupying Petersburg and Richmond, guarding supply lines, and holding railheads. Similarly, Lee had had more than 60,000 men at Petersburg and Richmond, but many deserted or were captured on the way to Appomattox.[1] U.S. forces did outnumber Confederate forces by almost two to one throughout Lee's flight from Petersburg to Appomattox, but those numbers weren't lopsided enough for the United Daughters of the Confederacy.

Someone, perhaps enraged at the claim that Grant had 118,000 men at Appomattox, chiseled the letters and numbers off the last line of the plaque.[2] Even that line could still be read as of 1999, but the passage of two more decades has made it illegible. Of course, if Union soldiers outnumbered Confederates thirteen to one, as the Daughters would have it, no wonder the Confederacy lost the war! So that's the motive for getting the numbers wrong. Ironically, although many Confederates were conquered in spirit in 1865, by the time this plaque went up in 1926, the UDC was unconquered in spirit. By then, as chapter 15 tells, the Confederacy had won!

In 1615, poet John Harington wrote the famous lines,

> *Treason doth never prosper,*
> *What's the reason?*
> *For if it prosper,*
> *None dare call it treason.*

The U.S. Constitution defines treason specifically and narrowly: "Treason against the United States, shall consist only in levying war against them, or in adhering to their enemies, giving them aid and comfort." Levying war against the United States, beginning at Sumter and ending for Lee and his men at Appomattox Court House, is precisely what the Confederates did.[3]

When this book first appeared, Virginia was so far from defining secession and the Civil War as treason that its governor annually declared April "Confederate Heritage Month"![4] The United Daughters of the Confederacy had several times as many members as its Union counterpart, the Women's Relief

Corps. The Sons of Confederate Veterans was still a vibrant if misguided organization. The Grand Army of the Republic, limited to Union Civil War veterans, had gone out of existence; its tiny museum in Springfield, Illinois, was hosted by a neo-Confederate when I visited! In 1999, none dared call the Confederacy treason, at least not on the landscape—not even at the very site where the United States won, a site owned by the American people under the stewardship of the National Park Service.

By 2019, this sorry state of affairs had finally begun to change. While Republican governors continued to proclaim the Confederate Month tradition, Democratic governors of Virginia let the tradition lapse. In 2010, however, when Republican governor Robert McDonnell proclaimed it again, his proclamation did not mention or condemn slavery. This prompted a storm of criticism, to which the governor, astoundingly, replied, "There were any number of aspects to that conflict between the states. Obviously, it involved slavery. It involved other issues. But I focused on the ones I thought were most significant for Virginia."[5] McDonnell later apologized for omitting slavery and never proclaimed Confederate Month again. The National Park Service now does mention slavery as the cause of secession, hence war, at most Civil War sites. But we still have a long way to go to get the war right.[6]

Equally in error is the marker erected by the Sons and Daughters of Confederate Soldiers to mark the first Virginia casualty of the Civil War almost four years earlier (chapter 60). Chapters 15 and 53 tell more about the UDC.

1. Most of Lee's cavalry was outside the surrender lines. They pulled out and went to nearby Lynchburg. There, they disbanded; most went home, but a few joined up with Gen. Joe Johnston's forces in North Carolina just in time to be paroled there.

2. No one I reached at NPS or the UDC knew who did this chiseling or when.

3. The Confederated States of America also attempted to create enemies of the United States with which to exchange aid and comfort. It did this by supporting undemocratic regimes in Latin America, which worked particularly well in Mexico, where the Confederacy supported France's attempt to put Maximilian on the throne as emperor.

4. Nevertheless, some neo-Confederates damned him because he also declared slavery wrong and implied the two might be linked.

5. McDonnell's reference to "that conflict between the states" of course referenced the neo-Confederate term for the conflict. No one called it that while it was going on. He also referenced "the insurmountable numbers and resources of the Union Army" as the reason for the Confederacy's defeat, echoing this marker at Appomattox.

6. Reid Mitchell, "The Creation of Confederate Loyalties," in Robert Azug and Stephen Maizlish, eds., *New Perspectives on Race and Slavery in America* (Lexington: UP of KY,

1986), 101–102; Tony Horwitz, *Confederates in the Attic* (NY: Pantheon, 1998), 268–69; Carol Bleser, ed., *The Hammonds of Redcliffe* (NY: Oxford UP, 1981), 131–32; Carleton Beals, *War Within a War* (Philadelphia, PA: Chilton, 1965), 73; Gabor Boritt, ed., *Why the Confederacy Lost* (NY: Oxford UP, 1992); Anita Kumar and Rosalind S. Helderman, "McDonnell's Confederate History Month Proclamation Irks Civil Rights Leaders," *The Washington Post*, 4/7/2010.

———————— ✯ ————————

66. A Sign of Good Breeding

VIRGINIA *Stickleyville*

Near Stickleyville, in the far southwestern corner of Virginia, a marker informs visitors that "In this valley, in June, 1785, Indians led by the notorious half breed, Benge, massacred the family of Archibald Scott . . . " "Notorious half breed," while insulting, tells its own history once one realizes the context. And as is so often the case, it tells more about Virginia in the 1930s, when the sign went up, than about the 1785 event.

"Half breed" on a historical marker "otherizes" the person thus described. Animals "breed"—particularly livestock—under human guidance. People "marry," or at least "cohabit." To use "breed" is to emphasize the physical act and the genetics of the process, implicitly denying the human story involved. This is particularly inappropriate when dealing with American Indian societies, which did not and for the most part, do not define people as "Native American" based on race but on history and culture.

Robert Benge was culturally Indian but multiracial physically. Possibly, he was Melungeon, a group that spread throughout the United States but is still concentrated in western Virginia and eastern Tennessee. Melungeons are what sociologists call "triracial isolates," or mixed-race peoples—people of European, Native, and African descent who have lived by themselves through most periods of American history because they refuse to take part in America's rigid system of racial categorization.[1]

Racial categorization has been particularly oppressive in Virginia, and intermarriage was discouraged in the Virginia colony. Alliance through marriage is a common way for two societies to deal with each other, and American Indians repeatedly suggested such a policy. Spanish men married Native women in California and New Mexico and converted them to Spanish ways. French fur traders married Native women in Canada and Illinois and converted to Native ways. Not the British. In their very first years in Virginia, the British encouraged intermarriage to promote alliances with nearby Native Americans, even offering a bribe to any white Virginian who would marry an Indian, but this offer lasted only briefly and few colonists took advantage of it. Thereafter, English colonists quickly moved to forbid interracial marriage. Pocahontas stands as the first and almost the last Native to be accepted into British-American society, which we may, therefore, call "white society," through marriage. After her, most interracial couples, like Benge's parents, found more acceptance in Native society. In fact, their children often became chiefs because their bicultural background was an asset in the complex world the tribes now had to navigate. In Anglo society, "half breeds" were not valued but stigmatized.

"Breeding" or eugenics was very much on the minds of political leaders and biological and social scientists in Virginia when the Benge sign went up. Chapter 63 noted that interracial marriages were legal in Virginia during Reconstruction. But Congressional Reconstruction lasted just two years in Virginia. In 1869, white Democrats returned to power. Four years later, they made black-white marriage a felony punishable by a year in jail and a fine of $100. In 1878, they made the jail term two to five years. The next year, Virginia declared any marriage between white and black void and defined "Negro" as a person possessing one fourth or more black parentage. By 1910, this was no longer stringent enough for the Virginia General Assembly, which redefined "Negro" to mean one-sixteenth black blood. Finally, in 1930, a person with "any Negro blood shall be termed a colored person."

W. A. Plecker, Virginia's first registrar of vital statistics, supplied the rationale for Virginia's increasingly rigid system of racial categorization in a 1925 address and article he titled "Virginia's Attempt to Adjust the Color Problem." He wrote, "[Whites] came to make homes, to create a nation, and to found a civilization of the highest type; not to mix their blood with the savages of the land; not to originate a mongrel population combining the worst traits of both conquerors and conquered." Complete racial separation was the answer, Plecker believed. He went on to discuss the mixed-race peoples in Virginia, including the Melungeons and mixed-race Indians, whose existence threatened such strict segregation. He foresaw the end of civilization if they continued to intermarry with whites but claimed Virginia had the remedy: "her recently enacted law 'for the preservation of racial integrity.'"

Under this act, "clerks are not permitted to grant licenses for white persons to marry those with any trace of colored blood." Plecker cited another authority who called this Virginia law "the most important eugenical effort that has been made during the past 4,000 years." His office was instrumental in getting hundreds of what he called "near-whites" thrown out of white schools or denied marriage licenses.

Virginia was hardly alone in its pursuit of "racial purity." "Good breeding" became a vulgar way for rich wasps to rationalize their good fortune (chapter 81). Crediting genetics for success fit with the "scientific racism" that stemmed from Social Darwinism—the "rise of the fittest." Eugenicist Madison Grant, a stalwart in the American Breeders Association and author of *The Passing of the Great Race in America*, framed the law restricting immigration that Congress passed in 1924. The ideology was nonempirical, even circular, for in the absence of any way to measure the genes that supposedly governed success, the only way to "prove" that heredity caused achievement was by assertion. Nevertheless, in the 1920s and 1930s, many state legislatures passed sterilization laws for people of "dubious stock" including isolated rural folk, the poor, and those with low IQ test scores. The Vermont eugenics program, for example, sterilized several hundred such people including many Abenaki Indians. Virginia sterilized more than 7,500 people, many without their knowledge or consent. As late as 1940, two-thirds of the states still outlawed marriage between whites and blacks; most of those also outlawed marriage between whites and "Orientals."

Today, most Americans no longer use "breed" for what human beings do, reserving that term for laboratory rats, livestock, and the like. Nor does Virginia still attempt to breed people by restricting whom they can marry. What happened to change white American thinking?

Mostly, it was World War II. Before the war, Hitler's scientists consulted with Plecker and other American eugenics authorities. Germany's defeat coupled with the horrors of the "master race's" death camps gave a bad name to eugenics from which it has yet to fully recover. Around the same time, nations that white colonial powers had controlled—India, the Philippines, Ghana, and many others—won their independence. Suddenly, white supremacy was embarrassing rather than customary on the world stage.

Partly in response to these developments, fourteen states dropped their opposition to interracial marriage. Plecker was quietly allowed to retire after the war, but Virginia would not change its segregation laws. Black Virginians brought one of the five cases that the U.S. Supreme Court decided in its 1954

Brown v. Board of Education ruling, outlawing racial segregation in schools. Even after 1954, however, Virginia judges still adhered rigidly to eugenics practices. In 1958, Richard Loving, Caucasian, and Mildred Jeter, part Native American and part African American, married in Washington, DC. Natives of Virginia, they returned to Mildred's parents' home in the eastern part of Caroline County for a wedding reception with their relatives. That night, police arrested them and expelled them from the state. "Notorious half breed" was still in the officers' minds.

In 1963, after living in Washington for a time, the Lovings filed suit against Virginia. Judge Leon Bazile, in a lecture combining pseudo-religion and pseudo-anthropology, told them, "Almighty God created the races white, black, yellow, Malay, and red, and he placed them on separate continents. The fact that he separated the races shows that he did not intend for the races to mix." Bazile had never read or chose to ignore what the *Bible* says about interracial marriage in *Numbers* 12, verses 1–15.[2]

The judge also seems not to have understood the implications of the *Brown* decision. In 1967, the U.S. Supreme Court reversed Bazile and struck down the Virginia law, simultaneously rescinding similar laws in all other states. Thus, the Lovings' victory not only resolved their own situation but also freed thousands of other people to marry the partner they pleased without regard to race. In Virginia alone, sixteen additional interracial couples married before the end of 1967 and thousands since then.

Now, so far as race was concerned, the state was no longer in the business of circumscribing choices made by the human heart. In 1982, Virginia finally again recognized its indigenous people as "Indian," not "colored." Shortly after the original publication of this book, Virginia took down its "half-breed" marker and replaced it with a much more accurate one that also avoids the word "massacre."[3] In 2017, Virginia put up two truthful markers about the Lovings. Plecker also deserves a marker, for he wrecked hundreds of lives and popularized an ideology that still lives today.

In 2002, Virginia did put up a marker about the first victim of its eugenics law, Carrie Buck, ordered sterilized after her lawsuit reached the U.S. Supreme Court but failed. At its dedication, Governor Mark Warner issued a formal apology for the state's sterilization program, noting that the marker "would remind us of past events and assist us to strive to do better." Meanwhile, the words "breed" and "half breed" continue to lie on markers across America from Georgia and New York to South Dakota, still reinforcing eugenics thinking.[4]

Chapters 7, 21, 24, and 35 describe additional markers and monuments inscribed with words that "otherize" American Indians.

1. N. Brent Kennedy in his book *The Melungeons* tells how the Melungeons may also trace their origins to early Portuguese, Turkish, or other immigrants from the Mediterranean area.

2. In the "Revised Loewen Translation," we read that Miriam and Aaron "spoke against Moses because of the black woman whom he had married." And the Lord told Moses, Aaron, and Miriam to "Come out to the tabernacle tent." And the Lord came down in the pillar of the cloud and called forth Aaron and Miriam. And he said, "Hear now my words: when I speak to *you*, I do so only in dreams. But when I speak with my good servant Moses, we speak face to face. Why then were you two not afraid to speak against my good servant Moses? Miriam, you think it's so important to be white? I'll make you white!" And the anger of the Lord was kindled against them. And the cloud departed from off the tabernacle tent, and, behold, Miriam became leprous, white as snow! And Aaron said unto Moses, "Alas, my lord, I beseech thee, we have done foolishly, and we have sinned. But let her not be as one dead, of whom the flesh is half consumed." And Moses cried unto the Lord, saying, "Heal her now, O God, I beseech thee." And the Lord said unto Moses, "All right, I'll give her leprosy just for a week, so let her be shut out from the camp seven days, and after that let her be received in again."

3. I do not know if my book sparked the change. Virginia has been revising bad old markers for some time.

4. Robert Beverly, *The History and Present State of VA* (Chapel Hill: U. of NC Press, 1947 [1705]), 38; Peter A. Thomas, "Cultural Change on the Southern New England Frontier, 1630–1655," in William Fitzhugh, ed., *Cultures in Contact* (DC: Smithsonian, 1985), 141; Jane Dailey, email, 3/99; W. A. Plecker, "VA's Attempt to Adjust the Color Problem," from Darlene Wilson, "Melungeon Home Page," clinch.edu/appalachia /melungeon/melung.htm#Archive, 12/97; Stephen Jay Gould, "Ideology in Practice," in John Trumpbour, ed., *How Harvard Rules* (Boston: South End Press, 1989), 263–64; J. Leitch Wright Jr., *The Only Land They Knew*, (NY: Free Press, 1981), 235; Gary Nash, *Red, White, and Black* (Englewood Cliffs, NJ: Prentice-Hall, 1974); E. Digby Baltzell, *The Protestant Establishment* (NY: Random House, 1964), 97; James Axtell, *The Invasion Within* (NY: Oxford UP, 1985), 302–27; N. Brent Kennedy, *The Melungeons* (Macon, GA: Mercer UP, 1997); Peter Wallenstein, "Race, Marriage, and the Law of Freedom," *Chicago-Kent Law Review* 70 no. 2 (1994): 394–409, 421–22; "Richard and Mildred Loving," hmdb.org/marker.asp?marker=119182; Jennifer R. Loux, "Virginia's Historical Marker Program: Its History and Growth," *Notes on Virginia* 54(2016): 9.

THE ATLANTIC STATES

67. Is California West of the Alleghenies?
WEST VIRGINIA *Union*

Along West Virginia 3, two miles east of Union in Monroe County, a marker commemorates

REHOBOTH CHURCH

> *Indians were still about when Rehoboth Church was dedicated by Bishop Asbury in 1786, and rifles as well as Bibles were carried by the worshipers. This is the oldest church building west of the Allegheny Mountains.*

Rehoboth Church may be west of the Alleghenies, but so is California, and by 1786, Franciscans had founded ten missions in California alone. Catholic churches in Texas date back another century: in 1681, Tiguan Indians and Franciscan fathers built Ysleta Mission near El Paso. Ysleta is still a functioning church. In 1682, Mexicans completed Nuestra Señora de Socorro Mission, which today calls itself the oldest continuously active Catholic parish in the United States. Older still are the astonishing Native American apartment houses in the Southwest. Pueblo kivas house religious ceremonies that have been performed since long before Rehoboth Church was built.

One reason *Lies Across America* begins in the West is to combat Protestant Anglocentric "thinking" and to remind readers that American Indian and Spanish settlers played major roles in the American past. The United States is an Anglophone nation to be sure, but overemphasizing its Anglo roots does violence to the past. When we begin with Plymouth Rock we fall into the trap of imagining that the English were first—first to "settle" the Americas (chapter 89) or first to build a church "west of the Allegheny Mountains."

In all, Spaniards and Mexicans explored and settled one-third of what is now the United States, from northern California to Arkansas and Louisiana to Florida. They left indelible imprints not only in place names and missions but also in our culture. The horse and the Latino culture connected with horses gave rise first to a new Plains Indian culture and then a new Anglo cowboy culture. Mission architecture and style are still potent forces in American design, and not only in the Southwest. And like the Socorro Mission, the Catholic Church lives on and is the dominant church in much of the formerly Spanish domain.

But if the Spanish dominated the southwestern United States in the first half of the nineteenth century, Anglos dominated in the second half. Anglo historians have told the story ever since, and largely from the viewpoint of New England. Until late in the 1950s, Catholic high schools in the United States did not use the same American history textbooks used in public schools. Catholic schools used Catholic American history textbooks, which emphasized the work of Father Junípero Serra and other Spanish explorers and missionaries throughout the Southwest. The idea of a Catholic version of U.S. history amused me until I realized that public school textbooks come from an equally biased Protestant Anglo Eastern viewpoint.

Here, the influence of Yankee historians can be seen on the West Virginia landscape. Literally false, the Rehoboth Church historical marker merely reinforces our conventional thinking of seeing the past from the vantage point of Boston, looking southwestward.[1]

1. Robert Broderick, *Historic Churches of the United States* (NY: Funk, 1958), 43–54.

--------------------------- ✯ ---------------------------

68. Juxtaposing Quotations to Misrepresent a Founding Father

DISTRICT OF COLUMBIA *Jefferson Memorial*

The Jefferson Memorial, dedicated in 1943, resembles the earlier Lincoln Memorial in its classical Greek architecture and the practice of putting words by its president on its stone walls. Saul Padover, assistant to the secretary of the interior under Franklin D. Roosevelt, chose the monument's quotations while writing an adulatory biography of Jefferson published in 1942. But while the Lincoln Memorial presents the Gettysburg Address and Second Inaugural in their entireties, the Jefferson Memorial juxtaposes fragments from widely scattered writings of Thomas Jefferson to distort his ideas and policies.

The first panel misquotes the preamble and conclusion of the Declaration of Independence, leaving out five words from within its selected excerpts. The architect requested the omissions so the text would fit better! Surely, *this* memorable text should not be altered for so petty a reason. We know Jefferson would not approve, for whenever he sent correspondents a copy of the Declaration, he took pains to show what the Continental Congress had added to his draft and what it had cut. The altered text reads,

> *We hold these truths to be self-evident: that all men are created equal,*
> *that they are endowed by their Creator with certain inalienable rights,*
> *among these are life, liberty, and the pursuit of happiness, that to secure*
> *these rights governments are instituted among men. We . . . solemnly*
> *publish and declare, that these Colonies are and of right ought to be free*
> *and independent states. . . . And for the support of this declaration, with*
> *a firm reliance on the protection of divine providence, we mutually pledge*
> *our lives, our fortunes, and our sacred honour.*

Omitting "that" before "among these are life, liberty, and the pursuit of happiness" may be minor though it does make Jefferson's parallel constructions seem less parallel and more awkward. Omitting "United" before "Colonies," however, alters the sense of the document to insinuate that thirteen separate states declared independence. One could argue that omitting "to each other" from the sentence, "We mutually pledge to each other our lives, our fortunes, and our sacred honour," removes a redundancy. Emphasizing that the 56 signers *were* talking to each other, however, as well as mutually to the embryonic nation and the world, suggests their lonely courage. They knew if they didn't hang together they might hang separately and worried lest some might break faith and betray the rest.

The second panel, on religious freedom, takes three quotations from Jefferson's Act for Religious Freedom, passed by the Virginia Assembly in 1779, and adds a sentence from a letter he wrote to James Madison a decade later. That final sentence is ripped out of context: "I know but one code of morality for men whether acting singly or collectively." In the context of religious freedom, preceded by phrases like "Almighty God" and "the Holy Author of our freedom," the sentence seems to imply that Jefferson held to an absolute moral code. Actually, a self-described Unitarian, Jefferson believed in the power of reason as a foundation of morality. Here, he was writing in the context of political economy; he and Madison were corresponding about such issues as whether institutions determine individual behavior and how then to shape those institutions.

I know no problem with the words on the fourth panel, a single extended quotation from a letter Jefferson wrote in 1816 on the need to change institutions "to keep pace with the times." The third panel, however, which the National Park Service brochure describes as "devoted to his ideas on freedom of the body and to his beliefs in the necessity of educating the masses of the people," is a hodgepodge of quotations from diverse writings by Jefferson from widely different periods in his life. The effect of this medley is to create the impression that Thomas Jefferson was very nearly an abolitionist. In their original contexts, the same quotations reveal quite a different Jefferson conflicted about slavery—at times its harsh critic, often its apologist.

The words on the wall read:

> God who gave us life gave us liberty. Can the liberties of a nation be secure when we have removed a conviction that these liberties are the gift of God? Indeed, I tremble for my country when I reflect that God is just, that his justice cannot sleep forever. Commerce between master and slave is despotism. Nothing is more certainly written in the book of fate than that these people are to be free. Establish the law for educating the common people. This it is the business of the state to effect and on a general plan.

By putting these fragments back into their wording and supplying their contexts, we can see what the monument leaves out.

The first fragment is based on the sentence, "The God who gave us life gave us liberty at the same time," part of the conclusion of *A Summary View of the Rights of British America*, a pamphlet written in 1774, where it follows a sentence objecting to taxes imposed on the colonies by the mother country. By grafting it onto sentences about masters and slaves, the Memorial implies that the passage was about slavery when it wasn't.

Padover took the second, third, and fourth sentences from a long paragraph, "Manners," in *Notes on the State of Virginia*, Jefferson's only book, published in 1785. The paragraph contains Jefferson's most important treatment of slavery, but Padover has rearranged its phrases to make a much tamer impression than Jefferson's original. Jefferson began by lamenting the harmful impact slavery had on *whites*:

> There must doubtless be an unhappy influence on the manners of our people produced by the existence of slavery among us. The whole commerce between master and slave is a perpetual exercise of the most boisterous passions, the most unremitting despotism on the one part, and degrading submissions on the other. Our children see this, and learn to imitate it . . . and thus nursed, educated and daily exercised in tyranny, cannot but be stamped by it with odious peculiarities. The man must be a prodigy who can retain his manners and morals undepraved by such circumstances.[1]

The panel's second sentence as arranged by Padover seems a pious plea to pay tribute to God as the giver of liberty; many visitors never realize that slavery is its topic. In context, Jefferson is prophesying that one of slavery's harmful effects on whites is to undermine political liberty. He has just lamented how slavery transforms slaveowners "into despots" and slaves "into enemies." "Can the liberties of a nation be secure when we have removed a conviction that these liberties are the gift of God?" refers to the former transformation, which prompts slaveowners to believe that liberty is theirs to give or take away. For a nation to remain free it is essential, Jefferson here implies, that its people and leaders respect freedom as one of man's God-given natural rights; here he recognizes, albeit obliquely, the inherent conflict between this theory and the practice of slavery.

The third sentence refers to the other transformation Jefferson has lamented, of slaves into enemies. As truncated by Padover—"Indeed, I tremble for my country when I reflect that God is just, that his justice cannot sleep forever"—it becomes a vague warning to the United States to shape up. Few readers would infer that slave revolt is its real topic, but Jefferson goes on to finish the sentence: "that considering numbers, nature and natural means only, a revolution of the wheel of fortune, an exchange of situation, is among possible events." This is the slaveowners' familiar fear of rebellion.

Padover's next sentence finally mentions slavery: "Commerce between master and slave is despotism." Padover distilled these seven words from the sentence that Jefferson had placed much earlier: "The whole commerce between master and slave is a perpetual exercise of the most boisterous passions, the most unremitting despotism on the one part, and degrading submissions on the other." Jefferson knew from experience how slavery corrupts relationships between people. He owned two plantations some 60 miles apart—a journey of several days back then—and was always absent from one of them. Often, he was absent from both for years on end, such as when he lived in Paris in the service of the United States. Like most planters, he relied on overseers and knew little about the day-to-day operation of his plantations when he was gone. So long as they operated profitably, he assumed everything was all right. Some of his overseers "were cruel," according to historian Lucia Stanton, "even by the standards of the day."

Slavery also contaminated sexual relationships "between master and slave," as Jefferson also knew firsthand. His father-in-law, John Wayles, after the death of his third wife, turned to his slave Betty Hemings for female companionship. Did Wayles love Hemings? Did she love him? The questions may not be answerable, not only because of a lack of available evidence, but also owing precisely to the authority structure of slavery about which Jefferson was writing. We do know they engaged in "boisterous passions," for they had six children. Jefferson's wife inherited them and they all came to live and work at Monticello. After her death, Jefferson, himself, fathered children by one of them, Sally Hemings.

The final statement on slavery at the Jefferson Memorial, "Nothing is more certainly written in the book of fate than that these people are to be free," comes from his "Autobiography," written in 1821 when Jefferson was an old man. To present a Jefferson who has such a sunny prognosis for slavery, again the memorial must take the words out of context, for Jefferson's next sentences in the "Autobiography" strike a chilling note: "Nor is it less certain that the two races, equally free, cannot live in the same government. Nature, habit, opinion has drawn indelible lines of distinction between them." Conor Cruise O'Brien points out, "The distortion by suppression has to be deliberate." Jefferson's fear of black revolt, his belief that blacks and whites could never live together in peace and equality, and his reliance on the money generated by slave labor fueled his support for slavery as an institution, support that increased as he aged. Jefferson never suggested fixing the problems he diagnosed by ending slavery; on the contrary, he repeatedly advised his fellow Virginia slaveowners against freeing their slaves and never freed any of his own, not even at his death, except for a handful of Hemingses.

The last two sentences, from 1786 letters to Jefferson's mentor, George Wythe and to George Washington, make it sound as if Jefferson would include African Americans among "the common people" to be educated. His actions would suggest otherwise. Thaddeus Kosciusko, the Polish hero of the Revolutionary War, made Jefferson the executor of his American estate. His will directed Jefferson to sell about $17,000 in government securities and use the money to buy, free, and educate young African Americans. According to historian John Miller, Jefferson "refused to execute this project," so the money went "to other purposes which had nothing to do with furthering the education of blacks."

Thomas Jefferson was a great and yet a complex man. The Jefferson Memorial does not do justice to his complexity. The Park Service brochure states, "Although his efforts to abolish slavery were not successful, he was one of the first Americans to argue forcefully the inconsistency of slavery in a democratic state." But Jefferson made no consistent effort to abolish slavery. While he was an idealist who hoped slavery would somehow end, he was also a slaveowner, a white supremacist, and, as his Revolutionary fervor receded, an advocate for slavery's expansion.

Like too many historic sites, the Jefferson Memorial covers over the blemishes on the hero it celebrates. It would be nice if Jefferson *were* the proto-abolitionist that the memorial and the park service brochure pretend he was. Jefferson scholar Paul Finkelman writes, "As someone committed to racial equality, I would in fact be far happier to find in Jefferson a model for a usable past, rather than a source of our present woes." Since Jefferson was more complex than that, his memorial needs to be more complex than it is. Instead of continuing to misrepresent Jefferson, the National Park Service could supply the contexts missing from the juxtaposed quotations on its panels. Then visitors could see Jefferson as a man who not only envisioned but also betrayed the hopes of mankind. Americans would be enriched by learning how Jefferson wrestled with slavery, even though in the end he "lost." We can live with this understanding. Indeed, since the United States has on occasion acted to realize and at other times to betray the hopes of mankind,

Americans *need* this understanding of Jefferson, better to understand "our present woes."[2]

Chapter 71 tells how guides at Independence Hall used to tell quaint stories about Jefferson's Declaration of Independence, neglecting its contradictions and its revolutionary import.

1. Here, I omit four sentences and parts of two others that comprise an excursus on imitation.

2. Thomas Jefferson, *The Portable Thomas Jefferson* (NY: Viking, 1975), 21, 214–15, 251–52, 517; Douglas L. Wilson, "Thomas Jefferson and the Character Issue," *The Atlantic* (11/92), www.theatlantic.com/issues/current, 8/98; "Biography of Samuel Johnson," justus.anglican.org/resources/bio/20.html, 8/98; Rebecca Bowman, correspondence, 7/98, 9/98; Lucia Stanton, *Slavery at Monticello* (Charlottesville, VA: Thomas Jefferson Memorial Foundation, 1996), 29; Conor Cruise O'Brien, "Thomas Jefferson: Radical and Racist," *The Atlantic* 278 no. 4 (10/96): 56; Leef Smith, "Tests Link Jefferson, Slave's Son," *The Washington Post*, 11/1/98; Paul Finkelman, *Slavery and the Founders* (NY: M. E. Sharpe, 1966), 144–45, 163–65; John C. Miller, *The Wolf by the Ears* (NY: Free Press, 1977), 77, 256; Thomas Jefferson, *The Writings of Thomas Jefferson, vol. 12*, ed. A. A. Lipscombe and A. E. Bergh (DC: Thomas Jefferson Memorial Association, 1904), 321–22.

✯
---

69. "No History to Tell"

MARYLAND *Hampton*

A generic National Park Service (NPS) brochure promises children, "Hidden within each national park is an exciting story waiting to be discovered. Learning the secrets of each national park is easy. Simply ask your teacher or Park Ranger. . . ." In 1999, when this book first came out, this wouldn't have worked at Hampton, an estate built just after the Revolutionary War and located just north of the beltway that circles Baltimore. The staff at Hampton insisted it had no story to tell and merely presented the architecture. Rangers would begin by saying something like, "Every National Park Service site has a historical reason to be in the Park Service, except this one." The NPS website groups its many sites under about 40 different topics. Many properties get multiple listings, but Hampton occurred only once, under "architecture."

The Georgian mansion *is* impressive. However, impressive antebellum plantation houses are so commonplace that their brochures have to engage in a battle of superlatives to lure the tourist dollar. Perhaps, as a result, the NPS home site no longer lists Hampton under architecture. As of July 2019, it doesn't list Hampton under *any* topic!

A lot of history happened at every plantation, however, including Hampton: the story of the site itself and its people, which mostly means the story of slavery. When this book first came out, very few plantations even touched upon enslavement Instead, they mainly talked about the rich white plantation owners, their silverware, and their wallpaper. The silence of antebellum homes about the nature of slavery is a crime against the public. It makes us stupid. Frederick Douglass understood that in 1855 when he wrote, "I expose slavery in this country, because to expose it is to kill it. Slavery is one of those monsters of darkness to whom the light of truth is death."

It was astounding how lopsided plantation tours were. For example, nine of every ten people living at The Hermitage, Andrew Jackson's mansion near Nashville, were enslaved African Americans. The audio tour gave these enslaved people just one sentence, mentioning their number: 130. At the gate to Magnolia Plantation in South Carolina stood a huge billboard offering "The Complete Plantation Experience"—yet Magnolia told next to nothing about the experience of most of the people who lived there. Indeed, things happened at antebellum home sites in the passive voice. At Hampton, guides told that the right-hand wing "is where the laundry was done" while the left wing "was for the cooking."[1] The brochure "Gardens and Grounds" said, "Construction of the terraces or 'falls' took place during the late 1790s and probably involved moving greater volumes of earth than in any other early American garden." Who moved it? No clue!

"Let me show you the builders of the house," said a guide in 1999. I imagined we'd learn something about the slaves, perhaps also the free artisans, white and black, who labored here. Instead, he led us to stand beneath the portraits of Charles Ridgely, the first owner, and his wife. The rhetoric was identical to the old slave song, only without the latter's derision:

> *Oh, Mr. Ridgely is a mighty fine man.*
> *He plants all the wheat, He plows all the corn,*
> *He weighs all the cotton,*
> *And blows the dinner horn.*
> *Mr. Ridgely is a mighty fine man.*

In fact, at every plantation, slaves built their own houses and the owner's too, grew their own corn and the owner's too, butchered the hogs, picked the cotton, and made their own clothing—or they raised the crops for sale that paid for the corn and nails and clothing. Nevertheless, most plantations made them invisible.[2]

When workers *were* mentioned, guides and brochures went to extraordinary lengths to avoid the s-word. Slaves become "servants" or even "antebellum workers." Owners become "masters." The booklet for Magnolia said a photograph of a slave cabin housed "domestic workers prior to the Civil War. It has been refurnished to show plantation workers' living conditions of those pre-Civil-War days."

Many plantations did tell about one favorite slave, a "Tonto" figure. By recognizing "the good" in one African American—always loyal to the white side—guides imply that the system was fair and that "good Negroes" liked their "masters." At Magnolia, it was Adam Bennett, who saved the silverware when Union soldiers demanded it. At The Hermitage, "Uncle Alfred" was born in slavery but "chose to stay on after emancipation."[3] He gets no last name, even on his tombstone, which says only,

UNCLE ALFRED

died Sept. 4, 1901
Aged 98 years
Faithful servant of Andrew Jackson

Here at Hampton the guide and brochure told of Nancy Brown Davis, "born a slave in 1838. She chose to stay on as a servant after she received her freedom."

All that visitors learned about the lives of Bennett or Alfred or Davis was their choice to throw in their lot on the white folks' side. That choice, in turn, prompted guides to claim that *their* master was kindly. Most historic houses still follow the "Lake Wobegone principle of owners"—everyone was above average! As an African American who visited George Washington's plantation in 1998 reported to me, "They give the impression that the slaves at Mount Vernon lived quite well. If you were going to be a slave, that was the place to be one." The assertion is hardly new; historian Jon Butler points out that planters themselves "constantly claimed that their own slaves were

In 1992–93, the Maryland Historical Society presented *Mining the Museum*, an installation by Fred Wilson that shocked museum-goers by raising questions about how and what museums usually display, particularly regarding race relations. Here, with the simple label "Metalwork 1793–1880," Wilson juxtaposed ornate silver works and slave shackles, leaving visitors to make the connection that the

one depended on the other. By showing only the silverware, Hampton and most other antebellum homes omitted this connection. Hampton now exhibits shackles and chains in its overseer's house, but this building is rarely open to visitors.

well fed, well treated, and fairly employed even if other slaves were not." The failure of most plantations today to expose slavery shows the influence that the "peculiar institution" still wields in our culture while simultaneously helping to maintain this influence.

Since about 2005, however, many slave plantations have begun to reveal formerly hidden truths about slavery. Now, visitors are beginning to realize the incredible drama that life in slavery often entailed. One person can make a difference. Judith O'Brien, hired as education director in 1997, transformed the interpretation at Sotterley, in southern Maryland. She also forged a relationship with the county school system that improved their eighth-grade curriculum while helping the plantation to survive financially. Near New Orleans, one rich man, John Cummings, bought Whitney and transformed it after first engaging expert advice. According to a professor who routinely brings public history students to Hampton, the publication of this chapter in 1999 sparked improvement here. At its website, NPS now notes that "the Hampton estate was created and evolved through the actions of enslaved African Americans, European indentured servants and the Ridgely family." Nothing could be more obvious; the fact that saying it up front took so many years shows how biased slavery sites have been. An exhibit panel makes another obvious point: "The enslaved, along with indentured and paid servants . . . performed most of the labor required to run this enormous enterprise." Another panel is titled "Bondage was Bondage," rejecting the claim that Hampton was somehow better. In 2018, at the first stop of the tour, the guide goes on about the furniture and the wallpaper in the "morning room" and demonstrates the bell the Ridgeleys would have rung "to bring their servants in to this room if they wanted more tea or coffee." But then he makes a correction: "They called them servants, but that was a euphemism, because they were enslaved workers." Again, saying this out loud marks a significant advance. He goes on to point out why the various bells were never labeled: because it was against the law to teach enslaved people to read.

Until recently, antebellum houses did not show that slavery was a penal system resting ultimately on force and threat of force. Few displayed a whip, chains, fetters, branding iron, or any of the advanced technology of mobile human confinement that owners devised—bells that could not be removed from the neck and the like. If the U.S. Army did not remove the whipping post, usually ostentatiously located in front of the Big House or between it and the slave quarters, the family took it out before putting the house on display for modern tourists. But again, times are changing. Tour guides at Hampton now remind visitors that Pennsylvania is just a two-day walk from the plantation; the port of Baltimore, teeming with free people of color, was even closer; and at least 76 slaves escaped. Guides also point out that after Nat Turner's rebellion, the Ridgelys, like prison wardens, put bars on their windows and heavy metal locks on their thick exterior doors and required that even their house slaves sleep outside of the house each night. Simply saying this undercuts any notion about benevolent masters living in harmony with contented slaves.

Hampton boasts what may be the most solidly-built slave quarters extant in America. The owners of many antebellum homes tore down their slave quarters decades ago, finding them an aesthetic and moral embarrassment. Thus, Hampton is fortunate to have them, and NPS now uses them to present solid exhibits about the lives of the enslaved. However, guides do not take visitors down the quarter-mile road to the quarters, and the quarters are not open when the grounds are too damp, so only a fraction of all visitors ever see this information.

Although Hampton has improved, some plantations now do much better. Whitney Plantation, near New Orleans, interprets its beautiful architecture and grounds from the viewpoint of the majority of the residents—the enslaved. As a result, plantations near Whitney also have found that they have to tell more about their slaves, because visitors, fascinated by Whitney, demand it! Also, unlike other plantations, Whitney draws black tourists as well as white. Since all tourists spend green dollars, this gives other plantations another incentive to broaden their focus. In Virginia, Carter's Grove includes information about the enslaved, as does Kingsley in Florida, Somerset Place in North Carolina, and Sotterley in southern Maryland. Monticello, Thomas Jefferson's home near Charlottesville, now devotes a room to Sally Hemings, the house slave who probably bore five of his children. Even some stodgy plantations in South Carolina like Magnolia are beginning to add some truths about slavery to their standard tours.

Most plantations still display only the owner's lifestyle. Historians have identified four key problems of slave life that plantations *should* tell about. One is the sense of racial inferiority that most whites believed and many blacks half-believed. The dining table with elaborate place settings, the wallpaper, the impressive staircase on display at Hampton, encourage everyone then and now, slaves and tourists alike, to believe that no ordinary mortals inhabited these halls, but impressive elegant people worthy of our respect. Thus, Hampton's imposing Georgian mansion helped the Ridgelys and their class stay dominant politically over "lesser" whites and also helped forestall slave revolts.

So far as I know, neither Hampton nor any other plantation shows the table manners at the other end of the social spectrum. "The slaves had to eat with mussel shells for spoons, and we sopped our gravy with our bread," as an ex-slave told a Mississippi interviewer in the 1930s. Fanny Kemble, married to a South Carolina planter, wrote that their "slaves mostly ate with crude wooden spoons or by using their fingers, as the children did." Archaeologists of the Old South have recovered so few spoons or forks as to suggest that this was the pattern on most plantations. Sometimes, planters had slave children eat from troughs. As one ex-slave remembered 70 years later, "There was a trough out in the yard where they poured in mush and milk, and us children and the dogs would all crowd 'round it and eat together. We children had homemade wooden paddles to eat with, and we sure had to be in a hurry about it, because the dogs would get it all if we didn't." Even without dogs, children often competed with each other for basic sustenance. Meanwhile, the children of the owners were learning which fork to use with which course. Hampton does display a panel, "Two Worlds, Side by Side," but it's too soft.

If guides drew *this* comparison, it could lead to discussions of more serious concerns. Visitors might be led to imagine the response of white owners and their elegant guests witnessing enslaved children tussling over their morning or evening meal with their bare hands. The scene would reinforce whites' belief that slavery was right—"they eat like animals!" When one racial group has all the power and grace and the other lives in squalor, it is hard for both races not to internalize that the former is superior.

The second key problem for slaves was their lack of independence. Slaves could not decide for themselves what to eat, when to eat it, or how to eat. Of course, they could not decide whether to work, where, or how. They could not even make a simple bench or table without permission. Indeed, they could not choose what to do from moment to moment. Deciding what to do during the course of a day is fundamental to life. Even a squirrel has this capability—it is the basic condition of thinking creatures. Depriving people of this freedom is the underlying *un*naturalness of slavery. White writers who interviewed ex-slaves in the 1930s often tried to get these elderly African Americans to agree that there were positives in slavery, such as not having to be on one's own; ex-slaves simply wouldn't buy it.

A related third problem was the inability of slaves to control their own careers, decide whom to marry, or preserve relations with their families. Ironically, slavery forced slaves to be "on their own" in ways interviewers in the 1930s could never imagine. In narrative after narrative, slaves tell of having their parents sold away from them as children and being unable to plan for the future. On many plantations, this anxiety peaked every year around Christmas, when some slaves were rented out for a year to another employer beginning January 1, which meant it might be a year or even more before husband saw wife or child saw parent again. This may have been a particular problem for slaves at Hampton, since the Ridgelys owned an ironworks, enterprises in Baltimore, and other plantations, and probably transferred workers from one to another. Near the end of her life, "Old Elizabeth," who may have been owned by the Ridgelys, recalled the impact of such a relocation on her:

> I was born in Maryland in the year 1766. . . . In the eleventh year
> of my age, my master sent me to another farm, several miles from
> my parents, brothers, and sisters, which was a great trouble to me.
> At last I grew so lonely and sad I thought I should die, if I did not

see my mother. I asked the overseer if I might go, but being positively denied, I concluded to go without his knowledge. When I
reached home my mother was away. I set off and walked twenty
miles before I found her. I stayed with her for several days, and
we returned together. Next day I was sent back to my new place,
which renewed my sorrow. . . . " On reaching the farm, I found
the overseer was displeased at me for going without his liberty.
He tied me with a rope, and gave me some stripes of which I carried the marks for weeks.

Most slaves had no possibility of control over their ultimate destiny—
no way out of slavery, even for their children—no matter how hard they
worked.[4] Particularly in Maryland and Virginia, children were an important
crop, liable to be sold south at any time. "The Value of a Person," a panel in
the slave quarters at Hampton, touches on this by asking, "What was the value of an enslaved person?" It then invites visitors to compare the cash value
to the owner with the intrinsic value the person has to other family members.

The fourth key problem slaves faced was violence. Paul Escott studied over
2,000 slave narratives taken down during the 1930s. He found that when
interviewers asked ex-slaves to assess their owners, whipping was the most
important single attribute to which they referred. Whippings could be life-
shattering experiences—not at all like the punishments that parents give their
children. In the 1930s, an ex-slave still remembered a whipping he received
as a young boy, 70 years earlier: "I just about half died. I lay in the bunk
two days, getting over that whipping—getting over it in the body, but not
the heart. No, sir, I have that in the heart 'till this day." Some overseers
then rubbed salt in the wounds. Escott found that about 70% of the slave
narratives told of being whipped as slaves—and these narratives came from
people who averaged perhaps ten years old when slavery ended. No resistance
was possible; another old man told of the whipping given his young sister,
70 years earlier, who had accidentally broken a clock: "My old marster took
her and tied a rope around her neck—just enough to keep it from choking
her—and tied her up in the backyard and whipped her I don't know how
long. There stood mother, there stood father, and there stood all the children and none could come to her rescue." Hampton now offers a panel in
the slave quarters that quotes a description of a Hampton slave's back after a
whipping: "thirty-seven gashes, from half an inch to three and a half inches

in length." Hampton still shies away from the harsher examples of violence, however. Owners might cut the thumb or finger off slaves who could write, for example, or cut off a toe or even foot to punish running away and prevent its recurrence. Never have I heard any plantation discuss the appalling practice known as "seasoning," the forced resocialization imposed to break slaves' will to resist.[5] Never have I been told by a guide that owners sometimes castrated male slaves for running away or occasionally if they "had become their rivals for coveted black women," as Eugene Genovese writes in *Roll, Jordan, Roll.*

The literature on African American slavery—secondary works as well as slave narratives—stresses these four concerns. Although Hampton has improved, and some other sites have improved more, most historic sites Americans visit to learn about antebellum life still stress none of them. Despite these four problems, slaves created communities of their own, with leaders and customs partly independent from planter society. Field hands' time was their own from sundown to sunup, and even during the day, especially on Sundays, they carved out some time and space for community life. Antebellum plantation sites tell little about this effort either.

Slavery, by no means as terrible for the owner as for the owned, nevertheless caused problems within white culture. The first was, again, the racism it produced. Slaveowners told themselves that owning black people was ethical because blacks were not really human. As Montesquieu ironically observed in 1748, "It is impossible for us to suppose these creatures to be men, because, allowing them to be men, a suspicion would follow that we ourselves are not Christian." By the 1850s, many white Americans claimed that blacks were so inferior that slavery was proper for them. This view of African Americans did not just go away in 1863; our institutions are still infused with the idea that it is appropriate, even "natural," for whites to run things, blacks to sweep up. Hampton, where the architecture itself proclaims that whites were on top, blacks on the bottom, offers a perfect place to connect the physical structure of the mansion and quarters, the social structure of the plantation, and the cultural result, racism.

A second problem that slavery created in plantation culture was its anti-work ethic. As table manners separated white owner from black slave, so did labor itself. Blacks had to work. Owners didn't, exactly. Starting a plantation and creating an ironworks did require work, to be sure. Supervising these enterprises as they grew and prospered took more. So did supervising the house slaves who cooked and cleaned the mansion. Nevertheless, the belief system on the plantation devalued manual labor and looked down on hard work of any kind. In *The Theory of the Leisure Class*, Thorstein Veblen tells how "labor comes to be associated in men's thoughts with weakness and subjection to a master. It is therefore a mark of inferiority . . . " Wealthy planters demonstrated their social status by consumption, not work. Over time, the Ridgelys succumbed to this ideological malaise; the NPS brochure for Hampton tells that Charles Ridgely in 1908 was remembered as "the typical aristocrat of his day. He had the fortune that enabled him to live like a prince, and he also had the inclination."[6]

Slavery also infused into white culture a fear of new ideas. Between 1820 and 1860, slavery became an ideologically closed system. Southern states made *receiving* abolitionist literature a felony. Secure on top of their social system, the Ridgelys of the plantation world had little incentive to mechanize their agricultural practices or educate their labor force.

Finally, plantation slavery led to distorted history. Planters concocted pseudoscience and false history to justify enslavement. Today, antebellum homes still distort history to hide what plantations really were and how they really worked. This is particularly true when they go beyond the date when most of them are frozen—about 1858.

What happened at Hampton when the Civil War began?

Guides mention in passing that the Ridgelys favored the South; one member of the family got in trouble for blowing up bridges at the start of the war.

What did the Ridgelys do when Maryland voted slavery out in 1864? Did they offer wage labor to their hundreds of newly freed slaves? Did most African Americans leave? Did they go to Baltimore? This illustration from *Harper's Weekly* in 1865 is captioned, "Arrival of Freedmen and Their Families at Baltimore, Maryland—An Every Day Scene"; they may have come from Hampton. Descendants of Hampton slaves still live in the area, but the staff has not tried to involve them in telling this story.

What of the rest of the people? Did one or more Hampton slaves escape to Baltimore, Pennsylvania, or Washington, DC? Did any fight for freedom in the U.S. Army or Navy? Historians write that the behavior of "their blacks" during the Civil War and immediately after was a "moment of truth" to owners—a truth that most antebellum homes hide from today's tourists.

Since Maryland did not secede, it did not undergo Reconstruction, but an interracial Republican coalition did control the state for several years. Were the Ridgelys white supremacist Democrats? How did their labor force vote? Which party controlled politics in the town of Hampton and in Baltimore County? Did Ku Klux Klan activity play a role in returning Democrats to power? Were there lynchings in this area during the 1880s and 1890s? A guide at Hampton in 1999 cared about this period but only about its *things*. In the music room, he told visitors, "We're always trying to get things closer and closer to what they would have looked like. Each room has a target date." The music room's target is 1870 to 1900. "What was going on here then?" I asked him. "How did they make their money?" He didn't really know. I ask what happened politically; he didn't know. Of course, every Southern slavery plantation that still exists was also a plantation during the postwar period, but the staffs at other plantations are equally silent about it, offering not a word nor showing a single object that might tell what took place after slavery. In 2018, we entered the sesquicentennial of Reconstruction.[7] It's time to do better.[8]

Economically, every slavery plantation became a sharecropping, a wage labor, or a renter plantation, but most say nothing about those systems, socially or economically. Hampton does give some information; a panel shows a photograph of what looks to be gang labor but is captioned, "At Hampton, tenant farming was not profitable either for the tenants or the Ridgelys." Other plantations similarly say, "After the Civil War, the plantation became unprofitable." Thoughtful visitors will deduce that this is an indictment of slavery: their vast antebellum profits, on display in their huge mansions and gardens, were indeed wrung "from the sweat of other men's faces," to quote Lincoln's Second Inaugural. As soon as workers had to be paid, plantations were no longer cash cows.

To address the issue of racism in our time, we must acknowledge the importance of slavery in our past. Slavery was absolutely central to the world history of the past 400 years, according to historian David Brion Davis. "Those plantations were not some sideshow," notes Edward Ball, author of *Slaves in the Family*. "This was the trunk of American history, from which the current society has grown." Historian Steven Deyle points out that the monetary value of Southern slaves was more than twice that of all other work-related investments in the entire nation! And the slave system was *not* growing more humane, it was growing more rigid. After 1830, state after state eliminated manumissions entirely or required that newly freed people immediately leave the state. By 1860, Southern leaders were beginning to clamor to reopen the international slave trade. So, it is a good thing that Hampton and other plantations are beginning to tell the awkward truths about slavery. Hampton should lead the way. After all, it is in public hands. How can we expect the affluent white Southerners who control most plantation sites to tell the full and sometimes unsavory truth about their sites when the National Park Service doesn't? Hampton still needs to deepen its exhibits on slavery to make its impact on blacks and whites more obvious. Its staff must still do due diligence on the stories of the descendants of its newly freed residents. It should incorporate its slave quarters into its Big House tour, for all visitors. Then the NPS website could legitimately list Hampton under "African American Heritage," "Enslavement," and "Reconstruction," as well as, of course, "Architecture and Building."[9]

1. It wasn't just the guides' fault; *Hampton National Historic Site*, the book from which they took their information, offered 70 pages of passive verbs before finally giving the workers one sentence on its next-to-last page of text: "Slaves and servants performed an essential function in plantation culture."
2. Chapters 42, 55, and 70 show aspects of the lives of enslaved African Americans. Chapters 57, 62, and 63 tell of the dramatic changes in the lives of those who survived until freedom came.
3. Visitors may wonder who "Uncle Alfred" was the uncle of. The answer is no one. "Uncle" and "Aunt" or "Auntie" were terms of quasi-respect for older and more senior African Americans during the Nadir of race relations; whites wouldn't want to use "Mr." or "sir" because that would imply these people were fully human. Vestiges of this practice linger on; viz, Uncle Ben's rice, Aunt Jemima pancake syrup.
4. A few owners did make deals allowing some slaves to buy their freedom; it would be interesting to know if any Ridgelys ever did.
5. The television miniseries *Roots* showed a portion of seasoning when a slave is forced to acknowledge that his name is no longer his African name but "Toby."
6. To be sure, this ideology inheres in upper-class culture, not just the antebellum South, but in *The Lazy South*, David Bertelson shows how plantation ideology magnified the problem.
7. I refer to Congressional Reconstruction. Historians call 1866–67 "Presidential Reconstruction" or sometimes "Confederate Reconstruction." Reconstruction was also an ideological movement, favoring equal rights for African Americans nationally.
8. In 2018, Cheryl LaRochea announced results of a two-year project by researchers at the University of Maryland, Towson University, the University of Maryland Baltimore

County, the National Park Service, and the Nanny Jack & Co. archives, studying enslaved people at Hampton. This removes an excuse that Hampton staff used in the past, that they simply "didn't have the data" to do a better job telling of the people who lived and worked on the plantation. See Mary Carole McCauley, "Researchers Fill in Stories of Hampton Slaves, Link Them to Living Descendants Today," *The Baltimore Sun*, 10/26/2018, baltimoresun.com/features/bs-fe-hampton-plantation-slaves-20181019-story.html. Hopefully, Hampton staff members will now make slavery central to the interpretation of their site. The new information might also enrich the interpretation of the postwar years.

9. The rewrite of this entry depended substantially on a report by and conversations with a public historian at a nearby institution. Other sources include Lynn Hastings, *Hampton National Historic Site* (Towson, MD: Hampton National Historic Site, 1986), 69; Jon Butler, *Awash in a Sea of Faith* (Cambridge, MA: Harvard UP, 1990), 133; WPA, *The Negro in Virginia* (NY: Hastings House, 1940), 67–68; Edward D. C. Campbell Jr., ed., *Before Freedom Came* (Richmond, VA: Museum of the Confederacy, 1991), 86, 167–70; "Memoir of Old Elizabeth" in *Six Women's Slave Narratives* (NY: Oxford UP, 1988 [1863]); Paul Escott, *Slavery Remembered* (Chapel Hill: U. of NC Press, 1979); Jan Hillegas and Ken Lawrence, eds., *The American Slave, Supplement, Series 1, vol. 6* (Westport, CT: Greenwood, 1977), 79; George P. Rawick, ed., *The American Slave, vol. 18* (Westport, CT: Greenwood, 1972 [1941]), 43–44, 144; Kennell Jackson, *America Is Me* (NY: Harper Collins, 1996), 73–74; Mina Veazie, conversation, 6/98; Judith O'Brien, presentation to NPS workshop on slavery, 3/2000; Lisa Corrin, ed., *Mining the Museum* (NY: New Press, 1994), xx; Eugene D. Genovese, *Roll, Jordan, Roll* (NY: Pantheon, 1974), 66–67, 97, 532; John Michael Vlach, *Back of the Big House* (Chapel Hill: U. of NC Press, 1993), 184; Loewen and Charles Sallis, eds., *MS: Conflict and Change* (NY: Pantheon, 1980), 98; Tingba Apidta, *The Hidden History of Massachusetts* (Roxbury: Reclamation Project, 1995), 39; Thorstein Veblen, *The Theory of the Leisure Class* (NY: New American Library Mentor, 1953 [1899]), 41–42; David Bertelson, *The Lazy South* (NY: Oxford UP, 1967); David Brion Davis, "A Big Business," *The New York Review of Books*, 6/11/98, 51; Philip Burnham, *How the Other Half Lived* (Boston: Faber and Faber, 1995), 63–65; Roger A. Davidson Jr., "'They Have Never Been Known to Falter': The First United States Colored Infantry in VA and NC," *Civil War Regiments* 6 no. 1 (1998): 4; Edward Ball quoted in Lynne Duke, "This Harrowed Ground," *The Washington Post Magazine* (8/24/94): 22; Steven Deyle, "Competing Ideologies in the Old South," paper at American Historical Association, 1/99; Anders Greenspan, "Changing Views of Woman and African-Americans in Public History Settings" (New England Historical Association, 10/96); Lucia Stanton, *Slavery at Monticello* (Charlottesville, VA: Thomas Jefferson Memorial Foundation, 1996), 29; Stanton, conversation, 7/15/98; James Oliver Horton, review of *Before Freedom Came*, *The Public Historian* 14 no. 2 (spring 1992): 111.

———— ✫ ————

70. The Reverse Underground Railroad

DELAWARE *Reliance*

From Maryland to Kansas and north to Vermont, historical markers and house museums commemorate sites on the underground railroad. When this book came out in 1999, nowhere did a single marker or historic site recognize the stream of humanity forced to make a reverse passage from north to south, from liberty into bondage. Partly as a result, few Americans knew about this ignoble trade.

The closest thing to a memory on the American landscape of the "reverse underground railroad" was a Maryland state marker on State Highway 392 just across the road from the state of Delaware:

PATTY CANNON'S HOUSE AT JOHNSON'S CROSSROADS

Where the noted kidnap group had headquarters,
as described in George Alfred Townsend's novel, The Entailed Hat.
The house borders on Caroline and Dorchester Counties and the State of Delaware.

Other than "kidnap," however, this marker conveys no hint of the reverse underground railroad.

The Cannon-Johnson Gang ran probably the largest kidnapping ring in the history of the United States, with agents and property in Alabama and Mississippi as well as in Delaware and Maryland. The gang consisted of Patty Cannon, her husband Jesse Cannon, her son-in-law Joe Johnson, his brother Ebenezer and his wife, and other extended family members. They stole free blacks from as far north as Philadelphia and New Jersey and sold them into slavery in the Deep South. Logically, Delaware should put up a marker right across the road, which serves as the border between the two states. The marker should tell how the Cannon-Johnson Gang owned land and houses on both sides, so they could avoid arrest simply by crossing to the other side, where their legal pursuers had no jurisdiction.

It is impossible to know how many African Americans were kidnapped into bondage within the United States.[1] Carol Wilson, a principal historian of the illicit trade, tells of kidnappings from New Hampshire to Louisiana. Southern Illinois was another haven for kidnappers of free blacks. In 1816, white and black antislavery men formed the Protection Society of Maryland to combat kidnapping. Over the next two years, these men prevented more than 60 kidnappings, principally by challenging ship captains who had kidnapped African Americans in their holds. These 60 were "only a fragment of the kidnapping activity," according to historian Steve Whitman, but the society disbanded in 1819, leaving the kidnappers unopposed. In *Black Bondage in the North*, Edgar McManus tells of 33 cases of unlawful enslavement in just one year in New York City. He believes that the overall black population in many Northern states showed little increase between 1800 and 1860 owing in large part to the "forced migration organized by kidnappers."[2] An African American from Springfield, Illinois, whom Abraham Lincoln knew, was unlawfully enslaved in New Orleans in the 1850s after venturing there, as Lincoln had done earlier, down the Mississippi. Lincoln and his law partner raised money to obtain his release. This experience later informed a portion of his First Inaugural, where he suggests that federal law should introduce "all the safeguards of liberty known in civilized and humane jurisprudence, . . . so that a free man be not, in any case, surrendered as a slave."

Greed was the motive for the reverse underground railroad, of course. Adjusted for inflation, ordinary field hands brought the equivalent of $20,000 to $40,000—children less, skilled artisans more.[3] Moreover, kidnapping wasn't hard because African Americans enjoyed few legal rights. In the South, blacks were presumed slaves unless they could prove otherwise. Just as slaves had to have passes to show patrollers (chapter 55), free blacks rarely traveled without proof they were free—and kidnap victims were hardly able to preserve their papers. In most states, Northern as well as Southern, blacks could not testify against whites, so the victims and their families and friends could not mobilize the legal process on their behalf. The Fugitive Slave Law of 1793 permitted slaveowners or their agents to go into free states, seize African Americans who had escaped, and take them South without due process of law. Bystanders could hardly dispute the whites' claim unless they knew the African Americans personally, so once out of the victims' immediate neighborhood, the kidnappers had an easy time of it.

Any African American who got into a scrape with the law was liable to get sold into slavery if the sheriff or police officer was corrupt. In Southern states, laws sentenced free blacks and their families to slavery or to fines, which, if not paid, led to enslavement for petty offenses like traveling from county to county without authorization, failure to pay taxes, and even unemployment. In New York City, Philadelphia, and Baltimore, Irish Americans trying to evict African Americans from jobs on the docks shanghaied them onto ships going South and sold them there. Black sailors, especially from the West Indies, were favorite targets because they often had no white acquaintance to

The new Fugitive Slave Law passed as part of the Compromise of 1850 made African Americans even less secure. This broadside, distributed by abolitionists in Boston, warned that law officers were likely to kidnap them into slavery. In the 1850s, thousands of African Americans fled to Canada to avoid this threat. Beginning in the 1830s, Northern states passed "personal liberty laws" to protect their black citizens from kidnapping and enslavement. These laws were then sometimes used to make it harder for slaveowners to re-enslave runaways and were cited by South Carolina leaders as a prime reason to secede from the United States (chapter 74).

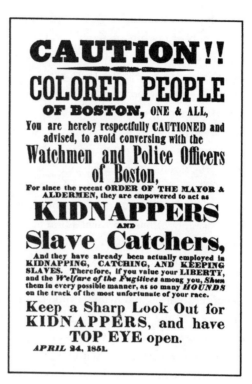

vouch for them and hence had no recourse once their papers were ripped up. According to historian Jeffrey Bolster, more than 200 sailors were kidnapped into slavery in one year. Children were also particularly vulnerable since they were easier to steal and less articulate on their own behalf.

To be sure, people also stole enslaved African Americans for resale. Slave stealing was not considered kidnapping, even when the victim was a child, because the law held slaves to be property, not people. Ironically, slave stealing was also less common than kidnapping, because an owner—a powerful *white person* with legal rights—was likely to come looking for his stolen slave. Thus, it was much less risky to kidnap a free black than to seize a slave.

One way we know about the Cannon-Johnson Gang is through an incident in which some of their victims were rescued. This complex legal event left a paper trail, including accounts of interviews with some of the kidnap victims. Samuel Scomp was one of these. A sixteen-year-old indentured servant in New Jersey bound to serve until he was 25, he ran away to Philadelphia in the summer of 1825. An African American in the pay of the Johnsons lured him onto a ship with the promise of a job unloading watermelons. Once on board, white men grabbed him, Joe Johnson tied his hands, and he was locked into the ship's hold. There, he met two other lads already captive; two more were added later that day.

That night, the boat sailed to Delaware. The five boys were marched to a carriage, taken to Joe Johnson's house, then transferred to Jesse Cannon's house. After a week there in chains, they were taken to a sloop along with two African American women who had been held at Patty Cannon's. Eventually, the sloop sailed to Alabama, where they were formed into a coffle and marched overland. In Tuscaloosa, one lad was sold. In the Choctaw nation in northwest Alabama, then independent, Samuel Scomp escaped, but an Indian caught him and returned him to Ebenezer Johnson, who flogged him with a hand saw, leaving "dreadful scars" on his back and head, according to Wilson.

Now the trip grew even more nightmarish for the African Americans. Ebenezer Johnson and his wife rode in a small carriage and the two smallest boys were in the one-horse wagon that accompanied them. The three older boys and the two women walked. In the words of Scomp's deposition, "They walked thirty miles a day, without shoes; when they complained of sore feet and being unable to travel they were most cruelly flogged; that deponent has received more than fifty lashes at one time . . . their feet became frosted in Alabama." Their journey finally ended a few miles from Rocky Springs in southwest Mississippi, where one of the boys died "in consequence of the frequent and cruel beating he received from Ebenezer Johnson."

Ebenezer Johnson stopped at the plantation of John Hamilton in Rocky Springs and offered to sell him the three boys and two women. Hamilton was unusual in that when one of the boys told him they were not slaves but had been stolen from Philadelphia, Hamilton took him seriously. Johnson produced a bill of sale, but Hamilton was unconvinced. He contacted Mississippi authorities, who cooperated with Philadelphia police; eventually, Hamilton returned the African Americans to Philadelphia.

This story had a positive ending for some of the victims, but Wilson tells of other documented abductees of the Cannon-Johnson Gang and other agents who ended up in bondage in North Carolina, Alabama, and Mississippi. In his famous autobiography *Twelve Years A Slave*, Solomon Northup, a farmer, hack driver, and entertainer who lived in Fort Edward, New York, told of being kidnapped from Washington, DC, in 1841 and sold in Louisiana. A Louisiana historical marker on U.S. 71 in Bunkie does mention Northup:

EPPS HOUSE

Built in 1852 by Edwin Epps. Originally located near Homesville on Bayou Boeuf about three miles away. From 1843 to 1853, Epps, a small planter, owned Solomon Northup, author of famous slave narrative Twelve Years A Slave.

The marker says nothing about Northup's kidnapping, but the Old Fort House Museum in Fort Edward includes Northup's house and tells the story. So does a fine feature film, *Twelve Years a Slave*, released in 2013.

No one knows how many undocumented cases of kidnapping the Cannon-Johnson Gang pulled off—Wilson estimates "scores and possibly hundreds." Gang members occasionally brought to trial usually got off or paid small fines. A Delaware court found Joe Johnson guilty in 1822 and sentenced him to a public whipping—39 lashes "well laid on"—but most members of the gang never faced a judge.

Eventually, however, Patty Cannon did run afoul of the law, not for kidnapping but murder. A tenant farmer discovered human remains buried on her farm. One gang member admitted that while he had lived with the Cannons, Patty, Joe, and Ebenezer Johnson had murdered a white Georgia slave trader having supper at the house. He led police to other places where bodies were uncovered, mostly unwary white travelers who had stopped at the tavern for the night. Driven to act by the murders of whites, Delaware authorities indicted Cannon and the Johnson brothers, but the Johnsons fled to Alabama and Mississippi. Cannon confessed to the murder of eleven people including a seven-year-old she had killed by striking in the head with a piece of wood, one of her own children, and the infant child of an African American woman owned by the Cannons. She also admitted to being an accomplice in at least twelve other deaths.

Residents of Johnson's Crossroads, the little community that straddles the Delaware-Maryland line, changed their town's name to Reliance to avoid the notoriety of the Cannon-Johnson Gang. They did not achieve amnesia, however. They still know about the kidnapping of blacks and that the gang was brought to justice only when their victims included whites. Patty

Cannon took poison while in jail to avoid hanging, but she lives on in the Reliance oral tradition. The woman who lived in Patty Cannon's house in 1999 told me that when they moved to Reliance, parents were still warning their children to be good "or else Patty Cannon will getcha!" In the 1980s, when her daughter was in elementary school, neighborhood children still feared to spend the night in the house.

It is not enough that residents of Reliance know about the kidnap ring. Kidnapping was one of the more monstrous facets of the slave trade all across America. All Americans need to understand the extent of racial kidnapping.

After this book came out, a fine Delaware historian, Kevin Brown, read this chapter and was astonished that he had not known of the reverse underground railroad and the Cannon-Johnson Gang. He determined to tell the story to the people of Delaware. Eventually, he mobilized people in the Delaware Archives, the legislature, and Delaware's premiere city, resulting in a marker near Amtrak in downtown Wilmington, where many people will see it. Its dedication led to a statement by the governor, commending "Kevin A. Brown, Esq., who originated the idea of the memorial, Senator Margaret Rose Henry, who sponsored the legislation, and Mayor James Baker, . . . as well as Russ McCabe from the Delaware Archives . . . for their efforts to bring this marker and the epic struggle of which it tells to Delaware."

In May 2012, Brown got Delaware to dedicate a second marker at Reliance, telling the story where it took place. Along with the movie *Twelve Years a Slave* and annual remembrances in upstate New York, our public history is now doing what it can, at least in two states, to help America end its amnesia about the reverse underground railroad.[4]

1. In a sense, as an abolitionist writing in William Lloyd Garrison's *Liberator* newspaper pointed out, "Every slave in the United States has been kidnapped."

2. I doubt that kidnapping one person or one family at a time can offset natural increase, migration to Canada or western states, and other macro forces. Nevertheless, it is interesting that New York and New England show declines or stasis in their black populations. Midwestern states show increases, however, and the reverse underground railroad operated there too.

3. Prices rose steadily from 1830 to 1860. In 1850 dollars, 1850–53 prices were $1,000 to $2,000. A website based on Consumer Price Index figures and the *Historical Statistics of the United States*, www.orst.edu/Dept/pol_sci/sahr (8/98), suggests a multiplication factor of 20. Chapter 81 would suggest a higher multiplier.

4. Carol Wilson, *Freedom at Risk: The Kidnapping of Free Blacks in America, 1780–1865* (Lexington: UP of KY, 1994), 10, 19–37; Nancy C. Curtis, *Black Heritage Sites: The North* (NY: New Press, 1996), 140; Curtis, *Black Heritage Sites: The South* (NY: New

Press, 1996), 137–38; Solomon Northup, *Twelve Years a Slave*, www.sunsite.unc.edu
/docsouth/northup/northup.html, 11/98; Alexander Davidson, *Complete History of IL*
(Springfield, IL: 1876), 230; John C. Miller, *The Wolf by the Ears* (NY: Free Press, 1977),
87; Jeffrey Bolster, "Black Sailors and Fugitive Slaves" (DC: National Museum of Amer-
ican History Colloquium, 2/8/98); Steve Whitman, *The Price of Freedom* (Lexington:
UP of KY,1997), 80–81; Edgar McManus, *Black Bondage in the North* (NY: Syracuse
UP, 1973), 1982; Richard E. Hart, *Lincoln's Springfield: The Early African American Popu-
lation of Springfield, Illinois (1818–1861)*, 2008; John Blassingame, ed., *Slave Testimony*
(Baton Rouge: LA State UP, 1979), 178–85; Stanley W. Campbell, *The Slave Catchers*
(Chapel Hill: U. of NC Press, 1970), 10; John Anthony Scott, *Hard Trials on My Way*
(NY: Knopf, 1974), 108–25; Rose Messick, conversation, 9/97.

★

---

71. Telling Amusing Incidents for the Tourists

PENNSYLVANIA *Philadelphia*

In Independence Hall, then the Pennsylvania colonial capitol, the two founding documents of the United States were discussed, adopted, and signed.
No historical markers tell about these nation-founding events. There are no
exhibits inside the Assembly Room, which the National Park Service (NPS)
keeps as it was in 1787 when delegates negotiated and adopted the Constitution of the United States. Instead, NPS relies on its staff to tell visitors the
history that makes this building so important.[1] Based on my four visits before
2000, the strategy didn't work—the history didn't get told.

It's not that the rangers were unprepared. They were animated and held
most of their audience's attention. Instead of revealing *what* happened here,
however, they told mildly amusing anecdotes about *how* it happened.

This worked fairly well for the Declaration of Independence. Guides told
about delegates keeping the windows shut because what they were up to was
treason from the British viewpoint. They told how delegates took months
to arrive at declaring independence. These are notable points, and besides,
one can argue that the prime importance of the Declaration of Independence
was the declaring, not the wording. Still, visitors might usefully be led to
contrast, for example, why Americans really fought for independence and
why they said they did. The Declaration attacks the British for inciting "the
merciless Indian Savages," when the colonials were actually upset with Great
Britain for precisely the *opposite* reason: the British had been "inciting" *peace*.

The Proclamation of 1763 had achieved peace with Native Americans by forbidding colonists from settling west of the Appalachian continental divide. This enraged many colonials.

Guides might also point out the contradiction between the famous phrase, "We hold these Truths to be self-evident, that all Men are created equal, that they are endowed by their Creator with certain unalienable Rights, that among these are Life, Liberty, and the Pursuit of Happiness," and the founders' practices of slavery and sexism. Guides said nothing so substantive.

If ignoring the content of the Declaration carries with it some costs, avoiding the "what" and telling the "how" did not work at all for the Constitution. That's because the substance of the Constitution *is* its significance. Guides didn't present substantive accomplishments of the Constitution. Nor did they present its failures. Had they pointed out some of each, visitors might leave thinking about the Constitution, not just feeling good about it.[2]

Instead of telling about the Constitution, guides described how long it took delegates to get to Philadelphia from South Carolina or New Hampshire. They pointed out how the delegates sat facing George Washington, whom they expected would be the first president. And they told how Ben Franklin observed to delegates sitting near him that the back of the president's chair had a sun painted on it. "I have often . . . looked at that behind the President without being able to tell whether it was rising or setting. But now at length I have the happiness to know that it is a rising and not a setting sun."

The framers faced a crucial sociological problem and faced it squarely: how to create a central government forceful enough to rule a large nation—the United States was already bigger than any European nation save Russia—and deal with European monarchies on equal terms . . . yet not create a monster. Part of their answer was to divide the government's power in various ways.

Most basic was the division between private life—private ownership of most land, housing, and most means of economic production—and the public sphere, the government. When the government owns the housing, it can evict people for expressing anti-regime thoughts. Similarly, when the state employs people, it can fire them for expressing anti-government opinions or reward them for their support. The greater the proportion of people on the public payroll, the smaller the economic base that might foster dissent.

The founders did not invent private ownership, having inherited the concept from the British. The United States was in the process of taking enormous tracts of land from the Natives to the west, however, and could have kept those lands public. Since the central government defeated the Indians and negotiated the land transfers, it started out owning the land. Under the Articles of Confederation, also passed in this building, Congress was already selling public land. After the Civil War, Congress would almost give it away to homesteaders, mining companies, and railroads. There have been important defects in this process, but individual ownership of land does provide the economic base that in turn facilitates private opinion.

The second balance is between the states and the central government. The United States is unusual among nations in that its fundamental laws in important areas differ from state to state. One state may routinely give mothers custody of children in divorce, while another usually awards joint custody. One state may provide low-cost college educations, while another boasts lower taxes but has smaller colleges with higher tuitions. States also provide points of leverage against the federal government—although not militarily, for the Civil War settled that. Various phrases in the Constitution, not just the Tenth Amendment, provide for this balance.

When schoolchildren speak of "the balance of powers," they refer to the third balance, within the federal government. The Constitution divides the government's power among three branches—Congress, the president and executive branch, and the Supreme Court and lower courts. Citizens who have been aggrieved by one may go to another for relief. The power of Congress is further divided between two bodies—the House and Senate, elected differently and for different periods of service.

The foregoing civics lesson has not even mentioned the most basic constitutional check of all: the Congress, president, and vice president are subject to periodic review by the people. Again, important defects disrupt the process—for example, the need for campaign funds that leads to distortions caused by wealth. Nevertheless, periodic elections not only let the people get rid of bad leaders, they also make political office less of a lifelong plum to be sought at any price and by any means necessary. Americans take periodic elections for granted today, but many countries in the world, from monarchies to Zimbabwe to the "People's Democratic Republic of North Korea," have not solved the problem of succession nearly as neatly.

Many other "minor" innovations in the Constitution help explain its success, including the difficult yet workable procedure for amending it, impeachment, the requirement that the Senate concur on presidential appointments, a narrow definition of treason, and the power-sharing by states that have allowed territories to organize as new states. It is now the world's oldest written constitution still in effect. All this is the "what" of the Constitution, and Americans need to be reminded of it because many do not understand it. Diane Skvarla, curator of the U.S. Senate, says many visitors to the Capitol have no understanding even of the three branches of government and are forever asking "Where is the president's office?" and "What does Congress do?" Their visit to Independence Hall won't help.

Some of the accomplishments of the Constitution have become doubtful. Consider the balance between the states and Washington. We have reached the point where the federal government dictates to states details of their traffic regulations, holding as carrot the federal share of highway appropriations. States can no longer stand up to the federal government even on minutiae like tests required for neighborhood-based water providers or the required staffing ratio for home-based daycare centers.

Or consider the relative power of the three branches of government. From the Woodrow Wilson administration, the federal executive has grown ever stronger. It now looms as by far the largest employer in the United States. Within that executive, some political scientists claim that a fourth branch—the CIA, National Security Council, and other covert agencies—has developed in the last 30 years. The Constitution cannot save democracy when officials in the FBI, CIA, State Department, and undercover agencies determine not only our policies but also how much the people, the Congress, and perhaps even the president need to know about them.

Guides do face time constraints. Twenty minutes is just not long enough to do justice to the "how" and "what" of both the Constitution and Declaration of Independence. In 2018, a student of mine took the Independence Hall tour yet again; he reported that the ranger spoke in more depth, particularly about the Articles of Confederation, but ran into the time problem. Guides might develop differentiated tours. Every other tour might focus on just the Declaration of Independence or Constitution. Then tour guides might have time to explain where the document's ideas came from, what it accomplished, and what remains problematic or has become problematic over time. Another tour might be labeled "biographical," featuring the charming stories about individual delegates that guides told in 1999. Still, another might focus on the effect of all three documents on African Americans, pointing out that the Constitution guaranteed their continued enslavement, forced their return to slavery if they escaped (chapter 74), and even guaranteed the continuation of the international slave trade for twenty years. This tour might emphasize the compromises required to get cooperation from South Carolina and Georgia, and the short-lived but important impact of the Declaration of Independence on ending slavery in the North and causing manumissions in the South. Yet another guide might take time to include Abigail Adams's now-famous 1776 letter to her husband, "Remember the ladies," tell that he ignored it because equal political rights for women were simply not on the table at the time, and explain the long road women had to follow to gain Constitutional protection. As one tour ends, some visitors might be intrigued to stay for the next, with its somewhat different focus.

The Constitution was never perfect and doesn't work perfectly now. Today, Americans from different political perspectives and social backgrounds make different criticisms of it. Nevertheless, we can hope that ours is still a rising and not a setting sun. In a democracy, the ideas within the most successful founding document in the history of the world shouldn't be concealed under a cloak of amusing anecdotes about the men who created it. If we cannot have brief civic dialogues in Independence Hall, where can we have them?[3]

1. The National Park Service website for Independence Hall has extensive resources for learning about what happened here, including a day-by-day summary of the debates about the Constitution.

2. In 1999, I also criticized tour guides for not talking about the Articles of Confederation, also ratified in this building in 1781. This important document established the first government of the United States, whose Congress passed the Northwest Ordinance, which set forth principles under which land north of the Ohio and west of the Alleghenies would become states. The Ordinance also banned slavery, although with lots of loopholes, and set aside land to fund public education. However, the NPS ranger my student heard in 2018 gave considerable attention to the Articles of Confederation.

3. J. Leitch Wright Jr., *The Only Land They Knew* (NY: Free Press, 1981), 78; William Bradford, *Of Plimoth Plantation*, rendered by Valerian Paget (NY: McBride, 1909), 284–87; Francis Jennings, *The Invasion of America* (Chapel Hill: U. of NC Press, 1975), 223.

---

72. George Washington's Desperate Prayer

PENNSYLVANIA *Valley Forge*

Valley Forge National Historic Park has subtle stories to tell about the nature of warfare in the eighteenth century, the politics of the American

Revolution, and the religion of the founding fathers. Through most of its history, however, the Valley Forge landscape has been marshaled in support of two uncomplicated morality tales.

The first fabrication Valley Forge used to inflict on visitors concerns the extraordinary suffering the men endured as they encamped there. "Valley Forge is the story of an army's epic struggle to survive against terrible odds, against hunger, disease, and the unrelenting forces of nature," said the brochure the National Park Service (NPS) used to give to visitors.[1] This hyperbole originated with George Washington himself, who wrote to the Continental Congress on February 16, 1778, "Naked and starving as they are we cannot enough admire the incomparable patience and fidelity of the soldiery." The brochure for the Valley Forge Historical Society Museum used to reproduce this sentence on its cover, but it is best viewed as propaganda by Washington to get better funding from Congress, not as an accurate account of the situation at Valley Forge.

At Valley Forge, the army was never in such extremities. Even in 1999, careful visitors could discern subtle corrections to this hoary storyline. "The troops were generally ill equipped to deal with the harsh winter before them," stated the NPS introductory film, *Valley Forge, A Winter Encampment.* A few seconds later, however, the narrator admitted, "The Valley Forge winter was generally moderate." The log huts the soldiers built were nice and warm, he went on. Although the food was often monotonous, supplies were available, especially if soldiers had money.

Perhaps owing to this chapter in the original version of the book, which did circulate through NPS, but more likely owing to the underlying scholarship, especially by Pennsylvania historian Lorett Treese, today, the Park Service website and brochure take pains *not* to repeat the old clichés about the suffering army. "The romantic image that depicts the troops at Valley Forge as helpless and famished individuals at the mercy of winter's fury and clothed in nothing but rags renders them and their commander a disservice," The NPS brochure now says, "The winter of 1777–78 was not the worst winter experienced during the war[.]" Immediately, NPS pulls its punches: "but constant freezing and thawing, and intermittent snowfall and rain, coupled with shortages of provisions, clothing, and shoes, made living conditions extremely difficult." From such pallid prose, few visitors will realize that the wintry ordeal was a myth. The Library at Mount Vernon, another major web resource on George Washington, mounts a more forceful debunking:

> Images of bloody footprints in the snow, soldiers huddled around lonely campfires, and Washington on his knees, praying that his army might survive often come to mind when people hear the words "Valley Forge." But truer images of the place would show General Washington using the time between December 1777 and June 1778 to train his men and to fight to maintain his position as the head of the Continental Army.

At the Morristown, New Jersey, National Historic Park, the Park Service points out that the winter of 1779–80, which Washington and the troops spent *there*, was the worst in a hundred years. Nevertheless, Morristown draws far fewer visitors, while "everyone knows" about the terrible winter the troops endured at Valley Forge. The NPS website now includes an "Epilogue: Valley Forge Past, Present, Future," which gives an interesting account of when and why Valley Forge became so dominant. Taken from Treese's book on Valley Forge, this essay is historiography at its best. It's hard to find on the NPS website, which nowhere credits its author, but Treese explains the relationships over time among the various organizations that have vied with each other to make Valley Forge a bigger myth. Three of these organizations ally to put forth the second morality tale that Valley Forge inflicts on visitors. The beautiful Washington Memorial Chapel, begun in 1903, sports two matched sets of dazzling stained-glass windows, one depicting the life of Jesus Christ, the other the life of George Washington. "Washington in prayer at Valley Forge is seen in the central opening over the door," explains the chapel's handout. The general kneels in prayer to Almighty God, seeking God's assistance when it seemed only He could aid the American cause, so desperate were its circumstances. The same kneeling general is on display in bronze at the nearby headquarters of the Freedoms Foundation, a nationalist organization whose heyday came during the Cold War, and in a painting in the museum of the Valley Forge Historical Society.

The image and the inspiration for the chapel, sculpture, and painting came from none other than Parson Weems, the Episcopal minister who published the first biography of Washington in 1800. Weems made up both the cherry tree story and the prayer incident, the latter in 1804 for a magazine article. Here is the Valley Forge tale in Weems's vivid prose:

> In the winter of 1777, while Washington, with the American army, lay encamped at Valley Forge, a certain good old friend, of the respectable family and name of Potts, if I mistake not, had occasion to pass through the woods near headquarters. Treading his way along the venerable grove, suddenly he heard the sound of a human voice, which, as he advanced, increased on his ear; and at length became like the voice of one speaking much in earnest. As he approached the spot with a cautious step, whom should he behold, in a dark natural bower of ancient oaks, but the commander in chief of the American armies on his knees in prayer! Motionless in surprise, Friend Potts continued on the place till the general, having ended his devotion, arose; and with countenance of angelic serenity, retired to headquarters.

Weems went on to relate how Friend Potts went home and told his wife about the incident.

> Thee knows that I always thought that the sword and the gospel were utterly inconsistent; and that no man could be a soldier and a Christian at the same time. But George Washington has this day convinced me of my mistake. . . . If George Washington be not a man of God, I am greatly deceived—and still more shall I be deceived, if God do not, through him, work out a great salvation for America.

Later authors added various details. Sometimes, tears flow down Washington's cheeks or down Potts's as he tells his wife what he saw. Sometimes, Potts's wife is "Sarah," sometimes "Betty" or "Martha." Potts himself sometimes becomes a preacher.

Regardless of the details, "the Valley Forge story is utterly without foundation in fact," according to historian Paul F. Boller Jr. A Quaker farmer named Isaac Potts did come into possession of a house in Valley Forge toward the end of the Revolutionary War, Boller says, "but he was nowhere near Valley Forge in the winter of 1777 when Washington was supposed to have been praying in the snow." Other lapses further discredit the story. Perhaps, we shouldn't be too hard on Weems, however, who probably never expected readers to take his fabulous biography, subtitled *Curious Anecdotes, Equally Honourable to Himself, and Exemplary to His Young Country*, so literally.

Nonetheless, aroused by the image, Herbert Burk, rector of All Saints' Episcopal Church in nearby Norristown, preached a sermon around the turn of the twentieth century that inspired his listeners to dig into their pockets to commemorate the yarn on the landscape. In 1903, they laid the cornerstone of the Washington Memorial Chapel at Valley Forge, a structure that would eventually cost more than a million dollars. The two parsons, Weems and Burk, doubtless felt that for Americans to believe that George Washington was a pious Christian would do no harm.

Washington's view of religion isn't easy to know. Some historians consider him a Deist, like many other leaders of the Revolution. He was a lifelong member of the Episcopal Church and believed that religion was "an indispensable basis for morality," in Boller's phrase, but he "was not given to praying on his knees or referring to Jesus in public or private." On the other hand, historian Peter Lillback points out that "Washington referred to himself frequently using the words 'ardent,' 'fervent,' 'pious,' and 'devout,'" and notes that more than a hundred different prayers in Washington's own hand can be found in his writings. But Gordon Wood, an authority on the Revolution, says that Freemasonry was more important to Washington than Episcopalianism. Indeed, for many leaders of that time, Wood notes, Masonry offered something of a surrogate religion complete with ritual, mystery, and fellowship.

In 1928, the U.S. Post Office endorsed the pious Washington by issuing a two-cent stamp of Washington on his knees as the focal point of America's remembrance of Valley Forge on its

Here is the Weems tale as illustrated by the U.S. Post Office Department in 1928.

150th anniversary. Rupert Hughes, a biographer of Washington, attacked the stamp as endorsing "what all historians know to be a downright lie," and denounced "the perpetuation of the tradition that he prayed at Valley Forge as the perpetuation of an idle, sanctimonious falsehood." Another citizen told the postal service, "Possibly Washington could not tell a lie, but Weems was not thus handicapped. Under a mass of silly moralizing, he nearly buried the real Washington." But despite the falsehoods that the first stamp brought to light, in 1977, the post office did it again. Honoring the 200th anniversary of Valley Forge, it adapted a 1935 *Saturday Evening Post* cover of the kneeling Washington for a Christmas stamp that is eerily reminiscent of Protestant Sunday School illustrations of Jesus praying in Gethsemane. In 1977, of course, the tale clearly differentiated the United States from "godless Communism," a comparison often made by the Freedoms Foundation. It also implied that God was on our side, not "theirs," whether "they" be Britain or Russia. And it allegedly happened *here*.

Such inaccurate imagery can have unfortunate consequences. Other important founders were less Christian than Washington. Thomas Jefferson called himself "an Unitarian," while Ben Franklin said, "I have found Christian dogma unintelligible. Early in life I absented myself from Christian assemblies." The United States was not founded as a Christian nation, even though a majority of its citizens have been Christians. People who don't know this, who think the United States is legally Christian, may be less tolerant of agnostics, atheists, Jews, Muslims, and others. Also, since many fundamentalists do not view the United States as a Christian nation today, misrepresenting Washington and other founders as devout Christians prompts some to blame the Supreme Court, the media, "liberals," our entire political leadership, or the devil for causing America's "fall from grace."[2] Notwithstanding the two parsons then, to believe that George Washington was a pious Christian may harm America.

Even if Washington never prayed here, even if that winter wasn't particularly severe, even if not much happened here, Valley Forge is still a beautiful park. Indeed, the absence of events there may be its most interesting story. The colonies were at war with the mother country, but no battles were fought from December 1777 through June 1778. Winter does not last until June in Pennsylvania. Nevertheless, the colonials stayed in their "winter" encampment at Valley Forge and the British stayed put in Philadelphia, and life went on without much fighting for six months. War was very different then.[3]

1. The old National Park Service material seems to still lie on the web at ScienceViews
   .com, scienceviews.com/parks/valleyforge.html
2. Other fundamentalists, it is important to point out, deny, on both historical and theological grounds, that the United States was founded as a Christian nation.
3. Lauren Kaminsky, label from "Myths of American History," Frances Tavern Museum,
   1995; clipping file of U.S. Postal Museum for 2¢ Washington-in-Prayer stamp, including Henry S. Ritter, 6/18/28 letter; Hughes quoted in "Prayer Stamp for Washington
   Called Baseless," *New York Herald Tribune*, 2/5/30; Paul F. Boller Jr., *Not So!* (NY:
   Oxford UP, 1995), 29–31; Peter Lillback, "Why Have Scholars Underplayed George
   Washington's Faith?" History News Network, hnn.us/articles/34925.html, 2/12/2007;
   Gordon S. Wood, *The Radicalism of the American Revolution* (NY: Knopf, 1992), 198,
   223; Rick Shenkman, letter, 10/95; Karal Ann Marling, *George Washington Slept Here*
   (Cambridge, MA: Harvard UP, 1988), 1–7; Fred E. Lange Jr., "Correction," *UU World*
   (May 1997): 9; Mary Stockwell, "Valley Forge," Mount Vernon, n.d., mountvernon
   .org/library/digitalhistory/digital-encyclopedia/article/valley-forge; Michael Novak
   and Jana Novak, *Washington's God* (NY: Basic Books, 2007); Lorett Treese, *Valley Forge:
   Making and Remaking a National Symbol* (State College: Penn State P, 1995); Treese,
   "Epilogue: Valley Forge Past, Present, Future," NPS, updated 2/2015, nps.gov/vafo
   /learn/historyculture/treeseepilogue.htm

---------------- ✷ ----------------

73. "You're Here to See the House"

PENNSYLVANIA *Lancaster*

According to *Out of the Past*, Neil Miller's survey of gay history, the first
openly gay person in the United States to run for public office was a candidate for the San Francisco Board of Supervisors in 1961. But the highest
office ever won by a *closeted* gay person was the presidency of the United
States more than a century earlier—by James Buchanan in 1856. Wheatland,
Buchanan's house in Lancaster, is open to tourists, but visitors won't learn
that he was homosexual—or much else about him.

In life, Buchanan was not very far in the closet. For many years in Washington, while serving as a Democrat in the U.S. Senate, he lived with William Rufus King, Democratic senator from Alabama. The two men were
inseparable; wags referred to them as "the Siamese twins." Andrew Jackson dubbed King "Miss Nancy," and Aaron Brown, a prominent Democrat,
writing to Mrs. James K. Polk, referred to him as Buchanan's "better half,"
"his wife," and "Aunt Fancy . . . rigged out in her best clothes."[1] When in
1844 King was appointed minister to France, he wrote Buchanan, "I am
selfish enough to hope you will not be able to procure an associate who will

cause you to feel no regret at our separation." On May 13, Buchanan wrote
to a Mrs. Roosevelt about his social life, "I am now 'solitary and alone,' having no companion in the house with me. I have gone a wooing to several
gentlemen, but have not succeeded with any one of them. I feel that it is
not good for man to be alone; and should not be astonished to find myself
married to some old maid who can nurse me when I am sick, provide good
dinners for me when I am well, and not expect from me any very ardent or
romantic affection."

King and Buchanan's relationship, though interrupted from time to time by
their foreign service, ended only with King's death in 1853. While Buchanan
was born and raised in Pennsylvania, William Rufus King was a Southern
slaveholder. Buchanan's proslavery politics may have stemmed in part from
their 23-year connection. Buchanan certainly thought highly of King: "He
is among the best, purest, and most consistent public men I have ever known,
and is also a sound judging and discreet fellow," as well as a "very gay, elegant
looking fellow."

Nevertheless, the staff at Wheatland never mentioned King when I went
there. Asked directly "was Buchanan gay?" a staff member replied, "He most
definitely was not," and pointed to a portrait of Ann Coleman on the wall
as evidence. Buchanan was in fact engaged to Coleman, the daughter of a
wealthy ironmaker, for several weeks in the late summer and autumn of 1819.
He showed so little interest in her, however, that rumormongers in Lancaster
suggested he was only in love with her fortune. She broke their engagement
because "Mr. Buchanan did not treat her with that affection that she expected from the man she would marry," according to a friend. Buchanan didn't
put up that portrait of her, either—it was hung there long after his death.[2]

Wheatland's coverup is bad history and has unfortunate implications. It is
important to recognize that some of our leaders in politics, the arts, and other
fields have been homosexual, including those whose leadership has been less
than estimable. Otherwise, the landscape implies that gays and lesbians have
never done anything.

Buchanan's sexual orientation is just one aspect of his life that those who
present this site resolutely refuse to talk about. Another is his politics! The
Wheatland brochure does not mention his party, slavery, or the Civil War!
A staff member said to our group, "We don't tell much about his politics,
because you're here to see the house." Well, no. Visitors come to see *this*
house because Buchanan lived here, which is why it is a historic site and

why its staff gives tours. For that matter, even if the owners and workers in a historic site had not included a president, most visitors would want to hear about the important events in the owners' lives, not just about their furniture.

This is a common failing of historic house sites, especially those connected with something "embarrassing" such as slavery or a less-than-successful president. Rather than reveal the history, guides retreat to talking about the silverware. At Wheatland, the introductory video shows how Buchanan served five courses at dinner, which candles and silver he used, the tumblers for water, his wine cellar. It and our guide made no mention of politics, not even revealing that he was a Democrat.[3] Yet Buchanan's complex involvement in Democratic Party machinations in Pennsylvania and the nation were probably the most important facet of his life, both to him and the country.

The video at Wheatland does mention that Buchanan was secretary of state under Polk and later sailed to England to be an ambassador under President Franklin Pierce. But its focus is on his travels, not what he did when he got there. Probably, they omit this because his statecraft was, to put it diplomatically, inauspicious. While minister to Great Britain, Buchanan was one of three key players in the gravest foreign policy crisis of the Pierce administration, the drafting of the Ostend Manifesto. Buchanan, along with John Y. Mason, U.S. minister to France, and Pierre Soulé, minister to Spain, all proslavery Democrats, drew up this document in October 1854 at Ostend, Belgium. It strongly suggested that the United States take Cuba by force if Spain refused to sell. Worried that Spain might not be able to control Cuba's toiling masses, the diplomats thus hoped to avoid a slave revolt there with "flames [that might] extend to our own neighboring shores," in the words of the manifesto. Some white Southerners, who had long feared that Cuba might become an independent black republic like Haiti, applauded the document. Most white Northerners denounced the manifesto as a plot to extend slavery, which it was. Spain regarded the pronouncement as an insult to its national integrity and refused to discuss the matter; eventually, the U.S. State Department disavowed the document. There is no mention of any of this at Wheatland, even though Buchanan was the primary author and editor of the manifesto.

As president, Buchanan continued the ruinous Kansas policies of Pierce, his predecessor (chapter 88). He appointed Robert Walker, a Mississippi slaveowner, as governor of Kansas Territory. Although proslavery, Walker was determined to have fair voting in Kansas on the slavery issue. When he

learned that proslavery forces had stuffed the ballot boxes, he threw out the
votes. Surprised by Walker's honesty, Buchanan withdrew his support and
Walker was forced to resign. Although supposedly operating under the principle of "popular sovereignty," Buchanan "did not intend to let Kansas solve
its own problem. He was determined to placate the slave power," according
to Civil War historian Jay Monaghan. Indeed, Buchanan himself probably
initiated bribes to try to get members of Congress to admit Kansas as a slave
state. Buchanan did oppose secession, but otherwise, he merits Teddy Roosevelt's description of him as a "truckling" politician in "obsequious subservi-
ence to the [South]."

The Kansas bribes were only one of several scandals that plagued the
Buchanan administration. Republicans in Congress discovered that Buchanan appointees used government printing contracts to overpay Democratic
newspapers in return for earlier campaign contributions. Buchanan was personally involved in granting a lucrative naval contract to a Philadelphia firm
that had helped reelect a friend of his to Congress. Abraham Lincoln was
nicknamed "Honest Abe" in contrast to his corrupt predecessor; after Lincoln's election, Republican Sen. James W. Grimes wrote, "Our triumph was
achieved more because of Lincoln's . . . honesty and the known corruption of
the Democrats, than because of the Negro question." Americans still remember Lincoln as "Honest Abe" but have forgotten why he was called that.

At the house, we learn none of this. As we depart, asked directly for
Buchanan's view on slavery, a guide replied, "He was against it. This whole
area was." She is right about the area: the Lancaster Presbyterian Church
refused Buchanan membership for years because of his proslavery views. Her
reply ensures a perfect record: Wheatland gives out false information about
Buchanan's homosexuality and his view on slavery, and it provides no information about their probable linkage, Buchanan's foreign policies, his politics,
and the role he played as the nation lurched toward secession.[4]

*Willa Cather (chapter 22) offers an example of a site beginning to treat sexual orien-
tations.*

1. "Gay" and "closeted" were not used in Buchanan's time to refer to matters of sexual
   orientation, of course. "Nancy" was a common term for effeminate men, usually (but
   not always) with gay connotations.
2. Ann Coleman died soon after breaking the engagement, possibly a suicide, a story
   Wheatland guides do tell.

3. The video does let slip that it was the Democratic Party that nominated Buchanan for President in 1856.

4. Philip S. Klein, *President James Buchanan* (Norwalk, CT: Easton, 1987), 30–31, 111, 130; Frederick M. Binder, *James Buchanan and the American Empire* (Selinsgrove, PA: Susquehanna UP, 1994), 202–209; John Howard, email, (6/16/97); Sol Barzman, *Madmen and Geniuses* (Chicago, IL: Follett, 1974), 91–94; Nigel Cawthorne, *Sex Lives of the Presidents* (NY: St. Martin's, 1998), 94–95; John Bassett Moore, *The Works of James Buchanan, vol. 6* (Philadelphia, PA: Lippincott, 1929), 1–3; letter from A. V. Brown to Mrs. James K. Polk, 1/14/1844 (thanks to Howard and the Polk Papers at the U. of TN); *America's Historic Places* (Pleasant, NY: Reader's Digest, 1988), 68; Neil Miller, *Out of the Past* (NY: Vintage, 1995), 347; William Hallahan, *Misfire* (NY: Scribner's, 1994), 107; Leslie W. Dunlap, *Our Vice-Presidents and Second Ladies* (London: Scarecrow Press, 1988); James McPherson, *Drawn With the Sword* (NY: Oxford UP, 1996), 42; Loewen and Charles Sallis, eds., *MS: Conflict and Change* (NY: Pantheon, 1980), 86; Jay Monaghan, *Civil War on the Western Border, 1854–1865* (Lincoln: U. of NE Press, 1955), 102; Carl Wheeless, *Landmarks of American Presidents* (NY: Gale Research, 1996), 144; Shelley Ross, *Fall from Grace* (NY: Ballantine, 1988), 84–91. A follow-up phone call in August 2018 revealed that guides still do not tell much about Buchanan's politics and nothing about his sexual orientation.

---------------------★---------------------

74. South Carolina Defines the Civil War in 1965

PENNSYLVANIA *Gettysburg*

Why did the South leave the Union? Since South Carolina left first, we might expect that its landscape would provide the clearest answer. Indeed, South Carolina's monument at Gettysburg, dedicated in 1965, claims to tell what the Civil War was about:

SOUTH CAROLINA

That men of honor might forever know the responsibilities of freedom,
dedicated South Carolinians stood and were counted for their heritage and
convictions. Abiding faith in the sacredness of states rights provided their
creed here. Many earned eternal glory.

Mississippi put up a monument with similar sentiments. These texts were intended to sway the Americans of the 1960s and decades to follow to the neo-Confederate viewpoint. As statements about the Civil War, they are absurd.

If this monument honored South Carolina's 5,500 volunteers to the *Union* cause, the first sentence would make sense. Those men, almost all African Americans, took up arms precisely to obtain "the responsibilities of freedom" for themselves and for their friends and relatives who still languished in slavery. Unionist South Carolinians never fought at Gettysburg, however. Nor would South Carolina have erected a monument to black South Carolinians or white Unionists in 1965, at the height of its white supremacist reaction to the Supreme Court's 1954 school desegregation decree. This monument is an attempt to do the impossible: to convert the Confederate cause—a war to guarantee that 3,950,000 people might *never* know the responsibilities of freedom—into a crusade on behalf of states' rights.

In 1860, South Carolinians were perfectly clear about why they were seceding. On Christmas Eve, leaders of the state signed a document to justify their leaving the United States. The "Declaration of the Immediate Causes Which Induce and Justify the Secession of South Carolina from the Federal Union" begins by emphasizing that thirteen separate colonies signed the Declaration of Independence. That was true, but at the same time as its delegates were discussing and signing the Declaration of Independence in 1776, South Carolina was adopting a state seal that expressed its view of the new United States. Twelve spears bound to a palmetto represented the twelve other original states and South Carolina. The band binding them together bears the inscription "Quis Separabit"—"Who shall separate?" Understandably, the Ordinance of Secession did not feature the State Seal.

The government set up under the Articles of Confederation provided little centralized control. In 1787, however, representatives met in Philadelphia to write a new document precisely because they felt they needed a more powerful union. South Carolina's delegates were quite active in shaping the resulting Constitution, which South Carolina fully supported. Like most slave state delegations, its emissaries demanded that the new compact deprive states of the power to impose import and export taxes, reserving that prerogative for the federal government. South Carolina's upper class needed a strong government to represent its rights in international trade and also in case of a slave revolt, always a fear in every planter's mind. The Ordinance of Secession briefly discusses the constitutional convention but never mentions that its purpose was to strengthen the unity of the new nation.

Instead, South Carolina's Confederates-to-be moved directly to their first grievance: "that fourteen of the States have deliberately refused, for years past, to fulfill their constitutional obligations," under Article Four of the U.S. Constitution. Article Four (Section 2, Paragraph 3) is the fugitive slave clause, which states, "No person held to service or labour in one State, under the laws thereof, escaping into another, shall, in consequence of any law or regulation therein, be discharged from such service or labour, but shall be delivered up. . . ." The South Carolina Ordinance of Secession approvingly declared, "The General Government, as the common agent, passed laws to carry into effect these stipulations of the States."

> But an increasing hostility on the part of the non-slaveholding States to the institution of slavery, has led to a disregard of their obligations . . . The States of Maine, New Hampshire, Vermont, Massachusetts, Connecticut, Rhode Island, New York, Pennsylvania, Illinois, Indiana, Michigan, Wisconsin and Iowa, have enacted laws which either nullify the Acts of Congress or render useless any attempt to execute them.

Thus, *opposition* to states' rights claimed by free states provided South Carolina's creed here.

The "Declaration of Immediate Causes" went on to condemn New York state specifically for denying "even the right of transit for a slave." Referring to the *Dred Scott* decision, the South Carolina document also denounced several northern states for "elevating to citizenship, persons [African Americans] who, by the supreme law of the land, are incapable of becoming citizens." Thus, South Carolina claimed the right to determine whether New York could prohibit slavery within New York or Vermont could define citizenship in Vermont. Carolinians also contested the rights of residents in other states to even *think* differently about their "peculiar institution," giving as a reason for secession the excuse that Northerners "have denounced as sinful the institution of slavery."

Political scientists know that the party that lost the last national election usually supports states' rights. In one sense, South Carolina Democrats followed this rule: the Ordinance of Secession expressed outrage at the victory of Abraham Lincoln the previous November. Ironically, Democrats from South Carolina and other Southern states had made Lincoln's victory possible by refusing to support the Democratic nominee, Stephen A. Douglas, precisely *because* Douglas had championed states' rights, or more properly, territories' rights to choose or reject slavery. In 1854, Douglas had pushed the Kansas-Nebraska Act through Congress. Southerners supported the act then because it potentially opened to slavery the Great Plains north of the Missouri Compromise line. By 1860, however, slaveowners had become more audacious. The 1857 *Dred Scott* decision encouraged them to believe that the federal government should guarantee slavery in all the land it controlled, but Lincoln's election changed all that. South Carolina seceded because Southerners, having lost control of the executive branch of the federal government, could no longer use it to crush attempts by individual states to avoid supporting slavery. The only "states' right" Carolinians demanded was the right to secede, because they saw they could no longer compel the national government to curtail the rights of *other* states and territories.

Southern leaders built no right to secede into the new nation that they controlled. Instead, the Confederate Constitution forbade states from ever "impairing the right of property in Negro slaves," and territories from ever prohibiting slavery, regardless of local sentiment.

South Carolinians in 1965 knew perfectly well that the desire to protect and extend slavery prompted their state to leave the United States. In a three-volume history published in 1934, David Duncan Wallace, himself a white supremacist South Carolinian, had emphasized slavery as the cause. In 1951, he came out with the condensed *South Carolina: A Short History*, in which he admitted, "The modern tendency to minimize slavery as the cause of secession is a natural reaction of writers weary of an oft-repeated disagreeable story." "The secessionists knew why they seceded," he pointed out, and they always cited the threat to slavery, real or imagined, as the cause.

Why would white South Carolinians in 1965 choose to obfuscate this simple fact so evident in the historical record? Clearly, in the 1960s, they were not comfortable with slavery and realized they could not convince Gettysburg visitors that slavery was a good thing. If they merely wanted to recognize the dedication South Carolina's troops showed at Gettysburg and commemorate those among them who died here, however, they would have erected a memorial like Tennessee's:

THE VOLUNTEER STATE

*This memorial is dedicated to the memory of the men
who served in [various corps in the Army of Northern Virginia].*

They fought and died for their convictions, performing
their duty as they understood it.

Instead, white South Carolinians wanted to convince those who read their stone that the Confederate cause was noble.

White Southerners seceded for slavery as the method to maintain white supremacy. In November 1864, the *Richmond Daily Enquirer* made this clear: "What are we fighting for? We are fighting for the idea of race." Writing about the antiblack and anti-Republican violence of the late nineteenth and early twentieth centuries, historian James Marten made the same point: "The overriding principle of the cause to which old rebels as well as Confederates-come-lately dedicated themselves was, of course, white supremacy."

The ideology of white supremacy had arisen during slavery to rationalize and legitimize "the peculiar institution"; it became slavery's legacy to the twentieth century. In the early 1960s, white supremacists still controlled South Carolina and strove mightily to keep African Americans in separate and unequal institutions. Public schools, for example, spent 50% more per white pupil than black pupil. Controlling the past, including how that past is told across the American landscape, helped white supremacists control the future. "States' rights" was just a subterfuge for those who wanted to take away individual rights. Converting the Confederate cause after the fact into a struggle for states' rights in the 1860s helped transmogrify the segregationist cause of the 1960s into a similar struggle for states' rights against an intrusive federal government. Celebrating those South Carolinians who stood most assuredly for black inferiority—Confederates—implied that white Carolinians in the 1960s who opposed civil rights ought likewise to be celebrated.

Glorifying the Confederacy in Pennsylvania, thus, had ideological consequences in South Carolina in 1965. Why did the United States allow the white supremacist leaders of South Carolina, Mississippi, and some other Southern states to say what they wanted regardless of historical fact? Wars are usually interpreted by their winners. Why would the North cede this prerogative to the South? And not only on the landscape but also in high school textbooks of U.S. history from the 1890s to the 1960s?[1] During those decades, our popular culture also celebrated the South, not the North, from minstrel shows (chapter 86) to movies like *Birth of a Nation* and *Gone with the Wind*. Why? What was in it for the North?

Between 1890 and about 1940, and lingering on to 1970, Northerners found it less embarrassing to let Dixie tell the story of the cause it lost than to reminisce about the cause they had abandoned. The Civil War had been about something other than states' rights after all. It began as a war to force or prevent the breakup of the United States. As it ground on, it became a struggle to end slavery. At Gettysburg in the fall of 1863, Abraham Lincoln was already proclaiming "a new birth of freedom"—black freedom. (Conversely, on their way to and from Gettysburg, Lee's troops seized scores of free black people in Maryland and Pennsylvania and sent them south into slavery. This was in keeping with Confederate national policy, which virtually re-enslaved free people of color into work gangs on earthworks throughout the South.)

By 1890, however, black freedom turned out to have been stillborn. In that year, Mississippi passed its new constitution, enshrining white supremacy in basic law, and Congress narrowly failed to pass the "Force Bill," a last gasp of Republican idealism on behalf of the rights of African Americans. In 1892, Grover Cleveland would win the presidency with a campaign that poked fun at Republicans as "nigger lovers." Four years later, the U.S. Supreme Court would grant official approval to racial segregation in *Plessy v. Ferguson*. Thereafter, segregation became required by custom if not law throughout most of the north, including Pennsylvania (chapter 81). Many towns expelled their black residents or decided informally not to allow any.

That is why monuments at Gettysburg mystify what the war was about. On Gettysburg's hallowed grounds, it would no longer do to delve too deeply into *why* so many men "here gave their lives," in Lincoln's words. The nation let South Carolina define what the Civil War was about, because for many decades after 1890, the United States was no longer "dedicated to the proposition that all men are created equal," as Lincoln had said it was, here at Gettysburg.

As recently as 2008, Gettysburg was less forthright than Lincoln had been in 1863. In 2005, historian Eric Foner told how he visited the battlefield with his family and his nine-year-old daughter said, "I feel so sorry for those Confederate soldiers." "You should," Foner replied, "because thousands of people died. But just remember, they were fighting to keep black people in slavery." "Oh yes," she said, "I forgot." "It's easy to forget," Foner agreed, adding that he could not recall seeing a single mention of slavery at Gettysburg.

In 2008, the new visitors center opened. In it, Morgan Freeman, chosen surely for his mellifluous voice but also appropriately named, narrates the new introductory video, "A New Birth of Freedom." The phrase is from the "Gettysburg Address," of course, and the new birth of freedom that Lincoln resolved we should have was, of course, black freedom. This was a reference to the Emancipation Proclamation, of course, which Lincoln had announced a few weeks earlier and which was set to go into effect a few weeks hence. It was the most controversial phrase in that speech in 1863. Many Northern Democrats denied that they were fighting for that purpose, but it proved true on the ground as well as eventually in the Constitution. The National Park Service also used "A New Birth of Freedom" as the name for their brochure for the park and placed it on the wall of the museum above the auditorium entrance. Slavery is more than mentioned at Gettysburg today. What should the National Park Service do about the South Carolina monument and other monuments that redefined the Civil War to meet the needs of white supremacists in 1965? Instead of toppling them, NPS needs to insert on the battlefield landscape (and in its video, audio tour, and guides' knowledge base) a candid analysis of how these monuments misrepresent the past and why their sponsors wanted them to. Then Gettysburg would help visitors understand not only the Civil War but also how Americans have remembered and misremembered it over time.[2]

Chapter 57 explains how the Civil War increasingly became a struggle to end slavery.

1. Vestiges of this treatment still muddle some American history textbooks today, as told in Loewen, *Lies My Teacher Told Me*, chapters 5 and 6.
2. *The Civil War Book of Lists* (Conshohocken, PA: Combined Books, 1993), 28; www. leginfo.state.scinfo/stateseal.html, 4/99; David Duncan Wallace, *SC: A Short History* (Columbia: U. of SC Press, 1951), 527; Drew Gilpin Faust, *The Creation of Confederate Nationalism* (Baton Rouge: LA State UP, 1988), 60; James Marten, *Texas Divided* (Lexington: UP of KY, 1990), 179; SC Department of Education data courtesy of Vernon Burton; James M. McPherson, *Battle Cry of Freedom* (NY: Oxford UP, 1988), 649; William Evans, *Beyond the Rivers of Ethiopia* (Pomona, CA: manuscript, 1997), 560; Janny Scott, "National Parks Get Low Marks in History," *The New York Times*, 11/15/97.

-------------------★-------------------

75. Remember the "Splendid Little War"— Forget the Tawdry Larger Wars

PENNSYLVANIA *Philadelphia*

At Penn's Landing in downtown Philadelphia is moored USS *Olympia*. Visitors can tour it and USS *Becuna*, a World War II submarine berthed nearby (chapter 76), as part of their admission to the Independence Seaport Museum.

According to *Olympia*'s brochure, "no vessel served the United States with more honor and distinction. And few participated in as many crucial world events." But the exhibits on *Olympia* barely hint at most of the history it witnessed in its 30 years of service.

The floating museum flaunts its role in the Spanish–American War. *Olympia* was Adm. George Dewey's flagship during the Battle of Manila Bay, fought on the morning of May 1, 1898. In this battle, called "the most one-sided victory in the annals of naval warfare," the U.S. Navy destroyed the Spanish fleet at anchor and left 381 Spaniards dead or wounded. Eight U.S. sailors were slightly wounded, and an engineer died of heatstroke. Thus began the Spanish–American War, which ended in total Spanish defeat 105 days later. No wonder John Hay, our ambassador to Great Britain, called it "a splendid little war."

Footprints in bronze on the ship's deck show where Dewey stood when he said, "You may fire when you are ready, Gridley." According to an exhibit on *Olympia*, "By noon on that day, the bombardment unleashed by Adm. Dewey's terse order had sunk or disabled every ship of the Spanish Pacific Fleet. From this victory, the United States gained possession of the Philippine Islands and became a world power."

Actually, to gain possession of the Philippines we had to fight the Filipinos. Dewey's victory didn't even get us Manila. Rather than risk American lives, Dewey met with Filipino leaders in Hong Kong in April before the United States declared war on Spain. He persuaded them to return to the Philippines from exile to lead the struggle against the Spanish on land. Aboard *Olympia* in Hong Kong harbor, he promised Gen. José Alejandrino that the United States had no interest in becoming a colonial power: "America is rich under all concepts; it has territories scarcely populated, aside from the fact that our Constitution does not permit us to expand territorially outside of America. For these reasons, the Filipinos can be sure of their independence and of the fact that they will not be despoiled of any piece of their territory." Both Dewey and Alejandrino knew that President William McKinley had told Congress on December 6, 1897, "I speak not of forcible annexation, for that cannot be thought of. That by our code of morality would be criminal aggression."

Believing Dewey and McKinley, Filipino troops regarded Dewey's forces as allies. The Filipinos overran all of the main island, Luzon, capturing thousands of Spanish soldiers, and surrounded Manila. Gradually, they took

Manila's suburbs and cut off the city's water supply. The Spanish commander in Manila then arranged to surrender to U.S. forces after a sham battle rather than to the Filipinos.

President McKinley's negotiators then used this surrender to force Spain to sell the Philippines to the United States in the Treaty of Paris, ending the Spanish-American War in December 1898. Even after the treaty formally ended the war, the U.S. Army continued to pour reinforcements into Manila. Our Filipino allies grew anxious, inferring that Americans intended to settle in for good. An uneasy border divided Manila, under U.S. control, from the rest of the island, controlled by Filipinos. Then on the night of February 4, 1899, U.S. sentries fired on Filipino soldiers, killing three. A plaque in a Manila suburb marks the spot where "at 9:00 o'clock in the evening of February 4th, 1899, Private Robert Grayson of the First Nebraska Volunteers fired the shot that started the Filipino-American War." Even though the U.S. Army had opened fire, American officers used the incident as a pretext to trigger a full-scale assault on Filipino troops in the Manila suburbs. In this attack, the United States suffered 59 killed and 278 wounded. Filipino forces lost five to ten times that, partly owing to punishing bombardment from Dewey's ships.

This was no sham war. By the summer of 1900, two-thirds of the entire U.S. Army was engaged in the Philippines; chapter 25 tells how the war dragged on for years. According to historian Leon Wolff, the Philippine-American War became "a moral issue almost unparalleled in American policy and politics."[1] This moral issue originated here on *Olympia*, among other places. Emilio Aguinaldo, soon to become president of the Philippine Republic, let Adm. Dewey know that he was worried about U.S. intentions after Spain was defeated. Dewey hosted Aguinaldo aboard his flagship and assured him that he had sent to State Department officials a telegram "recognizing Philippine independence under the temporary shelter of the U.S. Navy," according to Wolff. *Olympia* says not a word about any of the historic meetings between Dewey and Filipino leaders on its decks. In the officer's mess room, a display case houses seven dusty bayonets and spears, labeled simply "The Philippine Insurrection II." Some old Filipino clothing lies in another case, unlabeled except as to donor. Asked about the Philippine-American War, our guide assured us, "She [*Olympia*] didn't play any role in it."

Olympia has not even a display case to represent another controversial escapade in which it played a key role. According to its brochure, "On June 8,

1918, she was given the task of landing a peace-keeping force at the turbulent port of Murmansk in Russia." The brochure says nothing else about this episode; nothing in the ship hints it ever went to Russia. However, an exhibit in the museum in 2018 does cover this, saying we sent *Olympia* to Russia to combat Bolshevik influence, protect allied war material, and rescue "White Russian" refugees. That's reasonably accurate.

It wasn't peacekeeping. The 150 Marines from *Olympia* were the first U.S. combat troops that landed in Russia. They were followed by more than 5,000 additional American soldiers in Murmansk and Archangel, 500 miles southeast, and joined more troops from Great Britain, France, and even Italy, all under British command. The Wilson administration gave our troops no believable explanation as to why they were fighting Russia. Supposedly, our purpose was to coax Russia back into the war against Germany. Under its new communist government, Russia had dropped out of World War I and negotiated a separate peace with Germany. How an Allied attack in north Russia, along with a larger American-Japanese invasion in Siberia to the east that eventually reached Lake Baikal, might persuade Russia to rejoin the Allies and reopen its front against Germany was never explained. Moreover, although Germany signed the armistice that ended World War I on November 11, 1918, the United States fought on in Russia. That same day, *Olympia* arrived back at Murmansk after a trip to Archangel; two days later, the ship removed the first 47 wounded U.S. soldiers to Scotland.

Actually, our intervention had little to do with Germany. It began in 1917, shortly after the Communist takeover, when Wilson started sending secret monetary aid to the "White" Russians who had declared war against the Bolsheviks under Lenin. When Americans fought alongside White Russians in the north, however, they discovered that their allies—who retreated when attacked and defected when on patrol—had little enthusiasm for the cause. Worse, Whites who secretly favored the Red side tipped off the Red Army about Allied battle plans, keeping the Americans always at a disadvantage.

Like many of our undeclared wars, this enterprise ended as a fiasco. When U.S. troops started coming home in body bags, Americans started asking questions. Since Wilson had kept Congress out of the loop, its members could hardly defend his decisions. Moreover, like most other regimes and factions that the United States has covertly supported over the years, the White Russians were despots. About all they offered Russia's impoverished ex-serfs was a program of anti-Semitism.[2] The White Russian forces disintegrated by the end of 1919, and the last of our troops finally left Russia on April 1, 1920.

Woodrow Wilson kept this invasion secret from Congress and the American people as long as he could. By neglecting to tell about it aboard ship and by calling our soldiers a "peace-keeping force" in its brochure, *Olympia* does what it can to keep it secret today.[3]

Chapter 25 tells more about the Philippine-American War.

1. Parallels would be the Mexican and Vietnam wars.
2. The Red Russians were also despots but with an ideology and program.
3. Leon Wolff, *Little Brown Brother* (Garden City, NY: Doubleday, 1961), 40–48, 67–69, 227–28; David Wallechinsky and Irving Wallace, *The People's Almanac no. 3* (NY: Morrow, 1981), 270–71; Polar Bear website pages, www.acs.oakland.edu/~cjbeckro/Polar /backgrnd.htm and www.acs.oakland.edu/~cjbeckro/Polar//339th.htm, 8/98; Bentley Library website, www.umich.edu/~bhl/bhl/mhchome/polarb.htm, 8/98; Loewen, *Lies My Teacher Told Me* (NY: New Press, 1995), 14; Dennis Gordon, *Quartered in Hell* (Missoula, MT: Doughboy Historical Society, 1982), 56.

★

---

76. Celebrating Illegal Submarine Warfare

PENNSYLVANIA *Philadelphia*

Next to USS *Olympia* at Penn's Landing in Philadelphia, connected with the Independence Seaport Museum, floats a typical World War II submarine, *Becuna*. Submarines make popular museum exhibits; Chicago's Museum of Science and Industry has long featured a German U-boat. The sub's design necessitated interesting downsizing of living spaces and kitchens. Children enjoy traipsing through the watertight doorways and imagining they are at the controls. The snug juxtapositions of bunks and torpedoes remind visitors that men do sleep in war, and then they must wake up to fire. Seeing the artifacts used for domestic chores aboard a vessel of such savage purpose seems weirdly incongruous.

Becuna adds an important historical dimension to the usual emphasis on nuts and bolts. "In five war patrols, *Becuna* is credited with destroying thousands of tons of Japanese naval and merchant ships," says the museum brochure. In the process, it received four battle stars and a presidential unit citation. A bumper sticker in the forward torpedo room reads, "There are *only* two types of ships: Submarines and Targets." Our guide, a retired submarine crew member, told us, "On December 8, 1941, we got the word: fire at anything, without warning. If it was in our zone, it went down."

This history, though quite accurate, is contrary to international law. According to the *Encyclopedia of International Law,* "In war, a submarine may not sink a merchant ship without first having placed the crew and passengers in safety." During World War I, German submarines sank merchant vessels without allowing passengers and crew to evacuate. Germany's refusal to end "unrestricted submarine warfare" as we called it was a significant factor in America's decision to declare war on Germany in April 1917.

Until December 8, 1941, the United States maintained a "strict legalistic interpretation of this law," according to Janet Manson, whose dissertation, *Unrestricted Submarine Warfare, The Change in U.S. Policy, and German-American Relations, 1939–1941,* is the major work on the topic. Then, the Navy "completely reversed itself within hours." This was not a hasty reaction to Pearl Harbor; according to Manson, U.S. naval authorities had long planned to conduct such warfare before Pearl Harbor provided the excuse. She claims, "There has been no other foreign policy reversal in the history of the United States of this magnitude."

John D. Hayes, rear admiral of the U.S. Navy (ret.), admits that this amounted to "unrestricted submarine warfare." Heretofore, Hayes maintains, "American traditions and doctrine . . . had required submarines to be used in accordance with international law and primarily against combat ships." Our reason for starting unrestricted submarine warfare was the same as Germany's: Japan, like Great Britain, an island nation, depended on shipping for survival.

Meanwhile, Japan made no such change: "The Japanese used their submarines almost exclusively against combat ships," in Hayes's words. Our *Becuna* guide agreed: "They used their subs basically as part of their fleet, against our fleet." This amounted to wearing moral or tactical blinders, according to Hayes: "[Japanese submarines] could have constituted a dangerous threat to United States victory if Japanese naval leaders had not been blind to the reality of modern war."

Proud of the role he played in helping win World War II, our guide handed out a sheet of "Submarine Statistics." It tells that submarines sank some

201 Japanese warships "plus 1,113 merchant ships of more than 500 tons." "Why were merchant ships so important???" it asks. "The Japanese empire was an *island* empire," so cutting their supplies helped end the war sooner and decreased American casualties. "In all our submarines sank more than 55% of all ships sunk. More than surface ships, Navy air, and the Air Corp. combined."[1]

The handout begins on a plaintive note, however: "Many U.S. Submarine Veterans feel that their activities were not made public enough to let the population know how much they accomplished during World War 2." Perhaps that lack of recognition owes to some ambivalence in the United States about our conduct of submarine warfare. After all, our actions were identical to those for which we had condemned Germany. Highlighting them now would make for some cognitive dissonance; after all, we *still* call the Germans the bad guys in World War I, owing in large part to their policy of unrestricted submarine warfare. Emphasizing our submarine policy might also invite the inference that perhaps we won in the Pacific in World War II because we played by the same rules we earlier condemned.

Why should Americans today examine these moral complexities of World War II? Why not just commemorate the war as the nation did a few years ago on the 50th anniversary of victory over Japan? In the words of Adm. Gene La Rocque, "World War II has warped our view of how we look at things today. We see things in terms of that war, which in a sense was a good war. But the twisted memory of it encouraged the men of my generation to be willing, almost eager, to use military force anywhere in the world." One result, according to La Roque, was America's tragic intervention in Vietnam, which he called "a senseless waste of human beings." As World War II slowly passes from the memory of the living, the nation runs out of witnesses like my guide at *Becuna*. Indeed, when two students of mine toured *Becuna* in 2018, there were no guides. If Americans are to learn about war, we must have war museums that raise the tough questions—precisely the issues *Becuna* ducks.[2]

---

1. Among the 1,113 was the *Awa Maru*, a merchant ship carrying 2,000 tons of relief supplies from Singapore to Japan for American soldiers in Japanese prisoner of war camps. It was sailing with white crosses painted on its hull under a safe-conduct pass from the U.S. Navy when the submarine *Queenfish* sank it in the Taiwan Strait. Afraid that the Japanese might retaliate against the POWs, the United States formally apologized and offered to replace the *Awa Maru* with a similar ship.

2. Janet Manson, *Unrestricted Submarine Warfare, The Change in U.S. Policy, and German-American Relations, 1939–1941* (WA State U., PhD, 1987) and *Diplomatic Ramifications of Unrestricted Submarine Warfare, 1939–1941* (NY: Greenwood, 1990); John D. Hayes, "The War in the Central and Northern Pacific," www.grolier.com/does/wwii/wwii_10.html, 9/98; Carl Boyd and Akihiko Yoshida, *The Japanese Submarine Force and World War II* (Annapolis, MD: Naval Institute Press, 1995), 5; *Encyclopedia of International Law,* vol. 2 (Amsterdam: Elsevier, 1989), 327; Studs Terkel, *The Good War* (NY: New Press, 1995? [1984]), 3; Irving Wallace, David Wallechinsky, and Amy Wallace, *Significa* (NY: Dutton, 1983), 175; Gene LaRocque, www.cdi.org/adm, 11/97.

———— ✶ ————

77. The Pilgrims and Religious Freedom

NEW JERSEY *Trenton*

Of only two historical subjects treated at the New Jersey State Capitol in Trenton, one is the Pilgrims—and they never got to New Jersey![1] On the executive side is this marker:

THE MAYFLOWER

December 1620
This tablet is placed to honor the Pilgrims of the Mayflower.
In an age of intolerance and of bigotry, the Pilgrims of the Mayflower
laid the foundations of this mighty nation
wherein every man, through countless ages, shall have liberty to worship
God in his own way.

At the bottom the plaque reads, "Erected by the Society of Mayflower descendants in the State of New Jersey, November, 1932."

A great nation needs a great beginning, which is why Americans have latched so tightly onto the Pilgrims. A booklet put out by the Massachusetts Office of Travel and Tourism brags, "When the Pilgrims arrived on the *Mayflower* in 1620 and cast anchor in Provincetown harbor off Cape Cod, American history began." But it didn't. Starting here leaves out American Indians, the Spanish, and the Dutch. Nor did the Pilgrims "lay the foundations of this mighty nation," having come thirteen years after other English landed in Jamestown, Virginia.

This Protestant New England-biased history is not limited to the eastern seaboard. Pilgrim plaques identical to New Jersey's are in other state capitols, including Ohio's. An otherwise accurate historical marker in Kansas, "The Emigrant Tribes," begins, "When the Pilgrims landed at Plymouth Rock it is estimated there were 200 Indian tribes in what is now the United States." The process of dispossession it describes began well before 1620, however, with the Spanish, the Dutch, and the Virginians.

Choosing 1620 as America's founding date is an example of what historians call American exceptionalism. It makes the United States look exceptionally *nice*, for of all the founding legends, the Pilgrims' is the most pleasant. Emphasizing how nice we are helps make Americans ethnocentric. The related Thanksgiving story further reveals American ethnocentrism as our presidents annually thank God for the blessings He [*sic*] has bestowed upon our nation. While it is comforting to think that God is on our side, such assurance does not help Americans become thoughtful about their past.

Millions of American schoolchildren have been taught that the Pilgrims came here for religious freedom, but they did not. They already exercised complete freedom of religion in the Netherlands. Holland had long been a haven for the persecuted minorities of Europe, among them the Jews, the French Huguenots, the Belgian Walloons, and the English Separatists. That is why the last group, whom we now call Pilgrims, had gone there in the first place. They didn't need to come to America for religious freedom. Historians agree that they came here to escape poverty and avoid being assimilated into Dutch society.

Finally, the Pilgrims hardly let everyone "worship God in his own way" once they arrived. They immediately set up a quasi-theocracy and expelled or imprisoned their own believers who spoke against ministers. In 1658, Plymouth passed a law against "Quaker rantors." The Puritans to their north were even worse. It took decades before Massachusetts granted Catholics and Jews the same freedom to worship as other colonies. Roger Williams in Rhode Island and William Penn in Pennsylvania led the way. Maryland also briefly showed leadership in allowing freedom of worship. But representing the Pilgrims as pioneers of religious tolerance is preposterous.[2]

1. The other New Jersey plaque honors Woodrow Wilson, but don't get me started! (See Loewen, *Lies My Teacher Told Me* [NY: New Press, 1995], 11–25.)
2. Leo Bonfanti, *The Pequot-Mohican War* (Wakefield, MA: Pride, 1971), 6; Gustavus Myers, *History of Bigotry in the United States* (NY: Capricorn, 1960 [1943]), 5, 22; George F. Willison, *Saints and Strangers* (NY: Reynal and Hitchcock, 1945), 351.

---- ★ ----

78. Making Native Americans Look Stupid

NEW YORK *Manhattan*

In Battery Park at the lower tip of Manhattan stands a monument to the legend we all learned in elementary school—how the Dutch bought Manhattan for $24 worth of beads and trinkets. Incorporating a huge flagpole, on its base is a bas-relief depicting the transaction. It is captioned in stone, ". . . The purchase of the Island of Manhattan was accomplished in 1626. Thus was laid the foundation of the City of New York."

It's time to rethink this little fable. First, consider the price. My father bought the home in which I grew up, in 1937, for $8,000. It sold in 1983 for six times that. No surprise there; prices go up. But my father learned the $24 story in school in about 1911. So did I, in 1949, and so did my children, in the 1980s. Teachers still teach it today. It makes no sense! This $24 for Manhattan is the only figure in the Western World that has never been touched by inflation!

So, we have to rethink the purchase price. I estimate it was about 100 times higher—$2,400, perhaps. But even at $2,400, the statue invites us to smile indulgently at the Indians. What a bargain! Today, $2,400

A well-dressed Dutchman, perhaps Peter Minuit, leader of New Amsterdam in 1626, is handing a string of beads to a Native American wearing only a breechcloth and a full feathered headdress. If the transaction happened in August, the Dutchman is sweating; if in February, the Native is freezing. The sculptor has not striven for realism, of course; he simply follows an artistic convention about clothing that makes the Indian seem primitive.

wouldn't buy a site large enough to pitch a pup tent in Manhattan! What silly Indians, not to recognize the potential of the island!

Rather than deriding the Natives as foolish, history textbooks today lament the cultural gap that caused a basic misunderstanding. Native Americans held a pre-modern understanding of land ownership: buying and selling land wasn't part of their culture. This is the social archetype of the haplessly pre-modern Indian. Natives just could not understand that when they sold their land, they transferred not only the right to farm it but also the rights to its game, fish, and sheer enjoyment.

Although kinder than merely making American Indians foolish, that archetype is still wrong. Native American and European American ideas about land ownership were not so far apart. Most land sales before the twentieth century, including sales between whites, transferred primarily the right to farm, mine, and otherwise develop the land. *Access* to undeveloped land was considered public, within limits of good conduct. Moreover, tribal negotiators often made sure that deeds and treaties explicitly reserved hunting, fishing, gathering, and traveling rights to Native Americans. Natives were correct when they believed they still had the right to hunt on the land they had sold. Nevertheless, Europeans often then accused them of trespassing and jailed and sometimes killed them for the offense.

Even if they understood that they could continue to use Manhattan, it still seems surprising that American Indians would trade away their very homeland—sell their villages and gardens, their fishing grounds and hunting land—for $24 or even $2,400 worth of beads and trinkets. Peter Francis Jr., director of the Center for Bead Research in Lake Placid, points out that no documentary evidence even suggests that European trade beads were used to buy Manhattan.

If by now, the story seems hopelessly implausible, it should—because it didn't happen. It turns out that the Dutch paid *the wrong tribe* for Manhattan— the Canarsies. Today, visitors can take the subway from Battery Park to Canarsie—the name lives on in Brooklyn.[1] And indeed, the Canarsies lived in what is now Brooklyn. So why *wouldn't* they sell Manhattan to the Dutch? Especially since the Dutch probably paid a substantial sum in the form of blankets, kettles, steel axes, knives, and perhaps guns—goods American Indians valued highly and would go to great lengths to obtain. No doubt the Canarsies were as pleased with the bargain as the New Yorker who sold

Brooklyn Bridge to some later Europeans—they got paid for something that wasn't theirs in the first place.

The apocryphal Brooklyn Bridge sale invites us to laugh at the tourists—stupid bumpkins! Similarly, the Dutch were bumpkins in the "New World." As Reginald P. Bolton, who wrote most widely on the sale of Manhattan, put it, "The colonists do not appear to have made themselves acquainted with the native situation . . . [The Canarsies'] wily leaders conveyed the impression of their ownership of the whole island, and thus secured for themselves and their own people all the goods which the white men were offering."[2] But the conventional Manhattan sale tale invites us to laugh not at the tourists but at the Natives. It all depends on who has the power. The Dutch and their European American successors won, so the story is told to make the Indians the bumpkins.

Actually, the Dutch were happy to have bought Manhattan from the wrong tribe because they weren't really buying Manhattan but the *right* to Manhattan in the eyes of other Europeans. In short, they were buying respectability—in their own eyes too. With this monument, inscribed "In testimony of ancient and unbroken friendship, this flagpole is presented to the City of New York by the Dutch people, 1926," the Dutch were still in a way buying world esteem three centuries later.

The purchase also made allies of the Canarsies, who otherwise might have joined with the Weckquaesgeeks, the Indians who lived on Manhattan and owned most of it.[3] The Netherlanders didn't try to buy off the Weckquaesgeeks, a more difficult task since they knew, loved, and made their homes on Manhattan. Instead, they waited as a succession of inter-Indian wars, some instigated by the Dutch, and a series of epidemics weakened the Weckquaesgeeks. Then in the 1640s, with the aid of the Canarsies and other Native Americans on Long Island, the Dutch exterminated most of the Weckquaesgeeks.

Manhattan was only the beginning. Europeans were forever paying the wrong tribe for America or paying a small faction within a much larger nation. Often, like the Dutch, they didn't care. They merely sought justification for conquest. Fraudulent transactions might even work better than legitimate purchases, for they set one tribe or faction against another while providing Europeans with the semblance of legality to stifle criticism.

The biggest single purchase from the wrong tribe took place in 1803. Louisiana was not France's to sell—it was Indian land. The French never

consulted with Native owners before selling it; most Native Americans living there never even *knew* of the sale. Indeed, France did *not* sell Louisiana
for $15,000,000. The French foreign minister couldn't even tell the Ameri-
can negotiators its boundaries. France merely sold *its claim* to the land. In
short, like the Dutch with the Canarsies, the United States bought from the
French the right to respectability in the eyes of other Europeans. That's why
the government continued to pay Native American nations for Louisiana
throughout the nineteenth century. We also fought them for it: the *Army
Almanac* lists more than 50 Indian wars in the Louisiana Purchase from 1819
to 1890. Similarly, as late as 1715, Europeans were still paying the Reckga-
wawancs, tributaries of the Weckquaesgeeks who somehow escaped their
extermination and still claimed upper Manhattan. Despite the $24 story
then, Europeans were still paying for Manhattan almost a century after Peter
Minuit.

Treating Native Americans as ignorant, as this monument does, is part
of the fantastic history European Americans constructed to convince themselves they did not simply *take* the land. The statue and the story also help to
convince whites that Native Americans aren't very bright, at least compared
to European Americans. It was one of the latter, however, who put a Plains
Indian, complete with incongruous headdress, on a Manhattan monument.[4]

1. It's the final stop on the "L" train.

2. Bolton makes the best of what turns out to be scant evidence that this "sale" ever took
    place at all. "No deed has survived," Peter Francis notes, "although the West India Com-
    pany specifically instructed that a deed be secured."

3. Although many writers call the Indians who lived on Manhattan Weckquaesgeeks, like
    most Indians in the East before Europeans arrived, they lived in small kinship groups
    only loosely organized into tribes. Some were probably members of smaller groups such
    as the Reckgawawancs and were tributaries of the Weckquaesgeeks, who also lived in
    the Bronx and Westchester County. No Indians may have been living on the southern
    tip of the island, for the Dutch moved in with no difficulty and lived there for a year with
    no treaty.

4. So far as I know, the only evidence for the purchase of Manhattan written at the time is
    one sentence in a letter by Peter Schagen, 11/5/1626: "They have purchased the Island
    Manhattes from the Indians for the value of 60 guilders." I rely on these secondary
    sources: Irving Wallace, David Wallechinsky, and Amy Wallace, *Significa* (NY: Dutton,
    1983), 326; Robert S. Grumet, "American Indians," in Kenneth T. Jackson, *Encyclopedia
    of New York City* (New Haven, CT: Yale UP, 1995), 25–28; Reginald Pelham Bolton,
    New York City in Indian Possession (NY: Heye Foundation, 1920), 240–45; Bolton, *Indian
    Life of Long Ago in the City of New York* (NY: Joseph Graham, 1934), 127; Peter Francis
    Jr., "The Beads That Did *Not* Buy Manhattan Island," *New York History* 67 no. 1 (1/86):
    5–20; Robert S. Grumet, *Historic Contact* (Norman: U. of OK Press, 1995), 219; James

Finch, "Aboriginal Remains on Manhattan Island" (NY: American Museum of Natural History, 1909 Anthropological Papers, vol. 3), 72; and E. M. Ruttenber, *History of Indian Tribes of Hudson's River* (Saugerties, NY: Hope Farm Press, 1992 [1872]),71–78.

———— ★ ————

79. Which George Washington?

NEW YORK *Alabama*

In northwest Genesee County, on Ledge Road just east of the Tonawanda Indian Reservation, a 1932 New York State Historical Marker states,

FORDING PLACE ON GRAND CENTRAL TRAIL

Said to have been used by George Washington during the French and Indian War.

The Founding Father never set foot in Genesee County, however. It turns out that the George Washington mentioned was a local Native American, not the president! In 1934, this was pointed out to the state of New York, but they never got around to removing the marker.

Of course, the marker is not precisely untrue, and it does open up new possibilities for signs all across the United States. Not only are dozens of George Washingtons alive today, but at least four John Adamses reside in Seattle alone.[1] In 1999, Thomas Jefferson lived on in Anniston, Alabama, while in central Mississippi, John Quincy Adams was a college professor—of political science, naturally. Moving closer to the present, Lyndon B. Johnson lives in South Gate, California. They have all lived storied lives, I am sure, and if this New York marker offers any precedent, we may soon be reading bronze markers about them.[2]

1. The central park of Centralia, Washington, is named for another George Washington, an African American who founded the town in 1872! In the center of the park is a bronze plaque on marble that tells of Centralia's George Washington, so people can know for whom the park is named.

2. Susan L. Conklin, Genesee County Historian, "Historical Markers in Genesee County" (talk in Genesee County, c. 1995), 16; Nancy C. Curtis, *Black Heritage Sites: The North* (NY: New Press, 1996), 212.

*

80. John Brown's Plaque Puts Blacks at the Bottom!

NEW YORK *North Elba*

This peaceful farm is the final resting place for John Brown's body. Inadvertently, it also shows what happened, in American history, to his soul.

John Brown's farm is in beautiful country near Lake Placid's Olympic ski jumping towers. The house and even the pond are much as Brown left them. The site has additional historic significance for its relationship to the "Committee of Six," also known as "The Secret Six"—prominent abolitionists who gave financial support to Brown as he worked against slavery in Kansas, Missouri, and finally Harpers Ferry. One of the committee, Gerrit Smith, gave nearby farmland to African Americans to homestead. In 1849, Brown with two of his sons bought 244 acres and moved here. After Virginia executed John Brown for treason on December 2, 1859, Smith and others helped his widow and children survive here.

John Brown is buried under two tombstones. In the late 1850s, Brown asked that an old family gravestone, originally for his grandfather Capt. John Brown, who died in 1776, be moved to this place.[1] On the morning of his execution, Brown asked that three more names be added to the stone: his own, his son Oliver's, killed in the Harpers Ferry raid on October 17, 1859, and his son Watson's, who was wounded in the Harpers Ferry raid and died two days later. This was done, and their bodies rest here with his. The stone also commemorates a third son who lies elsewhere: "In memory of Frederick, son of John and Dianthe Brown, Born Dec. 21, 1830, and murdered at Osawatomie, Kansas, Aug. 30, 1856, for his adherence to the cause of freedom." This frail stone still stands, protected now with a plexiglass enclosure.

Brown and his children and followers lie at the foot of an imposing boulder. Keepers of Brown's memory decided to add a more impressive memorial, so in 1916, they put a beautiful bronze plaque on the boulder. Graced at the top with a portrait of Brown, it proclaims in large type, "Here lies buried John Brown." It continues with three paragraphs that tell of Brown's fight against slavery at Osawatomie and Harpers Ferry. Large letters then add, "Here lie buried with him twelve of his followers."

John Brown, put to death in 1859, went insane during the Nadir of race relations, 1890–1925. His image suffered accordingly. On the left is the photograph of himself he preferred, here signed "God Bless." Above is John Steuart Curry's portrait, part of Curry's mural, "Bleeding Kansas," in the Kansas State Capitol. Brown wore a beard only during the last months of his life, as a disguise—a federal price was on his head because he had helped eleven slaves escape from along the Kansas-Missouri border and escorted them to Canada. During the Nadir and to about 1970, artists and authors thought the beard was appropriate because it made Brown look like a religious fanatic, which is how Curry portrayed him, with blood on his hands and a tornado in the background.

The rest of the plaque mocks John Brown's life and mission. The ten men killed at Harpers Ferry are listed first—the last two identified as "Negro."[2] Then a separate box tells of four who escaped but were captured and hanged two weeks after Brown—the last two identified as "Negro."[3] A final box tells of six who escaped—again the last two identified as "Negro."

The racial designation does inform visitors that African Americans participated in the raid, although the plaque would certainly "feel" quite different if "Caucasian" were placed after each white person's name. The real crime of the plaque, however, is the placement of the names of blacks at the bottom in each category.

John Brown would be outraged. In 1838, the Brown family was living in Franklin Mills, Ohio, and had joined the nearby Congregational church. It held a summer revival, and on the second day, some African Americans attended. Ushers told them to sit by the door in the back, in the spot where the stove stood in the winter. According to Stephen B. Oates, a Brown biographer, "such discrimination in the House of God made Brown blazing mad." The next night he escorted some of the African Americans down to the Brown family pew. The deacons were upset and admonished Brown for what he had done, but the next night he again led the blacks to his pew.

John Brown lived perhaps the most integrated life of any white man in the nineteenth century. Many African American leaders of the day—Martin Delaney, Frederick Douglass, Henry Highland Garnet, Harriet Tubman, and others—knew and respected him. He deliberately chose to live at North Elba in part to be near black neighbors, and he lost not only his own life but the lives of three of his sons in the struggle for racial equality. It is heartbreaking that this man should get a segregated marker in the twentieth century.

The tentacles of white supremacy still linger across America, from the provincial streets of Alba, Texas (chapter 37), to the sophisticated meeting rooms of Manhattan's Union League Club (chapter 81). They clutch at the throat of the America we could be. Even so, it is astonishing to find them here at the epicenter of antiracist idealism in American life. John Brown's body lies a-moldering in the grave *here*. Immediately above, his symbolic meaning is desecrated.

Just as disturbing was the fact that the two staff persons who had worked at John Brown's Farm for a combined total of more than 40 years had never noticed the segregation until I pointed it out to them in 1998. They care about the site and the man. Unlike many U.S. history textbooks, they do not portray Brown as crazy; they respect his idealism. Nevertheless, listing the blacks last was just normal discourse to them, as it was to those who put up the plaque in 1916.[4] John Brown would have noticed. John Brown would never have permitted it, the way we do.[5]

1. After the captain's widow died, the family had erected a larger stone for them both, making the earlier one surplus.
2. A separate paragraph lists two others who were hanged in March of the next year and are also buried here.
3. These men, Shields Green and John Anthony Copeland, are memorialized on a cenotaph in Oberlin, Ohio.

4. When I visited again in 2018, the (new) curator toured us around Brown's house with obvious sympathy for his racial views. He had noticed the segregation on the plaque; indeed, he had read this chapter. He suggested putting blacks last might result from the order being in order of enlistment; the African Americans were the newest; but that wouldn't explain why they were each marked "Negro."

5. Stephen B. Oates, *To Purge This Land With Blood* (Amherst: U. of MA Press, 1984), 43; W. E. B. Du Bois, *John Brown* (NY: International, 1987 [1909]); Barrie Stavis, *John Brown: The Sword and the Word* (NY: A. S. Barnes, 1970); Truman Nelson, "Thoreau and John Brown," in William J. Schafer, ed., *The Truman Nelson Reader* (Amherst: U. of MA Press, 1989), 195–214; Richard Warch and Jonathan Fanton, eds., *John Brown* (Englewood Cliffs, NJ: Prentice-Hall, 1973).

────── ✯ ──────

81. The Union League Club: Traitors to Their Own Cause

NEW YORK *Manhattan*

On East 37th Street at the corner of Park Avenue stands a handsome building of brick and stone. "Of the many professional, political, and social clubs in this section," said *The WPA Guide to New York City* in 1939, "the most famous is the Union League Club." The building boasts this bronze marker:

UNION LEAGUE CLUB

Founded in 1863
This building its fourth home Erected in 1930

Such a bland plaque! The convoluted history of this private club deserves much more.

For more than a century, the Union League Club was virtually synonymous with the leadership of the Republican Party in New York and to a degree nationally. Indeed, in 1880, the club required prospective new members to "agree with the principles of the Republican Party as hitherto expressed." What happened in the Union League Club, exemplified in its changing membership policies, reflected and even helped cause the decay of idealism in the Republican Party. That decay sapped the will of the party to carry out the principles that prompted its birth in the 1850s and still hung on as late as 1890.

Professor Wolcott Gibbs, Rev. Henry Bellows, and other public-spirited citizens organized the Union League of America to combat the pro-secession sentiment that dominated New York City early in the Civil War. During the so-called New York City Draft Riot in July 1863, Democrats targeted its first home overlooking Union Square. Members of the Union League had to gather at their clubhouse to protect it from the arson and looting these thugs visited upon other pro-Union institutions and African Americans. According to Will Irwin's history of the Union League, members decided then "if they got out of this thing alive they would make the Club defy public sentiment by raising and equipping a regiment of Negro troops and sending them to the front. More than that, they would march these freed men through the city streets."

This illustration, from *Harper's Weekly*, shows the "presentation of the colors to the First Colored Regiment of New York by the ladies of the city in front of the old Union League Club in 1864." The "Mothers, Wives, and Sisters of the members of the New York Union

League Club" signed the "Presentation Address" as "Subscribers to the Flag." In part, they said, "When you look at this Flag and rush to battle or stand at guard beneath its sublime motto: 'GOD AND LIBERTY!' remember that it is also an emblem of love and honor from the daughters of this great metropolis, to her brave champions in the field, and that they will anxiously watch your career, glorying in your heroism, ministering to you when wounded and ill, and honoring your martyrdom with benedictions and with tears." In 1864, this was a remarkable statement across lines of gender, race, and social class. First on the list of signers was Mrs. John Jacob Astor, wife of perhaps the richest man in America!

The next year, the club did precisely that. Public sentiment had changed so rapidly, however, that white New Yorkers now lined the streets to cheer the regiment. A few months later, when white segregationists removed the widow of an African American soldier from a streetcar, the Union League Club came to her defense. When the club prepared to take the case to court, the streetcar lines caved in and dropped their discriminatory policy. The club then brought its antiracist ideals even closer to home. Like all other Northern black regiments, the Union League Club's was headed by white officers, but it boasted an African American chaplain and an integrated officers' dining hall. The club did not admit African Americans to membership, but it did host a reception for the officers of the regiment and, against the wishes of a few members, included the chaplain among the invited guests.

Throughout the rest of the war, the Union League Club hosted fundraising activities to provide decent hospitals for wounded soldiers. It played an important role in helping Lincoln carry New York State in 1864, although he again lost the city, as it was still a Democratic stronghold. During Reconstruction, the club helped start majority-black but interracial Union League chapters across the South that helped African Americans organize politically.

The club's idealism, like that of the larger Republican Party in the 1860s and early 1870s, stemmed from the "natural rights" tradition that Thomas Jefferson had enshrined in the Declaration of Independence. Abraham Lincoln referred to that tradition repeatedly, and after he died, the Union League Club and Republican Party sought to bring about the "new birth of freedom" foretold at Gettysburg. In Congress, Republicans had already passed the Homestead Act and Morrill Act, making farmland and higher education more accessible to the people. Now, Southern Republicans wrote imaginative progressive provisions into the new constitutions for the "reconstructed" states. These constitutions decreased the number of capital crimes and replaced flogging and branding with time in the penitentiary. They allowed Catholics and Jews to vote freely and run for office, and they also let married women hold property in their own right. In Florida, they granted the Seminoles one seat in the house and one in the senate. They started free, state-funded public school systems in the South for both races—previously, education had been costly for whites, while teaching African Americans to read and write had been a felony. Other clauses allowed a family to hold onto their house when declaring bankruptcy. According to historian William Evans, "Many of their provisions were immensely popular." In New York City, the Union

League Club's heady mixture of idealism and strong local organizing proved irresistible: the club had 1,400 members within ten years. Similar clubs grew in Boston, Philadelphia, and Chicago.[1]

Why wouldn't the Union League Club want to tell this marvelous story on its own historical marker? For that matter, why not tell it on its own website? As of 2019, the club says merely that it was founded "to help preserve the Union" and that some members "were instrumental in establishing The Metropolitan Museum of Art in 1870." Nothing about its role in the Civil War or Reconstruction!

The answer is straightforward, if heartbreaking: because nearly everything the club has done in the last 120 years has betrayed the ideals of its founding.

How could this happen?

Throughout Reconstruction, Democrats used violence to undermine the political rights of African Americans and white Republicans in the South, targeting Union Leaguers. According to Michael W. Fitzgerald, who studied the Union League in Mississippi and Alabama, "Of 362 individuals identified as League activists, at least 15 met violent deaths from the period 1868 to 1871, and another 7 were shot but lived. 26 were assaulted or fired upon, 22 seriously harassed, and 4 driven into exile. These categories together total 74, over one-fifth of the identified activists in Alabama and Mississippi."

After 1871, Democrats grew even bolder. Chapter 43 tells how white supremacists used force and fraud to take back control of the Southern states. The end of Reconstruction in 1876–77 gave rise to the uneasy "fusion" period. African Americans still voted, although not freely, and white Democrats were never sure they could keep control of state governments against coalitions of black voters and white Republicans and Populists. What were Northern liberals to do in this situation? Two solutions seemed possible: appeal to white voters in the North to preserve citizenship for all, thus maintaining the interracial Republican coalition in the South, or appeal to whites South and North on grounds other than race, such as Republican economic policies. The former group was called Stalwarts; the latter, including some former Democrats, got dubbed Mugwumps, Half-Breeds, or Liberals. Both factions contended for control of the Republican Party; the arguments went on into the night at the Union League Club.

President Ulysses Grant supported civil rights in the South and humane policies toward Native Americans in the West, but he undermined his own moral authority by allowing scandals to spoil his administration. The

Mugwumps cultivated a reform reputation. The next Republican candidate, Rutherford B. Hayes, promised both civil rights and clean government. When he thought he had lost the disputed election of 1876, Hayes initially bemoaned the loss of black rights that he knew would follow. But during months of negotiations, he gave up on the Stalwart view and sought the support of Southern Democrats, both to get confirmed and to build a new white Republican coalition in the South. He agreed to recognize white Democrat governments in the South in return for their pledges to respect the rights of African Americans.

Within months, his agreement with white Democrats collapsed, because they continued their campaign of terror against Republicans. Prosecution proved futile since white Democrats on juries would not convict other whites. What happened during the 1878 Congressional elections shocked members of the Union League Club. In Caddo Parish, Louisiana, whites killed upwards of 75 African Americans on election day. Fairfield County, South Carolina, was 75% African American, yet counted not a single Republican vote! Of 294 Southern counties with African American majorities, only 62 voted Republican compared to 125 in 1876 and most of them in 1874. It was clear to everyone that terror and fraud were responsible. President Hayes said, "I am reluctantly forced to admit that the experiment was a failure." In 1879, Republicans returned to Stalwart antiracist principles with Hayes's blessing.

But in the 1880s, the ideas of the Stalwarts began to sound shopworn, particularly to new members of the Union League Club who had not fought in the Civil War. Benjamin Harrison, elected president in 1888, ran a Mugwump campaign and ignored the aspirations of African Americans during his first year in office. But like Hayes, he grew so frustrated by Southern white outrages that he again took up the cause of black voting and civil rights promised by the Fourteenth and Fifteenth Amendments. With his blessing, in 1890, the Stalwarts reasserted themselves one last time in the Republican Party and the Union League Club. Under the leadership of Henry Cabot Lodge, senator from Massachusetts, Republicans introduced the Federal Elections Bill to promote honest elections in the South and publicize unfair elections.

White Democrats labeled it the "Force Bill" and pulled out all the stops to defeat it. Governor John Gordon of Georgia, ex-Confederate general and Ku Klux Klan leader (chapter 53), threatened a Southern white boycott of

Northern businesses, which worried Union League Club members. Demo-cratic senators got some Republican senators to defect in return for their votes on the McKinley tariff and got others to defect in return for their votes for free silver. The result was breathtakingly close: after passing in the House, the elections bill lost by one vote in the Senate.

The defeat was hardly novel. From the Civil War to the end of the century, not a single Democrat in Congress, North or South, ever voted for a single piece of civil rights legislation. Unless Republicans held large majorities in both houses or maintained perfect party discipline, they could never pass civil rights bills.

In 1892, Democrat Grover Cleveland's campaign made an issue of Repub-lican support for the "Force Bill." Democrats said it would lead to "Negro domination in the South" which would be "bad for the country." Republi-cans were tarred as "nigger lovers" and lampooned for "waving the bloody shirt," referring to their repeated accusations that Southern white Democrats had violently attacked Republicans to win elections fraudulently. Again, this was nothing new. What was novel was the response in the Union League Club and the Republican Party—they now backed away from the subject.[2]

This was the clear signal that the Republican Party and the Union League Clubs had abandoned the cause of equal rights. Emboldened by the defeat of the Lodge bill, white Democrats in Mississippi responded by passing a new constitution that used innovative "legal" devices to keep African Americans from voting.[3] All other Southern and border states emulated Mississippi by 1907. In 1894, Democrats repealed the remaining federal election statutes. In the Deep South, it now became too dangerous to claim membership in the Union League, and it disintegrated across the South. In 1896, in *Plessy v. Ferguson*, the U.S. Supreme Court declared racial segregation legal as the country descended further into the Nadir of American race relations lasting from 1890 until beyond 1920. Chapters 45 and 54 tell how desperate became the position of African Americans in the South. Chapters 15 and 86 tell how whites as far north as Vermont and Montana came to commemorate white supremacy during this time.

Northern and Southern whites now reunited under the banner of white supremacy. In the 1890s, Memorial Day celebrations organized by Union League members no longer stressed the need for vigilance against Southern attempts to overthrow the Union victory. Often, they invited white South-erners to speak, who admitted they had been wrong to secede but right to oppose "Negro domination." In 1891, Lodge suggested that the United States should keep out "Slovacks" from Eastern Europe because they represented "races most alien to the body of the American people," and he did not mean African American people. When Republicans retook the White House in 1896, the McKinley administration made no significant efforts on behalf of African American rights beyond appointing a few blacks as postmasters in Southern towns. Instead, it "made a number of gestures to honor the Confederate dead," in the words of historian Kurt Piehler. Soon, McKinley and Lodge too were involved in rationalizing the Philippine-American War by demeaning the capabilities of these "little brown brothers." The Republican Party lost what little authority it still had to improve the lot of minority races. From then on, whenever Republicans brought up the attacks white Southerners inflicted on African Americans, Democrats retaliated by citing outrages the Republican administration had visited upon Filipinos. The unfortunate result was to stifle antiracist idealism in *both* parties until the 1940s.

The Union League in the 1860s had stood for equal opportunity, and if the club honored rich Americans who had made the most of their opportunities, it still honored the principle of upward mobility. Plutocrats like J. P. Morgan and John D. Rockefeller joined for the club's prestige, however, not because of what it stood for. Soon it stood for nothing. After the Mugwumps took over in the early 1890s, in Irwin's words "the Union League Club went to the right of right." Now the club began to stand for ideas antithetical to its founding ideals, for example, refusing to admit upwardly mobile Jews, Italians, Catholics, and others of "incorrect background." Joseph Seligman, a Jew, leading banker, and friend of U. S. Grant, had been a founder of the club. His son Jesse became a member in 1868. In 1893, after 25 years of membership, fourteen as a vice president, Jesse Seligman resigned when members blackballed his own son Theodore because he was a Jew. A representative of the "Anti-Semitic Party, as it is called at the Union League," according to a *New York Times* report, blamed Jews for their own exclusion: "Opposition is not based upon any dislike of particular individuals, but upon the general belief that men of the Jewish race and religion do not readily affiliate in a social way with persons not of their own persuasion."

Abraham Lincoln had predicted that once Americans started reading the Declaration of Independence as "all men are created equal, *except Negroes*," it would not be long before they read it as "all men are created equal, *except*

Negroes, and foreigners, and Catholics." Ironically, the organization founded to promote his principles now proved his prediction all too accurate.

In *The Protestant Establishment*, sociologist E. Digby Baltzell concluded that the upper class in Northern cities "degenerated" into a caste at this point in U.S. history. The Union League Clubs led the way; upper-class clubs around the country followed suit.[4] The most elite in New Orleans was the Boston Club, the key organizer of Mardi Gras. Some of its founders were Jews, including Judah P. Benjamin, secretary of the treasury in the Confederacy, and the club had a Jewish vice president as late as 1904. But by the 1920s, the Boston Club had no Jewish members. A similar irony occurred at Harvard, which barred an African American student from the very dormitory where his father had lived decades earlier when attending the university. All across America country clubs quietly began keeping Jews, blacks, and sometimes Catholics away from their golf courses and swimming pools.

Having put their caste principles in place regarding membership, some in the Union League Club now turned to its employees. The management committee decided to fire the club's black servants and replace them with an all-white staff. At this point, ex-Union general Wager Swayne, a long-time member, intervened. During Reconstruction, Swayne had headed the Freedmen's Bureau in Alabama, helped found Talladega College, and was appointed the military governor of Alabama. After Reconstruction ended, Swayne became a lawyer in New York City and vice president of the Union League Club. "Here, just before his death in 1902, he fought a last battle for his youthful principles," in Fitzgerald's words. According to the *New York Times*, Swayne was "one of a few who got up a petition" to bring the matter to an open vote. "He spoke in favor of the Negroes, and after several others had talked on the same side the . . . decision was overthrown."

This victory was Pyrrhic, however, because it led to making *all* the wait staff black, which it still was at the Union League Club in the late 1990s. This pattern perpetuates plantation race relations, implying that the races should be separate and blacks should serve whites. Other clubs and elite restaurants adopted this practice, including George Pullman for his Pullman sleeping cars. Most whites in these institutions adopted Southern etiquette as well, calling black servers by their first names while demanding that blacks use courtesy titles like "sir" or "madam" for whites (chapter 45). Pullman went a step further: he required all Pullman porters to take on *his* first name and wear little badges showing it! That way passengers didn't have to interact with their social inferiors learning their real first names but could show the disrespect implied by unequal nouns of address simply by calling for "George."

Desegregating elite social institutions in New York City has taken decades and is still incomplete. Although whites have long agreed that many African Americans sing and dance well, the Metropolitan Opera engaged no black opera singers until after the Supreme Court had made segregation illegal,[5] and the Rockettes, Radio City Music Hall's famed chorus line, were exclusively white until 1987! "[Blacks] would destroy the purity of the line," claimed Russell Markert, its founder, in the 1970s. Markert would not even let a white dancer get a tan, as, "It would make her look like a colored girl." The Links Club, even more elite than the Union League Club and a key meeting place for national corporate leaders, continued to exclude Jews at least into the 1980s.

After years of acrimony, the Union League Club finally let an African American join in the 1990s. He was Earl Graves, owner of the magazine *Black Enterprise.* Across the United States, many country clubs have done the same thing, especially after the Professional Golfers' Association refused in 1990 to sanction tournaments at segregated golf clubs. Sportswriters then pointed out that many clubs refused to admit a second person of color.

Letting in one person of color was a step in the right direction for the Union League Club, but it was a little step taken very late. For a century, the Union League Club had made itself irrelevant to the hopes of mankind. As a waiter said to me, "It's just rich people making connections, man." Of course, the Union League Club is hardly irrelevant to its members. In 1996, for example, it hosted a "Career Fair" which "accommodated the 36 corporate representatives and 200 candidate attendees in an atmosphere conducive to networking and career advancement." Such connections help keep opportunity unequal in America. That's why Americans should care when a private organization like the Union League Club segregates itself by race, gender, religion, and class. And that's why New Yorkers should place a more explanatory historical marker in front of its entrance, telling how the elite turned their backs on the rights of all in favor of promoting the privileges of the rich. If members used their considerable social and economic power to prevent such a marker from going up, the effort—and resulting discussion—might still be salutary for the city and even for the club.[6]

Chapter 83 shows how the New York elite extended antiblack and anti-Jewish exclusion into the Connecticut suburbs in the 1920s and 1930s. Chapter 86 shows how antiblack symbols became part of the culture in all-white northern Vermont in the 1890s.

1. The Philadelphia Club boasts a historical marker out front that tells how it was founded "to preserve the Union" and "recruited and financed troops during the Civil War." However, it says nothing about race, even though the League had specifically helped organize five "colored" regiments. During Reconstruction, the League worked to end streetcar segregation in Philadelphia and favored civil rights, but the marker says nothing about these things either, surely because the Club turned away from racial equity thereafter.

2. Republican ideology had been strained by the three I's: Indian wars (flattening the last independent tribes in the West), immigrants (voting Democratic), and imperialism (the emerging clamor to annex Hawaii, for instance). In the face of these anti-democratic pressures, Republicans found it hard to invoke the old natural-rights tradition on behalf of African Americans. The new "scientific racism" deriving from Darwinism (chapter 68) provided an antithetical intellectual tradition to rationalize abandoning the doctrine of equal rights for all.

3. The 1890 Mississippi Constitution was illegal under any reasonable interpretation of the Fourteenth and Fifteenth Amendments, but the U.S. Supreme Court was hardly reasonable in the 1890s.

4. The Union League Club in Philadelphia took the same journey, from financing a black regiment in the Civil War to sanctioning overt racism in the 1890s.

5. The first African American opera singer was Marian Anderson in January 1955, more than fifteen years after her headline-making concert at the Lincoln Memorial.

6. Federal Writers' Project, *The WPA Guide to NY City* (NY: New Press, 1996 [1939]), 214–15; Will Irwin, et al., *A History of the Union League Club of NY City* (NY: Dodd, Mead, 1952), 8, 31–32, 78; William Evans, *Beyond the Rivers of Ethiopia* (Pomona, CA: manuscript, 1997), 542; James M. McPherson, *Battle Cry of Freedom* (NY: Oxford UP, 1988), 688; Ernest A. McKay, *The Civil War and New York City* (Syracuse, NY: Syracuse UP, 1990), 178, 239–43, 287, 301; Philip T. Drotning, *Guide to Black History* (Garden City, NY: Doubleday, 1968), 139; Kenneth T. Jackson, *Encyclopedia of New York City* (New Haven, CT: Yale UP, 1995), 1016, 1210; Union League, "About the ULC," 8/2018, unionleagueclub.org/Default.aspx?p=dynamicmodule&pageid=390621&ssid=311686&vnf=1; Michael W. Fitzgerald, *The Union League Movement in the Deep South* (Baton Rouge: LA State UP, 1989), 222, 234–42; Stanley P. Hirshson, *Farewell to the Bloody Shirt* (Chicago, IL: Quadrangle, 1962), 24–26, 126–27, 181, 206, 219 238–41, 251; Joseph T. Glatthaar, *Forged in Battle: The Civil War Alliance of Black Soldiers and White Officers* (NY: Free Press, 1990), 45–49, 58; J. Morgan Kousser, *The Shaping of Southern Politics* (New Haven, CT: Yale UP, 1974), 29–31; Horace Samuel Merrill, *Bourbon Leader: Grover Cleveland and the Democratic Party* (Boston: Little, Brown, and Co., 1957), 144; Alexander H. Stephens, *Recollections of Alexander H. Stephens: His Diary Kept When a Prisoner at Fort Warren* (NY: Doubleday, Page, 1910), 172–74; Mary R. Dearing, *Veterans in Politics: The Story of the GAR* (Baton Rouge: LA State UP, 1952), 435; Matthew F. Jacobson, *Whiteness of a Different Color* (Cambridge, MA: Harvard UP, 1998), 77; Kurt Piehler, *Remembering War the American Way* (DC: Smithsonian Institution Press, 1995), 65–66; Eric Anderson, *Race and Politics in NC* (Baton Rouge: LA State UP, 1981), 243; David Dunlap, "Council Panel Debates Bill to Bar Club Discrimination," *The New York Times*, 12/23/83; Maxwell Whiteman, *Gentlemen in Crisis* (Philadelphia, PA: Union League of Philadelphia, 1975), 228–29; E. Digby Baltzell, *The Protestant Establishment* (NY: Random House, 1964), 56,

138–40, 374–79; "Mr. Seligman Blackballed," *The New York Times*, 4/15/1893; John M. Barry, *Rising Tide* (NY: Simon and Schuster, 1997), 218; Irving Kolodin, *The Metropolitan Opera* (NY: Knopf, 1967), 547; Charles Francisco, *The Radio City Music Hall* (NY: Dutton, 1979), 69; "Day by Day," *The New York Times*, 3/30/83; Gregory J. Peterson, "What's All White, and Dances in NY?", *The New York Times*, 5/31/85; Robert Fikes Jr., ed., *Racist & Sexist Quotations* (Saratoga, CA: R & E Publishers, 1992), 69; Tom Callahan, "Golf Country-Club Dilemma," *US News and World Report*, 8/20/90, 60; John McCormick and Sharon Begley, "How to Raise a Tiger," *Newsweek* (12/9/96): 52–59; Peter Finch, "Racism: Golf's Intolerable Handicap," *Business Week* (8/13/90): 112; B. Clay, "Breaking Par Against Racism: Beyond Shoal Creek," *Black Enterprise* 27 (9/96): 100–104; Otis L. Graham, "The One and Only Tiger Woods," *The New York Times*, 8/31/96, 21; "Motive Questioned in Admittance of Black Doctor to Golf Club," *Jet* (7/12/93): 50; www.bergen.com/golf95/bergpri.html.#Alpine, 6/96.

------------------ ★ ------------------

82. Selective Memory at USS *Intrepid*

NEW YORK *Manhattan*

The aircraft carrier USS *Intrepid* is probably the largest object on display in any museum in America. After seeing extended duty in World War II and Vietnam, it's now serving another tour as the *Intrepid* Sea, Air, and Space Museum on the west side of Manhattan. The *Intrepid* is a feel-good museum that would rather exhibit anything but the realities of war. Since war isn't a feel-good subject, *Intrepid* can't say much about even "The Good War," World War II. And since the Vietnam War isn't a feel-good war, *Intrepid* simply ignored it in 1999, when I was there. Since I have not revisited, I shall retain the present tense, but I invite visitors to let me know if it has improved.

The *Intrepid* Museum avoids giving visitors more than the briefest glimpse of the reality of the Second World War. Its brochure describes *Intrepid* as "the battle-scarred veteran of World War II," but it isn't any longer. The Navy repaired all World War II damage decades ago. The museum does not even mark the locations where three Japanese kamikaze attacks hit the ship. *Intrepid* also imitates the practice of *Time-Life's* series on World War II, which Paul Fussell derides for its reluctance to show a dead American. The closest the museum comes are two photographs in one corner, several feet above viewers' heads. The first shows sailors cleaning up damage from an air attack and removing a dead crewman whose body is not fully visible. An adjacent photograph shows a dozen clean white body bags, awaiting burial at sea. The "Self-Guided Visit" material *Intrepid* distributes to schoolchildren omits even these glimpses of death. No wonder every visitor in the dozens of photographs in its advertising brochure is smiling. Everyone looks entertained. No one looks thoughtful. The *Intrepid* Museum has not given them a thing to think about.

Intrepid served three tours in Vietnam from 1966 through 1968, winning "best ship in fleet" on its third tour, but no display in the museum covers the Vietnam War or the ship's involvement in it. This is a grotesque misrepresentation, not least because *Intrepid* no longer *is* a World War II aircraft carrier; between World War II and Vietnam, the ship was rebuilt, and her entire configuration is now that of a Vietnam-era carrier. Nevertheless, apart from half a dozen aircraft from the Vietnam era visitors can inspect on *Intrepid*'s flight deck, the museum teaches nothing about naval and air combat in our longest war. A docent told me that a segment in one of the videos treated Vietnam, but I could not find it. In "The Politics of Public History," historian Michael Wallace agrees that the museum's videos omit *Intrepid*'s role in Vietnam; according to the board of retired admirals that vets the museum's interpretive programs by order of the Navy, Vietnam is too "political."

Aircraft from *Intrepid* flew 13,407 sorties against civilian and military targets in North and South Vietnam throughout its three tours. These attacks raise at least two important moral and strategic questions that would seem to be critical for any museum seeking to explain the role of an aircraft carrier. First, is it right to deliberately bomb civilian targets? Second, do such attacks work? Are they effective in bringing a war to a victorious end? Neither question is raised—let alone answered—in the *Intrepid* museum.

When accused of making attacks on civilian targets, the Pentagon simply denied it was doing anything of the kind in Vietnam. These claims lent drama to the reporting that proved them untrue. In December 1966, Harrison Salisbury of *The New York Times* went to Hanoi, capital of North Vietnam, and Haiphong, its port city, and sent back written accounts and visual proof of hospitals and houses destroyed by U.S. bombing. As they learned these facts, many U.S. citizens changed their mind about the morality of the Vietnam War and started to question statements made by government officials.

Deliberate bombing of civilian targets was not limited to North Vietnam. During *Intrepid*'s tours in Vietnam, our "pacification camps" in South Vietnam became so full that units were ordered not to "generate" any more refugees. "Now peasants were not warned before an air strike was called in on their village," in the words of Robert Buckhout. Unannounced air strikes on civilians then became routine, even though they killed the people we professed to be helping. "They were killed in their villages because there was no room for them in the swamped pacification camps."

In "Public History after Charlottesville," I used the terms *wertrationalität* and *zweckrationalität* to describe differing human reactions to morally complex situations like Vietnam. People display *zweckrationalität* when their acts are in accord with the demands of an organization to which they belong, even if the demands don't accord with their own sense of right and wrong. Our bombing policy disgusted some American sailors including, according to Buckhout, half of the non-aviation junior officers aboard *Intrepid*'s sister carrier *Hancock*, who lodged an official protest against the war with the ship's captain. Four sailors from *Intrepid* famously deserted in October 1967, when the ship was docked at a U.S. naval base in Japan. A Japanese peace organization helped them get to Russia, where they were awarded the Lenin Peace Prize, and they wound up in Sweden. There, dubbed "The Intrepid Four," they advocated for an end to the war.

All we get from the *Intrepid* Museum on these matters is a prideful label about the A-6 attack bomber: "A-6 attacks on Haiphong were so devastating that North Vietnamese believed they were being bombed by B-52 Stratofortresses instead of by two-seat naval attack bombers." Taking pride in such a job well done provides a perfect example of technical rationality. "Only following orders" is one meaning of *zweckrationalität*. At the Nazi war crime trials in Nuremberg, the United States held that doing what the organization requires is no excuse when the required acts violate moral values.

Even by the standards of technical rationality, however, the A-6 attacks had a counterproductive effect on public opinion throughout Vietnam, stiffening the people's resolve to resist the American attackers. According to Fussell, based on his own World War II combat experience and his extensive reading of the literature, the same thing happened in Germany in World War II: American (and British) bombing gave German civilians and troops a morally sound reason to fight on. Freeman Dyson, who interviewed American pilots during World War II, agreed that Allied bombing had little to do with defeating the Nazis. American flight crews bragged ruefully, "We made a major onslaught on German agriculture."[1] On the other hand, bombing was effective in Japan in 1945 and Yugoslavia in 1999, which may now persuade Americans that air power can be relied upon. A serious analysis of the failure of air power to lead to victory in Vietnam might prove useful to the American people in Kosovo's aftermath. A thoughtful military museum could raise this issue by asking visitors: if the United States were cruelly bombed, would Americans surrender? Such thoughtfulness is out of the question at *Intrepid*, however, which only in this one A-6 label even acknowledges that it was *in* Vietnam.

For two years, the museum did treat Vietnam in a special exhibit, "On the Line: Intrepid and the Vietnam War," which closed in 2017.[2] However, that exhibit seems to have left little residue on the ship or its website. Online, the museum's main treatment of the Vietnam War is this paragraph:

> *Intrepid* aviators attacked a range of targets, including transportation links, petroleum resources and industrial facilities. *Intrepid* pilots scored two shoot-downs of North Vietnamese aircraft. Three pilots became prisoners of war, and 21 men lost their lives in combat or in operational accidents.

How easy it would be simply to insert "four sailors famously deserted," into the middle of that last sentence!

Some Vietnam vets have expressed anger and sorrow that the *Intrepid* Museum omits their stories. Leaving out Vietnam does violence to the ship's past and brings no honor to its veterans. Indeed, it invites them to feel shame, for they know why they are unmentioned. Telling the story of their service in Vietnam complete with the conflicts built into that war would respect the airmen and sailors who were caught in the middle of *Intrepid*. But a feel-good museum cannot help visitors think about *any* issue about modern war—strategic, moral, or intertwined.[3]

Chapter 39 tells of another war museum that also avoids asking hard questions about war.

1. Dyson says the bombing units kept details of their raids secret, not so much to keep the Germans from knowing what was up as to keep the failures of the campaign from being known either back home or to the boys in the squadrons.
2. I think this exhibit may have treated the war seriously. It did note the "Intrepid Four." As of September 2018, the website indicated (wrongly) that the exhibit was still open: "On the Line: *Intrepid* and the Vietnam War Now Open," intrepidmuseum.org/LatestNews /October-2015/On-the-Line--Intrepid-and-the-Vietnam-War-Now-Open. Online interviews with the former crew cover only shipboard activities, such as cooking for the men, and focus on technical details. Only one pilot speaks; he says nothing about the bombing.

3. Michael Wallace, "The Politics of Public History," in Jo Blatti, ed., *Past Meets Present* (DC: Smithsonian Institution Press, 1987), 47–48; Robert Buckhout, ed., *Toward Social Change* (NY: Harper and Row, 1971), 179; Ryuichi Kitano, "'Intrepid Four' Deserter Returns to U.S. Navy Base 50 Years On," *Asahi Shimbun*, 10/30/2017, asahi.com/ajw /articles/AJ201710300025.html; Peter Kelman, *Protesting the National Identity: The Cultures of Protest in 1960s Japan*; "Citizens' Activism and the Intrepid Four" (Sydney: U. of Sydney, 2001), ses.library.usyd.edu.au/bitstream/2123/2443/6/06chapter4.pdf; Freeman Dyson, *Disturbing the Universe* (NY: Harper and Row, 1979), 29; PBS Frontline video, *Remember My Lai* (1989); Studs Terkel, *"The Good War"* (NY: New Press, 1994? [1984]), 208–209.

NEW ENGLAND

83. Omitting the Town's Continuing Claim to Fame

CONNECTICUT *Darien*

Darien is a town of about 20,000, less than an hour's commute from Wall Street, where many of its heads of family work. In front of its town hall, a Connecticut historical marker put up in 1979 tells how, "Until the advent of the railroad in 1848, Darien remained a small rural community." Then, it relates how the railroad led to summer residents and eventually to a growing year-round population of commuters. But it leaves out Darien's principal claim to fame.

Darien used to be a sundown town—a town that forbade African Americans and Jews to remain overnight. Like traditional sundown towns (chapter 37), it even boasted a billboard: in about 1948, according to then-resident Larry Abbott, a sign reading "Gentiles Only" greeted visitors on Hollow Tree Ridge Road. After World War II, Darien won national notoriety for its exclusivity. Laura Z. Hobson's bestselling 1947 novel, *Gentleman's Agreement*, treated Darien's unwritten covenant that prohibited real estate sales to Jews. Gregory Peck starred in the film version, directed by Elia Kazan, which won the Academy Award for best picture.

In the 1940s, Darien kept even Roman Catholics out. Since then, according to residents and journalists, Darien hasn't changed its essence. "Darien seems really to be about exclusivity," according to writer Richard Todd, who researched Darien in 1985. "In a way, who doesn't live here seems to matter more than who does." Darien excluded Jews at least until the 1970s. Today, Jews can live in Darien, and a few do. But they're not welcomed. "It's an exclusionary town," one realtor said. "If I had a client who was Jewish and she said, 'Would I be comfortable there?' I'd say, 'No. Don't even look.'" In addition to Darien's overall racial exclusivity, its country clubs and other private clubs are arranged hierarchically to delineate further gradations of exclusion based on wealth, occupation, religion, ethnic group, and family ancestry. Several clubs still have no Jewish members; at least one has never let an Italian American join.[1]

Beginning in the early 1980s, perhaps to show the world that Darien was not racist, Darien High School let a few black girls, mostly from Harlem, attend under the aegis of A Better Chance (ABC), a program that sends disadvantaged minority teenagers to prep schools and affluent suburban high schools to prepare them to enter superior colleges. The program has been an educational success, "but not a social success," says Todd drily. As of 1999, the high school had never hired an Asian American, Latino, or African American teacher.[2]

Despite the ABC girls, according to Todd, "the overwhelming absence in Darien is the absence of black faces. If there was ever a time when a black householder lived here, no one seems to remember it. No black families at all live in Darien now. In the past there were a few black live-in servants, but there appear to be none today." Todd may have slightly overstated the case; the 1990 Census lists 58 African Americans in Darien. In 1998, however, the town's residents still confirmed the complete absence of black householders in most neighborhoods. Where the 58 lived was a puzzle. Five or ten were ABC students living in a house donated by the Congregational Church. A local Darien history expert speculated that some African Americans "may be live-in maids or gardeners"; others may be adopted children or occupants of a housing project for the elderly built in 1988.[3]

Why is Darien so white Anglo-Saxon Protestant (WASP)? Many residents affect puzzlement when the topic comes up, or cite social class. Indeed, Darien is so white partly because it is so rich. But Darien's economic segregation merely overlays and reinforces its racial segregation. African American families live in equally affluent parts of nearby Stamford—but not in Darien. Moreover, Darien's period of population growth—from World War II to 1960—coincided with a doubling of Connecticut's African American population. Yet Darien's black population dropped from 161 to 112 during those years, and of the 112, 89 were female, a startling imbalance reinforcing the speculation that most were live-in maids in white households. By 1980, Darien had just 27 African Americans, including not a single family.

The reasons Darien became even whiter were not unique to this town. Across the United States, in keeping with federal housing guidelines tout-ing segregation as good realty practice, hundreds of overwhelmingly white suburbs were built or expanded after 1945. These included Beverly Hills outside Los Angeles; Edina near Minneapolis; Oak Lawn southwest of Chicago; Grosse Pointe, Michigan; and the aptly named White Haven, Mississippi, just south of Memphis. In the 1970s, some of these once openly racist towns quietly let African Americans move in (chapter 53), especially in the South. Other "sundown suburbs" gave up their all-white policies after 2000 but remain overwhelmingly white, like Darien today.

Political scientist Andrew Hacker crystallized the reason for the whiteness of these suburbs: "If there is one sword which hangs over the heads of untold millions of white—and Northern—Americans it is that they cannot afford to live in close proximity to Negroes. The single social fact which can destroy the whole image of middle class respectability is to be known to reside in a neighborhood which has Negroes nearby." In short, one reason Darien's residents choose Darien is that living there tells the world that one has the money and social power to avoid African Americans and other people of lower social status. To be sure, there are good reasons to live in Darien. Its school system is excellent, the landscape is attractive, and the town beach is lovely. Status, however, is the primary drawing card.

Urban sociologists describe suburban segregation as a social problem rather than an achievement to be proud of. Indeed, it was the key fact behind the Kerner Commission's famous 1968 warning that the United States is divided "into two societies; one largely Negro and poor, located in the central cities; the other, predominantly white and affluent, located in the suburbs." Thus, the Dariens in the world make a profound difference, as their example drives the entire system of residential segregation that still divides northern cities and suburbs along lines of caste and class. Thorstein Veblen explained how the upper class typically influences Americans' values: "our standard of decency in expenditure . . . is set by the usage of those next above us in reputability; until . . . all canons of reputability and decency, and all standards of consumption, are traced back by insensible gradations to the usages and habits of thought of the highest social and pecuniary class—the wealthy leisure class." This is especially true when it comes to choosing a place to live. So long as very WASP towns like Darien are the benchmarks of status, neighborhoods that are less WASP and less affluent cannot afford to welcome African Americans and Latin Americans—sometimes even Jewish Americans—without damaging their own social standing. Darien sets the standard.

Suburbs segregated by race and class contribute to the difficulties facing metropolitan areas in a second way: they literally do not take care of their own problems. Instead, they shunt them off on other communities, particularly onto the urban core. Like every community, even Darien with all its wealth creates some people who need help—alcoholics, the mentally ill, Alzheimer's victims, deviants, the homeless. They must leave. It is impossible to be homeless in Darien. Nor has Darien any group homes for people who need special care. Until recently, an aging parent who required a condominium, assisted living, or a nursing home could not live in Darien, for only expensive single-family homes were allowed there. Darien sends its people with social problems to Bridgeport or New York City and then looks down its collective nose at Bridgeport and "the City" for being unable to cope.

Residents of Darien hire maids whose families cannot afford to live in Darien. For that matter, Darien employs teachers, police officers, telephone linemen, and appliance repairers who also cannot afford to live there. Teachers commute for as long as an hour and maids come by train from Harlem. Inequality then becomes self-reinforcing: Harlem cannot tax where these maids work, only the modest apartments where they live. Harlem must educate its children but commands inadequate means to do so well. Darien ends up with higher-paid teachers, smaller classes, and better school equipment. In 2019, Darien had a lower property tax rate than other towns in Connecticut, while its schools and library were the highest rated because the tax base was so high. (Sometimes, Darien gets ranked the wealthiest town in the United States.) Students have high SAT scores, partly because the SAT correlates with social class. Thus, the academic disparities that help perpetuate the tradition of black maids working for higher-educated white homeowners get replicated in the next generation.

Darien contributes to America's urban problems in a third way. The town exemplifies what urban sociologists call "defended neighborhoods." Beginning around 2000, one couple, Christopher and Peggy Stefanoni, made a crusade and a living trying to build affordable housing in Darien and suing the town when it stopped them. City amenities are also restricted. No sign points to the town beach. Once found, signs mark it "Private" and a sentry checks even cyclists and pedestrians for beach stickers available only to Darien residents. Can anyone imagine New York City doing the same at Central Park? Even street signs are in short supply in Darien—the town marks only the side streets at most intersections, on the theory that drivers should already know the name of the main street they're on. When I suggested that visitors might find this confusing, one resident replied that Darien didn't really *want* a lot of visitors, and keeping Darien confusing for strangers might deter crime. Some residential streets are even posted "private."

Darien's ideology embodies a paradox. On one hand, Darien residents are happy that everyone knows their town is overwhelmingly WASP; its racial exclusivity is a sign of their good breeding. On the other hand, being overtly proud to live in an overwhelmingly WASP town would show bad breeding. The inhabitants of Darien take pride in imagining themselves to be very different from sundown towns out in the sticks. When opinion pollsters ask householders questions about race relations, Darien residents know to answer in a non-racist way.

Nevertheless, defended neighborhoods lead to defended hearts, and communities like Darien have plenty of these. People in defended neighborhoods keep their school systems separate and block attempts at metropolitan-wide desegregation. They strongly oppose what they view as intrusions by "outsiders"—people or governments from the larger metropolitan area—and maintain a strong "not in my backyard" philosophy. Usually, their political ideology blames the poor for creating their own poverty, perhaps because they don't really know any poor people. "We made it, why can't 'they'?" "Look at 'their' SAT scores!" Even the children are affected. A recent graduate of Darien High School told me that Darien's whiteness "allowed for the kids to joke and to maintain racist stereotypes. A lot of my friends came in with racist jokes, and you never had to worry about it." For example, students routinely say, "Don't Jew me." Children in Darien also grow up inexperienced in dealing with other races and feel uneasy when visiting "the City" as teenagers.

Of course, for Darien residents to imagine that their town has not been and is not racist requires considerable amnesia. The town has a museum, but its online presence never hints at anything remotely off-putting. Docents take fifth graders on "a guided journey by bus, to local historic spots in our wonderful town . . . " In these circumstances, proposing to revise Darien's historical marker might launch a useful civic dialogue. All the marker now says about the twentieth century is, "A few daily commuters to New York City then were forerunners of the many who have settled here and changed

Darien into a residential suburb of metropolitan New York." A possible revision might add,

> *Throughout the twentieth century, Darien excluded would-be residents*
> *on the basis of their race and religion. Laura Hobson's 1947 novel*
> *Gentleman's Agreement, made into a movie by Elia Kazan, tells how*
> *Darien used to keep out Jews. Darien is still overwhelmingly white; some*
> *clubs within it still keep out African Americans, Catholics, and Jews.*
> *Thus, Darien poses a problem for the New York metropolitan area and*
> *indeed for the nation.[4]*

1. In 2019, I did not check whether the clubs still exclude. The wealthiest of all, Wee Burn, no longer keeps women from being full members.
2. By 2018, the overall district's teaching staff was 1 % Asian American, 1 % African American, and 3 % Latino.
3. This project aroused major opposition.
4. Darien town website, www.darien.lib.ct.us/townhall/Tour/sign.htm, 8/98; Alice P. Hackett, *Sixty Years of Best Sellers* (NY: R. R. Bowker, 1956), 187; Richard Todd, "Darien, CT," *New England Monthly* (3/86): 43, 86; Bureau of the Census, *1990 Census, CT* (DC: GPO , 1992); Andre Cavalier, conversation, 7/98; ff col.com/towns/darien /darien1.htm, 8/98; David O. White, "Blacks in CT," in David M. Roth, ed., *CT History and Culture* (Hartford: CT Historical Commission, 1985), 202; E. Digby Baltzell, *The Protestant Establishment* (NY: Random House, 1964), 126; Andrew Hacker, "Sociology and Ideology," in Max Black, ed., *The Social Theories of Talcott Parsons* (Englewood Cliffs, NJ: Prentice-Hall, 1961), 289; Thorstein Veblen, *The Theory of the Leisure Class* (NY: New American Library, 1953 [1899]), 81; Mike Bryant, conversation, 11/97; Larry Abbott, conversation, 11/97; Loewen, *Sundown Towns* (NY: New Press, 2005); Lisa Prevost, "Snob Zones: Fear, Money and Real Estate,"*Salon*, 7/20/2013, salon.com /2013/07/20/snob_zones_fear_money_and_real_estate; Darien Historical Society, "Educational Programs," darienhistorical.org/education

---

★

---

84. The Problem of the Common

MASSACHUSETTS *Boston*

Boston marks its Common with a deliberately quaint sign quoting a deposition of "John Odin and others." Here it is, complete with its old-fashioned spellings:

In or about the year of our Lord 1634 the then present inhabitants of said
Town of Boston, of whom the Hon. John Winthrop, Esq., Gov. of the
Colony, was chiefe, did treate and agree with Mr. William Blackstone for
the purchase of his Estate and rights in any Lands lying within said neck
of Land called Boston, after which purchase the Town laid out a plan for
a trayning field which ever since and now is used for that purpose and for
the feeding of cattell.

It is amusing to imagine Boston Common, ringed now by busy streets and tall buildings, as a cow pasture. Its transformation from a common meadow is not merely a diverting story but points to a crucial twenty-first-century issue of individual betterment versus the common good. A marker telling about the historic problems on this common might provoke visitors to reflect on contemporary problems of the common worldwide.

In the 1630s, many Boston households owned a cow. Every morning a family member took the cow to the common, where it would join others and graze all day under the supervision of a cowherd paid by the town. To buy a second cow would be in the interest of an affluent family; if it did not need more milk and butter, the excess could be sold to cowless sailors and merchants. Expansion of this sort went on for only a few years, however, before the common pasture was hopelessly overgrazed. What was in the short-term interest of the individual family was not in the long-term interest of the community.

So many people visit Boston Common today that they cannot be allowed even to step on the grass, lest there be no grass. The city has far outgrown its common. Worse, Massachusetts has recently outgrown a larger common, an event of far graver economic consequence. In 1602, its common fishing ground, Georges Bank, was so rich in codfish that a British fisherman named the nearest peninsula "Cape Cod." Today, Georges Bank is in crisis. The total catch of cod, haddock, and flounder declined from just under 400,000,000 pounds in 1940 to about 26,000,000 pounds in 1993. During this decline, fisherfolk in Massachusetts responded the way people usually do when their standard of living is imperiled: they worked harder. Although this tactic may work for an individual family, it wreaked disaster on the common. According to writer Randolph T. Holhut, "Georges Bank is now considered commercially extinct, meaning that it cannot yield a sufficient amount of fish for fishermen to earn a living." In 1994, the U.S. Commerce Department

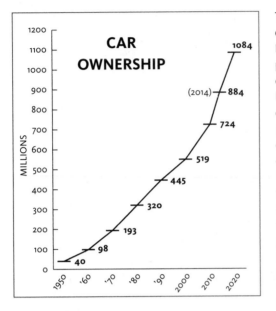

This graph shows car ownership around the globe. No sane observer would predict that such increases could continue for another lifetime without depleting our common pool of oil and polluting our common ocean of air. If nations like India emulate America's present-day level of resource use, the earth will become a desert. Tourists of the future will then consider the style of life in Boston in the year 2000 to be as quaint as we consider the idea of Boston Common as a cow pasture. "The problem of the common" has become the phrase by which economists refer to this tension between individual betterment and the good of all, so Boston Common is a proper place to raise this issue.[1]

closed Georges Bank to commercial fishing. In 2016, U.S. cod fishing hit an all-time low.

The problem of the common is larger even than Georges Bank. "Virtually every other fishing region in the world is also in peril," writes David E. Pitt in *The New York Times*. Indeed, the problem is bigger even than the oceans: because our economy has become global, our common has enlarged from a cow pasture to encompass the earth. Many insect populations, for example, vital to plant and animal species including ourselves, are crashing. Yet we continue to treat the earth as an inexhaustible resource.[2]

1. We are about to hit the billion-car mark. Depending upon whether pickup trucks, non-registered cars, etc., are included, some experts believe we have already reached it. Note, however, that car ownership and use cannot expand indefinitely, partly because space to park and drive is finite.

2. Randolph T. Holhut, "Strip-Mining the Oceans," from *The Written Word*, www.mdle .com/WrittenWord/opedc.htm, 8/96; David E. Pitt, "Despite Gaps, Data Leave Little Doubt that Fish are in Peril," *The New York Times*, 8/3/93; George R. Stewart, *American Place-Names* (NY: Oxford UP, 1970), 104; Loewen, *Lies My Teacher Told Me* (NY: New Press, 1995), chapter 10 cites and summarizes sources predicting ecocatastrophe and others suggesting we will avert it; Patrick Whittle, "Maine's Historic Cod Fishery

Had Worst Year in History in 2017," *Press Herald*, 7/27/2018, pressherald.com/2018/07/27/maines-historic-cod-fishery-had-worst-year-in-history-in-2017; Mary Hoff, "As Insect Populations Decline, Scientists Are Trying to Understand Why," *Scientific American* (11/1/2018); Stacy C. Davis, Susan W. Diegel, and Robert G. Boundy, "Transportation Energy Data Book," (DC: U.S. Department of Energy, Office of Energy Efficiency and Renewable Energy, various dates).

★
---

85. Celebrating Genocide

MASSACHUSETTS *Amherst*

The American landscape honors the ideas and actions of our ancestors—but *which* ancestors? Even the little town of Amherst offers many choices, from the reclusive poet Emily Dickinson to newspaper editor Horace Greeley. Above all others, however, Amherst chooses to honor Lord Jeffrey Amherst. What kind of ancestor was he?

Jeffrey Amherst was the commander in chief of the British forces in North America during the final battles of the French and Indian War. His victories against the French helped the British acquire Canada. As the French retired, defeated, their Indian allies fought on in what is now called Pontiac's Rebellion. The British under Amherst likewise fought on against the Indians. Indians were besieging Fort Pitt (present-day Pittsburgh, Pennsylvania) during the summer of 1763, and Capt. Simeon Ecuyer, one of Amherst's subordinates, "bought time by sending smallpox-infected blankets and handkerchiefs to the Indians surrounding the fort, which started an epidemic among them," according to historian Carl Walkman.

Because honoring a man for using germ warfare seems disgraceful, a mini-controversy has erupted over whether Amherst's underling knowingly gave the Native Americans smallpox and whether Amherst supported Ecuyer's actions. The evidence implicating Amherst has been clear for a long time, however. In the words of famed nineteenth-century historian Francis Parkman, "it was he who conceived and implemented the strategy to spread smallpox among them." According to Parkman, "in a 1763 letter to his colonel [Henry Bouquet], Amherst initiated the first known use of biological warfare in the 'New World': 'Could it not be contrived to send the smallpox among these disaffected tribes of Indians? We must on this occasion use every stratagem in our power to reduce them.'" And according to Walkman, "Amherst himself had encouraged this tactic in a letter to Ecuyer."

Smallpox fit with Amherst's larger mission, as he believed his task was "to annihilate the Indian population," wrote Parkman. The same summer Amherst wrote Sir William Johnson, superintendent of the Northern Indian Department, suggesting "measures to be taken as would bring about the total extirpation of those Indian Nations. . . . It would be happy for the Provinces [if] there was not an Indian settlement within a thousand miles of them." Amherst told his field commander that he viewed the Native Americans "not as a generous enemy, but as the vilest race of beings that ever infested the earth, and whose riddance from it must be esteemed a meritorious act for the good of mankind. You will therefore take no prisoners, but put to death all that fall into your hands."

Exterminating American Indians was precisely the charge that Britain and other nations had leveled at Spain in the 1500s—the so-called "Black Legend." The legend was true enough—under Spanish rule, war, slavery, and disease did kill Native Americans by the thousands. Nevertheless, many more American Indians remain today in those parts of the United States colonized by Spain than in the former British colonies, and Lord Jeffrey Amherst is one of the reasons.

Amherst returned to England later in 1763 and played no further role in what would soon become the United States. It seems outrageous to honor the man—whose most important connection with American history was to suggest and attempt "the total extirpation" of its Native peoples—by naming a town after him, and from time to time, Amherst residents do play down their town's namesake. From time to time, Amherst College tries to claim it was merely named for the town, not the man, but its museum displays a model of the man on a horse, planned for a time to be erected on the main campus hill. During the Vietnam War, the college quietly phased out its cafeteria dishes with images of Lord Jeff on horseback, sword drawn, chasing down American Indians after a student smashed several plates in protest. The school's mascot, a student dressed to evoke "Lord Jeff," went into hiding. During the Reagan years he came back, however, and students still sang "Lord Jeffery [sic] Amherst" as their fight song, which ends, "But give us our only Jeffery, he's the noblest and the best. To the end we will stand fast for him." Students in Amherst Middle School seemed more aware of the controversy about Amherst: way back in 1997, they debated the question "Lord Jeffrey Amherst—Hero or Monster?" and a majority favored the latter.

Since I have long believed it time to make some changes in the list of heroes our landscape commemorates, I made a modest try at such a change when I visited the Jeffrey Amherst Bookshop in downtown Amherst in 1998. "Do you know who your bookstore is named after?" I asked. The clerk laughed and said yes, all the employees know about Jeffrey Amherst and the smallpox story. So, I wrote to the owners and asked why they named their bookstore after him. They replied that they bought the store in 1978, already named. "However, since the town is called Amherst, the college Amherst, the inn across the common is the Lord Jeffrey Inn, the nickname of the college athletic teams the Lord Jeffs, and many other businesses named after him, it would have been an unwise choice to have changed the name," they replied. "Perhaps you would like to start a petition to have all these names changed—if so, you might also include Amherst, N.H., Amherst, N.Y., etc., etc."

Despite their biting reply, I did have a suggestion for a more appropriate namesake for the bookstore—Helen Hunt Jackson. She was even *from* Amherst—Lord Jeff never set foot in it—and she wrote books, too. If she is less well-known than Amherst, that is partly because nothing has been named for her. Ironically, Amherst College now owns her childhood home, at 249 S. Pleasant St. Its plaque reads simply, "The home of Helen Hunt Jackson, 1831–1847." Her life and work deserve more attention.

Helen Hunt Jackson was born in Amherst in 1830. By 1864, her husband and two sons had died, and she started writing. In 1879, she heard Standing Bear, a Ponca Indian from Nebraska, tell of his tribe's dismal forced eviction to what is now Oklahoma, and she decided to devote the rest of her life to promoting the cause of justice for Native Americans. She set furiously to work on a book that would do for the Indians, she hoped, what *Uncle Tom's Cabin* had done for the slaves. The result, published in 1881, was a scathing exposé of U.S. Indian policies titled *A Century of Dishonor.* According to historian Robert Utley, it "gained wide circulation and stirred the public conscience." Indeed, it is still in print and still well worth reading.

From her own funds, she sent copies of *Dishonor* to every member of Congress. One result was her appointment in 1882 as government investigator of the treatment of the Mission Indians of California, a generous response by President Chester A. Arthur to such an outspoken critic. She saw how California Indians were poor and abused both off and on their reservations, and she lamented the abandoned missions falling to ruin. Still wanting to transform America's Indian policies, in 1883 she began *Ramona*, her fictional account of an Indian woman who saw her husband murdered but could not testify against the killer because he was white and she was Indian.

Jackson died soon after completing her novel. *Ramona* became nineteenth-century America's most popular novel after *Uncle Tom's Cabin*, but never caused the transformation Jackson sought. *Ramona* did change American culture, however, helping trigger a rage for "mission style" architecture and furniture and leading to the preservation of the missions. Hollywood filmed *Ramona* four times, first by D. W. Griffith starring Mary Pickford and most recently starring Loretta Young and Don Ameche.

Helen Hunt Jackson exemplifies those Americans of all backgrounds who have tried over the centuries to change our policies and culture as they apply to the first Americans. Sometimes successful, more often not, they deserve recognition on the American landscape. Since the United States named its cities and counties during the age of imperialism, recognition all across America went to imperialists. In the post-imperialist age, African nations, which faced the same problem, have been doing some renaming; maybe America should, too.

The bookstore will never change; it went out of business years ago. In 2017, after the Amherst faculty voted unanimously and the students five to one to drop "Lord Jeff," he was gone, replaced by "the Mammoths." Renaming all the Amhersts would show that we no longer honor a man for his genocidal work.[1]

---

1. Francis Parkman, *The Conspiracy of Pontiac, vol. 2* (Boston: Little, Brown, 1886), 39; Carl Walkman, *Atlas of the North American Indian* (NY: Facts on File, 1985), 108; clipping file and student essays (Amherst, MA: Stephen Guy, Amherst Middle School, 12/97); Peter d'Errico, web.maxwell.syr.edu/nativeweb/subject/amherst/lord, citing microfilmed letters in the British Manuscript Project in the Library of Congress; Tingba Apidta, *The Hidden History of Massachusetts: A Guide for Black Folks* (Roxbury, MA: Reclamation Project, 1995); Alvin M. Josephy Jr., *The Patriot Chiefs* (NY: Viking Press, 1958); Howard Gersten, note, 11/95; Jessica Teters, letter, 7/96; KCET in association with Jon Wilkman Productions, "Ramona: A Story of Passion and Protest," videoplay by Nancy Meyer Wilkman, 1988; Robert M. Utley, *The Indian Frontier of the American West, 1846–1890* (Albuquerque: U. of NM Press, 1984),208; "Poll on Lord Jeff Results," amherst.edu /campuslife/aas/announcement; "Amherst College Replaces Lord Jeff Mascot with Mammoths," NECN, necn.com/news/new-england/Amherst--418263403.html

———— ☆ ————

86. Shards of Minstrelsy on a Far-North Campus

VERMONT *Burlington*

The landscape carries messages—open and covert—about black-white race relations all across America. The campus of the University of Vermont, just 50 miles from Canada, might seem to be about as far from this issue as possible while remaining in the United States. At the intellectual center of the campus, however, inside the entrance to Bailey-Howe Library, a bronze marker proclaims, "This university is especially indebted to the following for interest in Bailey Memorial Library." Among the plaques listing foundations and wealthy individual donors are two that signal an unusual connection to race relations. They say simply,

KAKE WALK DISBURSEMENT COMMITTEE 1964
and
KAKE WALK DISBURSEMENT COMMITTEE 1965.

Even their unusual spelling is part of their story, but that story remains hidden without further explanation.

For 80 years, Kake Walk was the most important student tradition on campus. In a contest pitting pairs of male dancers, one from each fraternity, the men performed a difficult routine involving elements of gymnastics, calisthenics, and dance, usually with arms linked, to the ragtime tune "Cotton Babes."[1] Although almost everyone at the college was white, the students performed in blackface and wore black kinky wigs. This bizarre competition was the centerpiece of the university's Winter Carnival from at least 1893 through 1969.

Cakewalks started on large antebellum slave plantations. In the evening, the owner might call on slaves to perform for the amusement of visitors. One might play the banjo while the rest danced or strutted around in a circle, each trying to outdo the others in inventiveness and outrageousness. The slave who was most comical won the prize, often a lump of sugar or a cake, from which we get the expression *"That* takes the cake!"

Two blackfaced dancers begin their Kake Walk as other pairs wait their turn on the sidelines of the University of Vermont gym, perhaps in the late 1950s.

Blackfaced minstrel shows appeared in American culture by 1830. They derived from blacks' song and dance on the plantation and from whites' need to picture African Americans as happy. Performers, more than nine-tenths of them white, sang, danced, and told stories in "Negro dialect." The evening needed a climax, and cakewalk filled the bill. The entertainers walked about in a circle, each in a unique style, then took a turn in the center while the rest formed a semicircle open to the audience. Robert Toll, the foremost historian of the form, tells that "minstrels emphasized Negro 'peculiarities'" because their white audiences "believed or wanted to believe that black slaves differed greatly from free white Americans."

In about 1890, white Southerners took from African Americans the last remnants of voting and civil rights. The Nadir of race relations set in. Northern whites sought to come to terms with this development, to which they had acquiesced. Minstrelsy "provided a nonthreatening way for white Americans to cope with questions about the nature and proper place of black people in America," as Toll put it. Minstrel shows became wildly popular, reflecting and reinforcing the lowly status of African Americans. "Heavily caricatured images of Blacks happy on the plantation and lost and incompetent off it remained the central message of minstrelsy," according to Toll. In Vermont, where few African Americans lived to correct this impression, the stereotype provided the bulk of white "knowledge" about African Americans. Second-class citizenship would be appropriate for such a sorry people.

In our electronic age, it is hard to imagine how prevalent minstrel shows were. Stephen Foster and James Bland's famous songs from the nineteenth century—"Old Black Joe," "My Old Kentucky Home," "In the Evening by the Moonlight," and many more—were written for minstrel groups. Minstrel shows were the rage of London; Commodore Matthew Perry introduced cakewalk to Japan. Thus, for Vermont students to turn to the blackface tradition to amuse themselves was not surprising. Minstrelsy was a product of white culture. No people of color needed to live nearby for it to work its peculiar magic. The period of Kake Walk's founding, 1888–93, saw more African Americans lynched than any other time in our history. The major leagues, which had included black ballplayers in the 1880s, expelled the last one in 1889. The Bronx Zoo displayed an African in a cage like a wild animal. *The Clansman* by Thomas Dixon was a bestselling book and a triumph on Broadway. "Coon songs," made popular on the minstrel stage, swept the nation in the 1890s. The coon, also called Jim Crow or Sambo, later immortalized on screen by Stepin Fetchit, "has always been used to indicate the black man's satisfaction with the system and his place in it," according to cultural historian Donald Bogle. In 1896, the U.S. Supreme Court legitimized "his place" in *Plessy v. Ferguson*, the decision legalizing segregation.

Repeatedly, up to World War II, students set "Kake Walk" programs in type that emphasized its three K's. Sometimes the competition was called "Kulled Koon's Kake Walk." The official name for the dance competition itself was "A Walkin' Fo' De Kake," the Vermont students' concept of black dialect. Skits became at least as important as the walking, and students often based their routines around racial themes including cannibals, lynchings, American Indians, "Orientals," Jews, and the Ku Klux Klan.

In the 1920s, reflecting the white supremacy of the Woodrow Wilson administration and the impact of the racist movie *Birth of a Nation*, Kake Walk became even more popular. Vermont students expanded it to two nights, each including skits and "walking." King and Queen were added in 1934, snow sculptures in 1940, again using dialect in their titles. Even after World War II, women students in blackface and raggedy dresses, called "pickaninny ushers" or "nigger babies," still ushered audience members to their seats. An editorial in the student newspaper written in 1948, and reprinted periodically later, sums up its importance: "When we think of college days, we will always remember Kake Walk. . . . The whole school becomes unified in one great surge of spirit." Downtown merchants ran special sales, and motel and restaurant owners braced for their biggest weekend of the year. The event itself usually made a large profit, a portion of which went for campus projects, prompting these plaques in the library.

Nonetheless, in the 1960s Kake Walk encountered turbulence. As early as 1950, Constance Baker Motley of the NAACP protested the blackface in a letter to the president of the university. The first hint that students saw a problem came in 1954. An editorial in that year's Kake Walk issue said,

PLEASE LOOK AT THE FRONT PAGE AGAIN LOOK AT THE
"BLACKFACE"
THIS IS THE TRADITION WE WANT TO SEE ENDED

Instead of getting rid of the blackface, some students tried to get rid of the newspaper!

The Civil Rights Movement had begun to change America. "If the Negro is being bombed in Alabama, then blackface in Vermont is no longer a joke," declared the president of the campus Interfraternity Council (IFC) in 1963. IFC made only a cosmetic change, however, choosing to have the 1964 walkers wear a light green makeup but retaining the title of the event as "Walkin' Fo' De Kake." Many fraternities were themselves racist; some national charters overtly limited membership to "Aryans" despite the notorious Nazi connotation of that term. When some students and townspeople denounced the change from blackface, IFC switched the next year to dark green, indistinguishable from black to spectators.

By 1968, in the context of campus protests, ghetto riots, the Tet offensive in Vietnam, the murders of Martin Luther King Jr. and Bobby Kennedy, the counterculture, and the beginnings of the women's movement, Kake Walk seemed anachronistic. After the 1969 performance, "The Black Students" at the university wrote to the student newspaper, "We realize that in the past this act could have been performed with complete ignorance of its effects. However, now that it has been brought out in the open, it can no longer be done out of ignorance." With exposure to black displeasure, white minds began to change. Elected student leaders had become convinced that the ritual was irretrievably racist. "Most of us have come a long way in less than a year in our thoughts about black people," wrote the director of admissions.

Some minds had not changed. "We'll recruit 'negros'," wrote President Lyman Rowell to several alumni, but "I am being careful to state in advance that we . . . do not intend to remake the University for their particular benefit." He denied that Kake Walk had any minstrel show origins and did "not feel that we have any reason for abandoning Kake Walk." Despite his view and a poll showing that two-thirds of the students still supported Kake Walk, the student senate voted 60/40 to end it. Vermont's governor and former governor spoke against it. Finally, on November 1, 1969, recognizing that "In these sensitive times it is possible to interpret this tradition as being racist in nature and humiliating to the Black people of this nation," the Kake Walk directors declared its demise. Today these plaques provide the only reminder of the event.

Nationally, influence from minstrel shows lingers on in the "fool" roles African Americans often play in television sitcoms and in Aunt Jemima pancake mix, named after a once-popular cakewalk tune. Otherwise, minstrelsy has left only a few shards on the landscape including the bizarre tombstone of blackface singer Al Jolson in Hillside Cemetery in Los Angeles (his statue in the pose he used to end "Mammy"), a statue of Bill "Bojangles" Robinson in Richmond, and a bust of blackface minstrel Billy West with his banjo in Greenwood Cemetery in Brooklyn.

Meanwhile, near the library stands Rowell Hall, named for the president who showed only negative leadership as the university went through the biggest convulsion of his administration. Even after students ended Kake Walk, President Rowell was still consoling distraught alumni, "I have no doubt that at some time in the future this whole area may be reexamined and Kake Walk could very possibly be re-instituted." The University of Vermont might instead reexamine his presidency by renaming Rowell Hall.[2]

1. "Independents" sometimes also entered a pair but rarely won.
2. Loewen, "Black Image in White Vermont: The Origin, Meaning, and Abolition of Kake Walk," in Robert V. Daniels, ed., *Bicentennial History of the University of Vermont* (Boston: UP of New England, 1991), 349–69; Marilyn Kern-Foxworth, *Aunt Jemima, Uncle Ben, and Rastus* (Westport, CT: Greenwood, 1994), 64.

---- ★ ----

87. Local History Wars

NEW HAMPSHIRE *Peterborough and Dublin*

A historical marker outside an old house in Dublin claims it to be the "First Free Public Library in America, supported by voluntary contribution," founded in 1822. Just eight miles to the southeast, a marker on the public library in Peterborough asserts that it is "The oldest free library in the world supported by taxation," founded in 1833.

The careful reader might notice that their subordinate clauses might make both markers true. Peterborough residents claim that their library, supported by municipal taxation, was a more important "first" than a free public library under a private board. But there are other claimants, including New Harmony, Indiana, in 1825. According to *The Whole Library Handbook*, "the first free public library was founded in Newington, Connecticut" back in 1787. But Newington librarians don't think their library was free back then.

The problem of local boosterism is evident everywhere across the American landscape. The "Hall of Fame for Great Americans" at Bronx Community College in New York City singles out William Morton as "the first to use ether as a general anesthetic." Morton also gets a monument in Boston Garden, although it never mentions him by name, being a monument to ether. Morton demonstrated the use of ether at Massachusetts General Hospital in 1846. This would seem an unusual, important, and appropriate "first" to commemorate, until one visits Bushnell Park in Hartford, Connecticut, where stands a bronze statue of Horace Wells, "the Hartford dentist who discovered modern anesthesia," according to a pamphlet in the Connecticut State Capitol nearby. At the corner of Main and Asylum Streets, Wells also gets a nice plaque including his portrait, "placed by 250 American dentists." It says that he, "upon this spot, December 11, 1844, submitted to a surgical operation, discovered, demonstrated, and proclaimed, the blessings of anaesthesia." Wells used nitrous oxide and his work inspired Morton.

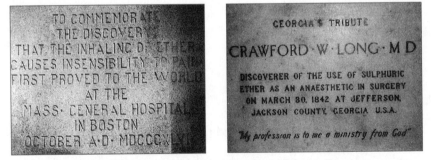

The inscription on the left comes from a monument on Boston Common commemorating the administration of ether by William Morton and Charles Jackson "at the Mass. General Hospital in Boston, October, 1846." The words on the right adorn the base of the statue of Crawford Long, one of Georgia's two contributions to the National Statuary Hall in the U.S. Capitol.

But maybe it wasn't ether of them! In the square in Jefferson, Georgia, an obelisk proclaims that "Sulphuric ether anaesthetic was discovered by Dr. Crawford W. Long on March 30, 1842, at Jefferson, Georgia, and administered to James M. Venable for the removal of a tumor." Another statue of Long is in the courthouse square in Danielsville, Georgia. To top it off, according to "A History of Anaesthesia at Harvard University," William E. Clarke, a student at the Berkshire Medical College in western Massachusetts, gave ether to a Miss Hobby while dentist Elijah Pope relieved her of a painful tooth some time before 1842.

Communities also vie with each other over the bones of dead people. Sitting Bull was killed at Fort Yates, North Dakota. A North Dakota historical marker is precise about what happened next: "He was buried here but his grave has been vandalized many times. This marker is directly over the gravesite." Another marker, near Mobridge, South Dakota, claims that Sitting Bull's bones are buried nearby, which is true, because Mobridge citizens stole them in 1953.

Kentucky and Missouri both claim Daniel Boone's bones. Boone died near Defiance, Missouri, in 1820 and was buried in nearby Marthasville. A group from Kentucky removed him, or so they thought, 25 years later and put him in the state capital. A Kentucky state historical marker reads "Daniel Boone's Grave" and tells that he was "reinterred with wife Rebecca in Frankfort Cemetery in 1845." Examination by a forensic anthropologist in 1983, however, proved that the crew from Kentucky got the wrong bones, probably those of a black slave who had predeceased Rebecca. Boone still lies in Missouri.

Perhaps the silliest of these local history wars is the dispute between Brunswick, Georgia, and Brunswick County, Virginia, over where Brunswick stew originated. For many years, Brunswick, Georgia, won this argument on the landscape, for it boasted a monument of a large cooking kettle with an inscription declaring that the first ever Brunswick stew was made there in 1898. In 1997, Brunswick County, Virginia, struck back, purchasing six Virginia state historical markers with the text,

"THE ORIGINAL HOME OF BRUNSWICK STEW"

*According to local tradition, while Dr. Creed Haskins and several friends
were on a hunting trip in Brunswick County in 1828, his camp cook,
Jimmy Matthews, hunted squirrels for a stew. Matthews simmered the*

squirrels with butter, onions, stale bread, and seasoning, thus creating
the dish known as Brunswick stew. . . . Other states have made similar
claims but Virginia's is the first.

The last four words seem unequivocal, but the phrase "according to local tradition" as well as the quotation marks around the title imply to discerning readers that less than absolute certainty characterizes this marker.

While who was first in stew may make little difference in the world, the historical distortions seen on other examples of local boosterism often have results that are by no means trivial. The next entry shows how Concord's desire to boost New Hampshire's only president helps to confuse those who read the state's public markers about the politics of the 1850s and the causes of the Civil War.[1]

The first airplane (chapter 38), first automobile (chapter 28), and the two springs
where Massasoit lived (chapter 90) offer other examples of local history wars.

1. Allen Kent, et al., eds., *Encyclopedia of Library and Information Science* (NY: Dekker, 1978), 86, 103–104, 273–88; George M. Eberhart, compiler, *The Whole Library Handbook* (Chicago, IL: American Library Association, 1995), 24; Robert Behre, conversation, 7/98; James F. Brennan, "The First Free Public Library," *Peterborough Transcript*, 7/26/1923; David Wallechinsky and Irving Wallace, *The People's Almanac No. 3* (NY: Morrow, 1981), 18–22; "Ether Monument," Celebrate Boston, celebrateboston.com /statue/ether-monument.htm; Rebecca Gray, "Stewing Over Stew," *U.S. Airways Attaché* (9/97): 94–95; "Anesthesia is Born," *American Heritage* (10/96): 116–17; staff, Crawford W. Long Museum, Jefferson Georgia, conversation, 8/98; "Inventory of American Sculpture," siris.si.edu/webpac-bin/wgbroker, 9/98; "A History of Anaesthesia at Harvard U.," hmcnet.harvard.edu/anesthesia/history/vandam.html, 8/98; Roadside America "Sitting Bull's Grave," roadsideamerica.com/set/hist, 11/97.

---------- ★ ----------

88. "Effective Political Leader"
NEW HAMPSHIRE *Concord*

What if a state wanted to commemorate its only native son president, but he wasn't very good at his job? In front of Old North Cemetery at the northern end of downtown Concord stands New Hampshire's answer: a historical marker honoring the only president from the Granite State.

FRANKLIN PIERCE 1804–1869

Fourteenth President of the United States (1853–57). Lies buried in nearby Minot enclosure. Native son of New Hampshire, graduate of Bowdoin College, lawyer, effective political leader, Congressman and U.S. Senator, Mexican War veteran, courageous advocate of State's Rights, he was popularly known as "Young Hickory of the Granite Hills."

Of course, no one has ever been "popularly known" by a nickname of nine syllables! Democrats concocted "Young Hickory of the Granite Hills" as a campaign slogan. Deeper problems invalidate this marker, however. Probably America's least popular president, Franklin Pierce was never "popularly known" as anything. To this day, he remains the only elected president ever denied renomination by his own party. Even his birthplace, Hillsborough, admits on its website, "He had left New Hampshire a hero in 1852. He returned in silence."

In a way, this Concord marker is merely another example of local booster-ism, like the Dublin and Peterborough markers both claiming the first library (chapter 87). This Pierce marker is not as benign as those gestures of local hubris, however, for it would defend Pierce by having us believe he stood for states' rights. The *New Columbia Encyclopedia* describes Pierce in precise-ly opposite terms: "a strong nationalist." His administration adopted what the encyclopedia calls "a vigorous expansionist foreign policy" on behalf of Southern slaveowners. Some planters wanted our government to replace Spain as the colonial power in the Americas, which would open new land for the growth of slavery. Accommodating this desire led the Pierce administra-tion into one of the larger fiascoes in the history of American foreign policy, the Ostend Manifesto, an attempt to bluff or force Spain to sell us Cuba as the beginning of an expanded Southern slave empire. It failed.[1]

The strongly negative domestic reaction to the Ostend Manifesto made clear that most Northerners would not support the extension of slavery. Nev-ertheless, Pierce supported the Kansas-Nebraska Act, which the Democratic party pushed through Congress in 1854. This law opened Kansas to slavery even though Kansas lay north of the Missouri Compromise line set up in 1820 to separate slave from free states. The result was a rush by slaveowners and free soilers to settle Kansas.

The antislavery settlers won. In 1855, their leaders met in Topeka and wrote a constitution in the first attempt to organize a state government. Although the Kansas-Nebraska Act supposedly allowed new territories and states to decide for themselves whether to adopt slavery, Pierce refused to allow states' rights. A Kansas historical marker in Topeka tells the result: "The next year their legislature was dispersed by U.S. dragoons under orders from President Franklin Pierce" Because the free-soil candidates won.[2] Then, in the next election, emboldened by support from the national government, pro-slavery forces in Missouri crossed over to vote illegally and intimidate free soilers from voting. Pierce approved these results even though his own appointees in Kansas criticized the election. The resulting Kansas legislature passed laws stating that only slaveowners could hold office, and that merely to declare slavery wrong was a crime. When Pierce endorsed these laws, the result was a civil war in Kansas.

As Theodore Roosevelt later summed up Pierce's time in office, "Pierce was completely under the control of the secession wing of the [Democratic] party." Jefferson Davis, Pierce's secretary of war, dominated his administration. He got Pierce to veto internal improvements except in the South. Like Democratic administrations before and after him, Pierce also opposed a homestead bill in the West simply because slaveholders saw that letting Americans get land cheaply was a threat to slavery. Cheap land would draw individual families who would work it themselves. Expensive land could only be afforded by the rich, who would then use slave labor to make it pay. Homesteading had to wait until the Lincoln administration a decade later.

After he left office, Pierce became even more of a Southern partisan. In 1860, he endorsed Jefferson Davis for president. When Lincoln issued the Emancipation Proclamation in January 1863, Pierce called it "an attempt to butcher the white race for the sake of inflicting freedom on blacks." Most northern Democrats, while opposing Lincoln on slavery, at least supported the North in the Civil War to hold the nation together. Not Pierce. In a speech on Independence Day, 1863, the day U.S. forces took Vicksburg, he attacked the idea of saving the Union. That was enough for New Hampshire residents. For the rest of his life, "he was reviled and repudiated . . . in his native state," according to Wilfred J. Bisson, his biographer.

Historians have called national leaders of the 1850s the "blundering generation," and Pierce was perhaps the worst of the lot. Indeed, a case can be made that he was the worst president in the history of the republic. Nevertheless, in the twentieth century, New Hampshire developed amnesia about Pierce. New Hampshireans erected his statue at the state capitol in 1914, called him an "effective political leader" on his marker, and put his name on Franklin Pierce College, which they founded in 1962. I asked the college receptionist, an undergraduate at the information desk, if a statue of the man existed on campus. "No," she replied. "We should have, because he was one of the founders of the college."[3]

1. James Buchanan was directly responsible; see chapter 73.
2. Topeka retaliated when it named its streets after the presidents: it left out Pierce!
3. William Harris and Judith Levey, eds., *The New Columbia Encyclopedia* (NY: Columbia UP, 1975), 726, 2027, 2146; "The Life of Franklin Pierce," on Historic Hillsborough, NH, website, www.conknet.com/~hillsboro/pierce/Pierce.html, 8/97; Larry Gara, *The Presidency of Franklin Pierce* (Lawrence: UP of KS, 1991); Theodore Roosevelt, *Thomas Hart Benton* (NY: Scribner's, 1926[1887]), 220; Wilfred J. Bisson, *Franklin Pierce: A Bibliography* (Westport, CT: Greenwood, 1993), Introduction and Chronology; Howard Mansfield, *In the Memory House* (Golden, CO: Fulcrum, 1993), 57–75.

89. "Settlement" Means Fewer People!
RHODE ISLAND *Block Island*

A copper scroll on a boulder at the north end of Block Island reads,

1661–1911

. . . to commemorate the 250th anniversary of the purchase and settlement of Block Island . . .

Paradoxically, however, Block Island's population in 1911, after 250 years of "settlement," was 1,314, while its population in 1660 just *before* "settlement" was about 1,350.

The population history of Block Island tells, in miniature, the demographic history of North America as it was "settled" by Europeans, beginning in Mexico in 1519. In 1524, when Verrazano visited Narragansett Bay, he saw the island's shores ablaze with signal fires and estimated its population at 4,000. The drop to perhaps 1,350 during the next 136 years was caused by diseases spread (accidentally) by British fishermen coming ashore in Massachusetts and by pandemics sweeping up from the Spanish in Florida. During the century after 1661, the Native population of Block Island declined further, to just 51, caused by the attacks, deculturation, and additional microbes that Europeans (and Africans) brought to what is now Rhode Island. The last Native American on Block Island, Isaac Church, died in 1886 at the age of 101.

Settlement of Block Island hardly began in 1611. Native Americans "settled" too. Indeed, at the time of the first sustained European contact, 1493, the number of people living in what is now the United States was probably about the same as the population of Great Britain. Anthropologist William Denevan termed the ensuing decline in Native people throughout the Americas as "possibly the greatest demographic disaster in the history of the world." Second only to the European (and African) invasion itself, this population decline is surely the most important event in American history. Yet few Americans have ever heard of it. Although the British took over such lands as India and Nigeria, they were never able to "settle" them because too many people already lived there. Indians and Nigerians were not decimated by new diseases brought by the European newcomers because Eurasia/Africa was already connected. Not so in America. Block Island's marker would offer a fine place to start learning about all this—but it implies American Indians were never here at all!

All across America, historical markers reserve "settle" and "settlers" for Europeans. A stone marker in the center of Greenfield, Massachusetts, announces:

TOWN OF GREENFIELD

Settled 1686 . . .
Incorporated 1753.

This is simply bad history. The *History of Greenfield* written by Francis Thompson in 1904 tells of the Pocumtuck Indians who had lived around Deerfield and Greenfield for millennia. In 1637, 50 years before 1686, these Natives sent 50 canoes full of corn, amounting to 500 bushels, to feed the starving British settlers of Massachusetts. Then, disease and a big Mohawk attack killed the Pocumtucks.

Signs like Greenfield's reinforce the old "virgin wilderness" myth. The American landscape would have a very different feel if all such markers read like this:

TOWN OF GREENFIELD

Settled c. 9000 BP[1] Resettled by Europeans 1686
Incorporated 1753.[2]

Chapters 7 and 21 show related terminology problems.

1. Or whatever best guess archaeologists can supply. BP means Before the Present.
2. Bureau of the Census, *Statistics for Rhode Island* (DC: GPO, 1913), 572; Bob Downie, conversation, 9/98; Francis Jennings, *The Invasion of America* (Chapel Hill: U. of NC Press, 1975), 16, 27; Emmanuel Altham, letter quoted in Sydney V. James, ed., *Three Visitors to Early Plymouth* (Plymouth, MA: Plimoth Plantation, 1963), 29; William Denevan, *The Native Population of the Americas in 1492* (Madison: U. of WI Press, 1976), 7; Loewen, *Lies My Teacher Told Me* (NY: New Press, 1995), chapter 3; Francis Thompson, *History of Greenfield* (Greenfield, MA: T. Morey, 1904), 5.

---- ★ ----

90. Fighting Over the "Good Indian"

RHODE ISLAND *Warren and Barrington*

Throughout our nation's history, European Americans have told themselves that Native Americans *wanted* them to come over, settle, and bring them into the modern "civilized" world. The gentlemen of the Massachusetts Bay Colony chose as their official seal an American Indian wearing only a few leaves around his genitals—obviously a primitive. From his mouth flow the words, "Come Over and Help Us." The seal is nothing more than white settler propaganda intended for European consumption. In reality, nobody wants outsiders to come in, take their land, burn their crops, destroy their houses, force a new religion upon them, and confine them to worthless patches of ground.

On the conquerors' side, we must recognize that, as H. L. Mencken once wrote, "Nobody thinks of himself as a son of a bitch." Throughout the history of contact between European Americans (and African Americans) on one side and Native Americans on the other, a few Indians have always welcomed the newcomers, with some even choosing to live on the white "side."[1] To soften invasion narratives, conquerors often highlighted the stories of natives who helped them. Americans might call these "Tonto figures," after the Lone Ranger's famous sidekick—the archetypal "good Indian," always ready to help track down the "bad Indians" and outlaws who menaced whites on the frontier.

Massasoit was an early "good Indian" who lived in what is now Rhode Island. In the summer of 1621, when the Pilgrims needed to ally with their neighbors, the Wampanoags, they sent an envoy to meet with Massasoit. He welcomed them and sent a member of his village, Hobomok, to live among the Pilgrims for several years as a guide and ambassador.

Today, since whites *want* to claim "good Indians," towns on either side of the Warren River both use bronze plaques on large boulders to mark Massasoit's homesite.

On Baker Street in Warren, the State Committee on Marking Historical Sites put up this plaque in 1907: "This tablet placed beside the gushing water known for many generations as Massasoit's Spring commemorates the great Indian sachem Massasoit, 'Friend of the White Man,' ruler of this region when the Pilgrims of the Mayflower landed at Plymouth in the year of our lord, 1620."

This statue of Massasoit stands in front of the Utah State Capitol in Salt Lake City. Another adorns the campus of Brigham Young University in Provo. To be sure, the sculptor was from Utah and the commission originated at Plymouth (chapter 26), but we might still ponder why Utah wanted Massasoit rather than, say, a leader of the Utes. At least portraying Massasoit as a generic Eastern woodland Indian in Utah offers some balance to the several monuments depicting Plains Indians in the East. Of course, West or East, Native Americans always appear dressed for a hot day in August.

On Rumstick Road in Barrington, the Rhode Island Citizens Historical Society and the Algonquin Indian Association put up this plaque in 1926: "This boulder marks the site of Massasoit Spring and commemorates the great Indian sachem Massasoit, friend of the white man and chief of this region when the Pilgrims landed at Plymouth in 1620." It seems to plagiarize some of its text from Warren.[2]

Wilder Munro, the principal speaker at the Warren dedication in 1907, supplied the following documentation for that location: "If ever a fact was firmly established by tradition, the fact of Massasoit's connection with this spring is." Munro, possibly worried that his listeners might be skeptical of his blatant reliance on "tradition," added that "the Father of American Geography," Jedediah Morse, "caught the story from the lips of children who had lived in the days of Massasoit and transferred it to his *American Gazetteer* in 1805." Since Morse was born a full century after Massasoit died, this is hardly likely.

So much for Warren. I place my bets on the Barrington location because the Algonquin Indian Association seems to have been a Wampanoag organization.[3]

More interesting than the tussle over Massasoit's Spring is the spectacle of these two communities vying to claim this Wampanoag Indian—an ironic honor in a state that wiped out most of his descendants in King Philip's War, 1675–76, only fourteen years after his death. Moreover, Rhode Island displays similar historical markers for other "good Indians." Charlestown has a memorial to the "Narragansett and Niantic Indians, the unwavering friends and allies of our fathers." In Little Compton, a marker remembers a "Queen of the Sackonates and friend of the White Man."

Why would Rhode Islanders do this? Certainly not to appease its Native American population: in 1990, just 4,071 Native Americans lived in Rhode Island, less than half of 1% of the state's 1,000,000 people.[4]

Rhode Island is hardly alone in this practice. Its northern neighbor, Massachusetts, is full of historical markers to "good Indians," like this one in Lowell:

WANNALANCET

On Wickasee Island . . . dwelt Wannalancet, last sachem of the Pennacook Confederacy, and like his father Passaconaway, a faithful friend to the English.

To the west, Connecticut has only six historical markers that treat Native Americans. Of these, three honor Uncas, the Mohegan who allied with the Europeans. No marker treats the Pequots, the tribe the British all but exterminated in New England's first Indian war, the Pequot War of 1636–37. Further west, the mountain states honor other "good Indians" including Sacagawea, the Native American woman who helped Lewis and Clark cross the Plains and the Rockies. Washington state honors Chief Sealth, after whom Seattle is named.

A historical marker on U.S. Highway 12, west of Webster, South Dakota, glorifies Solomon Two Stars. The marker tells how some Dakota Indians had killed a white family in Minnesota and fled west.

> . . . Near the present site of Webster this murderous group were met and recognized by Solomon Two Stars, an Army scout, on May 16, 1865. . . . A renegade nephew of Two Stars was captured. The latter confessed that he and the others were guilty of the murder. Under strict orders to take no prisoners, Two Stars was faced with a terrible choice. Duty demanded his kinsman be killed. Should he order one of the scouts to shoot him or accept the responsibility? Fifty years later, he said, "I shot him before my tears should blind me." Can white men produce a better chronicle of integrity?

Markers like these redefine "renegade" and "integrity" in totally partisan ways. "Murderous" too might apply to the euphemistic phrase "strict orders to take no prisoners," an order that blatantly violated the army code of war. Imagine what a historical marker written by Dakotas would say about Two Stars!

Our national culture particularly heroifies the first two "good Indians," Pocahontas in Virginia and Squanto in Massachusetts, who became foundation figures in our origin myths. Some "white" Americans are proud to trace their lineage to Pocahontas, who married John Rolfe and had many descendants. Squanto had no "European" progeny, but his friendship and assistance led to the first Thanksgiving, our national origin banquet. As a translator, ambassador, and technical adviser, Squanto was essential to the survival of Plymouth in its first two years. William Bradford called Squanto "a special instrument sent of God for their good beyond their expectation." Not only were Squanto and Massasoit on the European Americans' side; by implication to men like Bradford, they were also on the side of God.

Tonto figures still play an important ideological role in explaining and excusing the elimination of Native peoples. When European Americans honor "good Indians" by putting up their statues or marking their homes, they are trying to define themselves as "good white people." Whites deserve the country, goes the implicit argument. Look—here are the Indians who welcomed us to it and helped us take it.

Honoring "good Indians" makes for poor history, however. For centuries, whites have been thankful to Massasoit. White accounts of his help do not usually include the demographic context in which he operated, however. Rather, whites viewed East Coast Indians as inexplicably and haplessly hospitable. Massasoit's hospitality was not an example of "noble savagery," nor did it imply that the Pilgrims had earned his kindness by treating Indians well. It was a rational response to the new and threatening situation the Wampanoags faced. Massasoit needed to ally with the Pilgrims because diseases brought by the newcomers had so weakened his villages that he feared the Narragansetts to the west. His hospitality created an obligation and helped ensure reciprocal aid, the function gift-giving plays in many societies. Massasoit was no fool. For that matter, Tonto was no fool, although some critics of "The Lone Ranger" television series have pointed out that "tonto" means "fool" in Spanish. Neither were Squanto or Pocahontas foolish. They all made defensible choices in difficult situations. The English just played by different rules and did not return the favor as Massasoit had expected. In the end, after the fur trade wound down and the British saw no further way to make money off the Indians, they had no further use for them. So, they pushed them further west or annihilated them, "good" and "bad" alike.[5]

Chapter 4 details quite a different approach to Indian relations. Chapter 26 tells of the memorials left across the United States by an organization whose purpose in part has been to remember the "good Indian."

1. Some European Americans chose to live with Indians as well.
2. "Sachem" means "chief."
3. The Algonquin Indian Association is a Wampanoag organization; see "12". Clarence Manter Wixon Jr." at ancestry.com/boards/thread.aspx?mv=flat&m=28&p=topics.ethnic.natam.nations.wampanoag and "Obituaries, Clinton Neakeahamuck 'Lightning Foot' Wixon," *South Coast Today*, 11/12/2003, southcoasttoday.com/article/20031112/NEWS03/311129998
4. The previous chapter tells that about the same number, 4,000, lived on tiny Block Island before Europeans arrived.

5. Historic property data sheets and files for both sites on file at Rhode Island Historical
    Preservation and Heritage Commission; William McKenzie Woodward, correspon-
    dence, 8/95; Neal Salisbury, "Squanto: Last of the Patuxets," in David Sweet and Gary
    Nash, eds., *Struggle and Survival in Colonial America* (Berkeley: U. of CA Press, 1981),
    228–46; William Bradford, *Of Plimoth Plantation*, rendered by Valerian Paget (NY:
    McBridge, 1909), 93; Lee Friedlander, *The American Monument* (NY: Eakins, 1976),
    unpaginated.

------------ ★ ------------

91. At Last—An Accurate Marker

MAINE *Bar Harbor*

Our monumental journey, from Denali in Alaska and Columbus in California to our easternmost state of Maine, has taken us past many historical
markers that tell false history and statues that show bad images.

Here in Maine, however, perhaps cleansed by unpolluted ocean breezes,
things are different. Great Gott Island lies just south of Mount Desert Island,
also known as Acadia National Park. There on a house not far from the
Atlantic is the marker

On this site in 1897 nothing happened.

So far as I know, this marker is absolutely accurate.

GETTING INTO A DIALOGUE WITH THE LANDSCAPE

We have finished our journey. En route, we saw many historical markers whose biased terminology and outright lies stand in desperate need of revision. Many monuments represent only one side of a conflict and misrepresent what really happened. And many historic houses simply avoid history altogether in favor of details about the silverware.

We have also seen that our dialogue with this landscape has increased in recent years. Perhaps the only appropriate way to close our survey of public history is by considering how we can continue that dialogue. Things are changing, for the worse and for the better. During the 1990s, the nation witnessed what some called "the history wars."[1] "Historical revisionism" and "political correctness" were the buzzwords in this war. My own book *Lies*

A tall marble column dominates a small family cemetery in Hazlehurst, Mississippi. It looks dramatic, broken off abruptly at its top, as if hit by an airplane. This turns out to be a nineteenth-century convention signifying a life cut short suddenly by violence. It marks the final resting place of John Prentiss "Print" Matthews, killed November 6, 1883, while in the act of voting. Matthews led the interracial Republican Party in Copiah County, which the white supremacist Democrats vowed to destroy. In 1997, these high school students from Boston visited his grave and were moved by it. "I was really surprised to learn there were white people like him in the South just after the Civil War," wrote one later.

My Teacher Told Me: Everything Your High School History Textbook Got Wrong
played some role in the controversy. More than a hundred radio talk shows
invited me to discuss the book in the late 1990s. Right-wing talk show hosts
were particularly likely to ask me, with suspicion, "Your book isn't one of
those works of revisionist history, is it?" Their question implied that history
used to be "just the facts, ma'am," until people like me muddled it up by
applying our transitory present-day concerns—stemming from our time—to
the past.

Actually, historians are always revising history. George Santayana will forever be remembered for his aphorism, "Those who cannot remember the past
are condemned to repeat it," but he also said something more complicated
and more accurate about the past: "History is always written wrong, and so
always needs to be rewritten." The past, of course, cannot be revised. What
happened happened. But the very first account of an event—whether in a
diary, newspaper, or told over the fence to a neighbor—selects some parts of
what happened for retelling and leaves others out. Historical revisionism, in
short, hardly started in the 1990s. Textbooks of U.S. history written in different eras generally tell very different versions of the same event. Sometimes,
even the same textbook gives different interpretations as it goes through different editions.

Unlike textbooks, historical markers are written in bronze or chiseled in
stone on the landscape. Nonetheless, as we have seen, revisions are necessary.
Markers lie. Unfortunately, trying to persuade people to remove or revise a
marker or monument can touch off defensiveness over wrongdoing in the
past. We still have a long way to go to undo our pro-Confederate public history. Every monument that venerates the Confederacy, whether by its hieratic scale, location, verbiage, or expensive materials, must come down. The
monuments should not be destroyed but might be placed in a "Nadir of Race
Relations Park" with signage explaining how each is a product of its time
and has something to teach about that time.[2] Every county, town, fort, street,
building, lake, and school named for a person whose fame stems mainly from
his service to the Confederacy needs to be named for someone else, after an
interesting civic dialogue.

Every takedown movement begins with a single individual. I think I may
have sparked one removal inadvertently with *Lies My Teacher Told Me*. The
last image was of a particularly wrong historical marker in southwest Mississippi, "Union Army Passes Rocky Springs."[3] To conquer Vicksburg, the

Confederacy's last major outpost on the Mississippi River, U. S. Grant con-cocted a bold plan: he would get his men *south* of the city, then march them to the northeast, take Jackson, then attack Vicksburg from the east. To do so, he would have to abandon all supply lines, relying on the land and the people for food and water. Since 80% of the people were African American, this proved remarkably successful. The text of "Union Army Passes Rocky Springs," however, mystified the matter, claiming the army encountered only "the icy stares of the people who gathered at the side of the road to watch." In reality, it was the happiest day of the spectators' lives, for at that moment, at least for a while, they were free. They hosanna'd the troops, gave them food, showed them the best route to Jackson, and told them where the Confederates were. Shortly after my book came out, the marker disappeared. No one in the marker office would tell me what happened to it; one person vaguely suggested maybe a mowing machine had hit it. No matter; it was gone, never to reappear.

Near the town of Woodstock, Virginia, in the Shenandoah Valley, a state historical marker used to say,

LAST INDIAN OUTRAGE

Here, in 1766, took place the last Indian outrage in Shenandoah County. Five Indians attacked two settler families fleeing to Woodstock. Two men were killed; the women and children escaped.

In 1994, a snowplow hit the marker.[4] When Virginia replaced it, its wording had undergone some revision:

LAST INDIAN-SETTLER CONFLICT

A series of conflicts between settlers and Native Americans, including the French and Indian War, the Cherokee War, and Pontiac's War, occurred along the western frontier of the colonies. The last documented clash in the Shenandoah Valley took place nearby in 1766. A small band of Indians attacked the Sheetz and Taylor families as they fled for safety to the fort at Woodstock. Matthias Sheetz and Taylor were both killed, but their wives used axes to fight off the Indians and escape with the children.

Most obvious of course is the change of "Outrage" to "Conflict" in the title. Before dismissing this rewording as merely "politically correct," we might note that "outrage" was bad history. It told not of the event but of the mentality of those who erected the sign before World War II. Historians call that "presentist"—a product of the period when the sign went up. "Conflict," although literally revisionist (the sign was revised), is not so dependent upon the sensibilities of the early 1990s when the new text went up. "Conflict" is simply more accurate.

The new text also tells *more* history. Before the snowplow, a reader might reasonably infer that this "outrage" was a random act of violence against whites. The new wording provides some context.

Both texts inaccurately use "settler" to mean "newcomer," however. American Indians had "settled" that part of Virginia for many centuries before the European intruders.[5] Also, Joseph Clower Jr., a local authority on Woodstock history, notes that both markers may err in stating that the women and children "escaped." He suggests that their "escape" may, in fact, show Native reluctance to harm them. Indeed, Eastern Indians did sometimes refuse to kill women and children in battle. Instead, they took them as prisoners or *let* them escape.

Despite these remaining problems with the text, the revision makes a strong case for errant snowplows (or mowing machines). From New England to Kansas to the West Coast, other markers make Native Americans the savages and deserve snowplow attention. At Arthur, in neighboring West Virginia, for example, a marker for Vincent Williams uses BS (Before Snowplow) terminology, calling him "an early settler and noted Indian fighter of the South Branch." The marker continues, "When his home was attacked, Williams killed five Indians before he was shot in the back by the two remaining savages." It is reasonable to ponder whether this "noted Indian fighter" deserves to be called "the settler" rather than "the savage," since he killed more people than they did and the land was theirs before it was his.

Marker managers in other states, on learning what happened to "Last Indian Outrage," have told me they wished similar mishaps might damage markers under their jurisdiction. They do not have intimate enough relations with their state highway departments to arrange such "accidents" themselves. But Virginia no longer waits passively for markers to be hit. Revising "Last Indian Outrage" was only triggered by the snowplow mishap. The revision was really made possible by changes in Virginian society stemming from the

Civil Rights Movement, the Lovings' lawsuit (chapter 66), and school deseg-regation. These developments paved the way for the victorious candidacies of African American Douglas Wilder for lieutenant governor and governor. They also allowed Virginia to write a more accurate history on its landscape. Since 1999, Virginia has replaced more than 150 markers with BS terminol-ogy and put up at least 150 new markers for topics, people, and groups for-merly disfavored. "The modern-day marker program does not avoid difficult subjects," according to Jennifer Loux, its manager.[6]

Some other states are doing likewise. Kansas took steps to make its mark-ers more accurate and less offensive. Montana has been rewriting markers "that contained offensive language." Chapter 7 shows how Michigan is revis-ing markers to eliminate nonsensical uses of "discover." More states should follow suit because all across America, untruthful and prejudiced texts on our historic markers and monuments cry out silently for revision. Just with regard to Native Americans, biased use of "civilized," "devil," "discover," "half-breed," "hostile," "massacre," "menace," "savages," "settler," "squaw," and "wander" all *otherize* the people described, making it harder to relate their pasts accurately or treat them with justice and respect in the present.

We have seen how, in the first two decades of the new millennium, citi-zens and public officials across the country have begun to question our cel-ebratory monuments to the Confederacy. We have also seen how people who did important things but went unrecognized owing to their sexual ori-entation are now finding their way onto our landscape. As they do, we may become more accepting of various others in the present. Depending on the level of social justice Americans build into our future society, the day may come when the last truly offensive marker will be retired from the American roadside, lest it be damaged by a snowplow or vandalized by affronted citi-zens. Curators will put that bronze plaque on display in a history museum on that happy day, in an exhibit about how Americans lived and thought in the first half of the 21st century, perhaps with the label "Last Marker Outrage."

Or maybe that day will never come. Changing the landscape is rarely easy. Some elements in our society have a vested interest in retaining and retelling certain falsehoods about our past; efforts to make our historic sites more accurate will always arouse their opposition. America has always been changing. Maybe the United States will never *become* a truly just society—but we can constantly move our country toward *becoming* a truly just society. So long as our society is in revision then, so will its historic sites need revision.

Happily, every marker has two surfaces! State historians and review boards can go crazy trying to write one master narrative (often in 25 words or less!) that satisfies all sides concerned with a controversial incident, such as a violent labor strike. Instead, a labor historian and one aligned with the company could each submit texts, and after vetting for accuracy, both might then go up, each signed by its author or institutional sponsor. Such markers would allow new voices to speak in place of the godlike monotone of the state.

Other types of additions to our public history need to go up, made possible by technology. "Hear, Here, La Crosse" offers an example in Wisconsin: small inexpensive signs signal passersby to use their mobile phones to dial a number to hear an account of the history that took place at that spot. One professor and her college students did the brunt of the work. At many sites, you hear excerpts from interviews with actual participants. With a little help, high school students can do this too. At present, few historical markers tell about the 1950s and 1960s, the Civil Rights Movement, the movement against the Vietnam War, the women's movement in your town, etc. This kind of public history can make available to everyone accounts from people now alive who lived through those times and participated in those events.[7]

High school students can research the history of their town or school, write a historical marker, raise the money, and get it vetted and erected through their state program. Such a project empowers students, helps them realize that people like them write history—and choose what to write about—and also that people like them *make* history. Selecting the most important graduates of a high school or the most important former residents of a community leads to serious contemplation of "importance." Thinking about the history of an educational institution—its role in the class structure, the changing position of girls, perhaps its racial desegregation—helps students understand how the social world works.

Individuals can make a difference, too. We have seen (chapter 70) how one person can spark new state markers. Two students in a high school American Indian class traced the derogatory meanings of "squaw" and sparked a movement that eventually led to a Minnesota law requiring place names containing the word to be changed.[8] For that matter, any individual with the money (between $500 and $2,000) and a place to put it can erect a historical marker.[9]

Citizens can also establish new traditions to bring forgotten monuments and markers back to life, so they might again influence civic discourse. Monuments look static—carved in stone and all—but their meanings change as the present changes and as people enact new rituals at them. Chapter 26 told how Native Americans have been doing this at Plymouth Rock in an attempt to change how Americans view the Pilgrims. The American past is full of humane role models like Print Matthews, as well as oppressors like the man who shot him. Our ancestors are still there for us and can still speak to our condition today. If we let them, if we in the present can portray a more complete and complex view of the past, then our children will have a better chance to build a future they will be proud rather than ashamed to remember.

We can also put up historical markers to explain absence. Every sundown town and every segregated private club deserves a public marker exposing its past racism, for example. Some of these markers outside towns or clubs that have transcended their white supremacist past deserve happy endings. That's fine, too; we have no reason not to mark and be pleased about success stories. At clubs and colleges, the absence of women cries out for an explanation.

Our landscape also suffers from an absence of Reconstruction, the era when African Americans briefly enjoyed equal legal and civil rights, after the Civil War. Partly as a result, many Americans don't really know what Reconstruction was. Reconstruction was not the rebuilding of the South (or any other section) after the Civil War. It was the political renewal of Southern state governments, and it was also the accompanying ideological movement favoring black rights across the nation. All across the country, therefore, there are sites to mark. It is time to fix their omission. Since Reconstruction lasted until 1876, until at least 2026, the United States will be marking its sesquicentennial. The National Park Service has already made this anniversary a priority in the South. It should be easy to do because every plantation mansion in the Confederacy was extant during Reconstruction. Instead of freezing their sites in 1859, staff could tell what actually happened there during the Reconstruction years.

New public history about Octavius Catto in Philadelphia supplies an example of what might be done elsewhere. Catto was a black native of Philadelphia who taught at its Institute for Colored Youth (later Cheyney University). During the Civil War, he helped recruit African Americans into the U.S. Army. In 1866, he helped lead successful protests against Philadelphia's segregated streetcars. In 1870, the Franklin Institute, still an important science museum, admitted him as a member, showing the influence of Reconstruction as an ideology. The next year, on his way to vote on election day,

Outside Philadelphia City Hall, part of an extensive public history of Octavius Catto, is this bronze bas-relief of a horse-drawn streetcar, illustrating Catto's protest of segregated public transit as Reconstruction got underway.

he was shot dead in front of the polling place by an Irish American Democrat. As of 1999, few people had heard of Catto; certainly, I had not. Beginning in 2007, however, citizens have put up three pieces of public history about him: a lengthy and accurate grave marker in nearby Collingdale, a historical marker at his house in south Philadelphia, and an extensive piece of public art and memory at City Hall.

Similarly, California has Reconstruction stories to tell. As the Civil War ended, it was perhaps the most Republican of all states, but when Republican leaders began to apply their anti-racist idealism to Chinese immigrants, Democrats rapidly gained support. This too is part of the story of Reconstruction and helps explain why President Grant in late 1875 said the "public was tired out with these annual autumnal outbreaks in the South" and refused to send federal troops to quell antiblack violence in Mississippi.

If we really know American history, we should not shrink from the prospect of this struggle. We can take back the landscape. It does not belong to the dead, but to the living. Monuments and markers are messages to the future, and the future does not belong to the rich alone but to all of us. We must not act in haste, but we must act to make the landscape ours. We must initiate a dialogue with the past from countryside to city square, which will also begin a civic dialogue with each other. We can no longer allow the "War Between the States" phrases of the United Daughters of the Confederacy to stand uncontested. Labor history cannot be written by unions alone, while mining history is written by corporations. The American Legion cannot be left to put up war memorials by itself. Our goal must be to write the history of America on the landscape in a way that represents the past more accurately; doing so may also help bring into being that "beloved community" spoken of by participants in the Civil Rights Movement.

With a landscape of truth, we can learn where we really have been as a nation and what we have done as a people. History—telling what really happened in the past—is an ongoing process, not a product, and on the local level, we all can play a role. We must tell what happened, without the public relations puffery of local boosters. We can persuade our war museums, so sanitized as to be fraudulent, to be more forthright. If we cannot correct private sites like the National Mining Museum, we can mount corrections on the Internet or even across the street. We can write gays and lesbians back onto the landscape as heroes *and* villains—as history makers. We can stiffen the spines of state marker officers to use candid active verbs even when describing abhorrent events, so Americans can realize not only what has been done but also who did it. We can write back into the American story those men and women whose heroic actions on behalf of justice for people of all races and social backgrounds have been omitted or falsified because they lost, but whose examples remain important for us as we act today in the civic arena. We can, in short, write into Lincoln's "mystic chords of memory" notes of equity, inspiration, and truth from our American past. It is our country, after all, our narrative, and our landscape upon which to tell it.[10]

1. The most famous battle took place over the *National Standards for United States History*, published in 1994 by the National Center for History in the Schools and denounced shortly after publication by the entire U.S. Senate. (The vote was 99 to 1; one Louisiana senator refused to go along because the denunciation of the *Standards* wasn't harsh enough.) Other skirmishes took place at the Smithsonian, whose Air and Space Museum in 1994–95 canceled most of an exhibit about the atomic bombing of Hiroshima, and at the Library of Congress, where a staff protest caused the library to take down "Back of the Big House: The Cultural Landscape of the Plantation" hours after it opened in December 1995.

2. I must make an exception for chapter 53, Stone Mountain—too big to come down! Georgia needs to make many changes at the park, from renaming its streets (now named for Jefferson Davis, Stonewall Jackson, etc.) to adding plaques telling its KKK history to figuring out something—an inflatable structure?—to symbolize a competing story in equal hieratic scale.

3. I was suggesting that students who left high school miseducated about the past might not be able to remedy their ignorance at historic sites. Subconsciously, I was presaging my next book, this one.

4. My two sources differed: a local informant says snowplow, while Katherine Long, historian in the Richmond marker office, says mowing machine.

5. Chapter 89 shows how widespread is this biased use of "settled."

6. Some local matching funds are required. Since some local governments are not participating, Long noted that some erroneous markers "will continue to stand until a snow plow strikes!"

7. Virginia is developing an app that will speak the text of every state historical marker when a phone passes it, eliminating the need to stop and pull over.

8. Several other states have since joined Minnesota in eliminating "squaw" from their landscape.

9. But don't put up a wrong one! We hardly need more!

10. George Santayana, *The Life of Reason* (NY: Scribner's, 1932), 45; Ken P'Pool, conversation, 6/96; Joseph Clower Jr., correspondence, 6/21/96; Katherine Long, correspondence, 8/98; Jon Axline, "Montana's Historical Highway Marker's" [sic], *Newsline*, 9/99, mdt.mt.gov/publications/docs/newsletters/newsline/1999/newsep99.pdf; WPA, *The Negro in Virginia* (NY: Hastings House, 1940), 237; Harry Ploski and Ernest *Kaiser, The Negro Almanac* (NY: Bellwether, 1971), 255–63; Jennifer R. Loux, "Virginia's Historical Marker Program: Its History and Growth," *Notes on Virginia* 54 (2016): 9.

SELECTING THE SITES

Hundreds of thousands of historic markers and monuments dot the American landscape. Historian Martha Norkunas found nearly 200 in Lowell, Massachusetts, a city of fewer than 100,000 people, a ratio which, if extrapolated, suggests more than half a million for the United States! The Bergen County (New Jersey) Historic Society has put up more than 130 official county historical markers since the 1970s; its cities, towns, and voluntary organizations may have erected scores more. No one could ever list all the historic sites in the United States, let alone read and think about them.

Official state historical markers form a smaller population, and early in my research, I determined to read all of them. Texas dissuaded me. The Lone Star state has 16,000 state historical markers—far more than any other state. To read and digest one marker per minute would require more than 260 hours—almost seven weeks in the Texas office. At the other end of the spectrum is Maine, whose assistant director of historic preservation flatly assured me, "Maine does not have historical markers along its highways." Maine *has* markers and monuments, of course, not put up by a state agency, so the only way to read them is to drive every road in the state, keeping a sharp lookout.

Most states have between 50 and 2,000 markers, researchable in compilations put out online by state historical societies, or less handily in filing cabinets in state capitols. Then there is New Jersey, which has a functioning marker office but misplaced its files some years back. If a marker goes down in New Jersey, the state will help replace it—but only if the old one is brought in so its text can be copied!

I read every state historical marker in 34 states: Alaska, Arkansas, California, Delaware, Florida, Georgia, Idaho, Indiana, Iowa, Kansas, Louisiana, Maryland, Michigan, Minnesota, Montana, Nebraska, Nevada, New Hampshire, New Mexico, New York, North Carolina, North Dakota, Ohio, Oregon, Pennsylvania, Rhode Island, South Carolina, South Dakota, Tennessee, Vermont, Virginia, West Virginia, Wisconsin, and Wyoming.[1] I read a good portion of the markers in 15 more: Alabama, Arizona, Colorado,

Connecticut, District of Columbia, Hawaii, Illinois, Kentucky, Massachusetts, Mississippi, New Jersey, Oklahoma, Texas, Utah, and Washington.[2,3] In Missouri, I read only a few. I have also read hundreds and perhaps thousands of local markers, but the universe of local markers is so enormous and uneven that I cannot estimate it.

The set of historic monuments is similarly huge and indeterminate. Thick books treat the outdoor sculpture of Washington, DC, and New York City; smaller books cover smaller cities like New Orleans or Fort Wayne, Indiana. The "SOS" (Save Outdoor Sculpture) files maintained by historic preservation offices in most states list thousands of monuments. This vast number dwarfs the few hundred that I have photographed and studied.

Although identifying the population of relevant sites would be hard, several worthwhile sociological research projects could be carried out on America's public history landscape. For example, I believe that monuments to the Union went up much earlier than those to the Confederacy and, over time, said less and less about the ideological meaning of the Civil War, while monuments to the Confederacy went up later and said more and more about the ideological meaning of the war. If true, such findings would help interpret both sets of monuments and the reasons for their erection (see chapter 15). Research on when and where historical marker texts include women might correlate with sociological measures of women's role in society—or might merely reflect the influence of individuals here and there who gallantly worked for inclusive public history (see chapter 30). Changes in historical perspective could be charted by showing how a famous person or event—John Brown, say (chapter 80), or the Dakota War in Minnesota—has been commemorated in different eras. In 2019, marker texts are widely available, often with dates and supporting documentation, making research projects like these quite feasible.[4] I have not attempted this kind of quantitative research here.

Lies Across America examines about a hundred sites where history is told across the United States. Half are historical markers and a fourth are monuments. The rest include outdoor museums, historic houses, forts, and ships. Included are four sites that had no markers in 1999 but where past events cry out for acknowledgment, four indoor museums, and six names, since the names across America also tell how Americans remember their history.[5] In no case was I interested in correcting minutiae like "Here the First Presbyterian Church was organized in 1881," while it actually happened in 1883. The very first printings included three exemplary sites to show that markers and monuments can be honest and to affirm that such sites can make a difference. I soon removed them, because they didn't really fit under the title of the book. I also removed an Arkansas entry that was flatly wrong. I mistakenly called Grant County more "hospitable" toward African Americans than nearby counties without realizing that Sheridan, its county seat, was actually a sundown town. My next book, *Sundown Towns*, told of my error.

I made a few changes to my sources. I capitalized "Negro" and corrected obvious spelling and punctuation errors. Ken Lawrence and Paul Escott, who worked extensively with the WPA slave narratives, show that writers use dialect inconsistently when transcribing speech depending on their race and the speakers', so in sources that employ it, I converted dialect to more standard English. I also repunctuated some monuments to let their words flow more easily on the page than the limitations of stone sometimes allowed. I do not believe I altered the content of any source, marker, or monument.

I visited or learned about each site at a specific moment in time, mostly between 1994 and 1998. Since then, I tried to stay in touch with each site as it changed or failed to change. In 2018, two interns, Jacob Conrad and Diara Urey, and a colleague, Betsy Nix, gave me considerable assistance in this task. I cannot vouch that the same items will be displayed, the same interpretive practices will be followed, or even that the marker or monument will be standing on the date that you visit. If you find major changes, please email Stephen A. Berrey, Professor of History, U. of MI, at the email he has set up for this purpose, PublicHistorySites@gmail.com. Professor Berrey has kindly agreed to assist in this work going forward. Also, please tell him of any errors in scholarship you find, for although I have striven for accuracy I am inevitably not expert on 50 state histories. Finally, if you have other sites to bring to our attention because they tell history particularly badly—or particularly well—again, please contact Professor Berrey.[6]

1. This sentence overstates slightly the thoroughness of my work. If a state's marker texts were collected in a book published in, say, 1990, I did not always read all the markers put up between then and 1998. Since 1999, I have not tried to read all new state historical markers; my hands have been full just keeping up with the sites herein treated.
2. Washington, DC, has no "state historic markers" but boasts a plethora of plaques and monuments, many of which I have studied.
3. Old New Jersey marker texts (pre-1951) were published, so are available.
4. Examples of such research before 2000 include Harold Gulley, "Roadside Reminders of the Civil War: Historical Markers in Georgia" (Oshkosh: U. of WI Department of Geography, typescript, 1995?); Gulley, "Women and the Lost Cause," *Journal of Historical*

Geography 19 no. 2 (1993): 127–35; James B. Jones Jr., "An Analysis of National Register Listings and Roadside Historic Markers in Tennessee," *The Public Historian* 10 no. 3 (summer 1988): 19–30; Robert R. Weyeneth, "Historic Preservation and the Civil Rights Movement of the 1950s and 1960s" (Columbia, SC: Applied History Program, typescript, 1995); and John Winberry, "'Lest We Forget': The Confederate Monument and the Southern Townscape," *Southeastern Geographer* 23 no. 2 (11/83): 109–10.

5. Generally, I avoided cemeteries. Cemeteries do tell history to be sure; especially they convey biography. But tombstones rarely result from the kind of civic discourse that is required before a state puts up a historic marker or a community decides to place a monument in front of its courthouse.

6. Martha Norkunas, email to Public History Discussion List, 4/97; Reginald McMahon, "The BCHS Marker Program and How It Evolved," www.carroll.com/bchs/marker program.html, 9/98; Robert L. Bradley, correspondence, 11/96.

TEN QUESTIONS TO ASK AT A HISTORIC SITE

1. When did this location become a historic site? (When was the marker or monument put up? Or the house "interpreted"?) How did that time differ from ours? From the time of the event or person commemorated?
2. Who sponsored it? Representing which participant group's point of view? What was their position in social structure when the event occurred? When the site went "up"?
3. What were the sponsors' motives? What were their ideological needs and social purposes? What were their values?
4. Who is the intended audience for the site? What values were they trying to leave for us today? What does the site ask us to go and do or think about?
5. Did the sponsors have government support? At what level? Who was ruling the government at the time? What ideological arguments were used to get the government to acquiesce?
6. Who is left out? What points of view go largely unheard? How would the story differ if a different group told it? Another political party? Race? Sex? Class? Religious group?
7. Are there problematic (insulting, degrading) words or symbols that would not be used today, or by other groups?
8. How is the site used today? Do traditional rituals continue to connect today's public to it? Or is it ignored? Why?
9. Is the presentation accurate? What actually happened? What historical sources tell of the event, people, or period commemorated at the site?
10. How does this site fit in with others that treat the same era? Or subject? What other people lived and events happened then but are not commemorated? Why?

TWENTY CANDIDATES
FOR "TOPPLING"

When someone topples a statue or monument in the United States, public officials usually denounce the act as reprehensible vandalism. However, we certainly didn't call it that when the people of Eastern Europe pulled down statues of Stalin and Lenin. The officials have a point, however: in a democracy, a civic dialogue is the proper way to create the groundswell of public opinion that can get a monument removed or revised.

Some people may argue that vandalism is appropriate when most members of a community still favor a monument, yet that monument distorts history. Topplers, at least, take the past seriously and take seriously the need to challenge what Americans tell themselves about it. Moreover, teaching accurate history can be difficult when memorials create a context of delusion. Surely, Americans would be surprised to see heroic statues of Adolf Hitler dominating the squares and parks of Germany today, and if they did exist, we would applaud German citizens for toppling them. Similarly, the proper response to some of our statues would be to topple them. Nevertheless, before resorting to extralegal toppling, citizens must realize that persons of very different convictions—Ku Klux Klansmen, for example—can mount similar arguments to justify toppling statues and monuments that *they* feel distort the past.

A better solution than toppling may be to remove the offending object to a museum. There, in a new context with explanatory labels, the monument can teach visitors about two topics at once: the person or event it portrayed and also the people who once commemorated that person or event. Organizations can put pressure on state historical marker offices to reword a marker if its language is offensive or its facts are wrong. If a monument cannot be removed—Stone Mountain comes to mind—then citizens can at least provide historically accurate material at the site in the form of new markers and printed material. Leaving layers like this on the landscape also shows visitors that history is a dynamic human construct and changes as social structure changes.

When this book first came out in 1999, this appendix was its most

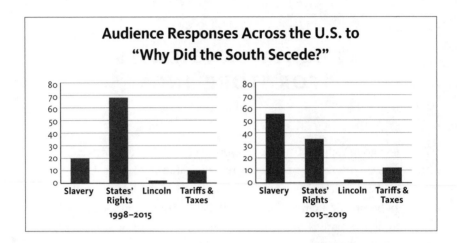

controversial part. Some people seized upon it to denounce the entire book. After the murders in Charleston, South Carolina, however, and especially after the white supremacy riot in Charlottesville, this appendix came to look somewhat more mainstream. The change shows how those two events changed the rhetorical landscape, leading to eventual changes in the actual landscape.

Still, accomplishing these revisions and removals can seem difficult, even after Charlottesville. Certainly, it can be hard to persuade people that what they have learned about the past is wrong and that the heroes commemorated on their landscape have feet of clay. It might be easier merely to bring down the offending icon. However, topplings worked in Eastern Europe because most members of the community supported them. The purpose of writing history more accurately on the landscape is to write it more accurately in the consciousness of our citizenry. For a lone individual or tiny "cell" to topple a statue or monument hardly accomplishes that goal, and hence is not an effective way to teach what happened in the past.

By now it should be clear that I use "toppling"—in quotation marks—as a shorthand for the kind of civic discourse suggested above. In that context, I offered my original list of top-twenty "toppling" candidates. It pleases me to tell the status of these terrible historic sites twenty years later, in 2019.

1. Perhaps the most hated monument in America was the only one I know that overtly praised white supremacy—the obelisk celebrating the White League in New Orleans (chapter 44). Even in 1999, citizens were

slowly toppling it; it had already lost two of its four columns. Then in 2017, Mayor Landrieu took it down, along with three Confederate monuments. I still hope that all four wind up in an exhibit somewhere about the Nadir of race relations, the period when they all went up. Such an exhibit would result in a fine learning experience for future generations of New Orleans visitors. But not the Rural Life Museum at Louisiana State University, as the next paragraph notes.

2. In Baton Rouge, Louisiana, "The Good Darky" is a symbol of black submissiveness. LSU's Rural Life Museum has elected not to use it as a tool to teach how African Americans had to comport themselves during segregation, or indeed to teach anything. Lacking any context, "Uncle Jack," as the museum "affectionately" calls him, still commemorates segregation and servility. In the process, the Rural Life Museum makes a case *against* trusting museums with offensive icons from the past. Since it is in the museum owing to a prior toppling incident, LSU has only to push it over again in its grassy ellipse. Museum officials can then put up a plaque explaining how the statue exemplified segregation, and its 1968 toppling symbolized segregation's overthrow. Then "Uncle Jack" will tell history instead of perpetuating a stereotype. Louisiana State is an institution of higher learning, so perhaps concerned students and professors in history, sociology, and other departments, joined by campus organizations, can bring this about. Or LSU's African American students might get the statue moved to one of Louisiana's predominantly black universities. Indoors, with suitable labels, "The Good Darky" would be a fine object for enlightening today's students about the Jim Crow years. That the statue still stands, proudly proclaiming white supremacy in 2019, indicts the faculty and student body of the university.

3. My next candidate lies all across America—statues of "the hiker" and their inscriptions reading "Spanish-American War, 1898–1902." Chapter 25 tells how these memorials conflate the Philippine-American War and the Spanish-American War. It also shows how citizens in Minnesota got a corrective plaque installed in their state capitol. Some memorials are even more confused, such as the statue in Memphis with the words "The Hiker. Typifying the American Volunteer who fought

Spain in Cuba, the Philippines, and Boxer Rebellion." Viewers who recall that the Boxer Rebellion involved Chinese attacks on American, British, French, German, Japanese, and Russian interests in and around Beijing will wonder what Spain was doing in China! Rather than topple him, citizens in every city where he still hikes might add a plaque explaining that he represents the Philippine-American War, not the Spanish-American War, and telling that the dates "1898–1902" refer to the Philippine-American War, while the Spanish-American War lasted only three months. The plaques could also provide a synopsis of the Philippine War to correct the fine sentiments often carved onto the base of the hiker. For instance, the Dover, New Hampshire, hiker tells that Americans fought "to succor the weak and oppressed against foreign tyranny and to give Cuba and the Philippines a place among the free peoples of the earth." The Spanish-American War did begin with a tinge of anti-imperialist sentiment, but in the Philippine-American War the United States *was* the "foreign tyranny." These plaques would help rescue the Philippine-American War from the historical amnesia in which it now languishes.

4. If any historical markers deserve toppling rather than just revision, first on the list is the marker for the "horrible Indian massacre" of 1861 in Almo, Idaho (chapter 12), since the event it describes never happened. Even so, displaying the really quite beautiful marker in a museum might make more sense; then labels could describe how people can and do falsify history. Also, a museum could make clear the climate of hostility toward Native Americans in 1938 that let the Sons and Daughters of Idaho Pioneers erect such a blatant historical fabrication.

5-6. At least *some* of the ubiquitous monuments and markers celebrating Christopher Columbus surely need to come down, I wrote in 1999. The process of deciding to raze them would increase the visibility and political efficacy of Native Americans. I suggested that we might begin by removing the two worst examples—those statues at the state capitols of California (chapter 3) and Ohio that falsify history by claiming that Columbus proved the world was round. Again, each would provide a nearby museum with a marvelous opportunity to teach Americans how sham stories have infiltrated our history textbooks as well as the American landscape. In 2018, a few communities did bring him down. Los Angeles removed his statue from a park.[1] San Jose took him out of city hall. Vandals rendered unreadable a monument to him in Baltimore. Citizen groups challenged him in New York City, Buffalo, St. Louis, and yes, Columbus, Ohio.

7. The career of John C. Calhoun shows a politician whose vision narrowed as his life went on, so his considerable powers ended in the service of slavery and treason. Clement Eaton, a white Southern historian, called Calhoun a "pernicious agitator" who "exploited the slavery issue and created stereotypes in the minds of the Southern [white] people that produced intolerance." I find him without redeeming characteristics, so I suggested removing him to museums from Marion Square in Charleston, the South Carolina State House, Calhoun College at Yale, the U.S. Capitol, and wherever else he sits in a place of honor. Indeed, Yale did rename the college, Minneapolis did rename Lake Calhoun, and even South Carolina is discussing what to do about Calhoun at various sites in 2019.

8. Even more honored than Calhoun is the leader of the Confederacy, Jefferson Davis. Every one of his many likenesses, so far as I know, honors his "service" as president of the Confederacy. Hence, every one should go. We can then put up plaques to explain what used to be here and where it is now (perhaps in a Nadir Park). These plaques need to tell that right after the Civil War the man was quite unpopular in the conquered South. African Americans and Unionist whites despised his cause. Many former Confederates blamed Davis and other "fire-eaters" for leading them into secession; even some who still believed in secession felt that Davis's poor leadership helped the Union win. Most Davis monuments went up only after his 1889 death, when white supremacy was locked in place all across America (chapter 81) and the Lost Cause was no longer lost.

Slowly we are moving toward toppling Davis. The University of Texas removed Davis's statue in 2015, two years before it removed Robert E. Lee. In 2019, even Richmond, where Davis presided over the

Confederacy for four years, has begun to consider removing Davis from Monument Avenue.

9. It would be a significant logistical achievement to vandalize Stone Mountain, let alone topple it. Surely, however, those who run it can find a way to tell every visitor about the connections between the Confederacy and all three incarnations of the Ku Klux Klan. This more complete history of Stone Mountain, whether told on new historical markers, in a brochure, or by guides, would help visitors realize the past power of the Klan in American life.

That said, after Charlottesville, some proposals for Stone Mountain actually take account of its hieratic scale. One is for a huge blimp to be moored permanently in front of it, conveying an anti-Confederate message. Another is a huge liberty bell to go on top of it, symbolizing Martin Luther King Jr.'s call to "let freedom ring" from Stone Mountain. And a third is, yes, to blast off the images entirely.

10. Also on the topic of the KKK and its connections with the Confederacy, whites of good will need to take the initiative to retire every statue of Nathan Bedford Forrest (chapter 52). Since I wrote the foregoing in 1999, African Americans in Memphis and Jacksonville, Florida, took the lead in removing Forrest from a park and a high school, respectively. Whites have yet to step up.

11. Albert Pike was another embodiment of the KKK and its links with the Confederacy. A Confederate leader of peculiar abilities and disabilities, he may have been a coward under fire. Certainly, his performance at Pea Ridge, the one battle in which he commanded troops, ended in near disgrace. Earlier, Pike had been the Confederacy's emissary to Natives in Indian Territory. He concluded treaties with the Cherokees, Comanches, Creeks, Osages, Seminoles, Senecas, Shawnees, and Wichitas, usually in such a way as to precipitate a civil war between the Confederate and Union factions within each tribe. After the war, according to histories of the Arkansas Ku Klux Klan written by insiders, he became a key leader of the organization. Nevertheless, Albert Pike gets a statue in Judiciary Square in Washington, DC, that describes him as "Author Poet Scholar Soldier Philanthropist Philosopher Jurist Ora-

tor." More appropriate would be "Bigot Coward Fomenter." Pike's is the only outdoor statue of a Confederate general in the District of Columbia. Only Forrest would be a worse choice. As of 2019, Pike's days on the landscape may be numbered. The city council and mayor of DC came out for his removal in 2017, after the Charlottesville race riot.

12. After the Civil War, the United States executed just one person, Capt. Henry Wirz, the notorious commander of the Andersonville POW camp, for war crimes. In 1909, the United Daughters of the Confederacy erected an obelisk in Andersonville, Georgia, to honor him! The monument maintains that Wirz was not at fault for the despicable conditions of the camp: "Discharging his duty with such humanity as the harsh circumstances and policy of the foe permitted, Captain Wirz became at last the victim of a misdirected popular clamor . . . " Georgia continued the apologia in 1956 by putting up a state historical marker claiming, "Had he been an angel from heaven he could not have changed the pitiful tale of privation and hunger unless he had possessed the power to repeat the miracle of the loaves and fishes." Such writing erases from memory the sympathetic white Georgians who brought food and clothing for his starving prisoners, only to have Wirz turn them away. The Sons of Confederate Veterans further dishonored the POWs who died here by awarding Wirz a medal of honor for "uncommon valor and bravery . . . " Every year, around November 10, the anniversary of his hanging, they stage a ceremony at the obelisk to revere Wirz. These acts by local whites sent a message to the staff at nearby Andersonville National Park, who responded with exhibits and videos that excuse the camp's conditions and focus instead on bad treatment of POWs by the Germans and Japanese during World War II. As one ranger said to Tony Horwitz, author of *Confederates in the Attic*, "I have to live in this community." The Grand Army of the Republic bitterly opposed the obelisk, and somewhere around 1950, someone tried to topple it and broke its base but failed to overturn it. It and the state marker need to go—perhaps to the museum at the park, once its staff musters the courage to speak truth to the neo-Confederates who now intimidate them.[2]

13. Finally, on the Confederates, every monument to "Afro-Confederates" which implies that many African Americans fought for the

Confederacy puts forth a lie. As chapter 56 points out, the Confederacy would not even permit African Americans to fight for it until March 13, 1865, almost at war's end. For starters, the obelisk to faithful slaves in Fort Mill, South Carolina, the monument to Henry "Dad" Brown in Darlington, South Carolina, the obelisk to Willis Howcott in Canton, Mississippi, and the phrases on other monuments elsewhere must all be corrected.

14. America's most toppled monument—the policeman with hand upraised at the Haymarket Riot—deserves one more removal (chapter 29). In a museum, labels could tell his interesting history as well as the story of the Haymarket Riot. I do concede, however, that the main issue with the Chicago Police Department no longer has anything to do with labor, but with race. I'm not sure that this figure, with his arm upraised, says anything to that issue, on either side.

15. "Pitchfork Ben" Tillman, one of the most racist people commemorated on the American landscape, should stand no longer at the South Carolina State Capitol. While he was a U.S. Senator, Tillman reacted to Teddy Roosevelt's hosting Booker T. Washington at the White House with these words: "The action of President Roosevelt in entertaining that Negro Booker T. Washington will necessitate our killing a thousand Negroes in the South before they will learn their place again." And here is Tillman on voting rights for African Americans: "We have done our level best. We have scratched our heads to find out how we could eliminate every last one of them. We stuffed ballot boxes. We shot them. We are not ashamed of it." State capitols are public buildings maintained by and intended for all the citizens of the state. Tillman's statue in a place of honor in Columbia says otherwise. In 2017, citizens of South Carolina started to demonstrate for his removal.

16. Mississippi's answer to Tillman is an ugly statue of governor and U.S. Senator Theodore G. Bilbo in the Mississippi State Capitol. At the end of his 40 years of public office, Bilbo was still shouting in 1946, "Do not let a single nigger vote. If you let a few register and vote this year, next year there will be twice as many, and the first thing you know the whole thing will be out of hand." Mississippians likewise need to haul his visage far from a place that purports to legislate for all citizens of

Mississippi. They have made a sort of beginning by moving it from the rotunda of the Capitol to a side room often used by the Black Caucus, some of whom use his outstretched arm as a coat rack.

17. The American Museum of Natural History in New York might leave Teddy Roosevelt where he sits on his horse, so long as it removes the African American and Native American standing subserviently beneath him.

18. Since Leander Perez cheated his white constituents as well as those residents he called "niggers," all citizens of Plaquemines Parish, Louisiana, might join in removing the three large bronze plaques that praise him at Fort Jackson (chapter 46). Closing Fort Jackson to tourists kind of takes care of the problem.

19. In 1999, I suggested that "removing the statue of Orville Hubbard in front of City Hall in Dearborn, Michigan, would be a giant step toward making Dearborn a nonracist city." Thankfully, as chapter 34 tells, Hubbard has been removed from City Hall; it seems unlikely he will go up again in a place of honor.

20. I do not recommend "toppling" the hieratic statue of Juan de Oñate north of Santa Fe because it would remove from the landscape a figure of huge historical importance and one of the few Spanish Americans now on it. But the public representation of history in New Mexico would only be improved if his foot were again removed (chapter 19). So, I don't suggest toppling this monument, only re-maiming it, preferably after public dialogue that includes Native Americans, Mexican Americans, and Anglos. In 2017, someone painted the statue's left foot red, again to bring attention to Oñate's cruelty.

Selecting this list was difficult: so many candidates clamored for inclusion. Any list can only be a beginning. The landscape is left to us, all across America. It is our responsibility to erect markers and monuments that tell what happened on it and to stop it from honoring "heroes" and events that deserve to be remembered but not commemorated. Since 1999, we have been making progress in that direction.[3]

1. He had only been there 45 years.

2. Even in 2019, a long article at the NPS website came to this bland conclusion about the horrors of Andersonville: "Over the years, the finger of blame has pointed in many directions, but the facts show that events of the time made this national tragedy happen" (nps.gov/parkhistory/online_books/civil_war_series/5/sec5.htm).

3. Oscar V. Campomanes, "Grappling with the Filipino as Primitive: The American Soldier in Love and War (1903)" (New Orleans: Society for Cinema Studies Conference, 1993); Clement Eaton, *The Freedom-of-Thought Struggle in the Old South* (NY: Harper, 1964 [1940]), 158; Tony Horwitz, *Confederate in the Attic* (NY: Pantheon, 1998), 322–39; Loewen and Charles Sallis, eds., *MS: Conflict and Change* (NY: Pantheon, 1980), 239; Andrew Glass, "Mississippi Sen. Theodore Bilbo Dies at Age 69, Aug. 21, 1947," *Politico*, 8/20/2016, politico.com/story/2016/08/mississippi-sen-theodore-bilbo-dies-at-age-69-aug-21-1947-227126; James M. McPherson, *Battle Cry of Freedom* (NY: Oxford UP, 1988), 404–405.

INDEX

PUBLISHING IN THE PUBLIC INTEREST

Thank you for reading this book published by The New Press. The New Press is a nonprofit, public interest publisher. New Press books and authors play a crucial role in sparking conversations about the key political and social issues of our day.

We hope you enjoyed this book and that you will stay in touch with The New Press. Here are a few ways to stay up to date with our books, events, and the issues we cover:

- Sign up at www.thenewpress.com/subscribe to receive updates on New Press authors and issues and to be notified about local events
- Like us on Facebook: www.facebook.com/newpressbooks
- Follow us on Twitter: www.twitter.com/thenewpress

Please consider buying New Press books for yourself; for friends and family; or to donate to schools, libraries, community centers, prison libraries, and other organizations involved with the issues our authors write about.

The New Press is a 501(c)(3) nonprofit organization. You can also support our work with a tax-deductible gift by visiting www.thenewpress.com/donate.